ETHICS OF CONSUMPTION

Philosophy and the Global Context
General Editor: Michael Krausz, Bryn Mawr College

This new series addresses a range of emerging global concerns. It situates philosophical efforts in their global and cultural contexts, and it offers works from thinkers whose cultures are challenged by globalizing movements. Comparative and intercultural studies address such social and political issues as the environment, poverty, consumerism, civil society, tolerance, colonialism, global ethics, and community in cyberspace. they also address related methodological issues of translation and cross-cultural understanding.

Titles in the Series

ETHICS OF CONSUMPTION

The Good Life, Justice, and Global Stewardship

Edited by
DAVID A. CROCKER
and
TOBY LINDEN

ROWMAN & LITTLEFIELD PUBLISHERS, INC.
Lanham • Boulder • New York • Oxford

ROWMAN & LITTLEFIELD PUBLISHERS, INC.

Published in the United States of America
by Rowman & Littlefield Publishers, Inc.
4720 Boston Way, Lanham, Maryland 20706

12 Hid's Copse Road
Cumnor Hill, Oxford OX2 9JJ, England

British Library Cataloguing in Publication Information Available

Library of Congress Cataloging-in-Publication Data

Ethics of consumption : the good life, justice, and global stewardship
   / edited by David A. Crocker and Toby Linden.
      p.   cm.—(Philosophy and the global context)
   Includes bibliographical references and index.
   ISBN 0-8476-8494-6 (cloth : alk. paper).—ISBN 0-8476-8495-4
(pbk. : alk. paper)
    1. Consumption (Economics)—Moral and ethical aspects.
   2. Conservation of natural resources—Moral and ethical aspects.
   3. Social justice. I. Crocker, David A. II. Linden, Toby.
III. Series.
HB801.E85   1998   97-14380
333.7′2—dc21   CIP

ISBN 0-8476-8494-6 (cloth : alk. paper)
ISBN 0-8476-8495-4 (pbk. : alk. paper)

Printed in the United States of America

♾ ™ The paper used in this publication meets the minimum requirements of
American National Standard for Information Sciences—Permanence of Paper
for Printed Library Materials, ANSI Z39.48—1984.

Contents

Tables and Figures

Tables

ix

Figures

Preface

The present volume brings to completion work that the Institute for Philosophy and Public Policy, a research unit of the School of Public Affairs at the University of Maryland, began almost five years ago. In 1992, members of the institute produced a series of working papers on ethical issues in population policy (many of which were published in the fall 1993 issue of the institute's report.) This research effort was undertaken with the generous support of the Global Stewardship Initiative of the Pew Charitable Trusts.

Susan Sechler, the director of the initiative, shared the institute's conviction that international attention to population trends and policies in developing countries should be supplemented by the examination of consumption patterns in industrialized countries. People and nature are affected not only by the sheer number of people in the world but also by the way people live. Central to individual and communal life is the consumption of materials, energy, and commodities of many sorts. Do we Americans and others in industrialized countries consume too much? Do we consume the wrong kinds of goods and services? How should we assess sufficiency and appropriateness? Should we change our consumption patterns? Why? How? What role, if any, should institutions such as governments play in instituting changes?

The institute seemed an ideal forum in which to confront these questions. Since 1976, its scholars have investigated the values and concepts that underlie public policy. Though they frame their research questions by looking carefully at empirical data, their own work is primarily conceptual and normative. It investigates the structure of arguments and the nature of values relevant to the formation, justification, and criticism of public policy. As the institute began to study consumption, it soon became clear that the subject required prudential and moral reflection as well as empirical information. For what we consume affects—

sometimes adversely, sometimes beneficially—our own lives, other people, our institutions, and the natural world.

The institute carried out its consumption research in three closely related steps, each of which made a contribution to the present volume. First, the institute's scholars sought to define the consumption landscape and address the ethical issues that it raises. Unlike population and environmental polices, consumption patterns and the political response to them had received scant attention. When scholars had addressed consumption, they had usually exhibited narrow disciplinary concerns and had largely neglected ethical evaluation and policy analysis. Through internal discussion and the preparation of working papers, institute scholars sought to rectify this situation.

Second, the institute hosted a conference on "Consumption, Global Stewardship, and the Good Life," at the University of Maryland, September 29–October 2, 1994. The conference, organized with the renewed support of the Global Stewardship Initiative, brought together philosophers and theologians, economists and environmentalists, sociologists, historians, political scientists, policy analysts, and social activists interested in understanding and assessing levels and patterns of consumption, especially in the United States. Six conference papers and five institute working papers were published in the institute's fall 1995 report. Fourteen of the conference papers and presentations were substantially revised and became chapters in the present volume.

Third, following the consumption conference, the institute commissioned five new essays or revisions of previously published essays from Robert Goodland, Nathan Keyfitz, Michael Schudson, Amartya Sen, and Paul E. Waggoner. These essays, supplementing both the conference and working papers, addressed the topics of diet, food and agriculture, population and consumption, and living standard. By enhancing the range of perspectives in this collection, the new essays increased the likelihood that the volume would serve as a touchstone for future discussions of consumption and global stewardship. Most of the volume's authors have extensively revised their initial essays to take into account other essays in the collection and to respond to editorial suggestions.

Throughout this lengthy and interactive process, a set of central themes (many of them discussed in the introduction to this volume emerged. As a result, the collection as a whole displays substantial thematic coherence. Although the authors frame the problem of consumption in a variety of ways, they agree on the importance of investigating the impact of consumption practices on the global environment, quality of life, and international justice.

We are pleased to acknowledge and thank the many individuals and institutions that contributed to this volume at one or more of the above stages. First and foremost, we wish to acknowledge the financial and moral support provided by the Pew Charitable Trusts through its Global Stewardship Initiative. Susan Sechler, and her deputy, David Devlin-Foltz, exemplify the finest traditions of philanthropic and civic leadership. From the institute's earlier work on the ethics of population, through the planning and execution of the conference, to the selecting and editing of twenty-eight essays, the Global Stewardship Initiative provided indispensable resources and encouragement. We also gratefully acknowledge financial support for this project from the National Endowment for the Humanities (NEH) Grant #RO-22709-94. The views expressed by the editors and contributors are, of course, their own and not necessarily those of the institute, the Pew Charitable Trusts, or NEH.

The Consumption Conference director, David A. Crocker, was ably assisted by the Conference Organizing Committee composed of L. Anathea Brooks, Teresa Chandler, Barbara Cronin, Maria Davila, Carroll Linkins, and Amanda Wolf. Throughout 1993 and 1994, each of them made essential contributions to the conference planning, execution, and follow-up. The following students at the School of Public Affairs or other units of the University of Maryland were helpful in attending to numerous details involved in mounting a successful event: Crystal Banks, Michaela Burger, Rita Collins, Tom Cox, Martin Domeski, Elizabeth Friedman, Debra Gonski, Brenden Harris, Colin Ross, Tracy Stanton, Fabiola Vethencourt, and Dea Whayland. Student rapporteurs of the conference proceedings included Dan Addess, Susan Baer, Crystal Banks, Hoosh Cott, John Duffy, Debra Gonski, Chris James, Garrett Ogden, Cheryl Rosenblum, Fredd Sapp, Naledi Saul, Ross Stern, and Dea Whayland.

We are also enormously indebted to William A. Galston, Judith Lichtenberg, Jerome M. Segal, and Mark Sagoff. Together with the volume's two editors, these four institute colleagues constituted the editorial committee for this volume. For well over a year, the committee rendered valuable service in reading, commenting on, and helping select the essays. Three other institute scholars—Robert K. Fullinwider, Peter Levine, and Xiaorong Li—contributed to the working papers series and thus helped to shape the institute's discussions and its evolving ideas on consumption.

Several students in the University of Maryland, all but one of them students in the School of Public Affairs, helped with the demanding tasks connected with preparing the manuscript for submission and final publication. These students, all of whom were carrying a full academic load, included Shamit Chakravarti, Henry Clifford, Natalie Lebeau, Seema Paul, Pavit Ramachandran, and Joe Sellwood.

We have been extremely fortunate to work with the fine team at Rowman & Littlefield and are grateful for the part they played in the publication of *Ethics of Consumption*. As editor of the series Philosophy and the Global Context, Michael Krausz supported the inclusion of our volume in a noteworthy list of publications. Philosophy acquisitions editors Jennifer Ruark and Christa Acampora were very helpful at various stages in the selection and promotion of the volume. We benefited from the highly professional editorial skills of Robin Adler, Julie Kirsch, Julie Kuzneski, and Deirdre Mullervy. We are indebted to Jonathan Sisk, senior vice president and editor-in-chief, for his overall leadership and for his commitment to philosophy in public policy and to *Ethics of Consumption*.

Finally, five members of the Institute for Philosophy and Public Policy are deserving of special mention. From beginning to end of the five year period, business manager Barbara Cronin, administrative assistant Carroll Linkins, and director William A. Galston supplied superb administrative support, often permitting "the consumption book" to take more than its fair share of such scarce goods as copying time and research assistants. The institute's exceptional editor, Arthur Evenchik, gave us wise counsel and much-appreciated editorial assistance at several crucial junctures in the volume's long gestation period. In April 1997, Peter Engelke became a graduate research assistant in the institute and was immediately thrust into all tasks connected with getting our volume to the finish line. He contributed immensely to all phases of our final effort.

DAC & TL

Acknowledgments

The author and publisher of this work gratefully acknowledge permission to use these previously published essays.

Chapter 2, "Carrying Capacity and Ecological Economics," by Mark Sagoff was originally published as "Roundtable: Carrying Capacity and Ecological Economics," in *BioScience* 45, 1995 American Institute of Biological Science.

Chapter 8, "A New Economic Critique of Consumer Society," by Juliet B. Schor was originally published in *Report from the Institute for Philosophy and Public Policy* 15, no. 4 (Fall 1995): 17–21.

Chapter 9, "Consuming Goods and the Good of Consuming," by Colin Campbell was originally published in *Critical Review* 8, no. 4 (Fall 1994): 503–20.

Chapter 10, "Consuming Because Others Consume," by Judith Lichtenburg was originally published in *Social Theory and Practice* 22, no. 3 (Fall 1996): 273–97.

Chapter 12, "Alternatives to the Consumer Society," by Paul L. Wachtel was originally published in another form in *Poverty of Affluence* (Philadelphia: New Society Publishers, 1989).

Chapter 13, "The Road Not Taken: Friendship, Consumerism, and Happiness," by Robert E. Lane was originally published in *Critical Review* 8, no. 4 (Fall 1994): 521–54.

Chapter 14, "Delectable Materialism: Second Thoughts on Consumer Culture," by Michael Schudson grew out of a lecture prepared for a conference on "Selling the Goods: Origins of American Advertising, 1840–1940" at the Strong Museum, Rochester, New York, in 1990. Revised versions of the lecture were published in *The American Prospect* 5, (Spring 1991): 26–35 and as the afterword to the British edition of *Advertising, the Uneasy Persuasion* (London: Routledge, 1992).

Chapter 16, "The Living Standard," by Amartya Sen is excerpted from the Hicks Lecture delivered by Amartya Sen at Oxford University in 1982 and published in *Oxford Economic Papers* 36 (1984): 74–79, 84–88. The 1987 postscript is excerpted from *The Standard of Living*, 1985 Tanner Lectures at Cambridge, with contributions by Keith Hart, Ravi Kanbur, John Muellbauer, and Bernard Williams, ed. Geoffrey Hawthorn (Cambridge, UK: Cambridge University Press, 1987), 17–19, 26–29, 36–38. The 1993 postscript is excerpted from "Capability and Well-Being," in *The Quality of Life*, ed. Martha C. Nussbaum and Amartya Sen (Oxford: Clarendon Press, 1993), 46–49.

Chapter 22, "On the Subversive Virtue: Frugality," by James A. Nash was originally published as "Toward a Revival and Reform of the Subversive Virtue: Frugality," in *The Annual* of the Society of Christian Ethics (1995).

Chapter 23, "Natural Resource Consumption: North and South," by Allen L. Hammond is adapted from "Natural Resource Consumption," by Allen L. Hammond et al., in *World Resources 1994–95*, (New York and Oxford: Oxford University Press, 1994), 3–26 and is based on work by the author and by Lawrence Klein of the University of Pennsylvania and Kirit and Jyoti Parikh of the Indira Gandhi Institute of Development Research in Bombay.

In Chapter 19, a portion of "The Journey of the Dead" from *The Afterlife and Other Stories* by John Updike, copyright © 1994 by John Updike, is reprinted by permission of Alfred Knopf, Inc. Portions of "The Return" by Frederick Turner, copyright © 1979, are reprinted by permission of the publisher, The Countryman Press.

Introduction

David A. Crocker and Toby Linden

Long before many of us began to think philosophically about consumption, we read our children stories that can be interpreted as parables of consumption, though we did not fully realize this at the time. Some of these stories told of characters who behave foolishly, like the fox hungering for grapes that hang beyond his reach. Others presented characters we might envy for their discernment and good luck. For example, when Goldilocks visits the three bears she has such a sure sense of what is too much, what is not enough, and what is "just right." Equally fortunate, the right stuff—although it belongs to the three bears and not to her—is readily available. The porridge is at the right temperature; a chair and bed are at the right degree of hardness. And Goldilocks, faced with an array of material goods, unerringly chooses the right thing.

Consumers in American society are not usually so lucky. With respect to many consumer goods, we don't know what is too much, what is not enough, and what is just right. Often the right goods are nowhere to be found. When they are available, we frequently fail to choose wisely, and, as a result, we have too much of some things and not enough of others.

Many of us realize that we need a better criterion for selection than advertising's image of the good life. That which is true for individuals also applies to our households, associations, enterprises, and governments. Our uncritical acceptance of Miss Piggy's dictum that "more is more" must give way to a society-wide deliberation about appropriate consumption.

The search for criteria for wise consumption choice, however, is not an easy one. This difficulty has several sources. First, the act or process of consumption has been understood and valued in very different ways.

1

Mainstream economists conceive (and approve) of consumption as the utilization of economic goods and services in the satisfaction of human wants. Radical environmentalists understand human consumption as the squandering of nature's resources and the destruction of its inherent value. Consumption can be defined so broadly that it includes production—"the processes by which consumer goods and services are created, bought, and used"[1]—and so narrowly that it is restricted to the purchasing of yuppie paraphernalia advertised in an airline's "buy while you fly" magazine.

Much contemporary debate about consumption has been vitiated and the search for reasonable consumption norms has been impeded because people are unclear about what they mean by *consumption* and *consumption goods* or use these terms in significantly different ways. Some moral disagreements about consumption can be resolved by showing that the erstwhile opponents are talking about different things. One aim of this volume is to distinguish and relate various understandings of consumption.

Even when people are talking about roughly the same thing, they often evaluate it in diametrically opposed ways. Hence, a second obstacle in the quest for a consumption ethic is that public debate has tended to polarize between strident indictment of American materialism and doctrinaire celebration of America's consumer cornucopia. Every holiday season is predictably accompanied by articles either roundly condemning Christmas commercialism and consumerism—"the curse of Christmas present"[2]—or uncritically applauding "the gift of excess."[3] The New Road Map Foundation, an activist group devoted to reducing what it sees as overconsumption in rich countries, kicks off the holiday season on the day after Thanksgiving by sponsoring "Planetary Buy Nothing Day"—a twenty-four-hour moratorium on consumer spending. But, in the countdown to Christmas, the news media supply frequent briefings about the volume of holiday sales and advertisers urge us to splurge in the shopping days that remain.

International forums also get locked into one-sided perspectives on consumption. On the one hand, transnational companies and international institutions advocating economic privatization triumphantly promise global access to the American Dream. On the other hand, critics from the North as well as the South not infrequently indict Northern consumption as an unsustainable global ideal and the chief cause of environmental and cultural destruction. Sometimes these rival positions hastily generalize from equally unbalanced but different sets of cases. Frequently they evaluate the same facts in contrary ways. In this collection we have sought to bring these opposing views into conversation with each other and, more importantly, to supplement them with writers who seek less one-sided positions.

A third impediment to moral reflection on consumption practices has been the ways in which consumption has been addressed academically over the past fifty years. Although earlier economists such as Adam Smith, Alfred Marshall, Thorstein Veblen, and James Duesenberry investigated and evaluated consumption practices, postwar neoclassical economists have largely ignored consumption as a topic. Mainstream economists—and often their critics—emphasize production of goods and services rather than their consumption. Consumers are conceived as insatiable preferences maximizers. Economists view particular consumer preferences either as "exogenous" and beyond criticism or as effects of production systems (for instance, supply, advertising, and marketing). With respect to developing countries, mainstream economists urge economic growth that is fueled by investment and savings rather than consumption. Until recently, those concerned with the limits of growth and the effects of human beings on the environment tended to blame production technologies or exploding populations rather than excessive or unbalanced consumption.

In recent years academics in many fields have challenged the mainstream economic approach to (and neglect of) consumption. Breaking out of narrow disciplinary concerns, a loosely allied group of social scientists has addressed consumption with keen awareness of work done in other fields.[4] Instead of describing consumers as insatiable utility-maximizers and making consumption an appendage of production, these scholars view consumers as expressing a variety of values and conceive consumption choices as having diverse sorts of consequences. My decision to buy a car, for example, has several dimensions that can only be separated artificially. My selection expresses something about the kind of person I am—adventurous, macho, patriotic ("Buy American"), cool, environmentally conscious, conservative, and so forth. Depending on such technical qualities as the vehicle's durability, repairability, fuel efficiency, and weight, my choice will have implications for the environment. Where the car was manufactured and/or assembled will make a difference to capital flows and employment. The very fact that I choose to own a car will also affect, when combined with similar choices of others, the future of transportation, both public and private. To understand personal and collective consumption choices requires knowledge of a variety of facts—noneconomic as well as economic—and values.

However, even this interdisciplinary approach to consumption has not been a clear gain in the search for reasonable consumption standards. For the new consumption scholars often uncritically assume doctrines

that impede the quest for a responsible approach to consumption—
value neutrality, consumer sovereignty, and/or moral relativism.

The value neutralist mistakenly believes that moral assessments of
consumption practices inevitably distort the scientific task of interpreting and explaining these practices. It certainly is true that we should
not permit our hopes and fears to interfere with the investigation, interpretation, and explanation of the empirical facts about consumption.
Before *assessing* consumption practices, we must *understand* their
causes, meanings, and consequences. This volume includes essays that
offer empirical analyses, explanations, and disagreements. For instance,
several authors differ over whether global production–consumption systems are surpassing the earth's carrying capacity and whether the latter
is a meaningful notion. Others disagree over whether the planet is running out of places to grow food and whether agro-business will be able
to continue to improve productivity without adverse environmental consequences. Authors in part II argue for various accounts of why we
consume (the way we do). Several authors in part VI compare Northern
and Southern consumption patterns, and pose important empirical questions about the global diffusion of a middle-class lifestyle. Having done
or availed themselves of empirical work, however, our authors go on to
deliberate about and to judge the worth of consumption choices and
practices. Our readers are urged to do likewise.

The doctrine of consumer sovereignty also blocks moral deliberation
and judgment about consumption choices. One not atypical advocate of
consumer sovereignty argues that no consumption norm is needed because either "an individual should be considered the best judge of his
economic welfare" or "even if [the individual] is not the best judge, he
should have the right to decide."[5] Yet even responsible adults, who arguably should have the legal right to make (most) consumption choices,
have reason to believe that consumption norms may enlighten and guide
their choices rather than reduce their liberty.

The moral relativist argues that since consumption patterns are relative to different societies and since societies differ, there is no objectively reasonable ethic of consumption. Even if we accept this highly
debatable premise that consumption patterns are culturally relative, the
conclusion does not follow that the search for general cross-cultural
consumption principles is impossible or undesirable, especially if the
resultant general principles call for diverse applications in different social contexts. And even if we abandon a full-fledged and *specific* ethical
universalism, we can argue that each person and culture—in the light
of some universal *general* principles—should critically evaluate its own
consumption ethic. It may be true that reasonable and agreed-upon consumption standards are, as Michael Schudson argues in this volume,

"more likely to be worked out in the thick of politics than in any clear-cut philosophical guidelines."[6] But, as Schudson acknowledges, "people should live by some set of moral rules for consumption." For "how much and what we consume can have moral consequences."[7] Most of the following essays, including those by social scientists, go well beyond moral relativism to at least implicit and often explicit moral judgments concerning consumption patterns and political responses to them.[8]

In summary, the essays in the present volume aim to understand and *normatively assess* the causes, nature, and consequences of American (and other) patterns of consumption from a variety of interacting perspectives. Furthermore, this collection examines and evaluates several explicit proposals for principles, and procedures for arriving at such principles, that would help Americans and people in other cultures distinguish good consumption from bad.

Completing the Question

Alan Durning, a critic of current American consumption, asks in the title of his 1992 book, *How Much is Enough?*[9] This question, however, is incomplete. We must go on to ask, "How much of *what?*," "Enough for *whom?*," and "Enough for *what purpose?*" What is insufficient for an opulent life might be too much for a spiritually austere life and just right for some other life (for instance, the good life as understood in Aristotelian terms). It all depends on what is being consumed, who is consuming it, and what are the purposes and effects of the consumption choice. Distinguishing and relating these questions will help frame the consumption debate and situate the essays collected in this volume.

Enough of What?

Approaches to consumption differ with respect to the objects consumed and what it means to consume them. In the mainstream economic or "national accounts" conception of consumption, what is consumed consists of goods and services produced for and purchased in the market, regardless of whether the purchasers are individuals, households, governments, or corporations and regardless of whether the items are used, altered, or used up.[10] Consumption, contrasted with both production and investment, is that part of economic output that includes everything from household groceries, corporate paper purchases, the services of public school teachers, and the clean up of oilspills. Something that is not purchased in the market or—on a more elastic version—cannot be assigned a shadow price, such as love, is not a consumption object. In this economic approach, consumption as a process contrasts with production, and controversy exists about which process is causally determinative.[11]

What can be called the "household conception" narrows this more general economic perspective so that consumers' goods "consist of goods and services bought by households for their personal use."[12] In this approach, consumer goods are limited to such things as dwellings, furnishings, transportation, clothing, food, medical care, child care, entertainment, water, energy, and so forth. Household consumption can be distinguished, on the one hand, from both household investments or savings and, on the other hand, from both government and corporate investment in replaceable goods such as highways, dams, factories, machines, office buildings, office furniture, and equipment. The latter goods "never end up in any consumer's possession"[13] and "typically last a long time and are replaced when they wear out."[14] An equally important distinction can be drawn between *household* or *personal* consumption and *public* consumption. Governments purchase goods, such as paper, and services, such as those of public school teachers and government lawyers.[15] Government agencies and nongovernmental joint enterprises—companies, clubs, and charities and other not-for-profit organizations—make consumption choices such as whether and how to recycle paper or increase energy efficiency. Although individuals may make the consumption choices, they do so on behalf of their group.

An even narrower definition of *domestic* consumption excludes services and subsistence goods and includes only those household commodities that bring nonessential convenience, enjoyment, or savings in labor—for instance, jewelry, Gucci boots, big-screen televisions, VCRs, microwaves, fragrance diffusers, electronic organizers, leaf blowers, and cellular phones. Although critics of consumerism sometimes denigrate these items as junk,[16] fans of consumerism affirm their importance for the American Dream or self-indulgently refer to them as toys.

Quite different than the definitions hitherto discussed is the environmental or the "energy and materials" conception of consumption objects. In this view (clarified and employed, for example, by Paul C. Stern), what is consumed are natural resources—energy, such as electricity and natural gas, and materials, such as air, soil, water, timber, and coal.[17] Consumption consists of any process by which humans interact with and alter the biophysical world. Not only the use of products after the point of sale but also investment activities, production processes, and marketing strategies "consume" insofar as they result in resource use and transformation. In this environmental conception, economic activity, for instance, buying an hour on the Internet, may not consume (very much) at all while a noneconomic activity, such as a wedding or religious ritual, may significantly transform materials and energy. The difference between the economic and environmental conceptions of consumption goods comes out clearly in their very different categorization of such things as federal dams and private factories. In the economic conception, these items are investment goods rather than consumption goods. In contrast, the environmental conception views the construction, use, and upkeep of these objects as kinds of consumption; for these activities, by using and altering physical materials and energy, transform the biophysical world.

In his essay in this volume as well as in his other writings, Herman E. Daly develops a metaphysical or foundational version of this environmental conception. For Daly, since nothing is ever produced or destroyed, consumption transforms matter and energy and thereby increases entropy or decreases the usefulness of resources. The true answer to the question "How much of what?" refers not to the goods and services bought and used but the more comprehensive notion of *throughput:* "the flow beginning with raw material inputs, followed by their conversion into commodities, and finally into waste outputs."[18]

A recent group of sociologists, anthropologists, historians, and other social scientists approach the objects and processes of consumption in a way that differs significantly from the economic/household and the environmental conceptions. From this perspective, what is consumed is *meaning.* When people shop for, buy, use, and display market goods and services, or when they accept governmental goods and services, they create, appropriate, modify, and express personal or social meanings. A cap with the logo of the Boston Red Sox is a material carrier of meaning. For the Red Sox fan living far from Boston, the hat expresses nostalgic identification with a geographical place, personal roots, and a regional way of life and differentiates the wearer from his neighbors. The same cap, worn by a native tour guide in the Costa Rican rain forest, may express entrepreneurial savvy and the ambition to live like a gringo. Rather than emphasize emulation and competition for social status as the motive for consumption, as Thorstein Veblen did, the new scholars attend to the ways that "individuals and groups objectify themselves and their values through their material culture and consumption acts."[19] By studying the meanings embodied in "objects of desire," these scholars seek to explain why individuals and groups consume the way they do and why changes occur in consumption patterns.

Enough for Whom?

To complete the question "How much is enough?" we also must ask "How much for whom or what?" A given consumption choice or practice may have effects—positive, negative, or neutral—on four distinguishable kinds of "recipients." First, a consumption decision or pattern may affect—beneficially, detrimentally, or indifferently—the consumer herself. Although we typically think of human individuals as the agents of consumption, we can also investigate the typical consumer activities of aggregates, such as housewives or Americans, and of groups, such as particular households, companies, not-for-profit organizations, or nations.

Second, in addition to affecting the consumer herself, consumption acts may have an impact on others; they may benefit or harm our fellow citizens, our descendants, or people in other countries. My freshly painted house may, depending on the color, gladden or sadden my neighbor's eye and affect her property's value. Depending on the brand, my purchase of fashionable sportswear may contribute to a retailer's and a manufacturer's profits but may also help maintain sweatshops in the United States and abroad.[20] The food, clothing, and crafts that Americans buy through corporations or nonprofit organizations may help artisan and agricultural cooperatives in developing countries but this dependence on foreign markets may distort the local economy.[21]

Third, individual or collective consumption practices may strengthen or weaken values and institutions deemed essential to our communities and nation. Some argue, for example, that widespread choice of private schooling weakens public education. Others, equally in favor of good education, contend that greater choice of private schools—made possible, for example, by publicly subsidized vouchers—would strengthen public education, since public schools would have to improve in order to compete for students. Another example: Robert Putnam has ignited an important public debate concerning the social significance of one household commodity—television. Putnam argues that television viewing is the decisive cause of the putative increase in American social isolation, public apathy, and incivility.[22] Whatever the facts of the matter, the general point is that individual consumption decisions, provided that a sufficiently large number of other people make the same decisions, can have significant effects on our institutions and ideals.

Finally, a given personal, governmental, or corporate consumption practice may have effects on the environment or the natural world. Automobiles deplete nonrenewable resources and, especially in large cities, pollute the air. Houses with solar heating conserve nature. Farmers, who degrade and erode soil, may plant hedgerows and restore nature. As the essays by Daly and Mark Sagoff demonstrate, controversy exists as to whether it is possible to measure the *totality* (scale or level) of environmental impacts or only the amounts of *particular kinds* of effects on, for instance, air and water quality. Both sides in this debate, however, recognize that it is often essential to disaggregate environmentally significant consumption in order to understand its impact on different sorts of nonrenewable and renewable resources.

Scientific research determines the causes, direct effects, and further consequences of the diverse consumption acts that different sorts of agents perform. Such research may resolve apparently intractable disputes—for example, the controversy concerning the greenhouse effect. Empirical investigation of the multiple causes and impacts of consumption, however, is not sufficient. Normative assessment is also called for. Ethicists, and, more broadly, citizens, should deliberate and decide which impacts are harmful, which are beneficial, and what should be our standards of assessment. To know how much is *enough,* we must know how to determine and apply reasonable criteria.

Enough for What Purpose?

Consumption choices serve many purposes and hence can be assessed by many standards. From ethical, aesthetic, and prudential points of view, citizens and ethicists evaluate the various impacts of consumption practices. They also deliberate about and choose various norms or standards. If we are going to proceed in accordance with our deepest normative convictions, what should we mean by the "harms" and "benefits" that consumption, in all its forms, produces? Among the normative concepts employed in the following essays are the following: utility (happiness, preference satisfaction), basic-need satisfaction, well-being, quality of life, seemliness, sustainable living, civic renewal, frugality, environmental health, environmental carrying capacity, and optimal scale. These concepts, sometimes competing and sometimes converging, are useful in making sense of what is normatively good, bad, and ugly. Consumption decisions, for instance, may be evaluated normatively insofar as they promote, undermine, or are neutral with respect to the well-being, quality of life, or moral duties of the individual consumers themselves. Consumption practices may responsibly help or impermissibly harm those who are distant in time and place. Consumption habits may enhance or damage such institutions and values as democracy, civic culture, or employment. Consumption choices—whether personal, governmental, or corporate—may be too much, too little, or of the wrong sort for a healthy and sustainable environment.

Standards employed to assess consumption also may be linked to the concepts of moral responsibility to formulate the obligations of various duty-bearers to others, both near and far. Several essays in our volume, especially those in parts III, IV, V, and VI take up the question of obligation in relation to consumption practices. What moral and prudential obligations, if any, do we have when we make consumption choices? Discretionary income that we spend on ourselves might have been better spent on others less fortunate. Do affluent individuals and nations have an obligation based on justice to consume less in order that destitute persons and societies may consume more or better? Or would such actions, however well-intentioned, be morally wrong or at least beyond the call of duty? Should I (or my group) do more than my (our) "fair share" if others persist in doing less than theirs?[23] How should we understand and weigh our sometimes conflicting duties to ourselves, our institutions, others, and the environment?

Which social institutions, if any, have obligations to reinforce or alter consumption practices and promote better consumption practices? In this regard, what are the responsibilities, unique or shared, of families, voluntary organizations (such as churches), businesses, the various levels of government, and international organizations? In particular, given the importance of individual liberty and the dangers of a paternalistic government, what role, if any, should government play in shaping consumer desires and consumption choices? How should we assess the various instruments that governments might use, including such domestic policy tools as legal prohibition of certain drugs, governmental inspection and regulation of the food and restaurant industries, consumption taxes on luxury items, presidential use of the bully pulpit, subsidies or tax breaks for homeowners, and trade restrictions on imported goods, or such international policy tools as global agreements for either voluntary or mandatory limits on greenhouse gas emissions?[24] It is not enough to know how much is enough. We also need to know what should be done about inappropriate consumption and who should do it.

Causal and Ethical Linkages

In distinguishing the four kinds of subjects or objects affected by consumption practices—the consumer herself, other people, institutions, and the environment—we do not wish to overlook the fact that they are often causally related to each other. If my gas-guzzling and smoke-belching car contributes unduly to the depletion of oil reserves and to environmental pollution, then my own quality of life and that of my grandchildren eventually may be lowered. Likewise, consumption choices that are good for the environment, other people, and the basic structure of our society in the long run may elevate my own well-being. But good things do not always converge. Reasonably priced consumer goods that appear to promote or protect the consumer's own well-being—sportswear, for example—may be produced by Central American children working for a pittance in deplorable conditions.[25] Likewise, consumption choices that decrease the consumer's well-being may be a boon to others. For example, instead of buying a more spacious and comfortable house, I might contribute to the restoration of the Chesapeake Bay.

An ethics of consumption coupled with relevant empirical information may facilitate consumption choice if and when our various responsibilities converge. Such an ethic, however, may also make matters harder as well as easier. Decisions may become more difficult as we become aware of our many and sometimes conflicting obligations—to ourselves, our compatriots, our institutions, those distant in time and space, and the environment—and recognize that we often lack surefire ways to resolve those clashes. But there is, we believe, no alternative to the approach adopted here: detailed empirical analysis, followed by careful normative reflection. Only then can genuine conflicts of principle be identified and resolved.

The Essays

We believe that the essays collected here will contribute to empirically informed and policy-relevant ethical reflection on consumption. The collection is divided into six parts.

Part I, "Consumption, Natural Resources, and the Environment," examines the impact of human and, especially, American resource use on the environment. As we have seen, whereas economists define consumption in relation to all goods and services purchased in the market, environmentalists and ecological economists conceive consumption as the human transformation of energy and materials. The centerpiece of this part is an exchange between Herman E. Daly and Mark Sagoff. Daly argues that there are physical limits to consumption and that a sustainable future requires that the United States lead the way in reducing consumption levels. Environmental philosopher Mark Sagoff criticizes the assumptions of Daly's ecological economics and argues that if we are to respect nature and live decent lives, we must consume not less but *differently*.[26] Allen L. Hammond, who is especially worried about the degradation of renewable resources, seeks to defend a middle ground between Malthusians, who believe we are running out of natural resources, and Cornucopians, who insist that more consumption is always better. Paul E. Waggoner examines the changing relationships among American diets, agricultural productivity, and cropland; he argues that increases in agricultural yields are the key to "sparing the land for nature."[27] Robert Goodland offers both prudential and environmental arguments for diets in which we eat lower on the food chain and eschew grain-fed meat. Part I concludes with philosopher and law professor David Luban's pessimistic speculation that both "safe-growth" and "no-growth" societies can be achieved only at the risk of destabilizing democratic institutions and replacing them with significantly more authoritarian regimes.

In part II, "Explaining Consumption," our contributors try to explain why individuals and households buy the goods and services they do. Each theorist also explores the import of his or her account for a moral assessment of consumption motives and practices. Juliet B. Schor criticizes neoclassical economics for its assumptions about consumption and advances "a new economic critique of consumer society." Colin Campbell, an English sociologist and representative of noneconomic consumption studies, stresses "imaginative pleasure seeking" as the key to the emergence and vitality of Western consumer culture. Judith Lichtenberg examines the phenomenon of "consuming because others consume," noting that much of our personal consumption is explained by a variety of "other-regarding" reasons. After providing an overview of household expenditure in the United States, Jerome M. Segal explains these consumption patterns by positing a core set of economic needs that consumers seek to satisfy. He then argues that the real income (adjusted for inflation) required to satisfy these needs has increased over the years and that policy tools might halt the growth of this "need-required income."

The essays in part III, "Assessing Consumption," examine the impact of current consumption practices on the lives of American consumers—on their happiness, quality of life, identity, or moral character—and make proposals for improving consumption practices. Before exploring new consumption alternatives, social psychologist Paul L. Wachtel criticizes American consumerism on the grounds that, while each purchase brings consumers some satisfaction, they are not satisfied with their lives as a whole. Political scientist Robert E. Lane contends that friendship and meaningful work, rather than money and consumer goods, bring happiness and that American consumerism frequently causes deep unhappiness. Recognizing the worth of many consumption choices, Michael Schudson finds fault with (and learns from) what he calls the Puritan, Quaker, Republican, and Antibourgeois critiques of consumer culture. Rather than succumb to a fashionable moral relativism, he endorses and contributes to the quest for a nonrelativist consumption norm. Drawing on Schudson's work and that of other recent consumption scholars, philosopher and legal scholar Alan Strudler and marketing professor Eleonora Curlo develop an expressivist theory in which consumption choices express one's identity and basic values.

They then apply this theory to assess expenditures on lawn care in the American Southwest.

Parts IV and V, "Consumption and the Good Life: The Capabilities Approach" and "Consumption and the Good Life: Religious and Theological Perspectives," not only assess consumption practices but also seek norms or general standards for evaluating personal and societal expenditures. In part IV, economist Amartya Sen and three philosophers—Martha C. Nussbaum, Jerome M. Segal, and David A. Crocker —explain, assess, and apply to consumption choices somewhat differing versions of Sen's seminal "capability approach" to the quality of human life. Sen argues against approaches to the standard of living that emphasize, on the one hand, commodities or opulence and, on the other hand, utilitarian happiness or preference satisfaction. In contrast, Sen contends that human well-being and, more narrowly, the living standard should be conceived in terms of certain valuable human functionings and capabilities to so function. In her chapter Nussbaum criticizes a coercive interpretation of Aristotelianism and defends a liberal—-capabilities—version. She then utilizes this perspective to identify appropriate and inappropriate state action with respect to consumption and other types of choices. Segal evaluates Nussbaum's arguments and sketches an alternative approach to good functioning in the economic realm. Crocker maintains that a functioning/capabilities interpretation of human well-being or enlightened prudence supplies a norm that avoids materialism and antimaterialism and offers guidance in making consumption choices that help our lives go well.

In part V representatives of three important American religious communities address, from the perspective of their respective traditions, the ethical and policy questions underlying consumption and stewardship. Drawing on both classic and more recent teachings, rabbi and theologian Eliezer Diamond offers a Jewish approach to personal and societal consumption. Economist Charles K. Wilber sets forth a Roman Catholic ethics of consumption. Finally, Protestant social ethicist James A. Nash endeavors to rehabilitate the personal virtue of frugality and employ it in assessing unjust and unsustainable economic and social practices.[28]

In addition to affecting the environment and our own lives, American consumption has diverse consequences for other nations and peoples. The chapters in part VI, "Consumption and International Justice," seek to understand and ethically assess the actual and ideal or just relations between, on the one hand, consumption in the North and, on the other hand, well-being in the South. Allen L. Hammond compares consumption in the United States and in poor countries, especially India, discusses the multiple consequences of Northern consumption on the

South, examines the environmental effects of poverty and population pressure, and explores policy options for responsible consumption and a sustainable future. Demographer Nathan Keyfitz clarifies the actual and ideal relations between consumption and population. Among other things, Keyfitz argues that a responsible global compact calls for changes in the level of both Northern consumption and Southern population. He further argues that the automobile is both the best symbol of a middle-class lifestyle and a leading cause of environmental degradation. Thomas W. Pogge argues that we bear a "negative responsibility" to reduce world poverty because "we participate in its unjust perpetuation." He also contends that those affluent nations that make more extensive use of the resources of our planet should compensate countries that, involuntarily, use very little. Legal scholar David Wasserman addresses the ways various moral considerations should constrain human appropriation and consumption of resources. Wasserman argues for establishing a positive foundation, based on doing good and avoiding harm, for protecting global resources and, to this end, assesses the merits of trusteeship and stewardship models of global responsibility. In the final essay of the section and the volume, Costa Rican philosopher Luis A. Camacho assesses the debate in his own country about consumerism and the issue of consumption as a theme in the North–South dialogue. Camacho argues that the slogan "the South has too many people and the North has too much consumption . . . hides a complex web of problems."[29] One lesson that can be drawn from Camacho's essay is that an ethics of consumption is not just timely in developed nations. Ethical reflection on consumption has an important role to play wherever citizens deliberate and decide on their society's development path and its relation to the global order.

Concluding Remarks

With respect to the following collection as a whole, three comments are appropriate. First, although consumption is important, it is not everything. Bad consumption is not the cause of all the world's problems, nor good consumption their cure. Just as earlier investigators often mistakenly paid attention to productivity, population, environment, ethnicity, and so forth in isolation from each other and from consumption, there is also the danger of a one-sided focus on consumption patterns to the exclusion of their links to other social factors and institutions. An ethics of consumption is meant to supplement and not replace such inquiries as an ethics of population, an environmental ethics, and an ethics of employment and poverty reduction.[30] It is only one—largely neglected—part of an ethic of personal conduct and institutional arrangements.

Second, we are keenly aware that more work is needed on consumption responsibilities, including their source, nature, bearers, and limits. Who should do what (and why) with respect to improving consumption choices and practices? What are the distinctive and shared consumption responsibilities of individuals, families, religious organizations, private associations, companies, governments on various levels, and international bodies of various kinds? In particular, attention should be given to consumption practices of governments and publicly oriented enterprises and to the multiple responsibilities and pressures that beset individuals within these organizations. Several of our essays tackle these issues, but as we move from ethics to policy and politics, much remains to be done in theory as well as practice.

Third, we hope that this volume contributes to cross-cultural discussions concerning appropriate consumption. Debates about the shape and limits of responsible consumption are occurring in both industrialized and developing countries throughout the world. As some American consumption patterns—cars, television, Levis, computers, and McDonald's hamburgers—spread around the globe, those patterns are being subjected to intense scrutiny. Sometimes American consumerist values are uncritically embraced; sometimes they are passionately rejected. More often, as Charles Mann points out, people around the world want what Americans have but also to be "aggressively themselves—a contradictory enterprise."[31] Most promising is the occurrence throughout the world of critical discussion, public deliberation, and social experimentation about how much is enough and what consumption is appropriate. A more nuanced American debate about the ethics of consumption—about the role of commodities in the good life, justice, and global stewardship—will benefit greatly from this global dialogue, and, we hope, contribute to it as well.

Notes

We gratefully acknowledge support for this research from the Global Stewardship Initiative of the Pew Charitable Trusts and from the National Endowment for the Humanities Grant # RO 22709-94. The views expressed are ours alone and not necessarily those of any association or funding agency.

1. Grant McCracken, *Culture and Consumption: New Approaches to the Symbolic Character of Consumer Goods and Activities* (Bloomington and Indianapolis: Indiana University Press, 1988), 139 n. 2.

2. Betsy Taylor, "The Curse of Christmas Present," *Washington Post,* 1 December 1996, C3.

3. Christopher Caldwell, "The Gift of Excess: Why You Can Indulge with a Clear Conscience," *Washington Post,* 1 December 1996, C3.

4. For critics of disciplinary isolation and of the hegemony of neoclassical economics with respect to consumption, see Ben Fine and Ellen Leopold, *The World of Consumption* (London and New York: Routledge, 1993); Daniel Miller, ed., *Acknowledging Consumption: A Review of New Studies* (New York: Routledge, 1995); and Neva R. Goodwin, Frank Ackerman, and David Kiron, eds., *The Consumer Society* (Washington, D.C., and Covelo, Calif.: Island Press, 1997). In the Miller volume, representatives of a variety of academic approaches, including anthropology, consumer research, geography, history, media studies, psychology, and sociology, provide overviews of the ways in which their respective disciplines approach consumption and what they have learned from other academic fields. The Goodwin volume consists of brief summaries of chapters from recent books and articles on consumption, many of which are interdisciplinary in character. Ten of the Goodwin collection's short essays summarize either much longer chapters in the present volume, *Ethics of Consumption,* or other writings by this volume's contributors.

5. S. K. Nath, *A Reappraisal of Welfare Economics* (London: Routledge & Kegan Paul, 1969), 9; quoted in G. Peter Penz, *Consumer Sovereignty and Human Interests* (Cambridge: Cambridge University Press, 1986), 14–15.

6. Michael Schudson, "Delectable Materialism: Second Thoughts on Consumer Culture," 266.

7. Schudson, "Delectable Materialism," 266.

8. Of those consumption social scientists not included in the present volume, Daniel Miller is most outspoken in calling for an ethics of consumption. "If we can rise to consciousness in our consumption activities . . . , then there is at least the glimmer of hope that responsibility could confront irresponsibility in citizenship, and morality could confront the amorality of the market. The task of the new study of consumption remains therefore the original goal of the Enlightenment, which is a rational morality born of consciousness." "Consumption as the Vanguard of History: A Polemic by Way of an Introduction," in *Acknowledging Consumption,* ed. Miller, 50.

9. Alan Thein Durning, *How Much is Enough? The Consumer Society and the Future of the Earth* (New York and London: W. W. Norton, 1992).

10. For summaries of both important mainstream and alternative economic approaches to consumption, see Goodwin et al., *The Consumer Society,* parts V and VI.

11. Marxists and those influenced by John Kenneth Galbraith (*The Affluent Society* [Cambridge, Mass.: Riverside Press, 1958]), argue that productive forces, including marketing and advertising, asymmetrically *determine* consumption preferences and consumer "behavior." Daniel Miller delights in turning this view on its head: consumption is "the vanguard of history," and the consumer is "the global dictator" (Miller, "Consumption as the Vanguard of History," in *Acknowledging Consumption,* 1–57).

12. Robert L. Heilbroner and Lester C. Thurow, *Economics Explained* (Englewood Cliffs, N.J.: Prentice Hall, 1982), 64.

13. Heilbroner and Thurow, *Economics Explained*, 64.

14. Heilbroner and Thurow, *Economics Explained*, 65.

15. Heilbroner and Thurow, *Economics Explained*, 65.

16. Alan Thein Durning, "Preamble: An Invitation to the American Dream," in *Redefining the American Dream: The Search for Sustainable Consumption,* Conference Report (Merck Family Fund, 1995), 1.

17. Paul C. Stern, "Toward a Working Definition of Consumption for Environmental Research and Policy," in *Environmentally Significant Consumption: Research Directions*, ed. Paul C. Stern, Thomas Dietz, Vernon W. Ruttan, Robert H. Socolow, and James L. Sweeny (Washington, D.C.: National Academy Press, 1997), 12–25. Cf. the similar definition of consumption in "Population and Consumption," *President's Council on Sustainable Development Task Force Report* (Washington, D.C.: Government Printing Office, 1996), 1–2. Our classification of different conceptions of consumption objects is indebted to Stern's essay. But while Stern's aim is limited to identifying scientifically researchable questions with respect to one kind of consumption, namely, the environmental consequences of the transformation of materials and energy, our interest is broader and includes normative assessment: How should we understand and assess the various sorts of consumption agents and patterns with respect to their impact on human well-being and institutions as well as the environment?

18. Herman E. Daly, *Beyond Growth: The Economics of Sustainable Development* (Boston: Beacon Press, 1996), 28.

19. Miller, "Consumption as the Vanguard of History," 54.

20. William Branigin, "Sweatshop Instead of Paradise," *Washington Post,* 10 September 1995, A1, A12.

21. See *Grassroots Development* 20, no. 2 (1996) for essays that document the ways in which small producers and craftspeople in Latin America are attempting, with more and less success, to find niches in the global marketplace. Pueblo to People is a nonprofit organization whose goal is to provide North American consumers with access to clothing, housewares, and food produced by Latin American artisan and agricultural cooperatives.

22. Robert D. Putnam, "Bowling Alone: America's Declining Social Capital," *Journal of Democracy* 6, no. 10 (January 1995): 65–78; and, "The Strange Disappearance of Civic America," *American Prospect* 24 (Winter 1996): 34–48. In "What If Civic Life Didn't Die?" *American Prospect* 25 (March/April 1996): 18–20, Michael Schudson challenges Putnam's argument that civic engagement is decreasing and, even if it were, that television viewing is the best explanation.

23. For a recent "hard line" argument that it is seriously wrong for affluent people—who are much better off and could easily lessen distant suffering—to refuse to sacrifice some of their time and wealth for the global poor, see Peter Unger, *Living High and Letting Die: Our Illusion of Innocence* (New York and Oxford: Oxford University Press, 1996). In part VI of the present volume,

Thomas W. Pogge argues that affluent world citizens have a responsibility to aid the global poor based not on our affluence but "on the fact that we participate in, and profit from the unjust and coercive imposition of severe poverty." For the classical statement of a less stringent conception of the demands of beneficence, see Susan Wolf, "Moral Saints," *Journal of Philosophy* 79 (August 1982): 419–39. General discussions of these issues occur in Catherine Wilson, "On Some Alleged Limitations to Moral Endeavor," *Journal of Philosophy* 90 no. 6 (June 1993): 275–89; and Liam Murphy, "The Demands of Beneficence," *Philosophy and Public Affairs* 22, no. 4 (Fall 1993): 267–92.

24. Jessica Mathews argues that mandatory controls are part of the solution to the problem "about how much to do to restrain the [global] warming, how fast, and by whom" ("Tricky Talks," *Washington Post*, 27 January 1997, A19). For an argument about the justice of an international comprehensive treaty covering greenhouse gases, see Henry Shue, "Subsistence Emissions and Luxury Emissions," *Law & Policy* 15, no. 1 (January 1993): 39–59.

25. American investments—whether or not we follow the environmental conception and count investments as part of consumption—also may enable us to increase our wealth by acts that cause the exploitation of workers in poor or newly industrialized countries: "The companies that can push workers hardest win the drive to the bottom, and with the right stocks I will participate, I will win" (Ted C. Fishman, "The Joys of Global Investment: Shipping Home the Fruits of Misery," *Harper's Magazine*, February 1997, 41).

26. See also Mark Sagoff, "Do We Consume Too Much?" *Atlantic Monthly*, June 1997, 80–96.

27. See Paul E. Waggoner, "How Much Land Can Ten Billion People Spare for Nature?" (Ames, Iowa: The Council on Agricultural Science and Technology, 1994).

28. For a highly critical conservative Protestant assessment of American consumerism, see Rodney Clapp, "Why the Devil Takes Visa: A Christian Response to the Triumph of Consumerism," *Christianity Today*, 7 October 1996, 19–33.

29. Camacho, "Consumption as a Topic for the North–South Dialogue," 559 (this volume).

30. "Ethics and Global Population," *Report from the Institute for Philosophy & Public Policy* 13, no. 4 (Fall 1993); J. Ronald Engel and Joan Gibb Engel, eds., *Ethics of Environment and Development: Global Challenge, International Response* (London: Belhaven Press; Tucson: University of Arizona Press, 1990); William Aiken and Hugh LaFollette, eds., *World Hunger and Morality*, 2d ed. (Upper Saddle River, N.J.: Prentice Hall, 1996).

31. Charles C. Mann, "Betting the Planet," foreword to *Material World: A Global Family Portrait*, by Peter Menzel (San Francisco: Sierra Club Books, 1994), 9.

1

Consumption: Value Added, Physical Transformation, and Welfare

Herman E. Daly

There are limits to the total amount of resources that the human economy can consume from the ecosystem that contains it; for the ecosystem—both as supplier of resources and as absorber of waste products— is itself limited. The earth ecosystem is finite, nongrowing, and materially closed. Though it is open to the flow of solar energy, that flow is also nongrowing and finite, even if quite large and currently underutilized. Historically, the limits of the ecosystem were not binding upon economic growth, because the economy was small relative to the total ecosystem. The world was "empty." But now it is "full," and the limits are more and more binding—not necessarily like brick walls, but more like tightly stretched rubber bands.

The total flow of resource consumption, or throughput, is the product of population times per capita consumption. John Stuart Mill, writing in 1857, foresaw that increasing the resource flow, and thus moving from an empty to a full world, would eliminate more and more of life's pleasantness and eventually lead to impossible demands upon the earth:

Nor is there much satisfaction in contemplating the world with nothing left to the spontaneous activity of nature; with every rood of land brought into cultivation, which is capable of growing food for human beings; every flowery waste or natural pasture plowed up, all quadrupeds or birds which are not domesticated for man's use exterminated as his rivals for food, every hedgerow or superfluous tree rooted out, and scarcely a place left where a wild shrub or flower could grow without being eradicated as a weed in the name of improved agriculture. If the earth must lose that great portion of its pleasantness which it owes to things that the unlimited in-

crease of wealth and population would extirpate from it, for the mere purpose of enabling it to support a larger, but not a better or a happier
population, I sincerely hope, for the sake of posterity, that they will be
content to be stationary, long before necessity compels them to it.[1]

Today there is widespread recognition of the importance of slowing
population growth and incipient attention to the challenge of limiting
the growth of per capita consumption. As the quotation from Mill demonstrates, concern about unlimited resource use is hardly new. Yet there
is also a history of wishful thinking on these matters. Consider, in this
light, the theory of the "demographic transition," which holds that population growth will stop if only per capita consumption reaches a certain level. Some believers in the demographic transition urge us to count
on economic growth alone to reduce population pressures and forestall
resource scarcities. But it is not very reassuring to hear that one term of
a product will stop growing if only the other term grows faster, when it
is the product of the two terms that must be limited. Will the average
Indian's consumption have to rise to that of the average Swede before
Indian fertility falls to the Swedish level? Can the eroded and crowded
country of India support that many cars, power plants, buildings, and
so on?
    One way out of this dilemma is the technological fix frequently re-
ferred to as "dematerialization." The Wuppertal Institute in Germany,
one of the places where interesting work is being done on the subject,
uses this somewhat extravagant term to mean "improved resource use."
The institute explicitly calls for technology to improve resource productivity by a factor of ten—a reasonable goal and a way to buy valuable
time to deal with more fundamental problems. But some technological
optimists get carried away with dematerialization; they seem to imagine
that soon we will have no use for material resources at all. To hear them
talk, one would think that McDonald's was about to introduce the "info-
burger," consisting of a thick patty of information between two slices
of silicon, thin as communion wafers so as to emphasize the symbolic
and spiritual nature of consumption. But in truth, though we can certainly eat lower on the food chain, we cannot eat recipes. The Information Reformation, like the demographic transition before it, expands a
germ of truth into a whale of a fantasy.
    While all countries must worry about both population and per capita
consumption, it is evident that the South needs to focus more on controlling population and the North more on controlling per capita consumption. This fact will continue to play a major role in North–South
treaties and discussions. Why should the South control its population if
the resources saved thereby are merely gobbled up by Northern over-

consumption? Why should the North control its overconsumption if the saved resources will merely allow a larger number of poor people to subsist at the same level of misery? Without for a moment minimizing the necessity of population control, it is nevertheless incumbent on the North to get serious about consumption control and not simply wish that dematerialization and the demographic transition will come to the rescue. Toward this end, a reconsideration of the meaning of consumption is offered in the following pages.

Consumption and Value Added

When we speak of consumption, what is it that we think of as being consumed? Alfred Marshall, the great synthesizer of neoclassical economics, reminded us of the laws of conservation of matter and energy and the consequent impossibility of consuming the material building blocks of commodities. "Man cannot create material things. . . . His efforts and sacrifices result in changing the form or arrangement of matter to adapt it better for the satisfaction of wants. . . . As his production of material products is really nothing more than a rearrangement of matter which gives it new utilities; so his consumption of them is nothing more than a disarrangement of matter, which diminishes or destroys its utilities."[2] What we destroy or consume in consumption is the improbable arrangement of those building blocks, arrangements that give utility for humans, arrangements that were, according to Marshall, made by humans for human purposes. Human beings add utility to matter/energy. This is what we mean by production; we do not create matter/energy itself. Useful structure is added to matter/energy by the agency of labor and capital stocks. The value of this useful structure imparted by labor and capital is what economists call "value added." This value added is what is "consumed," or used up, in consumption. That to which value is being added is the flow of natural resources, conceived ultimately as the indestructible building blocks of nature.

In the passage above, Marshall refers to "new utilities" added by human beings, thus leaving open the possibility that matter might have some preexisting utility. But subsequent economists, in emphasizing new utilities or value added, have neglected to consider any value that nature has already provided. In the standard economics textbook view, we consume *only* that value which we added to natural resource flows in the first place. And then we add it again, and consume it again, without end. This vision is formalized in the famous diagram of the isolated circular flow of exchange value between firms (production) and households (consumption) found in the initial pages of every economics text-book.

Thus, for all the focus on value added, modern economists have re-markably little to say about *that to which value is being added.* It is just "matter," and its properties are not very interesting. In fact, they are becoming ever *less* interesting to economists as science uncovers their basic uniformity. As Barnett and Morse put it in their classic study, *Scarcity and Growth,* "Advances in fundamental science have made it possible to take advantage of the uniformity of [matter/energy]—a uniformity that makes it feasible, without preassignable limit, to escape the quantitative constraints imposed by the character of the earth's crust."[3] That to which value is being added is merely homogeneous, indestructible building blocks—atoms in the original sense—of which there is no conceivable scarcity. That to which value is added is there-fore inert, undifferentiated, interchangeable, and superabundant—very dull stuff indeed, compared to the value-adding agents of labor with all its human capacities, and capital that embodies the marvels of human knowledge. It is not surprising that value added is the centerpiece of economic accounting, and that the presumably passive stuff to which value is added has received minimal attention.

Consumption and Physical Transformation

In fact, however, matter/energy is not at all uniform in the quality most relevant to economics—namely, the capacity to receive and hold the rearrangements dictated by human purpose, the capacity to receive the imprint of human knowledge, the capacity to embody value added. Physicists have recognized this quality of matter/energy in the famous second law of thermodynamics, the entropy law. One implication of the entropy law is that the capacity of matter/energy to embody value wears out and must be replenished. Thus, if the economic system is to keep going, it cannot be an isolated circular flow, as the textbooks suppose. It must be an open system, receiving matter and energy *from* outside to make up for that which is dissipated *to* the outside. What is outside? The environment. What is the environment? It is, again, a complex ecosystem that is finite, nongrowing, and materially closed, while open to a nongrowing flow of solar energy. Its limited capacities for renewal must be respected by the economic subsystem.

Consumption, then, involves not only disarrangement within the eco-nomic subsystem, but also in the rest of the system, the environment, as well. Taking matter/energy from the larger system, adding value to it, using up the added value, and returning the waste clearly alters the environment. The matter/energy we return is not the same as the matter/energy we take in. If it were, we could simply use it again and again in a closed circular flow. Common observation tells us, however, and the entropy law confirms, that waste matter/energy is qualitatively different from raw materials. We irrevocably use up not only the value we add to matter, but also the value that was added by nature before we imported it into the economic subsystem and that was necessary for it to be considered a resource in the first place. This irrevocable using up of the quality of usefulness of resources does not mean that resources cannot be replenished—rather it means that they *must* be replenished if the system is to continue. Since isolated circular flows are impossible, the replenishment must come from outside, from the environment.

This perspective does not deny that human beings add value to resources by labor and capital. But the value is added to the matter/energy that is most capable of receiving and embodying it. That receptivity might be thought of as "value added by nature." Carbon atoms scattered in the atmosphere can receive value added only with an enormous expenditure of energy and other materials. Carbon atoms structured in a tree can be rearranged much more easily. Concentrated copper can hold value added; atoms of copper at average crustal abundance cannot. Energy concentrated in a lump of coal can help us add value to matter; energy at equilibrium temperature in the ocean or atmosphere cannot. The more work done by nature, the more concentrated and receptive is the resource to having value added to it, the less capital and labor will have to be expended in rearranging it to better suit our purposes.

From a utility or demand perspective, value added by nature ought to be valued equally with value added by labor and capital. But from the supply or cost side, it is not, because value added by humans has a real cost in labor and an opportunity cost in both labor and capital use. We tend to treat natural value added as a subsidy, a free gift of nature. The greater the natural subsidy, the less the cost of labor and capital needed for further arrangement; the less the humanly added value, the lower the price, and the more rapid the use. Oil from east Texas embodied a much greater net energy subsidy from nature to the economy than does offshore Alaskan oil. But its price was much lower precisely because it required less value added by labor and capital. The larger the natural subsidy, the less we value it!

Thanks in part to natural subsidies, the economy has grown relative to the total ecosystem to such an extent that the basic pattern of scarcity has changed. It used to be that adding value was limited by the supply of agents of transformation, labor, and capital. Now, value added is limited more by the availability of resources subsidized by nature to the point that they can receive value added. Mere knowledge means nothing to the economy unless it becomes incarnate in physical structures. No low-entropy matter/energy, no capital—regardless of knowledge. Of course, new knowledge may include discovery of new low-entropy resources, and new methods of transforming them to better serve human needs. But new knowledge may also discover new limits, as when the recognition of damage to the ozone layer required us to reduce emissions of chlorofluorocarbons. At a more fundamental level, science may discover new impossibility theorems. It is useful to remind technological optimists that most of the basic laws of science are statements of impossibility: it is impossible to go faster than light; it is impossible to create or destroy matter/energy; it is impossible to have perpetual motion; it is impossible to have spontaneous generation of life from nonliving things; it is impossible for an organism to live in a medium consisting only of its own waste products; and so on. The success of science and technology is largely based on its intelligent refusal to attempt the impossible. Yet this very success is frequently pointed to by technological optimists as evidence that nothing is impossible.

The physical growth of the subsystem is the transformation of natural capital into manmade capital. A tree is cut and turned into a table. We gain the service of the table; we lose the service of the tree. In a relatively empty world (small economic subsystem, ecosystem relatively empty of human beings and their artifacts), the service lost from fewer trees was nil, and the service gained from more tables was significant. In today's relatively fuller world, fewer trees means loss of significant services, and more tables are not so important—at least not where most households already have several tables, as is the case in much of the world. However, continued population growth will keep the demand for tables up, and we will incur ever greater sacrifices of natural services by cutting more and more trees, as long as population and the number of tables per capita keeps growing.

There is both a cost and a benefit to increasing total consumption, and thus the scale of the economic subsystem. The benefit is economic services gained (more tables); the cost is ecosystem services sacrificed (fewer trees to sequester carbon dioxide, provide wildlife habitat and local cooling, prevent erosion, and so on). As scale increases, marginal costs tend to rise and marginal benefits tend to fall. The law of falling marginal benefits is simply a way of saying that, as rational beings, we satisfy our most pressing wants first; after that, we use resources to satisfy wants that are less pressing. The law of increasing marginal costs in like manner means that we first use the cheapest and most easily available resources; after that, we make use of less accessible and less concentrated resources. The intersection of falling marginal benefits and rising marginal costs defines the optimal scale, beyond which further growth would cost more than it is worth—would become anti-economic.

As we come to an optimal or mature scale of economic activity, production is no longer for growth but for maintenance. As Kenneth Boulding argued almost fifty years ago, "Any discovery which renders consumption less necessary to the pursuit of living is as much an economic gain as a discovery which improves our skills of production. Production—by which we mean the exact opposite of consumption, namely, the creation of valuable things—is only necessary in order to replace the stock pile into which consumption continually gnaws."[4]

Consumption and Welfare

The theoretical existence of an optimal scale of the economic subsystem is clear in principle. What remains vague is how to measure the costs and benefits of growth. If economic policy is anything, however, it is the art of reasoning with vague quantities in support of prudent action. We can have reasons for believing that an optimal scale exists, and that we are either above it or below it, without knowing exactly where it is. For policy purposes, a judgment about which side of the optimum we are on is critical.

What are our commonsense judgments about whether we are at, below, or above the optimal scale? To show that we have exceeded the optimum, it is not necessary to show that growth is physically impossible; nor that it has catastrophic costs; nor that it would have negative or zero marginal benefit, even if free. It is only necessary to show that marginal costs are greater than marginal benefits. It is quite logical and reasonable to argue that up to the present time, the total benefits of growth have, on the whole, been greater than the total costs, and yet to hold that growth should cease because, at the margin, costs have now begun to outweigh benefits.

It is worth emphasizing that benefits from qualitative *development*—technological, social, and moral improvement—are not in question, just those from quantitative *growth*. For example, no one objects to the invention of light bulbs that give more lumens per watt or the formulation of macroeconomic policies that provide more employment per dollar of GNP whenever we are faced with unemployment. (On second thought, people *do* sometimes object to the latter, in the interests of maximizing growth; but that is exactly the kind of growth idolatry I am complaining about.)

For rich, full countries, the marginal utility of extra growth is surely low. Great sums of money have to be spent on advertising to cajole people into buying more. As we have become goods-rich, we have become time-poor. In rich countries, people die more from stress and overconsumption than from starvation. Relative, rather than absolute, income seems to be the main determinant of self-evaluated welfare, and growth is powerless to increase everyone's relative income. The effect of aggregate growth on welfare in rich countries is therefore largely self-cancelling.

What about the poor? An increase in wealth from subsistence to middle-class level surely increases welfare, if all other things are equal. There is high marginal utility in resource use that improves the lot of the poor. Should this be paid for by cutting the luxury consumption of the rich (which is low in marginal utility), or by converting more natural capital into manmade capital? The rich favor the latter, and perhaps the poor do also, because they want to emulate the rich and because they doubt the political likelihood of redistribution or imposed limits to the takeover of natural capital. Inequality is converted into pressure for growth.

However, the growth that results from the pressure of inequality often does not go to the poor. Consider for a moment what, exactly, is growing in a growth economy. In the first instance, it is the reinvested surplus that grows. Who controls the surplus? Not the poor. They only get the trickle-down from growth (if that), and even if their absolute well-being increases, their relative position is more likely to worsen than improve as a result of growth. This is especially so in light of the far more rapid rate of population growth of the poor than of the rich (due to greater natural increase and frequently to greater immigration as well). A large and growing supply of labor keeps wages from rising and thereby also keeps profits up.

A large part of our national income is devoted to expenditures to protect ourselves from the unwanted side effects of increased production and consumption. Health care expenditures rise as a result of tobacco and alcohol consumption, as well as chemical and radioactive poisoning. We pay to clean up oil spills; we spend time and money on commuting. These expenditures should be subtracted from our national income as intermediate costs of the goods whose production or consumption imposes them; but instead we add them to our gross national product, and politicians, along with their academic magicians and media jesters, rejoice in the "improvement" of the economy.

Add to these considerations the corrosive effects of economic growth on community and on moral standards. Capital and labor mobility rips communities apart in the name of growth. Further, an economy that must grow must also sell. It is easier to sell in a community with low standards—if anything goes, then nearly anything will sell, no matter how tawdry or shoddy. Common prudence is now referred to negatively as "sales resistance."

We have plenty of landmarks to suggest that we have overshot the optimal scale of the human economy (not the least of which is the declining capacity of the earth to support life in the future). But many readers will consider that too impressionistic a judgment. They will ask for numbers. In the Middle Ages, holy thought had to be expressed in Latin; today it must be expressed in numbers. Aware that numbers can indeed be useful, Clifford and John Cobb and I developed the Index of Sustainable Economic Welfare (ISEW) for the United States.[5] What we found, briefly, is that there is very little evidence that welfare in the United States has been correlated positively with gross national product since 1947. There *is* evidence, however, that in the 1980s the correlation turned negative.

The consumer society must pay attention to what Al Gore said in his excellent but too-soon forgotten book, *Earth in the Balance*: "our civilization is, in effect, addicted to the consumption of the earth itself."[6] We absolutely must break that addiction.

Notes

Originally published as "Consumption and the Environment" in *Report from the Institute for Philosophy and Public Policy*, 15, no. 4 (Special Issue Fall 1995): 4–9.

1. John Stuart Mill, *Principles of Political Economy with Some of Their Applications to Social Philosophy*, bk. IV, chap. VI, sec. 2 (Fairfield, N.J.: Augustus M. Kelley Publishers, 1987 [1848]), 750.

2. Alfred Marshall, *Principles of Economics,* 9th ed. (New York: Macmillan, 1961), 63–64.

3. Harold J. Barnett and Chandler Morse, *Scarcity and Growth* (Baltimore: Johns Hopkins University Press, 1963).

4. Kenneth Boulding, "Income or Welfare?" *Review of Economic Studies* 17 (1949): 79.

5. See Clifford W. Cobb and John B. Cobb, Jr., *The Green National Product: A Proposed Index of Sustainable Economic Welfare* (Lanham, Md.: University Press of America, 1994), and Herman Daly and John B. Cobb, Jr., *For the Common Good: Redirecting the Economy toward Community, the Environment, and a Sustainable Future*, 2d ed. (Boston: Beacon Press, 1994).

6. Al Gore, *Earth in the Balance* (Boston: Houghton Mifflin, 1992), 220.

2

Carrying Capacity and Ecological Economics

Mark Sagoff

When the tempest arose, "the mariners were afraid . . . and cast forth the wares that were in the ship into the sea, to lighten it of them." This passage from the Book of Jonah (Jon. 1:5 King James) anticipates a strategy many environmentalists recommend today. Nature surrounds us with life-sustaining systems, much as the sea supports a ship, but the ship is likely to sink if it carries too much cargo. Environmentalists therefore urge us to "keep the weight, the absolute scale, of the economy from sinking our biospheric ark."[1]

This concern about the carrying capacity of earth, reminding us of the fearful sailors on Jonah's ship, marks a departure from traditional arguments in favor of environmental protection. The traditional arguments did not rest on prudential considerations. Early environmentalists such as Henry David Thoreau cited the intrinsic properties of nature, rather than its economic benefits, as reasons to preserve it. They believed that economic activity had outstripped not its resource base but its spiritual purpose. John Muir condemned the "temple destroyers, devotees of ravaging commercialism" who "instead of lifting their eyes to the God of the mountains, lift them to the Almighty dollar."[2] This condemnation was not a call for improved cost-benefit analysis. Nineteenth-century environmentalists, seeing nature as full of divinity, regarded its protection less as an economic imperative than as a moral test.

By opposing a strictly utilitarian conception of value, writers such as Muir saved what little of nature they could from what Samuel P. Hays called the gospel of efficiency.[3] Today, however, environmentalists themselves often preach this gospel. They have developed contingent valuation methodologies to assign what they call shadow prices to intrinsic values. They construct on-line, integrated, multiscale, ecological economic models and assessments using the results of interactive, interdisciplinary, adaptive, synthetic, multifactorial, multiscale, multifunctional, networked, computational, simulational, cross-cutting, externally funded research. They address uncertainties, vulnerabilities, and surprise scenario forecasts. Thus they adopt the very economic or utilitarian approach their predecessors deplored.

In this essay, I question attempts by today's environmentalists, particularly some of those who identify themselves as ecological economists, to vindicate environmental protection on instrumental grounds. I cast doubt on hopes that the utilitarian logic of ecological economics is any more able than that of mainstream economics to provide a strong foundation for the cause of environmentalism.

Mainstream versus Ecological Economists

Mainstream economists, such as James Tobin, Robert Solow, and William B. Nordhaus, typically state that nature sets no limits to economic growth. Trusting to human intelligence and ingenuity as people seek to satisfy their preferences and achieve well-being, these economists argue that people can "choose among an indefinitely large number of alternatives."[4] They believe that the earth's carrying capacity cannot be measured scientifically because it is a function or artifact of the state of knowledge and technology.

Ecological economists, in contrast, believe that sources of raw materials and sinks for wastes (what they call natural capital) are fixed and therefore limit the potential growth of the global economy. They reject the idea that "technology and resource substitution (ingenuity) . . . can continuously outrun depletion and pollution."[5] Growth faces limits, Herman E. Daly has written, and to "delude ourselves into believing that growth is still possible if only we label it 'sustainable' or color it 'green,' will just delay the inevitable transition and make it more painful."[6]

We may also characterize the difference between mainstream economists and ecological economists with reference to the concept of the limiting factor. According to Daly and his coauthors, we have "entered a new era" in which "the limiting factor in development is no longer manmade capital but remaining natural capital."[7] Mainstream economists argue, however, that if there is a limiting factor in economic production, it is knowledge, and that as long as knowledge advances, the economy can expand. "Where there is effective management," Peter

Drucker has written, "that is, the application of knowledge to knowledge, we can always obtain the other resources."[8] He adds: "The basic economic resource—'the means of production,' to use the economist's term—is no longer capital, nor natural resources (the economist's 'land'), nor 'labor.' *It is and will be knowledge.*"[9] From this perspective, the limits to knowledge are the only limits to growth.

The idea that knowledge is the key resource reflects theoretical and empirical results Solow presented in 1956 and 1957 and summarized in 1970. Solow found that economic growth depends "simply on the rate of (labor-augmenting) technological change," and that "most of the growth of the economy over the last century had been due to technological progress."[10] Economists following Solow have adopted a standard model of growth that contains only two factors: knowledge and the labor to apply it. This model differs from the classical models of Robert T. Malthus and David Ricardo[11] because "[natural] resources, the third member of the classical triad, have generally been dropped."[12]

Mainstream economists offer at least three arguments to show that knowledge and ingenuity are likely always to alleviate resource shortages. First, reserves of natural resources "themselves are actually functions of technology. The more advanced the technology, the more reserves become known and recoverable."[13] Recent examples of reserve-increasing technologies include the use of bacteria to leach metals from low-grade ore and the application of computer analysis to seismic vibrations to locate deposits of oil.[14] As a result of such advances, reserves of many nonrenewable resources have increased in recent decades, despite rising global consumption. Between 1987 and 1990, estimates of proven recoverable reserves of petroleum, for example, rose 11.4 percent, and those of natural gas by 17.9 percent.[15]

Second, advances in technology allow us not only to increase available reserves but also to employ substitutes for resources that may become scarce. When mainstream economists speak of substitutability, they generally refer to the substitution of one resource for another or "the ability to substitute away from resources that are becoming scarce."[16] As Solow explains, "Higher and rising prices of exhaustible resources lead competing producers to substitute other materials that are more plentiful and therefore cheaper."[17] Daly correctly ascribes to economists Nordhaus and Tobin the view "that in the aggregate resources are infinite, that when one flow dries up, there will always be another, and that technology will always find cheap ways to exploit the next resource."[18]

The third argument offered by mainstream economists is that the power of knowledge continually reduces the amounts of resources needed to produce a constant or increasing flow of consumer goods and services. "If the future is anything like the past," Solow writes, "there will be prolonged and substantial reductions in natural resource requirements per unit of real output."[19] Knowledge increases the productivity of natural resources just as it increases the productivity of labor. Glass fibers, for example, not only substitute for but vastly improve upon copper cables. The transmission capacity of an optical fiber cable increased by an order of magnitude every four years between 1975 and 1992. Today, a thin cable using optical amplifiers and erbium-doped fibers powered by laser diode chips can carry one-half million phone calls at any moment. Computers become stronger as they grow smaller; the world's entire annual production of computer chips can fit into a single 747 jumbo jet. Moreover, energy requirements continually decrease per unit of economic output; for example, the amount of energy needed to produce a unit of household lighting has decreased many fold since the time of candles and oil lamps. For reasons such as these, "virtually all minerals have experienced long-term declines in real prices during the last two generations."[20]

Reflecting on these trends, the World Resources Institute (WRI) questions the idea that shortages of nonrenewable resources will prove a limiting factor in the global economy. WRI states: "Even without more resource-sparing policies . . . the cumulative effect of increasing reserves, more competition among suppliers, and technology trends that create substitutes suggests that global shortages of most nonrenewable resources are unlikely to check development in the early decades of the next century."[21] WRI also dismisses "the frequently expressed concern that high levels of consumption will lead to resource depletion and to physical shortages that might limit growth or development opportunity." The evidence suggests "that the world is not yet running out of most nonrenewable resources and is not likely to, at least in the next few decades."[22]

Not all mainstream economists are convinced that there are no natural resource limits whatever to economic growth. Some mainstream analysts have proposed careful models for measuring price trends;[23] others have explained how difficult it is to obtain measures of scarcity;[24] and many others have explored problems created by externalities and common property resources.[25] Some ecological economists have tried to find common ground with mainstream economists with respect to residuals management (waste processing) and intertemporal equity (the due consideration of the interests of future generations).[26] Other ecological economists have emphasized adaptive management approaches to particular environmental and resource problems.[27] Not every ecological economist may agree with Paul Ehrlich and Anne Ehrlich[28] and Daly,[29] moreover, that we confront an age of scarcity in the near or, at best, the medium term.

While both mainstream and ecological economics comprise a variety of positions, sometimes intersecting, in this essay I single out for criticism a series of arguments that ecological economists, such as Ehrlich and Ehrlich, Daly, Robert Costanza, and Donnella Meadows,[30] have mounted against the growth model of neoclassical economics, as defended by Harold J. Barnett and Chandler Morse, Nordhaus, Tobin, Solow, Joseph E. Stiglitz, and others. To show that these arguments fail is to prove neither that the standard model is correct nor that there are no ecological or resource limits to growth. In fact, the thesis that there are significant natural limits to growth remains intuitively appealing. Accordingly, we should subject arguments for that thesis to friendly criticism, if by this means they can be strengthened and improved.

Energy and Entropy

In their dissent from the prevailing mainstream view, many ecological economists cite a theory put forward by Nicholas Georgescu-Roegen,[31] which depends on two premises to refute the standard model of economic growth. The first cites the second law of thermodynamics, which requires that in "entropy terms, the cost of any biological or economic enterprise is always greater than the product."[32] There is always an energy deficit. Second, the free or usable energy (what is called low entropy) that is used up to replace this deficit represents a fixed and dwindling stock. Because we are running down low-entropy terrestrial resources, ecological economists contend, "nature really does impose an inescapable general scarcity" and it is a "serious delusion to believe otherwise."[33]

The first premise is unexceptional: the global economy must consume energy. After running through its reserves of fossil fuel, it must therefore import power from some other source. The second premise, however, is controversial: Are energy resources limited to a fixed and dwindling stock?

If we ignore pollution problems, fossil fuels could subsidize the global economy for quite a while. According to John Holdren, "one sees no immediate danger of 'running out' of energy in a global sense. . . . At 1990 rates of use, resources of oil and natural gas would last 70 to 100 years," counting conventional sources only, and there is "a 1500-year supply of coal."[34] The World Bank estimated in 1992 that fossil fuel reserves are more than six hundred times the present rate of extraction. The World Bank concluded "fears that the world may be running out of fossil fuels are unfounded."[35]

The well-known problems associated with "greenhouse" gases, however, argue for a general conversion to nonpolluting energy sources, such as solar power and geothermal energy. These sources, which dwarf fossil fuels in the amount of energy they make available, seem so abundant that for practical purposes they may be regarded as infinite. Kenneth N. Townsend observes, for example, that "the spontaneous flow of energy on earth from low- to high-entropy states may be offset by solar flow."[36] Georgescu-Roegen himself recognizes that it may be possible "to make greater use of solar radiation, the more abundant source of free energy."[37]

The sunlight continually reaching the surface of the earth—not including vast amounts diffused in the atmosphere—is unimaginably immense. At the equivalent of 1.73×10^{14} kilowatts (kW) of power, it represents an annual energy income or subsidy of 1.5×10^{18} kW hours, about ten thousand times the amount of energy the global economy now consumes.[38] Even with today's technology, conversion efficiencies of sunlight to electricity are good—23 percent on sunny days and 14.5 percent on average annually for Luz solar trough systems,[39] and approximately 11 percent (with performance improving rapidly) for current advanced amorphous silicon, copper indium diselenide, and cadmium thin-film photovoltaic systems. Analysts who study the rapidly falling prices and increasing efficiency of solar energy tend to agree with Lester R. Brown that "technologies are ready to begin building a world energy system largely powered by solar resources."[40]

While photovoltaics currently enjoy the greatest interest, water, wind, and biomass also provide promising and cost-effective methods of harnessing the superabundant energy of the sun. Hydropower now supplies 24 percent of total world electrical-generating capacity.[41] Rapid gains in capturing wind power have made it competitive with other energy sources; in California, for example, wind machines now produce enough electricity to meet the residential needs of a city the size of San Francisco. Energy plantations, using fast-growing plants to remove carbon from the atmosphere, may build on the Brazilian fuel-alcohol program.[42]

One recent survey found that by "the middle of the 21st century, renewable energy technologies can meet much of the growing demand at prices lower than those usually forecast for conventional energy."[43] This survey brings together well-respected authorities who review enthusiastically the potential of hydropower, crystalline-and-polycrystalline-silicon solar cells, amorphous silicon photovoltaic systems, photovoltaic concentrator technology, ethanol and methanol production from cellulosic biomass, advanced gasification-based biomass power generation, wind energy, and various other power sources considered to be environmentally friendly. The survey also describes the exceptional prospects of nonsolar alternatives, such as tidal power, which captures gravitational energy, and geothermal power, which employs heat coming from the earth's core. The energy accessible to modern drilling technology from geothermal sources in the United States, for example, is thousands of times greater than that contained in domestic coal reserves.[44]

Amory B. Lovins, like others who study energy technology from the bottom up, has argued that advanced technologies are commercially available that can "support present or greatly expanded worldwide economic activity while stabilizing global climate—and saving money."[45] Lovins writes that "even very large expansions in population and industrial activity need not be energy-constrained."[46] If available geothermal, solar, and other sources of nonpolluting energy exceed global demand by many orders of magnitude, and if efficiency alone can greatly increase economic output with no additional energy inputs, it is not obvious how the second law of thermodynamics limits economic growth.

Rather than refute Lovins and other experts in their own terms (that is, with arguments showing the limited potential of solar and other technologies), ecological economists tend to rebuke them ad hominem. "This blind faith in technology," Carl Folke and his colleagues have written, "may be similar to the situation of the man who fell from a ten-story building, and when passing the second story on the way down, concluded 'so far so good, so why not continue?' "[47] Another writes that those unalterable to intractable scarcities "believe in perpetual motion machines" and "act as if the laws of nature did not exist."[48]

Complementarity of Natural and Human-made Capital

Ecological economists attempt to refute the mainstream position not only by citing the second law of thermodynamics but also by arguing that "the basic relation of man-made and natural capital is one of complementarity, not substitutability."[49] Extra sawmills, for example, cannot substitute for diminishing forests, more refineries for depleted oil wells, or larger nets for declining fish populations. Daly concludes that "material transformed and tools of transformation are complements, not substitutes."[50]

The problem with this argument, however, is that it fails to respond to the underlying contention of the mainstream model "that increasing resource scarcity would always generate price signals which would engender compensating economic and technological developments, such as resource substitution, recycling, exploration, and increased efficiency in resource utilization."[51] The examples Daly offers, indeed, seem to support the mainstream position. The use of solar energy increases when prices for petroleum rise. As prices for lumber or seafood increase, silviculture and aquaculture rapidly supplement and even underprice capture or extractive forestry and fishing. Food prices in general stand at historical lows because of continuous and continuing improvements in the science and practice of agriculture.[52]

The standard model of economic growth, as we have seen, assumes that human knowledge and ingenuity can always alleviate resource shortages so that natural capital sets no limit on economic growth. One may say that the standard model holds that knowledge can substitute for resources, then, in the sense that ingenuity can always find a way to get around scarcity—for example, by extending reserves, substituting between resource flows, and improving efficiency. This does not imply, of course, that nets can replace fish, saws replace trees, or that the economy can do without resources altogether. As Solow summarizes: "It is of the essence that production cannot take place without the use of natural resources. But I shall assume that it is always possible to substitute greater inputs of labor, reproducible capital [e.g., technology], and renewable resources for smaller direct inputs of the fixed resource."[53]

Daly concedes, in effect, that silviculture and aquaculture do alleviate scarcities just as mainstream economists would predict. When he considers what he calls "cultivated natural capital," including "agriculture, aquaculture, and plantation forestry," he writes that "cultivated capital does substitute for natural capital proper in certain functions—those for which it is cultivated. . . ."[54] The facts bear out this optimism. Tree plantations worldwide "spread rapidly in the 1980s, rising from 18 million hectares in 1980 to more than 40 million hectares by 1990."[55] The 1990s may become known as the decade of silviculture, as millions of hectares of land go into new industrial tree plantations each year, producing trees genetically engineered for various properties including rapid growth. During the 1990s, China plans to plant almost 60 million hectares of tree farms, for example, and India now plants four trees for every one it commercially harvests.[56]

The progress of aquaculture may be gauged from the fact that two of the top ten species harvested in the world today, silver carp and grass carp,[57] are farmed fish. Supplies of other species, such as salmon, are rising and prices are falling worldwide.[58] "We must realize that what is happening to the salmon industry in Europe now is similar to what happened in the chicken industry decades ago," the trade journal *Fish*

Farming International reports. "Salmon is becoming a low-cost food, and we shall just have to find ways to live with this."[59]

What kinds of scarcities, then, limit economic growth? In one passage, Daly suggests the limiting factor may be the earth itself—the stone and clay and sand from which bricks are made. Speaking of timber used in construction, he writes: "Of course, one could substitute bricks for timber, but that is the substitution of one resource for another, not the substitution of capital for resources." He then speaks enigmatically of the "inability of trowels and masons to substitute for bricks."[60]

To understand Daly's argument, one must place it in the context of Aristotle's discussion of the four causes: material, efficient, formal, and final.[61] The material cause in the example Aristotle uses, a statue of a horse, consists of the bronze of which it is made. The tools the sculptor applies to the materials are the statue's efficient cause. The formal cause consists of the idea, plan, image, or design—in short, the knowledge—that guides the artist. And the final cause is the reason or purpose—to celebrate a victory or pay off a debt—that led the sculptor to make the statue.

Daly has asserted his basic premise in clear and precise Aristotelian terms: "The agent of transformation (efficient cause) and the substance being transformed by it (material cause) must be complements."[62] All of Daly's examples—nets and fish, sawmills and trees, oil drills and oil reserves, trowels and bricks—illustrate the complementary relation between efficient and material causes, or, as he says, "the main relation between what is being transformed and the agent of transformation. . . ."[63]

Daly thus forcefully asserts what mainstream economists would never have thought of denying: one "cannot substitute efficient cause for material cause."[64] At the same time, he offers no argument to refute the principle that mainstream economists assert and defend: The formal cause of production (that is, design, knowledge, innovation, and ingenuity) can always overcome shortages in resources or materials. Thus, while mainstream economists know, for example, that harpoons and whales are complementary, they point out that advances in knowledge and invention have compensated for shortages of resources such as whale oil for uses such as lubrication and lighting. Similarly, while refineries cannot substitute for petroleum reserves, mainstream economists assert that human knowledge and ingenuity can find substitutes for petroleum—for example, by harnessing the inexhaustible resources of the sun. Nature need not limit economic growth, they propose, as long as knowledge increases and the sun shines.

The Question of Scale

When ecological economists speak of the limits of growth or caution that growth is unsustainable, they use the term growth in an idiosyncratic sense. "*Growth* refers to the quantitative increase in the scale of the physical dimension of the economy, the rate of flow of matter and energy through the economy, and the stock of human bodies and artifacts. . . ."[65] Daly adds: "*Scale* refers to the physical volume of the flow of matter-energy from the environment as low-entropy raw materials and back to the environment as high-entropy wastes."[66] Ecological economists also distinguish between *growth* and *development*. Economic growth, "which is an increase in quantity, cannot be sustainable indefinitely on a finite planet"; economic development, in contrast, "which is an improvement in the quality of life . . . may be sustainable."[67]

With respect to development, we must ask how ecological economists propose to measure improvements in the quality of life. If they adopt an economic measure, such as utility, preference-satisfaction, or macroeconomic indicators of prosperity, then what they mean by *development* simply collapses into what mainstream economists mean by *growth*. If they propose some other measure, they strike their tents as economists and set out on the high seas of moral philosophy.

What ecological economists mean by growth—an increase in physical scale, quantity, or volume—has no analog in mainstream economic thought. While growth is not a scientific term in mainstream economics, it is used generally to refer to the rate of increase of gross domestic product, defined as the value of everything the economy produces in a year at then-current prices. Quantitative increase in the physical dimension of the economy is neither necessary nor sufficient for economic growth in the conventional sense, which has to do with the value of production rather than the physical size of whatever is produced or consumed. If ecological economics possesses a central thesis, it is that the "term 'sustainable growth' when applied to the economy is a bad oxymoron."[68] Whatever ecological economists say about sustainability, however, has no apparent implications for what mainstream economists mean by growth.

If energy consumption or carbon emissions may serve as indicators of economic scale or quantity, as ecological economists use these terms, we can see that the scale of an economy may not vary with gross domestic product. Between 1973 and 1986, energy consumption in the United States, for example, remained virtually flat while economic production expanded by almost 40 percent.[69] Japan produces 81 percent more real output than it did in 1973 using the same amount of energy.[70] Primary energy demand in the United Kingdom in 1990 was less than it was sixteen years earlier, although the gross domestic product grew.[71] Since 1973, France and West Germany have decreased per capita emissions from fossil fuels as their economies have expanded. In France between 1973 and 1991, the economy grew by approximately 30 percent while per capita emissions declined by about 40 percent.[72] Although emissions sometimes increase with gross domestic product, no general relation holds between growth in the conventional sense and the scale ecological economists believe is unsustainable.

Ecological economists assert that economic growth, as they define it, is unsustainable because it stresses the carrying capacity of the earth. Economic growth in the conventional sense, however, bears no general relation to environmental stress. Societies with big gross domestic products, such as Sweden, protect nature, while nations in the former Soviet bloc with much smaller gross domestic products, such as Poland, have devastated their environments. The Scandinavian countries use their affluence to help countries with smaller economies, like Poland, clean up the environmental mess they have made.

In impoverished nations, as environment and development consultant Norman Myers observes, people may "have no option but to over-exploit environmental resource stocks in order to survive," for example, "by increasingly encroaching onto tropical forests among other low-potential lands."[73] The poorest of the poor, Myers writes, are often the principal cause of deforestation, desertification, soil erosion, and extinction of species.[74] It is the absence of economic growth rather than its presence, then, that is often responsible for rain forest destruction, desertification, erosion, and the loss of biodiversity.

No one believes that economic growth is likely to lead automatically to environmental protection. We have found no reason to agree with the contention of ecological economics, however, that growth in the sense of greater gross domestic product is unsustainable because it necessarily strains natural limits and leads automatically to resource depletion and ecological demise.

The scale or size of an economic activity, moreover, if measured in terms of the volume or quantity of the flow of matter-energy through it, seems to be a useless concept because it bears no clear relation to environmental quality. The physical quantity of detergents used to do laundry, for example, may be the same whether or not those detergents contain phosphates; the ecological consequences, however, will be vastly different. Similarly, a 12-ounce can of hair spray that uses chlorofluorocarbons will damage the environment much more than a 12-ounce can that uses a harmless propellant. Because quantities of water exceed those of any other material in our industrial metabolism, the most efficient way to limit scale might be to cut back on water, but no one believes we would thereby greatly protect the environment. One would cry over a gallon of spilled mercury but not over a gallon of spilled milk.

Presumably, ecological economists know that some forms of throughput are worse than others even in the same quantities or amounts. If ecological economists were to discriminate, however, on some basis other than quantity alone among kinds of throughput that harm the environment, they would find themselves embarking on a path at the end of which mainstream economists (such as those at the World Bank) are waiting for them. Rather than decry throughput in general, measured vaguely in terms of quantity, mainstream economists believe some pollutants and practices are worse than others, and so they address well-defined problems, such as chlorofluorocarbon loadings, rather than the size or scale of throughput as a whole. These economists reject the idea that the dose alone makes the poison; accordingly, they adopt a case-by-case approach that looks for regulatory solutions to specific market and policy failures.

If ecological economists were to relativize the concept of scale to kinds of throughput, they would also confront the problem of identifying and dealing with the pollutants, practices, and policies that are particularly harmful to the environment. They would have to decide which economic activities create greater risks than benefits, which externalities markets fail to price, and so on. If ecological economists conceded that water vapor is not as destructive as chlorofluorocarbons, in other words, even though industry releases a much greater quantity of the former, they would have to move on as economists to risk-benefit analysis, the pricing of externalities, and the correction of market failures. Thus the ecological economics paradigm would simply collapse into that of mainstream economics.

Co-opting Nature

To give empirical content to theoretical arguments about why the global economy can no longer grow, ecological economists often refer to what one describes as the "best evidence" of "imminent limits"[75] to economic expansion—an estimate by Peter M. Vitousek and his colleagues "that organic material equivalent to approximately 40% of the present net primary production in terrestrial ecosystems is being co-opted by human beings each year."[76] Vitousek and his colleagues also state that "humans now appropriate nearly 40% . . . of potential terrestrial productivity."[77] Commentators conclude: "If we take this percentage as an index of the human carrying capacity of the earth and assume that a growing economy could come to appropriate 80% of photosynthetic production before destroying the functional integrity of the ecosphere, the earth will effectively go from half to completely full during the next . . . 35 years."[78]

The argument that total net primary production limits gross domestic product or economic growth rests on two premises. First, the total amount of net primary production on which the global economy draws is fixed or limited by nature. Second, as economies grow, they must appropriate relatively more net primary production. Ehrlich and Ehrlich, for example, cite the scarcity of net primary production to refute the "hope that development can greatly increase the size of the economic pie and pull many more people out of poverty."[79] They call this idea "insane" because of "the constraints nature places on human activities."[80] Such an expansion of economic activity, Ehrlich and Ehrlich contend, "implies an assault on global NPP [net primary production] far beyond that already observed."[81]

Vitousek and his colleagues calculated the assault of the global economy on global net primary production in terms of three separate percentages. They estimated first the percentage of terrestrial net primary production that people directly consume and, second, the percentage they co-opt. By the term *co-opted net primary production*, Vitousek and his colleagues mean "material that human beings use directly or that is used in human-dominated ecosystems by communities or organisms different from those in corresponding natural communities."[82] The amount of net primary production that "flows to different consumers and decomposers than it otherwise would"[83] amounts to 42.6 Petagrams (Pg) of net primary production or approximately 19 percent of the terrestrial total. The 40 percent figure mentioned earlier—the one constantly cited—is the third percentage that Vitousek and his colleagues calculate. It refers to the percentage of net primary production that "human beings have 'co-opted' and potential NPP [net primary production] lost as a consequence of human activities."[84]

Vitousek and his colleagues calculate that the amount of net primary production people directly consume as food is equal to 0.91 Pg of organic material annually.[85] They estimate the combined consumption of plants by livestock and of wood by human beings at 4.4 Pg of dry organic material annually, resulting in a total of approximately 5.3 Pg of direct annual consumption of terrestrial net primary production by humans and their chattel.

The amount of direct consumption, a little more than 5 Pg of biomass, is less than the 15 Pg of organic material that the authors, using data collected in the 1970s, estimate is produced annually on cultivated land. We may conclude from the figures cited that, even by 1979, farmers produced much more biomass than people and livestock directly consumed. This is consistent with expert opinion, which estimates that world agriculture produces enough oilseeds and grain today to provide a vegetarian diet adequate in calories and protein for twice the world's population.[86]

Relying on 1970s data, Vitousek and his colleagues calculate present, not potential, net primary production; however, subsequent data suggest global net primary production need not be fixed at 1970s levels but may greatly increase, for example, in response to cultivation. For instance, in developing countries, wheat yields per acre doubled from 1974 to 1994, corn yields improved by 72 percent, and rice yields by 52 percent.[87] The potential for further increases is enormous. U.S. farmers now average approximately 7 tons per hectare (t/ha) of corn, but when challenged, as in National Corngrowers Association competitions, they have tripled those yields.[88] Varieties of rice developed recently are expected to boost average rice yields dramatically above the present 3.5 t/ha, with a conjectural biological maximum of about 15 metric tons per acre.[89]

Vitousek and his colleagues recognize that the net primary production output of cultivated land may exceed that of natural ecosystems—but when it does, "the amount of potential NPP [net primary production] co-opted by human beings increases."[90] The amount of net primary production farmers co-opt, then, becomes an artifact of the amount they create, not an indicator of a natural limit on productivity.

It is important to see that rising yields do not imply the co-option of more land but, in fact, may free land to return to nature. Between 1950 and 1989, the global output of major food crops rose by 160 percent, more than keeping pace with world population.[91] Most of the increase is attributed to improved yields, not to the use of more land. As a result of greater yields, the United States now idles 50 million acres of farmland in conservation reserves, and the nation is far more forested than a century ago, while remaining a major net food exporter.[92] Other industrialized nations, also net agricultural exporters, have also seen farms revert to forest.[93] The most telling examples of net primary production appropriation Vitousek and his colleagues present (for example, the "6 Pg of organic material [that] is consumed each year in fires associated with shifting cultivation"[94]) arise not as a result of economic growth but from human activity associated with the absence of economic growth—destitution.[95] Displaced peasants, driven by political and economic deprivation, are responsible for nearly three-fifths of current tropical deforestation.[96] This picture suggests that for the environment, destitution is far worse than economic development.

A similar doubt attends the second premise of the argument: net primary production and gross domestic product are related, so that as economies grow they must co-opt more and more organic matter. The great engines of economic growth—the service sector, information, communication, medical technology, education, and finance—do not draw heavily on net primary production. Why then should net primary production limit economic growth?

As early as 1854, pioneering conservationist and environmentalist George Perkins Marsh observed that humanity had long since completely altered and interfered with the spontaneous arrangements of the organic and inorganic world.[97] Other authorities agree that the landmass of the globe has been thoroughly co-opted,[98] as Vitousek and his colleagues define that term, for more than a century. If this is the case, however, then either there is no covariance between net primary production appropriation and increases in gross domestic product, or there has been no economic growth in the last century.

The Precautionary Principle

Ecological economists correctly point out that both ecological and social systems are complex, even chaotic, and that events in each—much less those that result from the interplay of the two systems—are inherently unpredictable.[99] Ecological economists argue that mainstream economics "lacks any representation" of the evolutionary nature of these systems and the nonlinear causation that is characteristic of them.[100]

We may distinguish two contradictory responses to this perceived failure of mainstream economics. First, ecological economists promote their own linear or Newtonian models, relating natural and man-made capital, throughput and ecological stress, and economic growth and net primary production co-option. The arguments examined in this essay suppose that within these pairs, each term varies with or complements the other in the simplest arithmetic way—so that economic growth, by filling up the world as cargo weighs down a ship, exceeds the carrying capacity of the earth.

Second, ecological economists propose a "precautionary principle" as one way "to deal with the problem of true uncertainty."[101] This principle recommends that society establish "safe minimum standards . . . for protecting Earth's life-support systems in the face of virtually inevitable unpleasant surprises."[102]

That the inevitable unpleasantness should nonetheless be a surprise reflects a belief, implicit in the writings of ecological economists, that nature is essentially benign—a loving mother cradling us with life-support systems. Ecological economists worry that technology may upset the womblike processes with which nature coddles us. The chief problem, as they understand it, is uncertainty. So far, nature's free gifts have sustained humanity, but as economies grow, we can no longer be certain of her continued largess.

In fact, mainstream economists also recognize uncertainties and surprises. They start, however, with the intuition that for almost all individuals of any species, nature is quite predictable. It guarantees a usually quick but always painful and horrible death. Starvation, parasitism, predation, thirst, cold, and disease are the cards nature deals to virtually every creature, and for any animal to avoid destruction long enough to reach sexual maturity is the rare exception rather than the rule.[103] Accordingly, mainstream economists reject the idea, implicit in ecological economics, that undisturbed ecosystems, such as wilderness areas, offer better life-support systems than do the farms, suburbs, and cities that sometimes replace them. Without technology, human beings are less suited to survive in nature than virtually any other creature. At conferences, we meet in climate-controlled rooms, depend on waiters for our meals, and sleep indoors rather than al fresco. Nature is not always a cornucopia catering to our needs; it can also be a place where you cannot get good service.

Mainstream economics, in subdisciplines involved with risk assessment, risk-benefit analysis, and decisions under uncertainty, identifies environmental hazards and recommends precautions against them. The Montreal Protocol (adopted in 1987 and strengthened in 1990), which controls chlorofluorocarbon emissions, illustrates one success of this mainstream approach. Mainstream economists focus on specific problems, such as ozone depletion and greenhouse emissions, rather than issue vague calls for safe minimum standards in general. A huge literature within mainstream economics responds to problems associated with global climate change.[104] Ecological economists might dispute this literature on technical grounds, but they cannot say it simply ignores scientific findings.

When ecological economists urge us to maintain a safe minimum standard or, as what they call an insurance policy, a number of uncoopted ecosystems and an adequate reserve of natural resources, questions arise as to which threatened life-support processes or systems and which resources in particular require protection. It is difficult to see how economists can address this question except with conventional cost-benefit analysis. In the context of radical uncertainty, there are many ways to cut back on the scale or size of economic activity. Which make the most sense? A current debate in Congress centers on the national helium reserve. Helium, presumably, is not the kind of natural capital that requires special protection. What is, then, and why?

To add more than a footnote to the vast literature about climate change, ecological economists must argue for something other than better cost-benefit analysis, smaller discount rates, or more attention to market failures and environmental externalities. To distinguish themselves from everyone else, ecological economists must identify threatened forms of natural capital that require special protection because they are the limiting factors in economic development or impose on the carrying capacity of the earth. The World Bank, representing the mainstream position, has described its view of the causes of ozone depletion, the greenhouse effect, and tropical deforestation and recommended solutions.[105] If the precautionary principle and the appeal to safe minimum standards are to add anything to the discussion, they must offer specific recommendations beyond those of the mainstream risk-benefit approach.

According to Costanza, however, the way the precautionary principle is to be applied is uncertain. The precautionary principle, Costanza concedes, "offers no guidance as to what precautionary measures should be taken."[106] The principle instructs us in general to save resources we might need and to avoid decisions with potentially harmful ecological effects. But "it does not tell us how many resources or which adverse future outcomes are most important."[107]

Conclusion

This essay has criticized five principal theses concerning the carrying capacity of the earth. These theses have been asserted by many ecological economists. The first thesis asserts that entropy limits economic growth. On the contrary, the entropy law shows only that economic growth requires abundant and environmentally safe sources of energy. Whether these sources exist is a question better answered by engineers than by economists. The engineering literature, especially with respect to solar power, suggests that safe, abundant, and inexpensive new sources of energy have already been found.

Second, mainstream economists believe and history confirms that knowledge, ingenuity, or invention—the formal causes of production— find ways around shortages in raw materials by increasing reserves, substituting between resource flows, or making resources go further. In reply, ecological economists answer that tools of transformation—the efficient causes of production—are complementary to and therefore cannot substitute for the material causes. While true, this reply is irrelevant.

Third, ecological economists define economic growth in terms of the physical dimensions of throughput, which, as they point out, cannot expand indefinitely. This tells us nothing, however, about growth as mainstream economists understand that term, which has to do with the value rather than the physical dimensions of production. The concept of throughput, moreover, is too amorphous to be measured; its relation to environmental deterioration therefore cannot be determined.

Fourth, ecological economists calculate that 40 percent of net primary production moves through the human economy or is in some way subject to human purposes. This calculation is said to represent the extent to which human beings and their effects fill up the world, as cargo might fill a ship. This argument rests on two premises: first, that total net primary production is fixed or limited in nature; and, second, that economies, in order to grow, must co-opt correspondingly more organic matter. Both premises are false.

Finally, ecological economists offer a precautionary principle that counsels us to play it safe but little instruction about what this means. As a historical matter, however, human beings have found it safer to control and manipulate nature than to accept it on its own terms.

The central principle of ecological economics—the concept of carrying capacity—fails to show that economic growth is unsustainable. Ecological economists are unable to point to a single scarcity of natural capital that knowledge and ingenuity are unlikely to alleviate. Moreover, the so-called carrying capacity of the earth for human beings is not a scientific concept and cannot be measured by biologists. It is an elastic notion depending on social, economic, industrial, and agricultural practices.[108]

Environmentalists a century ago pointed to the intrinsic rather than to the instrumental value of the natural world. Like Thoreau, they found heaven not only above their heads but also below their feet. They thought of nature as a divine mystery; the term *natural capital* would have been lost on them. If a leaf of grass, as Walt Whitman wrote in "Song of Myself" in his work *Leaves of Grass*, is no less than the journeywork of the stars, there is no need to conjecture about its medicinal benefits.

E. O. Wilson has correctly said that the destruction of biodiversity is the crime for which future generations are the least likely to forgive us.[109] The crime would be as great or even greater if a computer could design or store all the genetic data we might ever use or need from the destroyed species. The reasons to protect nature in general are moral, religious, and cultural far more often than they are economic.

To this reasoning, ecological economists may reply that morality and prudence teach the same lesson, so that one is likely to reinforce the other. Morality and prudence, however, teach very different lessons. Morality teaches us that we are rich in proportion to the number of things we can afford to let alone, that we are happier in proportion to the desires we can control rather than those we can satisfy, and that a simpler life is more worth living. Economic growth may not be morally desirable even if it is ecologically sustainable.

Prudence, in contrast, teaches that as long as you can get away with it, "More is more"—to quote the immortal words of Miss Piggy, a puppet diva created by Jim Henson. Advances in technology may one by one expunge the instrumental reasons for protecting nature, leaving us only with our cultural commitments and moral intuitions. To argue for environmental protection on utilitarian grounds—because of carrying capacity or sources of raw materials and sinks for wastes—is therefore to erect only a fragile and temporary defense for the spontaneous wonder and glory of the natural world.

We might, then, take a lesson from the mariners introduced at the beginning of this essay. When lightening the ship of its cargo failed to overcome the danger—the tempest only worsened—they looked for a moral rather than a physical explanation of their plight. They found it: Jonah confessed his crime in fleeing from God's commandment. When the sailors transferred Jonah from the ship to the whale, the seas became calm. Today, we are all aware that the seas may rise up against us. Like the mariners, however, we might consider not just the weight of the cargo but also the ethical compass of our biospheric ark.

Notes

I gratefully acknowledge support for this research from the Global Stewardship Initiative of the Pew Charitable Trusts and from the National Endowment for the Humanities Grant # RO 22709-94. The views expressed are mine alone and not necessarily those of any association or funding agency. I thank my colleague Herman E. Daly who, though he disagrees with much in this paper, provided many helpful criticisms and suggestions.

1. Herman E. Daly, "Elements of Environmental Macroeconomics," in *Ecological Economics: The Science and Management of Sustainablity,* ed. Robert Costanza (New York: Columbia University Press, 1991), 35.
2. John Muir, *The Yosemite* (New York: Century Co., 1912), 256.
3. Samuel P. Hays, *Conservation and the Gospel of Efficiency: The Pro-

gressive Conservation Movement 1890–1920 (New York: Atheneum, 1972 [1959]).

4. Harold J. Barnett and Chandler Morse, *Scarcity and Growth: The Economics of Natural Resource Availability* (Baltimore: Johns Hopkins University Press, 1963), 11.

5. Herman E. Daly, "Moving to a Steady-State Economy," in *The Cassandra Conference: Resources and the Human Predicament*, ed. Paul R. Ehrlich and John P. Holdren (College Station: Texas A&M Press, 1985), 274–75.

6. Herman E. Daly, "Sustainable Growth: An Impossibility Theorem, " in *Valuing the Earth: Economics, Ecology, Ethics*, ed. Herman E. Daly and Kenneth N. Townsend (Cambridge, Mass.: MIT Press, 1993), 268.

7. Robert Costanza, Herman E. Daly, and J. A. Bartholomew, "Goals, Agenda, and Policy Recommendations for Ecological Economics," in *Ecological Economics,* ed. Costanza, 8.

8. Peter Drucker, *Post-Capitalist Society* (New York: Harper Business, 1993), 45.

9. Drucker, *Post-Capitalist Society*, 8.

10. Joseph E. Stiglitz, "Comments: Some Retrospective Views on Growth Theory," in *Growth/Productivity/Unemployment: Essays to Celebrate Bob Solow's Birthday*, ed. Peter Diamond (Cambridge, Mass.: MIT Press, 1990), 53.

11. Robert T. Malthus, *Principles of Political Economy*, 2d ed., ed. J. Pullen (Cambridge, Mass.: Harvard University Press, 1989 [1864]); David Ricardo, *The Works and Correspondence of David Ricardo*, ed. P. Sraffa (Cambridge, England: Cambridge University Press for the Royal Economic Society, 1951 [1817]).

12. William B. Nordhaus and James Tobin, "Is Growth Obsolete?" Reprinted in *Economic Growth*, National Bureau of Economic Research (New York: Columbia University Press, 1972), 14.

13. T. H. Lee, "Advanced Fossil Fuel Systems and Beyond," in *Technology and Environment*, ed. Jesse H. Ausubel and Hedy E. Sladovich (Washington, D.C.: National Academy Press, 1989), 116.

14. M. Gianturco, "Seeing into the Earth," *Forbes*, 20 June 1994, 120.

15. World Resources Institute, *World Resources 1994–95* (New York: Oxford University Press, 1994), 169.

16. World Bank, *World Development Report 1992: Development and the Environment* (New York: Oxford University Press, 1992), 38.

17. Robert M. Solow, "Is the End of the World at Hand?" in *The Economic Growth Controversy*, ed. Andrew Weintraub, Eli Schwartz, and J. Richard Aronson (New York: International Arts and Sciences Press, 1973), 53.

18. Herman E. Daly, *Steady State Economics*, 2d ed. (Washington, D.C.: Island Press, 1991), 108.

19. Robert M. Solow, "The Economics of Resources or the Resources of Economics," *American Economic Review* 64 (1974): 10–11.

20. Vaclav Smil, *Global Ecology: Environmental Change and Social Flexibility* (London: Routledge, 1993), 57.

21. World Resources Institute, *World Resources 1994–95*, 6.

22. World Resources Institute, *World Resources 1994–1995*, 5.

23. D. C. Hall and J. V. Hall, "Concepts and Measures of Natural Resource Scarcity with a Summary of Recent Trends," *Journal of Environmental Economics and Management* 11 (1994): 363–79; Margaret E. Slade, "Cycles in Commodity Prices," *Journal of Environmental Economics and Management* 9, no. 2 (June 1982): 138–48; Slade, "Trends in Natural-Resources Commodity Prices: An Analysis of the Time Domain," *Journal of Environmental Economics and Management* 9, no. 2 (June 1982): 122–37.

24. Partha S. Dasgupta and Geoffrey M. Heal, *Economic Theory and Exhaustible Resources* (Cambridge, England: Cambridge Economic Handbooks, 1979); Anthony C. Fisher, "Measures of Natural Resource Scarcity," in *Scarcity and Growth Reconsidered*, ed. V. Kerry Smith (Baltimore: published for Resources for the Future by the Johns Hopkins University Press, 1979), 249–75; V. Kerry Smith and John V. Krutilla, "Toward Reformulating the Role of Natural Resources in Economic Models," in *Explorations in Natural Resource Economics*, ed. V. Kerry Smith and John V. Krutilla (Baltimore: published for Resources for the Future by the Johns Hopkins University Press, 1982), 3–29.

25. R. U. Ayres and A. V. Kneese, "Production, Consumption, and Externalities," *American Economic Review* 59 (1969): 282–97; M. I. Kamien and N. L. Schwartz, "The Role of Common Property Resources in Optimal Planning Models with Exhaustible Resources," in *Explorations in Natural Resource Economics*, ed. Smith and Krutilla, 47–66.

26. Talbot Page, *Conservation and Economic Efficiency: An Approach to Materials Policy* (Baltimore: Published for Resources for the Future by the Johns Hopkins University Press, 1977).

27. C. S. Holling, ed., *Adaptive Environmental Assessment and Management* (New York: Wiley, 1978); Michael Common, *Sustainability and Policy: Limits to Economics* (New York: Cambridge University Press, 1995).

28. Paul R. Ehrlich and Anne E. Ehrlich, *The End of Affluence* (New York: Ballantine Books, 1974).

29. Herman E. Daly, "Sustainable Development: From Concept and Theory to Operational Principles," in *Resources, Environment, and Population: Present Knowledge and Future Options*, ed. Kingsley Davis and Mikhail S. Bernstam (New York: Oxford University Press, 1991), 25–43.

30. Donnella H. Meadows, *Beyond the Limits: Confronting Global Collapse* (Post Mills, Vt.: Chelsea Greens Publishing Co., 1992).

31. Nicholas Georgescu-Roegen, *The Entropy Law and the Economic Process* (Cambridge, Mass.: Harvard University Press, 1971).

32. Nicholas Georgescu-Roegen, "The Entropy Law and the Economic Problem," in *Economics, Ecology, Ethics: Essays Toward a Steady-State Economy*, ed. Herman E. Daly (San Francisco: W. H. Freeman, 1980), 41–42.

33. Herman E. Daly, "Entropy, Growth, and the Political Economy of Scarcity," in *Scarcity and Growth Reconsidered*, ed. Smith, 69.

34. John P. Holdren, "The Energy Predicament in Perspective," in *Confronting Climate Change: Risks, Implications, and Responses*, ed. Irving Mintzer (New York: Cambridge University Press, 1992), 165.

35. World Bank, *World Development Report 1992*, 115.

36. Kenneth N. Townsend, "Is Entropy Relevant to the Economics of Natural Resource Scarcity? Comment," *Journal of Environmental Economics and Management* 23, no. 1 (July 1992): 98.

37. Georgescu-Roegen, "The Entropy Law and the Economic Problem," 47.

38. P. D. Dunn, *Renewable Energies: Sources, Conversion, and Application* (London: Peregrinus on behalf of the Institution of Electrical Engineers, 1986), 26.

39. Lester R. Brown et al., *State of the World 1995* (New York: Norton, 1995), 64.

40. Lester R. Brown, Christopher Flavin, and Sandra Postel, *Saving the Planet: How to Shape an Environmentally Sustainable Global Economy* (New York: W. W. Norton, 1991), 48.

41. Peter H. Gleick, "Water and Energy," *Annual Review of Energy and the Environment* 19 (1994): 290.

42. Harry Rotham, Rod Greenshields, and Francisco Rosillo Calle, *Energy from Alcohol: The Brazilian Experience* (Lexington: University Press of Kentucky, 1983).

43. T. B Johansson, H. Kelly, A. K. N. Reddy, and R. H. Williams, *Renewable Energy* (Washington, D.C.: Island Press, 1993), 1.

44. National Academy of Sciences, *Geothermal Energy Technology: Issues, R&D Needs, and Cooperative Arrangements* (Washington, D.C.: National Academy Press, 1987).

45. Amory B. Lovins and H. L. Lovins, "Least-Cost Climatic Stabilization," *Annual Review of Energy and the Environment* 16 (1991): 433.

46. Amory B. Lovins, "Energy, People, and Industrialization," in *Resources, Environment, and Population*, ed. Davis and Bernstam, 95.

47. Carl Folke, Monica Hammer, Robert Costanza, and AnnMari Jansson, "Investing in Natural Capital—Why, What, and How?" in *Investing in Natural Capital: The Ecological Economics Approach to Sustainability*, ed. AnnMari Jansson, Monica Hammer, Carl Folke, and Robert Costanza (Washington, D.C.: Island Press, 1994), 3.

48. Paul R. Ehrlich, "Ecological Economics and the Carrying Capacity of the Earth," in *Investing in Natural Capital*, ed. Jansson et al., 41.

49. Herman E. Daly, "Operationalizing Sustainable Development by Investing in Natural Capital," in *Investing in Natural Capital*, ed. Jansson et al., 26.

50. Herman E. Daly, "Toward Some Operational Principles of Sustainable Development," *Ecological Economics* 2, no. 1 (April 1990): 3.

51. C. W. Clark, "Economic Biases against Sustainable Development," in *Ecological Economics*, ed. Costanza, 320.

52. R. Heifner and R. Kinoshita, "Differences among Commodities in Real Price Variabilty and Drift," *Agricultural Economics Research* 45, no. 3 (Fall 1984): 10–20.

53. Robert Solow, "An Almost Practical Step toward Sustainability, " Occasional Paper (Washington, D.C.: Resources for the Future, 1992), 8–9.

54. Daly, "Operationalizing Sustainable Development," 30.

55. World Resources Institute, *World Resources 1994–95*, 131.

56. World Resources Institute, *World Resources 1994–95*, 79, 134.

57. Brown et al., *State of the World 1995*, 30.

58. N. Lord, "Born to be Wild," *Sierra*, November/December 1994, 73.

59. Erik Hempel, "Norway's Salmon Capacity is Now Nearly 300,000 tons," *Fish Farming International* (July 1994): 22–23.

60. Daly, "Operationalizing Sustainable Development," 26.

61. Aristotle, "Metaphysics: Book D.2," in *Aristotle's Metaphysics,* trans. H. G. Apostle (Bloomington: Indiana University Press, 1975).

62. Daly, "Sustainable Development," 36.

63. Daly, "Sustainable Development," 36.

64. Herman E. Daly, "On Wilfred Beckerman's Critique of Sustainable Development," *Environmental Values* 4, no. 1 (1995): 51.

65. Folke et al., "Investing in Natural Capital," 7.

66. Herman E. Daly and Kenneth N. Townsend, "Introduction," in *Valuing the Earth: Economics, Ecology, Ethics,* ed. Herman E. Daly and Kenneth N. Townsend (Cambridge, Mass.: MIT Press, 1993), 2.

67. Costanza et al., "Goals, Agenda, and Policy Recommendations," 7.

68. Daly, "Sustainable Growth," 263.

69. Michael Brower, *Cool Energy* (Cambridge, Mass.: MIT Press, 1992), 13.

70. Robert Goodland, "Growth Has Reached its Limit," in *The Case Against the Global Economy*, ed. Jerry Mander and Edward Goldsmith (San Francisco: Sierra Club Books), 216.

71. Department of Energy, United Kingdom, *Digest of United Kingdom Energy Statistics* (London: H.M.S.O., 1990), table A1.

72. W. R. Moomaw and D. M. Tullis, "Charting Development Paths: A Multicountry Comparison of Carbon Dioxide Emissions," G-DAE Discussion Paper #2, Global Development and Environment Institute (Medford, Mass.: Tufts University, 1994).

73. Norman Myers, "Population and Biodiversity," in *Population, the Complex Reality: A Report of the Population Summit of the World's Scientific Academics*, ed. Sir Francis Graham-Smith (London: Royal Society, 1994; Golden, Colo.: North American Press, 1994), 128.

74. Norman Myers, "The Question of Linkages in Environment and Development," *BioScience* 5 (1993): 306.

75. Robert Goodland, "The Case That the World Has Reached Its Limits," in *Population, Technology, and Lifestyle: The Transition to Sustainability*, ed. Robert Goodland, Herman E. Daly, and Salah El Serafy (Washington, D.C.: Island Press, 1993), 7.

76. Peter M. Vitousek, Paul R. Ehrlich, Anne H. Ehrlich, and Pamela A. Matson, "Human Appropriation of the Products of Photosynthesis," *BioScience* 36, no. 6 (1986): 368–73.

77. Vitousek et al., "Human Appropriation," 372.

78. William E. Rees and Mathis Wackernagel, "Ecological Footprints and Appropriated Carrying Capacity: Measuring the Natural Capital Requirement of the Human Economy," in *Investing in Natural Capital*, ed. Jansson, 383.

79. Paul Ehrlich and Anne Ehrlich, *The Population Explosion* (New York: Simon and Schuster, 1990), 269 n. 29.

80. Ehrlich and Ehrlich, *The Population Explosion*, 269 n. 29.

81. Ehrlich and Ehrlich, *The Population Explosion*, 37.

82. Vitousek et al., "Human Appropriation," 370.

83. Vitousek et al., "Human Appropriation," 372.

84. Vitousek et al., "Human Appropriation," 372.

85. Vitousek et al., "Human Appropriation," 369.

86. Paul E. Waggoner, "How Much Land Can Ten Billion People Spare for Nature?" Task Force Report 121 (Ames, Iowa: Council for Agricultural Science and Technology, 1994), 17.

87. J. Anderson, "Feeding a Hungrier World," *Washington Post*, 13 February 1995, A3.

88. Waggoner, "How Much Land Can Ten Billion People Spare for Nature?" 26–27.

89. Anderson, "Feeding a Hungrier World," A3.

90. Vitousek et al., "Human Appropriation," 372.

91. Brown et al., *State of the World 1995,* 7.

92. P. Crosson, "Is U.S. Agriculture Sustainable?" *Resources* 117, no. 10 (Fall 1994): 16.

93. World Resources Institute, *World Resources 1994–95,* 131.

94. Vitousek et al., "Human Appropriation," 371.

95. Myers, "The Question of Linkages," 306.

96. Myers, "Population and Biodiversity," 125.

97. George Perkins Marsh, *Man and Nature; or Physical Geography as Modified by Human Action* (reprint, with an introduction by David Lowenthal, Cambridge, Mass.: Belknap Press of Harvard University Press, 1965 [1864]), 3.

98. Aleksandr Maksimovich Riabchikov, *The Changing Face of the Earth: The Structure and Dynamics of the Geosphere, Its Natural Development and the Changes Caused by Man,* trans. John Williams (Moscow: Progress Publishers, 1975); Study of Critical Environmental Problems, *Man's Impact on the Global Environment: Assessment and Recommendations for Action; Report,* sponsored by the Massachusetts Institute of Technology (Cambridge, Mass.: MIT Press, 1970).

99. Folke et al., "Investing in Natural Capital," 11.

100. P. Christensen, "Driving Forces, Increasing Returns, and Ecological Sustainability," in *Ecological Economics*, ed. Costanza, 75–87.

101. Robert Costanza, "Three General Policies to Achieve Sustainability," in *Investing in Natural Capital*, ed. Jansson et al., 399.

102. Ehrlich, "Ecological Economics," 49.

103. G. C. Williams, "Huxley's Evolution and Ethics in Sociobiological Perspective," *Zygon* 23, no. 4 (1988): 383–407.

104. William R. Cline, *The Economics of Global Warming* (Washington, D.C.: Institute for International Economics, 1992); William Nordhaus, *Managing the Global Commons: The Economics of Climate Change* (Cambridge, Mass.: MIT Press, 1994); Thomas C. Schelling, "Some Economics of Global Warming," *American Economic Review* 82 (March 1992): 1–14.

105. World Bank, *World Development Report 1992.*

106. Costanza, "Three General Policies," 399.

107. Costanza, "Three General Policies," 399.

108. H. Schneider, "Climate and Food: Signs of Hope, Despair, and Opportunity," in *The Cassandra Conference: Resources and the Human Predicament*, ed. Ehrlich and Holdren, 42.

109. E. O. Wilson, "Resolutions for the 80s," *Harvard Magazine*, January–February 1980, 21.

3

Reply to Mark Sagoff's "Carrying Capacity and Ecological Economics"

Herman E. Daly

A General Reply

After a year and a half of friendly and sometimes instructive debates initiated by my University of Maryland colleague Mark Sagoff, shortly after I joined that faculty, I think I have finally discovered the key to understanding him: Sagoff is a Kantian ethicist, a deontologist, who fundamentally rejects utilitarian or consequentialist ethics. Consequently he rejects all economics, not just ecological economics, because it is all "the sordid lore of nicely calculated less or more" (to quote the English poet William Wordsworth)—it is utilitarian and consequentialist to the core and therefore irredeemable.

Although Sagoff's strategy is to use standard economics against ecological economics, his point is to show that there is not a dime's worth of difference between them, at least in terms of what is important to him. Both are consequentialist and utilitarian, whereas salvation is to come through direct spiritual intuition of what is inherently right and by acting accordingly.[1]

Alternatives to Economic Analysis

Sagoff tells us nothing about his preferred alternative; his direct or revealed spiritual insights into the inherent rightness of acts is not explained. He does not tell us what his perception of intrinsic value is, how to recognize it, how to distinguish more of it from less, or how we should go about increasing it, if in indeed we have such an obligation. All we are told is that nature is full of divinity, that heaven is below our feet as well as above our heads, and that John Muir thought we should look to the God of the mountains rather than to the Almighty dollar.[2]

Fine. Now in light of that philosophy, tell me how large the human population should be, what the proper level or range of per capita resource consumption is, and how much of the habitat of other species we are justified in preempting for human use. Sagoff does not try to help answer these major questions of ecological economics, but he does offer his professional services as a philosophical critic of this way of thinking, featuring yours truly as Exhibit A. Fair enough; the role of critic is surely legitimate—I am a critic of neoclassical economics. It is only fair that critics should be criticized—and the critic of the critic as well.

Because Sagoff uses the neoclassical economist's arguments against the ecological economist, while simultaneously rejecting both arguments, it is easy to get confused about whose voice one is hearing at any given moment. But it is clear that the technological optimism expounded with such enthusiasm in the article represents Sagoff's view as well as that of his otherwise disposable alter ego, the neoclassical economist. This point is important, because technological optimism mixed with Kantian deontology is an alchemist's elixir. It means that we do not have to be seriously concerned with consequentialist ethics, because technology can always neutralize any unfortunate consequences. No criterion is left but the inherent rightness of an act, because all offsetting negative consequences can be erased by technology. Life is made easy for a Kantian ethicist if he is also a technological optimist. Utilitarian economists are invited to go soak their consequentialist heads while deontologist philosophers decide everything on the basis of their deep intuitions of inherent rightness, secure in the faith that technology is likely to mop up whatever mess they make.

Outstripping Spiritual Purpose

Sagoff wants to arrive at the conclusion of the early environmentalists, as stated at the beginning of his article, namely, "economic activity had outstripped not its resource base, but its spiritual purpose."[3] In the time of Henry David Thoreau the economy had not yet outstripped its resource base, and instrumentalist arguments were naturally less pressing than they are today. I do not doubt that even then the economy was disconnected from spiritual purpose. Today, however, the instrumental arguments have become important as the growing scale of the human economy has indeed begun to erode its resource base. Does this situation mean that the intrinsic value arguments disappear? By no means.

Instrumental value is by definition instrumental to the realization of intrinsic value, and without intrinsic value it would not exist.

Sagoff is fond of the *not this, but that* construction: Not resource base, but spiritual purpose. Why not both resource base and spiritual purpose, especially after a century of exponential economic and demographic growth has changed Thoreau's world beyond recognition? Sagoff's fondness for this construction was noted also by Garrett Hardin, who, in a different context, quoted Sagoff's "remarkable assertion" that "pollution results not from our numbers . . . but from our life styles and rate of consumption."[4] The false denial of cause *a* in order more forcefully to assert cause *b* is faulty as logic and tiresome as rhetoric. It becomes ludicrous when the effect is caused by multiplying *a* and *b* together.

The population context is relevant to the point I am making. Because reproduction is a life-promoting act that our spiritual intuition tells us must be good, it is inconvenient to the deontologist to recognize negative consequences that could lead to too much of a good thing, lest he then be pushed into the consequentialist's camp. Therefore, it is convenient if population size has nothing to do with pollution. Only per capita consumption levels cause pollution, and because per capita consumption at currently desired levels is determined by greed rather than by conjugal love, we can escape the embarrassment of a utilitarian evaluation of the consequences of an excess of blessed events and remain on the high ground of direct spiritual intuition. Whatever base consequence of growth you can point to, our alchemist is likely to convert it into gold with his philosopher's stone of technology, aided by mercurial suspensions of the laws of thermodynamics.

It is instructive to revisit the story of Jonah, with which Sagoff both begins and ends his article. The reason for the tempest is that Jonah was running away, resisting God's command to preach repentance to the Ninevites. Toss Jonah overboard, purify the boat of sin, and all is well—no matter how many people or how much cargo we load on the ship. Our problems have moral causes—that is one lesson Sagoff draws for us from the story. I agree. He also suggests that physical factors have little or nothing to do with our problems. I disagree. I think the true lesson from the story of Jonah comes at the end: On a hill over looking Nineveh, Jonah sits in the shade, angry because God has forgiven the Ninevites. After hearing Jonah's presentation of God's message—"either repent or be smitten"—the Ninevites prudently decided to repent. But in Jonah's opinion their repentance was based too much on prudence (too consequentialist) and not enough on morality (insufficiently deontological). Jonah's standards were "higher" than God's. Jonah was so angry he wanted to die. God told Jonah to think about the improved well-being of the more than 120,000 Ninevites, and even that of their animals, and to remember that this outcome was a good consequence of Jonah's actions.

Some Specific Replies

Is Knowledge Key?

Citing many authorities, Sagoff argues that knowledge is the key, and resources are of minor importance. However, suppose that all manmade capital were reduced to rubble over night, but all knowledge in people's heads and in libraries remained intact. Suppose also that the natural capital remained as it was on the day that all manmade capital was destroyed. Could we, on the basis of our undiminished knowledge, reconstruct the destroyed manmade capital using the remaining natural capital? The answer is no, because we would have to begin again—not with East Texas oil that bubbles from the ground, but with undersea Alaskan oil that is inaccessible; not with Mesabi iron ore, but with leaner ores or recycled metals.

Knowledge, to mean anything for the economy, must be imprinted on the physical world. Not all parts of the physical world are equally capable of receiving and holding the imprint of human knowledge. The quality of matter/energy that makes it receptive to the imprint of human knowledge is low entropy: No low-entropy matter/energy, no manmade capital—regardless of knowledge; less low-entropy resources, less possibility of imprinting knowledge into physical structures (i.e., of making capital). Capital, as economist Kenneth Boulding said, is human knowledge "frozen" into physical structures. Entropy melts those structures, giving rise to the need for a continuous input of low entropy from the environment for maintenance. Organisms also represent information— the genetic knowledge imprinted in physical structures. The population of an organism is not limited by its genetic knowledge but rather by the availability in its environment of the forms of matter/energy needed to convert the genotype into a phenotype. Populations of capital are similar.

Knowledge and low-entropy matter/energy are fundamentally complements. Even though there are many possibilities for substitution of one source of low entropy for another, there is no substitute for low entropy (exergy) itself. Intelligent substitutions and technical adaptations should not blind us to the existence of the fundamental constraint to which they are still only adaptations. To those who get carried away with the independent power of knowledge and information, Frederick

Soddy, Nobel Prize-winning chemist and underground economist, provided a pithy reminder, "No phosphorous, no thought." If you are hungry, do not ask Sagoff for a sandwich—he is likely to just give you the recipe.

Economist Robert Solow is cited as having provided empirical evidence that most growth over the last century has come from technological progress—from knowledge, not from resources.[5] Solow used a two-factor aggregate production function (labor and capital) to explain production growth. The large, unexplained residual that he found might have been an embarrassment to some, but it was seen by Solow as an indirect measure of technological progress and a confirmation of his hypothesis that technology was of dominant importance. But if technological progress is a residual, then it includes the effect of everything that is not labor and capital, including, most notably, the contribution of increased resource use.

Other economists, using the more sensible approach of constructing an index of real inputs and seeing how much its variation explained the variation of real outputs, found small residuals and consequently not much that could be attributed to knowledge or anything else.[6] But Sagoff is convinced that technical knowledge is the "quintessence," fifth essence, through which the alchemist can transform the traditional four essences (earth, air, fire, and water), into each other, thereby fulfilling the quest for unlimited substitution—the shared dream of alchemists and neoclassical economists.

Different Types of Substitution

Sagoff fails to firmly grasp the distinction between the simple substitution of one resource for another (bricks for lumber in construction) and the not so simple, indeed impossible, substitution of capital in general for resources in general (saws for lumber in the construction of a wooden house, trowels for bricks in the construction of a brick house). Efficient cause (saws and trowels) cannot substitute for material cause (lumber and bricks). They are complements. Sagoff is wrong in his belief that neoclassical economists have never suggested the substitution of capital in general for resources in general. Because he finds my discussion enigmatic, let me quote the clear and precise critique by economist Nicholas Georgescu-Roegen (to which, as far as I can discover, Solow, Joseph E. Stiglitz, or other neoclassical economists have never replied).

Georgescu-Roegen (1979) wrote the Solow-Stiglitz variant of the Cobb-Douglas function as:

$$Q = K^{a1} R^{a2} L^{a3}$$

where Q is output, K is the stock of capital, R is the flow of natural resources used in production, L is the labor supply, and $a_1 + a_2 + a_3 = 1$ and, of course, $a_i > 0$.

From this formula it follows that with a constant labor power, L_0, one could obtain any Q_0 if the flow of natural resources satisfies the condition

$$R^{a2} = \frac{Q_0}{K^{a1}L_0^{a2}}$$

This shows that R may be as small as we wish, provided K is sufficiently large. Ergo, we can obtain a constant annual product indefinitely even from a very small stock of resources $R > 0$, if we decompose R into an infinite series $R = \sum R_1$, with $R_i \to 0$, use R_i in year i, and increase the stock of capital each year as required by the second equation. But this ergo is not valid in actuality. In actuality, the increase of capital implies an additional depletion of resources. And if K approaches infinity, then R will rapidly be exhausted by the production of capital. Solow and Stiglitz could not have come out with their conjuring trick had they borne in mind, first, that any material process consists in the transformation of some materials into others (the flow elements) by some agents (the fund elements), and second, that natural resources are the very sap of the economic process. They are not just like any other production factor. A change in capital or labor can only diminish the amount of waste in the production of a commodity; no agent can create the material on which it works, nor can capital create the stuff out of which it is made. In some cases, it may also be that the same service can be provided by a design that requires less matter or energy. But even in this direction there exists a limit, unless we believe that the ultimate fate of the economic process is an earthly Garden of Eden.

The question that confronts us today is whether we are going to discover new sources of energy that can be safely used. No elasticities of some Cobb-Douglas function can help us to answer it.[7]

Sagoff thinks that by putting R in the production function, neoclassical economists have given the physical world its due regard, without noticing that in their formulation R can be as small as one likes. This ever-shrinking R is mathematical fun and games with infinity rather than serious economics. To dismiss Georgescu-Roegen's argument by saying that engineers, not economists, are the ones to consult about new sources of energy is far too glib.

Clarifying Growth, Development, and Throughput

Sagoff considers the concepts of growth, development, and scale of throughput to be unclear. Let me attempt to clarify them. Growth is a physical increase in matter/energy throughput. Sagoff is right to point out that this concept is absent in mainstream economic thought, which is precisely the problem and the reason for introducing it and distinguishing it from development. Development is qualitative change; growth is quantitative physical increase. This usage is straight from the dictionary, so it is not idiosyncratic, as Sagoff claims. Because standard economics does not make this distinction, gross national product is a measure of growth and development. Because quantitative physical increase and qualitative improvements are different things, subject to different limits, conflating them can, and has, caused much confusion—a confusion in which growth economists, like rabbits in a briar patch, can hide under one bush and when discovered then scurry to the other.

Consider a given pattern or vector of throughput flows of matter and energy. Multiply that vector by a scalar. The result is an increase in scale of throughput. An increase in scale will surely result in a greater load on the environment. Of course, a different pattern of throughputs may be more environmentally benign. But a scale increase in that, or any other, pattern would still increase the environmental load relative to what it was. Sagoff mixes scale increase with pattern change.

"If we ignore pollution problems, fossil fuels could subsidize the global economy for quite a while," Sagoff explains.[8] Sure, but why ignore pollution, because that is the relevant constraint. Indeed, falling extraction costs, considered as evidence against scarcity in another context, make the pollution problem worse. It is in the context of a discussion of entropy that Sagoff considers it appropriate to ignore pollution problems. The implication that pollution is not a manifestation of entropy is part of Sagoff's alchemy.

Peter N. Vitousek and his colleagues' calculation is a reasonable attempt to put some quantitative dimension on the scale of the human economy relative to the total ecosystem.[9] Sagoff's riposte that the whole world has long been co-opted by humans and that therefore the relative size of the human niche is by definition 100% is not a reductio ad absurdum of Vitousek and his colleagues. It just calls attention to the need, recognized in practice by Vitousek and his colleagues, to determine how significant the chains of cause and effect have to be before we define them as part of human cooptation.

The precautionary principle advocated by Robert Costanza[10] and others should be compared to Sagoff's technological optimism, not to the savagery and inhospitality of nature, especially because in other contexts we are told that nature is divine, heaven is under our feet, and Muir's God of the mountains will take care of us. If one is a technological optimist and believes that resources are unimportant for the economic process, then one should not object to a policy of limiting the resource throughput, thereby raising its price. Such a policy would induce exactly the technological advances that use resources more efficiently—the very technology in which the optimists have so much faith. If a side effect of reduced resource throughput is to gain some insurance under the precautionary principle, as well as to preserve more of the earth as habitat for other species, then why object? Does the deontological, technological optimist have the courage of his convictions? If so, then join the ecological economists in advocating the policy of raising the price of natural resources and natural capital services, say through shifting the tax base away from income and onto throughput. If technology is the answer, why not actively promote its advance?

Many other ecological economists and I have long considered that the limits to growth stem from both possibility and desirability. We are not addicted to the *not this, but that* construction. Even so, one welcomes Sagoff's reminder that economic growth may be undesirable even if possible. We also recognize that, after some point, growth becomes impossible, even if still desirable. However, in most cases what should limit economic growth is neither pure desirability nor pure possibility. It is the economic interplay of these two considerations as reflected in the comparison of benefits (desirability conditions) with costs (possibility conditions). Exactly the "sordid lore of nicely calculated less or more" that has become Sagoff's bête noire.

If we believe that expanding the human niche a bit more is likely to, at the margin, increase intrinsic value by more than the consequent reduction of the natural environment is likely to diminish it, then we should grow a bit more. If we believe that a reduction in the human niche is likely to reduce intrinsic value by less than the consequent expansion of the natural environment is likely to increase it, then we should shrink. This approach is a consequentialist one without apology, although its demands far exceed the capacity of market prices to measure the relevant costs and benefits.

If Sagoff wants to tell standard economists not to be so anthropocentric in their concept of intrinsic value and to remember the welfare of other species in some appropriate way, then he should join ecological economists. If he wants to tell economists to consider the welfare of future generations, then more reason to join them. If he wants to remind economists that markets do a poor job of measuring full costs and benefits, still more reason to join them. If he also thinks that scale and distribution issues cannot be handled by markets alone, then he would be an ecological economist.

After we have recognized the intrinsic value of the natural world, then we have an obligation to protect and increase that value. That realization leads us to pay attention to instrumental value. From a philosopher, we might reasonably have hoped for enlightenment on the source and basis of intrinsic value. Instead Sagoff puts intrinsic and instrumental value in opposition to each other in another of his *not this, but that* formulations. But in this case the relation absolutely has to be *both/and*. Unless we have a notion of intrinsic value then there is nothing to which instrumental value can be instrumental. And unless we have a notion of instrumental value, we have no operational means of serving intrinsic value. It is a further mistake to identify intrinsic value with morality and instrumental value with prudence and then set up an opposition between them as Sagoff does.

Intuitions of Inherent Rightness

Prudential reasoning in terms of costs and benefits arising from the consequences of our actions, is, in my opinion, necessary to protect and enhance the intrinsic value of God's creation and its evolutionary potential. We must pay first attention to our intuitions of inherent rightness, especially as guided by religious tradition. I hope Sagoff helps us with that someday. But without cross-examination in the light of consequences, our intuition of inherent rightness can lead to fanaticism. Furthermore, I think those religious intuitions are in danger of being distorted, mainly by the alchemical heresy that technology is omnipotent, but also, paradoxically, by pantheistic sentimentality about the divinity of nature.

Notes

1. Mark Sagoff, "Carrying Capacity and Ecological Economics," *BioScience* 45 (1995): 610–20, reprinted as chap. 2 of this volume.

2. John Muir, *The Yosemite* (New York: Century Co., 1912), 256.

3. Sagoff, "Carrying Capacity," 28.

4. Garrett Hardin, "Paramount Positions in Ecological Economics," in *Ecological Economics: The Science and Management of Sustainability*, ed. Robert Costanza (New York: Columbia University Press, 1991), 53.

5. Robert Solow, "A Contribution to the Theory of Economic Growth," *Quarterly Journal of Economics* 70, no. 1 (February 1956): 65–94; "Technical Change and the Aggregate Production Function," *Review of Economics and Statistics* 39, no. 3 (August 1957): 312–20.

6. See, for example, D. Jorgenson and Z. Grilliches, "The Explanation of Productivity Change," *Review of Economic Studies* 34 (July 1967): 249–83.

7. Nicholas Georgescu-Roegen, "Comments on the Papers by Daly and Stiglitz," in *Scarcity and Growth Reconsidered*, ed. V. Kerry Smith (Baltimore:

published for Resources for the Future by the Johns Hopkins University Press, 1979), 98.

8. Sagoff, "Carrying Capacity," 32.

9. Peter M. Vitousek, Paul R. Ehrlich, Anne H. Ehrlich, and Pamela Matson, "Human Appropriation of the Products of Photosynthesis," *BioScience* 36, no. 6 (1986): 368–73.

10. Robert Costanza, "Three General Policies to Achieve Sustainability," in *Investing in Natural Capital: The Ecological Economics Approach to Sustainability*, ed. AnnMari Jannson et al. (Washington, D.C.: Island Press, 1994): 392–407.

4

Limits to Consumption and Economic Growth: The Middle Ground

Allen L. Hammond

All too many discussions of consumption and related issues tend toward the extremes: the Malthusian position that we are about to exceed the earth's carrying capacity, run out of resources, or exceed the earth's capacity to absorb pollution; or the Cornucopian position that the earth's bounty, coupled with human ingenuity and markets, will surmount all obstacles and provide an ever-rising stream of economic goods, food, technologies, and so on. These positions—stated in their most general and sweeping terms—are suspect on basic principles, as we shall shortly illustrate. The Malthusian argument suffers an additional burden; historically, it has been demonstrably wrong, so far.

The fallacy of both extreme positions is perhaps most easily exposed by considering what is meant by the term "consumption." When economists use the term, they have in mind all the economic value that is produced by human activity, less only that which is saved; all else is, in this usage, "consumed," even intangibles such as legal services or television shows. By this definition, economic growth automatically implies growth in consumption. This is true but meaningless, at least with respect to the environment. If the additional economic activity imposes no environmental burden, then neither does the consumption that results.

Physical scientists, on the other hand, use "consumption" to mean conversion of matter or energy to an altered state, as in the consumption of iron ore to produce steel or the consumption of coal to produce electric power. Whether economic growth implies rising consumption in this sense depends on the precise nature of the economic activity which is increasing, that is to say, on the pattern of consumption. Rising sales of software need not imply any increase in the consumption of iron or coal; indeed, they may imply a decrease, if software contributes to more efficient use of electricity. Thus economic growth may or may not face resource limits or place additional burdens on the environment—the case remains open, pending closer investigation.

Biological scientists, to give a third usage of the term, often focus on the consumption of food or other biologically produced resources and on carrying capacity—the presumed limit of the earth's ability to produce such resources. This third sense of consumption does have a certain resonance with today's circumstances: overharvesting of many marine fisheries has led to a peak in the world's fish catch, and overuse is visibly degrading some other biological resources. But it is worth remembering that carrying capacity depends on technology and social organization and hence changes over time. England supports far more people today than Malthus believed possible, and American farmers (less than 3 percent of the U.S. population, compared with 30 to 40 percent a century ago) feed a much larger population and regularly produce surpluses. It is increasingly possible, in principle, to decouple food production from the environment, wholly or partially (consider aquaculture, the source of the most rapidly growing portion of the world's fish catch). For all these reasons, the relation of economic growth to consumption, and of consumption to environmental harm, is more complex, and more context specific, than might first appear.

I suggest that a careful examination of actual consumption patterns and their environmental effects supports a middle position. We are not, the evidence suggests, running out of subsoil or "nonrenewable" resources—minerals, fuels, and so on. Proven reserves have increased over the past twenty years, and commodity prices are down. Substitution (of optical fibers made from abundant silicon for copper wires, for example) is occurring, recycling is rising, and markets appear to be performing their allocative function. No apparent "limits to growth" can be seen in this direction.[1]

But—Cornucopians, please take note—we *are* encountering scarcities of many "renewable" resources and degradation of the biological systems that produce or support them. In effect, we are mining many biological resources in ways that render them nonrenewable. Thus fish and fisheries, wood and the forests that produce it (wood is the one basic commodity for which prices have risen over the past twenty years), water and watersheds or aquifers (in many but not all regions), and fertile soils are all showing signs of stress and decreasing per capita availability. Even fresh air, the most basic of renewable resources, is becoming an endangered resource in some urban areas, where the scale of human activity overwhelms natural renewal processes.

Close examination of the pattern of degradation shows that some of it is associated with consumption by the wealthy. It is high-tech fishing boats from industrialized countries that are stripping the marine fisheries, and it is industrial use of oil and coal that is priming the earth's atmosphere with greenhouse gases. Such consumption may rise with economic growth, if human society does not take measures to prevent it; unaided, the market will not take such measures.

Some of the degradation, however, is associated with the unplanned consumption of the world's poorest populations, who must depend directly upon natural ecosystems for most of their food, fiber, fuel, and often shelter. Markets cannot work for the 20 percent or more of the world's population that has no money to buy things and that live at subsistence levels. Economic growth here, if it raised populations out of absolute poverty and gave them economic choices, might actually reduce consumption from, and degradation of, the most overstressed portions of the biological resource base. If they could afford it, poor people might burn kerosene or use electricity rather than burn trees. And it is trees (and the watersheds and forests they anchor) and other renewable resources that appear more threatened than nonrenewable resources.

The Future of Growth

What of the future? Suppose that we can reduce poverty, and the environmental damage associated with it, through jobs and economic growth. Such development would stabilize biological resources that are now at risk. But can a global industrial system expand indefinitely? Will economic growth and expanding human populations not rapidly consume all available energy and material resources and produce more pollution than living things can tolerate?

Perhaps. But notice that in the industrial countries, per capita use of materials and energy has not grown significantly in twenty years. Indeed, structural shifts under way in the economy—toward services and knowledge-based activities rather than manufacturing and materials-based activities as the primary source of economic value—coupled with rapidly advancing information (and other) technologies make it plausible, if not certain, that per capita consumption of materials and energy could decline radically over the next fifty years. Knowledge workers do not generate the same consumption patterns as steel workers; production and consumption of software worth one hundred dollars has a far smaller environmental impact than production and consumption of an equivalent value of steel.

Set against these optimistic trends, however, is the reality that per capita consumption of energy and materials in developing countries—now far lower than in the developed world—will inevitably rise, even as population continues to grow. So global consumption, and many kinds of environmental problems, will rise, at least in the short term. Use of fossil fuels and emissions of greenhouse gases may double or even triple by the middle of the next century, so that we are likely to find out the real environmental consequences of global warming. Other forms of pollution, concentrated by swelling urban populations, will cause increasing local and regional degradation.

Such trends will continue until population growth stabilizes and the basic infrastructure for urban and industrialized societies is built in developing countries. Progress toward these goals is occurring at different rates in different regions and, on current prognosis, is unlikely to be complete before the middle of the next century. How rapidly the process goes forward, and the extent to which developing countries can make use of emerging technologies to build more energy-efficient, less resource-intensive infrastructures and economic patterns, will determine the overall environmental impact of global development. Here, explicit policies, and the leadership example (or lack of it) in the industrial countries, will certainly play a crucial role.

The consequences of global warming and the resulting changes in climate are not known with any certainty. They may well be quite significant. But human societies have adjusted to other significant changes in climate; we are very adaptable creatures, especially over a half-century or more. And even though local and regional pollution may get worse before it gets better, the evidence suggests that as people's living standards rise, so do their demands for clean air, clean water, and other environmental amenities—things we do know how to achieve. Indeed, just such demands have resulted in reductions in pollution in most industrial countries over the past twenty-five years, even with economic growth. So the prospect that, over the next half-century, India and China may achieve living standards and consumption patterns of a typical European country today is hardly the end of the world. This is especially true if we continue to use energy and materials ever more efficiently, which is the trend in both advanced countries and in many newly industrialized countries as well. Eventually, if we are to stabilize the climate, all human societies will have to depend largely on energy sources other than fossil fuels.

The Sources of Wealth

One way to consider what human societies might aspire to is to inquire into the sources of wealth in the broadest sense of that term. A recent and unusually bold study by the World Bank dares to provide estimates of the real wealth of nations—that is, not just their material possessions or "built" capital, but also the "natural" capital represented by biological and mineral resources and the "social" and human capital represented by people, their abilities, and their social organizations. The World Bank finds that by far the greatest portion of national wealth in all but the poorest nations comes from human capital, and that developed nations differ from developing ones primarily in having a greater proportion of their wealth in the form of human capital.[2]

Consider each form of wealth separately. We are gradually depleting some of the earth's natural capital, such as oil deposits, but there are potential substitutes (solar energy, for example). And the earth replenishes other forms of natural capital, such as trees (provided we do not clear the forests faster than they can regrow). Built capital can continue to accumulate, but it appears that we have already seen a saturation point in the more industrialized countries—limits to the *demand* for more consumption of this type rather than limits to material growth. For human and social capital, however, there appear to be no limits—no limits to the knowledge we can accumulate, to aesthetic achievement, to the desirability of more effective social organizations. If we can organize our economies so that their consumption patterns favor accumulation of human capital rather than material capital, then the human future would appear to be unbounded. It may even be worth trading some of our original inheritance, natural capital, for increased human capital, if that is the cost of redeeming human assets out of poverty and degradation.

So I assert that the relation between economic growth, consumption, and the environment is neither clearly an unalloyed good nor a proven evil. Basic principles and the available evidence both suggest a rather more complex, and mixed, assessment. Meanwhile, our consumption patterns *are* changing. More than 70 percent of U.S. economic activity is already based on services, rather than on manufacturing, and the percentage is climbing in virtually all countries. By means of vigorous policy, consumption patterns can be induced to change even further, in ways that would secure a more environmentally promising future. Note, however, that I do not predict such a future—the issue is still in doubt, and it depends on decisions and actions still to be taken in many regions of the world.

Notes

Originally published in *Report from the Institute for Philosophy and Public Policy,* University of Maryland at College Park 15, no. 4 (Special Issue Fall 1995): 9–12.

1. For the data in this essay, see Allen L. Hammond et al., *World Resources 1994–95* (New York: Oxford University Press, 1994), 3–26; and my essay, "Natural Resource Consumption: North and South," in the present volume.

2. The World Bank, *Monitoring Environmental Progress: A Report on Work in Progress* (Washington, D.C.: World Bank, 1995).

5

Food, Feed, and Land

Paul E. Waggoner

In the mid-1980s, oracles forecast how Americans would use their agricultural resources.[1] They bravely grappled with tough questions: Will rising meat consumption overwhelm the production of the crops on which meat production depends, especially as the supply of land per person shrinks? Will set-asides exclude, erosion destroy, or urbanization devour cropland? Have yields reached a plateau of biological limitation? Will changing climate or water and energy shortages surprise and bedevil farming? And will genetic engineering finally work miracles outdoors or will Malthusian forces at last raise farm prices? These questions remain for us to answer.

Twelve years on, we know that, despite multiplying population, rising yields and other factors kept American farmers cultivating about the same area of cropland as they had since the Great Depression (fig. 5.1). We know that the American consumption of beef and the number of cattle peaked (fig. 5.2). We know that exports of meat, poultry, fruit, and vegetables grew while exports of grains and oilseeds only fluctuated.[2] How can we learn from the last twelve years and earlier forecasts?

Earlier Oracles

Malthus made the most enduring forecast: Population grows geometrically while farming production grows only arithmetically. Malthus Sr. believed in Rousseau's utopia of Nature. Impressed by a global population of one billion in 1798, Malthus Jr. wrote his *Essay on the Principle of Population* to disabuse his father.[3] If the global population of one billion in 1798 impressed Malthus Jr., today's five to six billion would

69

Fig. 5.1. The lowest segment shows the cropland harvested since the New Deal. The narrow segment shows the land idled by fallow, failed crops, and federal programs. The large top segment, labeled "spared" shows how much more farmers would have cropped if cropland per person in America had remained as high as in 1932.

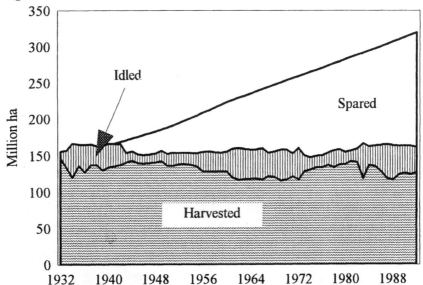

Source: Data from A. Dougherty, "Major Uses of Land in the United States," Resource and Technology Division, USDA ERS Agricultural Economic Report 643 (Washington, D.C.: USDA, 1987); and C. Sandretto (USDA), letter of 14 September 1994. The sum of the three segments in the figure was calculated as current population times the 1932 cropland per capita.

transfix him. People have nightmares that the looming population of ten billion will overwhelm Rousseau's utopia of Nature. They perennially predict higher food prices and prepare to stem the tide by, for example, legislating wilderness and posting signs on reserves.

But the tide of human needs overwhelms. Consider the letter Thomas Jefferson wrote James Madison after talking with a poor woman in the royal preserve of Fontainebleau: "I asked myself what could be the reason that so many should be permitted to beg who are willing to work in a country where there is a very considerable proportion of uncultivated lands? These lands are kept idle mostly for the sake of game. . . . Whenever there is in any country, uncultivated lands and unemployed poor . . . the laws of property have so far extended as to violate natural right."[4] Inspired by liberty, equality and fraternity, the mobs and guillotine of the French Revolution soon cut off the violation

Fig. 5.2. The number of beef cows in America reported by the U.S. Department of Agriculture (USDA) agricultural statistics and that number per 1000 human population.

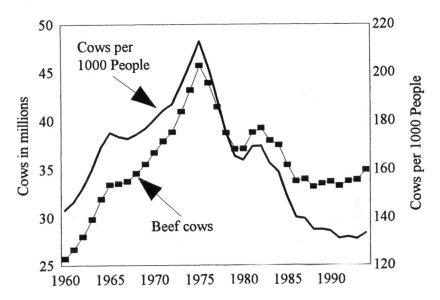

of natural right. And today Indonesians expand soybean fields, and impoverished Nordcstinos defeat good environmental intentions in Amazonia.

In the twenty-first century, proclamations in capitals and signs nailed to trees will not hold back billions of people if they need the reserved land. Nature's salvation lies not in proclamations and signs but in humanity having land to spare. Increasing crop yields, which will allow more food, feed, and fiber to be grown on the same or less area of cropland, are key to sparing the land.

Sparing Cropland per Person

Far and away the greatest threat to nature is lost habitat. First among the forces changing and consuming habitat is tillage, which turns over one-tenth of global and one-fifth of American land. A simple equation shows how to sparc cropland for nature.

$$A/P = (F+X)/Y$$

On the left stands the ratio that we wish to lower—hectares A per person P. The right-hand ratio suggests how to do it. Either lower the food and feed F per person, or raise the yield Y per hectare. For the globe, X is zero. For a nation, however, exports and imports per person X must be added to and subtracted from F. For an agricultural nation like the United States, freer trade gives a rising population in the rest of the world easier access to American food, increases X, and thus increases the American cropland per person A/P.

The blocks in figure 5.3 show that global cropland per person expanded from before Malthus until the mid-1950s. Each person took more land from nature than his parents did. Recently, however, cropland per person shrank. For the past forty-five years people have taken less from nature than their parents did.

Did people spare nature by reducing their consumption of food and feed F? No, just the opposite. From 1962 to 1989, the increase in the total calories in the world's food supply outpaced the growth in population, especially in poor countries. The supply of animal protein went up, too, especially in poor countries.[5] The triangles in figure 5.4 com-

Fig. 5.3. Three centuries of changing cropland per person.

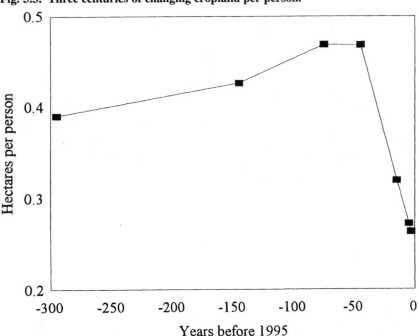

Years before 1995

Source: Data from J. F. Richards, "Land Transformation," in *The Earth as Transformed by Human Action,* ed. B. L. Turner et al. (Cambridge, England: Cambridge University Press, 1990), 163–78; and Food and Agriculture Organization of the United Nations, *FAO Yearbook,* vol. 45 (Rome: FAO), tables 1 and 3.

Fig. 5.4. The quantity of meat and feed produced in the United States and outside the United States compared to 1967.

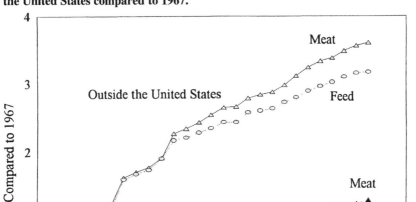

pare the production of beef, pork, and poultry in years since 1967 with production in that year. I separate production inside the United States (at the bottom) from production outside the United States (at the top). For a generation the American meat supply rose only 30 percent. Outside America the supply nearly quadrupled.[6]

In order to calculate how much land this production took, I first translated meat into feed. I neglected the savings of feed from cattle grazing and pigs eating waste, but I included in my calculations the fact that poultry convert feed to meat efficiently. Because Americans ate more poultry, they kept feed consumption almost constant while increasing total meat consumption by 30 percent. Outside the United States, a changing mix of beef, pork, and poultry consumption slowed the rise of feed consumption also. Nevertheless, quadrupling meat production outside the United States did take more feed.

But figure 5.3 showed that cropland per person fell despite more calories and meat per person. That means higher yields spared nature. The rising yields of maize exemplify the change. The long history of wheat yields tells the same story. After changing little from Babylon through Malthus's time to World War II, yields jumped in many nations, as shown in figure 5.5.

Fig. 5.5. The course of wheat yields in four nations on four continents.

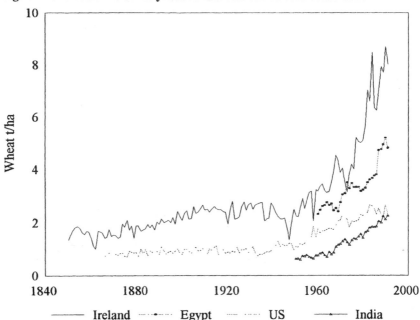

In figure 5.6, I repeat the rising amounts of meat and feed consumed outside the United States and add the area of coarse grains required to produce the meat. The repeated meat triangles and feed circles again show that the changing mix of beef, pork, and poultry caused feed production to rise more slowly than meat production. Blocks in the figure show that rising yields slowed the expansion of cropland even more. In twenty-five years outside America, meat more than tripled and feed tripled, but cropland to grow the feed only doubled.

The drama was unmistakable in America. Meat was up 30 percent, feed consumption was nearly unchanged, but land use was *down* 40 percent. Consumers spared some land by choosing different meat, but farmers did the heavy lifting with higher yields. Remember, my calculations neglected savings of cropland from cattle grazing and from pigs eating waste food, which exaggerates the savings of cropland by consumers choosing more poultry. Also, farmers spared land by growing higher yields of food crops, such as wheat and rice. Figures 5.4 and 5.6 report calculations, but a look at the actual figures for cropland growing feed tells the same story. Despite the rising meat consumption in and outside the United States, the percentage of the rather constant American cropland devoted to corn did not materially change (figure 5.7). The

Fig. 5.6. The quantity of meat, feed, and land needed to grow the feed outside the United States compared to 1967.

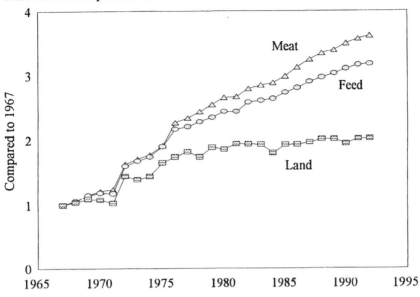

Fig. 5.7. The amount of cropland for exported and other corn in the United States as a percentage of all harvested cropland.

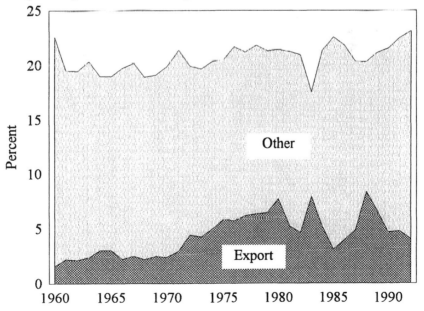

area for neither exported corn nor corn used in the United States changed materially, confirming that higher yields buffered the impact of increased meat consumption on land use.

Parenthetically, I remind the reader that, while farmers were sparing land for nature by lifting yields of feed crops, they were also sparing land by raising yields of such food crops as wheat and rice.

If the experience with yields and meat reported in figures 5.4 and 5.6 is prologue, the expansion of cropland projected for increased meat consumption as well as population must be tempered a little for a changing mix of meat and a lot for rising crop yields.

Can Research, Incentives and Farmers Keep on Lifting Yields?

Whether the rising yields since 1940 are prologue worried agriculture experts twelve years ago and must be faced before we can answer the question, "How much *more* land can farmers spare?" Have yields reached a plateau of biological limitation?

Those worried about biological limitations frequently cite the stubborn Japanese rice yields.[7] Because about half of American rice is exported, yields abroad can affect the extent of American cropland as well as provide evidence of biological limits. In figure 5.8, I compare the yields of Japan, which produces about 3 percent of the global crop, to those of three nations that together produce about two-thirds. Unlike Japanese yields of milled rice, which reached 4 tons per hectare (t/ha) in the 1960s and have scarcely risen for twenty-five years, yields in the other countries have risen considerably from the 1 to 2 t/ha yields of the 1960s. Nevertheless, a pessimist will easily perceive that all have risen slowly for five years. The 4 t/ha cannot, however, be a biological limit because in Australia and California *average* yields have touched or approached 6 t/ha, and in Morocco, Egypt, and Korea they have exceeded 4.6 t/ha. Further, yields of rice have exceeded 10 t/ha from large fields in China.[8] Assuredly, there is a ceiling. But where? I could locate the ceiling of production by the amount of photosynthesis the planet's sunshine could energize; its water, carbon dioxide, and fertilizer could supply; or its land and climate could sustain. That ceiling would feed multiples of ten billion.[9] Or, for a ceiling on yield I might calculate a maximum from plant physiology or call up visions of genetic engineering. Instead of calculation and vision, I choose a high yield already grown as a limit and plot in figure 5.9 the winning yield in the 1992 American corn growing contest.[10] U.S. farmers can keep on lifting their

Fig. 5.8. The course of rice yields in four nations.

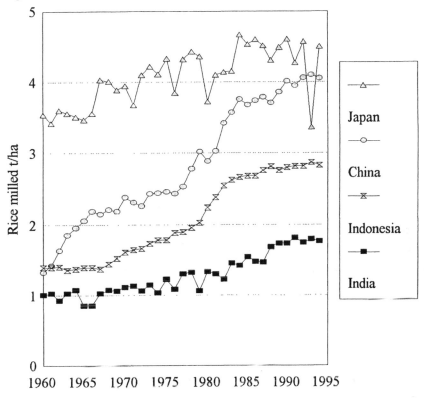

national average far before striking the limit of 21 t/ha grown in Pasco, Washington, in 1992.

In figure 5.9, fixing on the actual but single Pasco yield implies the limit is forever set, and plotting U.S. averages neglects the rest of the world. If the limit is set, then every rise in the average diminishes the gap of opportunity for further rises. The generation of experience in the Iowa Master Corn Growers' contest shows otherwise in figure 5.10.[11] Although the Iowa winners have yet to catch up with the yields in the brilliant sun and irrigation of Pasco, Iowa is the preeminent corn state. Since 1960, the doubling of the world average has not narrowed the gap between the world average and the Iowa average. Similarly, the winners of the Iowa Master Corn Growers' contest have kept open the gap of opportunity above the Iowa average by lifting the limit represented by their yields. Given research and incentives, farmers everywhere should be able to keep on raising yields.

Fig. 5.9. The course of American maize yields, projected toward a limit of the winning 21t/ha.

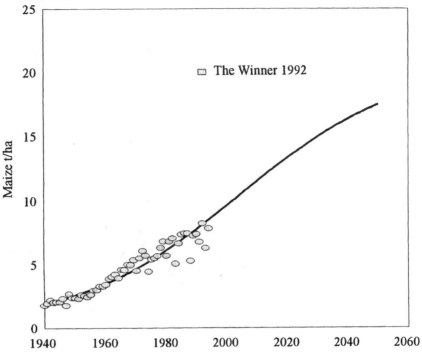

Urbanization

In the mid-1980s, there was also alarm about urbanization devouring cropland. A national appraisal placed the annual losses at over 1 million ha. Time would prove E. O. Heady[12] wise to suspect twelve years ago that the losses were much less than 1 million ha and to point out that, as large as the *relative* expansion of urban use was, it shrank cropland very little. Others voiced the widely held fear that urbanization devoured prime agricultural soils disproportionately, that is, faster than other soils.

We now have a clearer view of this subject. The USDA[13] undertook a painstaking study of changing urban use in 135 fast-growth counties. They compared aerial photographs at the same places over time, so-called paired points. The USDA found 0.4 to 0.6 acres converted per household during 1970–80, about the same as earlier USDA estimates, slightly less than the census estimate of 0.7 acres during 1970–80, and about a quarter of the 2.1 acres estimate published by the National Ag-

Fig. 5.10. World and Iowa average maize yields and the yields of the winners of the Iowa Master Corn Growers' Contest. Drought in 1988 and floods in 1993 cut yields.

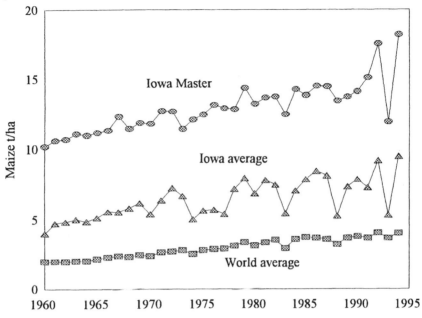

ricultural Lands Study during 1967–75. At three persons per household, the 0.4 to 0.7 acres becomes 540 to 940 square meters per person.

Highlights of the study of 135 fast-growing counties are:

- Prime agricultural land was *not* urbanized disproportionately;
- Conversions of forest and other rural land to cropland countered losses to urbanization; and
- Counties use *less* land per added household as population grows denser.

A study of twenty-nine counties[14] that grew rapidly from 1950 to 1987 produced the surprises that:

- Farmland shrank slightly *less* in these counties than in the rest of the country;
- Farmers in these counties shifted to more valuable products and actually sold *more* in terms of constant dollars.

The urbanization of farmland will continue to fascinate us. The spread of a great city strikes the eye as one lands at its airport or commutes to its center. The view from a plane over the world's busiest airport, O'Hare International in Chicago, cannot fail to impress, and E. W. Johnson recently wrote, "Consider the Chicago metropolitan area. While the region's population grew by only 4 percent from 1970 to 1990, residential land consumption increased by 46 percent, and suburban commercial and industrial land consumption increased by 74 percent."[15] Under the headline, "As Earth Day Turns 25, Life Gets Complicated," the *New York Times* anticipated that land-use issues would replace the antitoxics and wilderness preservation campaigns of the last twenty-five years.[16] The commentator added, "But protecting the landscape from the assaults of urban sprawl will demand something more than, and different from, the standard regulatory prohibitions." Further, Marchetti has speculated that, because people travel about an hour a day and expand their ambit as they travel faster, they enlarge their territories in proportion to the square of their speed.[17]

These warnings of urban sprawl are, however, softened by remembering that in the 135 fast-growing counties cited above, new households use less land as population grows denser. Similarly, the land developed per person in populous states like New York and New Jersey is much smaller than in less populous states like North Dakota or Montana. Although rising population will urbanize land, I expect development of land will not be proportional to the growing number of people. I expect that an increasing population density caused by a national increase in population plus concentration in metropolises will shrink the area developed per person.[18]

Unfortunately there is no precise moment at which nonurban land becomes part of the city. A pessimist would set the time when population reaches a certain density on a tract or an urban political boundary encloses it. An optimist might postpone the moment until the land no longer supports photosynthesis. So the definition of urban land can affect the calculation of the rate of urbanization, spreading alarm or complacency.

Fortunately, while we continue to be fascinated by the urbanization of land, especially in suburban states like Connecticut, the nation can continue secure for a while with Heady's conclusion that even *relatively* fast expansion of urban use shrinks America's wide cropland *relatively* little.

Reasonable Projections

Rising yields with headroom for still higher ones lead to projections of steady to moderately expanding cropland in America despite the burgeoning world population, its increasing meat consumption, and easier trade. For the U.S. Congress, experts projected adequate cropland irrigation for 2030.[19]

For the European Union (EU), R. Rabbinge and colleagues projected to A.D. 2015 the changes from the present 130 million ha of farmland in the EU. For Europe, free trade increases imports, and the Rabbinge free-trade scenario cuts cropland about two-thirds. A scenario spreading farm employment over Europe cuts cropland about 40 percent. A conservation scenario lowers cropland 80 percent. Even a scenario minimizing pesticides allows cropland to fall by half.[20]

Four years ago Resources for the Future (RFF)[21] assessed future American farming for the Environmental Protection Agency (EPA). Their business-as-usual scenario for A.D. 2010 envisioned growth in demand, modest at home and strong abroad, and continued competitive strength of American farmers. Business as usual expanded cropland, but not back to the area of the early 1980s. Water demand shifted production east. RFF wrote that the American commitment to wildlife might improve present habitat or get more habitat elsewhere rather than inhibit the expansion of cropland.

RFF's environmentally friendly scenario assumed that Americans would eat less meat, global population growth would slow, farmers abroad would raise yields, and less research and more rules would make American farming more costly. This would cut land and water use one-sixth and spare more for nature. In the end, diverse agricultural experts using diverse scenarios projected little expansion and perhaps possible contraction of American and European cropland.

Surprises

These are reasonable projections. Unfortunately, affairs conspire to surprise us and justify the title of C. Cerf and V. Navasky's *The Experts Speak: The Definitive Compendium of Authoritative Misinformation.*[22] So, while not crying "wolf" or "the sky is falling," I must allow for some likely surprises. I pick population, water supply, shifty pests, climate change, and breakthroughs. I reserve environmental cost for my conclusion.

Population

UN projections[23] for the twenty-first century run to the neighborhood of ten billion, which would surely affect demand for American food and feed and thus cropland area. But among the surprises could be a far smaller global population. Experts provide a range from six to nineteen billion around their central projection of eleven billion for A.D. 2100. Reasonable roots for surprises are found in a 1994 *New York Times* article, "Poor Lands' Success in Cutting Birth Rates Upsets Old Theories."[24] In addition to the reported success of contraception, a pandemic of AIDS and rapid economic gains in Asia provide other roots for a surprising slowing of population growth. Finally, the slower than expected rise of cereal and oilseed consumption since the 1970s[25] would temper the expansion of cropland for any increase of population.

Water

Although new varieties figure prominently in the Green Revolution, especially the public view, expanding irrigation helped. Two forces seem poised to cause a surprising slowing of the expansion. First, other uses compete with irrigation for water, and, in America, irrigated area is shrinking in every region but the East.

The second force is environmental opposition. Environmental harm, notably the salinization of soil, can follow poorly managed irrigation. The title of a campaign to discourage the World Bank financing a large project—"World Bank/IMF: 50 Years is Enough"—exemplifies the force of environmental opposition. The headline of the campaign, "World Bank's Arun Dam . . . Environmental Quagmire and Economic Folly," makes the opposition to global expansion of irrigation clear.

With expansion of irrigated area slowing, a slower increase of average yields seems almost too certain to be called surprising. The slower expansion challenges agriculture to grow more crop from each liter of water. Engineering to save water between canal and roots will help, as will higher yields on the watered land. Experiments spanning thirty years in Texas demonstrate more crop can be grown with less water: Because the evapotranspiration from soil and winter wheat changed little while the harvest doubled, the efficiency of water use doubled.[26]

New Pests

Pests are shifty. Unforeseen pests cause disastrous outbreaks. Surprising new fungi caused both the Irish potato famine of the 1840s and the Southern maize leaf blight of 1970. A National Research Council report summarizes: "History warns that new pests will appear but provides no data for a model that tells where and when newcomers will appear or what they will be like. The required warning system of sharp, exploring eyes in the field is old-fashioned but remains our most effective approach."[27] Although the generality that new pests will rise is sure, their specifics will surprise us, lower yield, and press on the supply of cropland until scientists and farmers bring the pests under control.

Maintenance Research

Rising yields represent progress that must be maintained. Dewey wrote "For certainly progress in civilization has not only meant increase in the scope and intricacy of problems to be dealt with, but it entails increasing instability. For in multiplying wants, instruments and possibilities, it increases the variety of forces which enter into relations with one another and which have to be intelligently directed."[28] As people enjoy the progressive rise of yield seen in figure 5.9, wants multiply, increasing the variety of forces that must be directed. For example, maintaining the gain in yield requires promptly replacing a variety that proves susceptible to a new pest. The replacement in turn requires keeping diverse genes at hand. Generally, as productivity rises, maintenance research is needed to uphold the gains and avoid unpleasant surprises.[29]

Unfortunately clues appear, as in the falling amounts of money granted to the International Agricultural Research Centers, that the world, perhaps lulled by success of past research, or thinking that yields lift themselves, may fail to maintain agricultural research. That failure would level yields, surprisingly and unpleasantly.

Climate Change

Although weather may have been surprising during recent decades, climate has not been. Nevertheless, modelers of global climate predict that within a century the known enrichment of the atmosphere with greenhouse gases will alter climate. Because their predictions disagree—especially about the critical factor, precipitation—I put climate change in the category of surprises.

The higher yields shown in figure 5.9 have further to fall than lower ones if unfavorable climate and weather surprise farmers. To explore whether yields are already becoming more variable, I plotted the change in yield from year to year in figure 5.11. For example, the Iowa average, which had suffered from the floods of 1993, rose 78 percent in 1994. The world average, which encompassed regions that did not suffer the floods, rose only 10 percent. The winning yield of the Iowa Master Corn Growers' contest fell relatively less in 1993 and rose an intermediate 52 percent from 1993 to 1994. Interest centers, however, on the growing variability as yields rise with time, providing more latitude for surprises. Climate change being one possible surprise, agriculture's practi-

Fig. 5.11. The change of average world, average Iowa, and winning Iowa Master Corn Growers' yields of figure 5.10 from one year to the next as a fraction of the first.

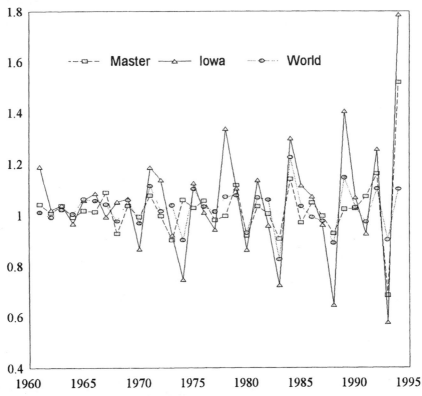

cal preparation is a diversified portfolio of responses to ease or exploit any changes and the flexibility to use the portfolio.[30] Diverse climates and genes, easy changes of land use, storage of food, and research are features of a flexible portfolio.

Breakthroughs

To preserve credibility, one must accede that some surprises are happy ones. It is optimistic but rational to hope that some breakthrough will become practice before world population reaches tens of billions. A breakthrough could jump yields and surprise us just as the leap after World War II would have surprised Malthus. The distance between average yields and the actual—not theoretical—winning 21 t/ha in figure 5.9 leaves room for a surprise. One can visualize that genetic engineering transferring genes from the winning maize to other crops might cause the surprise. The surprise would dislocate existing farming as did inventions such as railroads, cotton pickers, and higher-yielding varieties in the past, retiring old arrangements and opening opportunities for the venturesome. Still, the surprise would spare more land for nature.

Environmental Expense

The quotation from Jefferson calling fallow land a violation of natural right and the example of the French Revolution show the futility of reserving land for wildlife by signs and regulations when people are hungry and farmers are willing. For a given population and consumption, therefore, sparing land for nature comes down to raising yields. Contest winners can stir worriers' hopes that winning yields keep headroom open for raising yields. Still, worriers fear that externalities or environmental expense from higher yields will harm the very habitat spared. And their strictures could affect yield and thus expanse of cropland.

High yields require fertilizer, especially nitrogen, which makes protein in crops for human consumption. Without fertilizer, crops mine the soil and dwindle. Nevertheless, too much of anything can cause harm, and Kinzig and Socolow[31] wrote with alarm that in 1994 the use of nitrogen fertilizer had jumped to ten times its 1960 level, which I show in figure 5.12. Kinzig and Socolow showed only the explosive rise of nitrogen fertilization until 1985, which is shown by the solid curve in the figure.

Bringing the record of nitrogen fertilizer up to date, however, shows surprising results: The explosion from 1960 to 1985 ended in the 1980s. Boxes in figure 5.12 show the actual nitrogen use and circles show the projections by the World Bank and industry. After 1988, falling use in the former Soviet bloc lowered the global total. For the long run, other developed nations provide a window on the future. In France, use trended upward slowly until 1991 and then fell. In the United States, use has been level for fifteen years. Still, I shall use the example of fertilizer to explore whether the environmental expense or externalities of lifting yields will cancel the profit of sparing land for nature.

Integrating Expense and Reckoning It in Relation to Goals

Expense and profit remind me of that theoretical product, the widget. Freight bills would not obsess the manufacturer of widgets. She would

Fig. 5.12. Global use of nitrogen fertilizer (boxes) and its projected use (circles).

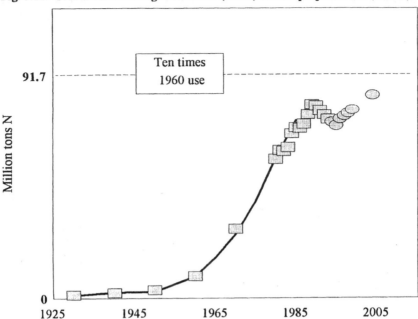

integrate all expenses. Also she would relate expenses to filling orders
for widgets rather than reckoning expense per square meter of factory
floor. I must be at least as wise as Boss Widgets, avoiding obsession
with, say, nitrogen and instead integrating several expenses into a holistic sum. I must relate expense to filling orders rather than reckoning it
per hectare of cropland.

The world orders tons of food and feed from farmers. In my example,
I integrate the environmental expense for land and fertilizer to fill humanity's order for 5 tons. The peculiarity of my choice of 5 emphasizes
that humanity places the order. The farmer's responsibility is minimizing the environmental expense to fill humanity's order.

To integrate quantities of land and fertilizer into the environmental
expense of growing humanity's 5 tons, I must take into account their
interrelations: More kilograms of fertilizer per hectare, higher yield,
and fewer hectares plowed and fertilized. In Iowa experiments, 10 kg/
ha nitrogen and 10 kg/ha phosphate yielded only 2 t/ha.[32] Raising nitrogen to 40 kg/ha with no increase in phosphate raised yield by only half.
Putting nitrogen and phosphate in step at 40 kg/ha lifted yield to 2.5
times the yield from 10 kg/ha each of nitrogen and phosphate. Finally,
80 kg/ha of each fertilizer yielded only a decreasing return in yield for
the extra fertilizer.

Farmers can fill the order for 5 tons on fewer hectares and spare land with fertilizer. But at what integrated expense of nitrogen plus phosphate plus land?

Because no market sets the environmental prices of hectares of land and kilograms of fertilizer, I shall invent a currency denominated in enviros (en) rather than dollars. I start with a price of 1 enviro per kilogram of each fertilizer element. I remember that habitat is preeminent and 1 ha requires about 100 kg of fertilizer. I say cropping 1 ha costs the same 100 en as 100 kg of nitrogen or phosphate. Although you may change my prices, you must ante up a set of environmental prices—enviros per hectare and enviros per kilogram—to play holistic environmental analysis.

In figure 5.13 I show the combinations of 10, 40 and 80 kg/ha fertilizer. Instead of yield, however, the vertical scale shows the enviros of expense to fill the order for 5 tons. In each bar, the bottom segment represents the enviros for land or habitat used; the middle segment

Fig. 5.13. Environmental cost of filling humanity's order for 5 tons of corn as nitrogen N and phosphate P fertilizer rates are raised.

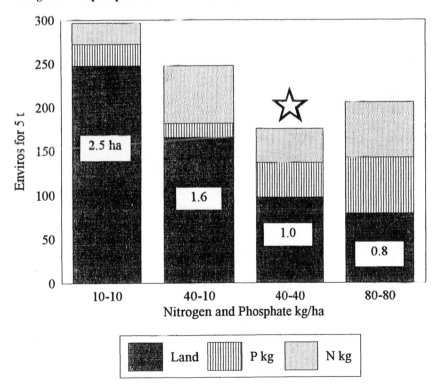

shows the enviros for kilograms of phosphate; and the top segment represents the enviros for kilograms of nitrogen. The first bar shows that with rates of 10 kg/ha nitrogen and phosphate, the farmer tilled 2.5 ha. At 100 enviros per hectare, 2.5 ha cost 250 enviros. On top of the 250 enviros for land stand 25 enviros for 10 kg phosphate/ha on 2.5 ha and the same for nitrogen. Growing the 5 tons with 10 and 10 fertilizer cost 300 enviros of integrated expense.

From the first to the second bar only the nitrogen rate changes, rising from 10 to 40 kg/ha. Although now limited by phosphate, which remained at 10 kg/ha, yield still rose and shrank area expense, the hectares to fill the order for 5 tons of corn. Shrinking the area fertilized lowered the phosphate quantity or expense and held nitrogen expense below the quadrupling that the change from 10 to 40 kg/ha might mislead one to expect. Remember, environmental expense is calculated from the kilograms of fertilizer to grow the order of 5 tons, not from rates of kilograms per hectare. So, less area to fertilize cut phosphate expense and tempered nitrogen expense from the quadrupled rate.

The star over the third, 40 and 40, bar signifies minimized integrated expense. One ha, just 40 percent of the 2.5 ha to fill the order for 5 tons with 10 and 10 fertilizer rates, filled the order. The 40 and 40 fertilizer rate cut land expense more than it raised fertilizer quantity and enviros. Going on to the fourth bar, 80 and 80, took a lot of fertilizer to save a little land.

What story does this chart tell? Improving the nitrogen rate from the first to second bar of figure 5.13 lowers the cost in land and phosphate. Getting phosphate in step from the second to third bar minimizes environmental expense. Optimizing production factors in step minimizes the integrated environmental expense of filling humanity's order for food and feed.

Intensive, precision farming[33] searches for the holy grail of that minimum for every square meter. The minimum integrated expense lies in the rational middle ground where land and fertilizer elements are in step.

You may still ask, "What about the environmental expense of other production factors, like pesticides, water, or silt?" The shade of lush crops makes weeds easier to control, and controlling weeds raises yields and shrinks the land tilled. Because insects and disease are controlled per hectare, higher yields lower the kilograms of pesticides required. Twice the yield per hectare, half the area, half the kilograms of pesticide applied at a constant rate. Shrinking the hectares to fill humanity's order lessens water consumption. Less sprawl of tillage means less erosion and silt. Optimizing all production factors in step minimizes environmental expense.

If we integrate environmental expense logically, including land, environmental strictures will not widen tillage or hinder the sparing of land.

What Will It Take for Ten Billion to Spare Land?

Earlier, I wrote a simple formula showing how food, exports, and yields set the cropland per person and thus land spared for nature. Rearranged, the formula calculates global cropland area.

$$A = P * (F+X) / Y$$

For the world, exports X are zero, and area A rises in proportion to population P and to food and feed F. Area A falls in proportion to yield Y. Because global demand profoundly affects American cropland, I shall examine the simple case of the globe, with an X of zero and a future population of ten billion.

In figure 5.14, the horizontal line at 1.4 billion ha or one-tenth of global land shows today's cropland. The upper margin at 2.8 billion shows how much more farmers will crop if population doubles with no change in food, feed, or yield. I arranged yields along the horizontal axis. Arrows mark typical yields in tons per hectare. They range from 1 for African wheat to 8 for Irish wheat or American corn. Near 5 I wrote *potatoes* because American potatoes produce as many calories per hectare as 5 tons of grain.

Farmers grow many crops: apples, coconuts, sisal, tea, broccoli, and wheat. The calories in all these divided by today's population come to six thousand calories per day for food, feed, and fiber. Divided by present cropland, the calories equal 2 t/ha of grain. I placed the star at 2 t/ha and today's 1.4 billion ha of cropland.[34]

The lower curve passing by the star shows how the land area farmers crop for today's population, food, and feed would explode if yields decreased to the left. Look at the higher curve marked by boxes to see how higher yields will spare land if population multiplies to ten billion.

If agriculture can push yields right to 4 t/ha or higher, ten billion people can spare as much or more land as today. If not, farmers will plow more and more land. If yields don't rise, farmers will help the ten billion postpone what Malthus called misery by taking land from nature to fill humanity's order for food and feed.

It Can Be Done

Two generations of American experience shown in figure 5.1 makes sparing land conceivable. Today in America alone, changes in yield

Fig. 5.14. Global cropland as a function of yield for present population (lower curve) and for ten billion provided the same six thousand calories per day for food, feed, and fiber (boxes).

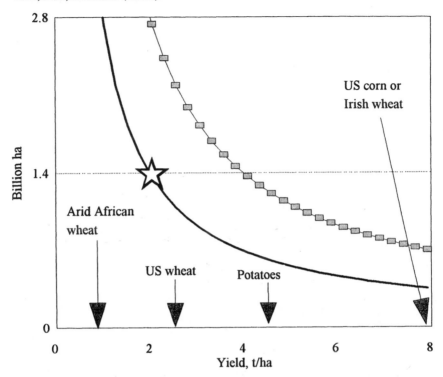

spare one-fifth of the expanse of the Amazonian basin. In American units they spare 177 times the acreage of Yellowstone. Lifted yields are the source of abandoned fields in New England, on the Great Plains, and elsewhere. In the Great Plains, this spared farmland is called the Buffalo Commons.[35]

In the end, proclamations and signs won't save nature. Higher yields spared nature, and they don't lift themselves. It takes vital research by agronomists, the right incentives from humanity, and venturing suppliers and farmers to spare land for nature.

Notes

An earlier version of this paper, "How Much More Land Can American Farmers Spare?" was originally presented at the RCA III Symposium on Crop and Livestock Technologies, May 1995. In addition to the Connecticut Station, I thank the Program for the Human Environment at Rockefeller University and the Council for Agricultural Science and Technology for their support. I thank Jesse Ausubel, Ed Runge, and Iddo Wernick for their suggestions.

1. B. C. English, J. A. Maetzold, B. R. Holding, and E. O. Heady, eds., *Future Agricultural Technology and Resource Conservation* (Ames: Iowa State University Press, 1984).

2. USDA, *Agricultural Statistics* (Washington, D.C.: USDA, 1993), table 371.

3. Thomas R. Malthus, *An Essay on the Principle of Population* (Cambridge: Cambridge University Press, 1992 [1803]).

4. Thomas Jefferson, letter of 28 October 1785 to James Madison, in *The Papers of Thomas Jefferson*, vol. 8, ed. J. P. Boyd (Princeton, N.J.: Princeton University Press, 1953), 681–83.

5. Food and Agriculture Organization of the United Nations (FAO), *FAO Yearbook*, vol. 45 (Rome: FAO, 1992), tables 106 and 107.

6. Consumers continue to be urged to forgo red meat in the name of the environment. (See for example, A. P. Kinzig and R. H. Socolow, "Human Impacts on the Nitrogen Cycle," *Physics Today* 47, no. 11 (1994): 24–31.) My intention is to show a maximum such a changing consumption or diet may cause. My foundation is the PS&D View database of the USDA ERS, 1 October 1994. I calculated meat consumption as the quantity of poultry meat, the head of cattle slaughtered times 300 kg in the United States and 200 outside, and the head of pigs slaughtered times 80 kg in the United States and 75 outside. I calculated the feed consumed to produce the meat with ratios of three for poultry, twelve for beef, and six for pork, which resemble the feed consumed per unit of production of broilers, beef, and hogs, reported by the USDA in *Agricultural Statistics*. Finally, I calculated the land by dividing the feed by the yields of coarse grains. Refining this simple process by recognizing that cattle consume roughage and pigs consume feed that would otherwise be wasted would lessen the conservation of cropland by the change from beef and pork to poultry. Differential improvements among animals in feed per production would modify somewhat the results of changing consumption from one animal to another. Improvements in conversion of feed to meat in all animals would slow the rise in demand for feed. The large features and conclusions would, however, remain.

7. B. Holmes, "A New Study Finds There's Life Left in the Green Revolution," *Science* 261 (1993): 1517.

8. S. Peng, "Report of Trip by Kush, Cassman, and Peng to Yunnan Province, 15 September 1993" (Manila: IRRI, 1993).

9. See Paul E. Waggoner, "How Much Land Can Ten Billion People Spare for Nature?" Report 121 (Ames, Iowa: The Council on Agricultural Science and Technology, 1994) (the full report is available at <http://www-forum1.stanford.edu/jmc/nature/nature.html>); Paul E. Waggoner, "How Much Land Can Ten Billion People Spare for Nature? Does Technology Make a Difference?" *Technology in Society* 17 (1995): 17–34; and R. Rabbinge, "The Ecological Background of Food Production," in *Crop Protection and Sustainable*

Agriculture, ed. Derek J. Chadwick and Joan Marsh (Chichester, N.Y.: John Wiley & Sons, 1993), 2–29.

10. Compared to theoretical computations of maximum yields, winning yields have the virtue of reality. The high yield in Pasco, Washington, in 1992 was reproducible; the same farmer grew about the same yield in 1993. High yields are widespread. In the 1993 contest, 92 of 922 entrants who irrigated produced more than 12.5 t/ha (200 bushels per acre) in places as diverse as Massachusetts, Florida, South Dakota, New Mexico, Louisiana, Washington, and California. Tabulation of the contestants in the 1992 and 1993 maize yield contest from the National Corn Growers Association, 1000 Executive Parkway, St. Louis, Mo., 63141-6397.

11. W. R. Hansen, Iowa Crop Improvement Association, Ames, Iowa, 1994, and the PS&D database of the USDA.

12. E. O. Heady, "Setting for Agricultural Production and Resource Use in the Future," in *Future Agricultural Technology*, ed. English et al., 8–30.

13. For comparison of various estimates, see M. Vesterby, R. E. Heimlich, and K. S. Krupa, "Urbanization of Rural Land in the United States," USDA ERS Agricultural Economics Report 673 (1994), 33. For studies of the 135 fast-growing counties see the same report.

14. M. Vesterby and K. S. Krupa, "Urbanization and Development Effects on the Use of Natural Resources," in Southern Rural Development Center Pub. 169, ed. E. M. Thunberg and J. E. Reynolds (1993), 85–114.

15. E. W. Johnson, "The Dispersed and Stratified Metropolis," *American Academy of Arts and Sciences Bulletin* 48, no. 7 (1995): 5–18.

16. K. Schneider, "As Earth Day Turns 25, Life Gets Complicated," *New York Times*, 16 April 1995, E6.

17. C. Marchetti, "Infrastructures for Movement: Past and Future," in *Cities and Their Vital Systems*, ed. J. H. Ausubel and R. Hermann (Washington, D.C.: National Academy Press, 1988), 146–74.

18. Evidence of slowing expansion with increasing density can be seen in figure 4.2.2 of "How Much Land Can Ten Billion People Spare for Nature?" A. Gruble, "Technology and Global Change: Land-use, Past and Present," WP-92-2 (Laxenburg: IIASA, 1992) adds further evidence: Even in Japanese metropolitan regions and Vienna, where densities reach 1 to 4 thousand people per km², buildings and infrastructure occupy only one-third of the land. For a comparison of American states, see Paul E. Waggoner, Jesse H. Ausubel, and I. K. Wernick, "Lightening the Tread of Population on the Land: American Examples," *Population and Development Review* 22 (1996): 531–45.

19. "The Second RCA Appraisal," Miscellaneous Publication 1482 (Washington, D.C.: USDA, 1990).

20. R. Rabbinge et al., "Ground for Choices," *Reports to the Government* 42 (The Hague, Netherlands: Science Council for Government Policy, 1992).

21. U.S. Environmental Protection Agency, "Agricultural Futures Project: Overview and Summary" (Washington, D.C.: U.S. Environmental Protection Agency, 1992).

22. C. Cerf and V. Navasky, *The Experts Speak: The Definitive Compendium of Authoritative Misinformation* (New York: Pantheon, 1984).

23. United Nations, Long-range World Population Projections, ST/ESA/ SER.A/125 (New York: United Nations, 1992).

24. W. K. Stevens, "Poor Lands' Success in Cutting Birth Rates Upsets Old Theories," *New York Times*, 2 January 1994, 1, 8. The headline encapsulates the report that, for example, the fertility rate of Bangladesh fertility declined 21 percent during 1970–91. For a full report see B. Robey, S. O. Rutstein, and L. Morris, "Fertility Decline in Developing Countries," *Scientific American* 269, no. 6 (December 1993): 60–67.

25. David Seckler, "Trends in World Food Needs: Toward Zero Growth in the 21st Century," Center for Economic Policy Studies Discussion Paper 18 (Arlington, Va.: Winrock International, 1991).

26. For regional courses of irrigated area in the United States, see "Preparing U.S. Agriculture for Global Climate Change," Report 119 (Ames, Iowa: Council for Agricultural Science and Technology, 1992), figure 5.6.1. The criticism of the World Bank is in Circular Letter, 13 September 1994 (Washington, D.C.: Environmental Defense Fund, 1994). Growing more grain with the same water is reported by M. E. Jensen, "New Technology Related to Water Policy-engineering," in *Water and Water Policy in World Food Supplies*, ed. W. R. Jordan (College Station: Texas A&M University Press, 1987), 43–49.

27. National Research Council, "Pest Management," *Climate and Food* (Washington D.C.: National Academy of Sciences, 1976), 128f. J. Goudriaan and J. C. Zadoks emphasize the scarcity of clear-cut examples where a climatic change of a few years shifted pests. See Goudriaan and Zadoks, "Global Climate Change: Modeling the Potential Response of Agro-Ecosystems with Special Reference to Crop Protection," *Environmental Pollution* 87 (1995): 215–24.

28. John Dewey, *Human Nature and Conduct: An Introduction to Social Psychology* (New York: Modern Library, 1930 [1922]), 286.

29. D. L. Plucknett and N. J. H. Smith, "Sustaining Agricultural Yields: As Productivity Rises, Maintenance Research is Needed to Uphold the Gains," *BioScience* 36 (1986): 40–45.

30. Council for Agricultural Science and Technology, "Preparing U.S. Agriculture for Global Climate Change." Report 119 (Ames: The Council on Agricultural Science and Technology, 1992).

31. Kinzig and Socolow, "Human Impacts on the Nitrogen Cycle," 24–31. For reported use, see Food and Agriculture Organization, *FAO Yearbook Fertilizer*. World Bank/FAO/UNIDO/Industry Fertilizer Working Group projections conveyed by Keith Isherwood, International Fertilizer Association, Paris, 5 January 1995. An exchange of letters was published in *Physics Today* 48, no. 8 (1995): 74–75.

32. E. O. Heady, J. T. Pesek, and W. G. Brown, "Crop Response Surfaces and Economic Optima in Fertilizer Use," Iowa Agricultural Experiment Station Research Bulletin 424 (1955): 292–332. 1 t/ha of corn is about 16 bushels per acre. I calculated the experimental results with the equation: Yield t/ha = N kg/ha / (N + 8) * P_2O_5 kg/ha / (P_2O_5 + 12). Costs shown in figure 5.13 were calculated using this equation.

33. Precision farming or soil crop management is described by P. C. Robert, R. H. Rust, and W. E. Larson, "Proceedings of Soil Specific Crop Management," (Madison, Wisc.: American Society of Agronomy, 1993).

34. For estimation of 2 t/ha see Waggoner, "How Much Land Can Ten Billion People Spare for Nature?" 47 and appendix A.

35. The Poppers coined "Buffalo Commons" for counties in the Great Plains where the human population is declining. See D. E. Popper and F. J. Popper, "Seasons of Boom and Bust," *Country Life*, July/August 1993, 25.

6

The Case Against the Consumption of Grain-Fed Meat

Robert Goodland

Introduction: Environmental Sustainability

This chapter argues that diet matters for environmental sustainability and is addressed to all concerned with accelerating the transition to sustainability in agriculture. Of all the important changes needed in order to approach environmental sustainability in agriculture, I choose to focus on diet for five reasons.

- First, there is little agreement that diet matters for agricultural sustainability or even that it is a legitimate issue for agricultural policy or economic development. Current global trends are moving away from sustainability. An increasing number of analysts report that we are moving toward the limits of global food production.
- Second, diet is a poverty and equity issue. The poor are mainly concerned with the quantity of their diet; the rich with the quality. The rich will always be able to buy what diets they want; but the consumption patterns of the rich may affect the poor.
- Third, much agriculture is not sustainable.[1] Worldwide topsoil loss, salination, waterlogging, depleting aquifers, overgrazing, deforestation, species extinctions, and agrochemical pollution exemplify lack of sustainability in the agriculture sector.
- Fourth, the adverse impact of the agriculture sector on the environment probably exceeds the impacts of all other sectors, even manufacturing and industry, in many countries. Agriculture has degraded more natural capital and caused more extinctions of species than any other sector, and agriculture uses more water than

other sectors of the economy in many nations. Many agricultural practices—such as feedlot runoff, abattoirs, effluent from oilpalm, rubber, and coffee processing—pollute. The energy consumption of agriculture is substantial in industrial countries and proportionately even higher in developing countries, considering the diesel used in tractors and pumps, the energy contents of fertilizers and biocides, and the fuel consumed in transport.[2]

- Fifth, within agriculture, the case against cattle is strong and intensifying. Cattle have arguably caused or are related to the most environmental damage to the globe of any nonhuman species through overgrazing, soil erosion, desertification, and tropical deforestation for ranches. Cattle numbers have increased 100 percent over the past forty years. Livestock now outnumber humans three to one.

These five reasons form a compelling argument to promote environmental sustainability in the agriculture sector through diet changes. Demand-side management, population control, and loss reduction also will be essential. As a quarter million more people must be fed each day, sustainability must be approached as a matter of great urgency. But there are also, as I shall show, health reasons for promoting environmental sustainability by adjusting diet.[3]

We have let the world become so full that there is, unfortunately, already a trade-off between human numbers and diet. H. W. Kendall and David Pimentel estimate that a world population of 7 billion could be supported at current levels of nutrition on a vegetarian diet, assuming ideal distribution and no grain for livestock, but without alleviating current hunger levels.[4] Joel E. Cohen writes that about 2,500 kilocalories of food are needed for a vegetarian diet, but this figure soars to 9,250 kilocalories if 30 percent of our diet is from animals.[5] If people eat some meat, only about 2.5 billion could be provided for; this excludes nearly two out of three people alive today. This is why it is so important for the world to remain low on the food chain, for those high to descend, and for us to discourage people from moving up.

The Global Food Crisis

Several factors are contributing to our current global food crisis, including rising grain prices, reductions in food aid, and undernourishment.

Grain Prices

There was no growth in the grain harvest during the first five years of the 1990s. At the end of 1995, grain carryover reserves dropped to 231 million tons, enough to feed the world for only forty-eight days, an all-time low. As a consequence, the price started to rise. For example, in 1995 wheat and maize prices hit fifteen-year and twelve-year highs respectively. Rice prices started to rise in 1987 and have maintained higher levels in the 1990s, with sharp upward volatility in 1993 and 1995 as carryover stocks fell to twenty-year lows.[6]

Food Aid

Reductions in food aid in 1995—25 percent less than in 1994 and far below the 1993 level—coincide with the increase in cereal prices, reduced availability of grain exports at concessional prices, and adverse conditions in food-importing nations. Low-income food-deficit countries would have needed to raise an additional $3 billion in 1996 for their food imports. Twenty-six countries face exceptional food shortages.[7]

Undernourishment

Between eight hundred million[8] and one billion people lack sufficient food to function minimally. About two hundred million children under five suffer from protein and energy deficiencies.[9] If adequate nutrients such as vitamins, iron, and iodine are considered, the number of malnourished may exceed two billion. Half of these people live in South Asia, one-quarter live in sub-Saharan Africa, and about one-tenth are in China (though China is rich enough to buy grain). The world's population may jump 50 percent to 8.3 billion by 2025. World food consumption also will have to jump by 50 percent by 2025 just to keep up with population increases, without reducing current hunger levels.

Ways to Increase the Availability of Food

Apart from reducing population or changing eating patterns, there are only three choices to increase the availability of food: extensification, intensification, and changing to grain-based diets. None of these choices is encouraging.

Extensification

Extensification is the expansion of cultivated area. There is substantial farmland lying idle in the countries of the Organization for Economic Cooperation and Development (OECD) either because such land has been taken out of cultivation through government policy, is uneconomic, or is fallowing. Possibly 25 percent of current cropland should not be cropped because it is degrading fast. The rate of land abandonment or degradation increases and may exceed the rate of cultivation of new land.[10] As most accessible and fertile soil already has been cultivated at some stage, thus destroying much of its original biodiversity value, practically all of what is not yet cultivated is less suitable or unsuitable for agriculture because it will be lower in quality and more prone to degradation. Much biodiversity will be lost by converting such land to agriculture if conventional management practices are used. It is not by accident that the remaining wildlands, especially tropical forests, are not cultivated. There are compelling environmental reasons why they were left in their natural state until now. These reasons differ from place to place—biodiversity values, habitat, erosion proneness, oligotrophy, inaccessibility, aridity. There may be up to 500 million hectares of potentially arable land; but its productivity will be well below today's average.

Abandonment of highly eroded or otherwise damaged land and the conversion of cropland to nonfarm uses are accelerating, thus further reducing the potential to increase cropped area. Some degraded lands can be fallowed, providing time for rehabilitation. But not much such land can be rehabilitated. Rehabilitation usually takes at least several decades, and such sites remain fragile after rehabilitation.

Thus there is little scope for expansion of agricultural area as a whole, although there is much regional variation. Expansion of cultivated area would probably impose too high an environmental cost for the meager increase in the amount of food produced.

Intensification

The second choice to increase food production is intensifying use of existing cultivated area. Here the outlook is not quite as bleak as for extensification. But the rise in grain yields per hectare during the late 1980s and early 1990s has slowed dramatically. From 1990 through 1993, worldwide grain yield per hectare declined. Japan's rice yields have ceased rising despite unlimited money and top-quality management. Although the International Rice Research Center's prototype rice variety, announced in 1994, may boost yields by 10 percent under field conditions in about five years, its own rice yields have plateaued or are falling, even under the world's most careful scientific management. There is little optimism in agricultural research centers.

Much of the Green Revolution's productivity increases came from increasing energy intensiveness—one hundred fold in some cases.[11] Fossil energy has now become too expensive for that to be repeated.

Part of the Green Revolution's success stemmed from using vastly more water, but water is an increasingly scarce resource.

Overgrazing is increasing on every continent. Rangeland beef and mutton production seems unlikely to increase much, leading to a steady decline in per capita supply. The cumulative effects of soil erosion has reduced the potential of perhaps one-third of the world's remaining cropland.

Most major ocean and freshwater fisheries are in decline. Unsustainable catch sizes have exceeded regeneration rates for so long that the fish resource itself is damaged. Pollution and destruction of estuaries, mangroves, wetlands, and other fish habitats intensify these trends. Per capita production of seafood probably peaked in 1989.

However, fish and other aquatic protein provide less than 1 percent of the world's food today and less than 5 percent of the world's protein. While this makes a big difference to many of the world's poor, it is much less significant for global food supplies. Moreover, in the next couple of decades, fish consumption seems likely to decline from 19 kilograms per person to about half that amount. Fish used to be cheap because their food source—plankton—is very widely spread and feeds on sunlight and water. Due to increasing depletion of fish stocks, however, fish prices are now much higher and often not affordable by the poor.

It is true that aquaculture—the "farming" of fish, mollusks, crustaceans, and aquatic plants such as seaweed—could substitute for some natural seafood and river fish. Although aquaculture is unlikely to produce anything like former tonnages of ocean fish catch, today's global aquaculture of 16 million tons could meet 40 percent of world fish demand within fifteen years.[12] In addition, aquaculture can also recycle sewage into protein.

Aquaculture, however, has two extremes. On the one hand, low-tech aquaculture depends for nutrients on autotrophs, such as green plants, plankton, and algae, and it is characterized by both low productivity and low environmental impact. No nutrients are added; harvests are low in amount and effects on the environment. On the other hand, modern aquaculture increasingly depends on high inputs of diesel and feed, such as grain, agricultural residues, and by-catch fish meal. Even so, fish farming is more productive than beef production, for fish need only 2 kilograms of feed per kilogram of liveweight gain, compared with 7 kilograms for beef. Aquaculture, then, merits more attention in the world food effort than does cattle raising.

Aquaculture protein is critical in many diets today—especially for the poor. Expanded aquacultural protein production could decrease the consumption of mammalian protein and reduce the financial and environmental costs that accompany the production and consumption of mammalian protein. Substituting plant protein for aquaculture and mammalian protein, however, would have even more beneficial human and environmental consequences.

The case is similar for irrigation: there is restricted scope for expansion of irrigated area, although much scope for improving current irrigation efficiencies—some 40 percent of water abstracted for irrigation never reaches the farmer's fields. Water is the main limiting factor for world agricultural production.[13] But irrigated area per capita has been falling since 1978.[14] Aquifer extractions in major food-production areas exceed replenishment rates; levels are falling, as much as 1 to 5 meters annually in major croplands of China and India. Irrigation water thus becomes more expensive and is also diverted from agriculture to cities: the world's cities are growing at the rate of one million people each week.

Grain-Based Diets

After extensification and intensification, the third choice to increase the availability of food is to feed grain and vegetables to people rather than to livestock. This could increase food consumption by humans without any increase in production. For a given quantity of grain, many more people could be fed well on grain-based diets, and become healthier, at much lower environmental and social costs than on meat-based diets. Most meat now comes from grain-fed animals. When farm animals were fed largely on surpluses and farm wastes, they acted as valuable buffers, evening out fluctuations in food supply, providing labor, and producing manure. But animals are increasingly the main consumers of grain that was formerly eaten directly by humans. Just as there is a hierarchy of efficiency in meat production (grain-fed beef at the top; krill or sustainably harvested mussels at the bottom), there is also a hierarchy in vegetable foods, with saprophytes (mushrooms and other fungi) above autotrophs (green plants). One could extend this ranking among categories of autotrophs too.

Only 17 percent of China's grain went to livestock in 1985; by 1994 this figure had risen to 23 percent. This compares with the 68 percent of grain fed to livestock in the United States. Because cattle convert grain to meat inefficiently, trends to carnivory exacerbate food deficiencies. This is not yet accepted in sustainability or development debates.

The prospects for increasing the supply of food by expansion of cultivated area are not promising. The prospects for intensification are somewhat more promising, and merit great attention. But we must also look at the demand side. Of course there is much recognized scope for reducing losses. But one underrecognized area for major gains is eating lower down the food chain. Vast amounts of food are wasted by inefficiently converting grains into meat. Eating lower down the food chain would improve health and food supply.

Why We Need to Eat More Sustainably

Every year, affluent people in OECD countries consume about 800 kilograms of grain indirectly,[15] much of it inefficiently converted into animal flesh, with the balance as milk, cheese, eggs, ice cream, and yogurt. Such diets are high in fat and animal protein and low in starch. In contrast, in low-consuming countries, annual consumption of grains averages 200 kilograms per person, practically all of it directly, with high efficiencies in conversion. Such diets are rich in starch and low in fat and animal protein; most protein in these diets comes from beans and grain. The grain consumption ratio between rich and poor countries is about four to one.[16]

The Food and Agriculture Organization (FAO) calculates that almost 50 percent of global grains are fed to livestock.[17] The two countries converting the most grain into meat are the United States and China—

Table 6.1. Annual Per Capita Grain Use and Consumption of Livestock Products.

| | | [kg rounded to the nearest 100 kg] Country | | | |
		U.S.	Italy	China	India
	Grain Use	800	400	300	200.0
	Beef	42	16	1	-
	Pork	28	20	21	0.4
Consumption	Poultry	44	19	3	0.4
	Mutton	1	1	1	0.2
	Milk	271	182	4	31.0
	Cheese	12	12	-	-
	Eggs	16	12	7	13.0

Source: Data from Lester R. Brown, *Full House: Reassessing the Earth's Population Carrying Capacity* (New York: W. W. Norton, 1994).

160 and about 100 million tons respectively.[18] Feedlot cattle consume 7 kilograms of grain to produce 1 kilogram of liveweight. Pork takes nearly 4 kilograms of grain per kilogram of liveweight. Poultry and fish are more efficient converters, needing about 2 kilograms of grain for each kilogram of liveweight produced. Cheese and egg production are in between, consuming 3 and 2.6 kilograms of grain per kilogram of product respectively.[19]

There are some encouraging as well as discouraging dietary changes. For example, annual U.S. beef consumption peaked in 1976 at 95 pounds per person; in the 1990s, it has stagnated around 66 pounds. U.S. beef consumption grew at only 1 percent between 1990 and 1995. European, especially U.K., beef consumption never reached those levels, but it is falling faster than in the United States. European Union (EU) consumption of beef and veal fell 6 percent between 1990 and 1995.

Developing countries' elites, in contrast, are eating increasingly high up the food chain. Such dietary shifts have long been regarded as an indicator of development; this view must change if sustainability is to be approached. Developing countries' animal consumption between 1960 and 1990 far outstripped human population increases, soaring 48 percent for large ruminants, 53 percent for small ruminants, 200 percent for hogs and 280 percent for poultry. Little of this increased consumption was by the poor. There is an additional undesirable feature in these countries: FAO calculates that increased grain importation into developing countries is to feed animals that are consumed by the minority higher-income sectors of society.[20]

Not only are mammals inefficient converters, but also their production is environmentally costly in terms of water used and greenhouse gas generated. The production of one pound of beef consumes more than 2700 gallons of water, whereas grain production consumes less than 200 gallons, and vegetables about half that. FAO points out that methane from cattle contributes 2.5 percent of global greenhouse gas (GHG) production.[21] Cattle contribute about 60 million tons of GHG per year, slightly less than rice paddies (70 million tons) but more than is caused by burning vegetation (55 million tons), gas drilling (45 million tons), termites (40 million tons) and landfills (40 million tons). As rice production is basically the same as rice consumption within months of harvest, the total rice cycle more or less balances its own GHG production (from soil bacteria) and consumption (from photosynthetic fixing of carbon dioxide).

Increased greenhouse gases—primarily from burning fossil fuel—have increased climatic instability. This reduces the prospects for a sustained series of good harvests and threatens the plankton fish food chain.

Milk consumption also has unfortunate consequences. In affluent countries such as the United States and Italy, milk consumption in its various forms exceeds meat consumption by weight (table 6.1). Its conversion efficiency is low, almost as low as grain-fed beef and much lower than poultry. There is a role for dairy products when they are produced mainly from the family draft cow. When a calf has been fed, there is not much surplus milk left over if its mother is working in the fields; so dairy would decline to low levels if environmental impact and efficiency were internalized. In addition, milk is not the healthiest of foods for adults. Cheese is dubbed "solid cholesterol" by health conscious physicians. Skim milk is more healthful, but it is still less efficient than foods lower down the food chain (fig. 6.1).

The solution is to avoid animal products as much as possible. One acre of cereals can produce two to ten times as much protein as an acre devoted to beef production. One acre of legumes can produce ten to twenty times more protein than an acre in beef production. As some cattle graze on semi-arid range, one cannot say that a specific acre used for beef production can be reallocated to grow cereals or legumes instead. But the UN World Food Council calculates that "ten to fifteen percent of cereals now fed to livestock is enough to raise the world food supply to adequate levels."[22]

Grain-Based Diet

Human diets vary enormously between and within countries. I do not advocate that certain diets be legally prohibited. However, we do need to produce food more sustainably and at lower environmental, social, and economic cost. People should always be allowed to choose the diets they want; but the full costs of their choices should be reflected in the price.

When people get richer, they tend to eat higher on the food chain and, more specifically, eat more meat. This partly explains why the world is moving away from sustainability. To achieve sustainability and help avoid hunger or starvation, in poorer societies, we need incentives to descend the food chain, eat less meat, and move toward a grain-based diet. The most-needed transition is toward eating mainly autotrophs (green plants) and saprophytes (mushrooms and other fungi), and consuming fewer products from heterotrophs (animals that cannot manufacture their own food), especially homeotherms (warm-blooded animals).

Fig 6.1. Environmental and Bioethical Food Chain Ranking

▼ WORST
Most Impact/Least Efficient/Least Healthy
—To be taxed highest—

1. Mammals:	Swine/Cattle/Goats/Sheep Rodents/Lagomorphs/Camelids/Deer [Eggs/Cheese/Milk/Butter]
2. Birds:	Chickens/Geese/Ducks/Pigeons/Turkeys

Homeotherms (warm-blooded)
_____
Poikilotherms (cold-blooded)

3. Other vertebrates:	Fish/Reptiles/Amphibians
4. Invertebrates:	Crustaceans/Insects/[Honey/Propolis]/Annelids/ Mollusks

Heterotrophs   Carnivory
_____
Vegan

5. Saprophytes:	Fungi/Yeasts/Other Microbes
6. Autotrophs:	Legumes/Grains/Vegetables/Starch Crops/Fruits/ Nuts/Algae

▼ BEST
Least Impact/Most Efficient/Healthiest
—Zero Tax—

Eating lower on the food chain reduces the environmental damage and suffering caused by overconsumption and excessive population. This is a lifestyle change that society can adopt if it wants to consume less of the earth's carrying capacity or reduce its "ecological footprint." Both our health and that of the planet would improve. Hunger, starvation, and malnutrition could be alleviated by such trends. Like voluntary population control, better diets are preferable to starvation, disease, and deteriorating environments.

Food and Agricultural Policy

This essay does not advocate immediate, universal adoption of grain-based diets. Instead, I seek an increased awareness of the importance of diet for deferring a solution to the global food crisis and meeting the challenge of sustainable development. A range of remedies will be needed, including education, improved advertising, incentives, internalization of the full costs of grain-fed meat production, and food conversion efficiency taxes.

Educational campaigns already emphasizing the health argument for eating more grains have begun but need to be intensified. Many incentives—for example, school feeding programs, education, improving maternal and child nutrition, and ration shops selling coarse grain—are available and have been tried on smaller scales than will be necessary to foster lifestyle changes. Removal of subsidies for livestock, both direct and indirect, should be an early step. Clearly, international development organizations and any groups seeking to reduce poverty should phase out of livestock production and should leave it to the private sector. Such groups should ensure that good economics prevail: full environmental and social costs should be used in calculating the prices of foods.

The changes I propose are incremental and relatively modest. The main change is the internalization of the costs of dietary preferences. People should continue to be able to choose to eat what they want. But if they choose to eat food with a large negative impact on the environment, they should pay the full costs of such a choice.

In calculating the best ways to promote efficiency in diet and to reduce environmental impact, we should look at direct and indirect subsidies currently enjoyed by the livestock sector. Such subsidies include full social and environmental costs of topsoil loss, erosion, siltation, biodiversity loss, and deforestation due to cattle; water prices (removal of water subsidies, it is said, would increase the cost of one pound of protein from steak to $89); sewage disposal from feedlots; medical costs associated with diets rich in animal products; the evolution of antibiotic-resistant infections caused by routine antibiotic feeding to cattle; transport costs; and internalization of GHG costs in transport, diesel, and fertilizers used for cattle feed production.

I leave the precise methodological nature of the incentives to economists. Taxes have to be shifted away from things we want more of—employment, payrolls, value added—and onto things we want to discourage—throughput, inefficiency, waste, pollution, overuse of renewable resources, such as overharvesting fish, and severance taxes on minerals and coal. Sumptuary taxes or ecotaxes are detailed by Daly and Cobb,[23] and von Weizsäcker and Jesinghaus.[24] Education campaigns and reallocation of research and development investments away from cattle and toward grains, starches, fruits, and legumes should be the start. Presumably the inputs to meat production, such as water, diesel, and grain, could be taxed.

Beef sales are the United States' largest revenue source in the agriculture sector. Just four meatpackers in the United States hold 82 percent of the market, suggesting a low-cost place to tax. Incentive methodology could address taxing feedlots, ranchers, or slaughter houses. The United States' 104 million-head cattle herd is the largest single user of grain, mainly in the form of winter feed cakes or pellets. Possibly that could be taxed. In some counties, livestock account for half the tax base. Presumably this could be raised. Or a land-use intensity tax could be designed to foster intensification, where appropriate, and demote extensification, such as ranching.

Presumably one could carry the argument further, as soon as the food/population outlook worsens, and tax crops based on how inefficiently they use water and fertilizer. If grain is taxed, it would be difficult to discriminate input for cattle from human food use. If taxing grain becomes necessary in the future in order to foster only its most efficient uses, such a regressive tax should be balanced by reducing income taxes and payroll taxes commensurately. Higher-priced grain would then automatically go to the more efficient uses, namely, feeding people.

The aim would be as follows: first, most people of the world, those already at the efficient, low-impact end of the food chain, would remain as they are. Second, affluent people now consuming much meat would consume more efficiently lower down the food chain. Third, people starting to move up the food chain, such as those in China and India, would be encouraged to stay where they are.

If such sustainability and poverty-alleviating measures become widely adopted, mammalian flesh consumption would decline and would consist mainly of males not needed for draft and females when they have finished producing milk. Hogs and poultry would be kept mainly to recycle wastes; their meat would be an occasional by-product. Ruminants would be restricted to natural range unusable for more intensive production. Aquaculture fish would become more widespread.

This conversion-efficiency sliding-scale tax should be refined by adding the "polluter pays" principle. Cattle feedlots and meatpackers would be taxed at the highest rate; domestically fed rodents and lagomorphs at the lowest. If biodiversity and habitat destruction is included in environmental damage, then cattle raised from pastures created from rainforest would be taxed the highest and natural range cattle would incur a lower tax.

No taxes would be paid on grains such as rice, maize, wheat, and buckwheat, starches such as potatoes and cassava, and legumes such as soy, pulses, beans, peas, and peanuts. Modest subsidies on coarse grains such as millet, pearl millet, and sorghum would alleviate hunger and are unlikely to be abused because the rich do not eat these grains. West African elites have abandoned indigenous grains like millet and sorghum, and have substantially converted to imported wheat and rice.

It would become far too complicated to tax crops differentially at the outset. No tax on plant foods and modest subsidy on coarse grains is enough differentiation. The main differentiation should be to tax consumption of mammals and other homeotherms.

Nonfood Agriculture

The same principles could be applied to nonfood agriculture. Alcoholic beverages divert much grain; they also should be taxed on conversion efficiency. Possibly zero tax on beer brewed from grain unsuitable for food; a low tax on beer brewed from excess grain; a higher tax on grain alcohols, such as gin and whisky, and starch alcohols, such as vodka. Grapes grown on rocky hillsides and not displacing food crops would be exempt, so some wine, brandy, and chacha (grape vodka) might escape taxation. Molasses, as a by-product of cane-sugar production, often is released into rivers where it is highly polluting. Therefore, one also might exempt potable spirits distilled from molasses like Cachaça, and rum which otherwise would be a pollutant.

Governmental and public research and development investments should be restricted to the zero-tax foods. Practically all such research and development should be focused on grains, especially coarse grains, starches, legumes, and vegetable oils. There are useful returns to research on fruits, nuts, seasonings, micronutrients and vitamins.

The environmental impact of obtaining cooking fuel can approach the impact of food harvesting, so substantial attention should be given to the environmental sustainability of cooking methods and its fuels. Using solar cookers, fuelwood hedges, efficient stoves, and pressure cookers would decrease the environmental impact of gathering fuelwood and burning agricultural residues. Recycling wastes merits higher attention too. Mulch, manure, agricultural residues, nightsoil, and carcasses are concentrated forms of nutrients. Their recycling decreases the need for fertilizer.

Other Dangers in a Meat Diet

OECD's wasteful and dangerous trend to convert herbivorous livestock to carnivory and even to necrophagy or cannibalism has backfired.

Many dead animals are now ground up for livestock feed. In July 1996, the EU banned the sale of brain, spinal cord, and spleen tissue from sheep, because cows develop bovine spongiform encephalopathy (BSE) if fed with brain tissue from BSE-infected sheep. BSE can also be transmitted from cows to sheep. No human is recorded to have contracted scrapie, which has been endemic in U.K. sheep for two hundred years, but few Britons eat sheep brains. BSE may eventually cost U.K. £5 billion sterling. As of mid-1996, 160,000 BSE cases in cows have been reported in the United Kingdom. Now many U.K. cattle are being incinerated. It is not easy to get rid of one million cattle. Burial is not an option because adequate landfill sites have run out. There are too few incinerators for immediate burning. Most of the destroyed cattle are disposed of by rendering the carcasses into tallow (formerly sold to soap powder and cosmetics industries) and grieves (meat and bone meal formerly sold for animal feed). Now such uses are banned; these wastes may be disposed of in power stations, but because this may clog the stations and the smoke will be smelly or unhealthy. Mountains of tallow and grieves are piling up.

The Impact of Reduced Meat Consumption on the Grain Market

Any decrease in the consumption of grain-fed flesh would not automatically free for human consumption the millions of tons of grain now fed to cattle, pigs, and poultry every year. Decreasing consumption of grain-fed flesh would cut the profits of grain farmers, who might then grow less grain. This trend is likely to be balanced to a certain extent by the countervailing trend of rising demand for grain and other plant products by people eating less flesh. While farmers would lose the higher profits from selling grain to feedlots, they may still produce grain or other vegetable products for direct consumption at increased efficiencies and with reduced environmental impacts.

With a decrease in the consumption of grain-fed meat, feedlots and slaughterhouses would decline, reducing water pollution substantially. So the world would be more sustainable and healthier. Marginal farmers would go out of business. Less marginal land would be cultivated, bringing immediate benefits to biodiversity. Less pasture and range grazed would free them for more sustainable uses, such as growing olives, many species of nut trees, and orchards. Raising buffalo and other less-risky animals could increase on natural dry range that has no alternative use, preferably at a stocking density well below carrying capacity.

Currently rising grain prices show demand is outstripping supply.

This is partly a short-term phenomenon resulting from a series of poor harvests but is also in part a long-term trend propelled by burgeoning populations, environmental degradation, increasing water scarcities, and rising incomes of some of the world's poor (e.g., in China). Grain diverted for meat intensifies this demand. Poor grain consumers will be increasingly unable to meet higher prices.

Will higher grain prices induce greater supply? A trend to more grain and less non-grain food may result, with costs for the poor. Increasing production and diversion of grains to feed tends to expand land allocated to grain and decrease land available for other crops whose prices are not rising as fast as those of grain. This will exert upward pressure on the prices of non-grain crops too. Increasing carnivory, as incomes rise, pressures agricultural prices in general. Since grain will command similar prices whether used for food or feed, it is the poor consumers of grain who are likely to suffer.

Reducing demand for meat will tend to lower grain prices or slow their rise. The precise effect on the grain markets will of course depend on the balance of the complex forces of supply and demand. But it seems reasonable to conclude that net decrease in carnivory would tend to moderate grain prices. Consider the likely effects in China, a grain-importing country. The decrease in grain-fed meat production could depress domestic grain prices, but demand for all foods is strong and likely to remain so because 14 million extra consumers are added each year, while arable land per person is scant, about 0.07 hectares, and decreasing. With a decrease in meat consumption, grain importers would allocate grain more efficiently and, hence, tend to import less. The money saved by importing less grain could be reallocated to domestic food production.

The Health Argument

The fact is that if energy needs are obtained from grain-based diets, then protein requirements are met. Cereals supply 50 percent of dietary protein and calories globally, and up to 70 percent in developing nations.[25] As most poor people worldwide are forced to eat grain-based diets and survive, there should be no argument that eating lower on the food chain risks health. Now even orthodox Western health authorities cannot muster arguments strong enough to satisfy meat lobbies. Italians eat less than half the amount of beef and poultry that Americans eat (table 6.1) and have a higher life expectancy. Part of this is related to diet: "Eat light and live longer" is supported by firm scientific evidence.

Problems arise when energy requirements are not met by grain-based diets, but by low-protein staples such as roots, tubers, bananas, and sweet potatoes. This highlights the importance of legumes and protein-aceous seeds (sunflower, sesame), particularly for vulnerable groups, such as infants. Many studies of extreme or vulnerable groups (such as pregnant women, infants, macrobiotics, athletes, the elderly, the wounded, and Trappists) reconfirm the adequacy of eating low on the food chain.[26]

The other side of the argument is increasingly clear. Western carnivory kills or maims increasing numbers of people. The links between serious health conditions—such as stroke, heart disease, cancer, obesity, hypertension, diabetes and food-borne illness—and high-meat diets are now inescapable. The message is clear: eating high on the food chain severely damages one's health. Heart disease in the United States alone costs $66 billion in 1996 according to the American Heart Association. Much of this can be attributed to high-meat diets. Cardiovascular disease need not be a consequence of living if one reduces carnivory. A low-fat grain-based diet has now become the main therapy for the 1.25 million annual preventable U.S. heart attacks. Heart disease can be reversed partly by moving lower on the food chain.

Conclusion

A change in diet is one of the measures urgently needed to approach environmental sustainability in the agricultural sector. Improving diets by moving down the food chain, eating less meat and more grains, would vastly improve food efficiency and reduce waste and environmental impact. Improving diet also improves health. Ethicists advocate diet shifts because equity is more likely to be improved, while pain and killing of animals are reduced. These are compelling arguments to move down the food chain.

Notes

Warm appreciation is offered for all the generous comments on earlier drafts and support received from Lester Brown, Cutler Cleveland, John Cobb, Herman Daly, and David Pimentel.

1. R. Sansoucy, "Livestock: A Driving Force for Food Security and Sustainable Development," *World Animal Review* vol. 84/85 (1995): 5–17; and "Integration of Sustainable Agriculture and Rural Development Issues in Ag-

ricultural Policy," *FAO 1995 Rome Workshop*, ed. S. Breth (Morrilton, Ark: Winrock, 1995).

2. C. J. Cleveland, "Resource Degradation, Technical Change, and the Productivity of Energy Use in U.S. Agriculture," *Ecological Economics* 13 (1995): 185–201; "The Direct and Indirect Use of Fossil Fuels and Electricity in U.S. Agriculture," *Agriculture, Ecosystems and Environment* 55 (1995): 111–21.

3. That diet has become a major opportunity to improve development is being recognized. See, for example, H. W. Kendall and David Pimentel, "Constraints on the Expansion of the Global Food Supply," *Ambio* 23, no. 3 (1994): 198–216; Lester R. Brown, *Full House: Reassessing the Earth's Population Carrying Capacity* (New York: W. W. Norton, 1994) and *Who Will Feed China?: Wake-Up Call for a Small Planet* (New York: W. W. Norton, 1995); Joel E. Cohen, *How Many People Can the Earth Support?* (New York: W. W. Norton, 1995); Paul R. Ehrlich, Anne H. Ehrlich, and Gretchen C. Daily, *The Stork and the Plow: The Equity Answer to the Human Dilemma* (New York: Putnam, 1995); and Robert Goodland, Catherine Watson, and George Ledec, *Environmental Management in Tropical Agriculture* (Boulder, Colo: Westview Press, 1984).

4. Kendall and Pimentel, "Constraints on the Expansion of the Global Food Supply," 199.

5. Cohen, *How Many People?*, 170.

6. J. M. Harris, "World Agricultural Futures: Regional Sustainability and Ecological Limits," *Ecological Economics* 17, no. 2 (1996): 95–116.

7. J. Diouf, Guest Editorial, *United Nations Non-Governmental Liaison Service*, 57 (April/May 1996): 16.

8. Sansoucy, "Livestock: a Driving Force," 5–17.

9. J. Diouf, Guest Editorial, 16.

10. David Pimentel, "Natural Resources and an Optimum Human Population," *Population and Environment* 15, no. 5 (1994): 347–70; and Kendall and Pimentel, "Constraints on the Expansion of the Global Food Supply," 199–200.

11. Kendall and Pimentel, "Constraints on the Expansion of the Global Food Supply."

12. Lester R. Brown, *Tough Choices: Facing the Challenge of Food Scarcity* (Washington, D.C.: Worldwatch Institute, 1996).

13. Kendall and Pimentel, "Constraints on the Expansion of the Global Food Supply," 200.

14. Sandra Postel, *Last Oasis: Facing Water Scarcity* (New York: W. W. Norton, 1992), 239.

15. Brown, *Full House;* Alan Thein Durning and Holly B. Brough, *Taking Stock: Animal Farming and the Environment* (Washington, D.C.: Worldwatch Institute Paper 103, 1991).

16. Brown, *Full House*.

17. Sansoucy, "Livestock: A Driving Force," 9.

18. Brown, *Who Will Feed China?* 163.

19. Brown, *Full House*.

20. Sansoucy, "Livestock: A Driving Force," 9.

21. Sansoucy, "Livestock: A Driving Force," 13.

22. Goodland et al., *Environmental Management*, 237.

23. Herman E. Daly and John B. Cobb, Jr., *For the Common Good: Redirecting the Economy toward Community, the Environment, and a Sustainable Future*, 2d ed. (Boston: Beacon Press, 1994).

24. Ernst U. von Weizsäcker and Jochen Jesinghaus, *Ecological Tax Reform: A Policy Proposal for Sustainable Development* (London and Atlantic Highlands, N.J.: Zed Books, 1992).

25. Harris, "World Agricultural Futures."

26. See S. I. Barr, K. C. Janell, and J. C. Prior, "Vegetarian vs Nonvegetarian Diets, Dietary Restraint, and Subclinical Ovulatory Disturbances: Prospective 6-mo Study," *American Journal of Clinical Nutrition* 60, no. 6 (1994): 887–94; A. D. Beardsworth and E. T. Keil, "Contemporary Vegetarianism in the U.K.: Challenge and Incorporation?" *Appetite* 20, no. 3 (1993): 229–34; J. Dwyer and F. M. Loew, "Nutritional Risks of Vegan Diets to Women and Children: Are They Preventable?" *Journal of Agriculture and Environmental Ethics* 7 (1994): 87–110; B. F. Harland, S. A. Smith, M. P. Howard, R. Ellis, and J. C. Smith, Jr., "Nutritional Status and Phytate: Zinc and Pmonks: 10 Years Later," *Journal of the American Dietetic Association* 88, no. 12 (1988): 1562–66; M. C. Herens, P. C. Dagnelie, R. J. Kleber, M. C. J. Mol, and W. A. Van Staveren, "Nutrition and Mental Development of 4–5-Year-Old Children on Macrobiotic Diets," *Journal of Human Nutrition and Dietetics* 5, no. 1 (1992): 1–9; K. C. Janelle and S. I. Barr, "Nutrient Intakes and Eating Behavior Scores of Vegetarian and Nonvegetarian Women," *Journal of the American Dietetic Association* 95, no. 2 (1995): 180–86; A. A. Jensen, S. A. Slorach, and A. Astrup-Jensen, "Factors Affecting the Levels of Residues in Human Milk," in *Chemical Contaminants in Human Milk*, ed. A. Jensen, S. A. Slorach, and A. Astrup-Jensen (Boca Raton, Fla.: CRC Press, 1991), 199–207; A. R. Mangels and S. Havala, "Vegan Diets for Women, Infants, and Children," *Journal of Agricultural and Environmental Ethics* 7, no. 1 (1994): 111–23; V. Sharma and A. Sharma, "Serum Cholesterol Levels in Carcinoma Breast," *Indian Journal of Medical Research* 94 (1991): 193–96; Gary E. Varner, "In Defense of the Vegan Ideal: Rhetoric and Bias in the Nutrition Literature," *Journal of Agricultural and Environmental Ethics* 7, no. 1 (1994): 29–40; and D. S. Weinstein, R. E. Austic, and R. Schwartz, "Cation Excess of Selected Omnivore and Vegetarian Diets," *Ecology of Food and Nutrition* 28, no. 1–2 (1992): 33–43.

7

The Political Economy of Consumption

David Luban

Begin with a fundamental clash between theory and political reality. Suppose, first, that there are good reasons for rich countries to limit consumption and for less-developed countries (LDCs) to set development goals more modest than current consumption patterns of rich countries. Suppose, second, that reducing rich-society consumption implies slowing economic growth within these societies and that stable levels of consumption imply a steady-state economy. Place these suppositions next to the view of every democratic politician in the world: that economies must grow robustly, that an economy growing at "merely" 1 percent annually is underperforming, that improving economic underperformance counts as the chief problem facing government, and that failure to solve this problem invariably turns a political leader into a former leader.

The contrast between theory and reality could hardly be more stark. It raises the chief questions explored in this chapter: Do existing political systems, and in particular liberal democratic political systems associated with largely capitalist economies, have the capacity to reduce or redirect existing consumption patterns? Conversely, can a society of reduced or redirected consumption be governed by liberal democratic regimes?

I say "reduced or redirected consumption patterns" because these may raise very different issues. Consider the three chief arguments against existing patterns of consumption, as summarized in Judith Lichtenberg's chapter in this volume. First, there are environmentalist arguments that we must not continue to impose strains on the biosphere by treating it as a mere resource trove and garbage dump. Such arguments can lead to two responses: the no-growth response developed two decades ago by the first generation of post–Earth Day environmentalists[1] and the more optimistic suggestion that a properly redirected economy can continue to grow unabated through a combination of recycling, technological efficiencies in production, soft energy paths, biotechnological advances, the replacement of environmentally unsafe technologies with environmentally safer ones, and the surprisingly greater resilience of ecosystems than gloom-and-doom prognosticators have suggested.[2] Let me call this latter vision the "safe-growth" vision. It implies rapid technological advances in environmentally safe directions coupled with the cultural changes implicit in transformed consumption habits.[3]

Second, there are arguments of international justice that begin with the observation that current consumption patterns combine a crisis of overconsumption by the wealthy Northern countries with a crisis of underconsumption by the poorer, Southern LDCs. If justice requires massive southward wealth redistribution, dramatically reduced levels of Northern consumption must result, for two reasons. First, southward migration of Northern capital, either through programs of aid or through private capital relocation to areas of the world with cheaper labor, will inevitably reduce consumption in the North. Second, even if the North could maintain current levels of consumption while the South also achieves consumption at these levels that would merely intensify the environmental concerns expressed in the first set of arguments. But, as in the first set of arguments, the response can point to either a no-growth pattern in the North, combined with a controlled-growth pattern in the South that stops far short of current Northern consumption patterns, or toward less draconian safe-growth patterns in all portions of the globe.

Third, there are moral and aesthetic arguments against extant Northern patterns of consumption—arguments captured in phrases such as "the acquisitive society" and the "throw-away culture"; in Thoreauvian suggestions that in consumerist society we lead lives of quiet desperation; and in Wordsworth's indictment: "Getting and spending we lay waste our powers."[4] As in the previous cases, adherents to these arguments may recommend lifestyles adapted to a no-growth regime, or, alternatively, safe growth that moves our culture and values in directions quite different from those we currently follow.[5]

One set of questions concerns the kind of political systems compatible with a no-growth society or a safe-growth society, when such a society is achieved in the long run. However, before the long run the gods have placed the short run, and a second set of questions asks how we are to get from where we are to the favored end-state.

The political question we began with thus decomposes into four questions: (1) How, politically, could the transition to a no-growth society be accomplished? (2) What, politically, does a no-growth society look like? (3) How, politically, could the transition to a safe-growth society be accomplished? (4) What, politically, does a safe-growth society look like?

No Growth

I begin with what is probably the most pessimistic answer to the first two questions, Robert L. Heilbroner's much-discussed 1975 speculation on the future of humanity in the face of the environmental crises that Heilbroner assumed will inevitably accompany rising population, expanding technology, shrinking resources, and the strains that managing all of these must impose on political systems.[6] According to Heilbroner, liberal-democratic politics cannot move us to a no-growth society; and the no-growth society could be maintained only under an autocratic authoritarian regime. Here are Heilbroner's conclusions:

> The problem is that the challenge to survival still lies sufficiently far in the future, and the inertial momentum of the present industrial order is still so great, that no substantial voluntary diminution of growth, much less a planned reorganization of society, is today even remotely imaginable. What leader of an under-developed nation . . . would call a halt to industrial activity in his impoverished land? What capitalist or socialist nation would put a ceiling on material output, limiting its citizens to the well-being obtainable from its present volume of production?[7]
> From [a] period of harsh adjustment, I can see no realistic escape. . . . Nor is it easy to foresee a willing acquiescence of humankind, individually or through its existing social organizations, in the alterations of lifeways that foresight would dictate. If then, by the question "Is there hope for man?" we ask whether it is possible to meet the challenges of the future without the payment of a fearful price, the answer must be: No, there is no such hope.[8]

In this section I shall summarize, but also supplement, the arguments leading Heilbroner to these remarkably gloomy conclusions.

The first argument concerns the difficulty of achieving a no-growth economy without severe economic crises. "As economists from Adam Smith and Marx through Keynes have pointed out, a 'stationary' capitalism is subject to a falling rate of profit as the investment opportunities of the system are used up. Hence, in the absence of an expansionary frontier, the investment drive slows down and a deflationary spiral of incomes and employment begins."[9] As Kenneth Boulding cautions, "It would be well for the no-growth enthusiasts to remember that the depression of the thirties was attributed to 'secular stagnation,' which is pretty hard to distinguish from no growth."[10]

By itself, this argument is not wholly persuasive. While it is true that a falling rate of profit in one sector of the economy leads to disinvestment in that sector as capital shifts to more profitable sectors, a no-growth economy would not contain more profitable sectors. Capital will continue to be invested, though at slow rates consistent with mere replacement of factors as they are used up, simply because capital has no more profitable place to go.

This implies, however, that no-growth must be achieved economy-wide, and indeed worldwide, or that legal barriers must be erected to prevent capital from migrating from no-growth economies to expanding economies. The latter prospect is unlikely: no-growth nations would have to be impossibly altruistic to erect barriers to exporting capital, since such barriers would amount to affirmative efforts to disadvantage constituents in favor of foreigners who have no such scruples. Nor would nations erect barriers to importing capital solely in order to keep their own economies from growing if other nations permitted growth. Thus, a no-growth capitalist economy could not exist unless it were established worldwide. Yet this would require a feat of international diplomacy and cooperation that seems wildly inconsistent with historical experience; perhaps it presupposes an end to the system of nation-states.[11]

A variant of this argument couches it in more familiar terms. Reduced consumption implies reduced production; reduced production implies increased unemployment; and, historically, widespread unemployment has proven to be a persistent source of political instability. Regardless of any other benefits, real or perceived, that high levels of consumption impart to members of a society, the connection between consumption and jobs provides an overwhelming political motive against limiting consumption. Plummeting employment levels typically launch societies into an all-too-familiar cycle of political extremism, scapegoating, and official repression, which often culminates in authoritarian regimes regardless of who wins.

A second point, noted by Mancur Olson, is that no-growth policies would most likely freeze not only the *level* of output, but also the *composition* of output. Suppose, for example, that in one year conditions warrant an increase in the production of some good—flu vaccine, for example. To maintain a no-growth policy, augmented flu vaccine production must be compensated for by diminished production of something else. But what else? And who decides what else? And what if consumers want the good for which production is deliberately reduced? Within market economies, fluctuations in demand affect supply through market mechanisms, though of course with some delay. What, then, if market response to increased demand for one good must be conjoined with a government-mandated decrease in the production of some other goods? Common sense tells us that governmental bureaucracies cannot possibly make thousands of coordinated production decisions quickly. The most practicable way of dealing with the problem is simply to ignore all but the most persistent and urgent fluctuations in demand and fix the composition of total output by fiat.[12]

The result is something like a command economy impervious to consumer demands. The collapse of European communism in 1989 suggests that such an economy is politically fragile, while the previous decades' experience with communism suggests that a command economy can be stably governed only by authoritarian means.

This is not to suggest that authoritarian governments cannot rule successfully, limiting consumption in the process. John King Fairbank has summarized Chinese history as "the world's longest tradition of successful autocracy"[13] and argues that the sempiternal stagnation of the Chinese economy and the astonishing stability of imperial-bureaucratic autocracy over three millennia are no coincidence (though the system periodically made China a pushover for more dynamic aggressors from abroad—the Mongols, the Manchus, and eventually the Western powers in the nineteenth century). Yet reflection on this and other examples suggests the disquieting conclusion that no-growth economies may not be able to sustain stable *democratic* rule.

A third point is that a no-growth economy is likely to experience bitter distributional struggles. After all, one person's upward mobility necessarily implies another's downward mobility.[14] We might expect increasing resistance on the part of the upper and middle classes to redistribution downward and increasing resentment and suspicion among different economic interest groups. Indeed, Lester C. Thurow argued compellingly in 1980 that even with economic growth America had become a "zero-sum society."

> For most of our problems there are several solutions. But all these solutions have the characteristic that someone must suffer large economic losses. No one wants to volunteer for this role, and we have a political process that is incapable of forcing anyone to shoulder this burden. Everyone wants someone else to suffer the necessary economic losses, and as a consequence none of the possible solutions can be adopted.[15]

Clearly, no-growth policies are analytically equivalent to a compulsory zero-sum society.

Moreover, no-growth levels of investment require that profits be distributed rather than reinvested. Ordinarily, this would imply enhanced levels of consumption—if I can't invest my money, then I must use it or lose it. But in a no-growth economy the additional consumer goods are unavailable. Prices for consumer goods would skyrocket in the face of increased demand, and it seems plausible that an unwholesome competition for scarce goods would inevitably result. Without enormous ideological and cultural change, we have every reason to expect that a no-growth society would not be a peaceful one.

This would be true internationally as well: efforts to achieve global no-growth status would confront the fact that the developed nations, with about one-third of the world's population, consume three-fifths of its resources, and it is as hard to imagine the wealthy nations voluntarily relinquishing their standard of living as it is to imagine other nations agreeing to freeze the status quo. As Justice Radha Binod Pal wrote in his famous dissenting opinion at the Tokyo War Crimes Tribunal, objecting to Allied attempts to outlaw war,

> Certainly dominated nations of the present day *status quo* cannot be made to submit to eternal domination only in the name of peace. . . . [T]here can hardly be any justification for any direct and indirect attempt at maintaining, in the name of humanity and justice, the very *status quo* which might have been organized and hitherto maintained only by force by pure opportunist "Have and Holders". . . . The part of humanity which has been lucky . . . can now well afford to have the deterministic ascetic outlook of life, and may think of peace in terms of political *status quo*. But every part of humanity has not been equally lucky and a considerable part is still haunted by the wishful thinking about escape from political dominations.[16]

Southern hemisphere nations have often responded with similar sentiments to Northern insistence that they protect their rain forests. In their view, the North has in effect given them an ultimatum: "We deforested ourselves in the process of getting rich; now we insist that you remain poor in order to maintain the last rain forests"—a kind of global chicken game that typically provokes resistance rather than acquiescence.

Indeed, a chicken game may very well define the politics of transition to a steady state. As Robert E. Goodin explains,

> Suppose the world's air, oceans or fisheries can afford for twenty nations to continue polluting. There will be a mad scramble in which each nation tries to lock itself inexorably into a policy of polluting, thereby forcing others to pay the costs of environmental protection that they have avoided. And this attempt to force the other to play cooperatively by locking your-

self firmly into a policy of noncooperation is, of course, the defining feature of a Chicken Game.[17]

What goes for pollution goes as well for consumption: national leaders who appreciate the importance of a fait accompli (the notorious "normative force of the actual") will attempt to lock themselves into the highest levels of consumption they can in order to set the bargaining baselines for constrained-growth agreements. Doing so will enable them to claim truthfully that redistribution would impose politically unacceptable sacrifices on the part of their constituents, sacrifices that would cost the leaders their influence and their jobs—the familiar negotiating tactic of painting yourself into a corner in order to lose the freedom to make concessions at the bargaining table.[18] As for leaders of have-not nations, they would plainly be foolish to accept constrained-growth accords that did *not* include substantial transfers of resources in their direction. As in the domestic case, where peace may need to be kept by force, an international steady-state regime would more likely than not be the culmination of a period of international strife.

The possibility of international and domestic strife may actually intensify already difficult allocative choices, by forcing guns-and-butter tradeoffs. In recent decades military expenditures have consumed roughly 5 percent of all expenditures on goods and services worldwide,[19] and this proportion would most likely go up rather than down. Nor is military consumption environmentally clean; on the contrary, armed forces are the single largest polluter on earth, and in the United States they produce more toxics each year than the top five chemical companies combined.[20] As the aftermath of the Gulf War demonstrated, the environmental consequences of actual warfare are more devastating still, so that in computing the expected environmental damage of military consumption one must factor in not only the actual production of toxics but the damage projected for a war multiplied by the probability of such a war—a probability that is quite substantial.[21] (Of course, a hard-hearted realist might point out that the reduction of population caused by war, coupled with the destruction of productive capacity and factors, would create space for postwar economic growth, at least for a while. This is precisely what Heilbroner meant when he spoke of "the payment of a fearful price" for meeting the challenges of the future.)

It is also worth speculating upon possible cultural adaptations to a no-growth regime. Because of its zero-sum character, we might expect not only intense competition between interest groups but also a series of very hard choices about resource allocation within individual societal budget lines. Thus, for example, one might well expect a general diminution of expenditures for unpopular "high culture": subsidies for operas and symphony orchestras may well dry up if their performances imply less money for rock concerts. Geriatric health care might come to seem like a waste of precious resources, and generational conflict over the directions of medical research and development seem plausible. Issues of patriarchy and sexism are likely to impart an ugly hue to other distributional conflicts. If it should turn out that every dollar devoted to treating cervical cancer means one less dollar devoted to treating prostate cancer, it is not hard to predict who will remain untreated; and it is likely that diminished employment opportunities will generate pressures for women to stay out of the workforce and return to traditional homemaking roles.

Moreover, a no-growth economy, with fixed composition of output, also suggests a loss of occupational mobility and choice. Only when a physician retires will a job open up for an aspiring physician. The modern idea of young people pursuing their interests may well give way to the premodern idea of following in the occupation of one's father or mother; a fluid social structure may evolve (or devolve) into a structure of castes and guilds. The pioneering, can-do spirit shared by economic enterprise and scientific or technological research may prove more frustrating and less adaptive to such a society than would the cautious incuriosity of Nietzsche's "last man." Hear Heilbroner once again:

> It is therefore possible that a post-industrial society would also turn in the direction of many pre-industrial societies—toward the exploration of inner states of experience rather than the outer world of fact and material accomplishment. Tradition and ritual, the pillars of life in virtually all societies other than those of an industrial character, would probably once again assert their ancient claims as the guide to and solace for life. The struggle for individual achievement, especially for material ends, is likely to give way to the acceptance of communally organized and ordained roles.[22]

Heilbroner cautions that such cultural characteristics, which obviously have their attractions, are by no means the stuff of utopia, and may indeed prove "deeply repugnant to [the] twentieth-century temper" insofar as they reject "the search for scientific knowledge, the delight in intellectual heresy, the freedom to order one's life as one pleases."[23]

Indeed, focusing on the freedom to order one's life as one pleases, historian Lawrence Friedman has argued persuasively that the postwar industrialized world increasingly represents a cultural commitment to *expressive individualism*, a worldview that "stresses self-expression, that is, . . . developing the special qualities and uniqueness of each person."[24] Symptoms of expressive individualism include the pride of place that the concept of *choice*, particularly lifestyle choice, occupies in Western political culture; the enhanced authority of "rights talk," the tendency to couch moral and political argument in the uncompromising terms of clashes between rights;[25] and the at-first-glance-contradictory combination of a desire to disown responsibility for others with a strong sense of entitlement to benefits provided by others. Our denial of responsibility flows from our sense that individual freedom to choose must be unconstrained; our sense of entitlement flows from our sense that we have a right to whatever it takes to express ourselves in the lifestyle of our choice. Friedman argues persuasively that these features of expressive individualism powerfully pervade the basic legal order of every Western society.

Yet it is precisely expressive individualism that seems so drastically incompatible, spiritually as well as materially, with a no-growth society. This suggests two conclusions: first, that democratic processes are likely to reject any efforts to halt growth and, indeed, to reject these efforts with a passion that derives not from narrow-sighted opportunism but from profound cultural commitments. Second, that efforts to halt growth would impinge on core features of contemporary legal orders—civil liberty and entitlements to social welfare—that there is no realistic chance of repealing altogether. Thus, efforts to halt growth may have to proceed extralegally and with very little democratic mandate—a polite way of describing what might be envisioned as a period of war and civil disturbance culminating in coup d'état and repressive rule. As Heilbroner speculates, "the passage through the gantlet ahead may be possible only under governments capable of rallying obedience far more effectively than would be possible in a democratic setting. If the issue for mankind is survival, such governments may be unavoidable, even necessary."[26] Just as a no-growth society may be a repressive and conflict-ridden one, the transition to such a society may well be impossible for any but an authoritarian government to manage.

Safe Growth

The disturbing cultural and political features of humanity's passage to a no-growth condition suggest that prudent planning should aim at safe growth rather than no growth. Safe growth, recall, consists in a combination of recycling, technological efficiencies in production, soft energy paths, biotechnological advances, and the replacement of environmentally unsafe technologies with environmentally safer ones.

As Robert E. Goodin observes, it may be merely the occupational prejudices of economists that imply a tradeoff between environmental quality and economic growth. Economists often equate increasing prosperity with expanding gross national product (GNP), and hence with augmented corporate profits, despite the weaknesses of GNP as an index of prosperity and the often-discussed fact that private profits often impose massive and unaccounted environmental degradation, injustice, and human misery ("external social costs," in the antiseptic language of economics).[27] Once we realize that, in Goodin's words, "the real goal is to maximize not growth rates but rather national well-being," and that "the indicators we use to measure growth, or prosperity, do not take into account all the factors which are genuinely relevant to people's sense of prosperity or well-being,"[28] the economists' spell begins to break. We can begin to imagine an economy that is growing in the most humanly relevant sense even though it is placing the least possible stress on the environment. Indeed, we can already see the glimmerings of such a transformation as we move from a "brown" manufacturing order to a cleaner, greener economy based increasingly on the transfer, processing, and utilization of information. It is a fallacy to assume that cleaner and greener inevitably implies leaner and meaner.

Yet even here enormous political obstacles must be overcome, obstacles that are likely to strain the capacity of democracies. Transforming an economy invariably costs jobs in the short and even medium run, a fact that creates enormous political repercussions. The trauma undergone by California immediately after the end of the Cold War cut into its defense industry is just a tiny example of what would happen in the move from current patterns of production and consumption to safe-growth patterns. Safe growth may require us to beat swords into plow-shares and plowshares into environmentally safer surrogates. Millions, perhaps billions, of workers worldwide will face threats to their accustomed livelihoods, and it is not at all clear that resources will be available to retrain and reemploy them. As we saw, the linkage of economic redirection with unemployment poses challenges that may be insurmountable by liberal democratic regimes.

This is particularly true in light of an argument offered by Mancur Olson in his 1982 book *The Rise and Decline of Nations*.[29] Olson begins by recapitulating a familiar consequence of his own and others' earlier work on collective action problems: even when it is in the interests of members of a group to organize themselves and provision themselves with some public good, free-rider problems systematically prevent them from doing so. Only relatively small groups, or groups able to offer their members special incentives for participating, are able to organize successfully. It follows that some interests will be better organized and better able to bargain for their own advantage than others.[30] The logic of selective interest-group formation explains familiar features of democratic regimes: the politics of special interests, and the capacity of special interests to frustrate societal interests that, though widespread, are too diffuse to organize effectively.

Ironically, long periods of peace amplify and accentuate this process. As David Broder summarizes Olson's argument:

> Stable societies, like the United States and Great Britain, which are spared the trauma of military defeat or social upheaval, almost inevitably tend to become barnacled with interest groups. The goal of these groups is not to increase national wealth but to claim a larger share of the pie for themselves and their members. As they assert their claims, they impede the society's ability to make needed policy changes and economic shifts, so growth slows and government becomes ever less responsive. By contrast, countries like Germany and Japan, which have had turbulent histories, are less interest-group encumbered, and therefore see their economies grow faster, their politics adapt more swiftly to change.[31]

Olson's primary point is that interest-group politics exerts a "drag" on economic growth. Yet precisely the same argument applies even if safe growth and not economic growth as such is our goal: peaceful democratic polities might not be able to attain that goal. Special interests aiming to defend their members' share of the pie will mobilize to stifle reallocation and realignment of the economy.

A second challenge is not so much structural as technological. If the chief challenge for democratic regimes aiming at safe growth is to transform consumption and production patterns while preserving jobs, we must realize that a move to an information society and a robotics-based society[32] is likely to cost jobs rather than create them. The most environmentally clean form of employment is in the service sector, which relies on human labor rather than the high technology that most progressive planners currently promote.

More daunting than either of these challenges, however, is the fundamental disparity between the rich North and the impoverished South. A sane consumption policy implies not merely safe or steady growth in the North, but vastly increased levels of consumption in the South. This requires immense wealth transfers from North to South, and it is hard to see how the political will can be mustered to effect such transfers. They imply, after all, not merely a transformed but a falling standard of living in the North.

One might respond that wealth transfers can be sold to a democratic public. Many observers noted that the same American public that views foreign aid with undisguised suspicion cheered rather than blinked at the Gulf War, despite the fact that it cost America tens of billions of dollars. Yet this is more a debater's point than a genuine response:

fighting a war is simply not the same thing as transferring native jobs overseas (as wealth transfers will inevitably be seen to do).

Hopes

Is the only conclusion Heilbroner's despair, then? Not necessarily. Though the political obstacles to safe growth (never mind the techno-logical obstacles) are daunting, they do not seem as insuperable as those facing the no-growth economy. Economic interest group politics need not be the last word in democracies, as Olson himself cautiously con-cedes:

> May we not then reasonably expect, if special interests are (as I have claimed) harmful to . . . coherent government . . . that students of the matter will become increasingly aware of this as time goes on? And that the awareness eventually will spread to larger and larger proportions of the population? And that this wider awareness will greatly limit the losses from the special interests? That is what I expect, at least when I am search-ing for a happy ending.[33]

Religious groups, though they themselves often indulge in destructive interest-group politics, can nevertheless play a role in marshaling public support for enterprises that have little to do with economic self-interest.

Indeed, shared belief, moral and spiritual commitment, and participa-tion in communities of principle can counteract the logic of interest-group formation. In one of the classic studies in rational choice theory, Michael Taylor demonstrates that under certain conditions diffuse groups can overcome the free-rider problem. That is, they can success-fully organize to provide themselves with a public good even absent special incentives or small, compact size. This occurs when group members decide to follow a strategy of *conditional cooperation*— intuitively, agreeing to cooperate in the group endeavor provided enough other members participate (either conditionally or uncondition-ally). I decide to participate in an interest group if, but only if, many of my fellows make similar decisions. Taylor demonstrates that, even if many members of the group fail to cooperate, a relatively small number of conditional cooperators can make cooperation a rational strategy, even from the standpoint of naked economic self-interest.[34] The attrac-tiveness of this approach is obvious: since each of us elects to cooperate only conditionally—we will cease cooperating if others do not cooper-ate—the approach does not depend on unrealistic assumptions of un-bounded human altruism.

The chief obstacle to conditional cooperation, Taylor notes, is that in large groups it is harder to monitor the behavior of other members.[35] Since the temptation to "cheat" by free-riding on other members is ever-present—it is, after all, the condition giving rise to collective action problems in the first place—it would plainly be foolish simply to assume that our fellows are cooperating. Yet monitoring their behavior is rather difficult. It becomes easier, however, if we have some basis for trusting them. Their known commitment to a community of principle, though it is an imperfect basis for trust, nevertheless may provide some basis. It sends a signal across the community that others are prepared to engage in conditional cooperation on matters of common concern. Shared and mutually transparent moral commitment can lead to the formation of organized groups able to counteract special interests aiming to protect their distributive shares.

The possibility of cooperation is not important only because it helps counteract the logic of selective interest-group formation, however. Conditional cooperation can play a direct role in reducing consumption. As Lichtenberg notes in her chapter in this volume, we consume many goods primarily because others consume them. She argues that our motivations for "consuming because others consume" are so deep-seated that such goods become the functional equivalent of necessities. In a telephone culture, one cannot unilaterally forgo owning a telephone. On the other hand, if many people are able to coordinate a cutback in consumption, no one incurs a real disadvantage; the goods change in status from necessities to dispensable luxuries. In that case, lower levels of consumption become practically possible and politically feasible. Regulating socially harmful luxury goods will still require coercion, but it may be coercion at levels compatible with liberal democracy. The elimination of tobacco consumption in public places is a perfect example. Once large numbers of people had come to see tobacco as a public nuisance, an enormous change in consumption patterns could be brought about by minimally coercive means.

Nor should the obvious painfulness of economic transitions be seen as an inevitable cause for despair. Workforces can be retrained, and democracies have survived hard transitions. As for the political necessity of aid to the impoverished South, Paul Kennedy has suggested that the interrelatedness of portions of the global environment gives rich societies a direct stake in the fate of those less developed: "The environmental issue, like the threat of mass migration, means that—perhaps for the first time—what the South does can hurt the North."[36]

Perhaps most importantly, we must realize that the connection between ever-increasing consumption and jobs, which has figured so prominently in our argument, is not a necessary connection. In my earlier arguments, I assumed that curtailing economic growth would create

massive unemployment, which history has indeed revealed as a breed-
ing ground of political instability and authoritarian government. There
is an alternative, however, to a society in which many are wholly unemployed while the fortunate cling fiercely to their jobs. The alternative,
which is currently under debate in Germany and elsewhere, is legislation to limit the workweek. In effect, such legislation equalizes unemployment, redistributing it throughout the workforce. Instead of a
workforce in which 350 workers hold forty-hour-a-week jobs while 50
workers are unemployed, we get a workforce in which all 400 workers
hold thirty-five-hour-a-week jobs.[37]

What makes this a feasible possibility is the finding—argued by Juliet
B. Schor in her book *The Overworked American*[38]—that many workers
in modern economies would prefer to trade some consumption for additional leisure time. Why, then, don't contemporary economic institutions reflect this preference? Many explanations may be offered. First,
of course, is the tradition of regarding more money and higher consumption as automatically valuable. Second is the phenomenon, discussed by Lichtenberg, that reductions in consumption will inevitably
impose genuine hardships unless they are collectively borne. Third is
an argument developed by Marc Galanter and Thomas Palay in a study
of large law firms:

> Why do big-firm lawyers insist on taking the gains of firm growth in the
> form of more money income rather than as sabbaticals, time for child-
> care, political involvement, greater work satisfaction, or whatever? . . .
> Money is not all that partners want. But as firms get bigger, securing and
> monitoring agreement about . . . the mix of "goods" they want as their
> return from practice becomes ever more complex. Since "money" is high
> (even if not first) on everybody's scale, it is almost always possible to get
> agreement on more money over any other competing good.[39]

The same is plainly true in other sectors of the economy: it is easier for
workers to agree on the importance of money and consumption than on
forms of nonmonetary compensation, so institutional inertia preserves
the long-week/high-pay/high-consumption value scheme. But if leisure/
consumption trade-offs were institutionalized and legislated, it is quite
possible that they would attract widespread political support, on largely
self-interested grounds, and at the same time remove much of the political sting of unemployment.

Of course, it is equally possible that limited-workweek proposals
would be regarded by many workers as unacceptable intrusions, de
facto transfer payments from them to their unemployed brethren. More-

over, such proposals presuppose that work can be parceled out among larger numbers of employees working shorter shifts. They presuppose, in other words, that tasks are endlessly divisible and workers largely fungible. This presupposition may be true of routine jobs, but it plainly makes no sense for, say, composing a symphony. Limited-workweek proposals thus run the political risk of legislatively enshrining status differences between routine and nonroutine work, thereby undermining the democratic acceptability of compulsory leisure/consumption trade-offs.

This should remind us that even in the rosiest scenarios the political tasks involved in achieving safe growth will be painful and daunting. To a dispassionate observer, the odds that democracies will be able to rise to the challenge must seem tragically slender. The connections between long-term needs and short-term consumer desires are far from transparent, whereas the connections must be made transparent if democratic consensus can be forged for meeting those needs. In the end, then, our attention must turn to the formation of public opinion: otherwise, sane consumption policies must be rammed down the throats of unwilling populations by central authorities, and that means the end of democracy.

At present, most Americans express a deep commitment to environmentalist principles and values; yet these do not translate into altered consumption patterns—we talk green but live brown. But talking green is a precious first step, and the possibility of drawing explicit bridges between our principles and our practice surely offers the greatest promise; it is an effort that will require herculean exertions on the part of public officials, religious and civic groups, educators, philanthropists, and the media.

A homely example will illustrate the problem, but also the promise: A currently popular children's cartoon is *Captain Planet*. The eponymous superhero teams up with children of different nationalities to fight pollution and save the earth, and each episode ends with the stirring slogan "Remember: the power is *yours!*" It is hard to miss the irony, however: *Captain Planet* airs in the midst of Saturday morning cartoons largely devoted to advertising My Little Ponies, Combat Trolls, and dozens of other toys and products on the wrong side of the environmental chasm. The audience is being turned simultaneously into conscious environmentalists and obedient subjects of the consumer society. These are the future citizens whose choices, both at the ballot box and at the shopping mall, will determine the fate of the earth; and every Saturday morning those choices hang in the balance.

Notes

1. See, e.g., Mancur Olson and Hans H. Landsberg, eds., *The No-Growth Society* (New York: W. W. Norton, 1973).

2. See Herman E. Daly, *Steady-State Economics: The Economics of Biophysical Equilibrium and Moral Growth* (San Francisco: W. H. Freeman, 1977).

3. Whether the optimistic assumptions underlying the safe-growth vision, or the pessimistic assumptions underlying the no-growth/slow-growth vision are empirically more plausible is a controversial and vexed question. It is discussed in some detail in Mark Sagoff's chapter in this volume.

4. William Wordsworth, "The world is too much with us," in *William Wordsworth*, ed. Stephen Gill (New York: Oxford University Press, 1984), 270–71.

5. Let us note that these alternatives imply corresponding alternative population policies. A steady-state economy must go hand-in-hand with a steady-state population or standards of living will nosedive as the same number of goods are divided among ever-increasing numbers of people. A safe-growth economy, on the other hand, may be compatible with a growing population.

6. Robert L. Heilbroner, *An Inquiry into the Human Prospect* (New York: W. W. Norton, 1974).

7. Heilbroner, *An Inquiry into the Human Prospect*, 133.

8. Heilbroner, *An Inquiry into the Human Prospect*, 136.

9. Heilbroner, *An Inquiry into the Human Prospect*, 84. Compare a more detailed version of the argument in Kenneth E. Boulding, "The Shadow of the Stationary State," in *The No-Growth Society*, ed. Olson and Landsberg, 96.

10. Boulding, "The Shadow of the Stationary State," 97.

11. On the anachronism of the nation-state, see Paul Kennedy, *Preparing for the Twenty-First Century* (New York: Random House, 1993), 122–34.

12. Olson, "Introduction," in *The No-Growth Society*, ed. Olson and Landsberg, 10–11. This argument remains equally valid regardless of the method government uses to regulate production, be it direct administrative ukase or indirect means such as tax manipulation.

13. John King Fairbank, *China: A New History* (Cambridge, Mass.: Harvard University Press, 1992), 1.

14. Heilbroner, *An Inquiry into the Human Prospect*, 85–86; Olson, "Introduction," 7.

15. Lester C. Thurow, *The Zero-Sum Society: Distribution and the Possibilities for Economic Change* (New York: Basic Books, 1980), 11.

16. Radha Binod Pal, *International Military Tribunal for the Far East: Dissentient Judgment of Justice R. B. Pal, M.A., LL.D.* (Calcutta: Sanyal, 1953), 114–15.

17. Robert E. Goodin, *Green Political Theory* (Cambridge, Mass.: Polity Press, 1992), 159; the argument that chicken games often "nest" in collective action problems is explored in technical detail in Michael Taylor, *The Possibility of Cooperation* (Cambridge: Cambridge University Press, 1987), 92–96.

18. Thomas C. Schelling, *The Strategy of Conflict* (Cambridge, Mass.: Harvard University Press, 1980), 27–28.

19. Ruth Leger Sivard, *World Military and Social Expenditures 1991* (Leesburg, Va.: WMSE Publications, 1991).

20. Sivard, *World Military and Social Expenditures 1991*, 5.

21. Suppose one asks this question: How many years, assuming a constant 3 percent likelihood per year of a major conventional war, would it take before the likelihood of war within that span of years was 75 percent? The answer is a surprisingly short forty-six years. Very few nations have managed to fight "only" three wars per century; thus, the 3 percent estimate is, if anything, a conservative one. At 3 percent annual likelihood of a significant conventional war, there is a 90 percent chance of one war each seventy-six years, and less than a 50 percent chance of avoiding a war within twenty-three years. Even a nation whose annual likelihood of war is only 0.1 percent runs a 50 percent chance of fighting a war within seventy-five years.

22. Heilbroner, *An Inquiry into the Human Prospect*, 140.

23. Heilbroner, *An Inquiry into the Human Prospect*, 140.

24. Lawrence M. Friedman, *The Republic of Choice: Law, Authority, and Culture* (Cambridge, Mass.: Harvard University Press, 1990), 35.

25. This tendency is, of course, decried by many contemporary communitarians. See, e.g., Robert N. Bellah et al., *Habits of the Heart: Individualism and Commitment in American Life* (Berkeley: University of California Press, 1985) and, more recently, Mary Ann Glendon, *Rights Talk: The Impoverishment of Political Discourse* (New York: Free Press, 1991).

26. Heilbroner, *An Inquiry into the Human Prospect*, 110.

27. As Herman E. Daly puts it, "We have . . . failed to make the elementary distinction between *growth* (physical increase in size resulting from accretion or assimilation of materials) and *development* (realization of potentialities, evolution to a fuller, better or different state). Quantitative and qualitative changes follow different laws. Conflating the two, as we currently do in our measure of economic activity, gross national product (GNP), has led to much confusion" ("Steady-State Economics: Concepts, Questions, Policies," *Gaia* 6 [1992]: 334). See also Goodin, *Green Political Theory*, 99–105.

28. Goodin, *Green Political Theory*, 103.

29. Mancur Olson, *The Rise and Decline of Nations: Economic Growth, Stagflation, and Social Rigidities* (New Haven, Conn.: Yale University Press, 1982).

30. Olson, *The Rise and Decline of Nations*, 36–37.

31. David Broder, "The Policy Paralysis That Grips Washington," *Chicago Tribune*, 27 September 1992, C3; summarizing Olson, *The Rise and Decline of Nations*, 36–74.

32. See Kennedy, *Preparing for the Twenty-First Century*, 82–94.

33. Olson, *The Rise and Decline of Nations*, 237.

34. Taylor, *The Possibility of Cooperation*, 88–99.

35. Taylor, *The Possibility of Cooperation*, 105.

36. Kennedy, *Preparing for the Twenty-First Century*, 96.

37. Such proposals, and the cultures they imply, are explored by Jerome M. Segal in chapter 18 of this volume.

38. Juliet B. Schor, *The Overworked American: The Unexpected Decline of Leisure* (New York: Basic Books, 1991).

39. Marc Galanter and Thomas Palay, *Tournament of Lawyers: The Transformation of the Big Law Firm* (Chicago: University of Chicago Press, 1991), 128.

8

A New Economic Critique
of Consumer Society

Juliet B. Schor

In contrast to growing numbers of scholars in other fields, economists have contributed relatively little to recent critiques of consumer society. With a few notable exceptions—among them John Kenneth Galbraith, E. J. Mishan, James S. Duesenberry, Tibor Scitovsky, and Amartya Sen—contemporary economists have been hesitant to entertain questions about the relationship of consumption to quality of life. Their reluctance is not difficult to explain. Most economists subscribe to a model that holds that as long as standard assumptions are satisfied, consumption *must be* yielding welfare; otherwise, it would not be occurring. (Actually the implications of the model are even stronger, as we shall see.) Economists, moreover, are typically unwilling to engage in critical discussion of values and preferences. In the absence of such discussion, it is easily assumed that the existing configuration of consumer choice is optimal.

To understand the peculiarity of this approach to consumption, we must recall that the field was once very different—that an earlier economics tradition in the United States had quite a lot to say about evaluative issues. Thorstein Veblen's *Theory of the Leisure Class*,[1] a work that exerted tremendous influence, is a classic in this tradition. Over the past hundred years, however, the discipline of economics has undergone a dramatic transformation, and a much more sanguine approach to consumer society has prevailed both within the profession and in society more generally.

Optimism and Resistance

Simon N. Patten, one of Veblen's contemporaries, was a central figure in initiating this process. Patten held a deep optimism about consumer

society. In his 1889 essay "The Consumption of Wealth," he argued
that it was time to emerge from the age of scarcity to the age of abundance. "We have built a new mansion on the hill," he wrote in a typical
exhortation, "but we still prefer the cottage in the valley."[2] Patten argued that consumers would have to change, to embrace the new consumer economy, and that this change was not only positive but also
ethically desirable.[3] Not incidentally, Patten was an advocate of mind
cure, a sunny religious movement that believed in "salvation in this
life."[4] As he saw it, much of that salvation was to come through material goods.

Optimists such as Patten met with considerable resistance. In addition
to critiques such as Veblen's, which questioned the desirability of consumerism, there was a long-standing fear among businessmen, economists, and others that consumer society might not be viable: it would
fail to generate sufficient consumer demand to grow and prosper. This
"stagnationist" view was based on the distinction between two types of
consumer goods: necessities and luxuries. It was thought that luxury
goods held limited appeal as compared to necessities. For this reason,
many economists believed that as wages rose, people would find their
needs for consumer goods satisfied and reduce their labor supply. The
reduction of labor supply at higher wages—the so-called "backward-
bending" supply of labor—was the basis of fears of stagnation brought
on by rapid productivity growth. If workers/consumers chose to take
increasing amounts of leisure, then there might not be sufficient consumer demand to keep the nation's expanding productive apparatus operating at full capacity. Prosperity might yield depression.

Paul H. Douglas's classic empirical study on the relationship between
wages and labor supply supported the existence of a backward-bending
supply curve.[5] And the idea of inadequate demand leading to stagnation
had a long if somewhat subterranean history within the profession,
going back to the debates between Robert T. Malthus and David Ricardo and to Karl Marx. This idea would of course eventually gain
many adherents with the onset of the Great Depression and the publication of John Maynard Keynes's *General Theory*.

Nevertheless, Patten's views did triumph. In the 1920s, as the mass
production economy boomed, economists such as Hazel Kyrk, Theresa
McMahon, and Constance Southworth criticized the needs/wants dichotomy; they presented the logical possibility of unlimited wants and
argued that a new type of consumer was (and should be) emerging.[6] In
the actual world of commerce, advertisers and marketeers began doing
their best to create such a consumer. Charles Kettering of General Motors invented the idea of the perpetually "dissatisfied" consumer, who
would always desire the new automotive model.[7] Advertisers began to

tie personal identity to products.[8] In a mass consumption society, this would eventually lead individuals to a continuous quest for new products and new identities in order to keep ahead of the crowd.

The Postwar Era and Beyond

Despite the eventual triumph of the "consumerist" vision, there were important and vibrant debates about its legitimacy and viability. Economists took seriously the question of how consumption relates to the quality of life. Even inveterate optimists such as Patten worried about "higher" and "lower" pleasures in consumption. Political movements for shorter working hours contributed to the national discourse about consumerism, for the alternative to "work and spend" was leisure time and public culture.[9] Empirical economists studied household budgets, looking at both "necessities" and "luxuries." Home economics was a serious scholarly field.

Over time, however, these issues virtually disappeared from the economics profession. As neoclassical theory came into its ascendancy, many previously important problems were ruled out of court, and economists came to accept the relationship between goods and satisfaction as straightforward and uninteresting. In neoclassical thinking, the consumer came to be characterized by a few simple principles, such as insatiability (more is always better) and independence (one's individual preferences are unaffected by those of others). The challenge became one of maximizing consumption subject to a budget constraint. If *homo economicus* could manage that problem right (and the Chicago school told us he always could), then his utility would be maximized. Economists stopped worrying about whether he would buy enough and left the field to marketeers. Indeed, by the last quarter of the century they were worrying about the reverse: why he was buying *so much* (and not saving enough).

In the contemporary period, economic theories on the role of competition have had important implications for the relationship between consumption and quality of life, providing the foundation for the twin doctrines of worker and consumer sovereignty. In the standard competitive model, workers' choices about how much to work and how much income to earn are said to represent their preferred choices, with competition ensuring that what workers want is available in the labor market. Similarly, consumers choose the goods and services that maximize their satisfaction, and competition ensures that the products they want are for sale. Production technologies and the cost of capital affect the prices of goods, but enterprising capitalists will be sure to supply those goods for which demand exists.

If worker and consumer sovereignty hold, then there is no ground for worrying about how goods affect satisfaction, well-being, or quality of life. If consumers aren't getting their monies' worth in these terms, they can simply change their buying patterns. Similarly, trade-offs between time and money are unproblematic; if people are working long hours, it is only because they prefer more money to more free time. In this worldview, leisure is just another commodity. Thus, although economists have spent tremendous effort testing theories about the *timing* of consumption, they have not often tested theories or critiques that abandoned the usual maxims about consumers or the assumptions of worker and consumer sovereignty. Once the neoclassical assumptions are relaxed, however, we are free to consider other possibilities for the conduct of economic life.

Market (and Other) Failures: Four Bases
for a Critique of Consumerism

Stanley Lebergott, who has dealt harshly with critics such as Galbraith and Scitovsky, argues that their objections to American consumption patterns are largely grounded on their own aesthetic preferences and, hence, are elitist.[10] There is some truth in this charge. Yet an economic critique of consumerism can offer important insights—not by making aesthetic judgments about specific consumer goods, but by raising questions about consumer society versus alternative ways of living. Consumer society has generated opposition throughout its existence and will continue to do so, because the consumerist path has real costs and precludes other, desirable possibilities. We can begin to explore the costs by considering the market (and other) failures that characterize the economy.

Market Failures in the Natural Environment

There is now widespread recognition that the market calculus fails to price and incorporate environmental or natural capital, a failure that results in the underpricing of goods and services. As a result, there exists "excess" consumption of goods and services *in general*, compared to what the optimal level of consumption would be if no external effects existed. (The extent of the excess consumption varies among goods and services, based on their respective environmental effects.) The intergenerational dimension of this market failure—future generations cannot express their preferences—increases the power of the environmental critique of consumer society.

Market Failures in the Constitution of Community

Robert D. Putnam's recent work on "social capital" shows that strong community ties yield substantial benefits in terms of efficient government, law-abidingness, and quality of life.[11] Has consumerism led to a weakening of community and, thus, to a loss of such benefits? Although there is little empirical evidence on this question, it has been argued that consumer society, by relying on marketized exchanges rather than reciprocity, reduces the bonds between individuals and makes community more difficult to sustain. Moreover, research indicating a decline of free time outside the workplace in modern consumer society[12] suggests a further, indirect link between consumption and a decline in community ties, which depend on people's ability to spend time with one another.

Failure to Meet Conditions of Worker and Consumer Sovereignty

New approaches to labor markets indicate that the standard model notwithstanding, conditions for worker sovereignty are not typically present. In the postwar United States, for example, employers did not offer workers the option of taking productivity increases in the form of increased leisure time.[13] Instead, employers routinely shared productivity gains as higher income. Employees (as consumers) then spent that higher income and, in the process, adjusted their preferences through a process of habit formation. This "work and spend cycle," as I have called it elsewhere,[14] led to an "inverse-neoclassical" world. In the neoclassical schema, workers get what they want. In the "work and spend world," they want what they get.

If employees do not have free choice in hours, one cannot infer that the current consumption path is desirable, much less optimal. It may be that people would be better off with shorter hours and less money. At present, however, that is an unattainable equilibrium.[15] If employers demand large penalties for shorter hours, they introduce a large proconsumerist bias into the economy. Under these conditions, worker preferences may remain latent, and thus fail to exert much pressure in the labor market.

Collective Action Failures

Almost a half-century ago, James S. Duesenberry formulated a theory of consumption based on relative position.[16] He argued that what mattered in terms of utility was not people's absolute level of income but their income relative to those around them. This phenomenon, colloquially known as "keeping up with the Joneses," has tremendous implications for assessing the welfare implications of consumer society. If it is relative income that really matters, then rising material standards of living do not necessarily yield rising welfare and quality of life.[17] Where status is relative, moreover, collective action problems arise that can only be resolved through the intervention of a central authority. Restraints on competition—rules requiring school uniforms, limits on spending in holiday gift exchanges, and zoning restrictions, for example—have a strong rationale when cooperation fails.

Toward a New Critique of Consumerism

I believe the four problems listed above are sufficient to serve as the basis for a new critique of consumerism. I say "new" because, insightful as they have been, existing critiques suffer from some serious flaws. The economists' critique, with its basis in aesthetics, has often been elitist. The environmentalists' critique, as it is usually made, relies largely on a moral appeal; but the centrality of consumer goods in American society blunts the effectiveness of a primarily ethical approach. In a society in which consumption is structurally positioned as the answer to so many needs, desires, and problems, and in which alternatives are structurally blocked, moral suasion is insufficient. Asking people to act ethically is important, but we must also analyze and transform the structures that make it difficult for them to do so.

In my view, a new critique should be positively oriented; that is, it should argue in favor of a better way of organizing the economy and society. For example, it should press for regulations and tax incentives that create genuine choice in working hours; it should promote community solidarity by suggesting alterations in the economic incentives for private and public consumption; and it should encourage us to think about sensible restrictions on consumption in order to solve collective action dilemmas. It should also avoid an error common to virtually all previous critiques—a failure to recognize both the allure of consumer goods and the ways in which "things" do meet needs.

For various reasons, I believe an attitudinal sea change has occurred in recent years, which makes the American people far more receptive to such a message than they have been previously. In part, this is a generational change, marked by the decline of material values and the rise of postmaterialist ones.[18] In part, it is a response to the macroeconomic climate, which has made the American Dream seem increasingly costly and out of reach, so that people are rationally adjusting their behavior to attain other goals. And in part it is the result of mounting social and psychological problems, problems that have not been solved by a half-century of growth in consumption. As a result, those who favor new approaches to consumption are presented with a tremendous opportunity.

Notes

First published in *Report from the Institute for Philosophy and Public Policy*, University of Maryland at College Park, 15, 4 (Special Issue Fall 1995): 17–21.

1. Thorstein Veblen, *The Theory of the Leisure Class* (New York: Dover Publications, 1994 [1899]).
2. Simon N. Patten, *The Consumption of Wealth* (Philadelphia: University of Pennsylvania, 1889), 62.
3. See also William Leach, *Land of Desire* (New York: Pantheon, 1993), chap. 8; Benjamin Kline Hunnicutt, *Work without End: Abandoning Shorter Hours for the Right to Work* (Philadelphia: Temple University Press, 1988); and Gary Cross, *Time and Money: The Making of Consumer Culture* (New York: Routledge, 1993).
4. Leach, *Land of Desire*, 228.
5. Paul H. Douglas, *Real Wages in the United States, 1890–1926* (Boston: Houghton Mifflin, 1930).
6. See Hunnicutt, *Working without End*, chap. 2.
7. Charles Kettering, "Keep the Consumer Dissatisfied," *Nation's Business*, January 1929: 30–31, 79.
8. Roland Marchand, *Advertising the American Dream: Making Way for Modernity, 1920–1940* (Berkeley: University of California Press, 1985).
9. See Hunnicutt, *Working without End*; Cross, *Time and Money*; Leach, *Land of Desire*; David Roediger and Phillip Foner, *Our Own Time: A History of American Labor and the Working Class* (London: Verso, 1989); and others.
10. Stanley Lebergott, *Pursuing Happiness: American Consumers in the Twentieth Century* (Princeton, N.J.: Princeton University Press, 1993).
11. Robert D. Putnam with Robert Leonardi and Raffaella Nanetti, *Making Democracy Work: Civic Traditions in Modern Italy* (Princeton: Princeton University Press, 1993).
12. Laura Leete and Juliet B. Schor, "Assessing the Time-Squeeze Hypothesis: Hours Worked in the United States, 1969–89," *Industrial Relations: A Journal of Economy and Society* 33, no. 1 (January 1994): 25–43.
13. Fred Best, *Exchanging Earnings for Leisure: Findings of an Exploratory National Survey on Work Time Preferences*, R&D Monograph 79 (Washington, D.C.: U.S. Department of Labor, Employment and Training Administration, 1980).

14. Juliet B. Schor, *The Overworked American: The Unexpected Decline of Leisure* (New York: Basic Books, 1991).

15. See Shulamit Kahn and Kevin Lang, "Constraints on the Choice of Work Hours: Agency versus Specific-Capital," National Bureau of Economic Research, Cambridge, Mass., Working Paper 2238, May 1987; William Dickens and Shelly Lundberg, "Hours Restrictions and Labor Supply," Working Paper 1638, National Bureau of Economic Research, 1985; Joseph Altonji and Cristina Paxon, "Labor Supply Preferences, Hours Constraints, and Hours-Wage Tradeoffs," *Journal of Labor Economics* 6, no. 2 (1988): 254–76; and Schor, *The Overworked American.*

16. James S. Duesenberry, *Income, Savings, and the Theory of Consumer Behavior* (Cambridge, Mass.: Harvard University Press, 1949).

17. Robert H. Frank, *Choosing the Right Pond: Human Behavior and the Quest for Status* (New York: Oxford University Press, 1985).

18. Ronald Inglehart, *The Silent Revolution* (Princeton, N.J.: Princeton University Press, 1977) and *Culture Shift in Advanced Industrial Society* (Princeton, N.J.: Princeton University Press, 1990).

9

Consuming Goods and the Good of Consuming

Colin Campbell

The tendency to denigrate consumerism derives from the widespread acceptance of sociological theories that represent consumers as prompted by such reprehensible motives as greed, pride, or envy. These theories are largely unsubstantiated and fail to address the distinctive features of modern consumption, such as the apparent insatiability of wants and the preference for the novel over the familiar. A more plausible view of consumerism regards it as an aspect of hedonism and links consumption to the widespread practice of daydreaming. Seen in this light, one can discern an idealistic dimension to modern consumption.

There has long been a tendency in both academic and intellectual circles to devalue, and often denigrate, that field of human conduct that falls under the heading of "consumption." This is due to the existence of a powerful tradition of thought that generally regards consumption with some suspicion, inclining us to believe that, even if it is not exactly "bad," it can have nothing whatever to do with that which is good, true, noble, or beautiful.

Two factors can be identified as largely responsible for this attitude of suspicion. One is the discipline with which the term "consumption" is most commonly associated: economics. For it is inherent in the basic paradigm adopted by economists that *production* is singled out as the activity that matters. Although in theory consumption is the sole end and justification for all production, it is quite clear that production, not consumption, is the more valued and morally justifiable activity. A second reason for the bias in favor of production is to be found in that Puritan inheritance that gave rise to modern economics (if indirectly, via utilitarianism), and that, more pertinently, also encouraged successive generations to place work above leisure, thrift above spending, and deferred gratification above immediate gratification. It is this general-ized asceticism that is largely responsible for the contemporary denigra-tion of consumption.[1]

However, even the Puritans did not condemn all consumption. What they accepted as legitimate was consumption directed at satisfying needs; what they fiercely condemned was any expenditure in excess of what was deemed necessary to meet these needs. In other words, it was luxury consumption that was roundly condemned, not consumption in general. One of the main reasons modern consumption has such a bad press is that it is generally seen to be mainly "luxury" or "want-based" in character. Consequently, even the little moral legitimacy consump-tion once possessed has today largely been swept away.[2]

In contemporary society, then, there are essentially two attitudes toward consumption. First, it may be viewed as a matter of satisfying "genuine" needs (what we may call "basic provisioning"), in which case, even if this is considered a mundane matter of routine, day-to-day decision making and habit, it is at least seen as a legitimate activity by most intellectuals. Alternatively, consumption is viewed as largely a matter of gratifying wants and desires by means of goods and services that are viewed as nonessential (that is, luxuries), in which case it is typically regarded as an arena of superficial activity prompted by ethi-cally dubious motives and directed toward trivial, ephemeral, and essen-tially worthless goals.

Now there are two distinct yet closely associated points to note about this latter attitude. The first concerns the idea that want-driven con-sumption concerns the "unnecessary" and, hence, the unimportant things in life; this leads to condemnations of consumption on the grounds that it involves people in superficial or frivolous activities. Consumption is thus contrasted with "real," significant activities such as work, religion, or politics. The second and related point is that involvement in trivial activities, and especially the tendency to take them seriously, is assumed to stem from questionable motives; no one guided by high-minded or noble concerns, it is assumed, would ever become involved in such dubious pursuits. Consequently, consumption is viewed as the realm in which the worst of human motives prevail— motives such as pride, greed, and envy. Any social scientist who wishes to understand consumption is forced to confront both of these moral judgments, since they are central to most theories of consumption.[3]

The question, therefore, is whether our understanding of the activities of consumption does indeed justify the condemnation which it gener-ally meets. In short, is consumption bad for us? In addressing this ques-tion, one is not concerned with whether consuming is harmful in the literal sense that our health or well-being is threatened by the nature of the items we consume. Rather, the focus is on the claim that consuming is deleterious because it is an activity (or a set of activities) that "brings out the worst in us" because it encourages us to behave in morally reprehensible ways. Does consumption lead us to be greedy, materialistic, avaricious, or envious? The predominant concern is with the motives (and to a lesser extent the goals) that are presumed to underlie modern consumption behavior.[4]

The thesis advanced here is that the usual antipathy toward the motives of consumption is, if not entirely without justification, extremely one-sided, if only because the social science theories that buttress it are hardly plausible. Close attention to why people actually do consume goods suggests the presence of an idealistic, if not exactly ethical, dimension. Therefore, we must first outline a somewhat different view of the nature of consuming in contemporary industrial (or postindustrial) society from those that currently prevail.

Modern Consumption

Why people consume goods is understandably a central question for social science. Essentially, there have been two general answers to this question, one economic, the other sociological. The inadequacies of the economic paradigm (in which the origin of wants is simply not explored) have been well documented elsewhere and will not be pursued here. On the other hand, the sociological model, which in practice means Thorstein Veblen's model, is still widely employed and its inadequacies are rarely noted.

In essence, Veblen's model assumes that consumption is a form of communication in which "signals" concerning the wealth (and thus, it is argued, the social status) of the consumer are telegraphed to others. In addition, it is assumed that individuals seek to use such "conspicuous consumption" as a way of improving their social standing, aiming ultimately to "emulate" that "leisure class" that, it is claimed, stands at the pinnacle of the class system. This view of consumption links it directly with an ethically dubious activity, social climbing. In assuming that consumers' main interest in goods is as symbols of status, Veblen asserts that consumers are motivated by a mixture of anxiety (over how others may view them) and envy (of those in a superior position). It is hardly surprising that, with the widespread acceptance of such a theory, consuming is commonly viewed as ethically suspect.

There are, however, many problems with Veblen's model, which generally can be said to be theoretically incoherent where it is not empirically false.[5] The key deficiency is that it does not account for the dynamism that is so typical of modern consumption. Status competition through conspicuous display does not require novel products; it coexists happily with an unchanging, traditional way of life.[6] In this respect, both the economic and the sociological models have the same central failing: they attempt to provide an ahistorical general theory that fails to recognize crucial differences between traditional and modern consumption. The question is not, Why do people consume? Rather it is, Why do we consume as we do? That is to say, why do *modern* individuals consume as they do?

The Problem of Consumerism

It is a fundamental mistake to imagine that modern consumption, or consumerism, is simply traditional consumption writ large, as if all that separates the two phenomena is a question of scale. Therefore, it is misleading to assume that modern consumption equals mass consumption. Consumption in modern societies may well be consumption "for the masses," something that could not occur until modern techniques made large-scale production possible; but what really distinguishes it from traditional consumption is its dynamic character. The very high levels of consumption typical of modern societies do not stem primarily from the fact that large numbers of people consume; rather, they stem from the very high levels of individual consumption, which in turn stem from the apparent insatiability of consumers. While technological innovation and planned obsolescence both play a part in keeping consumption levels high, the greatest contribution is consumers' almost magical ability to produce new wants immediately after old ones are satisfied. No sooner is one want satisfied than another appears, and subsequently another, in an apparently endless series. No modern consumer, no matter how privileged or wealthy, can honestly say that there is nothing that he or she wants. It is this capacity to continuously "discover" new wants that requires explaining.

What makes consumerism even more puzzling is that we typically discover that we desire novel products, ones with which we are unfamiliar. We cannot possibly know what satisfaction (if any) such products might yield when we desire them. Indeed, it would seem that it is principally this preference for novel goods and services that lies behind the apparent inexhaustibility of wants itself, as manifest, for example, in the central modern phenomenon of fashion.

These, then, are the features that distinguish the modern from the traditional consumer. The latter generally tends to have fixed needs rather than endless wants and, hence, consumes the same products repeatedly, as and when these needs arise. This pattern of consumption does not, as economists often seem to imply, simply result from the lack of resources to consume more. Rather, the pattern represents all the consumption that the "needs" dictated by traditional ways of life require.[7] The problem to be addressed when attempting to account for modern consumption, therefore, is how it is possible for inexhaustible wants—often wants for novel products and services—to appear with such regularity.

A Hedonistic Approach

It is possible to provide at least a partial solution to this problem by regarding modern consumption activity as the consequence of a form of hedonism. In saying this, it is important to recognize that what is meant by hedonism or pleasure seeking has nothing in common with that theory of satisfaction seeking, deriving from utilitarianism, that traditionally underlies most economic theories of consumption.

The latter model is built around the idea that human behavior is concerned with the elimination of deprivation or need. Consequently, it assumes that individuals interact with objects so as to make use of their "utility" to "satisfy" these "needs." Such conduct may bring pleasure to the individual, but this is not only not guaranteed but also not the reason the object was desired. Thus, economic theory is not centrally concerned with pleasure-seeking behavior. The principal reason for this is that while utility is a real property of objects, pleasure is a judgment that individuals make about stimuli they experience. As such, pleasure is not necessarily connected with extracting utility from objects. Trying to satisfy needs usually requires engaging with real objects in order to discover the degree and kind of their utility in meeting preexisting desires. Searching for pleasure means exposing oneself to certain stimuli in the hope that they will trigger an enjoyable response. Hence, while one typically needs to make use of objects in order to discover their potential for need satisfaction, one need only employ one's senses to experience pleasure. What is more, whereas an object's utility is dependent upon what it is, an object's pleasurable significance is a function of what it can be taken to be. Only reality can provide satisfaction, but both illusions and delusions can supply pleasure.

However, since the elimination of basic human needs is generally experienced as pleasurable (as in the experience of eating when one is attempting to eliminate the deprivation caused by hunger), pleasure seeking has traditionally been perceived as bound up with efforts to meet needs. This perception becomes less valid as the advance of civilization causes fewer people to experience the frequent deprivation of their basic needs, so that the pleasure associated with need fulfillment tends to become more and more elusive.[8] The traditional hedonist's response is to try to recreate the gratificatory cycle of need satisfaction as often as possible.

Traditional hedonism, hence, involves a concern with "pleasures" rather than with "pleasure," there being a world of difference between valuing an experience because (among other things) it yields pleasure and valuing the pleasure an experience can bring—that is, focusing upon a distinct aspect or quality of the experience. The former is the ancient pattern. Human beings in all cultures seem to agree on a basic list of activities that are "pleasures" in this sense, such as eating, drinking, sexual intercourse, socializing, singing, dancing, and playing games. But since pleasure is a quality of experience, it can, at least in principle, be judged to be present in all sensations. Hence the pursuit of pleasure in the abstract is potentially an ever-present possibility, provided that the individual's attention is directed to the skillful manipulation of sensation rather than to the conventionally identified sources of enjoyment.[9]

Modern Hedonism

All too often, then, it has been assumed that hedonistic theories of human conduct emphasize sensory pleasures. This, however, is not necessarily the case, for although all pleasure seeking can be said to have a sensory base, there is no reason that hedonism should concentrate exclusively, or even primarily, on the "baser" appetites. Indeed, while an emphasis on the sensory may have characterized traditional hedonism, it is not characteristic of its contemporary counterpart; modern hedonism focuses less on sensations than on emotions.

Emotions have the potential to serve as immensely powerful sources of pleasure, since they constitute states of high arousal. Any emotion—even the so-called negative ones, such as fear, anger, grief, and jealousy—can provide pleasurable stimulation. However, for the stimulation associated with such emotions to be experienced as pleasant, the extent of the arousal must be adjustable: it must be possible for the individual to "control" the emotion. An ability to self-regulate emotion is much more than a mere capacity to suppress (though this is its starting point), but extends to the "creation" of a given emotion at will.

Such emotional cultivation is achieved largely through the manipulation of what an individual believes to be the nature of his or her condition or environment, particularly through adjustments in the degree to which certain things are held to be the case. For example, to the extent that people can convince themselves that they have been harshly treated by life and do not deserve their bad luck, they will be able to enjoy the "pleasure" of self-pity. To a large extent, however, the deliberate cultivation of an emotion for the pleasure derived from experiencing it does not center around efforts to reconstruct what is believed about the real environment in this way. Rather, it tends to focus on the somewhat easier task of conjuring up imaginary environments that are sufficiently realistic to prompt an associated emotion. This modern, autonomous, self-illusory hedonism is called, in everyday language, daydreaming.

Daydreaming

Daydreaming is an integral part of the psychic lives of modern men and women, yet there is a tendency to ignore its presence or to deny its importance. Nearly everyone in modern society both daydreams and fantasizes; this is a regular, daily activity for people of both sexes and all ages.[10] Yet there has been little recognition of the importance of this phenomenon or of the fact that it is characteristically a modern practice, largely dependent on the development of individualism, literacy (that is to say, silent reading), and the novel. There is little doubt that the impulse behind daydreaming is a hedonistic one, as individuals turn away from what they perceive as an unstimulating real world in order to dwell on the greater pleasures imaginative scenarios can offer. In this context, the individual can be seen as an artist of the imagination, someone who takes images from memory or the immediate environment and rearranges or otherwise improves them so as to render them more pleasing. Such daydreams are experienced as convincing; that is to say, individuals react subjectively to them as if they were real (thereby gaining an emotional response), even while realizing that they are not. This is the distinctly modern ability to create an illusion that is known to be false but felt to be true.

Generally speaking, the way reality is typically adjusted by the daydreamer so as to give pleasure is by simply omitting life's little inconveniences, as well as by adding what, in reality, would be happy (if not extraordinarily unlikely) coincidences. In this way, imagined experience characteristically comes to represent a perfected vision of life, and from what are often quite small beginnings individuals may develop daydreams that become "alternative worlds"—that is, elaborate works of art—deviating more and more from what might reasonably be expected of reality.

Although daydreaming is commonly dismissed as an inconsequential phenomenon, there are grounds for believing that it has significant effects. For example, although daydreaming is typically prompted by boredom, the pleasures it supplies mean that daydreamers are likely to experience "real life" as more boring than they did before, increasing the probability that further daydreaming will occur. Thus, like all forms of pleasure, daydreaming can easily become addictive and result in a certain tendency to withdraw from ordinary life.

However, daydreaming differs from straightforward fantasizing in that it concerns events and scenarios that might actually occur at some point in the future. Indeed, daydreams often begin with simple, anticipatory imaginings surrounding real, upcoming events, such as holidays. This makes it more or less inevitable that actuality is going to be compared—in terms of pleasure gained—against the standard set by the anticipatory daydream and generally experienced as (quite literally) disillusioning. For no matter how pleasant the real-life experience turns out to be, it is impossible for it to resemble the perfection attained in imagination. Consequently, disillusionment is very likely to prompt still more daydreaming, and thus, inevitably, further disillusionment. This suggests that daydreaming creates certain permanent dispositions: a sense of dissatisfaction with real life and a generalized longing for "something better."

The Spirit of Modern Consumerism

Such an understanding of the dynamics of how dreams and experiences of real life interact may make it possible to explain those mysterious features of modern consumerism identified earlier in this chapter. These include not simply the question of where wants come from (and indeed go to), but also how it is that consumers have an inexhaustible supply of them and why it is that they have such a strong preference for novel, as opposed to familiar, goods. We can now suggest that modern consumers will desire a novel rather than a familiar product largely because they believe its acquisition and use can supply them with pleasurable experiences that they have not so far encountered in reality. One may project onto the novel product some of the idealized pleasure that has already been experienced in daydreams, but that cannot be associated with products currently being consumed (as the limits to the pleasure they provide are already familiar). For new wants to be created, all that is required is the presence in the consumer's environment of products that are perceived to be new.[11] Hence, we can say that the basic motivation underlying consumerism is the desire to experience in reality that pleasurable experience the consumer has already enjoyed imaginatively.

Only new products are seen as offering any possibility of realizing this ambition. But since reality can never provide the perfected pleasures encountered in daydreams (or, if at all, only very occasionally and in part), each purchase naturally leads to disillusionment; this helps explain how wanting is extinguished so quickly and why people disacquire goods almost as rapidly as they acquire them. What is not extinguished, however, is the fundamental longing that daydreaming itself generates. For the practice of daydreaming continues (and indeed may be strengthened), and there is as much determination as ever to find new products to serve as replacement objects of desire.

This dynamic interplay between illusion and reality is the key to understanding modern consumerism (and modern hedonism generally), for the tension between the two creates longing as a permanent mode, with the concomitant sense of dissatisfaction with what is and the yearning for something better. Daydreaming turns the future into a perfectly illusioned present. Individuals do not repeat cycles of sensory pleasure seeking (as in traditional hedonism) so much as they continually strive to close the gap between imagined and experienced pleasures. Yet this gap can never be closed, for whatever one experiences in reality can be adjusted in imagination so as to be even more pleasurable. Thus the illusion is always better than the reality, the promise more interesting than actuality.[12]

This theory of consumerism is inner-directed. It does not presume that consumption behavior is either guided by, or oriented to, the actions of others. In that sense, it breaks with the long-standing sociological tradition that presents consumption as an essentially social practice.[13] On the other hand, this theory does not present consumption as driven by material considerations. The idea that contemporary consumers have a magpie-like desire to acquire as many material objects as possible (the acquisitive society thesis) represents a serious misunderstanding of the basic motivational structure that leads consumers to want goods. The acquisitive society thesis is particularly at odds with the facts, for modern consumer society is characterized as much by the extent to which individuals dispose of goods as the extent to which they acquire them. Consumerism involves a high *turnover* of goods, not merely a high level of their acquisition. This fact is consistent with the claim that the true focus of desire is less the object itself than the experience the consumer anticipates possessing it will bring.

Consumerism and the Counterculture

By extricating modern consumption from its presumed connection with other-directed status striving and envy on the one side and crude materialism and acquisitiveness on the other, an understanding of this sphere of activity may be reached that does not automatically carry with it overtones of moral disapproval or condemnation. Unfortunately, this aim does not appear to have been achieved, since, by closely associating consumption with hedonism, it seems inevitable that consumerism will remain an object of moral disapproval. Indeed, one could claim that the present theory only makes matters worse, as, in some quarters at least, pleasure seeking is even more objectionable than the consumption of "luxury" goods. Certainly we can say that, on the whole, pleasure has been the one constant target of moralists over many generations, largely because of the hostile attitude originally taken by the early Christian fathers and typically still held in our own day by fundamentalists and other representatives of the religious right.[14]

There is, however, an alternative moral tradition that not only defends the pursuit of pleasure but also associates it directly with the highest moral and spiritual ideals. This tradition of thought was represented historically by antinomianism and then, in more recent times, by romanticism. It is still very much alive, with its last significant efflorescence occurring in the 1960s in the form of the movement we know as the "counterculture."[15]

Central to the romantic creed is the belief that the true and the good are both subsumed under the beautiful, and consequently that they, too, are to be discerned by means of the imagination. It also follows that these ideals, like beauty itself, can be recognized by their capacity to give pleasure, with the natural consequence that the path to virtue and enlightenment is identical with the pursuit of pleasure. This is recognizable as the faith that inspired many of the young counterculturalists of the 1960s; yet it is only fair to observe that they were hardly renowned for their defense of the consumer society. On the contrary, they launched the very critique of commercial and material values that has, to a large extent, laid the basis for much of our current unease about the state of modern life. While the counterculturalists defended pleasure seeking, they also attacked what they saw as the evil of consumerism. How is this paradox to be explained?

To some extent it can be accounted for by the fact that the counterculturalists, like the spokespersons for the conventional morality they claimed to reject, held that erroneous view of the nature of consumption mentioned above. Hence, they accepted the assumption that consumerism involved status envy, acquisitiveness, and materialism, while being

perhaps understandably reluctant to recognize that their own high valuation of pleasure might be connected in some way with their experience
as the first generation to be reared in a climate of widespread affluence.

In contrast to this explanation of the paradox, what one might call the
"official" explanation is that the romantic identification of pleasure
with the ideal realm of virtue and beauty means that there is an understandable hostility to any trivialization or "prostitution" of this central
dimension of human experience—hostility, in other words, to any tendency to treat the pursuit of pleasure as a simple end in itself, a mere
"recreation" in which push-pin could be regarded as on a par with
poetry. Thus, the Romantics' principal objection to consumption (it is
said) was not that it was prompted by a search for pleasure (even less
that it gave pleasure), but that pleasure seeking was not being taken
seriously enough. In other words, romanticism gives the highest possible legitimation to the pursuit of pleasure, especially the pursuit of
imaginatively mediated pleasure, while condemning not only simple-
minded and crass pleasures but also hedonism itself when it is not associated with a high moral purpose.

The Goods of Consumerism

However, to suggest that one can approve of pleasure seeking when it
is part and parcel of the pursuit of high ideals yet disapprove of it when,
separated from such ideals, it is engaged in simply for personal gratification presumes that it is possible to tell which is which. Unfortunately,
this is not so easy. For example, the practice of taking drugs, especially
LSD, was defended by many in the 1960s on the grounds that it was
an important means of attaining enhanced self-awareness and spiritual
enlightenment. But for many hippies and quasi hippies, drugs were
probably used with no such end in view but simply because of the
"high" they yielded. It is difficult to distinguish between these two
positions because, in practice, they often merge into one another; or
perhaps, more accurately, the one can easily become the other over
time. Individuals may set out to take drugs merely to gain a high, only
to find that their awareness is transformed; or, alternatively, those who
take drugs because they hope to attain enlightenment might merely develop an addiction to a particular form of intense physical stimulation.

It might be objected that this is to make heavy weather of what is
really a fairly simple matter, since as far as most consumption activity
is concerned, purely selfish, or at least self-interested, motives are obviously at work. Unfortunately for this argument, the presence of selfish
interests is not incompatible with more high-minded concerns. While

some consumption is merely a matter of mundane provisioning, much of it is of considerably less prosaic interest to those involved. Buying a house, a car, a boat, or a set of furniture is, for most people, an act of some moment, linked to what might be considered their "life projects." Understandably, then, major purchases of this kind often figure prominently in people's thoughts, where they play a crucial role as both incentives and rewards. In other words, such acts of consumption are critically interwoven into the motivational structures of individuals, providing the energy they need to carry through difficult tasks as well as the gratification necessary for them to believe subsequently that their efforts were worthwhile. In this direct and obvious sense, not only actual consuming but also imaginary, "anticipatory consuming" can indeed be said to be good for us, since without it, we might lack good reasons for doing anything at all.

It does not necessarily follow, however, that because purchasing goods plays such an important part in the reward system of individuals there is no idealistic or ethical dimension present in those projects around which individuals organize their lives. After all, although people's daydreams differ, a common factor, apart from the quality of pleasure, is the representation of the dreamer in an idealized manner. Thus, the pleasure people derive from daydreaming is not separate from their moral life; it is intimately associated with it. Doing good—or more accurately, perhaps, imagining oneself doing good and being good— often constitutes an important part of the pleasures of daydreaming.

In this respect, the pleasures associated with imagining perfect scenarios relate directly to imagining oneself as a perfect person, one who exemplifies certain ideals. This point can be illustrated by considering two important aspects of modern consumption: fashion and tourism.

The theory outlined above helps explain why modern consumers should be so eager to "follow fashion," without, however, having to resort either to the implausible suggestion that they are forced to do so or that they are merely striving to "keep up with the Joneses." Since fashion is an institution that guarantees the controlled introduction of a degree of novelty into goods with high aesthetic significance, the taste for novelty generated by the widespread practice of self-illusory hedonism helps explain the importance and persistence of this institution.

Unfortunately, there has been a consistent tendency for intellectuals to decry fashion, to treat it as a trivial, insignificant, even worthless phenomenon. Yet if we use the term properly, to refer to a consistent process of changes in style (rather than simply a synonym for custom or practice), opprobrium is entirely inappropriate. For fashion necessarily involves an aesthetic ideal, and those who dedicate themselves to keeping up with fashion—or even more interestingly, perhaps, to "taking the lead in fashion"—can be said, quite justifiably, to be striving to bring their lives into line with the ideal of beauty. That there may be an element of narcissism involved, or that the conduct in question may be strengthened by the presence of such motives as pride or vanity, does nothing to negate the ideal dimension of such behavior, since all forms of moral conduct probably require the helping hand of self-interest. "Following fashion" may indeed, in some instances, be little more than a mindless and morally worthless endeavor, but it can also be the high-minded pursuit of a serious ideal.

Much the same can be said of tourism, which is increasingly becoming a central component of not only modern consumerism but also modern life. Tourism involves the purchase of not products but experiences; yet, as with fashion, novelty is the most critical quality in defining the parameters of desire. Here, too, there has been a tendency in some circles to caricature and despise the "tourist" while celebrating, by contrast, the genuine "traveler." But this bias is hard to justify, since the acquisition of valued experiences is crucial to the goals that find favor in modern society (and especially, perhaps, in the contemporary United States). The human-potential and encounter-group movements of the 1960s and 1970s, as well as their successors, the quasi-religious and psychotherapeutic movements of the 1990s, stressed the importance of critical "experiences" in helping individuals to discover their "true selves" and maximize their potential. Such phrases are also often to be found in statements defining the goals of education, therapy, and art. If the acquisition of "experiences," especially those of a highly novel kind, is accorded such critical importance in contexts such as these, how is it that it should be denied this status when occurring under the heading of "tourism?"

Is Consumption Good for Us?

I do not know whether consumption is good for us. Such a question suggests both that we can agree on what constitutes the good life and that we know exactly what effects our current consuming practices are having on ourselves and our society. In addition, it is difficult to speak of consumption as if it were a single, undifferentiated activity. However, as I have tried to show, there is something distinctive about modern consumption. By elucidating this I have endeavored to shed some light on whether the motives and goals embedded in such activity can be considered good. Obviously there is no simple answer, for consumerism is a complex phenomenon.

However, it is clear that both self-interested and idealistic concerns are involved in consumerism. Indeed, consumerism is prompted by concerns and guided by values that underpin many other modern institutions, yet which, in those other contexts, are usually regarded favorably. It is not as if the theory I have outlined applies only to consumption. It applies with equal force to all forms of behavior in which imaginative pleasure seeking or desire plays a significant role. Romantic love is one such phenomenon, so one could ask, with equal justification, whether love is good for us.[16]

It is delusory to imagine that one can cordon off consumption from the larger moral and idealistic framework of our lives and dub it "bad" without, in the process, significantly affecting the total moral landscape of our world. Consumerism probably reflects the moral nature of contemporary human existence as much as any other widespread modern practice; significant change here would therefore require not minor adjustment to our way of life, but the transformation of our civilization.

Notes

An earlier version of this chapter was presented at the conference "Consumption, Global Stewardship, and the Good Life," at the University of Maryland, September 29-October 2, 1994.

1. Another moral dimension to this discussion is associated with gender. Much consumption activity (especially shopping) has long been seen as primarily "women's work," while production has been judged "men's work." This can also be seen as a major influence on the ethical judgments passed on consumption.

2. It has often been suggested that a new "ethic" has arisen that serves to legitimate consumerism. See William H. Whyte, *The Organization Man* (New York: Doubleday-Anchor Books, 1957); David Reisman et al., *The Lonely Crowd: A Study in the Changing American Character* (New Haven, Conn.: Yale University Press, 1950; reprint, New York: Doubleday-Anchor, 1966); and Daniel Bell, *The Cultural Contradictions of Capitalism* (London: Heineman, 1976). Tellingly, such claims are made by writers who do not themselves endorse the new ethic but, on the contrary, seek to condemn it, often from a perspective of apparent support for the old ascetic Protestant values. Consequently an attitude of suspicion, if not hostility, toward consumerism still typifies academic and intellectual discussions in this field.

3. This view sometimes places the blame on individuals for engaging in such practices, while at other times it exonerates them by arguing that consumers are typically coerced or manipulated into this form of behavior by others (usually manufacturers or advertisers). In either case, however, consumerism itself is judged to be bad, whether the source of the evil lies in individuals or in the organization of the society.

4. This extremely negative view of modern consumption is not typically shared by consumers themselves; indeed, one suspects that it is not shared by academics and intellectuals, either, when they are actually acting as consumers. In fact, there has recently been a movement among intellectuals and some academics to view consumerism as far more significant; see Steven Connor, *Postmodernist Culture: An Introduction to Theories of the Contemporary* (Oxford: Blackwell, 1989); David Harvey, *The Condition of Postmodernity* (Oxford: Blackwell, 1989); Mike Featherstone, *Consumer Culture and Postmodernism* (London: Sage, 1990); and Frederic Jameson, *Postmodernism, Or the Cultural Logic of Late Capitalism* (London: Verso, 1991). Here, there is a tendency to regard consumption as the central focus of the efforts of individuals to create and maintain their personal identities. However, despite this development, there is little evidence of any change in moral tone. For such conduct is still likely to be despised, if not actually condemned.

5. In the first place, the picture of a single, leisured elite that all other classes seek to emulate (either directly or indirectly) inaccurately portrays the complex stratification system of modern societies. Second, what determines the consumption habits of this elite remains a mystery, as *they* have no one to emulate. Third, new fashions in the consumption of goods do not always or even commonly originate with a social elite and then "trickle down" the status ladder as a result of imitation and emulation by those in inferior positions. In fact, fashions "trickle up" or even "across" just as often as they trickle down (see Paul Blumberg, "The Decline and Fall of the Status Symbol: Some Thoughts on Status in a Post-Industrial Society," *Social Problems* 21 [1974]: 480–98). Fourth, social standing is not determined simply by wealth (let alone only by conspicuously displayed wealth); other qualities, most obviously birth, can still be important. Finally, treating wealth and leisure as equivalents, both signifying "waste," is seriously misleading given the important Protestant tendency to applaud the first while deploring the second, as well as the Bohemian inversion of this view. For a full account of the emulation model of consumption see Thorstein Veblen, *The Theory of the Leisure Class: An Economic Study of Institutions* (New York: Dover Publications, 1994 [1889]. For a critique, see Colin Campbell, "The Desire for the New: Its Nature and Social Location as Presented in Theories of Fashion and Modern Consumerism," in *Consuming Technologies: Media and Information in Domestic Spaces*, ed. Roger Silverman and Eric Hirsch (London: Routledge, 1992); and, Colin Campbell, "Conspicuous Confusion? A Critique of Veblen's Theory of Conspicuous Consumption," *Sociological Theory* 12, no. 2 (March 1994): 34–47.

6. See, for example, Melville J. Herskovits, *Economic Anthropology: A Study in Comparative Economics* (New York: Alfred A. Knopf, 1960).

7. See Elizabeth E. Hoyt, "The Impact of a Money Economy upon Consumption Patterns," *Annals of the American Academy of Political and Social Science* 305 (May 1956): 12–22; and Kusum Nair, *Blossoms in the Dust: The Human Factor in Indian Development* (New York: Frederick A. Praeger, 1962).

8. See the argument in Tibor Scitovsky, *The Joyless Economy: An Inquiry into Human Satisfaction and Consumer Dissatisfaction* (New York: Oxford University Press, 1976).

9. These two orientations involve contrasting strategies. In the first, the basic concern is with increasing the number of times one is able to enjoy life's "pleasures"; thus the traditional hedonist tries to spend more and more time eating, drinking, having sex, and dancing. The hedonistic index here is the incidence of pleasure per unit of life. In the second, the primary object is to squeeze as much of the quality of pleasure as one can out of all the sensations one actually experiences during one's life. All acts are, from this perspective, potential pleasures, if only they can be approached or undertaken in the right manner; the hedonistic index here is the extent to which one is actually able to extract the fundamental pleasure that "exists" in life itself.

10. See J. L. Singer, *Daydreaming* (New York: Random House, 1966).

11. Products need not actually be new; they merely have to be presented or packaged in such a way that it is possible for consumers to believe they are new.

12. That there is a close relationship between people's daydreams and their selection, purchase, use, and disposal of goods and services is revealed, for example, by the nature of advertisements. But one should not assume from this that advertising *creates* daydreaming, as the latter appears to be an intrinsic feature of the mental life of modern humans and does not depend on external agencies to prompt or support it.

13. See Veblen, *The Theory of the Leisure Class,* and Riesman, *The Lonely Crowd.*

14. To suggest that consumerism is driven by pleasure seeking is to raise the possibility that ecological and anticonsumerist movements might have something in common with earlier Puritanical movements. Perhaps an important underlying (if not openly admitted) impulse behind such movements might indeed be a hostility to pleasure. Could such movements represent a new Puritanism in their calls for us to sacrifice our energy-expensive and "wasteful" way of life?

15. See, for the romantic nature of this movement, Colin Campbell, *The Romantic Ethic and the Spirit of Modern Consumerism* (Oxford: Blackwell, 1987); Frank Musgrove, *Ecstasy and Holiness: Counter-Culture and the Open Society* (London: Methuen, 1974); and Bernice Martin, *A Sociology of Contemporary Cultural Change* (London: Blackwell, 1981).

16. The question has of course been posed before and the answer much debated. See Jacqueline Sarsby, *Romantic Love and Society* (Harmondsworth: Penguin, 1983); Ethel Spector Person, *Love and Fateful Encounters: The Power of Romantic Passion* (London: Bloomsbury, 1989); and Stanton Peele, *Love and Addiction* (New York: Taplinger, 1975).

10

Consuming Because Others Consume

Judith Lichtenberg

Critics have long decried the levels of material consumption and indulgence prevalent in advanced industrial societies, but over the last several decades their voices have become more insistent. In the press and in the political arena, the matter came to a head during the 1992 Rio Earth Summit, when (to put it succinctly) the North accused the South of overpopulation, and the South accused the North of overconsumption.

Contemporary concerns about consumption and materialism have three different, although not mutually exclusive, roots. One is increasing international interdependence and the resulting sense that we inhabit a global community, which makes it hard to ignore the juxtaposition of so much wealth in some places with dire poverty elsewhere. Another is growing environmental awareness, which raises the possibility that our levels of consumption are irreparably harming the planet and its inhabitants. Finally, technological progress combined with the bombardments of the media have given us the sense that we are increasingly in the grip of having and owning—that we have more than anyone really needs, and that this excess is incompatible with virtue or true human flourishing.

Not everyone agrees, of course, that we middle-class North Americans and others similarly situated consume too much, and indeed it is not easy to say by what standards one decides how much is too much.[1] But the feeling that we might be living at a higher level of material dependence and indulgence than we ought to is prevalent enough in our culture, even if the dictum that "Action speaks louder than words" forces us to say it is not *that* prevalent. The concern has dominated moral philosophy over the last twenty years.[2] What has driven the philosophical debate, in addition to the reigning (but practically unbearable)

155

Judith Lichtenberg

interpretation of utilitarianism as requiring one to maximize the good, is the palpable presence of millions or perhaps billions of people worldwide who live in serious poverty, combined with the knowledge that we (individually, and even more collectively) could do something to alleviate that poverty if we chose. The question is whether or in what sense we ought to do something about it—whether, in particular, we are morally obligated to do something and, therefore, are morally blameworthy or deficient when we continue to live in relative or absolute luxury while others struggle to survive or subsist.[3]

I do not want to enter into this debate here, but rather to change its focus. This is partly because I think the debate is becoming stale, with one side arguing that we do have strong moral obligations to do more for others, even if it means lowering our own standards of living significantly, and the other side arguing that the threat to personal integrity, to the concept of a life with which one may, within certain crucial constraints, pretty much do as one chooses, would be too great if we acknowledged such demanding moral obligations. Each of these points of view pulls hard on us. The latter has "common sense" on its side, but it arouses our suspicions just because it is altogether too convenient to believe. The former, even if theoretically persuasive, moves too few people to action. This leads some, who assume ethics must be practical and take into account "human nature," to think that the morally strenuous view cannot be right; it leads others, committed to social change, to conclude that even if right, it is ineffective and thus irrelevant. But where do we go from here?

This debate turns out to be partly otiose if the general view set forth here is correct. I think we have been missing features of the social and psychological landscape with important implications for our moral and practical views. My aim in what follows is to go some way toward establishing the thesis that, to a large extent, people consume because others around them do. There are a variety of reasons for this relational feature of consumption. Among them are the aim of gaining status and superiority that the notion of "consuming because others consume" tends to evoke, an aim that has been cited almost to tedium ever since Thorstein Veblen published *The Theory of the Leisure Class* in 1899. Even this idea, I shall argue, is more complex, and less clearly damning, than is usually thought. But there are other reasons for consuming because others do—some having to do with the pursuit of status, but with the desire for equality rather than superiority, and some having nothing at all to do with status. In what follows I describe and evaluate the various other-regarding reasons for consuming.

This thesis about the relativity of the desire to consume has implications of two kinds, which I explore later in this essay. One is practical:

to the extent that a person consumes because others do, she could consume less if others did too without diminishing her well-being. It follows that the hand-wringing about how much we can reasonably demand that people sacrifice for the well-being of others is exaggerated, for reductions in consumption, when effected in a concerted way, need not involve deprivation in the way generally envisioned. It is not a matter of "sacrificing because others sacrifice," but rather of not having to sacrifice when material consumption falls collectively.

The other implication is moral. Critiques of consumption often amount to indictments of human character: the view that people consume because others do seems to suggest they are conformist, greedy, and preoccupied with material things, status, and one-upmanship. Although we should not discount these traits altogether, an appreciation of the complexities of consumption shows why it is often reasonable and respectable for a person to consume when others do; more generally, it illuminates certain puzzles about human desires and well-being.

The Relativity of Absolute Well-Being

How are people's desires for and consumption of things dependent on what others have? We can best answer this question by considering how their desires for and consumption of things are *not* dependent on what others have. It is natural to think here in terms of basic needs or minimum requirements—conditions that must be met if a person is to lead a minimally decent life. A person's need to consume some number of calories and nutrition, or to have clothing and shelter against the elements, exists independently of what other people have or do. Without food one dies; what other people do is irrelevant.

Even biological needs, however, are not wholly independent of context or circumstance. In a society in which strenuous physical exertion is important—either because physical activity is socially valued or because scarcity requires strength or speed to acquire necessities—a greater caloric intake might be needed to function effectively or well.

Whether all needs are partly relative to what others do, and thus in some cases to "ways of life," is a question we need not answer here. Two points are worth noting, however. First, a great deal depends on how we specify or describe needs. Suppose, for example, we agree that people have a basic need for enough food to survive or thrive. Stated in this way, the need is absolute in the sense of being invariant to circumstances, including the behavior of others. But how much food is enough to survive or thrive will vary depending on the circumstances. Thus, although we can describe the need absolutely, its satisfaction may depend on relational facts. As Amartya Sen argues, "the *absolute* satisfaction of some . . . needs might depend on a person's *relative* position vis-à-vis others."[4]

Second, some needs are much more relative than others. The need for air is quite nonrelative. Think, by contrast, of the ability to work, or, even more simply, to get around and do things (acquire food and the like) for oneself. In many contemporary communities, it is difficult to perform these tasks without private transportation. The need for a car is not "absolute" in the sense of existing irrespective of context. The economic system and the infrastructure could have evolved differently, so that a car would not be an indispensable item of modern life. A well-functioning system of public transportation creates and perpetuates demand: the larger and finer the net it casts, that is, the more places you can get to using it, the more people use it; the more people use it, the greater its economies of scale; the greater its economies of scale, the better and cheaper it gets. In such cases, people have purely economic and practical reasons for doing as others do.

In many communities today, however, a car *is* a virtual necessity. Indeed, for a suburban or rural family two cars are often required. A person's desire for a car, then, although dependent on what other people have and do, need not be rooted in greed, envy, or the desire for status.[5] Many items once thought of as high-tech luxuries—television, cable television, computers, on-line databases—are becoming increasingly necessary for the citizen in a technologically sophisticated society. Invention is the mother of necessity.

Just how far the point illustrated by this example extends is a difficult question. The danger on one side is being led to say that every deprivation relative to others in one's society is the frustration of a basic or important need. On the other side, critics of contemporary Western culture—those who decry "conspicuous consumption" and materialistic values—often pay insufficient attention to the significance of relative deprivation for absolute well-being.

Even when it would be an exaggeration to say that a particular item has moved from the status of luxury to necessity, new goods often become entrenched in a society—become more needlike—in a subtle and interesting process. We can observe this transformation with many recent innovations: microwaves, answering machines, VCRs, electronic mail. When first introduced, such items may have appeared frivolous, at least to those not mesmerized by gadgets. Gradually—but really very quickly—even the skeptics started to notice these items' uses. For example, while the benefits to owners of answering machines were immediately apparent, some callers at first found the devices awkward or even insulting. Soon, however, even skeptical callers began to notice the advantages to themselves: not having to call back repeatedly when no one answered or avoiding unwanted and unnecessarily prolonged conversations. Complaints about "talking to a machine" are rarely heard anymore. Similarly, car phones, which when first introduced were widely viewed as mere status symbols, are now recognized for their convenience and safety-enhancing features (in a dangerous world of carjackings and other crimes).

How does this phenomenon of the entrenchment of new products bear on the relational aspects of consumption? Acquisition of a good by many people can render it more necessary in an absolute sense, even if not always a "necessity." In some cases—public versus private trans-portation—this is a question of infrastructure: where others take buses, there will be buses, available to all, and I will have less need for a car. In other cases, such as electronic mail and on-line databases, we have what economists call networking effects: one lacking the service is made worse off by being cut off from the flow of information. Even the humdrum answering machine can affect how people conduct business, so that those lacking them may both suffer disadvantages themselves and also inconvenience others. So, for example, where it is assumed that most people have answering machines, it might be reasonable to ask someone to make a dozen phone calls, on the assumption that mes-sages can be left if no one answers. The person without an answering machine forces the messenger to work harder by calling repeatedly, and is more likely not to be reached at all. This may be more than an inconvenience: it may cost a businessperson her livelihood if the caller is a customer with alternative providers.

Salient Things

The process by which new goods get entrenched in a culture bears in a second way on the relational aspects of consumption: the acquisition of goods by others serves as a crucial form of publicity. Leaving aside for the moment questions about status and the need to "keep up with the Joneses," the fact that one's friends and neighbors have something new acts as a stimulus if the good has intrinsic appeal of any kind. Advertis-ers have always been fully aware of this phenomenon, which can be understood in terms of what cognitive psychologists call "salience": the physical presence of an item makes it more available to conscious-ness. The economist James S. Duesenberry describes this process in terms of what he calls "the demonstration effect":

> In given circumstances, . . . individuals . . . come into contact with goods superior to the ones they use with a certain frequency. Each such contact

is a demonstration of the superiority of those goods and is a threat to the
existence of the current consumption pattern. It is a threat because it makes
active the latent preference for these goods. . . . For any particular family
the frequency of contact with superior goods will increase primarily as the
consumption expenditures of others increase.[6]

In our zeal to find sophisticated or deep explanations for people's desires to raise their level of material well-being, we have neglected the
simple yet powerful effect of firsthand experience on wanting. It stands
to reason that a person is more likely to want something if he sees it
than if it exists for him merely as an abstract possibility. (Indeed, an
abstract possibility is usually an unconceived possibility, which moves
us not at all.) Familiarity breeds desire more often than contempt.

This desire-stimulating process seems perfectly respectable, as plausibly attributable to human curiosity or to being alive to one's surroundings as to greed or envy or status seeking—the explanations more
commonly offered by critics of consumption. Some might argue that,
on the contrary, this fact about human beings is precisely what terms
like *greed* and *envy* are meant to denote—wanting things when you see
them, being moved by the consumption habits of others. How are we to
resolve this dispute, where both sides agree on the evidence but disagree
about what it shows? It seems wrong to say the disagreement is merely
terminological (how you define *greed* or *envy*), since the two sides
make very different moral judgments about the human qualities in question. One solution is to have it both ways: to acknowledge an element
that is morally neutral or even praiseworthy (curiosity, aliveness to
one's surroundings), but also an element worthy of criticism (lack of
self-sufficiency, overdependence on material things). Yet whether moral
criticism is appropriate depends partly on other issues that await resolution. Under what circumstances, and for what reasons, does attraction
to material things constitute a vice? Some issues relevant to answering
this question are discussed briefly below.

However we resolve these questions, it is clear that as a matter of
fact, salience—here constituted by the possessions of my neighbors[7]—
acts as a powerful stimulus to the desire to consume. Now that the
world's poorest people have instant and constant access, through television and other mass media, to the lifestyles of their affluent "neighbors," the significance of the demonstration effect can hardly be
exaggerated.

This is not to beg the question of whether, all things considered,
having more things necessarily makes a person happier or better off.
We may acknowledge that getting what one's neighbors have enhances
one's welfare, without denying that everyone might be happier living

more simply. The explanation for these seemingly conflicting facts rests on the interaction of three phenomena: salience, opportunity costs, and collective action problems. Thus, if we assume (what the true ascetic presumably would not) that the life of things enhances one's well-being in certain respects, then, beginning from the status quo of a consumption-oriented culture and acquaintance with some new thing, having it may improve one's welfare, even though a different bundle of experiences inconsistent with having it (that is, beginning from a different baseline) might improve one's well-being even more. Given that my neighbors have it, and that the thing possesses at least some small utility or aesthetic virtue, I may be better off having it. It's hard to explain the pull that material things exert on most people's desires without acknowledging their intrinsic attractions, however shallow or transitory these might be.[8]

Other things being equal, then, more is often more. But the qualification is crucial. One can admit that if my neighbors have an item I will be better off having it and still maintain that a world in which I had fewer things and my neighbors did too would be better still—that in such a world we would all be better off. This claim involves a view about the overall worth of alternative ways of life—about how high-consumption "life packages" compare with others emphasizing different, nonmaterial goods instead. The present discussion of the benefits of consumption, however, is about micro, not macro; partial, not complete, compliance; the world of second-best: about the reasons for consuming when others around you do.[9]

Consumption and Self-Respect

Let us turn now to the reasons for consuming that probably loom largest when people think about consumption in modern society—and certainly if they hear of "consuming because others consume." We think of conspicuous consumption, keeping up with the Joneses, the ostentatious display of wealth, and the excessive reliance on material goods as a way of attaining status. But the contemptuous attitude revealed in these descriptions depends partly, I believe, on a misunderstanding of other-regarding consumption. I have already given two reasons for thinking so. First, because of a society's way of life or infrastructure, or because of networking effects, the satisfaction of needs and interests that most people would agree are basic depends in part on other people's consumption practices. And second, acquaintance breeds desire: it is not necessarily a sign of greed or envy to want things when you see them.

None of this is to deny that the desire to improve one's position vis-à-vis others plays an important part in the urge to consume. We want to have things, and to have others know we have them, in part in order to *say something* about ourselves to others. It is this expressive function that we now need to analyze more carefully.

First, we should note that not all expressive consumption need involve the desire to say something about one's worth. A person who wears one earring or long hair, or drives a Jeep Cherokee or rides a battered bicycle, is *expressing* himself—we might even say he is *making a statement* about himself and his values—but he need not be attempting to secure a place in a hierarchy.[10] It may even be questioned whether his behavior is communicative. Terms or phrases like *self-expression* and *making a statement* can be understood to imply communication to others, but they can also be understood in a more private way—perhaps as an outpouring of inner feeling. Let us assume, however, that for most people such forms of self-expression as fashion do include a crucial communicative component. In part, this communicative component is rooted in practical aims: it is useful to tell others what one is like in order to find those with similar interests. (This function is discussed further below in terms of ability signaling.)

But acts of consumption are sometimes designed[11] to communicate to others something about one's own *worth*, and it is this expressive function in which we are interested. Such status seeking has a bad reputation. A long tradition of moralists advises that what other people think of us is not important, that one should not base one's actions on the opinions of others, and so forth. If this were true, then all consumption aimed at sending a message, especially a message about one's worth, would be less than reputable. But although it is easy to describe situations where one shouldn't care what others think (for instance, where there is a right thing to do, and one must brave public opinion and do it), it seems too sweeping a judgment to say that it is always disreputable to care. The person wholly unconcerned with how others see her seems at best too saintly to serve as a model for the ordinary person; at worst, she may be pathological or contemptuous of other people.

At least in part, consumption designed to send a message about one's worth has a bad reputation because it masks a morally significant ambiguity. We imagine a world in which everyone is trying to outdo everyone else—trying not merely to keep up with the Joneses but to surpass them. Veblen certainly did much to promote this interpretation: "the end sought by accumulation is to rank high in comparison with the rest of the community in point of pecuniary strength. . . . However widely, or equally, or 'fairly,' it may be distributed, no general increase of the community's wealth can make any approach to satiating this need, the ground of which is the desire of every one to excel every one else in the accumulation of goods."[12] But although a person may consume to show that he is better than others, he may also consume simply to show that he is as good as others. Veblen fails to draw this distinction, which I believe is both morally significant and psychologically real. Let us first ask why it is acceptable and important for people to attain some measure of perceived equality with their fellows and then ask to what extent people want not merely equality but superiority.

For all but the most extraordinarily self-sufficient individuals, self-respect requires respect from one's fellows; it requires that one not be shamed before them. I take this kind of self-respect and the respect from others it implies to be fundamental human needs; a person cannot have a decent life without them.[13] As Veblen himself puts it: "Only individuals with an aberrant temperament can in the long run retain their self-esteem in the face of the disesteem of their fellows."[14] The satisfaction of these needs calls for a certain kind of equality, not superiority; it means having certain things that others have, not more than others have.

Adam Smith articulated this point—and its connection with consumption practices—two centuries ago, and his formulation has not been surpassed:

> By necessaries I understand, not only the commodities which are indispensably necessary for the support of life, but whatever the custom of the country renders it indecent for creditable people, even the lowest order, to be without. A linen shirt, for example, is, strictly speaking, not a necessary of life. The Greeks and Romans lived, I suppose, very comfortably, though they had no linen. But in the present times, through the greater part of Europe, a creditable day-labourer would be ashamed to appear in public without a linen shirt, the want of which would be supposed to denote that disgraceful degree of poverty, which, it is presumed, no body can well fall into without extreme bad conduct. Custom, in the same manner, has rendered leather shoes a necessary of life in England. The poorest creditable person of either sex would be ashamed to appear in public without them.[15]

Extrapolating from Smith's analysis, we might say that the need for self-respect—or, put negatively, the need to avoid shame—is basic and universal. But what it takes to satisfy that need varies widely from time to time and place to place. This point could have far-reaching implications. In Smith's society, self-respect meant leather shoes; in some circles in the 1990s it means Nikes.

Why some goods—such as shoes, of all things!—should have the kind of significance Smith describes is an interesting question, but one I shall not pursue here. We can see at least that goods functioning as markers of self-respect or other status must be "conspicuous"—visible and public—which explains the prominence of clothing and cars. What the inside of a person's house looks like matters less, for this purpose, since most others will not see it.

At the same time, it is plausible to think that in mass societies, the opinions and respect of subgroups, rather than the general public, assume greater importance. Two reasons might be offered in support of this claim. First, beyond the crudest indicators individuals are not noticed by the "general public." Second, it is psychologically difficult for individuals themselves to care about what "everybody" thinks; instead they focus on achieving respect from particular reference groups to which they compare themselves.

The path by which certain goods become "necessaries" must involve the processes of entrenchment discussed in the last section. It would seem that wherever there is material or technological progress, new goods will gradually assume the role of "signifying decency"—and others will assume the role of signifying superiority—that Smith describes. (This is not to say that in less dynamic societies no goods play this role, only that they are less often superseded.) This is important, for it suggests that technological progress combined with the need for self-respect tends to up the consumption ante.

Equality and Superiority

Two questions cast shadows over the foregoing account. First, how much equality does self-respect require? One might argue that all significant material inequalities are damaging to the self-respect of those who have less. The improbability of radical egalitarianism could render this point a reductio ad absurdum of the self-respect argument. But it would have to be shown that material inequalities generally do undermine self-respect. No doubt this is a matter of degree, and reasonable people will disagree about how damaging inequalities are. My point has been only that the absence of certain—circumscribed—goods undermines self-respect, and that it is therefore reasonable for people to want those things when others have them. How far-reaching the implications of this argument are remains to be seen.

The second question concerns the distinction between the desire for equality and for superiority. There are at least two reasons for thinking these differ in ways that matter. One is moral: to want to be (and to seem) as good as others seems clearly respectable; to want to be better than or to outdo others arouses our suspicions. In Kantian terms, it is possible to will everyone to succeed in their striving for equality, but not in their striving for superiority (or more simply, it is possible to will that everyone be equal but not that everyone be superior).[16] Some critics of egalitarianism would insist that to eradicate the desire for superiority would be to discourage excellence and individuality. Egalitarians can respond by distinguishing the desire to excel from the desire to outdo others: one can aim to do as well as one can or achieve a goal defined by the activity at hand rather than by the achievements of others.

Whether this argument can succeed in throwing out the bathwater (the desire to surpass others) without the baby (excellence and individuality)—and, more generally, whether the desire to surpass others is morally objectionable—are questions we cannot settle here. But there is another difference between the desire for superiority and the desire for equality. The first can lead to prisoner's dilemma situations, which are among the primary reasons for thinking consumption in the contemporary world problematic. (It need not always lead to them, however; whether it does or not will depend partly on the rate of technological change and changes in fashion.) We envision the ever-escalating spiral of acquisition among consumers all intent on proving their superior status. The desire for equal status does not appear to generate such vicious spirals.

Do people want merely to be equal to others, or do they want to be better? No doubt there is wide variation in this matter, both among people within a society and between cultures more generally.[17] Variation exists also within individuals: we are content to be merely as good as others in many respects, even if we want to excel in some. It would be foolish to deny the existence of the desire for superiority, but it is also a mistake to exaggerate its extent.

A classic social-psychological study conducted during and after World War II, *The American Soldier*, sheds light on these issues.[18] It was found that in the Military Police, opportunities for promotion were poor, yet satisfaction was higher than in the Air Corps, where opportunities for promotion were much better. The explanation is nicely summarized by W. G. Runciman:

> Those who were not promoted in the Military Police tended to compare themselves with the large number of their fellows who were also not promoted, while those few who had been promoted were likely to appear to themselves to have done relatively better. In the Air Corps, by contrast, the man who was not promoted would be likely to compare himself with the large number of his fellows who *had* been promoted, while these, though successful, would appear to themselves to have done relatively less well.[19]

This conclusion is intuitively plausible and borne out by casual observation. In a professional school with one endowed chair, the unendowed will be relatively content; where half the members of the department have endowed chairs, the situation of the unendowed will rankle. A person's position can seem tolerable and even satisfactory to her as long as most other members of her reference group—those to whom she compares herself—are in the same boat.[20] The sense of deprivation is largely relative to one's expectations, and these in turn depend on what others around one have.

This claim supports the view that equality is a satisfactory outcome for many people in many situations. Interestingly, the same line of reasoning suggests that even the desire for superiority can often be satisfied by superiority relative to one's reference group. This emphasis on relative endowment contrasts with a view of human beings as craving more and more, period. Even where people desire superiority and not just equality, the relativized view implies that consumption can be constrained. For to the extent that a person's aim is relative rather than absolute endowment, having more than others—rather than more and more and more—will suffice.

Both the moral concern about the desire for superiority (that it is reprehensible) and the practical concern (that it may escalate without surcease) will be more serious if there are reasons for doubting the stability of the distinction between the desire for equality and the desire for superiority. We turn now to this question. The discussion leads to more general questions about the extent to which the quest for status informs decisions about consumption.

Status and Other Goods

To think that by having or owning or showing certain things a person can demonstrate his status is to acknowledge that such things constitute the outward signs of some nonvisible condition.[21] This idea is so fundamental to the way material goods are viewed in our society that it is difficult to imagine not viewing them in this way.

The economist Robert Frank calls this crucial function of consumption *ability signaling*. It is worth quoting him at some length:

> In societies in which economic and social interactions between people are pervasive and important—that is, in every known human society—information about people with whom we might interact has obvious value. . . . Many of the most important decisions ever made about us depend on how strangers see our talents, abilities, and other characteristics.
>
>   . . . People's various talents and abilities are not like numbers tattooed on their foreheads, there for all the world to observe at a glance. Their assessment is a subtle and complicated task, which to accomplish with

reasonable accuracy requires a heavy investment of time and effort. Time and effort, however, are valuable for other purposes as well, and so we are led to seek ways of economizing on the evaluation process.

. . . The importance of consumption goods as signals of ability will be different for different occupations. Earnings and the abilities that count most among research professors are not very strongly correlated, and professors think nothing of continuing to drive a 10-year-old automobile if it still serves them reliably. But only in a very small town, where people know one another well, might it not be a mistake for an aspiring young attorney to drive such a car in the presence of his potential clients. Good lawyers generally earn a lot of money, and people with a lot of money generally drive fashionable new cars. The potential client who doesn't know better will assume that a lawyer with a battered car is not much sought after.[22]

If it is true that we need information about each other that would ordinarily be impossible or inefficient to acquire directly, we must read it off from more visible signs. We can, of course, argue about the reliability of different signs, but that is another matter. Individuals do not decide what the signs are or should be; they must pretty much take them as given. If you want to convey information, you have to speak the language. One decides to drive an Acura Legend or to wear Guess jeans, but one does not decide what information is conveyed by these choices. Sometimes, of course, the information will be misinformation. So if one cares what other people think, one must be sure to learn what different consumption choices are taken to signify.

The purely informational aspect of ability signaling obviously performs a useful function. Reading surfaces is a shortcut and, especially in mass societies where typically we are strangers to one another, we need shortcuts.[23] This function of consumption extends to its purely expressive aspects, unconnected with status considerations. How you dress, what kind of car you drive, what you eat—these choices tell people about your tastes, interests, and values. It is not necessarily a matter of status seeking to want other people to know such things.

Yet when consumption serves to signal abilities, the distinction between consuming to demonstrate one is as good as others and consuming to show one is better, and between either of these and consuming simply to convey information, begins to blur. Insofar as a person is attempting to convey information about his abilities, he is saying "I have these traits, these talents, I am *this* good (. . . so hire me, or let me into your university)." He is serving the useful function of providing information about himself, but he is also trying, in a competitive world, to obtain a scarce commodity.

The consumption of education provides illuminating examples of these complexities. (It also shows that the consumption of nonmaterial goods like education is in important ways just like the consumption of material goods.) What is the good that we desire, and that we hope to obtain for ourselves or our children, by enriched educational programs, private schools, prestige colleges, and advanced degrees? There are three kinds of possibilities. First, I may want my child to acquire the intellectual resources to appreciate Shakespeare or Einstein. What I seek here is a nonrelative good. To attain it, my child will need a certain quality of education. Theoretically, at least, everyone could have such an education; there is plenty of Shakespeare to go around, and my child's gain need be no one else's loss.

Perhaps, though—instead or in addition—the good I seek through education is a chance at one of society's better jobs. Better jobs are scarce, and we can assume that those with more and better education have an advantage in obtaining them. But better jobs can be scarce in two quite different ways. A job can be better because it is more interesting or rewarding (defined however one chooses), so that a person with a better job will have a better or richer life. Here again, what is wanted is a nonrelative good; it is a good that happens to be scarce, however, because of certain unfortunate accidents of the world we inhabit, and so one person's having the good excludes others from having it. There is no necessity that a person who wants a better job in this sense wants status—certainly not superiority, not necessarily even equality. Status may not enter as a consideration at all. Nevertheless, such a person will want to be better than others so that she will get the job.

A job can be better in a different sense: it can occupy a higher position in the social hierarchy. A person who wants a better job in this sense clearly seeks superiority over others; the good sought is what Fred Hirsch calls a positional good, one that is inherently scarce.[24] Only in this case do we find the concern with status that has so dominated thinking about consumption.

Of course, I have been arguing that the concern with status, insofar as it represents a desire for equality rather than superiority, is not reprehensible. Yet educational goods illustrate the instability of the distinction. We can further clarify this point with the example of so-called gifted and talented programs in the public schools. As a parent, I may believe that the educational needs of my children and of children generally are better served by an environment that deemphasizes tracking and that does not label academically talented students and segregate them from other students in special programs. I may hold this view even if my children are among those chosen by the elite system. Nevertheless, given the existence of a gifted and talented program, I will want my children to be selected for it. For once the system is in place, if my children are not labeled as better, they are thereby labeled as worse. It is simply rational to hope they are chosen, even if I disapprove of the system. A similar analysis can be given of the flight from public to private schools, "white flight" from integrating neighborhoods, and many other phenomena. In such situations, one who fails to practice what she preaches has at least a partial defense against the charge of hypocrisy.

We come back to the prisoner's dilemma situations mentioned in passing earlier. Just how large a range of consumption practices should be understood in these terms is a question that needs further investigation. But it is clear at least that some such practices do fall into this category: if you don't move ahead, you fall behind. So the decision not to acquire more of the good in question is not simply a decision not to improve one's well-being; it is in effect a decision to lower it. When high school diplomas are a dime a dozen, employers will start to require college degrees; even if the additional education is not necessary to do the job, it serves as a sorting device. When college degrees are a dime a dozen, employers will require MBAs or law degrees, even though the additional education is not necessary. As Hirsch puts it, when everyone stands on tiptoe, no one sees any better. But if you don't stand on tiptoe, you won't see at all. If you want to see better, you'll have to get stilts. But when everyone gets stilts. . . .

Another way in which the line between the desire for equality and the desire for superiority blurs emerges from a more careful examination of the idea of the reference group. It may be true that people often want only equality with respect to those groups to which they aspire or to which they think they belong. But sometimes it is part of the group's identity to derive satisfaction from what Veblen calls "invidious comparison" with other groups. A member of Mensa may be content so long as his IQ equals that of other members. But he may also derive satisfaction from knowing he is smarter than others who do not qualify for membership. Some would argue that class membership works similarly: a person's satisfaction with being middle class rests partly on knowing there is a lower class. The instability of the line between the desire for equality and the desire for superiority depends on how central invidious comparison is to a group's identity. It is probably safe to say that feeling superior is central to the identity of some groups but not others.

What's Wrong with Consuming, Anyway?

How much space do the relational aspects of consumption occupy in the totality of reasons for consuming? It is not easy either to interpret this question concretely or to know how to go about answering it. My own view is that the relational aspects of consumption are extremely important: the reasons people want things have a great deal to do with what others around them have. This proposition has not been fully established by the foregoing arguments; but I believe that observation of and reflection on social phenomena support the conclusion that consuming because others consume explains a great deal.

An important corollary is that to the extent that people's desires to consume depend on what others around them consume, collective reductions in consumption will be less painful to individuals than reductions individuals effect in isolation. And the reason is not simply that it is easier for people to make personal sacrifices if they know that others are doing likewise. It is also that, to the extent that consumption is relational, having less does not constitute a sacrifice if others also have less. We can put the point more strongly: to the extent that the desire to consume is relative, two societies could differ markedly in their overall level of consumption without differing in overall well-being, however well-being is understood.

This view helps explain the common observation that people in societies less affluent than our own are not necessarily worse off, and often do not seem less happy or satisfied, than we are. Relative deprivation—deprivation relative to those around you—is crucial. This is *not* to say that deprivation is wholly relative or that there are not certain privations that are absolutely bad and to be avoided. Such a conclusion would be comforting yet pernicious. Nevertheless, for a society acting in concert, the pain of reducing consumption should exceed the pain of reduced consumption, since what we are used to and what we are exposed to centrally affects our desires and degree of satisfaction. Collective, concerted efforts are less painful not simply because welfare is relational in the ways I have described but also because, typically, they do not require the same kind of full awareness that individual efforts do. Legally mandated taxes, deducted like clockwork from one's paycheck (and from everyone else's), do not hurt—because we do not notice them—in the way that individual choices to donate money often do. The latter may be purely voluntary, but because these acts are done deliberately and in full consciousness, we are constantly reminded of our sacrifice.

It is worth noting that I have not addressed the question of whether we ought to consume less or not. Partly as a result, this discussion might seem to have a certain ambiguous, "half empty or half full?" quality. Looked at in one way, it might appear to be an apology for consumption; looked at in another, it seems a call for the simpler life. It looks like the former because in explaining the relativity of consumption practices I have also been defending these practices to some extent. It looks like the latter because the questions raised get their force from the assumption that consumption is somehow problematic. Both impressions have some warrant. Let us see why.

First, the (partial) defense of consuming because others consume against the charges of conformity, greed, envy, or one-upmanship. I have argued that the desire to consume rests partly on factors that have nothing at all to do with status, and that even the desire for status is not always reprehensible—that we consume partly to satisfy the desire for a certain kind of equality that is essential to self-respect. Do these arguments commit the naturalistic fallacy? Just because people behave in a certain way or possess certain traits (assuming they do) does not amount to a justification. Perhaps we should conclude instead that human beings are contemptible or at least morally weak.

To some extent this dispute will remain immune to rational solution. When all is said there will still be serious disagreements about how much we can or should expect of mortal human beings—disagreements that cannot be analyzed further into soluble bits. But we can make some headway by distinguishing the different ways in which consumption is relational, for these differ morally. Consider the four categories that emerge from the foregoing discussion: (1) consumption dependent on infrastructure and networking effects; (2) consumption dependent on salience and the demonstration effect; (3) the status-related desire for equality; (4) the status-related desire for superiority. The first is least problematic morally, because it affects needs almost everyone will agree are basic and whose fulfillment therefore typically does not reflect vice. The last is most problematic, which is not to say that no defense of the desire for superiority can be made. I myself would not make it, however, and insofar as Veblen is right empirically I think he is wrong evaluatively: we should "depreciate" and "deplore" the tendency.[25]

It is the two intermediate cases that are most difficult to resolve. As I argued above in the discussion of salience, one person's greed is another's openness to new experiences, and it is not easy to see what further information could get them to see eye to eye. What this may show is just that their disagreement does not depend on divergent factual beliefs but, rather, on differing judgments about the moral value of certain character traits or behavior. Similar things can be said about equality and self-respect: facts about human psychology aside, we may disagree about how much a virtuous person should care about what others think.

Facts about human psychology aside? Here, it seems clear, we cannot dispense with naturalism. What we count as virtue must take heed of psychology; if the great mass of people cannot thrive or be happy without a certain degree of respect from their fellows, then it is at best only the remotest kind of virtue, fit for the very few, to go without it. There is still room for disagreement, of course, about how much we should care about what others think. This disagreement is rooted partly in disputes about or ignorance of the psychological facts and partly in evaluative issues.

The moral heart of the question about what consuming because others consume indicates about our character may rest, finally, on the importance of self-sufficiency as a moral ideal.[26] Self-sufficiency can be viewed in terms of both things and people. Salience and the demonstration effect involve dependence on things; the desires for equality and superiority involve dependence on other people and public opinion.

In these matters I would urge moderation. With respect to both things and people, too much self-sufficiency is eerily inhuman and remote; too little is slavish. It is for this reason, among others, that I take the foregoing arguments to constitute a defense of human character, but only a partial defense. We are made to respond to the stimuli around us and to care about the opinions of others; but that does not mean that we do not often care more than we should. We do.

The preoccupation with status and the opinions of others can manifest itself, and often has, in value systems that place less emphasis on material goods. Are these other outlets superior? Some would argue that material inequalities constitute a more benign and democratic manifestation of inegalitarianism than other forms, at least in part because material things are more easily separable from a person's identity. Others would insist on the intrinsic superiority of spiritual, moral, and intellectual values, even if they do not solve the hierarchy problem and even if, because they are less separable from the self, they give rise to greater problems of self-respect and deep inequality.

These are large questions I cannot address here. They matter insofar as we are interested in the intrinsic moral value of material consumption and in the implications of consumption for character. But—to return to the beginning—we worry about consumption for other reasons too: because it seems wrong for some to have so much while others have so little, or because we think those who have so much are partly to blame for others having too little, or that by consuming so much ourselves we impoverish others. Insofar as we worry about consumption for these reasons—reasons of justice—or for environmental reasons, consuming less materially could make a big difference.

To know for certain whether consuming less will make a big difference would require us to analyze and evaluate these reasons carefully. I hope at least to have shown why such changes, once effected, might be less significant and traumatic than those of us who have become accustomed to a certain level of material comfort might suppose.

Notes

This essay was written with support from the Pew Charitable Trusts. I am grateful to audiences at the University of Illinois, the University of Connecticut, and Yale and Wesleyan Universities for helpful discussions. I especially want to thank my colleagues at the Institute for Philosophy and Public Policy and, in particular, Karla Hoff, David Luban, Thomas Pogge, Jerome M. Segal, Alan Strudler, Leonard Waks, and David Wasserman for their conversations and comments.

1. That is because, as I shall argue below, the concept of "too much" is partly relative to what others have. And so to know what is too much we first must decide on a frame of reference—on the community to which comparison is being made.
2. One might take Peter Singer's essay "Famine, Affluence, and Morality," *Philosophy and Public Affairs* 1 (1971): 229–43, to mark the beginning of the contemporary philosophical debate.
3. I am leaving aside questions about whether we have had a role in bringing about the situation in which the poor find themselves. If one thinks A is causally responsible for B's plight, that gives a strong (perhaps undeniable) reason for thinking A must do something to remedy it. But the question is raised and vigorously discussed in the philosophical literature, even where it is not assumed that A is causally responsible for B's plight. I shall describe both these situations as raising questions of justice, although some would reserve the term for the first situation, describing the second instead in terms of benevolence or decency.
4. Amartya Sen, "Poor, Relatively Speaking," *Oxford Economic Papers*, n.s., 35 (1983): 159, reprinted in Amartya Sen, *Resources, Values and Development* (Cambridge, Mass.: Harvard University Press, 1984), 325–45.
5. Of course, cars have acquired a great deal of significance apart from their utility. One may want a particular kind of car to express something about oneself or to demonstrate one's status. The point is simply that these motives could be entirely absent and one would still have reason to want a car.
6. James S. Duesenberry, *Income, Saving and the Theory of Consumer Behavior* (Cambridge: Harvard University Press, 1949), 26–27. Duesenberry describes some of the same phenomena discussed here in terms of the "interdependence of preferences." As I hope my discussion makes clear, no significant questions are begged by allowing Duesenberry's description of the new goods as superior.
7. Here and elsewhere the word "neighbors" must be understood partly metaphorically. What reference group we compare ourselves to varies from person to person and context to context. Sometimes it is literally our neighbors; sometimes our coworkers; sometimes those who share our occupation; sometimes the parents of our children's friends. Literal neighbors sometimes have a special significance because, particularly in the suburbs, one is confronted by their houses, yards, and cars. As the sentence immediately following shows,

there are, at least in the contemporary world, few constraints that can be imposed in advance on the class of neighbors.

The concept of a reference group to which one compares oneself, extensively analyzed in the sociological literature, is central to our understanding of the processes described here. See, for example, Robert K. Merton and Alice Rossi, "Contributions to the Theory of Reference Group Behavior," in *Social Theory and Social Structure*, 1968 enlarged ed., ed. Robert K. Merton (New York: Free Press, 1968).

8. For discussion and defense of the attractions of consuming, see Michael Schudson, *Advertising, the Uneasy Persuasion: Its Dubious Impact on American Society*, afterword to the new English edition (originally published in the United States by Basic Books, 1984); and Colin Campbell, "Consuming Goods and the Good of Consuming" (this volume).

9. This is one reason for thinking that, as Robert E. Goodin puts it, "voting green but living brown" is not necessarily hypocritical. See his *Green Political Theory* (Cambridge: Polity Press, 1992), 78–83, 120–23.

10. See Alan Strudler and Eleanora Curlo, "Consumption as Culture: A Desert Example" (this volume) for a discussion of non-status-related expressive aspects of consumption.

11. I do not mean to imply that these choices are consciously designed to impress other people; almost certainly the processes are less than conscious much of the time.

12. *The Theory of the Leisure Class: An Economic Study of Institutions* (New York: Dover Publications, 1994 [1899]), 20–21. Veblen describes the point of this kind of accumulation as "invidious comparison," although he hastens to add that "there is no intention to extol or depreciate, or to commend or deplore any of the phenomena which the word is used to characterize. The term is used in a technical sense as describing a comparison of persons with a view to rating and grading them in respect of relative worth or value" (22). Whether Veblen meant to "depreciate" or not, that is certainly the way his words have been taken. It is not hard to see why.

13. Self-respect is among the Rawlsian primary goods—things that anyone would want no matter what their values or their plan of life. See John Rawls, *A Theory of Justice* (Cambridge, Mass.: Harvard University Press, 1971).

14. Veblen, *The Theory of the Leisure Class*, 20. Veblen speaks of self-esteem, not self-respect. Although the terms are often used interchangeably, there are reasons for distinguishing them. See David Sachs, "How to Distinguish Self-Respect from Self-Esteem," *Philosophy & Public Affairs* 10 (1981): 346–60. Following what I take to be Sachs's main idea, I understand self-esteem to mean having a high opinion of oneself or one's accomplishments, while self-respect involves having a proper regard for one's rights, deserts, or entitlements—having a sense that one is a person of value whose interests and wishes ought to be taken seriously. These concepts are clearly related, and are not always easily distinguishable. Nevertheless, my point is about self-respect, and I employ Veblen's assertion in support of it.

15. *The Wealth of Nations* (New York: Modern Library, 1937 [1776]), book V, chap. 2, 821–22.

16. I owe this point to Thomas Pogge.

17. In addition, societies differ in the goods that serve as markers of status. The Veblenesque critique of consumption practices can mask two different (although not mutually exclusive) complaints: that people care about status and superiority, and that these concerns manifest themselves crudely, in the display of material things, rather than, say, in intellectual, aesthetic, or spiritual values. I discuss this point further in the final section of this chapter.

18. Samuel A. Stouffer et al., *The American Soldier, vol. 1: Adjustment During Army Life* (Princeton, N.J.: Princeton University Press, 1949). The authors of this study coined the central and now-common term "relative deprivation."

19. W. G. Runciman, *Relative Deprivation and Social Justice: A Study of Attitudes to Social Inequality in Twentieth-Century England* (Berkeley: University of California Press, 1966), 18. For a discussion of the significance of relative deprivation in envy, with references to the social-psychological literature, see Aaron Ben-Ze'ev, "Envy and Inequality," *Journal of Philosophy* 89 (1992): 551–81.

20. A full account of these matters would have to explain how the reference group gets chosen: how people decide which—that is, whose—boat they are in. Sometimes this will be fairly obvious, but not always.

21. Perhaps this is not strictly true: one might think that the possession of things was itself *tantamount* to status or superiority. But I believe that the relationship is commonly taken to be an evidentiary one: possessions (which of course may be thought also valuable and desirable in themselves) are taken as a *sign* of worth. Compare the Protestant idea that emerged during the rise of capitalism that economic enterprise and wealth (although not material display) were the signs of spiritual salvation. See Max Weber, *The Protestant Ethic and the Spirit of Capitalism* (New York: Scribner's, 1958), and R. H. Tawney, *Religion and the Rise of Capitalism* (New York: Penguin, 1980).

22. Robert Frank, *Choosing the Right Pond: Human Behavior and the Quest for Status* (New York: Oxford University Press, 1985), 148–50. I am indebted to Frank's book and to Fred Hirsch, *Social Limits to Growth* (Cambridge, Mass.: Harvard University Press, 1976) for stimulating my thinking generally about these matters.

23. Things are not quite so simple. The informational aspect of ability signaling is conjoined with a disinformational aspect. I may want to communicate my abilities, or I may want to fool people into thinking I have abilities that I do not.

24. My discussion of education owes much to Hirsch's account. See *Social Limits to Growth,* chapter 3. The distinction between the intrinsic and the positional advantages of a job can sometimes be hard to draw. A person who feels his work is unappreciated or unrecognized, because it lacks a certain status, may be unable to enjoy what would otherwise be an intrinsically rewarding job.

25. See note 13 above and the text accompanying it.

26. For a discussion of the virtue of self-sufficiency, see Michael Slote, "Virtue Ethics and Democratic Values," *Journal of Social Philosophy* 24 (1993): 5–37.

11

Consumer Expenditures and the Growth of Need-Required Income

Jerome M. Segal

In discussions of mass consumption and consumerism in the rich countries of the world, it is often assumed that the most fundamental economic needs of the population have long since been met. True, there may remain certain recalcitrant pockets of poverty, but those are people distinctly "left out" of the economic largesse that has been bestowed upon the overwhelming majority of the population.

Indeed, it is because it is assumed that our consumption levels far exceed our needs that it is possible to speak of overconsumption and of the problem that our consumption levels might be creating for us, for the environment, and for others less fortunate.

Insofar as people in rich countries continue to feel hard-pressed economically, this is seen as part of the problem and part of the mechanism of overconsumption. Along these lines, in *The Affluent Society* John Kenneth Galbraith identified the forces of advertising and emulation as central to the psychological dynamic that keeps the affluent consumer always wanting more, even when legitimate need has been met.[1]

In this essay, I advance a rather different thesis. While it would be absurd to deny the differences between levels of consumption in the United States and in the impoverished Third World, it does not follow that in countries such as the United States economic need has long been overcome. Rather, I will argue, most Americans legitimately feel hard-pressed economically. Fundamental economic needs are either unmet or can be met only at high levels of income and consumption. This, however, is not the result of some fixed universal feature of the human condition but, rather, emerges from the socioeconomic conditions of a particular society at a particular point in time, and most importantly, from how that society decides to respond to economic need. In the United States, too often we address economic need through individual provision, that is, each household seeks to meet its needs by attaining higher levels of income for itself, even when we could much more efficiently meet our needs by acting collectively.

This essay looks closely at consumer expenditures in the United States. For each of the main areas of consumption expenditure, I identify some of the fundamental economic needs that such expenditures are intended to satisfy. The focus is on the questions, How much money does it take to satisfy these needs? and How has this level of need-required income (NRI) changed over time? I argue that over the years NRI has risen significantly in real terms and that this is the primary reason many people feel they purchase relatively little beyond necessities. Finally, I briefly consider why NRI has risen and the kinds of social policies that might stem or prevent the rise in NRI.

A primary purpose of this essay is to place this concept of need-required income in the center of discourse about consumption levels. Preventing the rise of NRI, that is, the rise in the amount of money needed to meet fundamental needs, is offered as a central policy objective. It is a goal that is particularly appropriate for Third-World countries, lest they find themselves repeating our own experiences. And it is a policy objective that must be embraced in rich countries if we are to free ourselves from the "money side" of life, if we are to create a space within which people might comfortably live a simpler, less harried existence.

Current Consumer Expenditures

Table 11.1 shows how in 1994 total consumer expenditures in the United States breaks down. These are averages, and some variation emerges when we examine different income groups and household types. Nonetheless, this broad spending pattern is remarkably uniform across the population. Consider table 11.2, which shows the percentage of expenditures devoted to various categories, for households at different income levels in 1994. With only minor exceptions, the rank ordering of spending categories is the same across the income spectrum. Moreover, across the income spectrum the areas of housing, clothing, and entertainment show almost no percentage variation. Transportation is also relatively stable, dropping off only with the highest income group. The largest difference is in the area of insurance, which includes personal insurance, pension contributions, and social security. For upper-income groups these "security" expenditures rise to a very sig-

Jerome M. Segal

Table 11.1. 1994 Total Consumer Expenditures in the United States

Category	Percent of Total Expenditures
Housing	31.8
Transportation	19.0
Food	13.8
Personal insurance/pensions (includes Social Security)	9.3
Health care	5.5
Clothing	5.2
Entertainment	4.9
Other	10.5

Source: Bureau of Labor Statistics, *Consumer Expenditure Survey* (Washington, D.C.: Government Printing Office, 1994)

Table 11.2. 1994 Consumer Expenditures by Income Group

	Pre-tax income of consumer units		
Type of Expenditure	$15,000--- 20,000 (percent)	$50,000--- 60,000 (percent)	Over $70,000 (percent)
Housing	32.7	29.0	30.0
Transport	19.5	19.0	16.8
Food	15.9	13.3	11.5
Insurance	5.0	13.0	15.3
Clothing	4.9	5.1	5.7
Health care	7.5	4.6	3.9
Entertainment	4.3	5.3	5.4

Source: Bureau of Labor Statistics, *Consumer Expenditure Survey* (Washington, D.C.: Government Printing Office, 1994)

nificant percentage of expenditures. This rise is made possible by decreases in other areas, most notably the areas of food and health.

Critics of American consumerism often envision an extremely wealthy, bloated society. A more modest image, however, is appropriate. In 1994, only 11.7 percent of households had an income of over $70,000, and for this upscale group average annual expenditures were $69,506. Over 75 percent of all households had incomes below

$50,000. The top quintile of households had an average pretax income of $76,660 and spent an average of $55,411 a year. For the second highest quintile, composed of households averaging 2.9 persons, the mean expenditure level was $34,247.

The term *households* includes single individuals, couples without children, and larger families. And the average levels meld together those on opposite ends of the income spectrum. It may be more informative to consider the social unit that remains at the core of our society (though less so than in previous generations): married couples with children. This group encompasses over 100 million people, about 41 percent of the total population.[2] If we look at median income, we find that in 1993 median income for married couples with children was $45,548; at this level of income, consumption expenditures are roughly $38,600.[3] It is useful to keep this figure in mind. If the median American two-parent family with children is spending $38,600 a year, then those who would advocate dramatically reduced consumption as an across-the-board prescription for Americans have to explain how such families are going to get by with expenditures of less than $30,000 a year—not an enviable task.

Another way of making the same point, that the potential for dramatically reduced expenditure levels may be less than critics of consumption assume, is to look at the income spectrum. If there is room for reductions in overall consumption expenditures, it lies primarily in the top quintile of households, which currently accounts for roughly 37 percent of the country's aggregate consumption. Suppose that it were possible to reduce the expenditures of this top fifth of American households to a level significantly closer to the national median, say to the level of the next highest quintile. Would this result in a dramatic reduction in overall consumption? Not really. If the expenditures of those in the top quintile fell to the expenditure level of the next highest quintile, this would only reduce total consumer expenditures by 13.4 percent.[4] What this tells us is that any general image that presents average Americans as imitating the *Dallas* model of consumption, and thus easily capable of cutting 25 or 50 percent of their expenditures, is seriously off the mark.

A seemingly very different picture of American consumption emerges if we look back in time. For instance, as table 11.3 shows, if we look at real per capita consumption expenditures over the past three decades, we find a 1994 level that is twice that of 1960 and three times that of 1929. Similarly, if we look at median family income for married couples (with and without children) over the years, we see a pattern of significant growth. In 1991 dollars, the pretax income of such families went from $17,498 in 1947 to $40,995 in 1991.[5] The historical picture

Table 11.3. Per Capita Personal Consumption Expenditures in Constant 1987 Dollars

Year	Expenditures ($)
1929	4,550
1940	4,505
1945	5,107
1950	5,764
1960	6,698
1970	8,842
1980	10,746
1990	13,093
1994	13,316

Source: Statistical Abstracts of the United States (Washington, D.C.: Government Printing Office, 1995), table 706.

suggests enormous increases in consumption, increases of such magnitude that it seems obvious that we would have been better off, as some have suggested, if we had exchanged some of this increase for more leisure (or more inherently rewarding work).[6]

We are faced, then, with two seemingly disparate pictures. On the one hand, over the broad historical period there has been marked growth in consumption. But when we look at where we are now, we find that for the typical family with children, consumption levels seem rather modest. Noting both the tremendous growth in consumption and the seeming impossibility of returning to earlier levels, many commentators argue that there has been a psychological inflation in our sense of what constitutes a necessity. For this reason, they say, we cannot see how to do with less, though what we now have would have seemed more than abundant from an earlier vantage point. This inflation in our sense of necessity extends the realm of what we feel we must have in two different ways. First, it introduces into that realm goods and services that we previously did without, including some that did not even exist (such as computer games, home videos, and microwave ovens). Second, with respect to those things that we did have before, we now feel the need to have better-quality versions of those items. We seek homes with larger rooms and more bathrooms, we require fancy restaurants, and elegant clothes. Moreover, as everyone else's income rises, we feel that ours must rise too, just so we can maintain our relative standing. As the economy grows, we feel we need more and more.

There is no doubt that these kinds of escalations in our sense of necessity exist and that finding ways to check this escalation must be part of an agenda for controlling ever-rising levels of consumption. However, we would also do well to consider another explanation for rising expenditures—that much of the rise in income and consumption has simply gone toward meeting the same needs we have always had (safe housing, transportation, care of children, and so on). Such needs have absorbed income growth in part because they were previously only partially met at low levels of income. But more interestingly, I will argue, *the real cost of meeting these fixed needs has grown substantially.*

Income Required for Core Needs

Assume the existence of a stable set of legitimate economic needs that can be met through the consumption of goods and services. At any given point in time, we can ask how much income is required in order to meet those needs. The answer is relative to a specific economy and a specific set of social policies and programs. This is most evident with respect to meeting basic needs in the Third World, where countries vary widely in the amount of household income needed to meet a given set of needs. For instance, consider the question, How much money does a family need to be relatively secure that a newborn child will survive? Let us interpret "relatively secure" as facing an infant mortality rate not greater than 30 deaths per 1000. In Sri Lanka in 1992 the infant mortality rate was 24 per 1000, but in Congo (with a similar income level) the rate was 83 per 1000, and in Venezuela the rate was 33 per 1000 even though the income level was more than triple that in Sri Lanka.[7] In some countries there is substantial social investment in clean water, inoculations, and government-provided primary health care. In other countries meeting health needs is more a matter of individual provision and requires that a family have the money for good food, clean water, sound health information, and adequate medical care in case of disease. Thus, the same need can be met at very different levels of family income. Basic needs development strategies have sought to find ways of satisfying human needs at particularly low levels of national and household income.

We can think of need satisfaction in terms of the following formula:

Need Satisfaction = Income X (Needs Satisfaction/Income)

The last term, Needs Satisfaction/Income, is a measure of efficiency, though not the kind typically investigated by economists. It tells us the extent to which income is being used effectively to satisfy needs. In Sri Lanka this efficiency measure was very high; in Venezuela it was far less so. In the United States our tendency has been to view needs satisfaction solely as a matter of the first term of the equation: the level of income. Little attention is given to the second term, how efficiently that income is utilized to satisfy needs.

The socioeconomic conditions and choices of any society are a major determinant of the personal consumption costs of meeting needs. Once we have identified a given set of needs, we can inquire about the cost of meeting those needs for a particular person at a particular time within a particular socioeconomic system. Then, by observing changes in these costs over time and adjusting for inflation, we can determine whether need-required income (NRI) is rising or falling.

Economists typically do not like to talk in terms of needs; they prefer the concepts of utility, want satisfaction, and preferences. Insofar as they do approach the issue of needs, they commonly work with a *fixed* basket of needed goods and services and consider whether these necessities have been subject to more or less monetary inflation than the economy as a whole. In this essay, I do not assume that a constant market basket of goods and services is required to meet the need in question. Instead, I argue that changes in the need-required basket of goods and services occur all the time and are a major cause of changes in NRI. It is not that new needs are being dreamed up but, rather, that the commodity specification, the goods and services required to meet long standing needs, changes rapidly. For instance, workers always needed to get from home to work. When they worked on farms, all they had to do was walk. Today, almost all employees require public or private transportation and the money to pay for it.

NRI in the United States has risen in real terms over the last several decades. If this rise has been significant, it will go a long way toward explaining why even with higher real incomes people continue to feel that they have little, if any, discretionary income.

Core Needs

There are many ways of characterizing the core needs that lie behind the need for income in rich countries. The following seem to work reasonably well.

1. *Housing*. Need for safe, minimally attractive housing located a reasonable distance from the workplace.
2. *Transportation*. Need for safe mass or private transportation that

allows family members to travel relatively quickly from home to work, schools, stores, and communal activities.

3. *Food.* Need for ample, healthy, reasonably diverse and enjoyable food, preparable or attainable within household time constraints.
4. *Health care.* Need for effective treatment of health problems.
5. *Clothing.* Need for socially acceptable clothing that is adequate to climate conditions.
6. *Education.* Need for effective and safe schooling (preschool through college and beyond) for children.
7. *Economic security.* Need for protection against large increases in NRI (e.g., as triggered by major illnesses) as well as protection against decline or loss of income.

There is nothing particularly elevated about these needs. They are relatively noncontroversial and serve to articulate a sense of necessity shared by people in middle- and low-income brackets. Let us now consider each of these individually.

Housing

NRI for housing has grown considerably, yet this need remains unsatisfied for many people. Many Americans, for all they may spend, simply do not have safe housing at a reasonable distance from work.

The explanation for the growth of housing NRI lies largely in two phenomena. The first is the rise in housing prices. Between 1970 and 1994 the median sales price of existing homes rose from $23,000 to $109,800;[8] adjusted for inflation, this represents an increase of 36 percent. However, this statistic glosses over substantial regional differences. In the Northeast and the West, the real increases in housing prices for existing homes were 57 percent and 71 percent, respectively, while in the Midwest and the South the real increases were relatively modest.

Compare two hypothetical families of modest means, one that entered the housing market in 1970 and one that entered in 1994. Assume they lived in an area where prices rose 60 percent in real terms. If mortgage payments constituted 25 percent of the household expenditures, there would be an increase in NRI of 15 percent from just this factor alone. To put this in perspective, note that from 1970 to 1993 real median family income for married couples rose only 17 percent.[9] Indeed, the situation is actually much starker if we look at median income levels of young households. Between 1970 and 1991, the real median income of families with householders aged 25 to 34 years actually declined. And in the age range of 35 to 44 it rose by a scant 11 percent.[10] For such families, the increase in NRI for housing explains a great deal about their sense of income pressure.

A second factor in the growth of NRI for housing is the continuing decline in personal safety, resulting in greater demand for housing in safe neighborhoods and smaller demand in unsafe neighborhoods. Thus, even in regions where aggregate housing costs have remained stable, *safe* housing has become progressively more expensive. To maintain a fixed level of safety people have had to move to progressively more expensive neighborhoods. The same is true of housing in locations where schools are safe and educationally sound. Because such housing is simply out of reach for many Americans, the high prices of homes in such neighborhoods do not fully reflect existing need. If middle- and low-income people had more money, they would increase the bidding war for housing that satisfies their needs.

Transportation

For most Americans, transportation needs are relatively well satisfied, but only at a markedly higher cost. Since the 1930s, the percentage of total consumption devoted to transportation has more than doubled for all income classes.[11] Given that real per capita consumer expenditures rose by more than 250 percent in the same period, we have something in the neighborhood of a 500 percent increase in real terms in the amount that families are spending on transportation.[12] There is good reason to think that nearly all of this represents an increase in NRI, not the growth of luxury.

What has happened is that first one automobile and then a second automobile has become a necessity for most middle-income families. This occurred not because of an inflated sense of necessity but, rather, because of underlying changes in our socioeconomic life. The shift to the suburbs, motivated in large part by the search for safe neighborhoods and decent public schools, has made the private automobile a necessity, and the emergence of the two-income family has tended to make a necessity of two cars. This trend has been reinforced by the relocation of stores outside of residential neighborhoods (often to malls five or ten miles away) and the shift of communal activities (especially for children) outside of their immediate neighborhoods.

To put it differently, in the early decades of the twentieth century people had the very same need for transportation that they have now, but they could and did satisfy this need quite well without automobiles. Today, in most parts of the country, a family without an automobile would be far more restricted in its activities than in times past. Thus, higher real income is required to meet the core need for transportation.

Consider as an example, a married-couple family in 1991. On the average that family spent $6,316 on the 2.6 vehicles it owned, or $2,429 per car.[13] Between 1960 and 1991, median income for married-couple families rose $16,153.[14] If consumption expenditures are assumed to be 85 percent of income, then they rose $13,730. If we assume that over those years, as women entered the labor markets, families moved to the suburbs, and so forth, annual transportation NRI went up one car's worth, or $2,429, then about 18 percent of the total consumption growth in that thirty-one year period was absorbed by an increase in the cost of meeting transportation needs.

Food

Though there are American families that fail to satisfy their need for ample, nutritious food, this need is reasonably well met for most Americans. Moreover, the income required to satisfy this need does not appear to have increased (in real terms) over the decades. In fact, there has been a major decline in the percentage of consumer expenditures allocated to food. Between 1935 and 1988–89, its share fell by half— from roughly one-third of household expenditures to only one-sixth. (At the turn of the century, almost 43 percent of the expenditures of urban wage earners went for food.[15])

In real terms, household expenditures for food increased only about 5 percent between 1935 and 1989.[16] This suggests that in real terms there has been virtually no increase in the income required to satisfy the core food need, and possibly there has even been some decline.

Health Care

The very concept of "basic needs" is logically related to questions of health. For instance, it is because the failure to meet minimum caloric requirements results in significant health damage (malnutrition, disease) that we say a person has a basic need for food with a particular level of caloric content. If there is an effective treatment for some significant health problem, then by definition a person with that problem has a basic need for that treatment. Here the need is derivative from a need for health itself, and is thus relative to the existence of effective treatments for health problems. In addition to the need for health care, people have a need for health-care security—an assurance that if they develop a health problem, they will have effective care.

In this essay, my primary focus is on household expenditures, particularly the extent to which today's vastly higher household expenditures go to cover growth in the cost of satisfying long-standing needs. However, unlike most of the other categories of need, the health area is one in which households' expenditures capture only a limited part of what is expended nationally in attempts to meet the need. In addition to out-of-pocket expenditures and household expenditures for medical insurance, much of the cost of health care is met through employer contributions to medical insurance and government expenditures. To a very large extent, the vast growth in national expenditures for health care and insurance has not been fully reflected in a growth of need-required household income. In real terms, the per capita level of total national health expenditures (public, business, and personal) almost tripled between 1970 and 1990. Yet as a society, we have been relatively successful in shielding our personal checkbooks from this explosion.

Over the long haul, health expenditures on the household level have risen roughly in line with the general growth of household income. Thus as a percentage of household expenditures, health expenditures have been relatively constant. In 1935–36 they constituted 4.4 percent of household consumption, in 1988–89 they constituted 5.7 percent, and in 1994 they constituted 5.5 percent.[17] Interestingly, health expenditures on the household level decline as a percentage of total consumption as we consider households in higher-income brackets. Part of the explanation for this is that as income levels rise, so does the adequacy of employer-financed health insurance.

The fact that a significant part of the burden for health-care costs has been shifted to the government and business sectors can be misleading. If, for instance, all health-care expenditures were paid for by the government, we would have zero consumer expenditures for health care and, thus, zero NRI for health care. Yet at the same time, collectively we would face an expanding need for growth in national income in order to finance the ever-expanding need-required national income for addressing health problems.

Does this mean that shifting the expenditure burden to employers and government is of no consequence? No, I would argue that it makes a considerable difference in that burden shifting can open up the possibility, for any given individual, of a life in which needs are satisfied at very low levels of household income. Collectively, the pressure is still there for the national economy to expand in order for these core needs to be met, but each individual family is relieved of the income pressure.[18]

In the health area, unlike other areas, the growth of NRI is potentially open-ended so long as there is an expansion in effective, but expensive, technologies. The underlying reason for this is the simple fact of the human condition—mortality and morbidity will continue to be with us, and we will have need of whatever works to postpone death and reduce the severity of disease. Unlike spending in other areas (such as transportation), where increased consumption (the second car that allows the second wage earner to get to work) represents little if any gain in well-being, spending for more effective health care does represent true progress. Nevertheless, we may well reach a point where we decide to put some limits on the growth of technologies that are generating an increase in health-related NRI. For example, we may conclude that the pace of change is simply too great for the social good, or that the marginal benefits of certain new technologies, especially if used widely, do not yield a welfare gain commensurate with the added economic strain they will place on households and society generally. This strain may become more evident as public financing and business contributions for health care reach their limits and as a greater proportion of the growth in health-related NRI devolves upon households.

Clothing

Over the last ninety years, spending for clothing and related services has shown a marked decline as a percentage of consumer expenditures. From a high point of 17.6 percent in 1917–18, it declined to 10.3 percent in the early 1960s and has fallen since then to between 5 and 6 percent. In real terms, per capita spending for clothing fell between 1960 and 1988. Yet there is little basis for believing that clothing needs are less adequately met today than thirty years ago. It seems clear that in this area, at least, we have not seen any increase in NRI. Nor does there seem to have been any inflation in people's sense of how much money (in real terms) they "must have" for clothing, even when we look at the possibility of inflated standards of decency and growth of NRI combined.

This is interesting, because it is clothing above all else that seems most powerfully in the grip of changing fashions and desires shaped by advertising. If one expected to find a powerful escalator of inflated desires, an escalator that makes people feel a need for more and more, it would be in this area. But apparently no such escalation has occurred. And if fashion, emulation, and advertising, all of which greatly affect what we wear, have relatively little impact in getting us to increase total clothing expenditures, then this strongly suggests that the strength of such factors in increasing expenditures for a given sector (rather than redirecting expenditures within a sector) has been overemphasized in other areas as well.

Education

The core need in this area is formulated in terms of the household's need for effective, safe schooling for children (preschool through college and beyond). There are other educational needs as well, but this is the most powerful and the one that accounts for most education-related spending. Here "effective" education is understood as schooling that equips a child or young person to succeed in the socioeconomic competition he or she will enter as an adult. To a large extent, it is effectiveness in these terms that motivates most families to seek educational opportunities for their children. The parents see their responsibility, and a good part of their own identity and fulfillment, as tied to how successful their children will be. When the disparities between socioeconomic winners and losers are very great, as they are in our society, the consequences of not receiving effective schooling are enormous. It is also true, however, that the magnitude of socioeconomic disparities and the relative scarcity of good jobs ensure that most people will not be successful; in principle, schools cannot equip most people to be winners in a competition with many contestants and few prizes.

This fact can result in more intense competition and in greater educational expenditures. In recent years, for instance, the elite colleges have experienced a very significant increase in applications and are rejecting ever-higher percentages of those that apply. As a result of the increased competition, a new specialist has emerged, the "educational consultant" whose job it is to both mold the high school student into the perfect applicant and to market him or her to the consultant's contacts at desirable colleges. The charge for this new service is $1,000 a year.[19] Similarly, as competition intensifies, the need for more extensive schooling increases, thus pushing up educational costs. This is one way of characterizing the phenomenon of overcredentialization.

In addition to schooling that is effective, parents have a clear need for schools in which their children will be safe. Years ago this was something that could largely be taken for granted. Today it is a major issue, and the pursuit of public schools that are both safe and good learning environments is a major reason people move to more expensive neighborhoods. These higher costs show up as housing costs, not education costs, even though they are satisfying schooling needs.

For the most part, our society finances schooling collectively, through free public schools up to the high school level. This was not always the case, and it is possible that this commitment will erode in the future. But what it has meant is that with the exception of preschool and college, the costs of schools have not fallen directly on the household budget. Typically, these expenses are paid locally, often financed through property taxes. Thus, schooling needs, which are powerful and expensive to meet, are only a minor part of consumer expenditures on the average.

Given the fact that public schools often fail to provide safe, effective schooling, an increasing percentage of parents find that they need income sufficient to send their children to private schools. From this, we might expect that there has been an increase in education-related expenses on the household level. This does not appear to be the case; at present there is no clear pattern of higher percentages of students enrolled in private schools. But, I suggest, this only means that most families lack the additional money to pay private school tuition.

There has, meanwhile, been explosive growth in NRI with respect to day care and prekindergarten schooling. This is directly related to the fuller entry of women into the paid labor force and is a clear example of the way in which a significant part of higher incomes and consumption levels goes to fulfill needs that were previously filled by different social arrangements.[20]

Between 1970 and 1993 the percentage of three- and four-year-olds enrolled in nursery schools rose from 20.5 percent to 40.5 percent.[21] The increase was greatest among three-year-olds—from 12.9 percent in 1970 to 27.1 percent in 1993, an increase of 110 percent. Between 1960 and 1994 the labor force participation rate of married women with children under six rose from 18.6 percent to almost 62 percent.[22] And between 1975 and 1994 the labor force participation rate for wives with a child one year old or younger rose from 31 percent to 59 percent.[23]

However, while there has been a vast increase in the need for child care, only a relatively small segment of the population meets this need by purchasing child-care services. While the percentage of children in organized child-care facilities has more than doubled since 1977, in 1991 these children accounted for only 23 percent of the children under five of employed mothers.[24]

The fact that three-quarters of the children of working mothers are not in organized day care explains why child-care expenses, which are staggering for families that incur them, typically do not clearly emerge in the aggregate statistics. Typical costs of day care in the Washington, D.C. area are $120 per week, or roughly $6,000 a year. Before-tax median income in 1993 for married-couple families with the wife in the labor force was $51,204.[25] Assuming annual expenditures of $42,000, the day-care bill for these families would constitute one-seventh of total expenditures. The $6,000 component of NRI incurred by families who pay for day care can also be put in perspective if we compare median income of married-couple families with wife not in the labor force in 1970 with married-couple families with wife in the labor force in 1993. In 1993 dollars, the difference in median income between these two different situations twenty-three years apart is a gain of about $18,700. If we assume that the 1993 family uses day care, while the 1970 family did not, roughly one-third of the income gain associated with the entry of the women into the labor force and two decades of income growth is absorbed by the day care expenditure.[26]

Higher education is the other major schooling expense that falls on the household budget. And here, too, there has been significant growth of NRI. In part this is because of an increase in the amount of schooling young people need in order to compete for employment. In addition, NRI has gone up because of the steep rise in tuition costs. In 1975 the annual cost of college tuition in four-year private schools was 19.1 percent of median family income. In 1993 it was equivalent to 33.2 percent of median family income.[27]

Economic Security

A key element of our security needs is protection against a sharp increase in need-required income itself. A serious health problem that requires expensive treatment is the most salient example of this, and the household expenses associated with protecting against such eventualities are included in the health-care expenditures discussed previously.

Typically, economic security issues have to do with protection against a severe drop in income. This typically emerges from loss or relinquishment of one's job as a result of physical disability, aging, or changed economic conditions.

Economic insecurity associated with possible loss of employment resulting from adverse economic conditions or corporate downsizing has become more pervasive in recent years. There are, of course, government programs designed to mitigate the associated loss of income, but these programs provide only limited protection. For most Americans the need for protection in this area is unmet. As a result, increasing numbers of people live in a state of heightened anxiety.

Because there is no form of private insurance that protects individuals against this loss, and thus no obvious purchase individuals can make to offset it, the need for economic security does not clearly translate into higher expenditures. Indirectly, however, there are a variety of things individuals might do to mitigate income insecurity associated with potential job loss. One strategy is to increase personal savings. Most people are unable to employ this strategy because they simply do not have sufficient income to do so. Insofar as the probability of job loss has risen, then the income needed to protect against future drops in the income stream increases as well. And if the savings necessary to provide security are enormous, then the increase in NRI will be similarly enormous.

Another strategy is to seek employment in occupations that are less vulnerable to economic contraction and dislocation. For those already in the labor force, this strategy requires devoting income to retraining costs; for parents with children and for young adults, it requires paying for an education that provides access to professions that have more secure income streams. In both cases, we confront an increase in NRI and, insofar as people adopt such security strategies, the higher spending may show up indirectly in educational and housing expenditures.

Perhaps the greatest source of economic insecurity is associated with a potentially devastating decline of income when one approaches old age. Household expenditures (contributions) to retirement plans are the typical private-sector approach to meeting this security need. Multiple factors, including an increase in life span and greater uncertainty regarding the viability of government programs such as Social Security, cause an increase in NRI. As in the area of health care, there are substantial numbers of Americans for whom this security need is unmet. Thus, increases in household expenditures for income insurance associated with retirement only tell part of the story with respect to the growth of NRI.

The data on expenditures for personal insurance and pensions (including life insurance, Social Security payments, pension contributions, contributions to IRAs, and so on) show that in higher-income households there is a very sharp increase in spending in these areas. Thus for households with incomes between $15,000 and $20,000, such expenditures constitute only 5 percent of total expenditures. This rises to 13 percent for households with incomes between $50,000 and $60,000 and reaches 15.3 percent—roughly what such consumers are spending on health and food combined—for those with incomes over $70,000.

How are we to understand this virtual explosion in security expenditures as income levels rise? If we had seen such a pattern when it came to expenditures for clothing, we would have interpreted it as indicating significant discretionary spending on the part of those better off. Yet here I would suggest that just the opposite is true. The fact that people who have more money spend higher percentages on security suggests that economic security is an unmet need for most people. One of the first things people do when they have the means is spend to increase security. For instance, of the $21,871 that consumers in the highest quintile spend beyond that spent by consumers in the next highest quintile, $4,689 (21.4 percent) goes for personal insurance and pensions.

One reason that NRI grows in the area of income security is simply that it is already growing in other areas. For example, if an individual is purchasing income protection for an income stream adequate to meet his needs, then as the latter increases, he has more to protect and the costs of the insurance rise accordingly.

A New Picture of the Affluent Society

Let us then pull together these various threads. Yes, over the years Americans have increased consumption expenditures considerably. Much of this increase in household expenditure has gone to meet fundamental needs, either because needs were previously unmet or because in real terms the cost of meeting these needs has increased dramatically.

What emerges is a quite different picture than that commonly portrayed with respect to our affluent society. For most Americans the subjective experience that they always need more money than they have is not to be explained by inflation in their appetites or their standards of decency ("I must have more square feet, a newer car, better furniture, new gadgets") but, rather, by socioeconomic conditions that have resulted in unmet needs or in increased cost of meeting long-existing needs. This is true of housing, transportation, education, and income security. Collectively these increases have kept us concerned about money despite income growth.

Let me conclude with an example that reenforces this picture from a different angle. Between 1970 and 1991 the income of married-couple families rose by 18 percent. There are two main reasons for the growth of income for these families: first, more women entered the labor market (in 1970 the wife was employed in 40 percent of these families and in 1991 the wife was employed in 59 percent of these families); second, over this period, the income of women has risen considerably faster than that of men. Indeed, married-couple families in which the wife was not employed showed no income growth at all over this period.[28] Let us then consider a married couple today in which the wife decides to take full-time paid employment. Assume that she earns $22,500 (median income for full-time female employees in 1993), and that on this marginal increment to the family income there is a combined federal and state income tax of 20 percent, and a Social Security tax of 7 percent. This leaves potentially $16,425 for increased consumption. Of this amount, some will be spent for existing unmet needs and some will be truly discretionary. But first, some must be spent for the increase in NRI associated with the change from a one-career to a two-career family. How great is this increase in NRI? It depends on the family situation. But let us assume that in this family the wife's working necessitates buying a second car and day-care expenses for one child (see table 11.4). In this not atypical example, almost all of the increased consumption generated by the wife's decision to seek paid employment (the single most important factor behind increased family income) goes toward meeting necessities incurred by the decision itself. Yes, income and consumption are up substantially. But the family continues to feel

Table 11.4. Additional Costs of Working Wife

Type of Expense	Amount Spent
Day care	$6,000
Annual cost of second car	$2,5000
Additional cost of lunch out	$1,000
Additional cost of ordering food in, or going out to dinner one night a week	$1,000
Cost of having home cleaned once a week	$2,500
Additional annual expense for work clothers	$500
Total additional costs	**$13,500**
Increase in NRI as a percentage of increments in disposable income	**82%**

pressed economically and now, with both parents working, is under far greater time pressure as well.[29]

Reflections on Policy

In the past we have seen little rise in NRI in the areas of food and clothing. And in the areas of health and education, the individual family has been largely shielded from increased spending as a percentage of income. It is the areas of transportation, housing, and income security that have increased the most.

If I were to hazard a prediction about future trends I would suggest that the situation with respect to food and clothing will remain stable and that transportation costs (barring some great increase in gasoline costs) will remain relatively fixed. On the other hand, we may have exhausted our society's willingness to shield households from future increases in health-related NRI; as the population continues to age and as new, expensive medical technologies continue to be developed, this potentially is an area of major NRI expansion.

Similarly, the dependence on day care can be expected to increase, and with time we will see greater and greater schooling competition. This may directly increase the costs of meeting schooling needs and will indirectly result in bidding up the cost of housing in safe neighborhoods with good public schools. Moreover, for most Americans the need for safe housing a reasonable distance from work with access to safe and effective public schools is unmet and likely to remain so.

Also in the area of income security needs are extensively unmet and this too may become an area of greater need for household income as our social mechanisms (such as Social Security) become both less reliable and less adequate for meeting the needs of retirees as that demographic group balloons twenty years from now.

It is beyond the scope of this essay to consider policies for either stabilizing or reducing NRI in these different sectors, but two points should be made. First, what may be needed in some areas is not a new government program or policy but a major redirection in the way our society thinks about our social life. For instance, meeting the need for income security may in the long run require rethinking our conceptions of old age, work, meaningful activity, and retirement.

Second, there will be little will and, thus, few resources for new directions if they are seen as discrete items on a new policy agenda. If major change is to be possible, we must rethink the most basic of questions: What is an economy for? I would like to close then with a word about the objective of having a society in which the level of NRI is low or, to put it differently, a society in which the efficiency of need satisfaction per unit of income is high.

In the Third-World context the rationale for working toward such a society with low NRI is simple and powerful—it allows the satisfaction of basic needs at low levels of income. Thus, some live who would otherwise die. To some extent, but with perhaps less power, the same argument can be made for high-income societies. But we may also seek a society with low levels of NRI for a different kind of reason: because it facilitates a distinctly valuable form of life. In a high-productivity society, if the amount of money a family needs to meet its core economic needs is rather modest, this allows the possibility of simple living. First it allows people to put in less time on the job. In particular for two career families, being able to meet core needs with two thirty-hour jobs, or two twenty-hour jobs rather than with two forty-hour jobs would be a blessing. It would enable us to restore some peace and harmony to our hectic, harried existence.

Second, a society with low levels of NRI is one in which we are largely freed from the economic realm. If our needs are met with limited income, we are freed from the money side of life. In choosing jobs we can focus more fully on the nonpecuniary aspects of a good job; if needs are met we can afford to experiment, to make changes in midcareer, to rethink a life plan, to reeducate, to take a bold plunge toward that thing we have always wanted to do.

And if needs can be met at low levels of NRI, then there is less to be anxious about if we suffer a drop in income, lose our jobs, or walk away from the production of goods and services that do not conform to our values.

In short, a high-productivity society with low levels of NRI is a society that makes possible lives that are less pressured and more centered on friends, family, and activities of inherent value and fuller dignity.

If a society seeks to check or perhaps even reverse the rise of NRI, then it will reconsider policies in many sectors, but the most significant shift will be in its definition of adequate social and economic performance. If a decline in the absolute level of NRI or a decline in the ratio of NRI to median income becomes the central objective rather than income growth, this will represent a fundamental change in orientation and it will reverberate through the culture and every phase of economic life.

Notes

I wish to thank Toby Linden for his assistance in obtaining and verifying statistical data and calculations.

1. John Kenneth Galbraith, *The Affluent Society*, 4th ed. (Boston: Houghton Mifflin, 1984).
2. *Statistical Abstracts of the United States* (Washington, D.C.: Government Printing Office, 1995), table 66.
3. Author's calculations based on Bureau of Labor Statistics, *Consumer Expenditure Survey* (Washington, D.C.: Government Printing Office, 1994), which shows that in two-parent families with children, expenditures are roughly 85 percent of pretax income.

Because single parent families have significantly lower income levels, many at or below poverty level, the median income for all families with children is considerably lower: $36,200 in 1993 (*Statistical Abstracts* (1995), table 737).
4. Author's calculations based on data in *Consumer Expenditure Survey*.
5. Bureau of the Census, *Money Income of Households, Families, and Per-*

sons in the United States (Washington, D.C.: Government Printing Office, 1991), table B-11.

6. For example, in *The Overworked American* (New York: Basic Books, 1991), Juliet B. Schor suggests that if we had taken all the productivity gains since the 1950s in the form of more leisure rather than higher income, we could have reduced the work week to half its present level. Her claim holds up if we focus on the income of any given person, but it may involve a fallacy of composition when applied to society as a whole. Given that some sectors had high productivity growth and others had low growth, cutting back on output in those with high growth and transferring labor to the low-growth areas (and thus allowing for more leisure for both sorts of workers) does not yield the full saving in labor inputs suggested by just looking at average productivity numbers.

The historical picture has not been one of steady growth, however. Indeed, median family income in 1994 ($38,782) is actually below that of 1979 ($39,227 in 1994 dollars) (*Economic Report of the President Transmitted to the Congress* [Washington, D.C.: Government Printing Office, 1996], table B-29). It is important to bear this sharp break in trend in mind. The thirty years following the end of World War II showed largely uninterrupted growth of income and consumption. In the last fifteen years or so years, this has not been the case. Per capita consumption figures still show some growth, while median family income figures do not. This difference is attributable to several factors, including an increase in income inequality as well as a reduction in family size. Nonetheless, the big picture for the last half-century is one of dramatic, steady growth in consumption for more than three decades following the war and relatively little for most people in the subsequent decade and a half.

The statistics often appear to show conflicting pictures of more recent years. For instance, hourly compensation of production and nonsupervisory employees increased 71 percent between 1959 and 1992, though it rose by only 5.7 percent between 1978 and 1992 (*Economic Report of the President* [1996], table B-43). But there is a very important difference between the compensation levels just cited and actual earnings. Compensation includes employee benefits paid as well as Social Security taxes. Between 1959 and 1995, hourly earnings went up by a modest 11 percent and actually fell by 11.7 percent between 1978 and 1995 (*Economic Report of the President* [1996], table B-43). While this explains some of the differences between competing images of American affluence, it does not alter the basic fact of increased consumption over the long historical view. For example, between 1950 and 1970 per capita consumption expenditures rose by 53 percent while distribution of income was relatively constant. We do consume at much higher levels than previous generations, but we do not feel much room for significant cutbacks.

7. United Nations Development Program, *Human Development Report 1994* (New York: Oxford University Press, 1994).

8. *Statistical Abstracts* (1995), table 1218.

9. *Statistical Abstracts* (1995), author's calculations from table 738.

10. *Money Income*, table B-10.

11. See Eva Sharp and Stephanie Shipp, "A History of U.S. Consumer Expenditure Survey: 1935–36 to 1988–89," *Journal of Economic and Social Measurement* 19 (1993): 59–96.

12. Author's calculations from data in *Economic Report of the President* (Washington, D.C.: Government Printing Office, 1993), tables B-5 and B-111.

13. Author's calculations from Bureau of Labor Statistics, *Consumer Expenditures in 1991* (Washington, D.C.: Government Printing Office, 1992), table 5.

14. This amount is in 1991 dollars. See *Money Income*, table B-11.

15. Eva Jacobs and Stephanie Shipp, "How Family Spending Has Changed in the U.S.," *Monthly Labor Review* (March 1990), table 2.

16. Author's calculations based on Sharp and Shipp, "A History."

17. Author's calculations based on Sharp and Shipp, "A History." The historical levels are from table 1.

18. The extent to which this is true depends on a number of factors, including how public expenditures are financed.

19. See Eric Wee, "Students Go the Extracurricular Mile for Admission to Elite Colleges," *Washington Post*, 8 May 1996, 1.

20. The point may well be made that prior to their entry into the labor force, women had critical unmet needs, or that over time new needs emerged. My point is more limited; it is simply that whatever the reasons for women's entry into the labor force, this brought with it higher NRI due to the need that employed persons have for child care so they can get to the workplace.

21. *Statistical Abstracts* (1995), table 243.

22. *Statistical Abstracts* (1995), table 638.

23. *Statistical Abstracts* (1995), table 639.

24. *Statistical Abstracts of the United States* (Washington, D.C.: Government Printing Office, 1992), table 600; *Statistical Abstracts* (1995), table 615.

25. *Statistical Abstracts* (1995), table 738.

26. *Statistical Abstracts* (1995), table 738.

27. Author's calculations based on *Statistical Abstracts* (1992), table 269; *Statistical Abstracts* (1995), table 287.

28. *Money Income*, table B-11.

29. This is not intended as an argument against dual career families, but to point out that in many situations the case for such patterns is not financial.

12

Alternatives to the Consumer Society

Paul L. Wachtel

The consumer way of life is deeply flawed both psychologically and ecologically. While pushing us to produce ever more goods, and thereby placing increasingly dangerous strain on the environment, it fails to offer the experiential satisfactions it promises. The system of growth and market-driven consumerism feeds off its own failure to satisfy our deeper needs. Like a cancer or virus, it inserts itself into what might be called healthy psychological tissue, substituting its own self-replicating program of needs for the pursuit of love, cooperation, nurturance, community, friendship, and dedication to higher purposes that have been the foundation of real satisfaction from the dawn of our species.[1]

Increasingly, we have come to define our needs in terms that stress purchases in the market and we have become increasingly alienated from and out of touch with the aspirations and endeavors that really make a difference in our lives. In acceding to the overriding goal of producing more and more goods to satisfy the artificial cravings of the marketplace, we create conditions that *diminish* our prospects for a satisfying life—increasing job insecurity and pressures to uproot ourselves from communities, for example, in order to compete and to maintain a mobile labor force; heightening the stresses endured during the many hours spent each week in the workplace in order to increase our productivity; placing increasingly greater strain on the family as parents work longer hours to be able to purchase the ever-larger stock of goods that feels "standard;" bearing the consequences of ever-growing inequality as we helplessly transfer the determination of social right and wrong to the market. Then, faced with these accumulating disamenities, we ironically try to quell the nagging sense that something is wrong by trying still harder to have (on an individual level) and to produce (on a societal level) even more consumer goods. This does little to resolve the source of the dissatisfaction, and it results in a further exacerbation of our distress and our failure to achieve a secure sense of well-being. Moreover, our *psychological* bind creates an accelerating *ecological* bind, adding still further to the sense that our lives are out of control.

The Connections between Psychological Well-Being and Ecological Balance

Most calls for limits to growth have stressed austerity in one way or another. They call upon us to get off the gravy train, to give up the joyride, to face up to a world of diminished expectations. But "tightening our belts" is an image unlikely to stir the imagination or encourage changes in an ecologically sound direction. So long as *deprivation* is what is implied—even in the service of preventing environmental disaster—most people will put off recognizing the unpleasant necessity; denial and temporizing will continue to be the order of the day until environmental abuse becomes so continuously and undeniably palpable that action cannot be avoided. At that point, it may be too late to prevent permanent damage, and it will certainly be much more costly.

What we need is an image of an alternative that is not just a bitter necessity but holds out promise of a genuinely better life. The image of belt-tightening is one that issues from within our *present* set of assumptions; it equates conservation, recycling, and fewer gadgets with having "less." A notion of "standard of living" more rooted in our actual psychological experience points in quite a different direction and challenges the idea that altering our present way of life means settling for less. It encourages us to think beyond material goods as the defining essence of the good life and to focus instead on the quality of our relations with others; on the clarity and intensity of our experiences; on intimacy, sensual and aesthetic experiences, and emotional freedom; and on the ethical, spiritual, and communal dimensions that give the entire enterprise meaning. In such a direction lies the path to a way of life that is at once more ecologically sound *and* more exciting and enjoyable.

The Interlocking Role of Social Structures, Values, and Basic Assumptions

The possibility of converting to such an alternative way of life requires that we understand the ways in which individual and societal values reciprocally interlock. Neither the individual's values nor those of the system are primary; each determines the other in continuous reciprocal interaction. People in a system with competitive values tend to become competitive, and in so doing they keep the system competitively oriented. Similarly, when people act cooperatively, they help to create or maintain a warm or cooperative system, which in turn brings out in them further cooperative behavior.

In a large system, such as a society or a corporation, the properties of the system predate the participation of the individuals currently part of it. These individuals' behavior is largely shaped by the prevailing climate as they are inducted into it. But it is nonetheless the case that the properties of the system cannot be maintained unless the *people* involved maintain it. If, because of whatever experiences they encounter—a shortage, a common experience of disappointment, even a persuasive book—they begin to change their values and assumptions, they will perforce begin to change the system as well. In mutually prompting each other and in interacting with others who have not yet changed their view, they can begin to create and stabilize a new structural arrangement with different consequences for everyone within the system.

For all the concrete changes I would like to see in our society, in many ways it is values and modes of thought that I wish most to address. This is not to argue, as many did in the 1960s, that changing the consciousness of individuals is sufficient; traditional political efforts and the creation of appropriate institutions and structures is crucial if a change in consciousness is not to be merely an ephemeral change in style while the substance remains unaltered. But I do believe that *without* a change in values and grounding assumptions, political and institutional changes will themselves be superficial and leave the basic structure of life unchanged. Some of the changes I advocate in this chapter clearly would not be possible under our present market economy without rather substantial modifications of the system. But I want to be clear that most basically I am addressing assumptions that will be important in *any* political and economic system.

Having More and Enjoying It Less

There is much reason to think that economic growth and the increases in consumption it brings do not yield an increase in feelings of satisfaction or well-being, at least for populations who are above a poverty or subsistence level. Why would this be? Why is the common perception that having more *does* make us feel better misleading? To begin with, that perception is usually based not on the absolute level of one's possessions but on a comparative sense of how one is doing relative to one's peers. We do seem to derive satisfaction from our standing in relation to those we regard as our reference group, and income and possessions are an easy way to "keep score."[2] The problem is that with regard to this source of well-being, economic growth helps not a whit. No matter how fast the economy grows or how large the overall pie, only 10 percent of the population can be in the 90th percentile. Economic growth may *result* from people jockeying for position on the economic hierarchy, but it cannot *resolve* the longings that are at the heart of a consumer society.

To be sure, there is another comparison for which growth, at least in principle, can provide salutary effects. People do derive some satisfaction, we may expect, from surpassing their own previous level. A prominent psychological theory, adaptation-level theory, teaches us that our perceptions are determined not by the absolute level of the stimuli we encounter but by how they compare to expectations and previous experiences.[3] If we have more this year than we did the year before, will we not feel our circumstances have improved?

Perhaps if all other things were equal, this would indeed be the case. But recent findings, along with countless other everyday observations, suggest that most often the overall impact of growth on the sense of well-being is nil or even negative. When Ronald Reagan was elected president in 1980, for example, few doubted that a key factor in his defeating an incumbent president was the widespread sense that Americans were experiencing "hard times" and that inflation had eroded the buying power of the average American. But in fact, the actual buying power of Americans *increased* during the Carter years. In strictly material terms, Americans *were* "better off than they were four years ago."[4] Moreover, comparing the actual stocks of material goods in the homes of Americans at the end of the Carter years to what American households had twenty years earlier—when survey indicators of subjective well-being were significantly higher—we find that, over a period when perceived affluence was declining, the increases in actual stocks of goods was utterly enormous, resulting in increases of hundreds of percentage points in such items as dishwashers, air conditioners, and the like.[5]

It seems that although we may often experience considerable pleasure or satisfaction with regard to particular items we have purchased—a pleasure from which I myself am certainly not immune—we encounter paradoxical consequences when we look at the overall impact of these purchases on our satisfaction with our lives. Each individual item seems to yield an increment in satisfaction or well-being, but when totaled up the whole is much less than the sum of its parts. Indeed, it is close to zero, in the sense that after all these improvements have been garnered, our life satisfaction as a whole is pretty much the same. Like a mountain of cotton candy, the seeming amplitude melts into thin air as we try to taste it.

Indeed the sum of all our efforts to improve our lives via purchases may actually be negative. Taking into account all of the experiences and requirements associated with continually increased consumption, we may well find ourselves worse off than before we began. For the ways we mobilize ourselves, both as individuals and as a society, in order continually to have "more," turn out to undermine some of the most important sources of enduring and sustaining satisfaction. The corrosive effects of the market, when unchecked by a commitment to more substantial and significant values, weaken and even destroy, for example, our sense of community and connection to others.

Deployment of Resources

In contemplating further what sorts of changes are required to achieve a more satisfying and sustainable way of life, it may be useful to begin by looking afresh at some of the ways in which resources of time, money, and effort are currently deployed. For example, the United States alone spends hundreds of billions of dollars each year on advertising and sales promotion.[6] The considerations advanced here suggest that not only is much of this huge sum being wasted—this money could be spent on education, medical research, or efforts to redress social inequalities—but it may actually *detract* from the sum of well-being, contributing both to increasing the sense of dissatisfaction with what we already have and to directing us further to enmesh ourselves in the vicious circle I have been depicting.[7]

A similarly enormous amount of effort and money is spent in the manufacture of products with planned obsolescence. These are of two sorts: products that will break in a relatively short period of time and products that, as part of a societal pattern, are rendered unappealing or even unacceptable by changes in style. Changes in hemlines, lapels, and so forth in clothing and the cosmetic model changes in automobiles that used to be an annual ritual that announced unmistakably to one's neighbors how many years it had been since you bought a new car are both instances of the latter type of obsolescence. For many years, auto model changes amounted to about a quarter of all that Americans paid to buy automobiles,[8] and a substantial proportion of the money we spend on clothing[9] is the result of perfectly good clothes having "gone out of style."

In a society more attuned to the ecological and psychological consequences of our pursuit of the good life through consumer goods, expenditures of this sort would likely be drastically reduced. Spending huge sums on efforts to induce us to spend still bigger sums on items we otherwise would not particularly want would scarcely seem a wise use of society's resources. If items were more durable and remained desirable longer, annual sales would go down, but, because they would need to be replaced less often, we would have similar stocks of goods with fewer produced each year. The resources now deployed in producing frequent replacements would be available for use elsewhere.[10]

In place of these various unproductive efforts, our resources could then be devoted to such things as health, education, scientific research, the arts, and recreational facilities. With regard to medical costs, the total expenditures might actually be reduced—but, importantly, not because of the reduction in services now borne by those forced to receive their medical services under the corporate rubric of managed care but, rather, because of greater attention to health in a broader, more systemic way. Our present system encourages competing firms in all industries to cut corners in ways that have numerous adverse effects upon our national health: diminished attention to worker safety and long-range environmental effects in the workplace; irresponsible dumping of chemicals into our soil, lakes, and rivers (both legally and illegally); resistance to adequate emission controls in cars; routine use of antibiotics in cattle, which threatens to create drug-resistant strains of bacteria; efforts to raise permissible levels of smoke and other pollutants; and so forth. These various policies, all motivated by the wish to save money, actually cost us all an enormous amount. A very substantial proportion of our medical expenditures are due to environmental factors. Samuel Epstein, a medical authority on cancer, writes that "a series of epidemiological studies have concluded that environmental factors cause from 70% to 90% of all cancers."[11] Many other illnesses are similarly attributable to manmade factors or factors potentially within our control. The sum total of our various efforts to save money by cutting corners on health, safety, and environmental standards may well yield a net national loss without even taking into account the more important consideration of pain, suffering, and premature death. When one considers the totals for excess medical bills and the productivity lost to missed workdays resulting from environmentally caused illnesses (not to mention such nonmedical effects of pollution as higher bills for cleaning clothes or maintaining buildings), our "bottom-line" oriented policies require a nearsighted accountant.

Interacting Solutions: An Illustration

In attempting to envision a way of life that is at once healthier, more satisfying, and more sustainable, it is useful to notice ways in which various solutions can interact. We suffer, for example, both from insufficient exercise and from air pollution caused by automobiles. Both problems could be greatly alleviated at once if large numbers of people biked to work instead of driving. This is an alternative that is available at present, of course. But biking to work on city streets or on highways, breathing the fumes of cars or fearing being hit by them, is not most people's idea of a pleasant, relaxing way to get exercise.

In New York City, dividers were built a number of years ago along certain streets to provide bike lanes separated from auto traffic. This did attract a greater number of bikers, but insufficient attention was given to how our entire system discourages such an alternative. The program was done poorly and halfheartedly, and public preparation was minimal. Before long it was declared a failure, and the dividers were ripped up.

Imagine instead an elaborate system of bike lanes segregated from auto and pedestrian traffic, with glass or clear plastic overhead protection from the rain and moderate amounts of heat for cold winter days (not much would be needed, because the exercise itself would warm people). Imagine as well an elaborate campaign to introduce the public to the benefits of such an alternative mode of transportation and to encourage enough people to use it so that reduced automobile-produced pollution would redound to the public at large, benefiting even those who did not bike to work as well as providing individual health benefits to each biker (and providing further benefits even to those who, because of health, age, disposition, or the number of packages they had to carry that day, drove on the now much less crowded streets and highways). Imagine as well greatly expanded parking facilities for bikes in all business centers and perhaps even the provision of showers for employees to freshen up after their exercise and before a day's work.

To most of us, such a scheme might evoke the adjectives healthful, invigorating, pleasant—and ridiculous. Our present mind-set makes such things seem impossible. Immersed in our habitual assumptions, we cannot see past or around them. But an alteration of values and assumptions along the lines suggested here would make such a scheme seem both appealing and practical. The resources required to implement it are far less than the resources we have devoted to our present transportation system, with all its negative consequences for our health. Whether, ultimately, reduced hospital bills for heart disease, lung cancer, and emphysema would completely offset the costs of constructing such a system, I cannot say (but I suspect that if we factored in as well the costs of gas, the greatly reduced costs of maintaining cars that were driven less, and the extra years each car would last, the balance would tip quite strongly in the direction of constructing the bike lanes). In any event, this is clearly a combined health and transportation solution that is well within our means and prevented at present only by our assumptions and habits.

Another scheme, which could complement the above one nicely, is already being tested in Europe. Developed by Angelo Dalle Molle, an Italian entrepreneur, it centers on electric cars and would greatly reduce energy consumption while diminishing noise and pollution.[12] The limiting factor thus far in the use of electric cars has been the long time it takes to recharge the battery and the relatively short distance the car can be driven between rechargings. Dalle Molle's plan, which seems well suited for urban transportation, provides for an integrated system using computers, in which many garages have the facilities to recharge batteries. Recharging time is relatively short if a partial recharge is given every forty or fifty miles. Most trips within a city are no longer than that, and the system is set up to provide drivers with an incentive to leave the car at their first destination for a quick recharge and pick up another when they are through with their shopping, visit, show, or whatever.

A key to the potential success of the plan is the absence of individual car ownership in the scheme. Customers unlock the electric cars with a special credit card and are charged for the time the car is out of the garage; thus it is to their advantage to return the car to the garage when any leg of their ride is finished. (Garages are distributed in such a pattern that any destination within the system's area is very close to a participating garage.) This arrangement enables a much higher percentage of the cars to be in use, since individual cars are not tied up for hours just sitting parked, as they are under a system of individual ownership.

Another potential advantage of such a system, if expanded and elaborated, is that it could enable drivers to use exactly the appropriate vehicle for any of a variety of uses. Instead of owning a particular car, used on all occasions, a participant in the plan would take out a station wagon when he had something large to transport, a small two-seater for a trip across town, and perhaps a convertible for a trip in the country. Since only as much car would be used as the purpose required, energy and pollution costs would be further minimized; and since, again, cars would not be kept out of circulation when their sole owners were not using them, fewer cars would be needed, resulting in lower costs and a further reduction in the energy use and pollution associated with the process of manufacturing the cars. At the same time, drivers would have the convenience of driving just the kind of car they need for any situation.[13]

Such convenience is not available under the present common versions of car rental. Long-term rentals are in essence an alternative form of car ownership. Short-term rentals, by the day or week, are available, but in significant respects even short-term rentals implicitly retain features of the ownership model. You still rent a particular vehicle for the entire period of the rental, have to find a parking space for it when it is not in use, and keep it parked waiting for you instead of available for general use. Part of the reason short-term car rentals are as expensive as they are is that one is paying not just for time of use but for "owning" it over that period—that is, for the exclusive right to it whether you are using it or not. Short-term rentals are also much less convenient than Dalle Molle's approach because there is usually a good deal of paperwork for each rental, reservations may be required, and there may even be a substantial wait for a vehicle. In Dalle Molle's scheme, one's credit card gives the same instant access that keys now do for car owners.

The preoccupation with owning that our present system breeds is expensive in both an economic and a psychological sense. Psychologically, a key feature of ownership is precisely the nonuse by others. Indeed, as Philip Slater has shown, *exclusiveness* of access is sometimes a more significant subjective meaning of ownership than access per se.[14] Of course, the wish for ownership is unlikely to disappear completely from our psychology or our lives. But its hypertrophy, a product of the exaggerated individualism and disparagement of shared possession that a market and consumer society breeds, yields a host of disamenities we are often too immersed in our prevailing assumptions even to notice—or at least to notice that there are options.

The Meaning and Nature of Work

Central to the changes I am advocating, and to the values associated with them, would be a different view of work. When income or production is our primary concern, other things are sacrificed in the effort to maximize this one abstract dimension. When the quality of subjective experience is the criterion, things look very different. Work, from this standpoint, is not just "input," to be manipulated in the service of some higher aim, but a part of life experience in itself, to be examined as an activity that occupies many hours of the day. Although in principle individuals even now can opt to seek work that is more pleasant and flexible, trading off some quantity of consumer goods for a less stressful and more humanly satisfying workday, in practice few people really experience this option. The social system has powerful effects, both in limiting the concrete options available[15] and in shaping the choices people recognize or see as desirable. Economic theory usually portrays decisions about trade-offs between work conditions and goods as a strictly individual matter; this is the best of all possible worlds because everyone has chosen precisely the trade-off he or she desires. Outside the mythical world of the economists' models, however, our very desires are socially shaped; what we regard as "standard" or "natural" things to want or have, what we think are the "basic" things we "need," depends a great deal on what our neighbors have. This is not simply a matter of conspicuous consumption or keeping up with the Joneses. It is how perception itself works in the social sphere.

In a culture less monolithically concerned with maximizing material product, very different choices might be made and very different considerations brought to mind. We might be pleased to produce a bit less in a fashion that made the workday for most of us more pleasant. And in considering whether social policy should facilitate or impede the relocation of factories to areas where efficiency and profitability would be increased by access to cheaper labor—and whether, as an individual, to move to a new location in order to have a higher income—considerably greater weight would be given to the value of remaining in a community where one has friends and a sense of belonging relative to the weight given to increasing income or production. There are indications that this is already beginning to happen on an individual basis. Increasing numbers of individuals (and their families), for example, are refusing to accept promotions that require them to move to another city.[16]

A number of other changes would follow as well from a greater recognition that we have made poor trade-offs by overestimating how much increased income and production contribute to our well-being. With less emphasis on criteria that maximize *economic* well-being alone, the choices we make might be very different. I recall vividly a cab driver who proudly told me that he bought his daughter a Buick when she started college—and who also told me that he had to drive fourteen to sixteen hours a day to make ends meet. The values that led him to try to be a good father by buying things for his daughter, at the direct expense of actually being able to spend time with her, may well have been a product of marital discord or personal conflicts; but his tale made an impression on me because it is not really so at odds with mainstream American experience. The cab driver's experience is per-haps an exaggeration of that experience, but his behavior is immedi-ately recognizable.

Few people would explicitly endorse the idea of being away from their children and then making it up to them by buying them things; nor did this man, in fact. We experience the feeling that there are things that, because of economic necessity, one simply "has to" do. There is no sense of having made a choice; we are not really aware of the trade-offs between economic criteria and personal, experiential criteria. To a considerably greater degree than we realize, with differing contents at different economic levels, economic criteria usurp our consciousness, as it were, and feel somehow natural or God-given. Other values recede without the explicit sense of a decision.

It is just such consciousness of choices and trade-offs that a heighten-ing of psychological values implies—asking oneself such questions as which will *really* feel better, a new car and a stereo or an extra hour a day with one's son or daughter; or being aware that when one says one *needs* a new car, it in fact can have more to do with one's learned sense of what one is supposed to have than with how reliably the old Ford handles the daily commute. Finally, what is entailed in the awareness of choices I am describing is that organizing one's life to meet such needs can have psychological consequences that we are usually discour-aged from noticing.[17]

With a different set of assumptions, we might well conclude that we would all be better off if less were produced and if the workplace, where we spend so much time, were a more pleasant place to be. Among the changes along these lines that might be sought—depending on particu-lar workers' desires and on the particular deprivations that currently exist in different workplaces—are greater opportunity for workers to engage in relaxed conversation on the job or more breaks to permit this; more recreational facilities attached to the workplace and provision of time to participate in recreational activities during the workday; and greater opportunity for workers and groups of workers to take responsi-bility for how things get done.

This latter change in traditional working conditions has been of par-ticular interest lately and has begun to be tried in some of the most productive factories in the world. There are indications that—in addi-tion to making work more interesting and enjoyable—it actually in-creases productivity as well.[18] But it is important in the present context to emphasize that even if it led to somewhat lower productivity, such a change might appear desirable in terms of the value orientation being discussed here.

If changes of the sort I am describing were embraced by a significant proportion of the populace, it would have an impact not only on how we think about work but also on how we think about unemployment. It is certainly the case—under *present* assumptions and arrangements— that if large numbers of people began wanting and buying less, began taking the fruits of our productivity not in material goods and purchasable services but in time to spend with friends and family or on personal interests and pursuits, unemployment would rise drastically. *If*, however, the unemployment arose from *such* a cause, it would have vastly different meaning and would permit vastly different remedies than the unemployment to which we are accustomed. For if the unemployment were the result of the majority of people wanting leisure more than additional goods, we could spread the work around to everyone's benefit. Rather than envisaging reduced purchases leading to three people working forty hours a week and one person unemployed, we could employ four people for thirty hours and—bearing in mind that we are discussing the consequences of people having *already* changed their values and preferences—*all would be better off*.

In discussions of the feasibility of such a solution, critics often suggest that most people will not be willing to share jobs in this fashion, that working only (say) thirty hours a week would mean making less money and having fewer things. In such objections, the critics engage in a tortured logic that denies the very premise of the problem they are addressing. There have been many sources of unemployment in our system, but one cannot logically object, in considering unemployment *specifically arising from people's decreased interest in goods*, that a solution that yields more jobs and leisure at the cost of fewer goods would be unacceptable.

"Equipping" People for a Better Life

It is important to be clear that what I am pointing toward is not just working less and taking less income. Nor is it a simple return to some hypothetical good old days when people were poor but happy. I do believe that we have lost some things of great importance in our frantic pursuit of economic growth. But we have also made significant gains in human welfare that I wish neither to deny nor to give up. The citizens of today's industrialized nations live longer and healthier lives than people did in the past; fewer of them are plagued by poverty and fewer still suffer malnutrition; they have greater opportunities for education and for entertainment than any population has ever had.

What I and other like-minded people are seeking is a synthesis of old and new: not a simple *return* to older amenities and patterns of living, but an *incorporation* and *transformation* of them so that they can be combined with the best of the new. Gearing up for greater efficiency was, in the long run, in the service of human needs (though for a long time at an enormous price for the poor and working classes). But the very advances in our productive capacities have *changed* our needs, and if we fail to recognize this we will fail to capitalize on the potential for human well-being these economic advances have put before us.

What many people are beginning to realize is that time is now more precious than goods, that indeed we hardly have time to consume what we already can afford. For a growing number of people, the problem is too little time to use their goods rather than too little in the way of goods to fill their time. Taking the surplus that modern technology offers in leisure rather than in goods would provide benefits both psychologically and ecologically.

Many, however, continue to opt for goods, at least in part because they are unsure how they would use the extra time. As Tibor Scitovsky has noted,[19] it takes certain skills to enjoy our panoply of consumer goods, and many people vaguely sense that they lack these skills. Even more fundamental is a deeper inability to enjoy life fully that we are unaware of because of our focus on dollars and cents and on goods. The lives of all of us—not just those who are ordinarily labeled as in need of psychological treatment—are limited both by restrictions and inhibitions that reflect social custom and by a key feature of human development: our prolonged dependency in childhood. This dependency, added to the fact that for years our cognitive capacities are so much more limited than they will be when we grow up, has a profound impact on our development. Our view of the world and its possibilities is largely shaped when we are helpless and uncomprehending, and this view is then acted out in our adult years, when many more possibilities are in fact available to us. Indeed, the differences between the cognitive capacities and life situation of the human child and the human adult are far greater than between many species. It is as though we learn how to live as one creature and then apply that lesson when we become something quite different.

If we are to take more of the fruits of our technological progress in the pleasures of play and leisure, rather than in accumulating still more material goods, we will need, among other things, to overcome the constrictions that derive from our early fears and fantasies. One valuable contribution of the human potential movement was the development of therapylike techniques that are directed not at those limitations we ordinarily label as neurotic but at the psychological forces that make "normal" people's lives less free or exciting than they could be. Such a therapy for the healthy, as it were, would hardly be the sole or defining feature of a more psychologically and ecologically oriented society, but it would have an important role to play.

If the ideas and methods that have arisen from the human potential movement are to play a useful role in enabling people to find an alternative to the consumer orientation to life, however, they will need to be recast in a less individualistic form. As formulated in the 1960s and 1970s, they were as much a symptom of as a challenge to the values and assumptions of our market-growth and consumer-dominated way of life. Both the promise of these methods and their limitations in the consumerist and individualist forms in which they have tended to be packaged are illustrated by the "marathon" sessions that were prevalent when the movement was at its zenith. For periods ranging from several hours to several days, participants encountered nearly continuous challenges to their customary patterns of relating, with the aim of eroding their social facade and enabling new perceptions and experiences to break through. Although such methods have significant risks that were often overlooked in the zeal of the times,[20] they also have the potential, especially if pursued wisely and humanely, to reveal to people possibilities in their lives that have been unrealized in the constraining net of convention and habit. They have been limited, however, as have most of the human potential approaches, by an excess of individualism that, ironically, reflects the very values many of the leaders of the human potential movement were attempting to challenge.[21]

People who go off on marathon weekends often come back high, experiencing the world in a fresh, exciting way. But usually it is not long before old patterns reassert themselves. The missing link is the person's context. He returns to an environment in which the expectations he encounters and the behavior of other people toward him is the same as it was before the marathon. His new behavior alters this somewhat, but the pull of other people's ingrained patterns is strong, and their behavior, like his own, is not readily modified by just one or two new experiences. Consequently, in thousands of interaction sequences each day, he encounters a force pulling him back to old patterns, and before long the effect of the marathon has dissolved.

This analysis suggests that for efforts at change to be maximally effective they should address whole networks of people who can mutually support the changes that come about until they become more stabilized. Such a contextually oriented approach—in contrast to an individualistic strategy that attempts to change "the person" essentially regardless of context—has affinities with the emphasis on interdependency that characterizes the science of ecology. It is another way in which the point of view being advocated here might be viewed as a "psycho-ecological" point of view.

Although the human potential movement has placed strong emphasis on the use of groups in its efforts, and thus to some degree has incorporated a contextual perspective, even the use of groups has tended to be influenced by individualistic assumptions. Frequently, each person in the group is regarded as individually responsible for his own experience. Moreover, even where the group's contextual effect is recognized—as when it is understood that certain kinds of behavior or experience are possible only with group support or possible for each only when all do it—there tends to be the lack of follow-up mentioned before in the context of marathons. Each individual in the group is assumed to have been changed by it, and each separately goes back to his or her original context to face its powerful conservative influence alone.

It is understandable that such an approach would have been taken by human potential practitioners. Dealing with the continuing contextual influences and/or working only with functioning networks of people is enormously more complex and demanding and often, in present circumstances, simply not practicable. Moreover, many of the human potential practices derive from work with patients with distressing symptoms or undeniably thwarting ways of life that produce motivation for change strong enough to enable some individuals to change with less attention to context than is required for the kinds of changes—at once more subtle and more extensive—that human potential work attempts with relatively healthy people.

The latter kind of change—change not just in psychological symptoms or disorders but in values, dreams, and people's fundamental orientation to the world and to each other—cannot be achieved by psychological means alone. Charles Reich's *The Greening of America*[22] captures well both the aspirations and the naïveté of the countercultural movements of the 1960s. A new consciousness does not spread through society like a virus, requiring little more than contact with those who have already been changed. Without fundamental changes in political and economic institutions, the countercultural virus is easily "cured," as it was in the 1960s. Young people who, at the time, looked like they would never adopt the habits of thought and way of life of their parents eventually moved into the suburbs and the corporate world. In essence, they had little alternative, because little had been done to develop new economic and social structures that could sustain what was, at the time, a sincere and sweeping change in their assumptive world.

Please note that I am not reversing what I said shortly above. It is not that psychological change is unimportant—attempting to change social and political structures without attending to the mindset that underlies the present structures is as naive and futile as is a psychological approach divorced from social and economic reality. Rather, what is required is attention to the *mutual* influence of each realm upon the other, resisting the temptation to treat either as less essential background or as an epiphenomenon.

Changes in broad societal values, changes in social institutions and structures, and changes in individual psyches are best viewed as mutually facilitative levels of change. As the one emerges, it is best pursued and amplified by working on the other two as well. Powerful psychological techniques can help to accelerate the changes—both by making alternatives clearer and simply by demonstrating that a shift in emphasis toward more intense and satisfying experience instead of accumulation of goods and income really does feel better—but these techniques per se hardly define or delimit the kinds of changes toward which the present analysis points.

The Renewal of Community

Few of us would explicitly avow that we have chosen to rely on products instead of other people, and, fortunately, the bonds of community and of interdependency are too important to be severed completely. Friendships, family ties, and sometimes even a genuine sense of community remain realities for a great many of us. But the widespread yearning for greater closeness to others suggests that for many there is a sense of superficiality about those connections, even when things look good "from the outside." In my own practice as a psychotherapist, such complaints predominate substantially over specific anxieties or symptoms.

Central features of the American value system run counter to a sense of communal solidarity and shared responsibility for each other. As Robert Bellah put it, "Personal freedom, autonomy and independence are the highest values for Americans. You're responsible for yourself. We place a high value on being left alone, on not being interfered with. The most important thing is to be able to take care of yourself. As soon as possible, we believe, a child should take care of itself. It's illegitimate to depend on another human being."[23] Not surprisingly, Bellah's research also revealed "an element of loneliness not far below the surface" and a sense of community as being "brittle, fragile, with a tremendous turnover."[24]

A key to developing a realistic and satisfying alternative to the culture of growth and consumerism is to help clarify and channel these vague longings and to make clearer the links between our present discontents and the goals we have embraced in both our public and our private lives. The modern version of an age-old human task—reconciling ourselves to the finite limits that frame our lives and to our dependence upon each other—is peculiarly difficult for us. We are faced with having to learn again about interdependency and the need for rootedness after several centuries of having systematically dismantled our roots, ties, and traditions. This will not be easy. But we have in our favor the very discontents I have been discussing. We are not rushing headlong into ecological Armageddon smiling all the way. The pleasure principle itself can be harnessed to help us change course. The contradictions in our way of life are ultimately our friends and allies: A more environmentally sustainable way of life will *feel* better.

Conclusion

There are many features of American life—the structure of our cities and suburbs, the nature of the expectations and temptations our children encounter daily, and so on—that make it difficult to persist for long, and even more difficult to thrive, in an alternative to the consumer culture. Without a great deal of continuing support from others, and without the creation of alternative structures that can provide the feedback that sustains change, people who have tried to change will begin to feel enormous pressure to go back to the patterns that society at large calls forth. They will begin to feel the needs they once spurned and will then conclude—as will those who watched them from the shopping center—that "human nature" was just too much to keep down.

The reader who is persuaded by the arguments of this chapter may be assured that the changes in his or her perceptions will be short-lived unless concrete steps are taken to create a structure of commitments. An individual decision to buy less, to strive less for higher income, and to concentrate instead on what really matters is likely to have all the impact and staying power of a New Year's resolution without support from others.

What is required are concrete actions that are at least semi-irrevocable: joining together, for example, with a few friends who have similarly come to understand the contradictions and self-deceptions of the consumer treadmill; making explicit and public commitments to each other about changes you will make in the next week or month; meeting regularly in consciousness-raising sessions to spur each other on to adhere to the mutually given promises; talking at those meetings about the difficulties of living differently when the rest of the society has not changed yet; and (crucially) considering how you might work to bring about the larger social changes that will make every step along the way easier.

Even if we avoid all the pitfalls discussed here, we may fail anyway. From the perspective of currently dominant assumptions, much of what I have been advocating can seem quite utopian. The forces aligned against change are formidable. But I believe that nothing is as naively utopian as continuing on our present course, using up nonrenewable resources, fouling our own air and water, stirring discontents we are increasingly unable to ease, and hoping for a deus ex machina by the name of "technology" to bail us out at the last minute. I do not know if we can make the changes we need to, but a hardheaded look at where we are now suggests we had better try.

Notes

This chapter is an edited version of chapters 7 and 8 of *The Poverty of Affluence: A Psychological Portrait of the American Way of Life* (Philadelphia: New Society Publishers, 1989), with some additional material from my presentation, "Consumption, Satisfaction, and Self-Deception," given at the conference "Consumption, Global Stewardship, and the Good Life," University of Maryland, 28 September–2 October 1994. A selection from my presentation, reprinted in part here, appeared in the *Report from the Institute for Philosophy and Public Policy*, 15, no. 4 (Special Issue Fall 1995): 20. My thanks to Toby Linden for his valuable assistance and input in the selection and editing of the material in this chapter.

1. For a good discussion of the primacy of these latter dimensions in generating happiness, see Jonathan L. Freedman, *Happy People: What Happiness Is, Who Has It, and Why* (New York: Harcourt Brace Jovanovich, 1978).
2. Cf. Robert H. Frank, *Choosing the Right Pond: Human Behavior and the Quest for Status* (New York and Oxford: Oxford University Press, 1985).
3. See, e.g., Harry Helson, *Adaptation-Level Theory: An Experimental and Systematic Approach to Behavior* (New York: Harper & Row, 1964) and P. Brickman and D. T. Campbell, "Hedonic Relativism and Planning the Good Society," in *Adaptation-Level Theory: A Symposium*, ed. M. H. Appley (New York: Academic Press, 1971), 287–302.
4. *Wall Street Journal*, 2 December 1980, 56.
5. See my *The Poverty of Affluence*, 14.
6. *Statistical Abstracts of the United States* (Washington, D.C.: Government Printing Office, 1994) lists a figure of $148 billion for advertising alone. The total for advertising and all other efforts at sales promotion is obviously much larger. One way of estimating the larger total would be to begin with an earlier analysis in Julian L. Simon, *Issues in the Economics of Advertising* (Urbana: University of Illinois Press, 1970), which yielded a figure of $60 billion in the late 1960s. Since it took four dollars in 1994 to purchase what cost one dollar in 1968 (*Statistical Abstracts*, 491), a conservative estimate would suggest a figure of $240 billion dollars. I say conservative because both the population

and the gross national product (GNP) have increased as well since then, almost certainly leading to a still further increase in the actual quantity of effort devoted to these activities.

7. See *The Poverty of Affluence* for a fuller account of the multiple interlocking features of the vicious circles in which we are caught.

8. Tibor Scitovsky, *The Joyless Economy: The Psychology of Human Satisfaction* (New York and Oxford: Oxford University Press, 1992 [1976]), 255.

9. Over $167 billion in 1993 for "Apparel and Services," *Statistical Abstracts of the United States* (Washington, D. C.: Government Printing Office, 1994).

10. The question of whether such a change in our patterns of production and use would greatly increase unemployment is clearly a crucial one. I discuss it later in this chapter.

11. Samuel S. Epstein, *The Politics of Cancer* (San Francisco: Sierra Club Books, 1978), 23. See also R. Doll and R. Peto, "The Causes of Cancer: Quantitative Estimates of Avoidable Risks of Cancer in the United States Today," *Journal of the National Cancer Institute* 66 (1981): 1191–1308.

12. *New York Times*, 30 April 1980, A2.

13. Similar schemes, some of them already in use on a trial basis, have been described by Emma Rothschild in *Paradise Lost: The Decline of the Auto-Industrial Age* (New York: Random House, 1973), 212–20.

14. Philip Slater, *Wealth Addiction* (New York: Dutton, 1980), 23–25.

15. See Juliet B. Schor, *The Overworked American* (New York: Basic Books, 1991) for an excellent discussion of the obstacles limiting people's opportunities to choose shorter or more flexible work hours.

16. "America's New Immobile Society," *Business Week*, 27 July 1981, 58–62.

17. Economists tell us that people rationally and calculatingly *choose* in such circumstances; that they weigh the subjective utility of leisure and work more only if what they buy is worth more to them than the leisure is. Self-deception is left out of this picture. Each party to the exchange is tautologically defined as better off (else he would not have chosen as he did). Clearly the present view differs.

18. See, for example, M. Bousqet, "The Poison Factory," *Working Papers* (Spring 1973): 2–27; M. Maccoby, "Changing Work," *Working Papers* (Summer 1975): 43–55; and D. Jenkins, "Beyond Job Enrichment," *Working Papers* (Winter 1975): 51–57.

19. Scitovsky, *Joyless Economy*.

20. Morton A. Lieberman, Irvin D. Yalom, and Matthew B. Miles, *Encounter Groups: First Facts* (New York: Basic Books, 1973).

21. See *The Poverty of Affluence*, especially chapter 6 where I argue that most of the flaws in the social and personal change efforts of the 1960s can be traced to an unwitting incorporation of many of the mainstream assumptions of the very growth-and-consumer society that these efforts were meant to transcend. Of particular significance in this regard was the persistence of highly individualistic modes of thought.

22. Charles Reich, *The Greening of America: How the Youth Revolution Is Trying to Make America Livable* (New York: Random House, 1970).

23. Quoted in L. Bernikow, "Alone: Yearning for Companionship in America," *New York Times Magazine*, 15 August 1982, 26–27.

24. Quoted in Bernikow, "Alone," 27.

13

The Road Not Taken: Friendship, Consumerism, and Happiness

Robert E. Lane

Since the mid-1960s in advanced and rapidly advancing economies, there has been a rising tide of clinical depression and dysphoria, a decline in mutual trust, and a loosening of social bonds. Most studies show that above a minimal level, income is irrelevant to one's sense of well-being but companionship and social support increase well-being. Since shopping and consumption are increasingly solitary activities, and watching television is not genuinely sociable, the increased time devoted to these activities may be responsible for rising levels of depression. Advanced societies are likely to increase "utility" if they maximize friendship rather than the getting and spending of wealth.

This essay addresses the question, Does the market economy, with its "rage to consume" (Émile Durkheim's "dreams of fevered imagination"), contribute to the growing prevalence of depression? After exploring the evidence regarding the increase in depression and its substantial costs, I will examine what seems to be a most important cause of depression: lack of friends or confidants, that is to say, a decline in "social support." I look at the other side of the coin, as well: how the presence of friends one can count on influences happiness. The crucial influence of family solidarity on happiness is not discussed here.

Turning to the relationship between markets and friendship, I will explore the costs and benefits of assigning priority to friendship over commodities and examine whether the market inhibits friendship and other kinds of social support and if so how. Both materialist and affiliative motives drive people to pursue commodities and friendship; each motive has its advantages and defects. Examining these motives, I ask if there is any type of demand for more friendships comparable to the demand for more commodities. Finally, I explore reasons for and solutions to the friendship deficit that seems to be a principal cause of depression. Thus, the first part of this essay explicates the nature and causes of our debilitating social malady and the second examines how our patterns of consumption influence the malady and how social support might relieve it.

Lest my references to "happiness" (as the obverse of depression) lead to misunderstanding, I will note at the outset that in my cosmology there are *three* final goods, not one. Happiness (and the relief of that most unhappy state, depression) is the one treated here. But human development and justice are equally important. This essay is not an effort to rescue utilitarianism; the happy society is not necessarily the good society.

Affluence and Depression

Consider some evidence of the growing incidence of depression in economically advanced democracies. "In some [advanced] countries," it was recently reported, "the likelihood that people born after 1955 will suffer a major depression—not just sadness, but a paralyzing listlessness, dejection and self-deprecation, as well as an overwhelming sense of hopelessness—at some point in life is more than three times greater than for their grandparents' generation."[1] A nine-nation study finds that this epidemic is characteristic of rapidly modernizing countries, such as Taiwan, as well as such economically advanced countries as Germany and New Zealand.[2] Since World War II, each succeeding generation in these advanced and rapidly advancing economies is more likely to be depressed, for, as Martin Seligman has reported, "depression has not only been getting more frequent in modern times, but it occurs much earlier in life the first time."[3]

While the United States is not the most depressed country in the world,[4] it may be on its way to that infelicitous rank. On the basis of two earlier (1982, 1985) epidemiological studies funded in the United States by the Alcohol, Drug Abuse, and Mental Health Administration involving a total of about twelve thousand people in 1982 and 1985, a rate of increase in depression in the United States much higher than the rates of other countries seems evident: "People born after 1945 were 10 times more likely to suffer from depression than people born 50 years earlier."[5] Myrna M. Weissman and her associates report research covering five sites in the United States with similar, but less startling, results. These authors find "an increasing risk of depression at some point in life for younger Americans. For example, of those Americans born before 1955, only one percent had suffered a major depression by age 75; of those born after 1955 six percent had become depressed by age 24."[6] This finding corresponds to an earlier report of a six-year study tracking 956 American men and women: those under forty were three times more likely to become severely depressed than were older groups.[7] The Weissman study suggests that about a quarter of the population now experiences some of the clinical symptoms of depression at least once during a lifetime.[8] Because all mental illness is painful, it is relevant that Ronald Kessler reports evidence showing that during their lifetimes almost half of the population (48 percent) will experience some kind of mild or severe mental illness, of which major depression is the most common.[9]

Studies of mood disorders in children are even more disturbing. For example, one study in Britain finds a 42 percent increase of mood disorders from 1985 to 1990 among children under ten years of age.[10] Reports from the United States indicate similar increased childhood rates, adding that childhood depression is a strong indicator of later depression in adulthood.[11] Since children of the depressed are much more likely to be depressed themselves,[12] a malign, self-reinforcing cycle seems to envelop us.

Major depression is not just a matter of mood. The recently standardized test for depression used in the nine-nation study mentioned above includes such further criteria as insomnia, loss of energy, hypertension, "loss of interest or pleasure in usual activities," "feelings of worthlessness, self-reproach, or excessive or inappropriate guilt," and "recurrent thoughts of death, suicidal ideation, wishes to be dead, or suicide." One classic formulation focuses on the trinity of hopelessness, helplessness, and worthlessness.[13] Although depression and anxiety are separate illnesses, most research reports link the two. Hopelessness is said by some to be the key variable.[14]

Let us take a moment to question the reliability and validity of these studies of rising depression. One reason for questioning them is that although measures of subjective well-being (happiness, satisfaction with life-as-a-whole) are, as we might expect, closely and inversely related to depression at any one time,[15] over time they do not track the measures of rising depression. I believe that this discrepancy between simultaneous and diachronic measures occurs because the happiness measures are more sensitive to the adaptation phenomenon, whereby people take as a standard their current or very recent moods, whereas the depression measures are not similarly sensitive. In any event, the measures of depression are more reliable than the simpler measures of happiness (in general surveys, often tapped by a single question). Other reasons for believing that the measures of rising depression are both reliable and valid are these: (1) the reliability of self-reports of depressive episodes has been demonstrated in careful retests of depression assessments after a four-year period[16]; (2) the studies of depression do not rely on visits to therapists (which are contaminated by self-selection) but, rather, on massive surveys of the general public; (3) independent studies using the same standardized instruments come to the same conclusions; (4) physical symptoms (fatigue, eating disorders), which are less vulnerable to trends in the "fashionability" of mental illnesses, support the diagnoses; (5) studies of children, who are not aware of what they "should" report, also support the diagnoses; and finally, (6) instead of an overcount of cases of depression, there may well be an undercount due to the prevalence of "masked depression."[17]

Friendship, Social Integration, and Depression

The absence of friends and family solidarity is the crucial explanatory variable for depression, just as their presence is a central explanatory factor for happiness. Citing a 1976 study published by the Department of Health, Education, and Welfare, James S. House argues that friendship and kin relationships, which provide "information leading the subject to believe that he is cared for and loved, that he is esteemed and valued, and that he belongs to a network of communication and mutual obligation, appear to reduce the levels of stress experienced, improve health, and buffer the impact of stress on health."[18] A major study focused specifically on depression finds that "depressives reported a lack of confidants both within and outside the household to a significantly higher degree than controls."[19] Both the *loss* of friends and the chronic *absence* of friends seem to have similar damaging effects on positive well-being, although the sudden loss of friends and family ties is more closely associated with the onset of depression. Depressives also have weaker social networks than the nondepressed.[20] A study of the elderly found that in addition to smaller friendship networks, the depressed had fewer associational memberships and weaker church affiliations.[21] Thus, although most studies find the lack of *confidants* to be a primary source of depression—and a primary buffer against the damaging effects of stress—weaker but more extensive relationships sometimes serve a purpose similar to that of confidants. Finally, since low self-esteem is both a symptom and a cause of depression, it is worth noting again that one important source of low self-esteem is the inadequate interpersonal relations that are, in turn, the source of the debilitating absence of friends and confidants.[22]

The causal sequence is important for the purposes of this study: if depression is a primary cause of loss of friendship and social networks, then our hypothesis that a society cultivating commodities instead of friends will cause depression is weakened, for the absence of friends and strong social networks would itself be caused by whatever caused depression. To some extent this is the case, inasmuch as it has been shown that as depressives recover their social relations improve, and when they relapse their social relations deteriorate.[23] On the other hand, some studies have shown that social networks, closely associated with the incidence and prevalence of depression, are themselves determined not by the skills and choices of the persons involved but largely by "culturally determined rules."[24] And others show that life events that reduce available social support *precipitate* onsets of depression.[25] The most conclusive evidence of the role of friendship (or other intimate relationships) comes from micro studies of the onset of depression: if a woman has even a single confidant she can survive, without depressive illness, the hardships and traumas that precipitate depression in other women not so happily befriended.[26] Finally, cognate studies of subjective well-being (happiness) find that when circumstances change so that a person is included in a social group, his mood and sense of well-being increase substantially,[27] and that number of friends is a far better predictor of subjective well-being than is level of income or wealth.[28] Thus, although there is much evidence that the depressed have poor social skills and that their very symptoms of helplessness and worthlessness inhibit their search for friends, when they are included in social groups or befriended by others, their symptoms improve. The same is true of the merely unhappy.

Apart from the decline of the family, has there been a decline in close friendships or a weakening of social networks during the postwar period of rising depression? There is little doubt that there has been a general postwar decline in intimate relationships, visiting among neighbors, and membership in secondary associations. House reports that as of 1976, consistent evidence "indicates that the prevalence of significant informal social relationships, networks, and supports has been declining over the last quarter century while people are increasingly calling on those same sources of support for help in dealing with personal problems."[29] We know that belonging to a variety of voluntary groups (such as fraternal orders, sports groups, church-related groups, and the League of Women Voters) is at least associated with a lowered vulnerability to depression, and these memberships have declined during the postwar period. For example, people with no such memberships increased from 25 percent in 1967 to 35 percent in 1993.[30] Church attendance is related to subjective well-being and to lower vulnerability to depression,[31] and in the 1960s there was a sharp decline in church attendance, followed by a plateau at a lower level.[32] And, while in 1974, 72 percent of those questioned said they visited with their neighbors more than once a year, in 1993 only 61 percent engaged in this form of socializing.[33] (One should note, however, that in a British study comparing neighbors to friends and members of the family, neighbors rated lowest in degrees of reciprocal help, warmth, and contribution to the enjoyment of leisure activities.[34])

We seem warranted in concluding that there has been an alarming increase in depression, with its associated feelings of helplessness, hopelessness, and worthlessness, in rapidly advancing and advanced countries, especially in the United States; that the loss of social support of all kinds is a cause as well as a consequence of depression; and that there has been a postwar decline in many forms of social support and of social integration. We must now consider how changes in income may influence both happiness and depression.

Income, Happiness, and Depression

In proposing to substitute friendship for commodities, we need to know what degree of well-being is lost by slighting the economic side of life. Devaluing economic pursuits in favor of greater companionship is likely to cause a loss of income, which, of course, is the means for buying and consuming commodities. Although earning, possessing, buying, and consuming have somewhat different hedonic statuses, by summarizing evidence from a variety of studies, we can say that for the nonpoor these economic activities have only a modest relationship to subjective well-being.[35]

There is ample evidence that within advanced economies, the rich are no happier than the less rich. In general, above the poverty line, happiness (or its pale, vulgar companion, average "utility") does not change much or at all as level of income increases. For most people above the poverty line, money does not buy (much, if any) happiness. Elsewhere I have documented this claim and called the assumed correlation between happiness and level of income (above the poverty level) "the economistic fallacy."[36] Put differently, if "utility" has anything to do with happiness, then above the poverty line, and even more so in the United States than in Britain, the long-term marginal utility of money is almost zero. Adam Smith knew this: "In ease of body and peace of mind, all the different ranks of life are nearly upon a level."[37]

But "mere" unhappiness is not depression. Is the relationship of income to depression the same as the relationship—or lack of it—between income and happiness? Among the poor, both unhappiness and depression are more prevalent than they are among those who are more affluent. The circumstances of poverty contribute to insecurity, stress, worry, and, for some, an inability to cope with unfavorable life events, and, hence, to helplessness and hopelessness. Whether depression is influenced by level of income *above* the poverty level is less clear, although at least one study reports that "the higher the socioeconomic status, the lower the level of [psychological] distress."[38] Another, smaller study reports the same relationship between socioeconomic status and depression but finds that all demographic variables together accounted for only 12.6 percent of the variance.[39] Earlier studies (which do not include the sharp increase in depression in the 1960s) tend to support the income–depression relationship,[40] but almost all observers add to the influence of inadequate material resources the possibly greater influence of the relatively impoverished social relations of the poor,[41] including a characteristic lack of intimacy in the working class[42] that inhibits working-class people from acquiring that single, all-important confidant.

Does depression tend to cause lower socioeconomic status (the "social drift" hypothesis), or does socioeconomic status cause depression? A longitudinal study using 1952 and 1968 data assessed this question and found that, on balance, the evidence favored the view that low social status was more a cause than a consequence of depression. It also found that, during those sixteen years, there was not much change in either factor: "not only did depression tend to persist, but its relationship to low SES [socioeconomic status] also tended to endure."[43]

Without conducting a thorough cross-cultural analysis here, we should note that although people in rich nations are happier than those in poor nations,[44] the current epidemic of depression seems to be striking the advanced countries more than the less developed countries (LDCs). Thus, Seligman reports that "on the whole, you do not find much in the way of depression as we know it—suicide, hopelessness, giving up, low self-esteem, passivity, and the like—in nonWestern cultures before they are modernized." He cites a 1984 study of New Guinea and an older study of the American Amish as evidence that the complex of things called "modernity," including the self-attribution and self-blame common to market societies, must cause some of the depression not experienced by LDC populations.[45] Similarly, Mexican-born immigrants to the United States have a lower incidence of depression than American-born Mexican-Americans.[46] (Earlier cross-national studies failed to find this Western–non-Western difference in mental illness, but they relied on pre-1965 data.[47])

Unhappiness and especially depression have social as well as personal costs: there is substantial evidence that unhappy people, compared to happy ones, are not only harder to live with but also less effective at school and at work.[48] The spouses, children, and friends of the depressed also suffer.[49] The depressed lose interest in everything but their misery; their judgment, understanding,[50] social responses, and capacity to work[51] are all impaired; they are more vulnerable to other disorders such as panic attacks;[52] their more frequent absences from work are costly to their firms;[53] and their treatment and occasional hospitalization impose heavy costs on their families, governments, and society in general.[54] I will not detail these costs and losses here, but, in addition to the intrinsic value of lost well-being, these burdens give urgency to the search for causes and cures of the social illnesses of market societies.

Conversely, let me suggest six reasons why a priority for friendship over commodities is a promising route to happiness, an effective protection against depression, and a step toward a more benign environment.

1. There is evidence that the pleasures of commodities are more satiable than the pleasures of friendship. Because people adapt easily to increased levels of commodity consumption, as Durkheim pointed out a century ago, consumerism dooms us to walk a hedonic treadmill that will never satisfy us. In contrast, the pleasures of friendship seem to increase with experience.

2. Although rivalry for friends is common, and among lovers has the unpleasant status of jealousy, in general, friendship is a variable-sum game: when I gain a friend, others do not necessarily lose one. Indeed, a friend of mine is more accessible to other friends of mine—a positive-sum game. Because friendship is almost infinitely expandable (the community may become a more friendly place), new friendships do not decrease the supply; and the "price" of friends does not tend to increase when the demand increases. Economic growth confers these felicitous properties upon some commodities, but the process is slower, such that in the short run, consumers are faced with a modified zero-sum game. Economics is said to be a science of coping with scarcity; it is not so with friendship.

3. Self-esteem, the most important disposition associated with happiness and a prime protector against depression, is unrelated to levels of income[55] (and therefore to levels of consumption) but it is closely related to friendship—or, rather, self-esteem has its most important source in intimate groups.[56]

4. While the reward system among friends has its drawbacks (conformity, risk-aversion, favoritism, fear of exclusion), it also has many advantages. Among friends the reward for effort or excel-

lence is praise, whereas market rewards are in money. Praise is more likely to be interpreted as information than as control and is, therefore, welcome, whereas money rewards are more often interpreted as control and, at least where the work being rewarded is intrinsically satisfying, control is often resented.[57]

5. Friendship is a known source of happiness and a protection against, and even cure for, depression while higher levels of income increase well-being only among the poor.

6. Finally, compared to material consumption, friendship is ecologically friendly.

Market Culture and Friendship

Assuming that we would rather be happy than depressed and accepting that it is the loss or absence of companionship, friends, and satisfying, enduring family relationships that account in substantial part for the rise of depression, what could have happened to keep us from pursuing the relationships that lead to happiness? One possibility is that we have been distracted not so much by manipulating merchants as by the gap between the abundance of goods capitalism has made available to us, on the one hand, and, on the other, the preoccupation with scarcity that is our inheritance from millennia of hunter-gatherer and peasant life. What is now true only of the poorest one-fifth of the population within advanced economies was once true of all but a tiny elite: more material resources are a prime source of happiness. But why do we not learn from experience that this is no longer the case?

The central assumption of market economics regarding consumer choice is that people pursue one line of goods until the "marginal utility" of some other line of goods is greater than that of the first one. At that point people switch, and they go on doing this until the marginal utilities of all goods they can afford are equal. Experience teaches them over time what the respective utilities of various goods may be; that is, the learning curve is such that people can equalize their utilities over a reasonably short space of time, short enough to avoid heavy sunk costs. If this picture is accurate, why would people pursue commodities that do not make them happy at the expense of friends, whose solace and joy would make them happier and reduce their chances of depression?

One fundamental problem is the perfect knowledge assumption of market theory. Economic theories of market-generated felicity fail to allow that *people often do not know* what makes them happy. Of course, the pursuit of happiness is not wholly blind—but it is myopic. Although resisted by almost everyone, the theory of a disabling myopia in the pursuit of happiness, with suitable specification of modifying conditions, is supported by very strong evidence.[58] Among other reasons for widespread resistance to the myopia theory is undoubtedly the fact that it violates both market and democratic theory and threatens the cherished tenets of individualism.

This is not the place for a review of the evidence of our ignorance of the sources of our own well-being, but some of the psychological tendencies that encourage our perverse preference for commodities over friendship may be briefly mentioned. People tend to prefer short-term to long-term gains—a familiar source of addiction. Thus, one inhibition to learning the true sources of happiness is the short-term pleasure caused by gains in income and consumption. The hedonic yield of money and commodities may be instantaneous, whereas the utility from friendships, and especially from intimacy, takes longer to become evident. Also, market comparisons require the "measuring rod of money." The lack of prices attached to friendship makes it difficult to compare the hedonic yields of friendship and commodities.

Moreover, friendship depends on intrinsic worth, but market exchange, of necessity, values only extrinsic, public worth. As Roy Harrod points out, friendships, unlike commodities and money, cannot be traded. Economics and, we might add, economic calculations performed by noneconomists are "concerned only with the goods and services of which the constituent items can be made alternatively available to one or [an]other of different persons. Thus goods like friendship and mystical experiences are excluded."[59] Again, market exchange places no value on sunk costs, but friendship is very often dependent on sunk costs, which, among friends, are valued in themselves and for the memories of good times or tribulations shared together. And finally, as Marx pointed out, people pursue money to compensate for failed friendships or disappointment in love, but under these circumstances money fails to satisfy. When people recover from their depression or other mental illness, they often give up their exclusive pursuit of money and goods and look to their relations with people.[60]

The priesthood of economists, whose vision is fixed by the model of priced market transactions, has allies in the advertisers who reinforce the belief that the good life is achieved only through consumption. These forces create a set of conventional beliefs through which we explain our actions to ourselves. It has been well established that we often interpret our behavior and even our moods by reference to conventional theories about what causes or should cause any given mood or behavior rather than by reference to independent causal theories developed through and tested against personal experience and privileged knowledge of our internal states.[61]

All of this may explain our fundamental ignorance of the sources of our own happiness—and, though less often, of our depressive feelings—that makes us willing to substitute commodities for friendships.

Are Markets "Cold Societies"?

Some, like Georg Simmel, hold that the market has created a "cold society" whose rationality undermines the emotional warmth necessary for friendship.[62] Marx, Lukacs, Fromm, and Marcuse believe in *commodification* theories: in market economies people are treated as commodities from which to extract as many utilities as possible. In the late 1970s and again in 1991 I argued against the view that markets had this effect on human relations.[63] New evidence has now changed my mind on this issue. Let us briefly examine the competing arguments and evidence.

Smith and Hume argued that markets free human relations from instrumental calculation by separating instrumental, self-interested relationships from what they called the "sympathetic" relationships in which people had previously been entangled. "If that is correct," writes Allen Silver, "commercial society promotes rather than discourages personal relations that are normatively free of instrumental and calculative orientations."[64] Indeed, it could be argued further that where the market allocates goods, human relations, freed of this burden, can concentrate on the emotional aspects of friendship. But, because sympathy and empathy are learned early in the family, the breakup of the family is likely to make this theory inoperative in modern societies.

A second line of defense against Simmel's indictment points to the inconclusiveness of the evidence of loneliness and the manipulative treatment of friends in modern society and highlights countervailing tendencies. Experts on city life have suggested that friendship networks are taking the place of neighborhoods and communities. Higher education is associated with better human relations; with the help of market-created affluence, educational levels have greatly increased over the years. While the geographical mobility encouraged by markets might be expected to undermine friendships, the fact is that people who move from one locality to another tend, after five years, to have as many good friends in the new place as in the old one—and often they move in order to be nearer members of their families. In any event, it is not at all clear that geographic mobility increased in the past century, and certainly not in the past fifty years. Finally, the evidence of suspicion and conflict in pre-industrial villages and traditional and primitive societies make a secular trend toward cold or conflictual relations seem unlikely. I examine all of this evidence below.

A failing of the Marx-Lukacs-Fromm-Marcuse theory that we treat each other as commodities is that its underlying theory of the easy transfer of (commodifying) behavior from domain to domain is weak. Although this issue has been much disputed, the current consensus among psychologists is that situational variation alters much behavior, such that people naturally change their behavior to meet the demands of different situations.[65] If people compartmentalize their behavior, market relationships need not contaminate friendships.

Additional arguments and empirical studies show that instead of demanding purely calculating behavior, markets require interpersonal trust. "Without an integrative framework," as Kenneth Boulding points out, "exchange cannot develop, because exchange . . . involves trust and credibility."[66] Empirical studies support this claim. They find that interpersonal trust is a condition not only for market exchange but also for economic modernization, industrial efficiency, and the delay of gratification and that it is at least associated with the sense of personal efficacy that contributes so much to well-being.[67] In spite of the extensive humanistic criticism of the market as the source of distrust, Alex Inkeles and Larry Diamond's comparison of human traits in modern and less modern countries finds "a strong positive association between economic development and a psychological disposition to trust other people."[68]

New Evidence against the Market

More recent studies, however, lend support to the market's critics. For thirty-three years the Harris poll has asked the following question: "Some say that most people can be trusted while others say that you can't be too careful in dealing with people. Which do you believe?" From 1960 to 1993 there was a steady downward trend in the percentage of respondents who said they trust "most people," from a high point in 1960, when 58 percent gave this response, to a low in 1993, when only 37 percent did so.[69] Can the postwar decline in interpersonal trust be laid at the doorstep of the market?

Two models of friendship—the reinforcement model and the social exchange model—interpret interpersonal affiliation as a series of marketlike processes.[70] If either or both of these marketlike models correctly interprets friendship relations in a market society, it is, indeed, likely that as Simmel believed, the market erodes the social support that is both a protection against depression and a source of happiness.

The reinforcement model has two versions, one inimical to the idea of friendship as a relation between people who intrinsically value each other, the other compatible with the idea of intrinsic worth but still making friendship contingent on other factors. The first, the operant contingency reinforcement theory made famous by B. F. Skinner, holds that "attraction [to another] is based on the positive affect accompanying reinforcement,"[71] where reinforcement is some act or expression by another that the self regards as favorable (flattering, helpful, value reinforcing, and so on). According to this theory, friendship can be seen as a modified market exchange: I do something and you pay me for it. The second reinforcement theory (one may think of it as Pavlovian, classical conditioning) is more compatible with nonmarket theories of friendship. It holds that if you are associated with another person under circumstances of pleasure, regardless of the source of that pleasure, you will like that person.[72] No exchange or payment is involved. This theory fits nicely with research on friendship emphasizing the pleasure of joint activities.

Unlike reinforcement theories, social exchange theories of interpersonal relations are deliberately modeled on concepts of economic exchange: They say that all human relations are based on cost-benefit analysis and survive only so long as the benefits exceed the costs. Benefits include sense of power, material rewards, ego enhancements, introductions to important persons, political favors, kindnesses to one's relatives, and so forth. Costs include deference and self-abasement, opportunity costs, sense of obligation, hypocrisy, and similar painful experiences.

Do market societies encourage contingent reinforcement and social exchange behavior to such an extent that they replace the idea that friends are to be intrinsically valued in favor of the view that, like other objects, they have only "exchange value?" Two examples help to illustrate, but not resolve, the problem. Leonard Berkowitz compared the helping behavior of the children of bureaucrats to that of the children of businessmen. He found that the children of businessmen would help others only in exchange for help to themselves but the children of bureaucrats helped others because they thought that was the right thing to do or that helping others represented a general social rule.[73] Here the influence on businessmen's children of market ideology and experience seems to support the development of human relations that are, in essence, exchanges. But in his study of "close friendships," Robert B. Hays found that the best predictor of closeness was not benefits *minus* costs, as exchange theory predicts, but benefits *plus* costs or sacrifices.[74] There is similar folk wisdom: one loves someone whom one has helped. (If, as in utility theory, one wishes to interpret sacrifices as benefits, on the grounds that they produce the benefits of a good conscience, social exchange theory will be as empty as is utility theory.)

I cannot say which model of friendship is more characteristic of advanced market societies. If Hays's subjects, who feel closer to those they help, are more characteristic, we might expect that in market societies there are abundant opportunities for people to counteract social isolation. If, on the other hand, the exchange model in Berkowitz's study is more characteristic, we will not be surprised to find market societies characterized by increasing depression. Michael Argyle writes that "people who simply try to maximize their rewards are liable to lose their friends; socially isolated adolescents have been found to have such childish ideas, and fail to realize that friendship involves loyalty, commitment and concern for the other."[75] In effect, if the contingency reinforcement and social exchange models accurately describe all social relations, including friendships, they prescribe a pattern of human intercourse already characteristic of the disturbed and depressed. No healing benefit comes from "social support"—if that is the term—of this kind.

That the practices and ideology of the market have pervasive effects on people is suggested by the effect that studying market principles has on economics students. Gerald Marwell and Ruth E. Ames gave economics graduate students and others the opportunity to choose either to contribute their earnings to a charitable pot or to keep the money for themselves. The economics students contributed about 20 percent of their earnings to the pot, whereas the others gave from 40 to 60 percent. On examination, the economists had no concepts or vocabulary to define the concept of "public interest."[76] Similarly, Gregory B. Brunk compared the voting intentions of a control group with the intentions of a group of students who had heard a lecture on Downs's theory of "rational ignorance" and the rationality of nonvoting. Those who heard the lecture showed a diminished intention to vote. Brunk speculated that the current positive effects of education on political participation might come to be reversed, "since those who are better educated will be more likely to encounter theories of rational [non]participation."[77] These examples address the reception of the implied or explicit message: do first whatever directly benefits the self. They do not speak directly to how to regard companionship—but they nevertheless have a message for that domain of life, as well.

The evidence of the rising tide of depression in market democracies, combined with the evidence that depression and unhappiness are caused in substantial part by lack of social support and that many forms of social support, along with the interpersonal trust that underlies social support, have declined in the postwar years, indicates that the market, in general, may inhibit friendship. But is there any reason to believe that, in particular, "the rage to consume" has crowded out or otherwise undermined friendship?

Consumer Culture and Friendship

We live in a consumer culture. One well-known text on consumer behavior imagines Rip Van Winkle's observations on waking from a very long sleep: he would "come to the conclusion that selling, buying, and consuming lie at the very core of life in most of the developed countries of the world."[78] An anthropologist calls this preoccupation a "rage to consume" and attributes it to the synthetic and fallacious "logic of scarcity" of the capitalist system, the "logic" that converts yesterday's concept of plenty into today's scarcity.[79] Calling modern man *Homo consumens*, Erich Fromm claims that "we, as human beings, have no aim except producing and consuming more and more."[80]

Although consumer lifestyles vary by national culture, the emphasis on consumption seems to have affected all advanced economies in much the same way.[81] Perhaps it is a general aspect of modernity. In his studies of the differences between urban, industrial workers and village traditionalists in developing countries, Alex Inkeles developed an index of modernity that included items on "consumer orientation": belief that possessions are the key to happiness, wanting more consumer goods of various kinds, striving to earn in order to possess more consumer goods, and so forth. There was, indeed, a tendency for those whose responses were characteristically "modern," rather than "traditional," to score higher on the consumer orientation items (although these moderns were less likely to think that possessions led to happiness), but the relationship was weak.[82] If there is a "rage to consume," it is more a product of advanced market societies than of modernity in its early stages. Very likely, consumerism is simply a function of disposable income.

The crowding-out hypothesis says that, given limited amounts of time and attention, people must choose between devoting time and attention to friends and devoting them to commodities. For each of these two goods there is a level of supply necessary for good health, including mental health, but beyond that level individual choices can mix the two goods in different bundles according to taste. The specific allegation of the crowding-out thesis is that, for many people in modern market economies, the hypertrophy of time and attention devoted to commodities has reduced the time and attention devoted to friends below the level necessary for both happiness and mental health.

Were less time devoted to market work,[83] more might be available for either shopping[84] or social activities. Yet might the newly available time be devoted instead to watching television? In order to be sure, we need data on work time, television viewing time, shopping time, and time spent in socializing with others. I know of only two studies that give these data. The first shows that from 1965 to 1975, when there was a decline in time spent on the job, the newly available time was devoted almost entirely to watching television (men by thirty-five minutes and women by forty-seven minutes), but that both men and women decreased their shopping (men much more than women) while they increased the time spent on such activities as visiting, letter writing, and informal social life.[85] The crowding out was mostly done by television, but in the remaining time, socializing increased while shopping decreased.

A second study, using comparable methods but with a better breakdown of activities, covered 1975 to 1981. Although both men and women spent about three times longer watching television than socializing, the time spent on socializing increased slightly, and "the overall impression is that uses of leisure time were slightly more interactive in 1981–82 than in 1975-76."[86] For men the new time released by marginally declining work hours—about one hour per week—was, after a general increase in household work is accounted for, devoted about equally to television, shopping, and socializing. In reverse, the increased time women spent on their jobs came from decreasing housework and from watching less television (about fifty minutes per week), rather than from reductions in social entertainment or conversation.

If attention to commodities were crowding out social interaction, we would expect to find any increase in time spent shopping accompanied by a decrease in socializing. The 1965–1975 study shows just the opposite, while the 1975–1981 study shows relative increases in both shopping and socializing of roughly the same magnitude. By these (inadequate) tests, the hypothesis that a "rage to consume" crowds out socializing fails. If the market has a destructive influence on friendship (and I now think it does), it must be through elevating instrumentalist and materialist values over social values, by eroding communities and neighborhoods, and by intermittently increasing the demand for overtime labor—as in the mid-1990s. In my opinion, a nonmarket influence, watching television, is also responsible for the decline in friendship, but that analysis would take us into new territory.

Shopping As a Social Experience

Has shopping become less of a social experience, more solitary, impersonal, and friendless? The days are long gone by when there were attentive counter-clerks instead of cashiers, when a neighborhood store was a social center and the storekeeper was everyone's friend. Can this change in the human relations of shopping serve to increase the sense of isolation experienced by depressives?

Before accepting this hypothesis, we must note that many companies are sensitive to the demand for "friendliness" and train their staffs to offer it: "the 'friendliness' of their staff may be crucial for airlines, hotel chains, or fast food outlets in establishing a market identity."[87] While a benefit to customers, "friendliness" does not lead to friendship or to the recruitment of the confidants so desperately needed by depressives.

There is, however, another dimension to shopping as a social experience: shopping with a member of the family. Some families make of shopping an intrinsically rewarding family experience.[88] A "family gatekeeper" (a psychographic marketing category) revealed a source of pleasure in her role as an opinion leader: "People come to me more often than I go to them for information on brands." As a way of keeping her store of information up to date, she says "I shop a lot for specials."[89] Because it takes time to shop for specials and to do comparative shopping, working-class shoppers rely more on advice from family and friends, familiar stores, and what is called "face-to-face" shopping. In the working class, too, husband-and-wife shopping teams are more common,[90] and perhaps the increased time devoted to shopping by husbands in all social classes has increased this shared experience.

Yet the demise of the neighborhood store, the colder relations between shopkeepers and their clients, and the modesty of the growth of husband–wife shopping all suggest an increasingly unsociable climate for consumers. Shopping is still divided along lines of gender, with women doing most of the everyday shopping and men doing most of the shopping for consumer durables. Economic theories basing the division of domestic labor on relative market earning power and relative skills largely fail in the face of the overwhelmingly more important ideology of traditional sex roles.[91] Since the growth of impersonality in patron–client relations fails to find compensation in social shopping, the hypothesis claiming a colder shopping experience is tentatively supported.

Consumption As a Social Experience

The tentative hypothesis in this section is that there has been a shift from collective to individual consumption, with a consequent loss of social interaction. It has been alleged that "the number of products that an individual always buys for individual consumption must certainly represent a very small proportion of consumer expenditures." Spending money on collectively consumed goods requires extensive family discussion.[92] Beyond the family, people talk about their various consumption experiences. Elihu Katz and Paul Lazarsfeld's early analysis of "opinion leaders" found that women talked much more—and much more democratically—about articles of purchase than about politics. In discussing politics, there was a certain deference to the wife of someone who might be expected to be informed, but regarding commodities, everyone was her own expert.[93]

A variety of goods may invite or require social participation for their enjoyment: food and drink; playing baseball, cards, bingo, and bowling; attending sporting events, theater, and concerts. In each case the enjoyment of others is almost a condition for enjoyment by the self. The idea that consumption is primarily a solipsistic experience, where only one's own utilities count, and not a collective experience dependent on the utilities of others, could only be entertained by economists. Even taken singly, a large part of the pleasures of consumption are social.[94]

Is consumption more or less social than it once was? I suggest the following proposition: *beyond a certain level of income, increased disposable income is more likely to be spent on goods consumed individually than on goods consumed collectively by households.* The marked increase in disposable income in the 1960s coincided with decreased happiness, but this could well be because of unpleasant political developments such as the Vietnam War and urban riots. Whatever the causes, along with the rise in per capita income came the beginning of the wave of depression that now plagues all advanced economies. From the gross data it is not easy to know exactly how the greater disposable income was consumed, but we know that the proportion of income spent on food, which is often consumed in groups, and on housing declines as income rises. And there are suggestive items in recent accounts of household budgets: between 1985 and 1988, household expenditures for food and housing increased about 2 percent while expenditures for "personal care" increased about 6 percent. (Time spent on personal care also increased in recent years.)[95] Similarly, between 1988 and 1989 the expenditures for food, housing, and household operations and furnishings each increased by less than 4 percent while expenditures on the more individualized items in "apparel and services" increased 7.4 percent.[96]

To make the point more vivid, consider how the category of things associated with "home," that is, the house itself and certain familiar rooms, is uniquely capable of enhancing a sense of well-being, especially among children. These things are often cherished and are four times as likely to be positively than negatively "toned," a higher positive loading than any other set of objects.[97] Family objects also have evocative power, as Peter Laslett observes in *The World We Have Lost*: "Time was when the whole of life went forward in the family, in a circle of loved, familiar faces, known and fondled objects, all to human size. That time has gone for ever. It makes us very different from our ancestors."[98] Does it also make us more depressed?

In the welter of alleged causes for the loss of social support and friendship that is surely a prime contributor to the upsurge in depression, I have found some ambiguous evidence that markets, themselves, are an inherent cause of social isolation; I have questioned the idea that attention to buying and consuming necessarily crowd out the time and attention available for friendship, suggesting instead that television may have this isolating effect; and I have proposed that the increased impersonality of shopping and the increased use of individually, as contrasted to socially, consumed goods have played modest roles in the loss of a therapeutic community of friends.

The Motive to Affiliate versus the Demand for Goods

In this section I compare two motives: affiliative and materialistic. Although the general need for affiliation with members of our species is universal[99] and the absence of affiliation has been shown to make people unhappy and invite depression, it does not follow that in the United States (or elsewhere) there is a demand for more friends than people have now, since people may not be aware of their affiliative needs. The degree of conscious loneliness is a kind of test of the demand for affiliation.

A survey conducted in the early 1970s found very little loneliness: asked to rate their lives on ten dimensions ("boring—interesting," "hard—easy," "lonely—friendly," and so on), people rated the friendliness of their lives second highest.[100] Urbanism is said to increase loneliness, but a study of the variation in interpersonal relations by size of community found that "total isolation is only weakly, if at all, associated with urbanism."[101] (However, in cities the networks that take the place of neighborhoods favor the more mobile middle class. And rural places can be very lonely.)

Because of the social stigma of loneliness,[102] however, we cannot wholly trust self-reports. A little specific probing finds a higher number of lonely people,[103] and the in-depth reports of depressives in urban settings locate even more, although even among these people loneliness was consciously experienced as such only when someone they cherished left the home or neighborhood.[104]

Although the early-1970s survey found that those with the most friends were the most satisfied with their lives and that a large majority expressed *some* desire to make new friends, the urgency of this desire was minimal: only one-half of one percent said they were "very interested." As might be expected, those who had the fewest friends were the most likely to be "very interested," although those with the most friends were the most likely to show a modest interest in making new friends.[105] This pattern suggests the causal influence of personality, and, indeed, extroversion has been found to be both directly associated with general cheerfulness and productive of friendships that add to a person's happiness.[106] It is the introverted, the socially awkward, and those for whom friendship is a problem who would benefit from any institutional or cultural pattern that changes priorities among commodities and friends.

Whatever else may be said about the popular demand for friendship, it does not represent a "rage" for affiliation. Taking a cue from the studies of depression, we might suspect that the *idea* of new friends is generally attractive but that loneliness, the conscious feeling of a lack of friends, and an urgent desire to make new ones come when some person one counted as a friend leaves, quarrels, or dies (although grief is rarely, by itself, a cause of depression). In this sense, although it is well established that having a lot of friends contributes to a sense of well-being, *demand* for new friendships more closely resembles the demand for replacing a car or a refrigerator that collapses than the more "elastic" demand for other commodities.

Although materialist motives may be assumed by economists, they have been largely ignored by psychologists (or, as mentioned above, have been treated as compensatory for deficient social relations), possibly because they defy assessment in the same terms as the "need for affiliation." The *demand* for material goods, however, is apparent. On average, almost regardless of their current levels of income, people believe they would, finally, be happy with only 25 percent more income. But of course the fact that the same estimate is made by those who already have 25 percent more suggests its foolhardiness. Similarly, when asked to rate the desirable and undesirable characteristics of their jobs, people rank congenial workmates at the same level as rate of pay (and interesting work ahead of both). Yet the demand for jobs is more influenced by financial rewards than by anticipated social rewards, albeit partly because applicants know more about pay levels than friendship levels.[107]

Economists, believing that "needs" are inherently subjective and that only "revealed preferences" are real, are satisfied only with the evidence provided by actual choices. By these standards it may seem that the demand for income with which to buy goods and services is greater than the demand for more friends. But this is not quite right: the way people have used the new leisure time generated by (somewhat) shorter working hours since World War II "reveals" a demand for more television, not more income or commodities—even though people rank watching television seventeenth in importance among twenty-eight activities listed, much lower than their work, which, in turn, is ranked lower than various socializing activities.[108] Thus, as introspection tends to confirm, people spend hours watching programs they do not care for.

Revealed preferences favor marginal increments of wealth over increments of affiliation. But revealed preferences have very little to do with happiness and even less to do with protection against depression.

The Road Not Taken: Giving Friendship
Priority over Commodities

The evidence on the rising incidence of depression in advanced economies seems to confirm the belief that market solutions to the deficit of companionship in modern society have failed. Economic growth is unlikely to be a solution, since precisely those countries that have experienced or are currently experiencing rapid economic growth have the highest incidence of depression.

Democracy's solution to distress, the welfare state, has, at least in this respect, failed as well. Those financially dependent on public aid are three times more likely than similar others to be depressed.[109] Although the causal relationship between being a welfare client and being depressed is not clear, no one has suggested that welfare is a solution to friendlessness, for unemployment and welfare are known to be socially isolating experiences. (The contribution to family felicity of government pensions for aged parents is another matter.)

If we were to follow the indications of widespread need, rather than of demand, how would we give priority to the pursuit of friendship (and family solidarity) over the pursuit of commodities? The basic idea would be for governments and markets (that is to say firms) to make the loss of such companionship and family solidarity a cost and the gain of these things a benefit in their respective calculations. But people are chary of governmental intrusion in their most private lives. Therefore, lest governments become invasive and paternalistic, the authorities would have to focus on creating a "scaffolding" within which individuals would find new opportunities for the companionship and family solidarity that would genuinely increase their sense of well-being. And, since the market is responsive entirely to prices and the opportunities for monetary profit, governments would have to alter firms' cost and profit calculations so that they would themselves seek to foster companionship (if not workmen's solidarity!) and reciprocal affection in family life.

In conclusion, let us consider a possible individualistic solution to depression and boon to happiness that does not depend on greater friendship.

An Alternative Source of Happiness

Given the crucial contribution to well-being made by social support in general and by friendship in particular, social support seems almost (but not quite) to be a sufficient condition for the happy life. But is it also a necessary condition? Solitary and possibly quite happy academics, professionals, artists, and artisans who find their satisfaction in work, without benefit of affiliation, will be right to doubt the necessity of more extensive friendships.

In an important, somewhat neglected study of well-being, Antonia Abbey and Frank M. Andrews stumbled on findings that illuminate these common-sense observations. They found, as have others, that "performance" (a feeling of having done a task well), social support, and a sense of controlling one's own fate were the major positive sources of well-being. But they also found that the last two, social support and sense of control, were substitutes for each other. That is, if a person has a high sense of control over her life, social support adds nothing to her well-being, while if a person has a high sense of social support, it does not matter if he has a sense of personal control. "Experiencing high levels of both social support and internal control seems to be no more beneficial than experiencing high levels of either one alone."[110] This important finding is supported by a more recent study showing that "control and support can substitute for one another to decrease depression."[111] Because a sense of personal control is closely related to happiness and is a specific antidote to that helplessness associated with depression, it may be a much more individualistic possible therapy for the malaise of modern societies.

But any policy that depended on developing in the population at large, and especially among those individuals who are more vulnerable to depression, the sense that they control their own destinies— particularly in a society where this is only marginally true—is unlikely to achieve its end. We follow the course laid down by the biological nature of a social species only if we seek to cultivate the bonding instincts with which we are born.[112]

Notes

An earlier version of this essay was presented at the conference "Consumption, Global Stewardship, and the Good Life," at University of Maryland, 28 September–2 October 1994. I thank for their help and absolve from blame Michael Argyle, Patrick Dunleavy, Stephen Edgell, and Stein Ringen, who commented on an earlier version of this essay.

1. Daniel Goleman, "A Rising Cost of Modernity: Depression," *New York Times*, 8 December 1992, C1.
2. Cross-National Collaborative Group, "The Changing Rate of Depression: Cross-National Comparisons," *Journal of the American Medical Association* 268 (2 December 1992): 3098–105. This report states that: "the results show an overall trend for increasing rates of major depression over time for all sites" (3102). The authors of this cross-national study were the first to use a standardized instrument (Diagnostic Statistical Manual of Mental Disorders—DSM-III) for large-scale cross-national work.
3. Martin Seligman quoted in James Buie, "'Me' Decades Generate Depression: Individualism Erodes Commitment to Others," *APA Monitor* 19 (October 1988): 18. Seligman, a distinguished experimental psychologist, relies on both U.S. and foreign studies.
4. Myrna M. Weissman et al., "Sex Differences in Rates of Depression: Cross-National Perspectives," Special Issue: Toward a New Psychobiology of Depression in Women, *Journal of Affective Disorders* 29, no. 2-3 (October–November 1993): 77–84. Compared to samples in Germany, Canada, and New Zealand, both lifetime rates and one-year rates for both men and women were lower in the United States.
5. Seligman quoted in Buie, "'Me' Decades Generate Depression," 18.
6. Myrna M. Weissman and Philip J. Leaf, "Affective Disorders," in *Psychiatric Disorders in America: The Epidemiological Catchment Area Study*, ed. Lee N. Robins and Darrel A. Regier (New York: Free Press, 1991), 54–80.
7. Cited in Goleman, "A Rising Cost of Modernity," C3.
8. Weissman et al., "Sex Differences in Rates of Depression," 64.
9. Ronald C. Kessler et al., "Lifetime and 12-month Prevalence of DSM-III-R Psychiatric Disorders in the United States: Results from the National Comorbidity Study," *Archives of General Psychiatry* 51, no. 1 (January 1994): 8–19.
10. June McKerrow, director of the Mental Health Foundation, reported in Paul Lewis, "'Quarter of Children' Mentally Ill," *Observer* (London), 19 September 1993.
11. Peter M. Lewinsohn et al., "Age-Cohort Changes in the Lifetime Occurrence of Depression and Other Mental Disorders," *Journal of Abnormal Psychology* 102 (February 1993): 110–20; Gerald L. Klerman, "The Current Age of Youthful Melancholia: Evidence for Increase in Depression among Adolescents and Young Adults," *Annual Progress in Child Psychiatry and Child Development* (New York: Brunner/Mazel, 1989), 333–54.
12. Myrna M. Weissman et al., "Early-Onset Major Depression in Parents

and Their Children," Special Issue: Childhood Affective Disorders, *Journal of Affective Disorders* 15 (November–December 1988): 269–77.

13. Aaron T. Beck, *Depression: Clinical, Experimental and Theoretical Aspects* (London: Staples; New York: Harper & Row, 1967).

14. Aaron T. Beck, Maria Kovacs, and Arlene Weissman, "Hopelessness and Suicidal Behavior: An Overview," *Journal of the American Medical Association* 234 (December 1975): 1146–49.

15. Antonia Abbey and Frank M. Andrews, "Modeling the Psychological Determinants of Life Quality," in *Research on the Quality of Life*, ed. Frank M. Andrews (Ann Arbor, Mich.: Institute for Social Research, 1986), 85–110.

16. Brigitte A. Prusoff, Kathleen R. Merikangas, and Myrna M. Weissman, "Lifetime Prevalence and Age of Onset of Psychiatric Disorders: Recall 4 Years Later," *Journal of Psychiatric Research* 22 (1988): 107–17.

17. Joseph H. Talley, "Masks of Major Depression," *Medical Aspects of Human Sexuality* 20 (November 1986): 16–25.

18. James S. House, "Social Support and the Quality and Quantity of Life," in *Research on the Quality of Life*, ed. Andrews, 255.

19. Martin Eisemann, "The Availability of Confiding Persons for Depressed Patients," *Acta Psychiatrica Scandinavica* 70 (August 1984): 166–69.

20. Traolach S. Brugha, "Personal Losses and Deficiencies in Social Networks," *Social Psychiatry* 19 (1984): 69–74.

21. Lawrence A. Palinkas, Deborah L. Wingard, and Elizabeth Barrett-Connor, "The Biocultural Context of Social Networks and Depression among the Elderly," *Social Science & Medicine* 30 (1990): 441–47.

22. P. McC. Miller et al., "Self-Esteem, Life Stress and Psychiatric Disorder," *Journal of Affective Disorders* 17 (July–August 1989): 65–75.

23. Eugene S. Paykel and Myrna M. Weissman, "Social Adjustment and Depression: A Longitudinal Study," *Archives of General Psychiatry* 28 (May 1973): 659–63.

24. Palinkas, Wingard, and Barrett-Connor, "The Biocultural Context of Social Networks."

25. Miller et al., "Self-Esteem, Life Stress and Psychiatric Disorder."

26. George W. Brown and Tirril Harris, *Social Origins of Depression: A Study of Psychiatric Disorder in Women* (London: Tavistock; New York: Free Press, 1978), 180–81.

27. Ed Diener, "Subjective Well-Being," *Psychological Bulletin* 95 (1984): 556–57.

28. Angus Campbell, Philip E. Converse, and Willard L. Rodgers, *The Quality of American Life: Perceptions, Evaluations, and Satisfactions* (New York: Russell Sage Foundation, 1976), 374.

29. House, "Social Support."

30. Robert D. Putnam, "Bowling Alone: America's Declining Social Capital," *Journal of Democracy* 6, no. 1 (January 1995): 65–78.

31. Catherine E. Ross, "Religion and Psychological Distress," *Journal for the Scientific Study of Religion* 29 (June 1990): 236–45.

32. Putnam, "Bowling Alone," 69.

33. Putnam, "Bowling Alone," 73.

34. Michael Argyle, *Cooperation, the Basis of Sociability* (London: Routledge, 1991), 111.

35. Frank M. Andrews and Stephen B. Withey, *Social Indicators of Well-Being: Americans' Perceptions of Life Quality* (New York: Plenum Press, 1976), 287; Jonathan Freedman, *Happy People: What Happiness Is, Who Has It, and Why* (New York: Harcourt, Brace, Jovanovich, 1978), 136–38; Angus Campbell, *The Sense of Well-Being in America: Recent Patterns and Trends* (New York: McGraw-Hill, 1981), 56–58; Ronald Inglehart and Jacques-Rene Rabier, "Aspirations Adapt to Situations—But Why Are the Belgians So Much Happier than the French: A Cross-Cultural Analysis of the Subjective Quality of Life," in *Research on the Quality of Life,* ed. Andrews, 3.

36. Robert E. Lane, *The Market Experience* (New York: Cambridge University Press, 1991), chap. 26; and, "Does Money Buy Happiness?" *The Public Interest,* no. 113 (Fall 1993): 56–65; for the underlying evidence, see references in note 35 above.

37. Adam Smith, *The Theory of Moral Sentiments* (Indianapolis, Ind.: Liberty Classics, 1976), 305, quoted in Terence Hutchison, "Adam Smith and the Wealth of Nations," *Journal of Law and Economics* 19, no. 3 (1976): 526.

38. John Mirowsky and Catherine E. Ross, "Social Patterns of Distress," *Annual Review of Sociology,* vol. 12 (Palo Alto, Calif.: Annual Reviews, 1986), 23.

39. George J. Warheit, Charles E. Holzer, and John J. Schwab, "An Analysis of Social Class and Racial Differences in Depressive Symptomatology: A Community Study," *Journal of Health & Social Behavior* 14 (December 1973): 291–99.

40. Support of general social class differences in the prevalence of depression may be found in Brown and Harris, *Social Origins of Depression,* 151; Leo Srole et al., *Mental Health in the Metropolis: The Midtown Manhattan Study,* vol. 1 (New York: McGraw-Hill, 1962); Dorothea C. Leighton et al., *The Character of Danger,* The Stirling County Study of Psychiatric Disorder and Sociocultural Environment, vol. 3 (New York: Basic Books, 1963); and Catherine E. Ross and Joan Huber, "Hardship and Depression," *Journal of Health & Social Behavior* 16 (December 1985): 312–27. Opposing the proposition is, again, Brown and Harris, *Social Origins of Depression,* 75—but these authors point to the resolution of this conflict, as well.

41. See, for example, Michael Argyle, *The Social Psychology of Everyday Life* (London: Routledge, 1992), 259.

42. Brown and Harris, *Social Origins of Depression,* 153–82.

43. Jane M. Murphy et al., "Depression and Anxiety in Relation to Social Status: A Prospective Epidemiologic Study," *Archives of General Psychiatry* 48 (March 1991): 223–29.

44. Alex Inkeles and Larry Diamond, "Personal Development and National Development: A Cross-Cultural Perspective," in *The Quality of Life: Comparative Studies,* ed. Alexander Szalai and Frank M. Andrews (London: Sage Publications, 1980), 73–109.

45. Seligman quoted in Buie, "'Me' Decades Generate Depression," 18.

46. Jacqueline M. Golding and Audrey M. Burnam, "Immigration, Stress, and Depressive Symptoms in a Mexican-American Community," *Journal of Nervous & Mental Disease* 178 (March 1990): 161–71.

47. Bruce P. Dohrenwend and Barbara Snell Dohrenwend, *Social Status and Psychological Disorder: A Causal Inquiry* (New York: Wiley-Interscience, 1969). See also L. M. King, "Social and Cultural Influences on Psychopathology," *Annual Review of Psychology*, vol. 29 (Palo Alto, Calif.: Annual Reviews, 1978), 405–33. Note that the positive relationship between economic growth and sense of well-being, which I have elsewhere called "the affluence effect," is reversed for depression. See Lane, *The Market Experience*, 24, 27–28.

48. Alice M. Isen, "Feeling Happy, Thinking Clearly," *APA Monitor* 19 (1988): 6–7; and "Positive Affect, Cognitive Processes, and Social Behavior," in *Advances in Experimental Social Psychology*, ed. Leonard Berkowitz, vol. 20 (New York: Academic Press, 1987). But also see Andreas Knapp and Margaret S. Clark, "Some Detrimental Effects of Negative Mood on Individuals' Ability to Solve Resource Dilemmas," *Personality and Social Psychology Bulletin* 17 (1991): 678–88.

49. Rena L. Repetti, "Individual and Common Components of the Social Environment at Work and Psychological Well-Being," *Journal of Personality and Social Psychology* 52 (1987): 710–20.

50. Lauren B. Alloy, ed., *Cognitive Processes in Depression* (New York: Guilford Press, 1988). But depressives are less accurate when the outcome involves a negative reference to the self. See Carmelo Vasquez, "Judgment of Contingency: Cognitive Biases in Depressed and Nondepressed Subjects," *Journal of Personality and Social Psychology* 52 (1987): 419–31; John S. Gillis, "Effects of Life Stress and Dysphoria on Complex Judgments," *Psychological Reports* 72, no. 3, pt. 2 (June 1993): 1355–63.

51. Norma D. Feshbach and Seymour Feshbach, "Affective Processes and Academic Achievement," *Special Issue on Schools and Development, Child Development* 58 (1987): 1335–47.

52. Jeffrey H. Boyd et al., "Exclusion Criteria of DSM-III: A Study of Co-occurrence of Hierarchy-Free Syndromes," *Archives of General Psychiatry* 41 (October 1984): 983–89.

53. W. Eugene Broadhead et al., "Depression, Disability Days, and Days Lost from Work in a Prospective Epidemiologic Survey," *The Journal of the American Medical Association* 254, no. 19 (21 November 1990): 2524–25.

54. In Britain about one-seventh of the total inpatient cost to the National Health Service is devoted to treating anxiety and depression. *The Independent*, 6 July 1992, 3.

55. Campbell, *The Sense of Well-Being in America*, 56–58.

56. Morris Rosenberg and Roberta G. Simmons, *Black and White Self-Esteem: The Urban School Child* (Washington, D.C.: American Sociological Association, 1971).

57. Richard Koestner, Miron Zuckerman, and Julia Koestner, "Praise,

Involvement, and Intrinsic Motivation," *Journal of Personality and Social Psychology* 52 (1987): 383–90. But girls are more suspicious of praise than boys.

58. Lane, *The Market Experience*, chap. 27, "Misunderstanding Happiness"; Richard Nisbett and Lee Ross, *Human Inference: Strategies and Shortcomings of Social Judgment* (Englewood Cliffs, N.J.: Prentice-Hall, 1980), chap. 9.

59. Roy F. Harrod, *Sociology, Morals and Mystery* (London: Macmillan, 1971), 64.

60. Lane, *The Market Experience*, 555–56.

61. Daryl J. Bem, "Self-Perception Theory," in *Advances in Experimental Social Psychology*, ed. Leonard Berkowitz, vol. 6 (New York: Academic Press, 1972).

62. Georg Simmel, "The Metropolis and Mental Life," in *The Sociology of Georg Simmel*, trans. and ed. Kurt H. Wolff (Glencoe, Ill.: Free Press, 1950), 412.

63. Robert E. Lane, "Interpersonal Relations and Leadership in a 'Cold Society,'" *Comparative Politics* 10 (1978): 443–59. The arguments given in the text below are summarized in Lane, *The Market Experience*, 215–19. In addition, the interchangeability of commodities and friends violates the preference of exchanging like-for-like goods demonstrated in Uriel Foa, "Interpersonal and Economic Resources," *Science* 171 (29 January 1971): 345–51. Taboos against money gifts to family members are illustrative of the compartmentalization of exchange.

64. Allen Silver, "Friendship in Commercial Society: Eighteenth-Century Social Theory and Modern Sociology," *American Journal of Sociology* 95 (1990): 1474.

65. David C. Fundor and Daniel J. Ozer, "Behavior As a Function of the Situation," *Journal of Personality and Social Psychology* 44 (1983): 107–12; David Magnusson, ed., *Towards a Psychology of Situations* (Hillsdale, N.J.: Erlbaum, 1981).

66. Kenneth Boulding, "The Basis of Value Judgments in Economics," in *Human Values and Economic Policy,* ed. Sidney Hook (New York: New York University Press, 1967), 68.

67. See, for example, George M. Guthrie, "A Social Psychological Analysis of Modernization in the Philippines," *Journal of Cross-Cultural Psychology* 8 (1977): 177–206; Shlomo Maitel, *Minds, Markets, and Money* (New York: Basic Books, 1982), 63–65; Burkhard Strumpel, "Economic Life Styles, Values, and Subjective Welfare," in *Economic Means for Human Needs: Social Indicators of Well-Being and Discontent*, ed. Burkhard Strumpel (Ann Arbor, Mich.: Institute for Social Research, 1976), 63.

68. Inkeles and Diamond, "Personal Development and National Development," 73–109 at 97.

69. Putnam, "Bowling Alone," 73.

70. George C. Homans, *Social Behavior: Its Elementary Forms* (New York: Harcourt, Brace & World, 1961); Peter M. Blau, *Exchange and Power in Social Life* (New York: John Wiley, 1964).

71. Gerald L. Clore and Donn Byrne, "A Reinforcement-Affect Model of

Attraction," in *Foundations of Interpersonal Attraction,* ed. Ted L. Huston (New York: Academic, 1974), 144.

72. Albert J. Lott and Bernice E. Lott, "The Role of Reward in the Formation of Positive Interpersonal Attitudes," in *Foundations of Interpersonal Attraction,* ed. Huston, 171–92.

73. Leonard Berkowitz and Philip Friedman, "Some Social Class Differences in Helping Behavior," *Journal of Personality and Social Psychology* 5 (1967): 217–25.

74. Robert B. Hays, "A Longitudinal Study of Friendship Development," *Journal of Personality and Social Psychology* 48 (1985): 909–24.

75. Argyle, *The Social Psychology of Everyday Life,* 66, citing J. J. La Gaipa and H. D. Wood, "Friendship in Disturbed Adolescents," in *Personal Relationships,* vol. 3, *Personal Relationships in Disorder,* ed. Steve Duck and Robin Gilmour (London: Academic Press, 1981).

76. Gerald Marwell and Ruth E. Ames, "Economists Free Ride, Does Anyone Else?" *Journal of Public Economists* 15 (1981): 295–310, reported in Amitai Etzioni, *The Moral Dimension: Toward a New Economics* (New York: Free Press, 1988), 250.

77. Gregory G. Brunk, "The Impact of Rational Participation Models on Voting Attitudes," *Public Choice* 35 (1980): 549–64, quoted in Donald P. Green and Ian Shapiro, *Pathologies of Rational Choice Theory: A Critique of Applications in Political Science* (New Haven: Yale University Press, 1994), 69.

78. James F. Engel, Roger D. Blackwell, and David T. Kollat, *Consumer Behavior,* 3d ed. (Hinsdale, Ill.: Dryden Press, 1978), 3.

79. Stanley Diamond, *In Search of the Primitive* (New Brunswick, N.J.: Transaction Books, 1974), 11.

80. Erich Fromm, *The Revolution of Hope: Toward a Humanized Technology* (New York: Rinehart, 1968), 1, 28. Along lines similar to mine, Fromm then advises a more "humanistic" form of consumption (120). For a rejoinder to this and other criticisms of consumption, see George Katona, *Psychological Economics* (New York: Elsevier, 1975), 376.

81. Susanne C. Grunert and Gerhard Scherhorn, "Consumer Values in West Germany: Underlying Dimensions and Cross-Cultural Comparison with North America," *Journal of Business Research* 20 (March 1990): 97–107.

82. Alex Inkeles and David H. Smith, *Becoming Modern: Individual Change in Six Developing Countries* (Cambridge, Mass.: Harvard University Press, 1974), 97, 349.

83. Is this hypothesis untestable, because Americans have, over the last twenty years, increased the amount of time they spend working, as Juliet B. Schor claims in *The Overworked American: The Unexpected Decline of Leisure* (New York: Basic Books, 1991)? No, because the evidence of an increase in working time over twenty years is at best ambiguous. In gross terms, the average weekly period of nonagricultural employment from age sixteen to age sixty-four has gone from 38.3 hours in 1970, to 38.1 hours in 1975, to 38.7 in 1985, to 39.1 in 1988. By international standards the latter figure hardly represents "overwork." While it seems to be true that women, with their dual responsibili-

ties, are overworked, among men only the better educated are, as of 1994, working longer than they were twenty years ago, while those with high school or less education are working fewer hours now than in 1975. 1981–82 data show that if one adds household work to market work, men in the twenty-five to forty-four age group worked 61.4 hours, while women in the same age group worked 56.4 hours. But it certainly is true that Americans have shorter vacations and fewer holidays than Europeans. See Sylvia Nasar, "More Men in Prime of Life Spend Less Time Working," *New York Times*, 1 December 1994, A1, D15; F. Thomas Juster, "A Note on Recent Changes in Time Use," chap. 12 in *Time, Goods, and Well-Being*, ed. F. Thomas Juster and Frank P. Stafford (Ann Arbor, Mich.: Survey Research Center, Institute for Social Research, 1985), 318–19; and U.S. Bureau of the Census, *Statistical Abstracts of the United States* (Washington, D.C.: Government Printing Office, 1980), 394, and *Statistical Abstracts of the United States* (Washington, D.C.: Government Printing Office, 1990), 386, 379.

84. While it might be objected that income, rather than the availability of time, determines how much time one shops, the fact is that nationally, time spent shopping has *declined* as per capita income has increased; and, in any event, time spent shopping is unrelated to level of income.

85. John P. Robinson, "Changes in Time Use: An Historical Overview," in *Time, Goods, and Well-Being*, ed. Juster and Stafford, 289-311, at 305. While such gross figures are important, a more careful analysis would break down the figures by social group. For example, for the 1975–1981 comparison, elderly men increased their television watching by eight hours and decreased their "services, shopping" by half an hour, whereas young husbands did not increase their television watching at all and *increased* their shopping by about half an hour.

86. F. Thomas Juster, "A Note on Recent Changes in Time Use," 318–19. There was a modest decline in television viewing in the United States during the 1975–1982 period, mostly among young adults and more often among men than women. There was also a British decline, with an estimated average exposure of 27.1 minutes per day in 1985 declining to 25.1 minutes in 1990 (*The Independent*, 25 June 1992, 3).

87. Keith Dowding and Patrick Dunleavy, "Production, Disbursement and Consumption: The Modes and Modalities of Goods and Services" (paper presented at the conference "The Marketization of Consumption: Public and Private," University of Salford, U.K., 8 July 1994), 3.

88. Engel, Blackwell, and Kollat, *Consumer Behavior*, 12–13.

89. Joseph Plummer, "Applications of Life Style Research in the Creation of Advertising Campaigns," in *Life Style & Psychographics*, ed. William D. Wells (Chicago: American Marketing Association, 1974), 166.

90. Engel, Blackwell, and Kollat, *Consumer Behavior*, 135–36.

91. Martha S. Hill and F. Thomas Juster, "Constraints and Complementarities in Time Use," in *Time, Goods, and Well-Being*, ed. Juster and Stafford, 461. It should be noted that Hill and Juster believe that the force of gender roles found in their study is changing, but that the current pattern still reflects a

division between the sexes. Married women who work for wages average between 3 and 18 more hours per week in total work than do married men. (Hill, "Patterns of Time Use," in *Time, Goods, and Well-Being*, ed. Juster and Stafford, 147.) And women with jobs spend almost as much time shopping as do housewives. It is this dual role that creates strains leading to distress (Barbara Wolfe and Robert Haveman, "Time Allocation, Market Work, and Changes in Female Health," *American Economic Review: Papers and Proceedings of the Ninety-Fifth Annual Meeting of the American Economic Association* 73, no. 2 [May 1983]: 134–39).

92. Hill, "Patterns of Time Use," 151–52, 160–61.

93. Elihu Katz and Paul Felix Lazarsfeld, *Personal Influence: The Part Played by People in the Flow of Mass Communications* (Glencoe, Ill.: Free Press, 1955).

94. There is a large literature on "collective consumption" that I cannot discuss here. This literature deals in part with the public-private dimension and the government regulation of consumption, but not, I think, with the way collective consumption encourages companionship. I am greatly indebted to Dowding and Dunleavy, "Production, Disbursement and Consumption." See also Patrick Dunleavy, *Democracy, Bureaucracy, and Public Choice* (New York: Prentice-Hall, 1992).

95. Robinson, "Changes in Time Use," 299.

96. U.S. Bureau of the Census, *Statistical Abstracts of the United States* (Washington, D.C.: Government Printing Office, 1990), tables 699 and 713. Comparisons for earlier periods do not always confirm the thesis advanced.

97. Mihalyi Csikszentmihalyi and Eugene Rochberg-Halton, *The Meaning of Things: Domestic Symbols and the Self* (Cambridge: Cambridge University Press, 1981), 129.

98. Peter Laslett, *The World We Have Lost*, 2d ed. (New York: Scribner, 1971), 22.

99. See John Bowlby, *Attachment and Loss*, vol. 1, *Attachment* (New York: Basic Books, 1969); Steve Duck, *Understanding Relationships* (New York: Guilford Press, 1991); David C. McClelland, *Human Motivation* (Glenview, Ill.: Scott, Foresman, 1985). McClelland explores the need for affiliation along with both the fear of rejection *and* the fear of intimacy.

100. Campbell, Converse, and Rodgers, *The Quality of American Life*, 48. See also Peter K. Lunt, "The Perceived Causal Structure of Loneliness," *Journal of Personality and Social Psychology* 61 (1991): 26–33.

101. Claude S. Fischer, "On Urban Alienation and Anomie, Powerlessness and Social Isolation," *American Sociological Review* 38 (June 1973): 323.

102. S. Lau and Gerald E. Gruen, "The Social Stigma of Loneliness: Effect of Target Person's and Perceiver's Sex," *Personality and Social Psychology Bulletin* 18 (1992): 182–89.

103. Lunt, "The Perceived Causal Structure of Loneliness," 26–33.

104. Brown and Harris, *Social Origins of Depression*, 133.

105. Campbell, Converse, and Rodgers, *The Quality of American Life*, 358–50, 380.

106. Michael Argyle and Maryanne Martin, "The Psychological Causes of Happiness," in *Subjective Well-Being: An Interdisciplinary Perspective,* ed. Fritz Strack, Michael Argyle, and Norbert Schwarz (Oxford: Pergamon, 1991).

107. Robert P. Quinn and Linda J. Shepard, *The 1972–73 Quality of Employment Survey* (Ann Arbor, Mich.: Survey Research Center, Institute of Social Research), 1074, table 3.28. See also Christopher Jencks, Lauri Perman, and Lee Rainwater, "What Is a Good Job? A New Measure of Labor-Market Success," *American Journal of Sociology* 93 (1988): 1322–57.

108. Juster, "A Note on Recent Changes in Time Use," 335.

109. Weissman and Leaf, "Affective Disorders," 76.

110. Abbey and Andrews, "Modeling the Psychological Determinants of Life Quality," 108.

111. Catherine E. Ross and John Mirowsky, "Explaining the Social Patterns of Depression: Control and Problem Solving or Support and Talking?" *Journal of Health & Social Behavior* 39 (June 1989): 206.

112. Edward O. Wilson, *Sociobiology: The New Synthesis* (Cambridge, Mass.: Belknap Press of Harvard University, 1975). Wilson gives the following example of the affiliative instincts of our primate forebears: "Rhesus monkeys, like other higher primates, are intensely affected by their [social] environments—an isolated individual will repeatedly pull a lever with no reward other than the glimpse of another monkey" (7). But there is evidence that controlling one's environment, too, is a motive with biological roots: like affiliative motives, the need for control seems to be present in more than one species.

14

Delectable Materialism: Second Thoughts on Consumer Culture

Michael Schudson

On 31 January 1990, when McDonald's opened in Moscow, Soviet citizens seemed stunned by the politeness of the people behind the cash registers who smiled and said, "May I help you?" They were delighted at the efficiency of the service despite a wait of two hours, and many took home their logo-laden McDonald's refuse as souvenirs. Tongue in cheek, the *New York Times* wrote of hope-starved Soviet consumers won over to "delectable materialism." The *Washington Post*, similarly jocular, painted a portrait of a factory worker standing beneath the golden arches and said of him, "He had seen the future—and it tasted good."[1]

In the waning days of the Cold War, American journalists poked fun at the Soviet passion for American consumer goods because they could not consider consumerism in the United States without depreciating it. It takes an immigrant or outsider to speak of American abundance in beatific terms. Boris Yeltsin, back home from a nine-day American tour in the fall of 1989, was effusive about the extraordinary wealth of American life: "Their supermarkets have 30,000 food items," he told supporters. "You can't imagine it. It makes the people feel secure." Yeltsin urged that "at least 100 million Soviets must pass through the American school of supermarkets," to understand the American system. "The leaders must be first."[2]

The late Henry Fairlie, a British immigrant to America, waxed eloquent about his adopted country in a celebratory Fourth of July essay. The United States is the first country, he said, in which he felt free. He cited his experience, in 1965, on his first morning in America, when the wife of the English friend he was staying with "took me, not to the

Washington Monument, but to a supermarket—just to stare." What the
supermarket, the cafeteria, and various gadgets told Fairlie was that
"convenience is liberating" and that the chief conveniences of American life were democratic. "Like the Franklin stove or the Ford Model T,
these amenities were meant for all." And Fairlie, like Yeltsin later, held
that "there is a meaning to the material progress of America . . . beyond
the physical benefits which it bestows."[3]

This celebratory attitude toward American materialism is rarely
shared by homegrown journalists and intellectuals. They view American materialism skeptically and critically. In part, they draw on the
anticapitalism of the left and the antibourgeois values of the aristocratic
right. Even more, they trade on a distaste for consumerism that is as
close to the heart of the American tradition as consumerism itself. President Jimmy Carter, for instance, found in his own tradition of evangeli-
cal Protestantism the anxiety that "too many of us now worship self-
indulgence and consumption" and he affirmed that "owning things and
consuming things does not satisfy our longing for meaning."[4] Here Carter provided an echo of Franklin Roosevelt's rhetoric. Roosevelt criticized Americans' "obeisance to Mammon" and sought to bring people
out of "an era of selfishness." It was time, he urged, to "put faith in
spiritual values above every material consideration."[5]

Of course, Americans have often celebrated material abundance and
even worshiped it; at the same time, American tradition has a long-
standing distrust of material goods. I am not about to endorse the idolatry of goods, but the primary task of this essay is to hold up for examination the view that attachment to material goods is pathological. For
most intellectuals and social critics, this position is much more congenial than hearty praise of an acquisitive society. In its many variants, it
offers an opening attempt to construct an ethics of consumption. But it
is as often a reflexlike rejection of consumption as encomiums to abundance and free markets are an uncritical embrace of consumption. My
critique of the critics of material goods, then, is an effort to clear the
way for a more balanced assessment of consumerism.

Critics of Consumer Culture

Criticism of advertising and consumer culture today emerges not so
much from a single source as from at least five distinguishable traditions of criticism. Three of these lie within bourgeois culture and two
lie outside it, critical not only of the distinctive institutions of advertising and consumer culture but of middle-class society and capitalism in
general. Teasing out and examining these strands of thought may help

clarify the conflicted relationship to the world of goods that social critics, intellectuals, and others share today.

Most criticism of consumer culture shares a few basic assumptions, which should be questioned at the outset. The critiques of consumer culture all object, as Emerson did, that things are in the saddle and ride us. They all seem to hold that if we could live the simple life, where things satisfy natural, biological needs and little more, we could properly devote attentions to justice or comradeship or aesthetic pleasures. We could then bask in the spiritual satisfactions the natural world can provide. But "the simple life" expresses only one view of the good life, and not self-evidently the best.

The advocates of the simple life presume that we can neatly separate *necessary* from *artificial* needs and wants, and they hold that we should attach our desires to the former alone. But what is necessary to sustain human life? This is not an easy question. Its answer certainly does not lie in biology alone. People in all societies are biological and social at once. The infant's first sucking at the breast is an act both biological and social, both nourishing and attaching. From that point on, the infant will want to be not only a *living* person but also a living *person*, a socially creditable member of a society. Human biological functions, like eating, are culturally coded and socially organized. It is important in all human societies that people eat like human beings, not like animals. This requires adherence to social conventions for eating that differ from one culture to the next. In the American middle class, a person must eat a certain quantity of food so that it cannot be said that the person "eats like a horse," on the one hand, or "eats like a bird," on the other. More important still, one must retain a certain reserve about eating so as to acknowledge that the activity is one of eating a meal, not one of simply consuming food. Without that reserve, a person can be accused of "eating like a pig" or failing to engage in the social activity of eating altogether by "inhaling" food.

In Alexander Solzhenitsyn's *One Day in the Life of Ivan Denisovich*, prisoners in the Soviet labor camp are fed only a thin gruel with some fish heads and tails thrown in. Ivan Denisovich, weak from malnutrition and overwork, nonetheless organizes his own ritual for eating. He takes off his cap before he eats. He refuses to eat fish eyes. In a subsociety intended to animalize prisoners, Ivan retains his humanity by continuing to eat meals rather than simply consuming food. Even in the poorest societies, human needs and desires are culturally constituted and socially defined. Human needs are for inclusion as well as for survival, for meaning as well as for existence. And consumer goods, as Mary Douglas and Baron Isherwood argued and as most scholars who think on these matters have now fully accepted, are for modern societies central elements in the establishment and circulation of meaning.[6]

But what, then, is required to live a social and socially creditable life? And how much? This will differ from one society to the next. The requirements of personhood differ across societies as both philosopher of modern capitalism Adam Smith and capitalism's most severe critic, Karl Marx, understood. Smith defined "human necessaries" as "not only the commodities which are indispensably necessary for the support of life, but whatever the custom of the country renders it indecent for creditable people, even of the lowest order, to be without."[7] He observed that a linen shirt is not "strictly speaking" a necessary of life but that, in most of Europe in his day, "a creditable day-labourer would be ashamed to appear in public without a linen shirt, the want of which would be supposed to denote that disgraceful degree of poverty, which, it is presumed, no body can well fall into without extreme bad conduct."[8] Similarly, Smith judged leather shoes a necessity in England for men and women but for men only in Scotland and for neither in France.

Marx, like Smith, understood human needs to be socially and historically produced. In *Capital*, he distinguishes between two kinds of consumer goods, necessities and luxuries, but he does not assume that necessities are either biological or natural. True articles of luxury are items that only the capitalist class consumes. A consumer necessity is something that is in general and habitual use among the working class—such as tobacco—whether or not it is physiologically essential to life.[9] Like Smith, Marx fully appreciated that human needs are social and relative. In *Wage–Labour and Capital*, he wrote that an owner may find a small house adequate so long as other houses in the same neighborhood are the same size. Then someone builds a palace and "the house shrinks from a little house to a hut. . . . Our desires and pleasures spring from society; we measure them, therefore, by society and not by the objects which serve for their satisfaction. Because they are of a social nature, they are of a relative nature."[10]

For Marx, the frightening invention of capitalism is not the creation of artificial or new needs but the emergence of a concept that there *is* such a thing as purely physical or biological need. Other social systems had treated human beings as social entities, not biological machines. Only capitalism conceived of people as raw material and only capitalists dared calculate the minimum amount it would take to keep workers alive and healthy enough to work in factories and reproduce in families the next generation of laborers.[11]

Criticism of consumer culture may adopt more of this dehumanized understanding of the relation of persons and things than it realizes. It seems to me fundamental, in grappling with the ethics of consumption, to begin from that area of agreement between Adam Smith and Karl Marx—that human life is by definition social and cultural, that human needs are relative across societies, and that what counts as necessary in a given society has to be defined somehow in relation to what the poorest members of society require for creditable social standing. In the United States, for instance, this almost certainly means a television. It may even mean an automobile, except, perhaps, for residents of New York City and a few other places where public transportation is a passable alternative. The driver's license may be as close to a badge of full social membership as this society has.

Keeping in mind the fundamental socialness of human needs and insisting that we cannot get around a degree of relativism even in trying to define *basic* needs (but I will return to just how this relativism is constrained), let me turn to the five critiques of consumer culture in American social thought. I will first take up three bourgeois objections to consumer culture. Some critics, whom I shall call Puritans, attack people's attitudes toward material goods in pursuit of spirituality; some critics, whom I shall call Quakers, attack features of the goods themselves in pursuit of simplicity; and some, whom I shall label republicans, in pursuit of civic virtue attack the consequences of possession, notably complacency and the loss of civic engagement.[12]

The Puritan Critique

The Puritan critique worries about whether people invest an appropriate amount of meaning in goods. By Puritan, I refer to the conviction, symbolized by the sturdy and sober New England colonists, that people should invest less meaning in worldly possessions than in spiritual pursuits. In this view, pleasure should be subordinated to duty, the flesh to the spirit, and temporal concerns to religious obligations. Yet Puritan critics do not necessarily agree about what an appropriate degree of meaning investment in material possessions might be. Some critics have suggested that contemporary American attitudes toward goods are not crassly materialist enough, that people find goods insufficient without investing surplus meaning in them. British critic Raymond Williams writes that advertising is the very proof that people in modern capitalist societies are not materialist—because the job of the ad is to convey added value to the product itself. "If we were sensibly materialist, in that part of our living in which we use things, we should find most advertising to be of an insane irrelevance. Beer would be enough for us, without the additional promise that in drinking it we show ourselves to be manly, young in heart, or neighbourly."[13] Advertising, then, is magic, and it magically associates extra, non-essential meaning with perfectly ordinary, serviceable goods. For Williams, the trouble with contemporary attitudes toward goods is that goods, in themselves, are undervalued but, in their associations, are overspiritualized. In adopting this view, Williams accepts that there is such a thing as "goods in themselves." He implies that drinking beer is no more than consuming a beverage rather than, among other things, a rich expressive display of comradeship (a remarkably Puritanical assumption for someone coming from pub-strewn Britain).

In contrast, the late American historian and critic Christopher Lasch has argued that people underspiritualize goods. In *The Minimal Self*, Lasch complains that manufactured goods are inferior to handmade goods in that they cannot serve as "transitional" objects, that is, objects that bridge the gap between the individual's inner self and the social world.[14] He borrows here from psychoanalyst D. W. Winnicott's view that children often use physical objects to represent or stand in for the mother, even in the absence of the mother. Far from being regressive, this behavior helps the child develop autonomy from the mother. For Lasch, handcrafted goods have the mark of human activity upon them, while commodities are elements in a prefabricated dream world that cannot aid us in gaining a sense of mastery over our experience. Lasch is able to maintain this view only because he traces the beginnings of American consumer culture to the 1920s rather than recognizing, as many social historians now do, its eighteenth-century origins.[15] In *The True and Only Heaven*, Lasch again writes with admiration of craftsmanship or, at least, with resentment of intellectuals who fail to appreciate manual labor as he does.[16] But his larger point is that contemporary attitudes toward goods are more satanized than spiritualized, that we are possessed by our possessions, that we are, in a word, addicted. In his earlier work, *The Culture of Narcissism*, Lasch held that consumers are "perpetually unsatisfied, restless, anxious, and bored." Capitalism shapes in them "an unappeasable appetite" for new goods and new experiences.[17] This is not, Lasch emphasizes, conventional hedonism but something worse—a compulsion, an addiction, a sickness linked intrinsically to consumer capitalism.

So the heart of the Puritan critique is a utilitarian valuation of goods. Goods should serve practical human needs (or human social relationships, in Lasch's view). They should be valued for their capacity to fulfill human needs but they should not be ends of desire in themselves. The concept of needs here tends to be very limited. Certainly the Puritan critique is suspicious of the aesthetic dimension of human experience and has no place for someone who takes pleasure in the feel or look of a consumer good. It may be, as James Agee once wrote, that the sense of beauty is a class privilege—that only the comfortable have the leisure to contemplate the beautiful. But this is an argument for economic improvement or redistribution, not an argument that an aesthetic sense is unrelated to the good life. The original Puritans found offensive dancing, music, theater, nonreproductive sexuality, and other material and bodily pleasures. They at least had the virtue of consistency.

There are implicitly empirical claims in the notion that people overspiritualize or underspiritualize goods, with little proffered evidence one way or the other. Is Williams right to suppose people do not find most advertising "insanely irrelevant?" My reading of the evidence is that people ignore the vast amount of advertising they see and distrust much of the little advertising they take in.[18] Is Lasch correct that massproduced goods fail as transitional objects? I see no evidence, certainly not from my own children, that mass-produced blankets are inferior to grandma-made afghans as "transitional objects." I wished that my preschool daughter was as attached to the quilt my wife made or the afghan my grandmother made as to the cotton blanket we got from J. C. Penny, but she was not. Do I overspiritualize goods in this desire? Does my daughter underspiritualize? And what is the appropriate standard?

Of course, the preference for the handcrafted good may also betray an indifference to the burden of the laborer who does the handcrafting. In 1900, the American housewife did a great deal of handcrafting, spending more than forty hours a week in preparing meals. In 1975, the average housewife spent ten hours in food preparation and about one hour a week, rather than seven, doing laundry.[19] Is this to be regarded as progress and liberation? Or must we conclude that it represents the underspiritualization of food and clothing?

The Quaker Critique

The Quaker critique is less concerned with how people feel about goods than with objectionable features of the products themselves, usually their wastefulness or extravagance. Christopher Lasch, whose multifarious critiques of consumer culture fit into almost all of my categories, took up the old complaint that modern industry is dictated by "planned obsolescence" or Sloanism, the annual model change that Alfred P. Sloan introduced to General Motors more than half a century ago to coax people to buy new cars even when they have serviceable old ones.[20] Here critics take changes in products to be not only useless but also manipulative, aimed only at pointless product differentiation to which people will attribute unfounded meaning. The fashion industry is a regular target of such criticism, as it was for the Quakers themselves in their adherence to plain dress.

Critics, however, have too easily generalized from a few salient examples. Does Sloanism actually guide American industry? Does it even guide the automobile industry? While General Motors was developing the annual model change, other companies were producing washing machines, radios, single-family homes, bicycles, phonographs, and bathroom fixtures that were designed to last, and did last, for years. Sloanism is an aspect of the American economy, but it is more a marketing strategy for a particular set of conditions than a deep cultural force.

In the case of automobiles, consumers were not happily holding onto their cars for years until Sloan found a way to introduce wasteful fashion to utilitarian transport vehicles. Before Sloan dreamt of the annual model change, the used-car market was large and growing; people were obviously "buying up" as they could afford to, reproducing in the automobile an objective correlative of already existing systems of class and status distinction. They were resisting the implications of Henry Ford's one-model, one-price policy. So were many of Detroit's auto makers, for reasons no more calculating. Many of Detroit's entrepreneurs were building more expensive cars, pricing themselves out of the lucrative mass market, and ultimately bankrupting themselves in a status-driven effort to manufacture cars of a sort appropriate to their own station, or desired station, in Detroit society.[21] They went too far up-market while Henry Ford controlled the lower end of the market and Alfred P. Sloan looked to the middle.

The fashion consciousness Sloan helped institutionalize was the General Motors solution to a perceived problem for the industry—the expanding market in used cars.[22] Sloan himself understood General Motors to be using the annual model change to adapt to the existing trends of American life, notably the practice of trading up. "Middle-income buyers," he later wrote, "assisted by the trade-in and installment financing, created the demand, not for basic transportation, but for progress in new cars, for comfort, convenience, power, and style."[23] The problem for the industry was that the cars were in fact well made and lasted a long time. The annual model change may indeed be wasteful, but "planned obsolescence," as critics still call it, does not characterize most of American industry and it was in its origins as much a response to the desire of consumers to be fashionable as a cause of fashion consciousness.

Still, we can concede that some kinds of consumption are more practical, less ostentatious, and less wasteful than others and, by that measure, more morally defensible—perhaps a bicycle is better than a car. But what about a plain car rather than a fancy one? Volkswagen advertising used to be morally smug, emphasizing that the VW was plain, even ugly, simple, graceless, and unchanging year after year. Did this make the VW a more ethically satisfying choice of car? Or had VW just found a way to turn Puritan and Quaker sentiment into a marketing ploy?

What is the appropriate level of aesthetic interest a consumer good should evoke? What is the appropriate level of workmanship and luxury for products? How should we weigh the Cadillac against the subcompact Chevy? The former may use up more resources and be less fuel efficient but it may also be a better—and safer—car. Some practical and spartan products may not only be aesthetically unappealing but ecologically unsound. Paper plates and towels may be easier to use and dispose of than china and cloth towels that are designed for regular reuse, but they are wasteful.

Not that wastefulness is always easy to measure. Polyester has long been abused in some circles—because it is artificial and, so go the rationalizations, it does not last like cotton. But polyester manufacturers have pointed out that polyester takes less energy to produce and to maintain (it never needs ironing) than cotton and, over the lifetime of a garment, absorbs less of the earth's total energy and resources. A product that never needs ironing saves not only electricity but also human, almost invariably female, labor. Today polyester can even be manufactured from recycled soda bottles.[24] A similar case has been made for disposable diapers and other products that appear to be wasteful but, relatively speaking, may not be.[25]

The Quaker critique tends to suggest that consumption that is more practical, less ostentatious, and less wasteful is better. Goods should not be pointlessly differentiated. They should not be made useful, efficient, speedy, or convenient beyond some consensual standard of what level of usefulness is normative; they should not be multiplied if they can be made durable for sharing or personal reuse. They should husband the earth's resources with care. People should, as they produce and consume, have human posterity in view.

But what is the standard of appropriate convenience and who is to set it? In 1930 only one-half of American households boasted flush toilets while in 1980 more than 98 percent did.[26] In 1980, indoor plumbing was surely a necessity in Adam Smith's terms—it was required to be a socially creditable person, but clearly it was not "physically" necessary and surely it was quite wasteful of limited water supplies. On what grounds is the Boeing 747 acceptable but the Concorde wasteful? In my house, the electric blender is considered acceptable but not the electric can opener, the electric toothbrush but not the electric blanket. But on what grounds are such decisions made? How do we arrive at a baseline for consensus—and, if we cannot (and I think that we cannot), then what is the character of the moral objection to excessive consumption? The distinction between necessary and superfluous consumption is, as historian Lorna Weatherill suggests, "deeply misleading." The notion of luxury simply "does not provide a firm basis for examining the meaning of consumer behaviour."[27]

The Republican Critique

The last of the bourgeois objections to consumption, the republican perspective, is concerned not with attitudes toward goods nor with the wastefulness of goods themselves but with the corrupting influence on public life of a goods orientation in private life. This is perhaps the most trenchant and resonant of the critiques. In the republican vision, a goods orientation or consumerist orientation is debilitating in three ways. First, it is passive. People consume themselves, Stuart Ewen has written, "into social and political passivity."[28] Satisfaction with goods produces acquiescence in politics. People who transfer their passive orientation toward goods to the world of politics expect political life to be prefabricated and expect to participate in it simply by making a choice between predetermined alternatives. This idea of politics reduces a voting booth to a vending machine.

Second, a goods orientation gives priority to possession rather than to production as a defining feature of personal identity. In a consumer society, "lifestyle" surpasses a person's work life as the defining feature of existence. Republicans take this to be not only a misunderstanding of what human beings are but also a politically conservative misunderstanding that diverts attention from the task of making our work lives more vital and democratic.

Third, a goods orientation is privatizing. People abandon the town square for the front porch, and then later the front porch for the backyard or the television room. The town pump gives way to the commercial laundry or Laundromat, the Laundromat to the home washer and dryer. People seek comfort increasingly inside their domiciles, and their domiciles increasingly house only members of a nuclear family, not an extended family, servants, or boarders.

Is a consumerist orientation to goods necessarily passive? H. F. Moorhouse makes a strong argument to the contrary, as have many others who emphasize the "active" involvement of audiences in their consumption activities. Moorhouse examines the consumption of automobiles in the United States. He writes of the appropriation by young people of Detroit-made cars in the "hot rod" culture of the 1940s. Teenagers did not passively accept the automobile but decorated, redesigned, and even reengineered Detroit cars for their own purposes in racing (often illegally). The ethos of hot rod culture was not passivity but a commitment "to labour, to strive, to plan, to exercise skill, to compete, to succeed, to risk."[29] One does not have to look back to the 1940s, of course, to find people actively engaged with the things they consume, developing expert knowledge about goods they like even to the point of becoming manufacturers themselves. This may involve redesigning products for their own purposes or even directly entering the world of production, like women romance novel readers who turn to writing and publishing romances themselves.[30]

I do not mean to protest too much here. Certainly even active forms of watching baseball are, with respect to physical activity, more passive than the most passive ways of playing the game (the daydreaming elementary school right fielder at least stands erect and trots on and off the field). But it is important to note that there are degrees of activity in consumption just as there are degrees of disengagement in labor. A youngster may watch as a coach demonstrates a gymnastics routine or how to field a ground ball; watching of this sort is not likely to be passive at all.

The role of work in human identity is scarcely self-evident. Why must we assume that it is the defining feature of human identity? Many sociological studies of labor take it for granted that only in labor can "real" satisfaction in life be attained; all other satisfactions have to be regarded as substitutes, more or less unsatisfying, more or less illusory.[31] But why treat consumption, a priori, as peripheral to key matters of human fulfillment? Moorhouse holds that there is no empirical rationale for privileging workplaces as "the crucial sites of human experience and self understanding."[32] I agree. Labor and occupation are very important but it is some kind of metaphysics that makes labor the defining feature of human life.

As for the privatizing character of consumerism, this too is contestable. When are private satisfactions in consumer goods too private? When backyard swimming pools replace the community pools? When purchased books weaken public libraries? When a washer and dryer replaces the commercial Laundromat or commercial laundry, themselves replacements for hard domestic labor and household servants? When radio and television replace movies, theaters, and concerts, themselves rather recent commercial replacements for quilting bees and barbecues and social visiting on the front porch?

But the most serious riposte to republican critics is this: the rise of consumer culture has been a building block of a participatory, active, democratic society, not a barrier to it. Political activism in the years leading up to the American Revolution was organized around consumer identity and the nonimportation of British consumer goods. The anti-importation movement, as David Shi has suggested, was in part encouraged by the ethic of republican simplicity; the battle against Britain was seen also as a war for moral regeneration. Many colonial leaders saw frugality and patriotism linked closely together. Samuel Adams, though the owner of a brewery, was indifferent to his own economic well-being and took pride in the frugality and simplicity of his living while he devoted himself to political affairs.[33] But anti-importation was not a protest against commercial culture so much as an effort to regulate life within it. The rapidly growing consumer culture and improving living standards were widely welcomed. The anti-importation movement provided, as T. H. Breen has argued, a basis for the democratization of political protest. While traditional political action was available only to propertied white males, consumer-based protest could be much more widely shared. Basing protest on consumer identity was a radically egalitarian move and a novel one: "No previous popular rebellion had organized itself so centrally around the consumer."[34]

This is not a unique instance. Lizabeth Cohen has suggested that the growth of a national mass culture "helped unify workers previously divided along ethnic, racial, and geographic lines" in the 1920s and 1930s, and so contributed to the Congress of Industrial Organizations (CIO) organizing efforts.[35] Organizing around a consumer issue proved a potent force: ethnic working-class opposition to Prohibition, she argues, brought workers a new unity as Democrats and a new openness to state actions as solutions to their problems.[36] In the 1960s, political protesters certainly did not all use marijuana, but a common culture of protest was forged in part by a shared appreciation of rock music and the democratic aura of both rock and pot. It is clear, at the very least, that consumer culture cuts two ways in its effects on political protest and popular militance. Perhaps critics are right that consumerism may sometimes take people out of the public square, but clearly there are also powerful historical instances where consumer culture has provided the avenue and the engine for entrance into public life.

Antibourgeois Critiques

I will discuss more quickly the nonbourgeois or antibourgeois objections to consumer culture since, in a variety of ways, they have been bootlegged into the bourgeois self-criticism. The Marxist or socialist objection to consumer culture is that, however beneficent the economic system may appear from the side of consumption, it rests on the exploitation of workers in the capitalist system of production. Indeed, Ewen and Lasch have separately argued that the point of consumer society is to distract the minds and bodies of workers, to serve as an opiate of the people, submerging dissatisfaction with life in the exploitative workplace. "The tired worker," Lasch writes, "instead of attempting to change the conditions of his work, seeks renewal in brightening his immediate surroundings with new goods and services." Advertising, Lasch complains, "upholds consumption as an alternative to protest or rebellion."[37]

Twenty years ago, Lasch's hyperventilating prose seemed persuasive, at least for those already critical of American materialism. But he offers no evidence that the baubles of consumerism buy off discontent or that, if they do, we are nonetheless safe in dismissing them as baubles. A questionable assumption in his argument is that the satisfactions of the consumer world are illusory. Ordinarily, they are quite real. The critics may see goods as distractions, but they can also be seen as authentic sources of both utility and meaning. Moreover, as I have just suggested, they may be as often motivation for political activity as a substitute for it. The current social transformation of Eastern Europe, galvanized by economic aspirations as well as by political hope, is the most recent case in point.

The aristocratic objection to consumer society is primarily aesthetic. Where the socialist critique of consumer culture is a critique of exploitation on behalf of the goal of equality, the aristocratic or elitist objection to consumer society is an attack on ugliness in defense of culture. Mass-produced goods are ugly. The trouble with this critique is its anti-democratic bias; the attack on mass-produced goods is often a thinly veiled attack on the masses themselves. Mass-produced goods may be judged ugly by some, but they are often significantly cheaper than hand-crafted products. The evidence of this is not only before our eyes but available in the historical record. For instance, carpets were once available only to the wealthy; the power loom made them available to most citizens. Ready-to-wear clothing was available by the mid-nineteenth century to working-class people who could not have afforded items of such quality before.[38] A great amount of homemade wear was shoddy and ill-fitting.[39]

Again, the problem is one of standards and relativism. We cannot just smuggle in an assurance that we know what valid culture is: no one does. Worse, as economist Fred C. Hirsch argued, aesthetics are intrinsically implicated in hierarchical relations when "positional" goods like parks, vacation spots, and restaurants are found beautiful in part because of their exclusiveness, spaciousness, quiet, and seclusion—in short, because of the absence of other people.[40] Valuing what is exclusive, we call it fine or beautiful and so incorporate social distinction into our very definition of quality. Some of our terms of praise call attention specifically to scarcity, and scarcity becomes linguistically equated with quality—*rare, unique, one of a kind.* The problem of not having aesthetic standards on which we could all agree is compounded by the problem of having too readily at hand aesthetic standards that are intrinsically antidemocratic.[41]

Conclusion

Historian Daniel Horowitz, in his study of social science discussions about consumerism at the turn of the century, comes to a curiously modest conclusion. His book is critical of the "moralism" of the critiques of profligacy and self-indulgence he analyzed, but he says in the end that his work is "a critique of a view of consumption that I still hold to a considerable extent."[42] He lists what he takes to be pieces of an alternative and more positive view of consumption, including studies that demonstrate people's complex incorporations of commercial goods into their own lives. People make these goods serve their individual needs and, even when they use the goods in standard fashion, take them quite pragmatically, not attributing to them any of the spiritual or romantic qualities that advertising seeks to build up. He concludes of these and other arguments, "No one has yet pulled these scattered pieces of evidence and different modes of interpretation into a coherent counterargument."[43]

This remains true a decade later. What has changed, however, is the world scene, particularly the economic collapse and political disintegration of the Soviet Union and Eastern Europe. Communism's collapse does not justify capitalism's remarkable failures, at least in the United States, to provide citizens with basic needs of affordable shelter, health care, and economic security. But it does make more apparent the need to scrutinize the criticisms of consumer culture that have flourished among relatively affluent intellectuals in Western societies. It is time to criticize, as Michael Walzer has, the mistake of "rational leftism" in its critique of consumption, "as if it were not a good thing for ordinary men and women to possess useful and beautiful objects (as the rich and the powerful have always done)." When owning things becomes the exclusive aim of living, then something is clearly amiss, "but we need to mark off that moment from all previous moments of innocent desire and acquisition."[44]

There may be no way out for us yet. We may be stuck in our intellectual life as in our culture with ambivalence about goods. Albert O. Hirschman finds this ambivalence in Adam Smith himself.[45] David Shi finds it throughout American history: "From colonial days, the image of America as a spiritual commonwealth and a republic of virtue has survived alongside the more tantalizing vision of America as a cornucopia of economic opportunities and consumer delights."[46] Neil Harris finds even in Sinclair Lewis, that great critic of crass American values, an ambivalence about the commercial world: "Merchandising, then, occupied a curiously ambiguous place in Lewis' scheme of things: on the one hand, testimony to the commercialization of American culture, the triumph of mass-produced objects over personality; and on the other, evidence of taste, culture, artistic accomplishment, and sophistication. Buying could be either an act of subservience to manufacturers and advertisers or a demonstration of individuality."[47] Horowitz insists that it is inevitably and necessarily both.[48]

It is time to face up to that ambivalence en route to a political and moral position beyond the snickering, joking, and hypocritical posturing of most criticism of consumer culture. This does not mean we should forgo criticism of consumer culture, especially at a moment of growing concerns about environmental and ecological catastrophe and the distribution of consumption not only among rich and poor people within a society but among rich and poor nations within a world system. It is more difficult to take for granted, as Adam Smith did, that a clearly demarcated national society is the correct social world within which necessity and luxury are to be defined. We do need to think today of consumption in a global context. Issues such as "dumping" of products in the Third World, international agreements on fishing and whaling, or international policy on the production of ozone-depleting products all lift our moral horizons to the global level.

At the same time, the implications of a global vision are difficult to fathom. To live as well in Phoenix as one might in New York for a middle-income person requires air-conditioning, just as for a resident of Boston to live as well as a resident of Los Angeles requires substantial investment in fuel during the winter. If Americans all agreed to move to the more temperate climates of the country, we could save enormously in world energy resources. If we required everyone to live within a certain distance of their place of employment, we could also save enormously on gasoline. But people have investments in locale, even in a global age. It is one thing to question the political legitimacy of, say, Jewish settlers in the West Bank, whose presence, less than a generation old, has divided Israelis from the outset, but it is quite another thing to question the ecological legitimacy of the entire population of southern California, northern New York state, or Minnesota. Without any practical policy suggestions to justify massive redistributions of population and resources it is hard to know just where a global consumer ethic might end.

But a global consumer ethic should begin, and it should begin afresh. Freeing ourselves from biblical or republican or Marxist moralisms, we should recognize that there is dignity and rationality in people's desire for material goods. We should then seek to reconstruct an understanding of the moral and political value of consumption that we and others can decently live with.

What might that understanding look like? What principles might it be founded on? I have raised a host of questions about various existing standards of moral condemnation and I have suggested that the standards most frequently appealed to are inconsistent and ill considered. But I do not mean to say that *no* standards can be established.

Amartya Sen offers some guidance in his emphasis on human "capabilities." He writes of the same Adam Smith passage I cited earlier that Smith's example of the leather shoes is not an argument for moral relativism. It is only an argument that leather shoes may or may not be a human necessity. What particular consumer goods mean will vary from one society to another and one era to another. But what remains constant is the goal that people should have goods sufficient so that they will not be ashamed in society. Societies should be organized so that no one falls below a level that provides access to the consumer goods required for social credit and self-respect. The protection of human dignity or, more broadly, the ensuring of human "capability to function" is not relative.

If societies should be organized so that all inhabitants (or all citizens—there are important debates here about who counts as a society member) possess a "capability to function," this may suggest a moral and political baseline concerning consumption. It has to do most of all with the distribution of goods across classes. If some few consume so much bread that there are not enough crumbs left for others to have the capability to function, the society has failed.

Just what this means, practically, is an intensely difficult problem, on two grounds. First, to a large extent, people understand their own capacity to function locally, not nationally or globally. People's social reference groups, modern mass media notwithstanding, are the people they see face-to-face on a daily basis or the people they feel closely connected with by kinship or social location. These are the people who truly matter to their capacity to function. Think of the hundreds of tales, in novels, short stories, and films, of the young couple from different ethnic groups, religions, or social classes meeting each other's families for the first time. The young people anxiously fret that their parents will embarrass them—either because their material possessions are too humble and shabby or, on the other hand, because they are too extravagant and ostentatious. We still live in a multitude of differentiated social worlds and the goods that make a person creditable in one may be meaningless or even discrediting in the next.

Second, we have increasingly and paradoxically an opposite problem: that we have more and more information about how the other half lives, an other half from across the street or half way around the world. There is a sense, more than ever before, that we are all part of a single reference group. Humanity as a whole is not of daily concern to most people, but people in the developed regions of the world certainly have easy access to information about people all over the globe. We also know that we are globally connected more than ever and that economic and political decisions in one corner of the world influence daily life in other corners—the worldwide sensitivity to oil prices is a good example. Whatever people's particular religious or cosmological views may be, there is certainly a growing veneer, at least, of universalism. No one is an island, no one stands alone, as the John Donne-based song says, "each man's joy is joy to me, each man's grief is my own." Whether from universalistic ethical principles of traditional religions, from Enlightenment liberalism, or from growing awareness of the interdependence of people in a global economy on a planet with finite resources, it grows hard *not* to imagine that the whole of humanity is *my* reference group, *my* community.

On the one hand, then, there is the persistent localness of reference groups and the consequently local definition of what package of goods is required for the human capability to function. On the other hand, there is the growing globalness of human consciousness that compels universalistic standards. The former would seem to suggest a nearly boundless relativism, the latter a set of universal standards that would imply a redistribution so radical that even saints might hesitate to recommend it.

Somewhere in between the radically relativist and the hopelessly universal, there may be some standards, flexible but not spineless, for judging consumption. When we find a way to define them, they may resemble some of the standards I have found wanting here. It seems to me there is something to save from the heritage of Puritanism, which recognizes possession as an inappropriate aim of life, however valuable a means; from Quakerism, which recognizes the vanity of goods and, in a modern ecologized variant, moves from objecting to the vanity of goods before God to the wastefulness of goods before a resource-scarce and unequal world; from republicanism, which scouts out dangers of

private satisfaction in the face of public squalor—not that private satisfaction in itself is wrong but that it can dangerously remove people
from pitching in to maintain our public household, our common life;
from a Marxist or socialist vision, which sees that for every act of consumption there is an act of production and that a calculus that weighs
the moral worth of the consumption of goods must take into account
the human dignity of the work that went into their production; and from
aesthetic elitism, which, without making beauty a class privilege or
craftsmanship a religious cult, honors both utilitarian and aesthetic standards of grace and durability, form and function.

Certainly people should live by some set of moral rules for consumption—and, in any event, we do. How much and what we consume can
have moral consequences. Increasing awareness of environmental deterioration and ecological and economic interconnectedness makes this
more apparent than ever before. At the same time, I do not see any
likelihood of establishing a calculus that will enable us to reach agreement about whether our own or anyone else's uses of products are justified. Coming to agreement on such matters is more likely to be worked
out in the thick of politics than in any clear-cut philosophical guidelines.

Notes

This essay grew out of a lecture prepared for a conference on "Selling the
Goods: Origins of American Advertising, 1840–1940" at the Strong Museum,
Rochester, New York, in 1990. Revised versions of the lecture were published
in *The American Prospect* 5 (Spring 1991): 26–35 and as the afterword to the
British edition of my *Advertising, the Uneasy Persuasion* (London: Routledge,
1992). The present essay draws on those publications but is substantially revised.

1. Frances X. Clines, "Moscow McDonald's Opens: Milkshakes and
Human Kindness," *New York Times*, 1 February 1990, 13; and Michael Dobbs,
Washington Post, 1 February 1990, A1.

2. Associated Press, *San Diego Union*, 24 September 1989, A24.

3. Henry Fairlie, "Why I Love America," *New Republic*, 4 July 1983,
12–17.

4. "A Crisis of Confidence," *Weekly Compilation of Presidential Documents* 15 (15 July 1979): 1235–41.

5. From several different public addresses, cited in David Shi, *The Simple
Life: Plain Living and High Thinking in American Culture* (New York: Oxford
University Press, 1985), 233.

6. Mary Douglas and Baron Isherwood, *The World of Goods* (New York:
Basic Books, 1979).

7. Adam Smith, *The Wealth of Nations* (New York: Modern Library, 1937 [1776]), 821.

8. Smith, *The Wealth of Nations*, 822.

9. Karl Marx, *Capital*, vol. 2 (London: Penguin Books, 1978 [1885]), 479.

10. Marx, "Wage-Labour and Capital" in *Karl Marx: Selected Writings*, ed. David McLellan (Oxford: Oxford University Press, 1977), 259.

11. Marx, "Economic and Philosophic Manuscripts of 1844" in *The Marx-Engels Reader*, 2d ed., ed. Robert Tucker (New York: W. W. Norton, 1978), 94–96.

12. I borrow these labels, very loosely, from Shi, *The Simple Life*, and Neil Harris, "The Drama of Consumer Desire" in *Yankee Enterprise,* ed. Otto Mayr and Robert C. Post (Washington, D.C.: Smithsonian Institution Press, 1981), 189–216.

13. Raymond Williams, *Problems in Materialism and Culture: Selected Essays* (London: Verso, 1980), 185.

14. Christopher Lasch, *The Minimal Self: Psychic Survival in Troubled Times* (New York: W. W. Norton, 1984), 193–95.

15. See Lasch, *The Minimal Self*, 28. The key work that dates consumer culture to the eighteenth century is *Birth of a Consumer Society: The Commercialization of Eighteenth-Century England*, ed. Neil McKendrick, John Brewer, and J. H. Plumb (Bloomington: Indiana University Press, 1982).

16. Christopher Lasch, *The True and Only Heaven: Progress and Its Critics* (New York: W. W. Norton, 1991).

17. Christopher Lasch, *The Culture of Narcissism: American Life in an Age of Diminishing Expectations* (New York: W. W. Norton, 1978), 72.

18. For a full discussion, see Michael Schudson, *Advertising, the Uneasy Persuasion: Its Dubious Impact on American Society* (New York: Basic Books, 1984).

19. Stanley Lebergott, *Pursuing Happiness: American Consumers in the Twentieth Century* (Princeton, N.J.: Princeton University Press, 1993), 51.

20. Lasch, *The True and Only Heaven*, 63, 110, 520.

21. Donald Finlay Davis, *Conspicuous Production: Automobiles and Elites in Detroit, 1899–1933* (Philadelphia: Temple University Press, 1988).

22. John B. Rae, *The American Automobile Industry* (Boston: Twayne Publishers, 1984), 62.

23. Alfred P. Sloan, *My Years with General Motors*, ed. John McDonald with Catharine Stevens (Garden City, N.Y.: Doubleday, 1964), 163.

24. Martha M. Hamilton, "It's Not Your Father's Leisure Suit," *Washington Post National Weekly Edition*, 15–21 April 1996, 19.

25. Maura Dolan, "Disposable Articles of Faith," *Los Angeles Times*, 12 March 1991, 1; Reid Lifset and Marian Chertow, "Changing the Waste Makers," *The American Prospect* 3 (Fall 1990): 83–88.

26. Lebergott, *Pursuing Happiness*, 102.

27. Lorna Weatherill, "The Meaning of Consumer Behaviour in Late Seventeenth- and Early Eighteenth-Century England" in *Consumption and the World of Goods*, ed. John Brewer and Roy Porter (London: Routledge, 1993), 207.

28. Stuart Ewen, *Captains of Consciousness: Advertising and the Social Roots of the Consumer Culture* (New York: McGraw-Hill, 1976), 204.

29. H. F. Moorhouse, "American Automobiles and Workers' Dreams," *Sociological Review* 31 (August 1983): 411.

30. Janice A. Radway, *Reading the Romance: Women, Patriarchy and Popular Literature* (Chapel Hill: University of North Carolina Press, 1984).

31. H. F. Moorhouse attributes this view to Ely Chinoy in his classic study of American automobile workers, Moorhouse, "American Automobiles," 405.

32. Moorhouse, "American Automobiles," 407.

33. Shi, *The Simple Life*, 56, 60.

34. T. H. Breen, "Narrative of Commercial Life: Consumption, Ideology, and Community on the Eve of the American Revolution," *William and Mary Quarterly* 3d ser., 50 (1993): 486.

35. Lizabeth Cohen, "Encountering Mass Culture at the Grassroots: The Experience of Chicago Workers in the 1920s" in *Popular Culture and Political Change in Modern America*, ed. Ronald Edsforth and Larry Bennett (Albany: State University of New York Press, 1991), 99.

36. Lizabeth Cohen, *Making a New Deal: Industrial Workers in Chicago, 1919–1939* (Cambridge and New York: Cambridge University Press, 1990), 364–65.

37. Lasch, *The Culture of Narcissism*, 138.

38. Stuart M. Blumin, *The Emergence of the Middle Class: Social Experience in the American City, 1760–1900* (Cambridge and New York: Cambridge University Press, 1989), 140–41.

39. Daniel J. Boorstin, *The Americans: The Democratic Experience* (New York: Random House, 1973), 97.

40. Fred C. Hirsch, *Social Limits to Growth* (Cambridge, Mass.: Harvard University Press, 1976).

41. These issues are developed in comprehensive fashion in the work of Pierre Bourdieu, notably, in *Distinction: A Social Critique of the Judgement of Taste*, trans. Richard Nice (Cambridge, Mass., and London: Harvard University Press, 1984).

42. Daniel Horowitz, *The Morality of Spending: Attitudes toward the Consumer Society in America, 1675–1940* (Baltimore: Johns Hopkins University Press, 1985), xi. For a recent positive assessment of mass consumption, focusing on the resourcefulness of immigrants (Jewish immigrants, in this case) in making use of consumer goods to help themselves assimilate to American society, see Andrew R. Heinze, *Adapting to Abundance: Jewish Immigrants, Mass Consumption, and the Search for American Identity* (New York: Columbia University Press, 1990).

43. Horowitz, *The Morality of Spending*, 169.

44. Michael Walzer, "Only Connect," *New Republic*, 13 August 1990, 34.

45. Albert O. Hirschman, *Shifting Involvements: Private Interest and Public Action* (Princeton, N.J.: Princeton University Press, 1982), 48–50.

46. Shi, *The Simple Life*, 277.

47. Harris, "The Drama of Consumer Desire," 210.

48. Horowitz, *The Morality of Spending*, xii.

15

Consumption As Culture: A Desert Example

Alan Strudler and Eleonora Curlo

Once the southwestern desert was dry and brown (or perhaps light green). Now much of it is wet and deep green. New suburbs sprawl, with names like "Green Valley," "Evergreen," "The Lakes," and "Waterford Falls." In a large southwestern city, dolphins splash about in a 1.5 million gallon pool, endless lines of tract homes sport Bermuda lawns, and trees and bushes transplanted from the soggy and humid East Coast flourish in parks thick with sprinklers and fountains. Something happened. Southwesterners changed their consumption practices. They became consumers of large quantities of water, and used this water to transform their neighborhoods.

In this chapter, we examine the ethics of a consumption choice: the choice to change the color of the desert. In doing so we will avoid questions about the economics of this change. We will not be concerned with the question of whether, by changing the desert, people risk depriving themselves of natural resources that either they or their children will one day need. We stay away from the economic question for two reasons.

First, we doubt the cogency of worries about the consumer threats to the water supply, at least for the short run. Although individual consumers in the desert use more and more water, the sum of their use is tiny compared to commercial agricultural use. If anything threatens the water supply in the desert, it is commercial agriculture. But desert agriculture is declining. By insisting upon the development of elaborate devices for bringing water to the desert, agricultural industry drove up the price of water. As a result farmers can hardly afford to pay for the water they need, and the industry is moving to places where it is cheaper to grow fruit and vegetables. No matter how gluttonous individuals are in their use of water, they cannot soon replace the demand of the expiring agricultural industry. As a consequence, political leaders in Phoenix have recently made public calls for individual consumers of water to use more water. These leaders fear that unless water use in the Phoenix area at least remains stable, federal officials will cut back on the water allocation to Phoenix. Phoenix officials thus suggest that residents who wish to do good for their community should use more, rather than less, water.[1]

Our view on the economic modesty of consumer water use in the desert is at once empirical and speculative, and we know that some will see the facts and politics differently. But we have a second reason, which may prove appealing even to those who disagree with us about the facts and politics, for looking outside the economic consequences of consumer water use. We think it worth examining the ethics of consumption apart from its economic consequences. Many sociologists and anthropologists argue—and we think they are right—that people consume not only because of the practical advantages that consumption may provide but also because of the symbolic or expressive role of consumption acts, including their capacity for making a statement about one's identity or character, one's relationships with other people or with a community, and even one's intentions.[2] If the expressive function of consumption is important and legitimate, then we should understand how we can assess consumption practices by expressive criteria. We hope, then, that by reflecting on the specific case of water consumption practices in the desert, we may see how expressive criteria may enter into assessing a consumption practice.

The distinctive character of expressive concerns is a matter we think best explained in terms of examples developed throughout this essay, but it can be explained in a preliminary way now. Consider how two friends might share wine at a meal. The person closest to the bottle might pour a glass for her dining companion before serving herself. Yet serving one's companion first has efficiency disadvantages: for example, it is a bit cumbersome and hence raises the specter of spills, and it creates risk that one might misinterpret the drinking aims of one's companion (who, we presume, is capable of pouring her own wine). Still it seems plain enough why wine drinkers, from poor peasants in Basque mountain villages to wealthy Georgetown socialites, endure this ritual. Doing so helps make the meal more than a digestive event. It creates expressive possibilities, allowing one to confirm bonds of affection and respect for one's fellow diner. We suggest that consumption practices generally are rooted in an enormous array of expressive intentions and that reflection on these intentions, rather than reflection on the concern to satisfy biological needs or other low-level human needs, provides the best hope for understanding Western consumption practices and dissatisfaction with them.

Because our concern is with understanding expressive approaches to assessing consumption practices, our issue can be understood as prior to the economic issue. The economist asks how we might best achieve our consumption aims. We ask instead how to understand and assess the values that inform these aims. In doing so, we inquire how mass consumption practices affect not our ability to get what we want but rather the sensibilities that shape our judgments about what is worth wanting. We try to make sense of the claim that mass consumption sometimes coarsens individual sensibilities, so that although a person may get more of what he or she wants, he or she is worse off for getting it. We maintain that the questions we ask are at root ethical because they are questions about what is a good way to live.

Toward a Noneconomic Critique

Water consumption rates vary in the desert.[3] People in Phoenix and Las Vegas use two to three times as much water per capita as people in Tucson. In the past this difference was solely a function of personal taste. People in Phoenix and Las Vegas, who were mainly transplanted easterners, decorated their landscape in ways that made them feel as if they were still easterners; people in Tucson, who also included transplanted easterners, showed more of a taste for the desert and were thus happy to live on grounds that did not require much water. More recently, these differences in taste have expressed themselves in government action: local authorities in Tucson have approved relatively harsh landscaping and plumbing regulations and have imposed water billing rates designed to inhibit the gluttonous.

People in Tucson thus chose, both individually and as a community, to use substantially less water than their Phoenix neighbors. Economic implications aside, is there a way to understand their choice? In this essay we assume that Tucsonans did the right thing and Phoenicians the wrong thing so that we can assess how norms of consumption might discriminate between these cases. No doubt this assumption oversimplifies the differences between Tucsonans and Phoenicians. But the use of simplifying assumptions often forms part of fruitful explanatory processes in both philosophy and social science, and we think that it will help us in identifying what is attractive in Tucson consumption practices.

The best known noneconomic critiques of consumption practices derive from John Kenneth Galbraith, who has been scorned by colleagues in economics for moving away from their discipline and into morality and aesthetics. While Galbraith does not address issues of water consumption specifically, he provides a critique of consumption that is general enough in its scope that we should be able to infer its implications for water consumption.

Galbraith argues that many of the consumption choices that people make are flawed by what he calls the *dependence effect*. Indeed, by appeal to the dependence effect, Galbraith hopes to discredit the neoclassical position in economics that advocates social deference to the consumption choices individuals make in the market. While, Galbraith suggests, many economists seem to think that economics must take consumer preferences as given, so they might examine the efficiency of competing paths to the satisfaction of these preferences, Galbraith hopes to show that some preferences, including those vitiated by the dependence effect, are problematic in ways that may make their satisfaction not worthwhile.

Galbraith's target—the idea that consumer preferences, particularly those of competent adults, must be viewed as given—seems important not only in contemporary economics, but also in the leading work in consumer psychology. Hence in *The Adaptive Decision Maker*, John Payne and his colleagues devote several hundred pages to canvassing the different ways that consumer choice and consumer judgment can go wrong; but all the mistakes in their encyclopedia are calculation errors owing to the human need to simplify problems and adopt other cognitive shortcuts so that humans might more efficiently use scarce "decision-making resources."[4] If Galbraith is correct, then consumers commonly err in choosing their goals even when they are not misled by cognitive shortcuts. Galbraith's idea, that basic preferences (what might also be called preferences about "final ends") may be rationally criticized, while hardly popular in the social sciences, is not new. Indeed, it was prominent in John Dewey's theory of practical reasoning, and it may plausibly be attributed to all Kantian theorists holding that reason is practical.[5]

Galbraith's distinctive twist on the idea of rationally criticizing consumption preferences invokes the dependence effect, which he characterizes as follows:

> As a society becomes increasingly affluent, wants are increasingly created by the process by which they are satisfied. This may operate passively. Increases in consumption, the counterpart of increases in production, act by suggestion or emulation to create wants. Expectation rises with attainment. Or producers may proceed actively to create wants through advertis-

ing and salesmanship. Wants thus come to depend on output. In technical terms, it can no longer be assumed that welfare is greater at an all-round higher level of production than at a lower one. It may be the same. The higher level of production has, merely, a higher level of want creation necessitating a higher level of want satisfaction. There will be frequent occasion to refer to the way wants depend on the process by which they are satisfied. It will be convenient to call it the Dependence Effect.[6]

Suggestive as these remarks may be, it strikes us as still unclear what constitutes the dependence effect and what is so bad about it.

To make a stab at understanding what Galbraith might intend, consider the want for laundry detergent, one of his favorite examples. Suppose that two detergents, Glory and G, clean clothes equally well, but that Glory is heavily advertised, and hence prestigious and expensive, while G is a drab and cheap generic. Galbraith's argument requires that our want for Glory instead of G depends invidiously on the commercial processes that produce Glory and therefore that no particular value attaches to satisfying the want for Glory rather than G.

The operation of the dependence effect in wants for detergent, which involves the productive process "actively" creating wants through advertising or salesmanship, seems a bit easier to make out than the operation of the dependence effect in the wants of desert-dwellers for abundant water, if only because of our familiarity with the phenomena of advertising and sales pitches: we know what it would be like to see an ad for Glory or for a door-to-door salesman to urge Glory upon us. The passive production of wants, as Galbraith presents it, is comparatively obscure. It proceeds by "suggestion or emulation." Applying this to our Phoenicians, we suppose Galbraith might say that our commercially sustained television culture promulgates an ideal of homes behind white picket fences and green, well-manicured lawns, and that this ideal generates water wants that are no more worth satisfying than Glory wants. We buy lawns, as we buy Glory, in hopes of coming closer to an ideal of the good life passively imposed upon us by the commercial system; the realization of this ideal makes us no better off but costs much to pursue.

Galbraith's attack on the passive production of wants contains an obvious omission. It does not explain why we should doubt the value of satisfying those wants stimulated by or created by the commercial system. It does not explain how the dependence effect taints consumer preferences. Galbraith's critics suggest some possibilities that, as one might expect from offers of help coming from such sources, do not work. Nevertheless we think that insight may be gained by reflecting on the critical arguments on understanding dependence. The first, championed by F. A. von Hayek in his attack on Galbraith, sees dependence as nothing more than causation.[7] The second, urged by Robert Arrington, identifies dependence as a particular kind of causal relation, namely, a causal relation involving wrongful manipulation.[8]

Consider the simple causation interpretation of the dependence effect. According to it, a consumer's wants may have their causal locus either within the character of the consumer himself (they may originate in the personality of the consumer), or else outside the consumer, for example, in the consumption process. To the extent that wants do not originate in the personality of the consumer, they are not the consumer's wants, and satisfying them cannot be presumed to do the consumer any good.

As Hayek observes, the problem with the dependence argument, at least on his causal interpretation, is that virtually all of a specific person's wants originate outside his personality. A person's want for music, art, or a particular variety of food, for example, will have a source in his education. Indeed, the particular content of our desires generally depends on cultural and other environmental influences. If the mere occurrence of this kind of causal influence is enough to warrant the stigma of the dependence effect, then at most a tiny minority of our desires—the most instinctual or atavistic—are worth satisfying. Plainly this cannot be the result that Galbraith is after in proposing the dependence effect.

For Galbraith's account to be plausible, we might narrow it so that it counts among wants blemished by the dependence effect not all wants that show some external causal influence but, instead, those wants that show causal influence that is somehow morally problematic. The dependence effect would then consist not simply in commercial processes causally *influencing* a person's wants but in these processes *manipulating* a person's wants.

On this interpretation of the dependence effect, Galbraith's position still fares poorly, however, because manipulation is a charge difficult to make stick. One person manipulates another when he gets him to do something by preying on an emotional weakness, such as fear, or by knowingly getting the person to choose on the basis of false information. For example, a salesman who gets you to buy a special vacuum cleaner by telling you that it will save your children from some environmentally induced cancer may manipulate you both by preying on your emotions and by getting you to act on false information. The root idea seems to be that when you are manipulated, you do not act autonomously; you act on wants that have been cultivated (in a strong sense of that term) by someone else—wants that you would disown if you had your wits about you. Indeed, when a person's action results from manipulation, it provides grounds to excuse him for what he does, by at least mitigating the responsibility that we ascribe to him. It seems doubtful that many consumer choices are marred by this kind of compromise of autonomy. The advertising process and the more subtle forms of commercial persuasion that Galbraith calls "emulation and suggestion" are often rather straightforward appeals to a person's vanity. In these cases, we think a person remains in control: he knows what he is doing; he is no marionette; it is implausible that he is not responsible for his purchase because he was incited by an advertisement. Indeed, if the mere appeal to vanity counts as manipulation, then telling someone that he should buy a pair of pants because he might appear more attractive in them is manipulation, which is absurd.

One other possibility is to find some adverse moral relation weaker than manipulation that characterizes the causal relation linking commercial processes and wants. We suggest, against Galbraith's critics, that he is correct in identifying an invidious dependence effect. We maintain that its invidious character does not lie simply in its causing people to have wants not rooted in their biology but, instead, in its causing people to consume goods with impoverished symbolic significance. An obvious corollary of our view is that not all preferences that seem tainted under Galbraith's original characterization of the dependence effect are in fact tainted.

The Expressive Function of Consumption

Sometimes the production process affects how one thinks about one's wants but there seems to be no illicit dependence effect. There are at least two cases in which the commercial process may causally but innocently affect deliberation about and formation of wants. In both cases, the dependence effect seems benign. The first case is Hayek's; it occurs when the commercial processes help inform and educate. The other case is more difficult. In this case, the commercial process does something other than inform or educate: it helps constitute the value of the object of our wants.

Consider fashion. Fashionable clothing is valuable (at least in the lives of some people), we think, but the existence of advertising, an aspect of the commercial process, is the background condition that makes much fashion possible. It is a cliché but nonetheless true that people make statements with their clothing. Some of these statements are very familiar. A motorcycle jacket, Levis, and a torn T-shirt express that a person conceives of himself as a rebel; a dark blue suit expresses that a person is conservative; and bell-bottoms combined with a tie-dyed shirt once expressed that one was a dope-smoking free spirit but now may express that one is nostalgic or burned-out. It is no doubt useful to have clothes available as devices to express character; explaining your character takes a lot more effort than putting on a suit. But more than convenience is gained by the expressive value of clothes. For many people, clothes also serve to exercise aesthetic sensibilities.

Consider bell-bottom pants. They became stylish again a few years back. We believe that their wearers wanted them in part as a consequence of the commercial process that has nothing to do with education or information but that value derived from wearing these pants may nonetheless be real and untainted.

Bell-bottoms were first popular during the hippie era. The bells on these pants served no useful purpose and thus marked the person who wore them as liberated from the austere and puritanical conventions of his parents. Bell-bottoms, along with tie-dyed shirts and polka-dot scarves, did not express militant, hostile, or even violent rebellion—as might the combination of leather motorcycle jackets, Levis, and T-shirts—but instead it expressed rebellion against violence; it expressed the idea that freeing the happy side of ourselves was good.

Bell-bottoms are no longer hippie garb. When people wear them now, it is with a less ethereal vision. Indeed, the frivolous element of bell-bottoms, while still a symbol of a lack of seriousness, may be combined with other items of clothing that have a techno-industrial look in order to articulate how important it is for us as busy people to cultivate a schizoid life in which one can, for example, shift quickly from entering data into our computers to getting a dose of pleasure at the local fast-food "gourmet" shop; bell-bottoms now confirm the compartmentalization of pleasure.

The present meaning of bell-bottoms is made possible by the fact that bell-bottoms had a meaning fixed in the sixties. Choosing clothes today provides an occasion for elaborating on this system of meaning. If it were not for the production system promoting images and producing clothes, we might have a thinner stock of expressive tools. By picking and choosing among these devices and elaborating on the themes thereby evoked in their own idiosyncratic ways, people make themselves into aesthetic objects, fashion themselves, launch their own more or less intelligent fantasies. Consumption items thus acquire their significance by virtue of their history. To consume an item may thus be to express one's connection to its past. The commercial process sometimes fosters this connection and sometimes, as we suggest, makes the connection difficult.

The expressive use of commodities is not restricted to clothing. It also occurs with most of the other goods we buy. People buy cars because they want to identify with an image of power (Mustang), rationality (Honda), responsibility (Taurus and Volvo), sophistication (BMW), fun (Camaro), wealth (Mercedes), or machismo (pickup truck). Styles of household furniture and computers may also be valuable for the images they convey. Again, we do not propose here to defend buying any of these particular commodities because of their expressive value, or to assert that their expressive value is less crude than that contained in the personalized license plate that reads "I'M TOUGH." Instead, we claim: first, that the expressive function of goods is often important for understanding their appeal; second, that this expressive function is partly determined by the commercial process, which helps fix the images that we associate with goods; and third, that the expressive function of a good is ordinarily tied to its history.

Michael Schudson confirms the importance of the expressive value of goods. In his account of a famous passage from Alexander Solzhenitsyn's *One Day in the Life of Ivan Denisovich*, Schudson explains the importance of expressive activity in consumption when even more basic biological needs make themselves strongly felt.

> Prisoners in the Soviet labor camp are fed only a thin gruel with some fish heads and tails thrown in. Ivan Denisovich, weak from malnutrition and overwork, nevertheless organizes his own ritual for eating. He takes off his cap before he eats. He refuses to eat fish eyes. This description is among the most moving and poignant in the novel. And why? Because here, in a society intending to animalize prisoners, Ivan continues to eat [ritualized] meals as he consumes food and so retains, literally, his humanity.[9]

Schudson thus suggests that a "human being, to be human, must show that he or she is not just an animal or brute, not just biological, and must in some manner make that nonanimal nature visible."[10] As Schudson sees it, symbolic activities, including the use of a wide variety of goods whose meanings are fixed for us culturally, are a vehicle for making our "nonanimal nature" visible.

Suppose, now, that the expressive function of goods is often important for understanding their value for us. That value is fixed, it seems plain, not only by the intrinsic nature of these goods but also by facts about how the goods exist in our minds or how we conceive of them. Moreover, how we conceive of these goods is determined culturally by the role of these goods in the lives of other people and by their images in art (at least popular film), television, and advertising. Honda, because of its historical role in bringing engineering innovation to the automobile industry, has the image of making a well-engineered car. Suppose that this image has been legitimately earned but that, as Lee Iacocca maintains, Honda is now losing its edge. One might still choose to buy a Honda to express one's commitment to engineering; Hondas, because of their history, may symbolize good engineering even if they are no longer especially well-engineered.

In the case of Honda as we have presented it, one wants the car, at least in part, because of its image, because of what it would symbolize to have it, and not simply because of the car's functional merits. Similarly, for our bell-bottoms wearer, it is in part the image of the pants that constitutes their value. Images, of course, are encouraged and developed by the commercial process through advertising and other marketing activities. Images constitute the symbolic meaning of goods or establish a convention whereby a good has a particular meaning. Precisely because trade in images seems to be such an important human activity, we should be reluctant to dismiss it. In any event, it seems that wants caused by the production process in its capacity as sustainer and producer of images need not thereby be tainted by anything like a dependence effect.

Culture and Consumption

Jean Baudrillard argues, against Galbraith, that, instead of regarding the consumption process as undermining the value in consumer choice, one should regard the process as an ally: by helping to establish symbolic meaning in goods, the process enables the consumer to make choices that have value otherwise unavailable to him or her.[11]

Baudrillard's attack on Galbraith brings out a possible oversimplification in Galbraith's conception of consumption choice. The picture coming from Galbraith, at least as we have been interpreting him, is that either a consumption choice originates entirely within a person, as a matter of his biology, and is thereby legitimate, or it is imposed from without and is thereby illegitimate. This dichotomy seems obviously false. Consumer choice possesses a cultural dimension. The character of a consumer's desires for food, clothing, recreation, and shelter are often realized in culturally specific and commercially driven expressions of taste. A consumer's biological constitution may contribute to his choices on these matters but cannot wholly explain them.

Can commercial processes affect consumer choice in a way that undermines the value of that choice? The symbolic significance of goods suggests one possibility. When a good derives at least part of its value symbolically, acquiring the good enables a person to make a statement about his own character, situation, identity, and relationships with others. This raises the possibility that the good may vary in its capacity or appropriateness as an expressive device and that commercial processes may contribute to the variance. Indeed, it raises the possibility that a good may be impoverished in meaning in a way that makes its use stand as an obstacle against a person's using the object to mean something about his life. We suggest that one should search for invidious aspects of the dependence effect in the possibility that the commercial process habituates a person to consuming goods with impoverished expressive value. For simplicity, it may be useful to now take a stand on the dependence effect. We say that the dependence effect obtains when advertising or other commercial processes causally contribute to the formation of consumer preferences but that the effect need not be bad unless it occurs in such a way as to habituate a person to consuming goods with impoverished expressive significance. The idea of impoverished expressive significance remains to be explained.

We suppose that just as there are many ways in which a good may have expressive value for a person there are also many ways in which the expressive function may succeed or fail. As an illustration, return to the case of a water consumption choice in the desert. Consider the differences one might find in the symbolic significance connected with the objects of these wants. We maintain that important differences lie in the historical richness of the things people want. One want—the Tucsonan's want—allows a person to place himself within the distinctive context of local history, as a person identified within the historically defined local community. The Phoenician's want, on the other hand, is ahistorical and generic, placing him outside local history.[12] It commits him to a landscape ideal that lacks connection to any particular place. The Phoenician's choice thus seems to mark him as placeless.

Let us continue to indulge ourselves in the assumption that Tucsonans have simply made a better consumption choice than Phoenicians have. How does the idea of the expressive significance of consumption acts explain that distinction? The Tucson consumption choice, one might say, is an elaboration of desert themes, going some way toward signifying the dignity and complexity of membership in the local geographical community. The Phoenix choice, on our interpretation, seems oblivious to the possibility of making a statement that forms part of a coherent desert story. By embracing a landscape that lacks connection to the cultural history of the land in which she lives, a person separates herself from the past that surrounds her. In the absence of a relation of continuity with the past, a person's moral character ordinarily loses something.

So far we have been trying to understand the moral difference between the choices of the Tucsonan and the Phoenician in cultural terms or, more specifically, in terms of how these choices can be regarded as more or less thoughtful elaborations of themes rooted in local cultural geography. In these terms, we have suggested, Tucsonans may come out ahead. Before considering more carefully the plausibility of the claim of an advantage for Tucsonans, it may be useful to state more plainly the basis of our evaluative claims. Consumption choices, we maintain, often have expressive implications. They may enrich one's expressive life or they may leave one expressively impoverished. We suppose that when a consumption choice ranges over goods whose value includes a substantial expressive component, it counts in favor of the choice that making it leaves a person with a comparatively rich and full set of culturally fixed meanings that might be expressed in consumption acts. The past is an obviously important source of cultural significance or meaning. It follows that, other things being equal, there is good reason to engage in consumption practices that safeguard one's link to the past, and it counts in favor of the Tucsonan's landscaping choice that it preserves this link.

One might think it rash to declare, on the basis of the kinds of expressive considerations so far adduced, the triumph of the Tucsonans. One might object, for example, that we underestimate the expressive power of the Phoenician landscape choice. Thus one might argue that the Phoenician choice, contrary to our claims, retains the possibility of strong expressive connection with local geography. Or one might argue that the Phoenician choice retains the possibility of other adequate expressive connections. These arguments are worth attention.

Desert tradition contains many themes besides peaceful community. Humans and animals have a history of plunder and destruction in the desert, and one might say that by engorging themselves with water, Phoenicians show distinctive fidelity to this entrenched set of desert themes. In trying to make sense of the contention that there is something better about the Tucsonan's choice, then, it may seem overly simple to appeal to historical continuity. For one thing, history—even history of local geography—seems far too heterogeneous to permit simple inferences about the constraints that local geography imposes. The history of the desert contains ancient oases, cactus forests, parched ground, cemeteries, garbage dumps, and groves of imported olive trees. Since all of these form part of history, it is hard to say why any one of them gets privileged status as a prerequisite for historical continuity. Further, even if one could somehow establish the centrality of some particular theme, it is not clear why it must get deference. Why care more about continuity with spartan desert themes than with themes of oases or garbage dumps?

The problem of the heterogeneity of the past is illustrated by the fact that the idea of cool green lawns is not the invention of Phoenicians but is itself historically rooted. Scholars trace the idea of the lawn to various origins including the Tudor bowling alley, the village green, and the British adaptation of French formal gardens. Kenneth Jackson, a historian of the American suburb, suggests that in early American history, the lawn represented a refuge from the terror and anarchy of nature, and that after the development of large cities, the lawn served as a "verdant moat separating the household from the threats and temptations of the city." Jackson explains that settlers regarded the "wilderness as the dark and terrifying home of Satan's missions."[13] The "verdant moat" of Phoenicians might be viewed as the American version of a desert oasis.

To the extent that any of these ideas of the past animate Phoenician choices about watering their lawns, we suppose they would have to be subjected to a different variety of criticism than that they are simply ahistorical: Phoenicians still would be cultivating some version of the past by cultivating their lawns. But whether Phoenicians are in fact cultivating the past cannot be determined simply by considering what is in their front yards. One must also consider what is in their minds. We doubt that Phoenicians really fancy themselves as plunderers or moat makers. Their desire for cool green lawns, on our assumptions, arose not from sadistic urges, postmodern aesthetic anarchy, or the desire for isolation from swarming wilderness or its urban counterpart but from fixation on images that lack a connection with the local geographical history that forms the context in which the choice is made. It follows that Phoenicians do not self-consciously develop a theme of plundering or anything similarly ambitious, even if they are plundering. This suggests some reason to doubt the expressive power in the Phoenician's choice. An expressive choice is an intentional act. To the extent that one is unaware of the symbolic significance of the choice, its symbolic significance is diminished. Because the Phoenician landscape choice, as we depict it, does not consciously confront the geographical culture that constitutes its context, the choice seems expressively empty. In short, we cannot credit Phoenicians with the culture of plundering because they do not conceive of themselves as plunderers.

Continuity with the past isn't everything. Some breaks with the past may be viewed as valuable. Plainly rebellious acts, deliberate rejection of the stale or repugnant, are more worthwhile than the embrace of obsolete tradition. We do not wish to insist on the invariant supremacy of a norm of historical fidelity. Creative rebels deserve respect. One might even conceive of Phoenicians as rebels against desert themes. One might then suppose that their break with local history should be viewed not as loss but as gain. But we think that this supposition would be a mistake, which we think can be seen by contrasting the Phoenician landscape choice with our earlier reconstructed hippie choice for bell-bottoms. The hippie choice and the Phoenician choice both mark a break with the elements of the past: hippies broke with the traditional military image associated with bell-bottom pants and Phoenicians broke with the southern Arizona image of landscape. But the hippie rejection aimed, however successfully, at open rebellion against the rigidity of military ideals, and the traditional meaning of bell-bottoms could be used as a means toward attaining this aim. Phoenicians, as we see it, simply ignore the significance of their landscape; they neither consciously reject this landscape nor comment on it ironically, sarcastically, or otherwise. Unlike the hippies, Phoenicians fail to confront the meanings that lurk around them and instead embrace a landscape ideal drawn from memory and commercial images of the generic suburban home. Ignoring something differs from rebelling against it and lacks the expressive potential of rebellion. Earlier we said that it counts in favor of a choice if it enhances one's expressive vocabulary. It is a corollary of this notion that such choices must be consciously reflective; because a vocabulary is valuable to a person only if it is available to her, and vocabulary can be available only if one is conscious of it, the availability of a vocabulary requires appreciation of its history and complexity. Hence, even though a postmodern cultural rebel might choose the very same lawn as our typical Phoenician, his reasons would differ, and so the value of the choice, too, would differ.

If, as we suggest, the Phoenician consumption choice limits the cultural connection to local desert geography, one might think that it doesn't matter. What the Phoenicians really treasure, it may seem, is their tie to the eastern landscape. It may also seem that the choice for smooth green lawns increases the Phoenician's prospects for success on this front. We view a Phoenician choice that favors a tie to the landscapes of the East as on par with the choice of an immigrant not to learn the language of his new country. Both leave a person without the cultural resources to engage and appreciate the good that one confronts in ordinary day-to-day experience. A person who does not learn the language of his new land is limited in his ability to appreciate what goes on there and is limited in the extent to which he can belong there. He alienates himself from the people that might have formed his community. In a small way, one who plops down a lush green lawn on desert ground also inhibits his appreciation of a community—a community with nature and not simply a community with humans. We regard that as a loss to avoid.

As we said at the beginning of this essay, our picture of Phoenicians is oversimplified. No doubt it would be denied by the Phoenix Chamber of Commerce. We paint the picture as we do on the basis of various pieces of evidence: our own visits to the city, discussions with residents and academics from Phoenix, and newspaper accounts of landscape practices and rationales. Nevertheless, our picture purports to be about something empirical, and hence might be wildly false: perhaps, for example, the landscape of Phoenicians corresponds to an ingenious and subtle aesthetic sensibility that we are just too dull to appreciate. If our picture of Phoenicians is wildly false, we owe the people of Phoenix an apology; but the point of our essay remains. The example of Phoenix lawns is intended to typify the use of consumption symbols whose meaning has gone flat. If this is not a problem in the Phoenix landscape, it is nonetheless a potential problem in some places and, we hope, an illuminating contrast with the Tucsonan choice.

We do not mean to suggest that the choice of Phoenicians, even according to the simplification that we construct, is wholly devoid of symbolic value. To the contrary, as Michael Schudson urges, humans seem almost compulsively to inhabit a symbolic world. Hence no matter what we consume, we will engage in symbolic acts. Even in the most wretched of conditions, even if you force people to live inside a garbage dump, they will talk, classify, and argue about the things they see.[14] One should, therefore, not be much encouraged by the fact that contemporary mass culture, including the culture of lawn care, engages the attention and interest of so many people. It is the integrity of this culture, and not individual enthusiasm for it, that is open to question. Our concern so far has been to show how that culture might undermine one kind of value in consumer choice. We suggest that this process of undermining value distinguishes the malignant instances of Galbraith's dependence effect. Such loss of value matters, but it is not all that matters. Indeed, for all we know, the civic leaders of Phoenix may be correct in asserting that increasing their use of water through lush gardening is an effective way for Phoenicians to secure economic and political advantages for their community.

The initial case of the dependence effect that we discussed concerned Galbraith's example of laundry detergent. It presented the possibility that people would pay much more for one brand of detergent than for another simply because the first was seductively presented in advertising. If it really seems plausible that people are somehow tricked by advertising and related processes into getting a raw deal, then we should think that users of laundry detergent suffer a fate similar to that which we attribute to Phoenicians. People consume with expressive aims, whether it is to demonstrate their membership in a glamorous community through the use of Glory detergent or to convey eastern (or generically American) landscape ideals through the use of alien landscaping practice in the desert. Even though these expressive acts can be made to appear apt through promotion in advertising and other devices of mass culture, sometimes this appearance is illusion and the expressive acts are flat or even empty. In that case, we see an invidious version of what Galbraith calls the dependence effect.

Implications

Understanding the norms of consumer choice in terms of their symbolic or cultural significance raises several issues of public policy. We may look at policy options in terms of their cultural consequences and not simply their economic consequences. The fact that limiting home use of water in the desert will encourage people to develop local vegetation and landscape provides a policy reason for limiting water use, and this reason operates independently from economic concerns regarding the allocation of scarce resources. We mean to suggest not that economic consequences do not matter but that one cannot understand what matters, even at an individual level where no issues of distributive justice are at stake, simply in terms of economic consequences.

The idea that symbolic issues matter in the realm of consumer choice has policy implications outside of water use. Consider food. European nations have long protected traditional foods with laws, regulations, and tariffs. Germans have enacted purity standards to limit what can be sold as beer in their country; Italians have placed limits on what can be sold as pasta; and the French similarly impose restrictions on cheese, wine, and bread. While skeptics may dismiss these actions as attempts to protect local producers from foreign competition, we may instead plausibly regard many of them as attempts to enhance the prospects that individual consumers will make choices for goods whose cultural significance depends on preserving their locally idiosyncratic character. It is, we think, a common mistake to regard European concerns about defending its food culture against Americanization as somehow elitist. One may imagine a snob in an expensive Parisian restaurant looking down his nose at people who eat at McDonald's and resent the snob for denying the common people of France who cannot afford haute cuisine a chance at an evening out. But this image of European snobbery is an American conceit. There are millions of lower-income people and a huge number of very poor peasants in Western Europe who could not tolerate, even if they could afford, the food, beer, or wine that rich Americans consume as daily fare. The attempt to defend the richness of life of these modest people does not seem aptly characterized as elitism or snobbery. Now perhaps if the European market were made wide open to competition from industrialized American agriculture bolstered through the right advertising campaigns, even the poor peasants would succumb to the convenience of American fast food and cheap agriculture. It does not follow, however, that these people would be better off.

The etymology of the word "consumption" suggests the idea of destruction; to consume something is to destroy it. If, as we have suggested, the ethics of consumer choice in this area must be understood in symbolic and cultural terms, then wise consumption choices involve a departure from this etymology. To consume is to keep alive the past from which we construct our present selves. This places us in the role of stewards rather than destroyers. Notice that we are not making the circular suggestion that consumers should be stewards of the past simply because we as consumers have an independent obligation to be good stewards. Instead, we are suggesting that because worthwhile consumption requires the existence of a vital past upon which people can draw, our consumption practices can flourish only if we act as good stewards, preserving that past.

In their recent book, *Redesigning the American Lawn*, F. Herbert Bormann, Diana Balmori, and Gordon T. Geballe report on a growing movement in the United States and Canada in which people are replacing their lawns with indigenous vegetation.[15] The result is that people waste less water and introduce fewer harmful chemicals into the environment. People who adopt the role of steward of a cultural tradition, we suggest, have reason to preserve our cultural resources, including nature, in ways that work to the common advantage.

Notes

1. Interview with Professor Heather Campbell, School of Public Affairs, Arizona State University, 21 March 1996.

2. For a review of this literature, see Colin Campbell, "Consumption: The New Wave of Research in the Humanities and Social Sciences," *Journal of Social Behavior and Personality* 6 (1991): 57–74; see also Grant McCracken, *Culture and Consumption: New Approaches to the Symbolic Character of Consumer Goods and Activities* (Bloomington: Indiana University Press, 1988). Perhaps the finest statement of the anthropological view occurs in Mary Douglas and Baron Isherwood, *The World of Goods* (New York: Basic Books, 1979).

3. Curt Suplee, "The Lawning of America: A Brief History of Our Peculiar Mania for Grass," *Washington Post Magazine*, 30 April 1989, 16–24.

4. John Payne, James Bettman, and Eric Johnson, *The Adaptive Decision Maker* (New York: Cambridge University Press, 1993).

5. For a good discussion of Dewey's approach to practical rationality, see Henry Richardson, *Practical Reasoning about Final Ends* (New York: Cambridge University Press, 1994); for a Kantian approach, see Christine Kors-

gaard, "The Sources of Normativity," in *The Tanner Lectures on Human Values*, vol. 15, ed. Grethe B. Peterson (Salt Lake City: University of Utah Press, 1994).

6. John Kenneth Galbraith, *The Affluent Society*, 4th ed. (Boston: Houghton Mifflin Company, 1984), 126.

7. F. A. von Hayek, "The Non Sequitur of the 'Dependence Effect,' " *Southern Economic Journal* (April 1961).

8. Robert L. Arrington, "Advertising and Behavior Control," *Journal of Business Ethics* 1 (February 1982): 3–12.

9. Michael Schudson, *Advertising, The Uneasy Persuasion* (New York: Basic Books, 1984), 132.

10. Schudson, *Advertising*, 133.

11. Jean Baudrillard, *Selected Writings*, ed. Mark Poster (Stanford: Stanford University Press, 1988), 37–43.

12. We recognize that neither all Phoenicians nor all Tucsonans are the same: there are dissenting and dominant voices in each community. And we also recognize the difficulty of drawing inferences from any individual consumption choice. Our concern is with the dominant community choice.

13. Kenneth Jackson, *Crabgrass Frontier* (New York: Oxford University Press, 1985).

14. Victor Perera; photographs by Daniel Chauche, *Unfinished Conquest: The Guatemalan Tragedy* (Berkeley: University of California Press, 1993), chap. 1.

15. F. Herbert Bormann, Diana Balmori, and Gordon T. Geballe, *Redesigning the American Lawn* (New Haven: Yale University Press, 1993).

16

The Living Standard

Amartya Sen

In an illuminating analysis of "the scope and status of welfare economics," Sir John R. Hicks makes the apparently puzzling remark: *"The Economics of Welfare* is *The Wealth of Nations* in a new guise."[1] In explaining the connection between A.C. Pigou and Adam Smith, Hicks shows that Pigou was "taking over" much of "the *classical* theory of production and distribution" and "turning" it into "the economics of welfare."

There is, in fact, a remarkable similarity even in the motivations behind Smith's and Pigou's works and their respective views of the nature of political economy and economics. Adam Smith starts his inquiry (in the *Wealth of Nations*) by referring to what will determine whether "the nation will be better or worse supplied with all the necessaries and conveniences for which it has occasion."[2] Pigou begins by arguing that "the social enthusiasm which revolts from the sordidness of mean streets and joylessness of withered lives" is, in fact "the beginning of economic science."[3] The central place given to the determination of the standard of living is a part of their common view of the nature of the subject.

Editors' note: This essay is excerpted from the Hicks Lecture delivered by Amartya Sen at Oxford University in 1982 and published as "The Living Standard," *Oxford Economic Papers* 36 (1984): 74–79, 84–88. To this essay, the editors have added postscripts from two of Sen's later essays. The 1987 postscript is excerpted from *The Standard of Living,* 1985 Tanner Lectures at Cambridge, with contributions by Keith Hart, Ravi Kanbur, John Muellbauer, and Bernard Williams, ed. Geoffrey Hawthorn (Cambridge, U.K.: Cambridge University Press, 1987), 17–19, 26–29, 36–38. The 1993 postscript is excerpted from "Capability and Well-Being," in *The Quality of Life,* ed. Martha C. Nussbaum and Amartya Sen (Oxford: Clarendon Press, 1993), 46–49.

This essay is concerned with investigating the *concept* of the living standard. The topic falls within "welfare economics" in a broad sense, but it is a somewhat specialized problem within that subject. In fact, in recent years, there has been a tendency for attention to move a little away from this specialized problem because of greater concern with the analysis of overall social welfare, systematized in the notions of "social welfare functions."[4] But the original problem of living standard remains interesting and important—and one of much general interest.

I begin by making two preliminary points about the concept of the standard of living. First, insofar as the living standard is a notion of welfare, it belongs to one aspect of welfare, not unconnected with what Pigou called "economic welfare." Pigou defined "economic welfare" as "that part of social welfare that can be brought directly or indirectly into relation with the measuring-rod of money."[5] Hicks notes that "the distinctions which . . . [Pigou] draws, on this basis, are unquestionably interesting," but goes on to say, "yet the concept of Economic Welfare, on which Pigou in fact based [the distinctions], or thought he was basing them, has nevertheless been very generally rejected."[6] Hicks has clarified, in "The Scope and Status of Welfare Economics" and elsewhere,[7] the main issues involved—including Pigou's rationale and the critics' reasoning. He does not provide an overall judgment, but in his own economic analysis, Hicks opts for the "decision to treat the Social Product as primary, and to banish 'economic welfare.' "[8]

The distinction between welfare and economic welfare is indeed problematic. But the approach is also, as Hicks says, "unquestionably interesting." The function that the distinction serves in Pigou's analysis can indeed be met in many exercises by the concept of the "social product." Nevertheless, there are other problems—notably those concerned with individual welfare and individual standards of living—in which a distinction closer to Pigou's own (between economic welfare and overall welfare) may well be necessary.

Let me illustrate. I have not seen you for many years—since I was chucked out of school, in fact. I run into you one day in the West End waving at me from your chauffeur-driven Rolls Royce, looking shockingly prosperous and well-heeled. You give me a ride and invite me to visit you at your mansion in Chelsea. I remark that I am pleased to see what a high standard of living you are enjoying. "Not at all," you reply. "My standard of living is very low. I am a very unhappy man." "Why so?" I have to probe. "Because," you reply, "I write poems—damn good ones too—but nobody likes my poems, not even my wife. I am always depressed about this injustice, and also sorry that the world has such deplorable taste. I am miserable and have a very low standard of living." By now I can see no reason to doubt that you are indeed unhappy, but I feel obliged to tell you that you do not know the meaning of "standard of living." So you drop me off at the next Tube station (remarking, "My standard of living high/ What a plebeian lie!" adding to the set of people who do not think much of your poetry).

I think Pigou would very likely be right in maintaining that your "economic welfare" is high even though you are unhappy and quite possibly have a low overall welfare. That would be right not because welfare or utility or happiness can plausibly be split into distinct self-contained parts, of which "economic welfare" happens to be one. Rather, it can be argued that "economic welfare" is an interesting concept of its own, which relates to—but is not necessarily one separable part of—welfare or utility or happiness. A person's material well-being can be a sensible subject of study without our being able to split the sense of overall well-being into several separable bits, of which material well-being is one. A "plural" approach to utility[9] permits the coexistence of various distinct concepts of utility, which are *interdependent*, without one being a separable part of another. While I shall presently argue that living standard is best seen not as a utility concept at all (roughly speaking, it can be said that it deals with material well-being and not with the *sense* of material well-being), it *is* an "economic" concept (roughly speaking, being concerned with *material* well-being). More will be said on this presently.

The second point concerns the motivation underlying studies of standard of living. It can be part of the objectives of policymaking (for example: "we plan to raise the standard of living fastest!"). But that need not be the only motivation. We may be primarily concerned with a cognitive question, such as comparing standard of living between two actual persons, or two actual nations, or the same person or nation at two actual points of time. The use of "counterfactuals," if any, may not, therefore, take the rather straightforward form it tends to take in the usual "virtual displacement" (or marginalist) analysis (such as what *would have* happened if this person had a different bundle of commodities at the *same* point of time, with the *same* utility function?). In making comparisons of actual living standards, there may be no reasonable basis for assuming the same utility function—the same desires, wants, temperament, and so forth.

This distinction concerns the contrast between "comprehensive comparisons" and "situational comparisons."[10] Comparisons of standard of living need not be confined only to situational comparisons (such as "I am better off this year than I would have been if I had last year's commodity bundle this year"). They may call for comprehensive comparisons ("I am better off this year than I was last year"). We cannot, then, just vary the commodity bundles and keep the utility *functions* (and related correspondences) *necessarily* unchanged. If the utility-functional characteristics are indeed unchanged, then this would be a further fact and not just a part of the standard counterfactual exercise.

Alternative Approaches

There are at least three general approaches to the notion of the standard of living of a person. The first is to see the living standard as some notion of the *utility* of a person. The second is some notion of *opulence.* The third is to see the standard of living as one type of *freedom.* The first two approaches have been more explored than the third, although—to put my cards on the table—it is the third that I would argue for in this essay.[11] But I begin with utility and opulence.

The utility view of the standard of living is well presented by Pigou himself. In fact, Pigou uses "economic welfare," "the standard of living," "standard of real income," and "material prosperity" as more or less synonymous.[12] Economic welfare is defined, as was already stated, as "a part of welfare as a whole,"[13] and "the elements of welfare" are seen as "*states of consciousness* and, perhaps, their relations."[14]

It is fair to recognize that the notion of "utility" has, by now, several distinct meanings. Pigou himself distinguishes between "satisfaction" and the "intensity of desire," referring to the latter as "desiredness."[15] As a loyal "consciousness-utilitarian," Pigou does not dispute the claim of satisfaction to be the *authentic* version of utility or welfare, and he defends the desiredness view (and the willingness-to-pay measure) *contingently* by asserting that "it is fair to suppose that most commodities, especially those of wide consumption that are required, as articles of food and clothing are, for direct personal use, will be wanted as a means to satisfaction, and will, consequently, be desired with intensities proportional to the satisfactions they are expected to yield."[16]

It would appear that the more dominant schools of utilitarianism today take a "desire" view of utility rather than the "satisfaction" view and put value on the fulfillment of what is desired rather than on the amount of satisfaction it generates.[17] The battle is by no means over,[18] and there are indeed many complex issues involved.[19] But this need not detain us here, since it is necessary, for our purpose, to discuss *both* the "satisfaction" view and the "desiredness" view of utility and, related to this, to examine the two corresponding views of the standard of living (seen in terms of utility).

The identification of the living standard with *overall* utility as such is obviously open to the problem that was discussed in the last section—the problem that had led Pigou to introduce the notion of "economic welfare" in the first place. If the standard of living has to be seen in terms of utility, then distinctions of Pigou's type would have to be made.

The second approach—that of living standard as *opulence*—goes back at least to Adam Smith. The concern with a nation being "better or worse supplied with all the necessaries and conveniences for which it has occasion"[20] is a concern with the opulence of the nation. Indeed, Adam Smith thought that the two objectives of "political economy, considered as a branch of the science of a statesman or legislator" were "first, to provide a plentiful revenue or subsistence for the people, or more properly to enable them to provide such revenue or subsistence for themselves; and secondly, to supply the state or commonwealth with a revenue sufficient for the public services." "The different progress of opulence in different ages and nations has given occasion to two different systems of political economy with regard to enriching people."[21]

The modern literature on real income indicators and the indexing of commodity bundles[22] is the inheritor of this tradition of evaluating opulence. Since this evaluation is often done with respect to an indifference map, it is tempting to think of this approach as the utility approach in disguise. But there is an important difference even when the evaluation of real income is done in terms of an indifference map representing preference, since what is being evaluated is not utility as such (in the form either of desiredness or of satisfaction), but the *commodity basis of utility*. The two approaches will be congruent only under the special assumption of constancy of the utility *function* (not to be confused with the constancy of tastes). As was discussed in the first section of this essay, this is a bad assumption for measuring the standard of living (even if it is acceptable for rational choice or planning involving counterfactual comparison of alternative possibilities). The distinction will be discussed further in the next section.

The third approach—that of freedom—is not much in fashion in the literature on the standard of living, but I believe it has much promise. Freedom here is interpreted in its "positive" sense (to be free to *do this* or *be that*) rather than in its "negative" form (not to be interfered with).[23] In this approach, what is valued is the *capability* to live well, and in the specific economic context of standard of living, it values the capabilities associated with economic matters.

To illustrate the contrast involved, consider the problem of food and hunger. In the capability approach a person's ability to live without hunger or malnutrition may be valued. This does not amount to valuing the possession of a given amount of food as such, except indirectly through causal links, in a contingent way (since the impact of food on nutrition varies with such factors as metabolic rates, body size, climatic conditions, sex, pregnancy, lactation, and work intensity). Nor does it involve equating the value of the freedom from hunger or from malnutrition with the *utility* (happiness, pleasure, or desire fulfillment) from that achievement. More will have to be said on these contrasts presently, because some complex issues are involved.

I should like to assert that focusing on capability as freedom in the context of judging living standard is not a new approach. Its lineage certainly goes back to classical political economy, even though it may not have been explicitly stated in this form. Freedom was very much a classical concern. In fact, even in the statement about opulence that I quoted from Adam Smith earlier in this section, Smith modifies his reference to providing "a plentiful revenue or subsistence for the people" by the statement, "more properly to enable them to provide such revenue or subsistence for themselves."[24] In a different context (dealing in fact with the value of negative freedom), Hicks has pointed out that the classical backing for "economic freedom" went deeper than justifying it on grounds of "economic efficiency." The efficiency proposition, as Hicks notes, "was no more than a secondary support," and Hicks is certainly right to question the justification for our "forgetting, as completely as most of us have done, the other side of the argument" dealing with the value of economic freedom as such.[25]

When it comes to evaluating what counts as "necessaries," with the supply of which Adam Smith was so concerned, Smith does go explicitly into certain quite complex capabilities, such as the freedom to appear in public without shame:

> A linen shirt, for example, is, strictly speaking, not a necessary of life. The Greeks and Romans lived, I suppose, very comfortably, though they had no linen. But in the present times, through the greater part of Europe, a creditable day-labourer would be ashamed to appear in public without a linen shirt, the want of which would be supposed to denote that disgraceful degree of poverty which, it is presumed, no body can well fall into without extreme bad conduct. Custom, in the same manner, had rendered leather shoes a necessary of life in England. The poorest creditable person of either sex would be ashamed to appear in public without them.[26]

Following Smith's reasoning, I have tried to argue elsewhere[27] that *absolute deprivation* in the space of capabilities (such as whether one can appear in public without shame) may follow from *relative deprivation* in the space of commodities (such as whether one possesses what others do, such as linen shirts or leather shoes in Smith's example). Some of the apparent conflicts in defining poverty (the "relative" versus the "absolute" views) may be avoided by seeing living standards in terms of capabilities and assessing the value of commodity possession in terms of its contribution to capabilities and freedoms.

The possibility of judging advantage in terms of the extent of freedom also has been discussed by Karl Marx[28] and John Stuart Mill.[29] The roots of the capability approach and freedom-based evaluation of the standard of living, thus, go back to Smith, Marx, and Mill, among others. The standard of living—and economic freedom in the "positive" sense—can be seen as relating to "positive freedom" in general in ways that are not altogether dissimilar to the relationship between "economic welfare" and "welfare" in general. The standard of living, on this view, reflects the "material" aspects of freedom.[30]

Functioning, Capability, and Freedom

The distinction between commodities, utility, functioning, and the capability to function, may not be altogether transparent, and it calls for some explanation.[31] Consider a good, such as bread. The utilitarian will be concerned with the fact that bread creates utility—happiness or desire fulfillment—through its consumption. This is, of course, true. But creating utility is not the only thing that bread does. It also contributes to nutrition, among other things. In modern consumer theory in economics, the nature of the goods has been seen in terms of their "characteristics." Gorman, Lancaster, and other economists have systematically explored the view of goods as bundles of characteristics.[32] Bread possesses nutrition-giving characteristics (calories, protein, and so on) but also possesses other characteristics, such as providing stimulation, meeting social conventions, and helping get-togethers.[33] A characteristic—as used in consumer theory—is a feature of a good, whereas a capability is a feature of a person in relation to goods. Having some bread gives me the capability of functioning in particular ways, such as being free from hunger or living without certain nutritional deficiencies.

Four different notions need to be distinguished in this context. There is the notion of a *good* (bread); *characteristic of a good* (calories and other nutrients); that of *functioning of a person* (the person living without calorie deficiency); that of *utility* (the pleasure or desire fulfillment from eating bread or from being well nourished). A utility-based theory of living standards concentrates on the last item of the four—utility. Analyses of living standards in terms of opulence or "real income" tend to concentrate on the first item—commodities. Egalitarians concerned with income distribution worry about the distribution of goods, and they, too, will focus on the first item. These two approaches can be refined by taking explicit note of the second item, the commodities' characteristics.

"Characteristics" are, of course, abstractions from goods, but they do relate ultimately to *goods* rather than to *persons*. "Functionings" are, however, personal features; they tell us what a person is doing or achieving. "Capability" to function reflects what a person *can* do or *can* achieve. Of course, the characteristics of goods owned by a person would *relate* to the capabilities of that person. A person achieves these capabilities through—among other things—the use of these goods. But the capabilities of persons are quite different from (though dependent on) the characteristics of goods possessed. Valuing one has *implications* on wanting the other, but valuing one is *not the same thing* as valuing the other.

If, for example, we value a person's ability to function without nutritional deficiency, we would favor arrangements in which the person has adequate food with those nutritional characteristics, but that is not the same thing as valuing the possession of a given amount of food as such. If, for example, some disease makes the person unable to achieve the capability of avoiding nutritional deficiency even with an amount of the food that would suffice for others,[34] then the fact that he or she does possess that amount of food would not in any way "neutralize" the person's inability to be well nourished. If we value the capability to function, then that is what we do value, and the possession of goods with the corresponding characteristics is only instrumentally valued and that again only to the extent that it helps in the achievement of the things that we do value (namely, capabilities).

Consider now one more example, to explain the motivation behind looking at capabilities for assessing the standard of living. Take two persons, A and B. A is rather less poor than B, eats rather more food, and works no harder. But he is also undernourished, which B is not, since B has a smaller body size (coming from Kerala rather than Punjab, say), has a lower metabolic rate, and lives in a warmer climate. So A eats more but B is better nourished. However, it so happens that A is religious, contented with his fate, and happier than B, and has his desires more fulfilled than has B, who keeps grumbling about his lot. In the way this example has been constructed, A is doing better than B *both* in terms of commodity-index and utility (in fact, under *each* interpretation of utility: satisfaction and desire fulfillment). That is for sure, but does that imply that A has a higher standard of living? Rickety old A, chronically undernourished, riddled with avoidable morbidity, and reconciled—by the "opium" of religion—to a lower expectation of life? It would be hard to claim, under these circumstances, that A does indeed have a higher standard of living than B. He may earn and eat more, and may be less dissatisfied, but he does not have the capability to be well nourished in the way B is, nor is he free from malnutrition-related diseases. Indeed, it would be hard not to say that it is B who has a higher standard of living despite *both* his unhappiness and lower income than A.

The issue of capabilities—specifically "material" capabilities—is particularly important in judging the standard of living of people in poor countries. Are they well nourished? Are they free from avoidable morbidity? Do they live long? Can they read and write? Can they count? And so on. It is also important in dealing with poverty in rich countries (as I have tried to argue elsewhere).[35] Can they take part in the life of the community?[36] Can they appear in public without shame and without feeling disgraced (to return to Adam Smith's question)?[37] Can they find worthwhile jobs? Can they keep themselves warm? Can they use their school education? Can they visit friends and relations if they choose? It is a question of what the persons can do or can be and not just a question of their earnings and opulence nor of their being contented. Freedom is the issue, not commodities, nor utility as such.

It is, however, worth reemphasizing that the thesis here is not that there is no distinction between freedom—even "positive freedom" in general—and the living standard. That would be an absurd claim. It is, rather, that the living standard can be seen as freedom (positive freedom) of particular types, related to material capabilities. It reflects a variety of freedoms of the material kind (such as to be able to live long, to be well nourished, to take part in the life of the community). Some of the others may be very important, but not a part of the normal concept of the standard of living. Indeed, the living standard may be seen as corresponding to positive freedom in general in the way that Pigou's "economic welfare" may be seen as corresponding to welfare as such. It is in this sense that the living standard can be seen as "economic freedom."

It may, of course, be pointed out that the rejection of opulence or utility as the basis of assessing the standard of living does not establish the relevance of freedom as such. There is scope for ambiguity in the arguments presented. We may well value what a person *does* (or actually *achieves*) rather than what he *can do* (or *can achieve*), which is what freedom has to be concerned with. Should we not, for example, look directly at *nourishment* as such rather than the *capability to be nourished*?

There is, I believe, substance in this line of questioning, but it is not as persuasive as it may first appear. What about the wealthy ascetic who decides to fast and becomes undernourished despite being rich and having the means to be excellently nourished? It seems rather odd to see him as deprived, with a low standard of living. He has chosen to fast; he was not forced to fast.

Capability *is* of importance. To take another example, the *capability* to visit friends and relatives may be important for standard of living. However, a person who chooses not to make use of that capability, and curls up instead with a good book, may not be sensibly seen as being deprived and having a low standard of living.

It does seem plausible to concentrate on a person's capabilities and freedoms as indicators of living standard. Variations of tastes can be accommodated more easily in a format that focuses on the capability to function in different ways rather than just on particular functionings. Also, uncertainty about our own future tastes makes us value freedom more. But, on top of that, some importance may be attached to the power a person has over his or her own life—that a person is not forced by circumstances to lead a specific type of life and has a genuine freedom to choose as he wants. The standard of living has much to do with what Marx described as "replacing the domination of circumstances and chance over individuals by the domination of individuals over chance and circumstances."[38]

Difficulties

I am not under any illusion that the capability approach to the standard of living would be very easy to use. It is particularly difficult to get an idea of a person's positive freedom of choice—what he or she could or could not have done or been. What we observe are the actual choices and realizations. But the case for using the capability approach is not, of course, logistic convenience but *relevance*.

In some practical exercises with the capability approach, the logistic problems have not proved to be quite so hard as to make the effort to use existing data worthless. For example, in an exercise on checking the nature and extent of "sex bias" in living standards in India,[39] the approach has proved to be quite convenient. In fact, even the informational problems have been, if anything, eased by moving attention away from food consumption data of *particular members* of the family (almost impossible to get) to observed nutrition, morbidity, mortality, and so forth. Indeed, the move from individual *commodity consumption* to individual *functioning* would often tend to make the data problem easier, even though much harder data requirements would have to be imposed in order to identify *capability sets* fully.

I end by noting three important issues that are particularly difficult to deal with. First, when there is diversity of taste, it becomes harder to surmise about capability by simply observing achievement. For extreme poverty this problem is less serious. Valuing better nourishment, less illness, and longer life tends to be fairly universal; these objectives are also largely consistent with each other, despite being distinct. But in other cases—of greater relevance to the richer countries—the informational problems with the capability approach can be quite serious.

Second, if capabilities of different sorts have to be put together in one index, the issue of aggregation may be quite a difficult one even for a given person. There is, in addition, the problem of group aggregation. I have tried to discuss these issues elsewhere,[40] and the picture is far from hopeless. But I must confess that they are indeed hard problems to tackle, requiring a good deal of compromise. It is, however, worth mentioning that, for many problems, an *aggregate* ranking is not needed, and for most a *complete* aggregate ordering is quite redundant.

Third, freedom is a set (rather than just a "point") in the sense that it refers to various alternative bundles of things one could have done and not just to the particular bundle one did do. This makes the evaluation of "capability sets" rather unlike that of evaluating utility or indexing commodity bundles. Often it will indeed make sense to identify the value of the set of capabilities with the worth of the "best" element in the set, and this reduces the set-evaluation problems to a derived element-evaluation exercise. But in other contexts, the value of the "best" element does not capture the value of freedom adequately. For example, if we remove from the feasibility set all elements other than the best one, the utility level that can be achieved with a given utility function may not be affected, but in a very real sense the persons' freedom *is* reduced. In interpreting standard of living in terms of freedom (related to material capabilities), a different range of complex issues has to be faced that does not quite arise under the utility or the opulence approaches.

Nevertheless, if standard of living is best seen in terms of capabilities (as positive freedoms of particular types), then these complexities simply have to be faced. The standard of living is one of the central notions of economics. And it is one of the subjects that interests the general public, specifically in the context of policy. In directing attention to these questions, economists such as Smith, Pigou, and Hicks have taken on issues that are complex *as well as* of deep and lasting importance.

Even if data limitations may quite often force us to make practical compromises, conceptual clarity requires that we must not elevate such a compromise to a position of unquestioned significance. Hicks has explained his attitude toward welfare economics thus: "I have been trying to show that 'welfare economics,' as I would now regard it, is composed of a series of steps, steps by which we try to take more and more of the things which concern us into account. None of our 'optima' marks the top of that staircase. We must always be prepared to push one, if we can, a little further."[41] It has been argued in this paper that the capability approach to the standard of living will be a step forward—certainly conceptually and perhaps even in actual empirical application.

1987 Postscript

The Relative and the Absolute

I now make a few remarks on international variations in what is taken to be poverty and the use of minimum living standards for the identification of the poor. There has been a lively debate on the relative nature of the standards of poverty and the need to revise upwards the cut-off line as we go up the ladder of general opulence. Some have tried to give this variation a fairly simple and direct form. For example, Peter Townsend has argued: "Lacking an alternative criterion, the best assumption would be to relate sufficiency to the average rise (or fall) in real incomes."[42] Others have seen in such relativity a confounding of poverty and inequality, arguing that poverty would then appear to be pretty much impossible to eliminate. If the poverty line is fixed entirely relatively to the "average" income, there are always some who are relatively poor.[43] Still others have gone on to seek peculiar psychological explanations for the popularity of the relativist view. For example, Dr. Rhodes Boyson, as minister of social security in the United Kingdom, had the following to say in Parliament in 1984: "Those on the poverty line in the United States of America earn more than 50 times the average income of someone in India. That is what relative poverty is all about. . . . Apparently, the more people earn, the more they believe poverty exists, presumably so that they can be pleased about the fact that it is not themselves who are poor."[44]

The mystification involved in this extraordinary speculation can be substantially eliminated if we see the standard of living in terms of functionings and capabilities. Some capabilities, such as being well nourished, may have more or less similar demands on commodities (such as food and health services) irrespective of the average opulence of the community in which the person lives. Other capabilities, such as the ones with which Adam Smith was particularly concerned, have commodity demands that vary a good deal with average opulence. To lead a life without shame, to be able to visit and entertain one's friends, to keep track of what is going on and what others are talking about, and so on, requires a more expensive bundle of goods and services in a society that is generally richer and in which most people have, say, means of transport, affluent clothing, radios or television sets, and so on. Thus, some of the capabilities (relevant for a "minimum" level of living) require more real income and opulence in the form of commodity possession in a richer society than in poorer ones. The same absolute levels of capabilities may thus have a greater relative need for incomes (and commodities). There is, thus, no mystery in the necessity of having a "relativist" view on the space of incomes even when poverty is defined in terms of the same *absolute* levels of basic capabilities. Boyson's far-fetched psychological explanation is completely redundant.

There are, of course, other variations as well in the comparative picture. Sometimes the same goods may cost relatively more, in terms of exchange rates of currencies, in the richer countries than in the poorer ones, as has been well discussed by Dan Usher.[45] Also the level of *capabilities* that are accepted as "minimum" may themselves be upwardly revised as the society becomes richer and more and more people achieve levels of capabilities not previously reached by many.[46] These variations add further to the need for more income in the richer countries to avoid what is seen as poverty in terms of "contemporary standards."

There is no great difficulty in sorting out the different elements in the relativity of the poverty line in the space of incomes (and that of commodities) once the conception of the standard of living is given an adequate formulation in terms of capabilities. A difficult, but central, issue in studying poverty is the concept of the standard of living itself.[47]

Living Standard and Well-Being

I have so far not discussed explicitly the distinction between the concept of well-being and that of the standard of living, and that issue should now be faced before proceeding further. Well-being is the broader and more inclusive of the two related notions. Pigou tried to draw a distinction between "economic welfare" and "total welfare," defining the former as "that part of social welfare that can be brought directly or indirectly into relation with the measuring rod of money."[48] His distinction is ambiguous and rather unhelpful, and it may not serve the purpose for which Pigou devised it. In fact, some of the obviously "noneconomic" aspects of well-being may also, in some sense, "be brought directly or indirectly into relation with the measuring rod of money," for example, through such "vulgar" questions as: How much would you be willing to pay to be loved by your granddaughter? These payments may not actually be made, but nor are some obviously "economic" ones (such as, how much would you pay to eliminate urban air pollution that adds to the cost of keeping your house clean?). The interpretation of the information content of answers to these questions is deeply problematic. Similarly, other payments that happen to be actually made may not be geared to one's own well-being at all, and thus not figure in one's "economic well-being," for example donations made to OXFAM for famine relief possibly without any direct or indirect benefit to oneself. While it is easy to be sympathetic to the reasons that prompted Pigou to make the distinction between "economic welfare" and "total welfare," the nature of that distinction is confusing and its usability quite limited.

One way of amending Pigou's distinction in line with his evident motivation is to separate out "material" functionings and capabilities (such as being well-nourished) from others (such as being wise and contented). I have tried to argue elsewhere[49] [pages 287–98 in this volume] that this may be a good way to proceed, but I am less sure of this now. Being psychologically well-adjusted may not be a "material" functioning, but it is hard to claim that achievement is of no intrinsic importance to one's standard of living. In fact, any achievement that is rooted in the life that one oneself leads (or can lead), rather than arising from other objectives, does have a claim to being directly relevant to one's standard of living. It is possible that this way of drawing the line is a little too permissive, but the alternatives that have been proposed seem clearly too narrow. For example, the "economic test" of whether a deprivation can be eradicated by more affluence is tempting enough, but it is hard to claim that the standard of living of a person dying of an incurable disease (not remediable by affluence) is not directly reduced by that particular predicament. The living standard may, often enough, be influenceable by economic means, but that is more plausibly seen not as the basis of a sound *definition* of the standard of living, but as an important *empirical* statement about the typical relationship between economic means and the living standard.

If the line of distinction proposed here is accepted, then the contrast between a person's well-being and living standard must arise from possible influences on personal well-being coming from sources other than the nature of one's life. For example, one's misery at the sorrow of another certainly does reduce *ceteris paribus* one's well-being, but in itself this is not a reduction in the person's living standard. This contrast has featured in practical discussions for a very long time. For example, in the third century B.C., Emperor Asoka in India noted the distinction clearly enough in one of his "rock edicts" in the context of clarifying the idea of an injury being done to a person: "and, if misfortune befalls the friends, acquaintances, companions and relations of persons who

are full of affection [toward the former], even though they are themselves well-provided for, [this misfortune] is also an injury to their own
selves."⁵⁰ One's well-being may be affected through various influences,
and it is the assessment of the nature of the life the person himself leads
that forms the evaluation of the living standard.

It may be useful to see the distinction in the context of another contrast, to wit that between a person's overall achievements (whatever he
wishes to achieve as an "agent,") and his personal well-being (elaborated in my Dewey lectures).⁵¹ Three different notions may be distinguished: (1) agency achievement, (2) personal well-being, and (3) the
standard of living.⁵² The distinction between agency achievement and
personal well-being arises from the fact that a person may have objectives other than personal well-being. If, for example, a person fights
successfully for a cause, making great personal sacrifice (and perhaps
even giving his or her life for it), then this may be a big agency achievement without being a corresponding achievement of personal well-
being. In the second distinction, namely that between well-being and
the living standard, we are restricted in both cases to looking at achievements of personal well-being only, but whereas for well-being *tout
court* there is no further qualification as to whether the achievement
relates to the nature of the person's life, the notion of the standard of
living does include exactly that qualification.

In an earlier paper⁵³ I distinguished between "sympathy" and "commitment" in the context of analyzing motivations for action. In helping
another person, the reduction of the other's misery may have the net
effect of making one feel—and indeed *be*—better off. This is a case of
an action that can be promoted on grounds of "sympathy" (whether or
not that is why the action is actually chosen), and this falls *within* the
general area of promotion of one's own well-being.⁵⁴ In contrast, a case
of "commitment" is observed when a person decides to do a thing
(such as being helpful to another) despite its not being, in the net, beneficial to the agent himself. This would put the action outside the range
of promoting one's own well-being (linking the action with *other* objectives). At the risk of oversimplification, it may be said that we move
from agency achievement to personal well-being by narrowing the
focus of attention through ignoring "commitments," and we move from
personal well-being to the standard of living by further narrowing the
focus through ignoring "sympathies" (and, of course, "antipathies,"
and other influences on one's well-being from outside one's own life).
Thus narrowed, personal well-being related to one's own life will reflect
one's standard of living.

The lines of distinction can, of course, be drawn in other ways as
well, but the system outlined here seems to be both interesting in itself

and well-related to the motivations underlying traditional concerns with the concept of the standard of living. The curiosity and interest that made William Petty, Antoine Lavoisier, Joseph Louis Lagrange, and others take up their investigations into real income and living standards were related to the assessment of the nature of people's lives. The view of the living standard taken here fits in fairly well with that motivation.

Capability and Functioning

I have left one difficult general issue for discussion until almost the very end, and that is the question of the respective roles of capabilities and functionings in the assessment of living standard. A functioning is an achievement, whereas a capability is the ability to achieve. Functionings are, in a sense, more directly related to living conditions, since they *are* different aspects of living conditions. Capabilities, in contrast, are notions of freedom in the positive sense: what real opportunities you have regarding the life you may lead. [55]

Given the close connection of functionings with actual living, it might seem reasonable to concentrate on functionings rather than capabilities in evaluating the living standard. I believe that this is, to a great extent, right. But it is not fully right. Capabilities have a direct role, too, since the idea of a living standard has an aspect that is not quite independent of the perspective of freedom. Suppose I can choose various styles of life—*A, B, C,* and *D*—and I choose *A*. Consider now that the other styles of life—*B, C,* and *D*—become unavailable to me, but I can still choose *A*. It might be said that my standard of living is unchanged, since *A* is what I would choose anyway. But it is not absurd to argue that there is some loss in my living standard in this reduction of freedom.

One way of putting this is to argue that the value of the living standard is given by the capability to lead various types of life, and while special importance is to be attached to the actual lifestyle chosen, the availability of the other options has some value too. Another, perhaps more illuminating, way of seeing this question is to demand that the functionings be "refined" to take note of the alternatives available. Choosing *A* when *B* is also available is a different "refined" functioning, it can be argued, from choosing *A* when *B* is not.

An illustration may help to bring out the contrast. Consider two people, both of whom are starving—one without any alternative (since she is very poor) and the other out of choice (since he is very religious in a particular style). In one sense, their functioning achievements in terms of nourishment may be exactly similar—both are undernourished (and let us assume that they are so even to the same extent). But one is "fasting" and the other is not. The religious faster is *choosing to starve,* whereas the poor starver is exercising no such choice over whether to starve or not. In the space of *refined* functionings, alternative opportunities could thus figure in the characterization of functionings themselves.[56] The notion of capability is, then, partly reflected in the identification of the refined functionings.

In fact, the relations between functionings and capabilities are much more complex than they might at first appear. Living conditions are, in a sense, states of existence—being this, or doing that. Functionings reflect the various aspects of such states, and the set of feasible functioning bundles is the capability of a person. But among the beings and doings are activities of choosing, and, thus, there is a simultaneous and two-way relationship between functionings and capabilities. It is, of course, true that once the functionings have been suitably richly characterized then we can again ask the question: What alternative "refined" functioning bundles are open to this person? But in the process of getting to that point, considerations of alternative functionings (and thus of capabilities) have already been taken on board.

The formal problems of characterization, while interesting, are perhaps not ultimately very important, and what is really significant in all this is to accept the legitimacy of certain freedom-type considerations as part of the conditions of life.[57] Thus the capability approach, broadly defined, is concerned not only with checking what set of bundles of functionings one could choose from but also with seeing the functionings themselves in a suitably rich way as reflecting the relevant aspects of freedom. The constitutive plurality of the capability approach to the living standard has to take note of this as well.

1993 Postscript

The Aristotelian Connections and Contrasts

In earlier writings I have commented on the connection of the capability approach with some arguments used by Adam Smith and Karl Marx.[58] However, the most powerful conceptual connections would appear to be with the Aristotelian view of the human good. Martha Nussbaum[59] has discussed illuminatingly the Aristotelian analysis of "political distribution" and its relation to the capability approach. The Aristotelian account of the human good is explicitly linked with the necessity to "first ascertain the function of man," and it then proceeds to explore "life in the sense of activity."[60] The basis of a fair distribution of capability to function is given a central place in the Aristotelian theory of political distribution. In interpreting Aristotle's extensive writings on ethics and politics, it is possible to note some ambiguity and, indeed, to find some tension between different propositions presented by him, but his recognition of the crucial importance of a person's functionings and capabilities seems to emerge clearly enough, especially in the political context of distributive arrangements.

While the Aristotelian link is undoubtedly important, it should also be noted that there are some substantial differences between the way functionings and capabilities are used in what I have been calling the capability approach and the way they are dealt with in Aristotle's own analysis. Aristotle believes, as Nussbaum notes, "that there is just one list of functionings (at least at a certain level of generality) that do in fact constitute human good living."[61] That view would not be inconsistent with the capability approach presented here but would *not*, by any means, be *required* by it.

The capability approach has indeed been used to argue that while the *commodity* requirements of such capabilities as "being able to take part in the life of the community" or "being able to appear in public without shame" vary greatly from one community to another (thereby giving the "poverty line" a relativist character in the space of commodities), there is much less variation in the *capabilities* that are aimed at through the use of these commodities.[62] This argument, suggesting less variability at a more intrinsic level, has clear links with Aristotle's identification of "nonrelative virtues," but the Aristotelian claims of uniqueness go much further.[63]

Nussbaum, as an Aristotelian, notes this distinction, and also points to Aristotle's robust use of an objectivist framework based on a particular reading of human nature. She suggests the following: "It seems to me, then, that Sen needs to be more radical than he has been so far in his criticism of the utilitarian accounts of well-being, by introducing an objectivist normative account of human functioning and by describing a procedure of objective evaluation by which functionings can be assessed for their contribution to the good human life."[64]

I accept that this would indeed be a systematic way of eliminating the incompleteness of the capability approach. I certainly have no great objection to anyone going on that route. My difficulty with accepting that as the *only* route on which to travel arises partly from the concern that this view of human nature (with a unique list of functionings for a good human life) may be tremendously overspecified and also from my inclination to argue about the nature and importance of the type of objectivity involved in this approach. But mostly my intransigence arises, in fact, from the consideration that the use of the capability approach as such does not require taking that route, and the deliberate incompleteness of the capability approach permits other routes to be taken that also have some plausibility. It is, in fact, the feasibility as well as the usefulness of a general approach (to be distinguished from a complete evaluative blueprint) that seems to me to provide good grounds for separating the general case for the capability approach (including, inter alia, the Aristotelian theory) from the special case for taking on *exclusively* this particular Aristotelian theory.

In fact, no matter whether we go the full Aristotelian way, which will also need a great deal of extension as a theory for practical evaluation, or take some other particular route, there is little doubt that the kind of *general* argument that Aristotle uses to motivate his approach does have a wider relevance than the defense of the particular form he gives to the nature of the human good. This applies, inter alia, to Aristotle's rejection of opulence as a criterion of achievement (rejecting wealth and income as the standards), his analysis of *eudaimonia* in terms of valued activities (rather than relying on readings of mental states, as in some utilitarian procedures), and his assertion of the need to examine the processes through which human activities are chosen (thereby pointing toward the importance of freedom as part of living).

Incompleteness and Substance

The Aristotelian critique points toward a more general issue, namely, that of the "incompleteness" of the capability approach—both in generating substantive judgments and in providing a comprehensive theory of valuation. Quite different specific theories of value may be consistent with the capability approach and share the common feature of selecting value-objects from functionings and capabilities. Further, the capability approach can be used with different methods of determining relative weights and different mechanisms for actual evaluation. The approach, if seen as a theory of algorithmic evaluation, would be clearly incomplete.[65]

It may well be asked, why pause at outlining a general approach, with various bits to be filled in, rather than "completing the task?" The motivation underlying the pause relates to the recognition that an agreement on the usability of the capability approach—an agreement on the nature of the "space" of value-objects—need not *presuppose* an agreement on how the valuational exercise may be completed. It is possible to disagree both on the exact *grounds* underlying the determination of relative weights and on the *actual* relative weights chosen,[66] even when there is reasoned agreement on the general nature of the value-objects (in this case, personal functionings and capabilities). If reasoned agreement is seen as an important foundational quality central to political and social ethics,[67] then the case for the pause is not so hard to understand. The fact that the capability approach is consistent and combinable with several different substantive theories need not be a source of embarrassment.

Interestingly enough, despite this incompleteness, the capability approach does have considerable "cutting power." In fact, the more challenging part of the claim in favor of the capability approach lies in what it denies. It differs from the standard utility-based approaches in not insisting that we must value *only happiness* (and sees, instead, the state of being happy as one among several objects of value) or *only desire fulfillment* (and takes, instead desire as useful but imperfect evidence—frequently distorted—of what the person herself values).[68] It differs also from other—nonutilitarian—approaches in not placing among value-objects *primary goods as such* (accepting these Rawlsian-focus variables only derivatively and instrumentally and only to the extent that these goods promote capabilities), or *resources as such* (valuing this Dworkinian perspective only in terms of the impact of resources on functionings and capabilities), and so forth.[69] A general acceptance of the intrinsic relevance and centrality of the various functionings and capabilities that make up our lives does have substantial cutting power, but it need not be based on a prior agreement on the relative values of the different functionings or capabilities, or on a specific procedure for deciding on those relative values.

Indeed, it can be argued that it may be a mistake to move on relentlessly until one gets to exactly one mechanism for determining relative weights, or—to turn to a different aspect of the "incompleteness"—until one arrives at exactly one interpretation of the metaphysics of value. There are substantive differences between different ethical theories at different levels, from the meta-ethical (involving such issues as objectivity) to the motivational, and it is not obvious that for substantive political and social philosophy it is sensible to insist that all these general issues be resolved *before* an agreement is reached on the choice of an evaluative space. Just as the utilization of actual weights in practical exercises may be based on the acceptance of a certain *range* of variability of weights (as I have tried to discuss in the context of the *use* of the capability approach[70]), even the general rationale for using such an approach may be consistent with some ranges of answers to foundational questions.

Notes

1. John R. Hicks, "The Scope and Status of Welfare Economics," *Oxford Economic Papers*, vol. 27, no. 3 (November 1975), 312, reprinted in Hicks,

Wealth and Welfare, Collected Essays on Economic Theory, vol. 1 (Oxford: Blackwell, 1981), 223.

2. Adam Smith, *An Inquiry into the Nature and Causes of the Wealth of Nations* (New York: Modern Library, 1937 [1776]), lvii.

3. A. C. Pigou, *The Economics of Welfare*, 4th ed. (London: Macmillan, 1952), 5.

4. See A. Bergson, "A Reformulation of Certain Aspects of Welfare Economics," *Quarterly Journal of Economics*, 52 (February 1938): 310–34; Paul A. Samuelson, *Foundations of Economic Analysis* (Cambridge, Mass.: Harvard University Press, 1947); and Kenneth J. Arrow, *Social Choice and Individual Values* (New York: Wiley, 1951).

5. Pigou, *Economics of Welfare*, 11.

6. Hicks, "Scope and Status," 219.

7. John R. Hicks, "Valuation of Social Income," *Economica* 7, no. 26 (May 1940): 105–24, reprinted in Hicks, *Wealth and Welfare*; "The Measurement of Real Income," *Oxford Economic Papers* 10, no. 2 (June 1958): 125–62, reprinted in Hicks, *Wealth and Welfare*; and *Wealth and Welfare*.

8. Hicks, "Scope and Status," 230–31.

9. Amartya Sen, "Plural Utility," *Proceedings of the Aristotelian Society* 81 (1981): 193–215.

10. Amartya Sen, "Real National Income," *Review of Economic Studies* 43, no. 1 (February 1976): 19–39, reprinted in Amartya Sen, *Choice, Welfare and Measurement* (Oxford: Clarendon Press; Cambridge: MIT Press, 1982); Amartya Sen, "The Welfare Basis of Real Income Comparisons: A Survey," *Journal of Economic Literature* 17 (1979): 1–45, reprinted in Amartya Sen, *Resources, Values and Development* (Oxford: Blackwell; Cambridge, Mass.: Harvard University Press, 1984).

11. I have tried to do this in greater detail, namely, in my Hennipman Lecture (April 1982), published as *Commodities and Capabilities* (Amsterdam: North Holland, 1985).

12. For example, Pigou, *Economics of Welfare*, 100–1, 622–23, 758–67.

13. Pigou, *Economics of Welfare*, 12.

14. Pigou, *Economics of Welfare*, 10, italics added.

15. Pigou, *Economics of Welfare*, 23.

16. Pigou, *Economics of Welfare*, 24.

17. See Henry Sidgwick, *The Methods of Ethics*, 7th ed. (London: Macmillan, 1907); F. P. Ramsey, "Truth and Probability," in F. P. Ramsey, *Foundations: Essays in Philosophy, Logic, Mathematics and Economics* (London: Routledge, 1978); John Harsanyi, *Essays on Ethics, Social Behaviour and Scientific Explanation* (Dordrecht: Reidel, 1976); R. M. Hare, *Moral Thinking* (Oxford: Clarendon Press, 1981); J. A. Mirrlees, "The Economic Uses of Utilitarianism," in *Utilitarianism and Beyond,* ed. Amartya Sen and Bernard Williams (Cambridge, U.K.: Cambridge University Press, 1982), 63–84. There is a third view, quite popular among economists, that definitionally identifies the utility ranking with the binary relation of choice. As an approach it begs more questions than it answers. See Hicks, "The Measurement of Real In-

come," and Sen, *Choice, Welfare and Measurement*. It is also particularly unsuited for interpersonal or intertemporal comparison so essential for studies of living standards, since people do not actually face the choice of being someone else or living at some other time.

18. See J. C. B. Gosling, *Pleasure and Desire* (Oxford: Clarendon Press, 1969); Richard Brandt, *A Theory of the Good and the Right* (Oxford: Clarendon Press, 1979); among others.

19. Sen, "Plural Utility"; James Griffin, "Modern Utilitarianism," *Revue internationale de philosophie* 36, no. 141 (1982): 331–75.

20. Smith, *Wealth of Nations,* lvii.

21. Smith, *Wealth of Nations*, 297.

22. The literature has been surveyed and critically examined in Sen, "The Welfare Basis of Real Income Comparisons."

23. See Sir Isaiah Berlin, *Four Essays on Liberty* (Oxford: Clarendon Press, 1969) for the contrast between "positive" and "negative" views of freedom. Berlin's own focus is on the "negative" approach because of his concern with liberty as such. The nature of the contrast is further discussed in Amartya Sen, "Rights and Agency," *Philosophy and Public Affairs* 11, no. 1 (Winter 1982): 3–39; Amartya Sen, "Rights and Capabilities," in *Morality and Objectivity: A Tribute to J.L. Mackie,* ed. Ted Honderich (London: Routledge, 1985), 130–48.

24. Smith, *Wealth of Nations,* 397.

25. Hicks, "A Manifesto," in *Essays in World Economics* (Oxford: Clarendon Press, 1959), reprinted in *Wealth and Welfare,* vol. 1, 138.

26. Smith, *Wealth of Nations*, 821–22.

27. Amartya Sen, "Poor, Relatively Speaking," *Oxford Economic Papers* 35, no. 2 (July 1983): 153–69, reprinted in Sen, *Resources, Values and Development.*

28. Karl Marx with Friedrich Engels, *The German Ideology* [1846] in *Karl Marx: Selected Writings*, ed. David McLellan (Oxford: Oxford University Press, 1977 [1846]); Karl Marx, *Grundrisse*, trans. Martin Nicolaus (New York: Vintage Books, 1973 [1858]); Karl Marx, *Critique of the Gotha Program* [1875] in *Karl Marx: Selected Writings*, ed. David McLellan.

29. John Stuart Mill, *On Liberty* in *On Liberty and Other Essays*, ed. John Gray (Oxford, New York: Oxford University Press, 1991 [1859]); Mill, *On the Subjection of Women* in *On Liberty and Other Essays* (1991 [1869]).

30. Note, however, that the test of whether something "can be brought directly or indirectly into relation with the measuring-rod of money" (Pigou, *Economics of Welfare*, 11) may be a misleading one in examining the basis of "material prosperity." Many "public goods," such as roads or parks, are not purchasable, but are quite important for material prosperity (and presumably for economic welfare). So is the absence of crime or pollution, though none of these things is offered for sale in the market. There are many complicated issues in deciding what counts as "material" but it can be argued that the measuring-rod of money is not central to the idea of "material prosperity."

31. See also Sen, *Choice, Welfare and Measurement*, 29–31, 353–69.

32. W. M. Gorman, "The Demand for Related Goods," *Journal Paper J*

3224 (Ames, Iowa: Iowa Experimental Station, 1956); Kelvin J. Lancaster, "A New Approach to Consumer Theory," *Journal of Political Economy* 74, no. 2 (April 1966): 132–57.

33. See Tibor Scitovsky, *The Joyless Economy* (London: Oxford University Press, 1976); Mary Douglas and Brian Isherwood, *The World of Goods* (New York: Basic Books, 1979); Angus Deaton and John Muellbauer, *Economics and Consumer Behaviour* (Cambridge, U.K.: Cambridge University Press, 1980), and other explanations of different types of characteristics associated with consumption.

34. On the variability of the relation between food intake and nutritional achievement and the existence of multiple equilibria, see, among other works, P. V. Sukhatme, *Nutrition and Poverty* (New Delhi: Indian Agricultural Research Institute, 1977); N. S. Scrimshaw, "Effect of Infection on Nutrient Requirement," *American Journal on Clinical Nutrition* 30 (1977); T. N. Srinivasan, "Hunger: Defining It, Estimating Its Global Incidence and Alleviating It," in *The Role of Markets in the World Food Economy*, ed. D. Gale Johnson and G. Edward Schuh (Boulder, Colo.: Westview Press, 1983), 77–108.

35. Sen, "Poor, Relatively Speaking."

36. Cf. Peter Townsend, *Poverty in the United Kingdom* (London: Penguin, 1979).

37. Smith, *Wealth of Nations*, Bk. V.

38. See Marx, *The German Ideology*, 190.

39. See J. Kynch and Amartya Sen, "Indian Women: Well-Being and Survival," *Cambridge Journal of Economics* 7 (1983): 363–80.

40. Sen, "Real National Income," "The Welfare Basis of Real Income Comparisons," and *Commodities and Capabilities*.

41. Hicks, *Wealth and Welfare*, xvii.

42. Peter Townsend, "The Development of Research on Poverty," in *Social Security Research: The Definition and Measurement of Poverty*, Department of Health and Social Security (London: HMS, 1979); and *Poverty in the United Kingdom* (Harmondsworth, U.K.: Penguin, 1979). See also G. C. Fiegehen, P. S. Lansley, and A. D. Smith, *Poverty and Progress in Britain*, 1953–73 (Cambridge, U.K.: Cambridge University Press, 1977); Wilfred Beckerman and S. Clark, *Poverty and Social Security in Britain Since 1961* (Oxford: Clarendon Press, 1982); Peter Townsend, "A Sociological Approach to the Measurement of Poverty: A Rejoinder to Professor Amartya Sen," *Oxford Economic Papers* 37, no. 4 (December 1985): 659–68; Amartya Sen, "A Reply to Professor Peter Townsend," *Oxford Economic Papers* 37, no. 4 (December 1985): 669–76.

43. This is not, strictly speaking, correct. Even if the poverty line is defined entirely relatively to the median income (say, 60 percent of it), it is still possible for poverty to be eliminated, though that would depend on the elimination of a type of inequality. If, on the other hand, the "poor" are defined as those in, say, the bottom decile of the population, then poverty will obviously not be eliminable.

44. *Parliamentary Debates*, Commons, 6th ser., vol. 62 (1984), 1241. These and other views on poverty are critically discussed by J. Mack and S. Lansley, *Poor Britain* (London: Allen and Unwin, 1985).

45. Dan Usher, *The Price Mechanism and the Meaning of National Income Statistics* (Oxford: Clarendon Press, 1968).

46. Amartya Sen, *Poverty and Famines: An Essay on Entitlement and Deprivation* (Oxford: Clarendon Press, 1981), chaps. 2, 3; see also E. J. Hobsbawm, "Poverty," in *Encyclopedia of the Social Sciences* (New York: Collier-Macmillan, 1968); and D. Weddeburn, ed., *Poverty, Inequality and the Class Structure* (Cambridge: Cambridge University Press, 1974).

47. This is discussed in Sen, "Poor, Relatively Speaking."

48. Pigou, *Economics of Wealth*, 11.

49. Sen, "The Living Standard," *Oxford Economic Papers* 36, supplement (November 1984): 74–90, reprinted in part in this volume.

50. "Rock Edict XIII at Erragudi, Statement VII," in D. C. Sircar, *Asokan Studies* (Calcutta: Indian Museum, 1979).

51. Amartya Sen, "Well-Being, Agency and Freedom," *Journal of Philosophy* 82, no. 4 (April 1985): 169–221.

52. I am grateful to Bernard Williams for suggesting this way of clarifying the distinction between well-being and living standard (though he would have, I understand, drawn the boundaries somewhat differently).

53. Amartya Sen, "Rational Fools: A Critique of the Behavioral Foundations of Economic Theory," *Philosophy and Public Affairs* 6, no. 4 (Summer 1977): 317–44, reprinted in Sen, *Choice, Welfare and Measurement*.

54. It is, however, important to distinguish between the possibility that one's well-being is being promoted by one's action and the possibility that the action is being chosen for that reason; on this, see Thomas Nagel, *The Possibility of Altruism* (Oxford: Clarendon Press, 1970). Here we are concerned primarily with effects rather than with motivations, and, thus, the use of distinction between "sympathy" and "commitment" is rather different here from its use in Sen, "Rational Fools."

55. Note that the extent of freedom must be judged not only by the number of alternatives but also by the goodness of the alternatives. To take a simple case, if the functioning bundle x is superior to bundle y, and y to z, then the capability set $\{x,z\}$ is superior to set $\{y,z\}$. Also, in an important sense, set $\{x\}$ is superior to set $\{y\}$. The argument involves the relevance of "counterfactual" choice to freedom ("what would you choose given the choice over x and y?"). On this, see Sen, *Commodities and Capabilities*, and "Well-Being, Agency and Freedom."

56. See Sen, *Commodities and Capabilities*, chap. 7, and "Well-being, Agency and Freedom."

57. The importance of freedom in judging a person's life was sharply emphasized by Marx. His liberated society of the future would make it "possible for me to do one thing today and another tomorrow, to hunt in the morning, fish in the afternoon, rear cattle in the evening, criticize after dinner, just as I have in mind, without ever becoming hunter, fisherman, shepherd or critic" (Marx and Engels, *The German Ideology*, in *Karl Marx: Selected Writings*, 169).

58. See particularly, Smith, *Wealth of Nations*, and Marx, "Economic and

Philosophical Manuscripts*" in *Karl Marx: Selected Writings*. The connections are discussed in Sen, *Resources, Values and Development*, "Well-Being, Agency and Freedom," and *The Standard of Living*, 1985 Tanner Lectures at Cambridge, with contributions by Keith Hart, Ravi Kanbur, John Muellbauer, and Bernard Williams, ed. Geoffrey Hawthorn (Cambridge, U.K.: Cambridge University Press, 1987). [Editors' note: portions of *The Standard of Living* appear as the 1987 postscript to Sen's essay in the present volume.]

59. Martha C. Nussbaum, "Nature, Function, and Capability: Aristotle on Political Distribution," *Oxford Studies in Ancient Philosophy* suppl. vol. (1988): 145–84; and Nussbaum, "Non-Relative Virtues: An Aristotelian Approach," *Midwest Studies in Philosophy* 13 (1990): 32–53.

60. See particularly Aristotle, *The Nicomachean Ethics*, Bk. I, s. 7, trans. David Ross (Oxford: Oxford University Press, 1980), 12–14.

61. Nussbaum, "Nature, Function, and Capability," 152.

62. For example, Sen, "Poor, Relatively Speaking" and *Resources, Values and Development*.

63. On this see Nussbaum, "Non-Relative Virtues."

64. Nussbaum, "Nature, Function, and Capability," 176.

65. This relates to one part of the critique presented by Charles Beitz, "Amartya Sen's *Resources, Values and Development*," *Economics and Philosophy* 2 (Fall 1986), 282–91.

66. On this see Sen, *Commodities and Capabilities*, chaps. 5–7.

67. On this question, see John Rawls, *A Theory of Justice* (Cambridge, Mass.: Harvard University Press, 1971); Thomas Scanlon, "Contractualism and Utilitarianism," in *Utilitarianism and Beyond*; and Bernard Williams, *Ethics and the Limits of Philosophy* (Cambridge: Cambridge University Press, 1985).

68. For comparisons and contrasts between the capability approach and utilitarian views, see Sen, *Resources, Values and Development* and "Well-Being, Agency and Freedom."

69. See Rawls, *A Theory of Justice* (Cambridge, Mass.: Harvard University Press, 1971); Rawls, "Priority of Right and Ideas of the Good," *Philosophy and Public Affairs* 17, no. 4 (Fall 1988): 251–76; Rawls, *Political Liberalism* (New York: Columbia University Press, 1993), 182–87; Ronald Dworkin, "What is Equality? Part 2: Equality of Resources," *Philosophy and Public Affairs* 10, no. 4 (Fall 1981): 283–345; Amartya Sen, "Equality of What?" in *Tanner Lectures on Human Values*, vol. 1, ed. S. McMurrin (Salt Lake City: University of Utah Press, 1980), 197–220; Sen, *Resources, Values and Development*; Sen, "Justice: Means Versus Freedoms," *Philosophy and Public Affairs* 19, no. 2 (Spring 1990): 111–21.

70. See Sen, *Commodities and Capabilities*; on the general strategy of using "intersection partial orders," see Amartya Sen, *Collective Choice and Social Welfare* (San Francisco: Holden-Day, 1970; Amsterdam: North Holland, 1979); Sen, "On Weights and Measures: Informational Constraints in Social Welfare Analysis," *Econometrica* 45, no. 7 (October 1977):1539–72.

17

The Good As Discipline,
the Good As Freedom

Martha C. Nussbaum

The freedom which we enjoy in our political association extends also to our ordinary life. There, far from exercising a jealous surveillance over one another, we do not feel called upon to be angry with our neighbour for doing something that pleases him, or even to indulge in those injurious looks which cannot fail to be offensive, although they inflict no positive penalty. But all this ease in our private relations does not make us lawless as citizens . . . particularly as regards laws protecting the injured and those which, although unwritten, cannot be violated without evident disgrace.[1]

—Thucydides, *History of the Peloponnesian War*

But stamp a man like Debs or a woman like Kate O'Hare as felons, and you dignify the term felony instead of degrading them, and every thief and robber will be justified in feeling that some of the stigma has been taken from his crime and punishment.

—Ernst Freund, "The *Debs* Case and Freedom of Speech," 1919[2]

Politics and the Good

"A person who is going to make a fruitful inquiry into the question of the best political arrangement must first set out clearly what the most choiceworthy life is. For if that is unclear, the best political arrangement must also be unclear" (Pol. 1323a14–17). So Aristotle defended an idea that has recently enjoyed a revival in political debate. His claim is that political arrangement cannot proceed intelligently unless it uses an account of human flourishing to guide it. The reason he plausibly gives for this claim is that the goods distributed by politics, such as money, honors, and entitlements, are not good in and of themselves. They are good insofar as they are tools of human functioning. It would appear, then, that political planners cannot judge their role well, or distribute goods appropriately, if they do not set them in this context of functioning, saying what they are good for and how much people need.

This seems to mean taking a stand on what the most important human functions are, at least for political purposes. The task of political planning is to get the tools of functioning to the people who need them; that is why it requires taking a stand on the functions for which these goods will be used. Only such an account will tell us what people need, informing us, for example, about the ways in which resources go to work to promote health, mobility, or learning. Equally important, only such an account will tell us what people may like but really do not need— telling us, for example, that there is a morally important difference between a rich person's interest in additional accumulation and a poor person's interest in getting what it takes to live a decent life. The theory of the good functions as a limit in these two distinct ways. Up to a certain point, resources are necessary tools of human functioning; beyond that point, they are just heaps of stuff being accumulated. Politics is interested in the good for both of these reasons.

The case for using a theory of human flourishing in politics looks strong. But liberal objections quickly arise. How can we base political planning on a theory of the human good that is reasonably comprehensive, covering many of the most important areas of human life, without violating the moral integrity of citizens as choosers? If citizens are pursuing their own diverse conceptions of the good, won't public policy, in choosing its own substantive account, unacceptably advantage some and disadvantage others? These anxieties are legitimate. Any good-based theory needs to address them, and neo-Aristotelian theories have done so in a variety of different ways. It is my purpose in this chapter to make clear the extent to which my own approach to a neo-Aristotelian account of human functioning is in essence a liberal approach, in which the account of the good is seen as a benchmark for various human freedoms, rather than a source of discipline for the wayward. After presenting the rationale for using a rich account of human functioning and laying out the elements of the account, I shall introduce, for purposes of contrast, two nonliberal versions of a neo-Aristotelian position. One derives from conservative Catholic neo-Aristotelianism; it focuses on the role of the state in promoting virtue and discouraging vice. The other derives from radical environmental and anticonsumption thought; it focuses on the role of the state in curbing a wasteful lifestyle. After contrasting my account with these two in a schematic way, I shall comment on a variety of cases, including political speech, drug regulation, safety standards, and redistributive taxation. All of these topics are important for the issue of consumption.

The Need for the Good

No prominent liberal thinker has denied that politics needs at least some account of the good. As John Rawls says, justifying his account of what he calls the "primary goods," we need to have some idea of what we are distributing, and we need to agree that these things are good.[3] Rawls's well-known answer to the problem was to introduce in this connection a "thin theory of the good," a list of items all rational individuals would desire as prerequisites for carrying out their plans of life. He added that these individuals would prefer more of the relevant goods rather than less, whatever else they wanted. More recently, he has qualified the view by stating that the primary goods are to be seen not as all-purpose means but as citizens' needs understood from a political point of view, in connection with the development and expression of their moral powers. The account of the moral powers (of forming and revising a life plan) is itself an important part of the political theory of the good.[4] Rawls stresses that in no case do these items provide a theory of what is most valuable in life or what gives life meaning: "When seen as rights, liberties, and opportunities, and as general all-purpose means, primary goods are clearly not anyone's idea of the basic values of human life and must not be so understood, however essential their possession."[5]

Rawls's list of primary goods already includes a number of items that look like capabilities to function: rights and liberties (of conscience, speech, assembly, political exercise, and so on), powers and opportunities, and the social bases of self-respect, along with more obvious resource type items, such as income and wealth. More recently, Rawls has included freedom of movement and the free choice of occupation,[6] thus tilting the list further in the capability/function direction. Nonetheless, he draws the line at making the basis for interpersonal comparisons of well-being an index of capabilities rather than of resources. The suggestion is that any further movement in this direction would jeopardize the priority of liberty, telling citizens in an unacceptable way what they should value in life. The ultimate bearers of personal and ethical value may be forms of human functioning, but politics, in developing the basic structure of society, takes no stand on what those functionings are.

How, in response to these weighty considerations, does the "capabilities approach" argue that political planning needs a more comprehensive theory of the good? Four arguments have been made.[7] First, individuals have widely varying needs for resources if they are to achieve the same level of functioning. Nutritional needs vary with age, occupation, and gender. A person whose limbs work well needs few resources to be mobile, whereas a person with paralyzed limbs needs many resources to achieve the same level of capability. A child needs more protein than an adult, a pregnant or lactating woman needs more nutrients than a nonpregnant woman. Many such variations may escape our notice if we live in a prosperous nation that can afford to be lavish with nutritional resources; in poorer nations we must be alert to these variations. Again, if we wish to bring all citizens of a nation to a similar level of educational attainment, we will have to devote more resources to those who encounter obstacles to personal development from traditional hierarchy and prejudice; thus women's literacy in many parts of the world will require more resources than men's literacy. This means that if we operate only with an index of resources, we will frequently miss inequalities that are highly relevant to well-being. If, instead, we ask how individuals are actually doing in the various areas of human life, using a list of basic functions as a guide, we will find out to what extent resources have been able to engender capabilities.

Second, a closely related point, the approach that measures quality of life in terms of possessions frequently will fail to go deep enough to diagnose obstacles to functioning that can be present in a society even when resources are spread around adequately. Hierarchical patterns of labor, gender relations that undercut self-esteem and autonomy—these and other socially shaped conditions can cause individuals to fail to avail themselves of opportunities that they in some sense have, such as free public education, the vote, or the right to work. In such cases, we get much more information about the total life quality in that society by asking about what individuals are actually able to do and to be than by asking only how many primary goods they can command. Rawls's approach acknowledges this point in the area of the basic liberties and opportunities, stressing that we must ensure not only equal liberty but also the equal worth of liberty, not only formal equality of opportunity but also fully fair equality of opportunity. Extending these considerations to other areas of life—for example, health and education—seems consistent with the basic spirit of Rawls's proposal, although he has not taken this step.

Third, the mere fact that individuals choose conceptions of the good does not entail that their selections are reliable indicators of what that individual would choose on reflection, with full information about alternatives and in circumstances favorable for choice (for example, ones free from intimidation and with adequate experience of options). For the desires and preferences of individuals—including their desires and preferences in the matter of choice of a conception of the good—are socially and politically shaped and can frequently be deformed by deprivation and hierarchy. Thus if the liberal thinks that refraining from evaluating people's choices is somehow neutral or apolitical, she is mistaken—she has simply opted in favor of the status quo rather than in favor of change. To give just one illustration of this point, if we hand around education-related resources to individuals in a traditional gender-divided society, allowing them to use those resources in keeping with their conception of the good in each case, then—even if we suppose that women are free to choose in the matter, something that is not always the case—we will find that in the absence of education and knowledge of alternatives women themselves will frequently endorse a conception of the good in which they remain subordinated and ill-educated. Have we dealt with them more justly here, when we allow them their alleged freedom to choose in accordance with the conception of the good they happen to have than we would if we instituted compulsory primary and secondary education for women, making up our own minds on the question of the good in the conviction that their condition is unfavorable for deliberation on this question? In other words, too quick a flight from the question of the good ensures the victory of time-honored conceptions, which are not necessarily those that the parties would endorse on fullest reflection. Rawls was among the first recent political thinkers to address this problem of preference deformation: so, once again, the observation would appear to be entirely in the spirit of his basic idea.[8]

Finally, political planning cannot and does not focus on resources alone—this is simply impractical. Governments are not simply in the business of allocating cash to citizens; typically they must choose to target their funds one way or another, supporting education, health, family leave, child care, or whatever. The real-life political debate takes the form of asking how much we should be devoting to each of these areas and whether some service should be added to or subtracted from government support; thus, it presupposes some reflection about the importance of these areas in citizens' lives. Rawls handles this through his complicated series of stages, beginning with the choice of basic principles of justice, moving through the constitutional to the legislative stage. In each phase, somewhat more information is permitted. For real-world deliberation about policy, however—frequently in international settings—we have difficulty recapitulating any such neat division, so we must be satisfied to make our case in a way that is only roughly comparable to Rawls's ideal theory (and therefore, on this point at least, does not contradict it).

The central objection made by Rawlsian liberalism against comprehensive theories of the good is that they remove choice from citizens and are unfair to those who do not share the comprehensive theory being supported. As I have already indicated, this question of choice is itself complex, if one wants from choice something more than unreflective assertion of tradition. But the objection must still be confronted if the Aristotelian capability-based approach is to commend itself in our pluralistic world. At this point, however, we must examine the Aristotelian proposal itself, since only then will we be able to see how far the charge holds against it.

The Central Human Capabilities

The list of basic functions is generated by asking a question that from the start is evaluative: What activities characteristically performed by human beings are so central that they seem definitive of a life that is truly human? In other words, what are the functions without which (meaning without the availability of which) we would regard a life as not fully human? We can get at this question better if we approach it via two somewhat more concrete questions that we often really ask ourselves. First is a question about personal continuity. We ask ourselves what changes or transitions are compatible with the continued existence of that being as a member of the human species and what are not. Some functions can fail to be present without threatening our sense that we still have a human being on our hands; the absence of others seems to signal the end of a human life.[9] This question is asked regularly when we attempt to make medical definitions of death in a situation in which some of the functions of life persist or to decide, for others or (thinking ahead) for ourselves, whether a certain level of illness or impairment means the end of the life of the being in question.[10]

The other question is a question about kind inclusion. We recognize other humans as human across many differences of time, place, custom, and appearance. We often tell ourselves stories, on the other hand, about anthropomorphic creatures who do not get classified as human, on account of some feature of their form of life and functioning. On what do we base these inclusions and exclusions. In short, what do we believe must be there if we are going to acknowledge that a given life is human?[11] The answer to these questions points us to a subset of the common or characteristic human functions, informing us that these are likely to have a special importance for everything else we choose and do.

Note that the procedure through which this account of the human is derived is neither ahistorical nor a priori. It is the attempt to summarize the empirical findings of a broad and ongoing cross-cultural inquiry. As such, it is open ended and humble; it can always be contested and remade. Nor does it claim to read the facts of "human nature" from biological observation: it takes account of biology as a relatively constant element in human experience. Nor does it deny that the items it mentions are to some extent differently constructed by different societies.[12] It is because the account is evaluative from the start that it is called a conception of the good.

It should also be stressed that, like Rawls's account of primary goods, this more comprehensive list of the good is proposed as the object of a specifically political consensus. The political is not understood exactly as Rawls understands it, since the nation-state is not assumed to be the basic unit,[13] and the account is meant to have broad applicability to cross-cultural deliberations. Nonetheless, the point of the account is the same: to put forward something that people from many different traditions, with many different fuller conceptions of the good, can agree on, as the necessary basis for pursuing their good life. This is why the list is deliberately general—the "thick vague conception of the good," I have called it. This means that each of its components can be more concretely specified in accordance with one's origins, religious beliefs, or tastes. In that sense, the consensus that it hopes to evoke has many of the features of the "overlapping consensus" described by Rawls.[14]

Having isolated some functions that seem central in defining the very presence of a human life, we do not rest content with mere bare humanness. We want to specify a life in which a kind of basic human flourishing will be available. For we do not want politics to take mere survival as its goal; we want to describe a life in which the dignity of the human being is not violated by hunger or fear or the absence of opportunity. The list of basic capabilities is an attempt to specify this basic notion of the good: citizens should have all these capabilities, whatever else they have. Politically, we may think of this as an account of what quality of life measurements should measure.

Central Human Functional Capabilities[15]

1. *Life.* Being able to live to the end of a human life of normal length[16]; not dying prematurely, or before one's life is so reduced as to be not worth living.
2. *Bodily Health and Integrity.* Being able to have good health; to be adequately nourished[17]; to have adequate shelter[18]; having opportunities for sexual satisfaction and for choice in matters of reproduction[19]; being able to move from place to place; being

secure against violent assault, including sexual assault, marital rape, and domestic violence.

3. *Pleasure and Pain.* Being able to avoid unnecessary and nonbeneficial pain, so far as possible, and to have pleasurable experiences.

4. *Senses, Imagination, Thought.* Being able to use the senses; being able to imagine, to think, and to reason—and to do these things in a way informed and cultivated by an adequate education, including, but by no means limited to, literacy and basic mathematical and scientific training.[20] Being able to use imagination and thought in connection with experiencing and producing spiritually enriching materials and events of one's own choice (religious, literary, musical, and so forth). Being able to use one's mind in ways protected by guarantees of freedom of expression with respect to both political and artistic speech, and freedom of religious exercise.

5. *Emotions.* Being able to have attachments to things and persons outside ourselves; to love those who love and care for us, to grieve at their absence; in general, to love, to grieve, to experience longing, gratitude, and justified anger. Supporting this capability means supporting forms of human association that can be shown to be crucial in their development.

6. *Practical Reason.* Being able to form a conception of the good and to engage in critical reflection about the planning of one's own life. This includes, today, being able to seek employment outside the home (in a regime protecting the free choice of occupation) and to participate in political life.

7. *Affiliation.* Being able to live for and to others, to recognize and show concern for other human beings, to engage in various forms of social interaction; to be able to imagine the situation of another and to have compassion for that situation; to have the capability for both justice and friendship. Protecting this capability means, once again, protecting institutions that constitute such forms of affiliation, and also protecting the freedoms of assembly and political speech.

8. *Other Species.* Being able to live with concern for and in relation to animals, plants, and the world of nature.

9. *Play.* Being able to laugh, to play, to enjoy recreational activities.

10. *Separateness.* Being able to live one's own life and nobody else's. This means having certain guarantees of noninterference with certain choices that are especially personal and definitive of selfhood, such as choices regarding marriage, childbearing, sexual expression, speech, and employment.

10a. *Strong Separateness.* Being able to live one's own life in one's own surroundings and context. This means guarantees of freedom of association and of freedom from unwarranted search and seizure; it also means a certain sort of guarantee of the integrity of personal property, though this guarantee may be limited in various ways by the demands of social equality, and is always up for negotiation in connection with the interpretation of the other capabilities.

The "capabilities approach," as I conceive it,[21] claims that a life that lacks any one of these capabilities, no matter what else it has, will fall short of being a good human life. So it would be reasonable to take these things as a focus for concern in assessing the quality of life in a country and asking about the role of public policy in meeting human needs. The list is certainly general—this is deliberate, in order to leave room for plural specification and also for further negotiation. But like (and as a reasonable basis for) a set of constitutional guarantees, it offers real guidance in the ongoing historical process of further refinement and specification. The capabilities approach claims, furthermore, that the guidance offered by such a list is superior to that offered by several rivals on the development scene. It is superior to that offered by a focus on gross national product (GNP) per capita, since that measure of life quality does not even tell us about the distribution of resources, far less about other areas of human functioning, such as life expectancy, political liberty, and education, which are not always well correlated with GNP per capita. It is superior to a focus on utility, construed as the satisfaction of desire or preference, since it cannot be seduced by the tendency of human psychology to adapt to a bad state of affairs, lowering aspiration to reflect a lower level of opportunity.[22] Finally, as already suggested, it is superior to a focus simply on the distribution of resources, since it enables us to ask how resources do or do not perform the task that gives them their point.

The list is, emphatically, a list of separate components. We cannot satisfy the need for one of them by giving a larger amount of another one. All are of central importance and all are distinct in quality. (Practical reason and affiliation, I have argued elsewhere, are of special importance because they both organize and suffuse all the other capabilities, making their pursuit truly human.[23]) This limits the trade-offs that it will be reasonable to make and, thus, limits the applicability of quantitative cost-benefit analysis. At the same time, the items on the list are related to one another in many complex ways. For example our characteristic mode of nutrition, unlike that of sponges, requires moving from here to there. And we do whatever we do as separate beings, tracing distinct paths through space and time. Notice that reproductive choices involve both sexual capability and issues of separateness and bind the two together in a deep and complex way.

Capability As Goal

We have spoken both of functioning and of capability. How are they related? Clarifying this is crucial in defining the relation of the capabilities approach to liberalism. For if we were to take functioning itself as the goal of public policy, the liberal would rightly judge that we were precluding many choices that citizens may make in accordance with their own conceptions of the good. A deeply religious person may prefer not to be well nourished but to engage in strenuous fasting. Whether for religious or for other reasons, a person may prefer a celibate life to one containing sexual expression. A person may prefer to work with an intense dedication that precludes recreation and play. Are we[24] saying that these are not fully human or flourishing lives? And are we instructing government to push people into functioning of the requisite sort, no matter what they prefer?

Here we must answer *no*: capability, not functioning, is our political goal. This is so because of the very great importance we attach to practical reason as a good that both suffuses all the other functions, making them human rather than animal,[25] and figures, itself, as a central function on the list. It is perfectly true that functionings, not simply capabilities, are what render a life fully human: if there were no functioning of any kind in a life, we could hardly applaud it, no matter what opportunities it contained. Nonetheless, for political purposes it is appropriate for us to shoot for capabilities, and for those alone. Citizens must be left free to determine their course after that. The person with plenty of food may always choose to fast, but there is a great difference between fasting and starving, and it is this difference that we wish to capture. Again, the person who has normal opportunities for sexual satisfaction can always choose a life of celibacy, and we say nothing against this. What we do speak against, for example, is the practice of female genital mutilation, which deprives individuals of the opportunity to choose sexual functioning (and indeed, the opportunity to choose celibacy as well).[26] A person who has opportunities for play can always choose a workaholic life; again, there is a great difference between that chosen life and a life constrained by insufficient maximum-hour protections and/or the "double day" that makes women unable to play in many parts of the world.

The issue will be clearer if we point out once again that there are three different types of capabilities that figure in the analysis.[27] First, there are what we call *basic capabilities*: the innate equipment of individuals that is the necessary basis for developing the more advanced capability. Most infants have from birth the *basic capability* for practical reason and imagination, though they cannot exercise such functions without a lot more development and education. Second, there are *internal capabilities*: that is, states of the person herself that are, so far as the person herself is concerned, sufficient conditions for the exercise of the requisite functions. A woman who has not suffered genital mutilation has the *internal capability* for sexual pleasure; most adult human beings have the *internal capability* to use speech and thought in accordance with their own conscience. Finally, we have *combined capabilities*,[28] which we define as internal capabilities *combined with* suitable external conditions for the exercise of the function. A woman who is not mutilated but is secluded and forbidden to leave the house has internal but not combined capabilities for sexual expression (and work, and political participation). Citizens of repressive nondemocratic regimes have the internal but not the combined capability to exercise thought and speech in accordance with their conscience. The aim of public policy is the production of combined capabilities. This means promoting the states of the person by providing the necessary education and care; and it also means preparing the environment so that it is favorable for the exercise of practical reason and the other major functions.[29]

This clarifies our position. We are not saying that public policy should rest content with internal capabilities, but remain indifferent to the struggles of individuals who have to try to exercise these capabilities in a hostile environment. In that sense, we are highly attentive to the goal of functioning and instruct governments to keep it always in view. On the other hand, we are not pushing individuals into the function: once the stage is fully set, the choice is up to them. (Below I shall comment on some acceptable uses for public persuasion in steering the functioning of mature adults.)

The approach is therefore very close to Rawls's approach using the notion of primary goods. We can see the list of capabilities as like a long list of opportunities for life functioning, such that it is always rational to want them whatever else one wants. If one ends up having a plan of life that does not make use of all of them, one has hardly been harmed by having the chance to choose a life that does. (Indeed, in the cases of fasting and celibacy it is the very availability of the alternative course that gives the choice its moral value.) The primary difference between this capabilities list and Rawls's list of primary goods is its length and definiteness, in particular its determination to place upon the list the social basis of several goods that Rawls has called "natural goods," such as "health and vigor, intelligence and imagination."[30] Since Rawls has been willing to put the social basis of self-respect on his list, it is not at all clear why he has not made the same move with imagination and health.[31] Rawls's evident concern is that no society can guarantee health to its individuals—in that sense, saying that our goal is full combined capability may appear unreasonably idealistic. Some of the capabilities—some of the political liberties, for instance—can be fully guaranteed by society, but many others involve an element of chance and cannot be so guaranteed. We respond to this by saying that the list is a list of political *goals* that should be useful as a benchmark for aspiration and comparison. Even though individuals with adequate health support often fall ill, it still makes sense to compare societies by asking about actual health capabilities, since we assume that the comparison will reflect the different inputs of human planning and can be adjusted to take account of more and less favorable natural situations. (Sometimes it is easier to get information on health achievements than on health capabilities; to some extent we must work with the information we have while not forgetting the importance of the distinction.)

In saying these things about the political goal, we focus on adults who have full mental and moral powers—what Rawls calls "normally cooperating members of society." In the case of adults with severe mental impairment, the goal should probably be some well-judged level of functioning, not capability, and therefore we will have to make choices about which functionings we deem important. Children are different, since we are trying to promote the development of adult capabilities. We may in some cases be justified in requiring functioning of an immature child, as with compulsory primary and secondary education (see below); but we must always justify coercive treatment of children with reference to the adult capability goal.

Earlier versions of the list appeared to diverge from the approach of Rawlsian liberalism by not giving as large a place to the traditional political rights and liberties—although the need to incorporate them was stressed from the start.[32] This version of the list corrects that defect of emphasis. These political liberties have a central importance in making well-being human. A society that aims at well-being while overriding these has delivered to its members a merely animal level of satisfaction.[33] As Amartya Sen has recently written, "Political rights are important not only for the fulfillment of needs, they are crucial also for the formulation of needs. And this idea relates, in the end, to the respect that we owe each other as fellow human beings."[34] This idea of freedoms as need has recently been echoed by Rawls: primary goods specify what citizens' needs are from the point of view of political justice.[35]

The capability view justifies its elaborate list by pointing out that

choice is not pure spontaneity, flourishing independently of material
and social conditions. If one cares about people's powers to choose a
conception of the good, then one must care about the rest of the form
of life that supports those powers, including its material conditions.
Thus the approach claims that its more comprehensive concern with
flourishing is perfectly consistent with the impetus behind the Rawlsian
project, which has always insisted that we are not to rest content with
merely formal equal liberty and opportunity but must pursue their fully
equal worth by ensuring that unfavorable economic and social circumstances do not prevent people from availing themselves of liberties and
opportunities that are formally open to them.

The guiding thought behind this form of Aristotelianism is, at its
heart, a profoundly liberal idea[36] and one that lies at the heart of Rawls'
project as well: the idea of the citizen as a free and dignified human
being, a maker of choices. Politics here has an urgent role to play, providing citizens with the tools that they need, both in order to choose at
all and in order to have a realistic option of exercising the most valuable
functions. The choice of whether and how to use the tools, however, is
left up to the citizens, in the conviction that this is an essential aspect
of respect for their freedom. They are seen not as passive recipients
of social patterning but as dignified free beings who shape their own
lives.[37]

The Good As Discipline: Two Nonliberal Aristotelians

There are many Aristotles. His thought about functioning and capability
continues to inspire divergent approaches, as it has throughout history.
Thomas Aquinas, Karl Marx, and T. H. Greene—all these people took
themselves to be following the lead of Aristotle, and all developed accounts of human functioning that underwrote their political goals. They
were not all liberals, clearly. In areas such as heresy and religious liberty, Aquinas clearly thought that producing virtue and truth was more
important than protecting the liberty of conscience (if he could even be
said to have had that concept). Marx, too, was interested in getting to
truly human functioning by the most effective route, whether or not this
involved protection of political liberties.[38] Descendants of these two
approaches are still influential on the political scene. The defender of a
liberal form of Aristotelianism should, then, clarify its requirements by
contrasting them with other neo-Aristotelian proposals. For the sake of
economy, let us henceforth refer to the liberal Aristotelian capabilities
view as *L* and to its rivals (yet to be introduced) as *A* and *B*.

In what follows, the defender of *L* has no further interest in what

Aristotle actually said. *L* invokes Aristotle not in order to appeal to authority, but in order to acknowledge a source of illumination. But *L*'s proponents never thought Aristotle very helpful on the question of rights and liberties.[39]

We now confront two illiberal Aristotelians. Both are schematic creations: although each is related to real arguments, the aim here is to clarify the capabilities approach, not to engage in exegesis of any individual's position. Opponent *A*, in some respects the heir of Aquinas, is related to the views of contemporary conservative natural-law thinkers, such as John Finnis, Germain Grisez, and Robert P. George, and also to some aspects of the thought of Alasdair MacIntyre.[40] Opponent *B*, in some ways an heir of Marx, is related to a bundle of arguments being advanced in environmental circles, and also to arguments that give economic well-being pride of place over political liberty. Let us hypothesize, for the sake of argument, that both opponents concur—at least for the most part—with our list of basic human functions and capabilities.

Opponent *A*, agreeing in general with *L*'s account of what is most basic, urges that we use a list of basic functions rather than a list of the associated capabilities. We are to use this list as a fully comprehensive conception of good functioning that will enable us to evaluate the choices that individuals make. If a person makes a choice that prevents her from actualizing a good on the list, or even chooses simply not to actualize some good on the list, the list will enable us to criticize that choice. If she makes a choice that actualizes some function other than the ones on the list, this too may be criticized: the fact that the activity in question is not a basic human function is reason for judging it morally subpar. When individuals make such choices, it will be appropriate for the state, in its role as educator and promoter of virtue, to change the person's behavior—both by persuasion and by many types of coercive legal action. Opponent *A* will use the list, then, to scrutinize and in many cases to render illegal various forms of activity that do not appear to inflict harm on third parties; he will favor paternalistic legislation of many kinds, in areas such as drug and alcohol use, sexual morality (homosexuality, abortion, contraception, prostitution, obscenity), and violence in the media.

Supporters of *A* may also favor certain limits on political speech outside the context of an imminent threat to public order. Thus, to take a historical example, it would be consistent with *A*'s general position to endorse the 1919 U.S. Supreme Court decision that upheld the conviction of socialist Eugene Debs for obstructing draft recruitment after he gave a speech expressing a general abhorrence for war and a sympathy with workers who fight wars to serve their masters' interests. (Debs was given a ten-year prison sentence.) As in the cases of morals laws and obscenity, so with allegedly seditious speech: *A* will not shrink from making a convicted felon of someone on account of a personal expressive act. For it is *A*'s view that the law is the teacher of virtue, and branding such a man as a felon is a way of reinforcing patriotic dispositions in the nation as a whole. In contemporary American terms, *A* would be likely to be a strong supporter of laws against flag burning.

When position *A* is instantiated in a liberal constitutional regime, its supporters' advocacy of morals legislation faces tight constraints imposed by the constitution. On contraception, abortion, flag burning, political speech, a good deal of artistic speech, and recently, in some limited respects, homosexuality, many positions favored by *A* have been found unconstitutional in the United States and are to that extent no longer live options. Where the regime's shape is more elastic, however, we may imagine supporters of *A* going much further, legislating a highly specific idea of the correct forms of sexual and familial functioning and providing criminal sanctions for departures. The Islamic regime of Iran is an extreme example of such law-backed moralism, defended by appeal to a norm of human functioning. Women who wear makeup outdoors or who show a lock of hair, who are surely seen as perverted in functioning by the regime, will be punished as felons for their degenerate acts.

Clearly it is just this sort of interference with other people's conceptions of the good that Rawls and other liberals are worried about when they urge politics to eschew comprehensive theories. Their worries are well grounded, since such comprehensive theories are playing an increasing role in both domestic and international politics. And often, indeed, they do seem to have the inhibiting role Rawls fears, clamping down on the choices of citizens who for sincerely held reasons of their own see things differently.

However, there are a number of obvious differences between *L*'s capabilities approach and *A*'s program for a politics of virtue.

1. *L*'s list is open-ended and nonexhaustive. It does not say that these are the only important things or that there is anything nonimportant (far less, bad) about things not on the list. It just says that this is a group of especially important functions, on which we can perhaps agree to focus for political purposes when we assess the quality of life.
2. The aim of *L*'s list is to tell politics to do certain things for people, not to tell people that they are going to get political disabilities unless they come up to a certain moral mark.
3. The goal of *L* is full capability; after that, choice is free. Choices may be morally evaluated, and of course if they are harmful to

others they may be politically constrained. But a person will not be politically constrained just on the ground that he or she, having been given the chance to actualize the goods on the list, fails to do so. The goal is enabling, not policing.
4. In many specific ways, as we have seen, *L* builds this respect for choice into the list itself, with the central role it gives to the traditional political liberties and to privacy and liberty with respect to sex and speech. In these areas it is, after all, not only the use of the list that diverges from opponent *A*, it is the list itself, which enshrines these freedoms as humanly central and forbids government to pursue well-being in ways that undercut or remove these liberties. Thus it is only up to a point and only in appearance that *A* is able to endorse the same list; what *A* more concretely means by "freedom of speech" is not the same as what *L* means by it.

Things, however, are not so clear as that, for two reasons. First, even an account that makes choice central still does some policing, still takes a stand on what choices are permissible and what choices are not. The pro-choice position on abortion is not the straightforward antithesis of the anti-abortion position, since it leaves room for individuals to make choices both for and against abortion in accordance with their individual consciences. But it still takes a stand in this way: it says that this choice is one that individuals are permitted to make, and in this way it differentiates abortion from murder. A law protecting homosexuals from discrimination leaves ample room for choice—it does not tell anyone to be or become a homosexual. It expresses an attitude of respect for the homosexual, making the judgment that his or her choices are within the permissible range of sexual conduct, at least so far as public policy is concerned, and it distinguishes homosexual conduct sharply from marital rape, child seduction, and other forms of sexual conduct that the public sphere agrees to police. So *A*'s legitimate question is, isn't the liberal list really closer to his in purpose than the defender of *L* has let on, and isn't the advocacy of choice in certain areas expressive of a different moral or ideological judgment concerning the value of the acts in question, not just of a hands-off liberal policy? Even *L*'s judgment that bodily pleasure is a good per se is deeply at odds with many considered religious views of the good, which see such feelings as expressive of a fallen and sinful nature and urge the good person to police such inclinations in him or herself.

Second, making citizens capable of choice in some area is frequently a matter that requires extensive preparation and education. This preparation is frequently unidirectional and irreversible, foreclosing the choice of returning to the status quo ante; therefore it can involve taking a stand on the good and tilting the process in one direction rather than another. Again, there is room for suspicion that a liberal ideology may creep in to skew the way things go. In some areas the skewing may be uncontroversial. We want citizens who are capable of reasoning well rather than poorly, even though we are aware that education can produce both results and even though we know that a person who once learns to add numerals correctly will not easily become capable of doing it another way. We want people who are capable of affection and affiliation rather than people who are capable only of hate, even though we know that producing the capacity for love makes a certain sort of sociopathic behavior impossible. But in other areas there is more room for controversy—especially when producing capabilities seems to involve altering time-honored conventions and the preferences that go with them. Learning to be an autonomous planner of one's own life means unlearning or not ever learning dispositions of subordination and acquiescence that in many parts of the world have traditionally defined the good woman and wife. Learning to be literate makes it impossible to choose illiteracy, and many deeply entrenched conceptions of women's roles are threatened by this development.

What the defender of *L* should say in response to the first question is that there are genuinely hard cases, especially where metaphysical and religious traditions disagree about the status of the being in question. Abortion is among these very hard cases, and this may well mean that it is not a right that should be protected by appeal to notions of privacy and choice. (I think it can be sufficiently protected by considerations of equality, in that we do not require men to donate life support even to their born children, who are certainly full human beings. So an anti-abortion law would impose an unequal burden on an already disadvantaged group.[41]) One can, however, distinguish this case from cases in which metaphysical traditions hold that women are lesser beings, less suited for education or political participation, by showing that such arguments are bad arguments, with an inadequate empirical basis and faulty reasoning. Again, one can insist that the opponent of rights to consensual homosexual activity has not made out an empirically convincing case for any harm caused to others by this activity and has very likely argued in an internally inconsistent way—if, for example, he uses an argument based on the centrality of procreation in acceptable sex and yet extends acceptability to the sterile or elderly married couple. And if one insists on these virtues of argument one can defend certain sorts of policing as legitimate—laws against marital rape and domestic violence, for example—while acknowledging that in some cases the moral and legal issues will be difficult ones for reasonable people.

On the second point *L* should grant that indeed some capabilities do preclude some choices. The literate person cannot become illiterate. But that is far from being the end of the issue of capability and freedom. Literacy is a capability connected with the enhancement of choice in many areas of life; illiteracy entails deprivation of information and therefore of reflection about the good. The defender of L is not neutral about the capability for deliberation and reflection about the good. Like Rawls, she takes a firm stand on practical reason, insisting that satisfactions without choice have no moral worth. (It would appear that A should follow her, given the tremendous value accorded to choice and practical reason in the entire Aristotelian tradition.)

If, then, we can show that a certain controversial capability is a precondition of the exercise of practical deliberation, we have offered these two thinkers a very powerful reason to endorse that capability as a good in the terms of their own conception. Support for practical reasoning and its social prerequisites commands a broad political consensus, even among people who differ about the good in many important ways. Thus, at the Cairo population conference, parties who differed in many ways about women's lives and their reproductive rights—in part because some were supporters of A and some of L—still found it possible to agree on the value of female education.

In short, A believes that legal disabilities are justified by the very fact of diverging from the official good; L says that this is a violation of the dignity and integrity of the person. L's focus on the good does not license punishing people, except when they do harm to others. If A suggests that they are being punished de facto, by the very definiteness of the capabilities on the list, which may not reflect their own views, L should answer as Rawls answers, by saying that this is a list that seeks and can command a wide political consensus among reasonable people, which permits much latitude for personal and group choice about the good.

If A sees the state as a protector and producer of virtue, B sees the state as aggressive enemy of excess. Let us suppose, once again, that B agrees with us, at least initially, about the contents of the list of basic capabilities. Focusing on the idea of the good as setting an upper as well as a lower limit on the need for resources, B now claims that the free and open style of life in contemporary America leads to accumulative behavior that is highly injurious to the environment, to other species, and also, indirectly, to the well-being of other human beings who do not enjoy the same living standard and must cope with the damages of pollution. B also notes that population increases threaten the globe's future and the internal living standard of its constituent societies. B sees the state as a vigilant protector of the good of all and with this rationale favors mandatory controls on population and on the consumption of resources. *B* will also be inclined to favor strong environmental curbs on industry, product safety standards, and curbs on certain types of commercial speech. In connection with the priority given to material well-being, *B* will frequently advocate measures, from redistributive taxation to land reforms, that will strike some as interfering with property rights. Because *B* focuses on the material conditions of human well-being, giving these pride of place, supporters of B will be willing to subordinate political liberties to material well-being if only a strong top-down approach seems capable of handling the problems of greedy and diseased choice.

Both *B* and *A* are a family of positions, but *B* is even more clearly heterogeneous, since it contains a variety of different views on the morality of redistribution between nations, the status of the claims of future generations, the question of anthropocentrism in ethics and politics, and, finally, the relationship between the political liberties and economic and social well-being. (We could identify two distinct subfamilies here, which are rarely combined: *B1*, radical environmental anticonsumption positions that urge the state to curb wasteful and environmentally degrading lifestyles, and *B2*, authoritarian forms of socialism that accept the state's use of coercion to guarantee that everyone has material well-being.[42]) But *B* captures intuitively a general "left" good-oriented view that insists on the good precisely in order to criticize, with Aristotle, the unlimited greedy accumulation of mere stuff, which frequently does violence to human functioning.

A and *B* have a good deal in common. Both focus on functioning rather than capability as goal; and they do so because neither trusts the judgments of fallible individuals about how and whether to move from one to the other. Though both positions are found in liberal democracies, both show some sympathy for the rule of wise guardians who will take thought for the good of all, criticizing in the process such diseased preferences as individuals are likely to have. Both countenance some governmental interference with the choices of individuals, so long as the good is the goal. Neither one regards the political liberties and the liberty of conscience as having an absolute priority. They differ primarily in the other goals to which they do assign priority: moral perfection in the case of *A*, equal economic well-being in the case of *B*.

But, equally clearly, *B* is a close relative of *L*. The two positions share a central insight (and one that Marx derived from his reading of Aristotle): that choice has material conditions. Truly human functioning is not created by simply telling people that they can choose; instead, it requires a complex active adjustment of the whole life context of people, in such a way that their context creates full combined capabilities. And this frequently requires government intervention.[43] Whereas *A* and

L differ fundamentally—*A* seeing the goal as a kind of disciplined moral perfection, *L* seeing the goal as an interlocking set of freedoms—*B* and *L* would not appear to differ quite so fundamentally. They share a basic intuition about the role of political action: that its central task is getting people what they need so that they can live well,[44] not, as *A* would have it, regimenting their activities so that they do not step out of line. However, once we see that *B* is willing to subordinate choice and liberty to a definite vision of good functioning, we see that its difference from *L* is also quite fundamental. Both *B* and *L* use the list of capabilities as a guide for the project of getting people what they need and thus promoting full equality of opportunity and capability—not, with *A*, as a way of passing moral judgment on the lives individuals actually choose to lead. And yet, in neglecting the priority of liberty, *B* neglects an absolutely central part of the account of capability as *L* characterizes it.

How should the liberal Aristotelian respond to opponent *B*? She should begin by making two big concessions in *B*'s direction. First, she should concede that the capabilities view has yet to respond to legitimate concerns about the claims of the environment and other species. The capabilities view is an anthropocentric view and, as such, will certainly need supplementation from other views of our moral obligations.[45]

Second, she should observe, agreeing with *B*, that there is no liberty of choice without state action. Therefore the appearance that *B* is in favor of all kinds of state intervention with choice in areas of property and environment, and that liberals are not, must be misleading. There is no system of property rights, or political liberties, without state action, indeed without a strong state; so a liberal could not be a general opponent of state "interference" with choice. The difference between the liberal and *B* will lie in the specific limits of state action that are endorsed, not in the support for the fact of such action.[46] Indeed, the entire distinction between state action and inaction is slippery, for such demarcations typically reveal the assumption of a "baseline" concerning which ways of doing things (which actions, one might well say) are taken to be natural and normal.[47]

The liberal should also emphasize an important basis of agreement with *B*. On the liberal-Aristotelian view, property rights do not enjoy the same priority that is enjoyed by liberties of conscience, thought, speech, and assembly. It seems plausible to think that all of those liberties are themselves basic human capabilities, constitutive of a person's full humanity. To abridge them is to violate the person at her core. Property, the Aristotelian view holds, can be at most a tool of such capabilities for functioning, some stuff a person uses to get on with her activities. This means that it is not at the core in the same way, and interference with it will properly not be seen as violating personal dignity and integrity in the same way. Aristotle himself thought that basic questions of ownership, including the question whether there should even be private property, could be settled only by looking at the role of property in supporting human flourishing.[48]

Beyond this point, *L* must part company with *B*. When *B* urges us to subordinate political liberties to the production of economic well-being, *L* must reply that this fails to grasp the whole point of producing capabilities, which is to show respect for the powers of individuals to fashion a life. We simply have not produced truly human functioning, as *L* understands it, if we have pushed people around in ways that violated central aspects of their personhood.

The Good As Freedom: Capability and Limit

The best way of carrying these contrasts further is to talk about specific issues. Obviously each of them is complex enough to generate an essay of its own, and what can be said here will be both incomplete and insufficiently justified. Nonetheless, a more concrete idea of the differences between *L* and the opposing views should begin to emerge.

1. Education. Here we have one area of agreement among all three Aristotelian positions, for all will stress the fundamental role of education in promoting all the other capabilities, and all will be likely to favor free and compulsory primary and secondary education. To this extent, the good appropriately limits choice, in the process vastly expanding the set of choices for the future. *L*'s agreement here, however, is motivated by a distinction between mature adults and children; this distinction is not so crucial to *A* and *B*, who to some extent think of adults the way *L* thinks of children.

2. Political Speech. *L*, like the Rawlsian liberal, gives this liberty an extremely strong degree of priority, holding that it can be limited only in the case of an immediate and clear threat to public order. Thus *L* would side with Ernst Freund against Oliver Wendell Holmes on antipatriotic and antiwar speech, would oppose the legal regulation of flag burning, and would support the right of unpopular groups to political protest. Concerning hate speech, *L* will probably leave some latitude for nations to decide things in accordance with their own special history: thus Germany may be right to judge that the regulation of Nazi speech is essential to promoting the other human capabilities in the context. On the whole, however, only hate speech that is targeted at an individual and similar to a threat would appear to be a candidate for regulation under *L*'s understanding of the priority of liberty.[49] *A* will attach less value to this liberty and a greater priority to morally correct functioning. *B* will be focused on well-being issues, not morality, but will similarly be inclined to accord this liberty less priority.

3. Other Political Liberties. The freedom of assembly, the right of political participation, and, in particular, the liberty of religious belief and exercise will, similarly, be given an extremely strong degree of priority in *L*. They can, once again, be qualified only in the case of a clear and immediate threat to public order—although religious liberty may not be construed to permit the infringement of basic rights and liberties of members of the religious group, since for *L* the basic bearer of capabilities is emphatically the individual and not the group as such.[50] Once again, both *A* and *B* will be likely to tolerate more compromises with these liberties in pursuit of their other goals.

4. Population: Law and Reproductive Choice. *L* holds that the choices people make with regard to reproduction and the shape of a family are among the most intimate and definitive of selfhood and, thus, among those where it is especially important to protect the capability of choice.[51] *A* and *B*, in their different ways, are not so attached to choice in this area. *A* will likely favor legal interference with abortion and possibly also contraception; *B* will favor mandatory limits on family size and penalties for divergence from these limits. *L* should probably permit government to promote by persuasion and perhaps even some limited use of tax incentives policies that are deemed conducive to realizing the full capability set for all citizens.[52] But it should certainly stop well short of policies such as China's aggressively interfering one-child rule and the practices of mandatory sterilization for certain groups that have been favored elsewhere in the developing world.

Notice a complexity in this position. The fundamental bearer of capabilities for *L* is an individual person, not a group. (Here again, *L* is close to the Rawlsian liberal.) But sometimes individuals are oppressed within their families, and the active help of government is their only way of ensuring the equal worth of their liberty. Thus, aggressive government action to promote condom use, for example, may be the only way in which women in many parts of the developing world can attain the capability of choice within their marriages, with respect to both pregnancy and disease. For government to get out of the area completely would not be a good way of promoting choice. In such cases *L* will favor such measures as aggressive advertising and subsidizing of condoms on the theory that, rather like education, such policies expand the genuine capability set of all individuals.

5. Family Law. *L* will favor a uniform secular system of family law that is dedicated to promoting and protecting the capabilities of individual family members. Unlike some upholders of *A*, *L* will reject the argument that the liberty of conscience requires giving religious groups the right to make the law for their own members in such matters as marital consent, divorce, marital rape, and domestic violence. *L*'s rationale here is that families are composed of individuals who all have their needs for and rights to functioning. The only way to guarantee the protection of these individual rights will be for the basic constitutional structure to take a stand in defense of women's equality in all that relates to marriage and divorce. In a similar way, a uniform criminalization of marital rape and domestic violence is the only way to ensure to all citizens the equal capability for bodily integrity. *L* will therefore be highly critical of the situation in nations such as India, Bangladesh, and Israel, which have a liberal constitution with all sorts of guarantees of equality but then turn many important matters over to religiously based courts of family law that do not accord the same level of protection to human capabilities.[53]

6. Morals Legislation: Sex and Drugs. Here there is a fundamental split between *L* and *A*. *A*, focusing on the role of the state as teacher of virtue, will favor a wide range of morals laws, even without a showing of harm to others. *L*, focusing on capabilities as goal, will refuse to intervene unless there is a clear and immediate showing of harm. There will be gray areas, and the decision in some areas, such as prostitution and hard drugs, will properly turn on empirical information. If prostitution can be shown to be reformable in ways that do not involve harms to women of the kind now associated with the control of pimps, *L* will be likely to support its decriminalization.[54] If the decriminalization of hard drugs can be shown to reduce harms associated with their illegality, *L* will consider such policies, though not without special protection of the interests of minors. Regulation of adult smoking will be supported by *L* only on the grounds of harm to the health of nonsmokers—although, here again, minors can be treated differently and although here, as in the case of population control, the use of public persuasion by government is a perfectly legitimate way to advance healthy functioning without interfering with capabilities. *A* will typically support aggressive legal controls in all of these areas.

7. Safety and Environment. *L* and *B* will support a good deal of government control over such matters as product safety, drug testing, medical licensing, housing codes, and the protection of individuals from harms caused by pollution and environmental contamination; since this is not really related to *A*'s focus on virtue, *A*'s position is not clear. *L* and *B* will be likely to strike the balance somewhat differently in the environmental area, but the capability for a fruitful relationship with the world of nature is on *L*'s list as well as *B*'s,[55] and promoting this capability will certainly require legal regulation of individual choices.

Product safety standards and housing codes are different from the morals laws favored by *A*, because their rationale is not primarily to prevent risky personal choices but, rather, to prevent harm to others (the ignorant general public, the poor) that would be caused by the absence of such regulation. Compulsory recycling and other policies aimed at preserving the environment for the long-term future will be more difficult for *L* to handle, but if *L* follows the lead of Rawlsian liberalism she may favor such policies as appropriate in the light of the interests of future generations. Once again, the issue will be whether a convincing showing of harm to others can be made.

8. Work and Occupational Choice. *L*, like the Rawlsian liberal, makes the right to work and the free choice of occupation central features of human functioning. In this *B* may not agree (and to that extent will not agree with a part of the list). *B* may be convinced that a market economy is bad for people on other grounds and be persuaded by these thoughts to favor an economic system that does not protect free choice of occupation in the way that a market economy does.[56] All three positions will probably admit some form of military conscription or required national service, but it is significant that this will be morally complex for *L* in a way that it will not be for either *A* or *B*.

9. Taxation, Land Reform, and So On. *A* does not appear to have a definite position on these issues. *L* and *B* would both support redistributive measures designed to promote capability equality if empirical information indicates that they really will promote that goal better than other policies, and *L* will not think this necessarily involves a grave interference with liberty. (*L* does not have as clear a sense of who rightly owns what as some property libertarians do and would regard the use of the term "taking" as begging many questions in the absence of a theory of just ownership.) If some citizens find themselves thwarted with respect to expensive preferences or tastes they have developed, *L* and *B* will remind them—concurring here with Rawls—that the political conception of citizenship they have agreed to adopt is that of an active shaper of a life plan, one who takes responsibility for his or her own tastes and preferences.[57] Thus the fact that someone's strong taste for a second home is thwarted by a policy of land reform in West Bengal should not be seen as necessarily involving a violation of that person's liberty. For the person's liberty, as understood by the conception, involves precisely a power of shaping and reshaping tastes, and this liberty is not at all violated by a reasonable redistributive policy.

Unlike *B*, however, *L* will insist on constraints imposed by the idea of strong separateness, which mandates a limited inviolability of personal property and possessions. Certainly *L* will insist on protections against unwarranted search and seizure as among the fundamental liberties, whereas B might not.

If anything has emerged clearly from this sketch, it is that each of these areas needs further investigation and argument from the proponents of *L*. Meanwhile, however, the hope is that a working sketch has emerged of a stance that further clarifies the basic motivations of *L* and its implications.

Citizens As Choosers

L's opponents will charge that by focusing on capability as goal *L* lets people get away with a lot of substandard functioning. *A* will say that in the absence of firm control people diverge from the path of virtue. *B* will say that in the absence of control they indulge in extravagance and greedy accumulation. This is true. But the defender of *L* has a final reply to make: that there is a distinctive human good expressed in the freedom we give our fellow citizens to make choices that we ourselves may hold to be profoundly wrong. Respect for the ethical separateness and the good faith searching of our fellow citizens is built into *L*'s list, in the basic role it gives to traditional political liberties, especially in matters of speech and sexuality. *L* urges that this ought to be recognized as a distinctive human good, even by people who hold that the choices many citizens will make when they have those freedoms are profoundly mistaken. Mutual respect does not imply uncertainty or skepticism about the good; it implies, instead, a certain higher-order good, a vision of the citizen as an active searcher for what has worth, whose sincere engagement in that search should be allowed to unfold in freedom, even if it should lead to what seems to be error—unless it inflicts manifest harms on others. This conception of the citizen is not peculiar to Aristotelian and Kantian liberalism: it is also deeply rooted in the Catholic tradition, ancestor of *A*, and in the Marxian tradition, ancestor of *B*. To that extent there may be internal inconsistency in both *A* and *B*, insofar as they build respect for practical reason into their conceptions and then suppress its workings at crucial junctures. At least we may urge them to see whether, from their distinctive starting points, they could not accept the conception of liberty in position *L*, as the basis for a working political consensus. It would appear that they must accept it unless they wish to depart radically from a picture of the dignity and inviolability of the human being that guided them both in shaping their own distinctive conceptions. But if they accept this conception, they should accept the political consequences that flow from it—unless they can show us that such consequences do not follow.

This is the beginning of a further argument, not its end; on every issue that divides the positions, as well as the foundational questions, concrete arguments must be thrashed out in detail. But ultimately, *L* claims, in our use of the good in domestic political action and in the many international deliberations in which the capabilities approach may play a role, the good as discipline must yield to and be illuminated by the good as freedom.

Notes

I am very grateful to David A. Crocker, Amartya Sen, and Cass Sunstein for their comments on an earlier version of this paper. This essay is continuous with several others I have published: "Nature, Function, and Capability," *Oxford Studies in Ancient Philosophy*, suppl. vol. 1 (1988): 145–84; "Non-Relative Virtues: An Aristotelian Approach," in *The Quality of Life*, ed. Martha C. Nussbaum and Amartya Sen (Oxford: Clarendon Press, 1993), 242–76; "Aristotelian Social Democracy," in *Liberalism and the Good*, ed. R. Bruce Douglass, Gerald M. Mara, and Henry S. Richardson (New York: Routledge, 1990), 203–52; "Aristotle on Human Nature and the Foundations of Ethics," in *World, Mind, and Ethics: Essays on the Ethical Philosophy of Bernard Williams*, ed. E. J. Altham and Ross Harrison (Cambridge: Cambridge University Press, 1995), 86–131; "Human Functioning and Social Justice: In Defense of Aristotelian Essentialism," *Political Theory* 20 (1992): 202–46; "Human Capabilities, Female Human Beings," in *Women, Culture, and Development: A Study of Human Capabilities*, ed. Martha C. Nussbaum and Jonathan Glover (Oxford: Clarendon Press, 1995), 61–104; "The Feminist Critique of Liberalism," in *Women's Voices, Women's Lives: The Amnesty Lectures 1996*, ed. M. Forey and J. Gardner (Boulder: Westview, forthcoming).

1. I have followed Crawley's translation for the most part, substituting more literal renderings at several points throughout.
2. *New Republic*, 3 May 1919, 13; for the text of Freund's article and a discussion of the controversy in which it played a part, see Harry Kalven, Jr., "Ernst Freund and the First Amendment Tradition," *University of Chicago Law Review* 40 (1973): 235–47, with afterword by Douglas H. Ginsburg.
3. John Rawls, *A Theory of Justice* (Cambridge, Mass.: Harvard University Press, 1971), 62 ff., 90–95, 396–97.
4. See John Rawls, "The Priority of the Right and Ideas of the Good," *Philosophy and Public Affairs* 17, no. 4 (Fall 1988): 251–76; and *Political Liberalism* (New York: Columbia University Press, 1993), 178–90.
5. Rawls, *Political Liberalism*, 188.
6. Rawls, *Political Liberalism*, 181.
7. See Nussbaum, "Aristotelian Social Democracy" and "Human Capabilities"; also Amartya Sen, "Equality of What?" in *Choice, Welfare, and Measurement* (Oxford: Blackwell; Cambridge, Mass.: MIT Press, 1982) and

"Capability and Well-Being" in *The Quality of Life*, ed. Nussbaum and Sen, 30–53.

8. See Rawls, *A Theory of Justice*, 415–16; *Political Liberalism*, 185.

9. Notice that in respect of this question, the grouping of the functions is extremely important: being able to use the senses is considered something without which a life is not fully human, but lacking the use of one or more particular senses is not. On the other hand, when we move from mere human functioning to good human functioning, we will judge that lacking the ability to use even one of the senses is an impediment to good functioning; this gives us reasons to devote resources to assist those who are in jeopardy with respect to even one of these capabilities.

10. In "Aristotle on Human Nature" I discuss the treatment of this point in contemporary medical ethics.

11. In "Aristotle on Human Nature," there is a more extended account of this procedure, its cross-cultural origins, and how it is used to justify the list of human functions.

12. See Nussbaum, "Non-Relative Virtues."

13. For an excellent discussion of this question, and a revision of Rawls with which I largely agree, see Thomas W. Pogge, *Realizing Rawls* (Ithaca, N.Y.: Cornell University Press, 1989).

14. Rawls, *Political Liberalism.*

15. In most respects, this list is the same as the one I give in "Human Capabilities," with new attention paid to violence against the person, the presence of justified anger, and the role of free choice of occupation.

16. "Normal length" is clearly relative to current human possibilities and may need, for practical purposes, to be to some extent relativized to local conditions. But it seems important to think of it—at least at a given time in history—in universal and comparative terms in order to give incentives for change and redistribution. For instance, the *Human Development Report*, published by the United Nations Development Programme, uses a comparative notion of life expectancy to illustrate differences of performance between countries, showing, for example, that a country may have done well with some indicators of life quality, but badly on life expectancy. And although some degree of relativity may be put down to the differential genetic possibilities of different groups (the "missing women" statistics, for example, allow that on the average women live somewhat longer than men), it is also important not to conclude prematurely that inequalities between groups, for example, the growing inequalities in life expectancy between blacks and whites in the United States, are simply genetic variation and not connected with social injustice.

17. The precise specification of the health capability is not easy, but the work currently being done on health in drafting new constitutions in South Africa and Eastern Europe gives reasons for hope that the combination of a general specification of a health right with a tradition of judicial interpretation will yield something practicable. It should be noticed that I speak of health, not just health care: and health itself interacts in complex ways with housing, education, and dignity. There is controversy over whether levels of health and nutrition should

be specified universally or relatively to the local community and its traditions. For example, is low height associated with nutritional practices to be thought of as "stunting" or as felicitous adaptation to circumstances of scarcity? For an excellent summary of this debate, see S. R. Osmani, ed., *Nutrition and Poverty* (Oxford: Clarendon Press, WIDER series, 1992), especially the following chapters: on the relativist side, T. N. Srinivasan, "Undernutrition: Concepts, Measurements, and Policy Implications," 97–120; and on the universalist side, C. Gopalan, "Undernutrition: Measurement and Implications," 17–48. For a compelling adjudication of the debate, coming out on the universalist side, see S. R. Osmani, "On Some Controversies in the Measurement of Undernutrition," 121–61.

18. There is a growing literature on the importance of shelter for health. For example, the provision of adequate housing is the single largest determinant of health status for HIV-infected persons. Housing rights are increasingly coming to be constitutionalized, at least in a negative form—giving squatters grounds for appeal, for example, against a landlord who would bulldoze their shanties.

19. I shall not elaborate here on what I think promoting this capability requires, since there is a future volume in the WIDER series devoted to this topic: *Women, Equality, and Reproduction*, ed. Jonathan Glover and Martha C. Nussbaum (Oxford: Clarendon Press, WIDER Series, forthcoming).

20. A good example of an education right that I would support is given in the African National Congress South African Constitution draft, Article 11:

Education shall be free and compulsory up to the age of sixteen, and provision shall be made for facilitating access to secondary, vocational and tertiary education on an equal basis for all. Education shall be directed towards the development of the human personality and a sense of personal dignity, and shall aim at strengthening respect for human rights and fundamental freedoms and promoting understanding, tolerance and friendship amongst South Africans and between nations.

The public (or otherwise need-blind) provision of higher education will have to be relative to local possibilities, but it is at least clear that the United States lags far behind most other countries of comparable wealth in this area.

21. Amartya Sen has not committed himself to any such definite list of the basic functions and capabilities.

22. On "adaptive preferences," see Amartya Sen, "Gender Inequality and Theories of Justice," in *Women, Culture, and Development*, ed. Nussbaum and Glover, 259–73; also "Capability and Well-Being."

23. See Nussbaum, "Aristotle on Human Nature" and "Aristotelian Social Democracy."

24. Again, I do not mean "Sen and I," since Sen is not committed to this whole enterprise. This is just the academic "we," meaning "I, and anyone who is interested in pursuing this project with me."

25. See Nussbaum, "Aristotle on Human Nature," with discussion of Marx, 118–20.

26. See Martha C. Nussbaum, "Double Moral Standards?" Reply to Yael Tamir, "Hands off Clitoridectomy," *Boston Review* October/November 1996,

28–30, and "Religion and Women's Human Rights," in *Religion and Contemporary Liberalism*, ed. Paul Weithman (Notre Dame, Ind.: Notre Dame University Press, 1997).

27. See Nussbaum, "Nature, Function, and Capability," 160–72, referring to Aristotle's similar distinctions; and, on the basic capabilities, "Human Capabilities," 83–89.

28. My earlier essays called these "external capabilities," but David Crocker has suggested to me that this suggests a misleading contrast with "internal."

29. This distinction is related to Rawls's distinction between social and natural primary goods. Whereas he holds that only the social primary goods should be on the list, and not the natural ones, such as health or imagination, we say that the *social basis* of the natural primary goods should most emphatically be on the list.

30. Rawls, *A Theory of Justice*, 62.

31. In *A Theory of Justice*, Rawls comments that "although their possession is influenced by the basic structure, they are not so directly under its control" (62). This is of course true if we are thinking of health: but if we think of the social basis of health, it is not true. It seems to me that the case for putting these items on the political list is just as strong as the case for the social basis of self-respect. In "The Priority of the Right," Rawls suggests putting health on the list.

32. See Nussbaum, "Aristotelian Social Democracy."

33. See Nussbaum, "Aristotle on Human Nature."

34. Amartya Sen, "Freedoms and Needs," *New Republic*, 10 & 17 January 1994, 38.

35. Rawls, *Political Liberalism*, 187–88.

36. Though in one form Aristotle had it too. See Nussbaum, "Nature, Function, and Capability," 146–55, 181–84.

37. Compare Sen, "Freedoms and Needs," 38: "The importance of political rights for the understanding of economic needs turns ultimately on seeing human beings as people with rights to exercise, not as parts of a 'stock' or a 'population' that passively exists and must be looked after. What matters, finally, is how we see each other."

38. One might of course distinguish between the revolutionary situation and the envisaged goal: such distinctions were made with much plausibility by Robespierre in the French Revolution. But since Marx says so little about the life under communism, we cannot tell how far the traditional political liberties would be protected. Obviously many of his followers have not attached great importance to them.

39. See Nussbaum, "Aristotelian Social Democracy."

40. See John Finnis, *Natural Law and Natural Rights* (Oxford: Clarendon Press, 1980); and Robert P. George, *Making Men Moral: Civil Liberties and Public Morality* (Oxford: Clarendon Press, 1993). For related discussions, see Robert P. George, ed., *Natural Law Theory* (Oxford: Clarendon Press, 1992); Alasdair MacIntyre, *Whose Justice? Which Rationality?* (Notre Dame, Ind.: University of Notre Dame Press, 1988). For a collection that includes a variety

of interpretations of both natural law theory and philosophical liberalism, see Robert P. George, ed., *Natural Law, Liberalism, and Morality: Contemporary Essays* (Oxford: Clarendon Press, 1996).

41. See Cass R. Sunstein, *The Partial Constitution* (Cambridge, Mass.: Harvard University Press, 1993).

42. Examples of *B2* would be Chinese or Cuban socialism; examples of *B1* would include the position of Holmes Rolston III, "Feeding People Versus Saving Nature?" in *World Hunger and Morality*, 2d ed., ed. William Aiken and Hugh LaFollette (Upper Saddle River, N.J.: Prentice-Hall, 1996), 248–66. Since *B2* is far more influential in today's world than *B1*, I shall focus more on this subfamily.

43. For an illuminating and balanced account of such matters, see Jean Drèze and Amartya Sen, *India: Economic Development and Social Opportunity* (Oxford: Clarendon Press, 1995), which both gives the case for government intervention to promote human capabilities and criticizes some aspects of socialist and Marxist regional government for excessive economic control. See also Drèze and Sen, *Hunger and Public Action* (Oxford: Clarendon Press, 1989).

44. Some varieties of *B1* would not agree here, since their focus is on the environment as such, not on people; to that extent, here again, my arguments focus on *B2*.

45. These concessions apply primarily to *B1*. *B2* usually sees environmental quality as necessary for the well-being of people.

46. See Stephen Holmes and Cass R. Sunstein, *The Cost of Rights* (New York: Norton, forthcoming).

47. See Sunstein, *The Partial Constitution*, 71–75, 159–61, 204–5.

48. See Nussbaum, "Aristotelian Social Democracy," with reference to Ronald Dworkin's similar view.

49. See Cass R. Sunstein, *Democracy and the Problem of Free Speech* (New York: Free Press, 1993).

50. See Nussbaum, "Religion and Women's Human Rights."

51. See Amartya Sen, "Fertility and Coercion, *University of Chicago Law Review* 63 (1996): 1035–61.

52. Here I disagree with Sen's more libertarian version of *L*; see Sen, "Fertility and Coercion." On norm management, see Cass R. Sunstein, "Social Norms and Social Roles," *Columbia Law Review* 96 (1996): 903–68.

53. See Nussbaum, "Religious Discourse and Women's Human Rights."

54. See Sibyl Schwarzenbach, "Contractarians and Feminists Debate Prostitution," *New York University Review of Law and Social Change* 18 (1990–91): 103–30; Laurie Shrage, "Prostitution and the Case for Decriminalization," *Dissent* (Spring 1996): 41–45; Martha Nussbaum, " 'Whether From Reason or Prejudice': Taking Money for Bodily Services," *Journal of Legal Studies* 27, no. 2, pt. 2 (June 1998).

55. Note that *L* and *B2* think of environmental quality as instrumental to human capabilities, whereas *B1* thinks of it as good in itself.

56. On this reason for defending the market, see Rawls, *Theory of Justice*, 272. Rawls notes that this does not tell us whether to favor market socialism or capitalism.

57. See Rawls, *Political Liberalism*, 185.

18

Living at a High Economic Standard:
A Functionings Analysis

Jerome M. Segal

When we evaluate the economic performance of any particular society, be it our own, those of the former communist countries, or those of the Third World, a central criterion is whether or not there has been a general and sustained rise in the *standard of living*. If there has not been, or, if relative to the performance of other countries or its own performance in other periods the results have been mediocre, then this strongly suggests some problem with economic institutions or economic policy.

Implicitly or explicitly, such evaluations are constantly being made. They fill our news pages; they flesh out our sense of where progress is being made and where it is not; they serve as the backdrop for our ongoing policy discourse.

Of course, the validity of the evaluations and the use to which they are put rest on the adequacy of the concept of *standard of living*. If we are operating with a faulty conception of the standard of living (or of some analogous concept such as *economic well-being*), then the evaluations will be flawed and the policy prescriptions misguided.

Given the impact of how we understand the fundamental concepts, it is striking that more attention is not paid to them. Both Amartya Sen and Martha C. Nussbaum have played a significant role in insisting on the importance to public policy of alternative conceptions of the good and in challenging the dominant notions of the good that are implicit within mainstream economic discourse.

Specifically, both Sen and Nussbaum have argued against conceiving of the individual good (or well-being or standard of living) either in terms of utility or preference satisfaction, or in terms of levels of income or possession of goods. Instead, drawing on earlier thinkers, in

342

particular Aristotle, they have articulated a general approach that emphasizes human functioning—what people actually do, feel, and experience—and their capabilities to function. In this approach, having a good life is above all else to live (and experience) in particular ways.

In her essay in this volume, "The Good as Discipline, the Good as Freedom" Nussbaum opens with a quotation from Aristotle: "A person who is going to make a fruitful inquiry into the question of the best political arrangement must first set out clearly what the most choiceworthy life is. For if that is unclear, the best political arrangement must also be unclear" (Pol. 1321a14–17). She writes, "The reason [Aristotle] plausibly gives for this claim is that the goods distributed by politics, such as money, honors, and entitlements, are not good in and of themselves. They are good insofar as they are tools of human functioning."[1]

This is a perspective with which I agree, and my primary concern is with these goods: money, honors, and entitlements, not as distributed by politics but rather as generated and distributed through economic life. In this essay, I seek to use a version of the capabilities/functionings approach to shed light on one of the most fundamental questions of economics: What is the relationship between higher levels of income and increased standard of living (or economic well-being)? This question can be posed on two levels, that of each person taken individually and that of the society as a whole. For the individual the question emerges as: Does my standard of living go up as my money income rises? And for the society as a whole, the question might be posed as: To what extent does a general rise in the level of income increase economic well-being?

These crucially important questions do not even get formulated if we start off on the wrong foot, conceptually speaking. Thus, if we understand *standard of living* as identical to the income or consumption level of the individual, then economic growth that results in a general rise in the income level or in the level of consumption will have produced—by definition—a rise in the standard of living. Our question will have been answered before we even start. It is a central virtue of the capabilities/functionings approach, which understands well-being as a pattern or variety of patterns of human functionings and/or capabilities, that it blocks any automatic transition from increased consumption to increased well-being. Thus, what the dominant economic discourse approaches as a matter of logical truth is on the capabilities/functionings approach revealed to be an empirical matter of considerable complexity and subtlety.

In what follows I first review Nussbaum's explication of what she terms "the central functional capabilities" to consider the usefulness of her specific approach to the question at hand. Second, I introduce a different approach within the larger capabilities/functionings orientation, one that I believe can shed considerable light on the relationship of income growth to higher standards of living.

Nussbaum's List of Central Human Functional Capabilities

Here then is Nussbaum's list of central human functional capabilities.[2]

1. *Life*. Being able to live to the end of a human life of normal length; not dying prematurely, or before one's life is so reduced as to be not worth living.
2. *Bodily Health and Integrity*. Being able to have good health; to be adequately nourished; to have adequate shelter; having opportunities for sexual satisfaction and for choice in matters of reproduction; being able to move from place to place; being secure against violent assault, including sexual assault, marital rape, and domestic violence.
3. *Pleasure and Pain*. Being able to avoid unnecessary and nonbeneficial pain, so far as possible, and to have pleasurable experiences.
4. *Senses, Imagination, Thought*. Being able to use the senses; being able to imagine, to think, and to reason and to do these things in a way informed and cultivated by an adequate education, including, but by no means limited to, literacy and basic mathematical and scientific training. Being able to use imagination and thought in connection with experiencing and producing spiritually enriching materials and events of one's own choice (religious, literary, musical, and so forth). Being able to use one's mind in ways protected by guarantees of freedom of expression with respect to both political and artistic speech, and freedom of religious exercise.
5. *Emotions*. Being able to have attachments to things and persons outside ourselves; to love those who love and care for us, to grieve at their absence; in general, to love, to grieve, to experience longing, gratitude, and justified anger. Supporting this capability means supporting forms of human association that can be shown to be crucial in their development.
6. *Practical Reason*. Being able to form a conception of the good and to engage in critical reflection about the planning of one's own life. This includes, today, being able to seek employment outside the home (in a regime protecting the free choice of occupation) and to participate in political life.
7. *Affiliation*. Being able to live for and to others, to recognize and show concern for other human beings, to engage in various forms of social interaction; to be able to imagine the situation of another and to have compassion for that situation; to have the capability for both justice and friendship. Protecting this capability means, once again, protect-

ing institutions that constitute such forms of affiliation, and also protecting the freedoms of assembly and political speech.

8. *Other Species.* Being able to live with concern for and in relation to animals, plants, and the world of nature.

9. *Play.* Being able to laugh, to play, to enjoy recreational activities.

10. *Separateness.* Being able to live one's own life and nobody else's. This means having certain guarantees of noninterference with certain choices that are especially personal and definitive of selfhood, such as choices regarding marriage, childbearing, sexual expression, speech, and employment.

10a. *Strong Separateness.* Being able to live one's own life in one's own surroundings and context. This means guarantees of freedom of association and of freedom from unwarranted search and seizure; it also means a certain sort of guarantee of the integrity of personal property, though this guarantee may be limited in various ways by the demands of social equality, and is always up for negotiation in connection with the interpretation of the other capabilities.

Nussbaum has presented a list of capabilities to function. Each is claimed to be necessary for the good human life. She says that "a life that *lacks any one* of these capabilities, no matter what else it has, will fall short of being a good human life."[3] And while Nussbaum is open to the possibility that the list might need to be further augmented or revised, I believe her intention is to be comprehensive, to have identified *all* of the capabilities that are necessary for the good life.

Since for every capability term there is a correlate functioning term (for instance, for the capability "being able to live a normal life span" there is the correlate functioning "living a normal life span"), Nussbaum easily could have presented her list as a set of functionings. Her reason for not doing so is that "capability, not functioning, is our political goal. . . . For political purposes it is appropriate for us to shoot for capabilities, and for those alone."[4] At the same time Nussbaum states, "It is perfectly true that functionings, not simply capabilities, are what render a life fully human: if there were no functioning of any kind in a life, we could hardly applaud it, no matter what opportunities it contained."[5]

While fear of excessive state interference might lead one to specify the specific targets of what Nussbaum refers to as "political planning" in terms of capabilities (enabling the citizenry to function in certain ways) rather than in terms of their actually functioning in a desired way, it does not seem to me that the needs of public policy can be met fully by an analysis that remains on the capabilities level.

For instance, when we seek to define and measure actual standards of living, we are legitimately concerned with the actual lives that people are living, not just what potential they might have to be living at any given standard. Thus, a family might have an income that enables them to live free from avoidable diseases, but our concern for well-being extends to at least knowing the extent to which they are doing so. What the state decides to do about it, if anything, is a separate matter.

This concern for the actual functionings on the individual level is similar to what is now a commonplace with respect to evaluating overall economic performance on the societal level. For instance, in looking at socioeconomic performance in Third World countries, we are not just concerned with whether or not the economy has the potential to reduce infant mortality to negligible levels but whether or not it has actually done so. Thus, I would argue that for policy purposes we need information not only on capabilities but also on actual functionings as well.

This point brings me to a particular problem I have in understanding how functionings and capabilities are related on Nussbaum's account. Given what she has said, that "it is perfectly true that functionings, not simply capabilities, are what render a life fully human," one might infer that in her view the good life consists of functioning in a certain manner, and the various capabilities deemed "necessary" for the good life derive their status from the logically prior necessity of the correlate functionings to the good life.

Yet, from specific passages in her account it would seem that this is *not* what she is saying. Thus, she has made clear her view that not all of the correlate functionings are necessary. She writes:

> A deeply religious person may prefer not to be well nourished but to engage in strenuous fasting. Whether for religious or other reasons, a person may prefer a celibate life to one containing sexual expression. A person may prefer to work with an intense dedication that precludes recreation and play. Are we saying that these are not fully human or flourishing lives? And are we instructing government to push people into functioning of the requisite sort, no matter what they prefer?
>
> Here we must answer *no*: capability, not functioning, is our political goal.[6]

Given that she has asked two questions, one about whether these functionings are necessary for a flourishing life and one about whether the state should intervene, it is not fully clear whether her "no" applies to both questions or only to the latter. As I find it implausible that these correlate functionings are each necessary for the good human life, I will interpret her as having similarly recognized that people can flourish without all the functionings.[7] But if this is her position, then for those functionings that are *not necessary* it is hard to understand why the correlative capabilities are necessary.[8]

This is not merely a theoretical point about the logic of her claim that these capabilities are necessary; it emerges again and again when we ask of specific capabilities whether they are necessary for the good human life. Examples:

1. "Having opportunities for sexual satisfaction." Some people have very little or no sex at all—certain priesthoods, certain nineteenth-century utopian communes, some people who are impotent, some people who are faithful to one who has died. Nussbaum would agree that we cannot say that none of them are living a good life. But if it is not necessarily important that these people have sexual activity, why is it necessary for their living a good human life that they have opportunities for such activity? Is the life of the monk with reduced opportunities less good than that of the priest facing daily temptation?

2. "Being able to move from place to place." If this merely means the ability to walk around, then almost everyone has it. I assume Nussbaum means something more, such as the ability to travel within one's country, a freedom that serfs did not have and that is generally lacking among the poor. But if so, then while this capability may be important to many people, it would seem excessive to say it is a necessary feature of the good life. Some people live well without ever leaving their valley; indeed if life is good, they have less incentive to roam.

3. "Being able to live with concern for and in relation to animals, plants, and the world of nature." I'm not sure what it means to not *be able* to live in this way. Consider this first on the level of functioning. Is it really the case that people who do not like animals, or who take little interest in them, do not live a good life? How did Shakespeare, Aristotle, Descartes, or Balzac live in relation to animals and nature? Does it matter? Suppose we find that they lacked the capability "to live with concern for animals and plants," perhaps because they believed that animals were mechanisms without consciousness. Would this show that they did not have good human lives?

4. "Being able to laugh, to play, to enjoy recreational activities." On the level of functioning, why is it necessary that every good human life must contain play and recreation? There are good lives of dedication and devotion to ideals of religion, service to others, knowledge, political transformation, or art. Some people are very serious—and they may not be well-rounded individuals. Playing, laughing, and recreating may be absent in their lives; yet it seems that they can have a good life. Indeed, they may find pleasure,

satisfaction, meaning, and even joy in what they do without playing, laughing, or recreating at all. Suppose that they not only do
not play or recreate but also lack the capability of doing so—either
because of the time demands of what is vital to them or because
of psychological disposition. It would seem odd to maintain that
because they lack this capability (which need not be actualized in
any event) their lives fall short of being good human lives.

5. "Being able to live one's own life and nobody else's. . . . having
certain guarantees of noninterference with certain choices that are
especially personal and definitive of selfhood, such as choices regarding marriage. . . ." Is it really true that no one who had an
arranged marriage ever had a good life? Are entire cultures ineligi-
ble? We may want to protect the right of people to choose for
other reasons—after all, everyone has an inalienable right to make
mistakes—but that is very different from saying that being able to
choose is a necessary feature of any good life.

6. "Being able to live one's own life in one's own surroundings and
context." By this Nussbaum "means guarantees of freedom of association and of freedom from unwarranted search and
seizure. . . ." Such freedoms are unfortunately rather rare in
human history. Are we saying that no one who lives in a society
without freedom of association lives a good life?[9] For some people
this lack of freedom is utterly irrelevant; for others it may mean
they are thwarted. But even for those who chafe and struggle
against it, can one not find the good life in the political struggle
against injustice? Many people have found that they flourished
most intensely in political struggle—over the Vietnam war, for
example, or in the civil rights movement. Such struggle can be the
most meaningful part of someone's life, a kind of high point of
creative energy and common cause with others against injustice.

I see no reason to deny that people may flourish without significant
freedom (political or psychological) to move about, to marry whomever
they wish, to participate in political activity, or to enjoy nature. We can
have good lives without freedom from potential unwarranted search and
seizure and without freedom from suppression of political speech or
assembly. Indeed, people who have these freedoms may ask, with some
despair and emptiness, "Where have all the causes gone?" This is not
to say that as a general matter such capabilities and freedoms are not of
great importance to the human good. It is merely to say that there are
many ways and circumstances in which people can flourish. We cannot
assume that those capabilities and freedoms are necessary for every
good life or even that they matter in every life.

The significance of the foregoing points is this: If the list of capabilities is truly a list of necessary capabilities for the good life, then it is an extremely powerful tool. It allows us to look at societies or situations in which these capabilities are lacking and say that whatever else may be going on, these people are being denied the opportunity of the good life and, thus, that things must change. If, on the other hand, the list is, as I believe, a list not of necessary capabilities but of generally important capabilities, then it has less power. Where one or another capability is missing, the good life might still be possible, might even be compensated for by the availability of another capability. Nonetheless, if Nussbaum has provided a menu of clearly defined "building blocks" of the good life such that any concept of the good life worthy of respect is constituted by selections from the menu, she has accomplished a great deal.

Let me then turn to another question: Do these capabilities, even if one has them all, add up to the good life? Or has something important been left out?[10]

One difficulty that we encounter in trying to answer this question is that many of these functionings (or capabilities) are matters of degree. And often enough matters of degree can be very important. Thus, if someone has a great capability to love and to make friends and enjoy them—and if such capabilities are realized in his life—then one is tempted to say that he has a good life. But the case would be much less convincing if either the capacities or the functionings existed to a very limited degree. Because she is committed to explicating the good human life and not just human life per se, Nussbaum has, I believe, an intention to specify a *minimal threshold* of capability that is required. Yet, quite a few of these capabilities are articulated without any minimal threshold being evident. If there is no minimal required level, however, then nearly everyone has the capability in question, whether they are impoverished or rich, flourishing or languishing. Examples: "having opportunities for sexual satisfaction" (Nussbaum list #2); "being able to move from place to place" (#2); "being able . . . to have pleasurable experiences" (#3); "being able . . . to participate in political life" (#6); "being able . . . to engage in critical reflection about the planning of one's own life" (#6); "being able to laugh, to play, to enjoy recreational activities" (#9).

I would suggest that, at least to a minor degree, virtually everyone has such capabilities. If this is true then, without any minimal threshold being identified, the possession of all of these capabilities (and their minimal expression in the actual living of life) cannot be sufficient for the good life unless we are prepared to say that virtually everyone now leads such a life. The obvious corrective would be to identify substantial thresholds for each valuable capability. The problem with this, however, is that while having (or exercising) all of these valuable capabilities might be sufficient for the good life, it would be very implausible that it was necessary to have each capability to such a high degree.

The question of a threshold emerges from another direction as well. As I understand it, Nussbaum wants her account to accommodate a wide variety of specific visions of the good life. She believes that it is an essential part of the good life that each person work out his own conception of the good life; if this is to be meaningful, then multiple forms of the good life must be possible. The problem is that on different concrete conceptions of the good life *very different* elements are emphasized. What minimal threshold may be necessary under one conception may be viewed as quite unnecessary, even excessive, under another.

Consider, for instance, the visions of the good life represented by Aristotle (contemplative), D. H. Lawrence (sexual/experiential), Leon Trotsky (revolutionary), Cotton Mather (religious), and Caribbean Cruise Lines (pleasure/play). I am not sure that Nussbaum would accept these as alternative forms of a good human life, but they seem plausible candidates to me. Each represents a vision that has had a powerful appeal to many. Each offers opportunities for a person to flourish, at least in some important domains of the human personality.

Suppose for a moment that we view these as acceptable alternative ways of having a good human life. Note that they all have a common structural feature in that they all agree that one key element constitutes the very heart of the good life and that others are secondary, optional, or even excluded altogether. But they disagree sharply on what that one central element is. Is it self-examination, sex, political engagement, religious devotion, travel, recreation, absence of pain, fun, or what? All of these elements are represented on Nussbaum's list, but the minimal threshold that would be necessary for any one of these visions might be excessive for the others. To remain open to all of them, the list could not require high thresholds. Yet from the perspective of each of these conceptions, if Nussbaum's list only requires the most minimal level of that which it treats as central, then the entire list is thoroughly inadequate, failing to capture the essence of the good life.

If this criticism is correct, then her list fails to provide in a meaningful sense the building blocks of the good life. It is not that someone else might do better than Nussbaum; rather, it seems that the project itself is not attainable. What were to have been the building blocks of any good life emerges only as a great menu offering the elements of the multiple incompatible visions. This, of course, does not get us very far.

Nussbaum might respond by saying that each of these conceptions represents an excessive concentration on one or another element, and that they are all flawed. But I do not see how she could demonstrate this. Moreover, it seems to me that often enough the good life is somewhat lopsided. A person can have most or all of Nussbaum's items in his or her life, and yet somehow it does not come together. The lopsidedness may emerge because the good life needs some central project or conception that pulls the pieces into a kind of coherence, so that it is in fact *a life* and not just a series of episodes: getting nourished, playing the piano, taking a walk in nature, visiting a friend, reflecting on the good life, choosing a mate, having sex. This integration is one dimension of what people refer to as "meaning."

Another aspect of "meaning," I believe, has to do with feeling that it all amounts to something. People typically experience a need for some element of transcendence, a connection to something bigger than our interests and tastes—a connection to something of enduring value. This often means a life that is devoted to some ideal, be it service to others, art, knowledge, political transformation, or religion. And in this devotion, there may often be much that is good that is given up.

Finally, and independent of the above, while Nussbaum emphasizes that the capabilities approach offers those concerned with public policy "guidance . . . superior to that offered by several rivals on the development scene,"[11] her analysis fails to provide much "guidance" just where one would look for it: with respect to questions of economic life.

One way of thinking about the economic realm is to consider that most adults participate in two distinct markets. First, in the labor market we are sellers of our time and skills. In exchange we receive income and diverse nonpecuniary benefits that come with employment. Second, we enter the marketplace as consumers, purchasing, in exchange for income, a wide variety of consumption goods and services.

With respect to the economic realm, understood in terms of these two kinds of market involvement, Nussbaum's version of the capabilities/functionings approach offers relatively little for those concerned with central categories such as work, time, and consumption.

Work

For most of us, one third of our life is spent at the workplace; there is in Nussbaum's essay a striking absence of discussion of work environments. Meaningful work is absolutely central and at the core of any serious consideration of alternatives to the consumerist vision of the economic good. If it appears at all within Nussbaum's list, it is in the brief reference to choice of employment within her category of "separateness."[12]

When we think of standard of living in terms of income levels, we completely miss the fact that the value we get from what we consume with our income is only half the story. The other half involves the work itself. Far from being neutral, work—for better or worse—represents a major component of our economic well-being. The work we undertake is a major determinant of our social status, individual sense of well-being, and self-fulfillment. So central are these elements to human well-being that a case can be made that, in societies in which basic elemental needs for food, clothing, and shelter have been met, economic activity's primary impact on well-being is not through higher levels of consumption but through the work experience itself.

If we focus on "authentic work"—work that is inherently rewarding and is deeply expressive of the individual—it is possible to argue for a fundamental reconceptualization of economic life. It would be excessive to maintain that to have this kind of work is to live well and to not have this work is to live poorly no matter what else one has in life, but authentic work is surely at the heart of the good life. Above the basic needs level, economies might reasonably take the provision of authentic work as their primary objective rather than the provision of consumption goods.

Time

The choices we make when we sell our labor time have a powerful impact on the larger place of time in our lives. In purely quantitative terms, for those who seek the good life outside the realm of paid employment (and, given the nature of work in the real world, this applies to most people), the amount of time devoted to work, to getting to work, and to preparing for work determines what we have left for work in the home and for so-called leisure.

The good life has much to do with our relationship to time. Life is a passage through time, and time itself has become part of our oppression. In part this has to do with the balance between time spent doing what is inherently valuable and that which is merely instrumental and often stultifying. Less subtly, the good life has to do with leisure. Aristotle was well aware of the impossibility of living the good life if too much time is devoted to the purely instrumental. To some extent, as a result, he saw slaves and servants as a necessary part of a sound household economy.

Our lives are often sadly overburdened. This is especially true of women who work at paid employment and—more than their fair share—at home, but it is true also of men. Our lives are harried to the point that there is no gracefulness to them at all. Among the supposedly successful middle class, many live at the point of exhaustion. Even when freed from odious work, in a rage to live the good life we can drive ourselves crazy just running around. With no gracefulness to it all, without some crafting of an aesthetic of time, even an agglomeration of good activities does not constitute a good life.

Consumption

At the core of the concern with the good life, from Aristotle to the present day, has been the issue of money and the things that money can buy. There has been a sense that our appetites are insatiable and that we are trapped in a never-ending escalation of our sense of the minimally necessary level of consumption. A central role for a concept of well-being, especially one grounded in the capabilities/functionings perspective, is to help us see such issues with greater clarity. Although Nussbaum believes that beyond a certain point additional consumption not only fails to improve life but may diminish it, only in a limited way does her list come into contact with things that we purchase.

When we get to areas of major consumer expenditure—food, housing, education, transport—we get little or no guidance as to how to think about how much is enough. Nussbaum speaks of being "adequately nourished," "having adequate shelter," and "having adequate education." But adequate for what? And in whose eyes?

Presumably, Nussbaum intends "adequate" to serve a critical purpose, distinguishing what is enough from what our runaway desires may seek. And here the functionings/capabilities approach can be very useful as "adequacy" can be explicated in terms of specific valued functionings. Unfortunately, Nussbaum does not take the capabilities/functionings approach in this more concretely economic direction.

What we need is a general analysis somewhat akin to that example from Adam Smith to which Sen has called attention in recent years:

> A linen shirt, for example, is, strictly speaking, not a necessary of life. The Greeks and the Romans lived, I suppose, very comfortably, though they had no linen. But in the present times, through the greater part of Europe, a creditable day-labourer would be ashamed to appear in public without a linen shirt, the want of which would be supposed to denote that disgraceful degree of poverty which, it is presumed, no body can well fall into without extreme bad conduct. Custom, in the same manner, had rendered leather shoes a necessary of life in England. The poorest creditable person of either sex would be ashamed to appear in public without them.[13]

Smith goes on to point out that in the Scotland of his day appearing without shoes was only shameful for men, while in France both men and women could appear without shoes and not suffer social stigma.[14]

The point is that living at a high economic standard does not consist of wearing a clean linen shirt or a pair of shoes. Rather it consists (in part) of a specific functioning: *appearing in public without shame.*[15] Exactly what clothing is required changes over time and differs from society to society. But in all or almost all societies there is some association between clothing, public appearance, and shame; and, thus, there is a valid cross-cultural formulation of this element of standard of living. And in any given culture in which one's ability to be clothed depends upon one's monetary income, a central driving force behind the pursuit of money would be that it enables one to be clothed at least to the level of being able to appear in public without shame.

For our purposes, the capability "being able to appear in public without shame" has a direct connection to economic life that other capabilities, such as "being able to laugh" or "being able to form attachments," do not seem to have, even though they are pertinent to human well-being in its broader aspects.

Can we then build upon Smith's example and formulate a set of functionings that collectively explicate what it is to live at a high economic standard? And can we use that analysis to shed light upon fundamental questions such as the role of growth of income within the individual and societal quest for a better life?

Focusing on the Economic Realm

I believe the capabilities/functionings framework can forcefully illuminate some of the central issues concerning consumption, economic policy, and economic performance. To see how this approach can be brought to bear on economic issues, let us consider that aspect of life that is distinctly economic. Rather than inquire about the good life or human well-being in all its richness, we limit our focus to the notion of *standard of living.* Typically, as mentioned earlier, economists think of a person's standard of living as identical with his level of income (or consumption). Or, if they make a theoretical distinction between income (or consumption) and standard of living, they will use income (or consumption) as a proxy for standard of living.

It is just this approach that Sen has criticized, and the great value of the linen shirt example is that it allows us to view income and consumption as tools that promote or facilitate central, and possibly universally valued, functionings such as "appearing in public without shame." Moreover, the desire to appear in public without shame emerges as a key motivational factor in explaining consumption expenditures and, to some extent, labor market choices.

In his essay "The Living Standard," partially reprinted in this volume, Sen calls for an explication of the concept of standard of living in terms of key capabilities to function rather than in terms of actual functionings.[16] Here, as with Nussbaum, I take issue with this emphasis. Merely having the capability to live well materially speaking (whether or not this is the limit of appropriate concern of the state) is not the same as actually doing so. To have a high standard of living is to actually live well economically.

Sen asks, "What about the wealthy ascetic who decides to fast and becomes undernourished despite his being rich and having the means of being excellently nourished? It seem rather odd to see him as deprived, with a low standard of living. He has chosen to fast; he was not forced to fast."[17] Sen is, of course, correct that there is a world of difference between the wealthy ascetic who decides to fast and the undernourished poor, even if both are undernourished. But this does not show that standard of living is best explicated in terms of capabilities. First, we want to keep open the possibility that a wealthy person might through choice or otherwise actually live at a very low standard. This would be foreclosed by definition if merely *being able* to live at a high standard were the same as doing so. Second, taken as functionings, fasting and starving are simply two different functionings. To fast is not to starve, even if nutritionally they come out the same. Understanding standard of living in terms of functionings does not mean that we obliterate the differences between different kinds of functionings.

Sen offers another example, saying "the *capability* to visit friends and relatives may be important for standard of living. However, a person who chooses not to make use of that capability, and curls up instead with a good book, may not be sensibly seen as being deprived and having a low standard of living."[18] Again, I do not believe Sen has made his case. It is impossible to undertake all valuable functionings at the same time. Merely forgoing one in favor of another does not show deprivation. But consider someone who, in favor of staying in his room with a good book, permanently gives up visiting relatives, or eating good meals, or any other valued functioning. At some point, I believe, we would want to say that he is living at a very low standard. Whether this is self-inflicted or a result of deprivation is yet another matter.

Whether standard of living is best explicated in terms of capabilities or functionings, or as a mix of the two, should remain an open question. Better to judge actual analyses than to foreclose alternatives. In the current essay, I offer an account based only on functionings.

One way to approach the task of isolating economic well-being is to focus on the individual as a consumer, as an agent in the marketplace making consumption expenditures. From this perspective, we might ask if it is possible to identify one or more key functionings for each of the major categories of consumption expenditure. Such functionings would capture the forms of life experience and activity that consumer expenditures enable.

Consider table 18.1, which pairs functionings with areas of consumption expenditure. Families spend most of their money on these six areas of consumption expenditure. And while the core functionings identified in table 18.1 do not exhaust the functionings that may be enabled through consumer expenditures in these areas, and which motivate these expenditures, they do offer a picture of a way of life or, let us say, a level of economic life that can serve as an alternative to the level of income or consumption in appraising the standard of economic life.

One of the virtues of identifying the level of economic life (or standard of living) with a set of functionings rather than with income or expenditures is that it allows us to inquire about the role of money or expenditures in bringing about the good economic life. It does this in two ways. First, we can ask for any given individual (or family) about the connection between income and the core functionings. For each of the core functionings above, income is necessary but not sufficient. Not

Table 18.1. Areas of Expenditure and Core Functionings.

Area of Expenditure	Core Functioning
Clothing	Appears in public without shame
Housing	Hosts with pride in a dwelling a reasonable distance from work and in a safe neighborhood
Transportation	Gets around relatively quickly among the central loci of everyday life (home, work, friends, schools, shops)
Food	Eats meals that are healthful, appetizing, and leisured
Health	Receives effective preventive and remediable health care
Education	Children are schooled effectively and safely

only must the money be spent for specific commodities but also the commodities must be utilized in a particular way. Thus, one may have the food but not the leisured meals. One may have the house and still fail to host or to host with pride. What then becomes clear is that, on the individual level, the translation of income into a high standard of living is itself an art form. It is very much a matter of knowing how to live and may involve a broad range of knowledges and psychological capabilities. To see things this way is a useful broadening of perspective on "the economic."

Second, however, once we begin to inquire about the set of functionings that make up a form of economic life, it becomes clear that those directly connected to expenditures are only part of the picture. There are other realms of concern than consumer expenditure that are central to our motivation as economic agents, in particular those that are central to our behavior in labor markets (where we are sellers) rather than the market for goods and services (where we are buyers).

Thus, a more complete notion of standard of living or economic functioning would have to go beyond these six areas of consumer expenditure to include the nonpecuniary labor market concerns shown in table 18.2.

These four areas, and the core functionings that are identified with them, enter into the decisions we make in labor markets. To a greater extent than with consumption expenditures, these functionings may be enabled by nonmonetary aspects of our economic involvement. With

Table 18.2. Nonpecuniary Labor Market Concerns and Core Functionings.

Nonpecuniary Labor Market Concern	Core Functioning
Security	Lives free from anxiety over the decline or loss of income
Beauty	Lives in an aesthetically rich human and natural environment
Leisure	Devotes ample time to enjoyment of friends and amusements
Work	Derives social esteem and personal self-expression through employment

respect to our desire to live in an aesthetically rich urban or natural environment, we make decisions about *which* labor markets to enter (we might look for work in Seattle, New York, or Aspen). And in pursuit of a life free from anxiety over loss of income, we may choose to trade off higher pay for greater security. (There are consumption expenditures—disability insurance policies, for instance—that also promote security functionings.) Similarly, we may prefer greater leisure to higher income. And in some circumstances the pursuit of social esteem and self-expression also may represent a trade-off against income, though clearly income level itself is a factor in attaining social esteem.

Taken together, these ten functionings offer a vastly richer understanding of standard of living than does the focus on income or consumption expenditure. Together they extend Smith's linen shirt example to a relatively comprehensive set of functionings that, if not universally valid, have widespread cross-cultural validity.

How, then, does this analysis compare to Nussbaum's analysis, and is it vulnerable to some of the same objections I raised when discussing her approach? First, of course, it should be clear that these are not competing analyses. Nussbaum is operating within the capabilities/functionings orientation to explicate what it is to live a good life. Within the same tradition, I have focused much more sharply on the economic realm, seeking to explicate a different concept: standard of living. Living a good life and having a high standard of living are not the same thing, and how they might be related remains to be clarified.

Second, there are some parallels and some important differences between the two approaches. Nussbaum has focused on capabilities, and I have focused on functionings. Because she has only articulated capabilities, Nussbaum's analysis cannot be sufficient for having a good life. Nor does she claim that it is. She claims, rather, that each capability is necessary for the good life. This I disputed. With respect to my analysis, I would maintain that these ten functionings, collectively, are sufficient. To live in this way is to live at a high economic standard. I do not, however, maintain that to live at a high economic standard it is necessary to function in each of these ten ways. I do, however, make a claim almost as strong: to live at a high economic standard (that is, to have a high standard of living) it is necessary that one function in *almost all* of these ways; one could not forgo more than one or two and still be living well, economically speaking.

In considering Nussbaum, I argued that she faces a problem with respect to specifying thresholds of capability. The minor problem is that she did not specify thresholds, and, thus, it could be maintained that everyone (whether their life is good or not) has to some degree most of the valued capabilities. In my analysis, the differences between high, medium, and low standards of living are captured in the way the functionings are characterized. In the specific instance, I have explicated what it is to live at a *high* economic standard. But by systematically recasting the level of functioning, for instance, by replacing "hosts with pride" with "hosts without shame," one could characterize a more moderate standard of economic life. And, presumably, Nussbaum could supplement her analysis so as to provide thresholds of capability that would allow her to distinguish between what is necessary for a very good life, a moderately good life, a minimally decent life, and so forth.

The real problem Nussbaum faces is that if she specifies thresholds, which she must, she will find that what is far below what is necessary in one vision of the good life may prove excessive in another vision. This, I argued, leads to a dilemma. Either Nussbaum accommodates a wide range of visions by keeping thresholds low, thus, from the point of view of each vision, missing its essence; or she excludes many such alternatives and faces the significant burden of showing that such exclusion is not a matter of arbitrary preference.

The analysis of standard of living does not get into these difficulties because what is being explicated is a more limited economic concept. Thus, it is quite possible, and indeed true, that in some conceptions of the good life, there might be disdain for living at a high economic standard, and, thus, these various functionings might not be a part of certain conceptions of the good life at all. However, it does not follow that the meaning of the concept *standard of living*, or *high economic standard*, would vary. A Trotskyite, for example, might have taken the stance that to live well economically is incompatible with living as a revolutionary in solidarity with the proletariat.

Similarly, there are multiple conceptions of the good life that would view it as involving life at a high (or at least a decent) economic standard plus something extra and more important that gives it its distinctive quality. Thus, it might be that D. H. Lawrence and Cotton Mather would both agree that the good life is not essentially economic, would disagree violently about the role of sexuality and piety in the good life, and yet would largely agree about the role of a moderately high economic standard.

The point, then, is that by limiting our focus to what it is to live well "economically speaking," it is possible to articulate a concept whose meaning is relatively stable across alternative visions of the good life, even though the place of economic well-being within the good life may vary.[19]

Policy Guidance and a Functionings Analysis
of Standard of Living

The functionings analysis of standard of living offers a new direction when it comes to measuring standard of living, comparing levels at different times or in different cultures, and investigating causal factors responsible for growth or decline in standard of living. Unlike expenditure levels, these ten items cannot be collapsed into a single number. But we could, for instance, compare the percentage of people at a given time or in a given society that have these levels of functionings (either one by one or all of them) and then consider how those percentage levels correspond to income levels.

A functionings analysis can be expected to reveal that differences or changes in the standard of living often do not correspond to changes in real income levels. To the extent that this is so, it will offer a way of measuring what might be termed "the standard-of-living efficiency of income" for different societies or a given society at different times. This yardstick would be a measure of the extent to which changes in income convert into changes in the standard of living. Potentially, radically different standards of living are possible at the same level of per capita income and with the same pattern of income distribution. It is one of the virtues of disaggregating standard of living that inquiry into these relationships is made possible.[20]

An appropriate and vital concern for any society is how the standard of living of all of its members can be raised. As suggested above, when we understand standard of living in terms of income levels, it is a near logical truth that equitable economic growth brings about a general rise in the standard of living.[21] But once we understand standard of living in terms of the ten types of functionings detailed above, we are faced with ten complex empirical questions, each of which asks about income growth and rising levels of human functionings. Such questions include:

- When everyone's income level rises, what is the impact on the general ability of people to quickly transport themselves to the central loci of personal life?
- When everyone's income level rises, what is the impact on the extent to which people are wearing clothing that supports pride in self?
- When everyone's income level rises, what is the impact on a sufficiency of leisure?
- When everyone's income level rises, what is the impact on the extent to which people have meaningful work?

Consider these questions for a moment. They have no easy answers. Each requires independent and extensive research. It is quite possible that there will be a tight relationship between general income growth and improved functioning, but there may be no relationship or there may be a negative relationship. The answer may depend not only on the specific component of standard of living being considered but also on the specific historical period and society in question.

Here, of course, we are not asking about a single individual. For a single individual, income growth can, in many instances, result in greater levels of functioning. But what works for a given individual may not work for all of us collectively. When we all stand on tiptoe, not only does no one see the parade any better, but we all end up less comfortable.[22]

At this point, I think we can safely venture that no one knows the answers to these questions. This situation in itself is interesting. What it means is that with respect to the most fundamental of reasons for pursuing equitable economic growth, no one, neither economists nor noneconomists, is currently in a position to say with authority whether or not economic growth is the key to increasing the general level of economic well-being.

While it is clearly outside the purview of this essay to attempt to answer these questions, it is striking how weak the intuitive link between income growth and improved functionings appears to be. To a significant extent, these collective improvement problems appear to be growth resistant. For instance, functionings that are tied to pride or shame, such as appearing in public without shame, hosting with pride, or deriving social esteem through employment, all seem vulnerable to what John Kenneth Galbraith called the "squirrel wheel" phenomenon. We may run faster but not make any progress—the standards for income and expenditures that promote pride, avoid shame, and engender esteem may rise in pace with growth in the income level.

In the search for "effective schooling," so long as this is understood as schooling that enables the child to succeed in the socioeconomic competition, there may be a similar problem. If broadly shared income growth does not increase the number of winners (as may happen if success is understood in relative terms), then here too there is little or no progress.

With respect to functionings such as devotes ample time to enjoyment of friends or gets around relatively quickly among the central foci of everyday life or hosts with pride in a dwelling a reasonable distance from work or lives free from anxiety over the decline or loss of income or lives in an aesthetically rich human and natural environment, a case can be made that economic growth has lowered rather than raised these dimensions of standard of living. Surely, if we were to measure standards of living in each of these dimensions, we would not expect consistently to find that those in rich countries live better than those in poor countries.

The value of the functionings analysis should be apparent. It opens the door to new questions and to possibly surprising answers. It demonstrates the importance, as Aristotle maintained, of clarifying what we mean by a better life before we embrace public policies in our collective pursuit of it.

In reflecting on the policy dimension we are brought to the question that Nussbaum emphasized: What is the appropriate role of the state? Nussbaum views the role of government vis-à-vis the good life as merely to enable good functioning. After that, it is up to responsible adults to choose whether or not to function in these ways. She opposes using the government to shape people's desires or employing the law to prod or (if necessary) force people to function in desirable ways.

But this dichotomy is too stark, as least if we are focused not on The Good Life writ large but on those functionings that—by and large—constitute what it is to live at a high economic standard. Here, there are many discrete smaller choices, some where it makes sense to use the law only to encourage, some where we might want to go beyond education and enablement to give a prod, and some where we do want to compel.

The reason, I believe, is similar to one I pointed out previously: across a substantial range of alternative visions of the good life, it is possible to have agreement on the meaning of economic well-being and, to a lesser degree, its general relationship to the good life. Thus, without doing violence to the autonomy of the individual in working out his or her conception of the good life, it is possible to have the state more forcefully involved in bringing about those actual functionings that constitute living at a high (or decent) standard of living.

I will conclude with examples of "functioning-promoting" as distinct from merely "functioning-enabling" policies that are within the American consensus of the appropriate role of the state in promoting a higher standard of living. This in itself does not prove that those who challenge this consensus, for instance libertarians, are wrong. But it does serve to identify what is actually involved in maintaining that the state should only enable good functionings and not go further and prod or compel them.

There would be considerable controversy about using the law to prod people to save because it is part of the virtue of frugality. Nonetheless, we do have mandatory Social Security. And while this "extraction" of income by the state can be justified in terms of preventing people from becoming a burden to others, there is substantial recognition that people may need to be forced in this way to provide for their own security. Moreover, even those who view Social Security as unduly paternalistic often enough support tax code provisions that encourage people to contribute to individual retirement accounts (IRAs) and 401 (k) plans.

Similarly, with respect to functionings in the area of health, the concern of the state is not merely with enabling people to be healthy but with their actually being healthy. True, the reason for this concern lies to a considerable degree in a concern that others might either be infected or burdened, but to some extent it lies in a concern with good functioning itself. Thus, when a decision was made to put fluoride in the water, the state was seeing to it that nonuse of fluoride would no longer be a live option.[23] Here, going beyond enabling good functioning (say by making fluoride pills available) was justifiable as an imposition not of the majority view of the good life but, rather, of the majority view of the causal relationship between fluoride and health functionings about which all share a common appraisal.

This illustrates two things. First, that the legitimacy that we accord to the state's prodding (or forcing) of a given behavior (such as saving) depends strongly on the reason for which the state is acting. And second, it illustrates that there is a line we draw between prodding in order to bring about functions that are constitutive of living at a high economic standard (such as living without anxiety over loss of income) and proddings that are designed to actualize a specific, but not shared, view of the good life.

Within this economic realm, there are also situations in which we might act to force individuals toward good functioning because when each makes his own choice the results come out in ways that collectively we judge to be inferior. Consider the decision over how many hours to work (and thus how much leisure to take). For any individual to choose more leisure and less income means a decline in his relative income standard. Left to resolution through individual choices, we have a pattern of life with too much work for good living (a lower standard of living). Thus, collectively (and democratically) we have passed legislation that prohibits consenting adults from entering into certain kinds of exchanges (for example, more than forty hours of work per week at standard pay). As a result, I would argue, we are all better off.

We might also ask, What does it mean for the state to "enable good functioning" if we are dealing with squirrel wheel problems? If the efforts of each to achieve good functioning work to thwart any collective progress toward good functioning, then perhaps a stronger role for the state is warranted. I myself would not be adverse to some kind of restraint that serves to limit what we spend on cars and houses. We have luxury taxes on yachts; perhaps we should have progressive property taxes on houses so as to prevent rapid escalation in "standards of decency" that keep us running after more affluent homes.[24]

Thus, I would argue that wisdom, at least with respect to attaining higher levels of economic functioning, lies not in adopting some general view about whether government should only promote capabilities or whether it should compel functionings. One can reasonably use police power to enforce an eight-hour day and taxing powers to prod people to give to charity (for a variety of reasons) and yet fully resist any temptation to force or even encourage people to read Henry James, though it would be good for them.

Notes

I want to thank David A. Crocker for some consistent prodding and valuable comments on earlier drafts of this paper.

1. Martha C. Nussbaum, "The Good as Discipline, the Good as Freedom" (this volume), 312–13.

2. This list reproduces Nussbaum's in "The Good as Discipline," 319–20.

3. Nussbaum, "The Good as Discipline," 320; my emphasis.

4. Nussbaum, "The Good as Discipline," 321.

5. Nussbaum, "The Good as Discipline," 321.

6. Nussbaum, "The Good as Discipline," 321.

7. If it is true that not all of the correlate functionings are necessary, one might wonder if any specific ones are. To this Nussbaum does not give an answer.

8. If her position is that these correlate functionings really are necessary, but the state should not intervene, then the account is vulnerable to the examples I present below, though they would need to be recast in functionings language.

9. David A. Crocker takes the position on this and the above issues not that their lives cannot be said to be good, but that they are "less good" than they would be if they had these and other freedoms. Obviously, this is sometimes true, but as a general claim I do not find it convincing.

10. I have previously maintained that no set of capabilities could be sufficient for the good life since it is possible that they would all remain mere potential. Here I assume that some or all of Nussbaum's valuable capabilities are actualized. I am asking if this is enough.

11. Nussbaum, "The Good as Discipline" 320.

12. In "Aristotelian Social Democracy," in *Liberalism and the Good*, ed. R. Bruce Douglass, Gerald M. Mara, and Henry S. Richardson (New York: Routledge, 1990), 203–52, Nussbaum calls attention to Aristotle's view that some forms of labor are incompatible with "good human functioning" because they harm the worker, leaving him unable to adequately undertake other functionings. However, an awareness of this potentially negative role that work can

play is quite different from viewing meaningful work as a central part of the good life.

13. Adam Smith, *An Inquiry into the Nature and Causes of the Wealth of Nations* (New York: Modern Library, 1937 [1776]), 821–22, quoted in Amartya Sen, "The Living Standard," in this volume, 292.

14. Smith, *Wealth of Nations*, 822.

15. In capabilities language, having a high standard of living would involve having clothing such that one *can* appear in public without shame. I stress *actually* appearing without shame (assuming that the person appears at all). Having the clothes so that one can appear without shame is only a step removed from having the money to buy such clothes so that one can appear without shame. Unless one actually buys the clothes *and* wears them, and thus *appears* without shame, one is not *living* at a high standard, despite the potential to live so.

16. In *The Standard of Living* (Cambridge: Cambridge University Press, 1987), Sen changes his position to include functionings as well as capabilities in evaluating the living standard. (See the 1987 postscript to Sen's essay in this volume, 298).

17. Sen, "The Living Standard," this volume, 295.

18. Sen, "The Living Standard," this volume, 295.

19. A similar point can be made about the relationship between economic well-being and well-being per se. It should not be thought that economic well-being is necessarily a part of well-being. If, for instance, the self is thought of as primarily spiritual, then much of what happens in the economic domain is largely irrelevant.

20. One of the reasons that focusing on the more narrowly economic "standard of living" offers more payoff than focusing on "the good human life" or "human well-being" is the greater consensus that exists when we focus on the narrowly economic. Thus, I would argue, when it comes to what people either want money for, or what they are seeking when they sell their labor, there is far more commonality among human beings than there is when it comes to how they understand a fuller notion of the good life.

21. I say "near" logical truth, for it remains possible that during some period (for example, a war) all of the economic growth would be channeled into increased government production and thus would not affect consumption levels.

22. Fred C. Hirsch may have been the first to use this image in his *Social Limits to Growth* (Cambridge, Mass.: Harvard University Press, 1976).

23. Those who wish to maintain a sharp line between acceptable and nonacceptable motives for state actions could respond that the good functioning that befell those who did not want to ingest fluoride was only a collateral benefit of a public health measure favored by the majority, but not appropriately its intended purpose.

24. In *The Affluent Society* (Cambridge, Mass.: Riverside Press, 1958), Galbraith took the position that almost all private spending has reached the point at which on the margin it brings no real increase in the standard of living. Thus, he argued for preventing private spending (using taxes) to increase public spending in areas where collective improvement in the standard of living is possible (such as parks or public safety).

19

Consumption, Well-Being, and Capability

David A. Crocker

In this chapter I ask how much and what kind of personal and house-hold consumer goods are appropriate if we Americans are to achieve individual well-being, if our lives are to go well. Consumer goods are those personal and household goods and services that individuals purchase for private use. Such goods—homes, furniture, automobiles, clothes, food, medical care, and recreation—are not insignificant portions of national output, accounting for about two-thirds of U.S. gross national product (GNP). Moreover, given our relatively low levels of savings and investment, such consuming takes up more than 95 percent of an American household's disposable income (compared to 85 percent in West Germany and 80 percent in Japan).[1] But while this essay is primarily concerned with addressing American consumers, it may be of relevance to people elsewhere, especially insofar as they are attracted to or actively imitate our consumption patterns.

Controversies concerning American household consumption frequently emphasize the impacts of our consumer choices beyond our own lives. Some consumption choices may harm our neighbors, weaken our democracy, or contaminate our rivers. Others might assist us in contributing to some cause—for instance, environmental conservation, the National Rifle Association, or famine relief—to which we are committed. But our consumption choices and patterns also may be beneficial or detrimental to *our own well-being*—apart from or in addition to their effects on other persons, institutions, or the natural world. My main purpose here is to investigate this fourth way of assessing consumption.

If our goal is to protect and promote our own well-being, what and how much should we consume? What role should goods and services play if our lives are to go well? What kinds of consumption are or would be good for us? Which would be bad for us? What evaluative criteria should we employ to assess the impact on our lives of our present consumption patterns and to evaluate alternative consumption patterns and ways of living? This sort of evaluation will be facilitated by employing a reasonable norm of human well-being.

It is of course true that the various objects affected by our consumption choices—the environment, other people, our institutions, and our own well-being—can be causally related to each other in complex ways. Sometimes, for example, what is good for us benefits others, and sometimes it harms them. It is beyond the scope of this essay to address—let alone resolve—the resultant perplexities, but most of us would hold that although our own well-being is only *one* normative consideration, it is *among* the norms that should guide us in our consumption choices. And some people's purchases are largely if not exclusively motivated by the goal of enhancing their own well-being. Hence, we do well to investigate the notion of well-being and how it can contribute to evaluating consumption choices.

Certainly we do not need a consumption norm to know that some consumption choices (high-fat foods, for instance) are generally bad for us, and others (certain life-saving medicines) typically good for us. An adequate conception of well-being, however, can help us interpret those considered judgments of which we are most confident, and offer direction concerning the appropriateness of other choices about which our judgments vacillate or falter.[2]

The norm of well-being that I offer in this essay will supply general rather than detailed guidance. After all, as Stanley Lebergott has remarked, no principle can tell us that five compact disks is the right number to buy each year, while six is too many and four is too few.[3] Any norm that presumed to set such specific limits would be arbitrary, even dictatorial. What we need is not an algorithm or calculus that issues in context-independent answers but rather a general orientation that has sufficient content to guide each of us and encourages choices appropriate to the distinctive character of our individual circumstances.

Materialism and Antimaterialism

A first step in arriving at a reasonable consumption norm is to assess widely held normative outlooks about the acquisition and possession of commodities and, more generally, about human well-being. Materialism and antimaterialism are two such perspectives. Getting clear on where and how these rival norms go wrong will help us arrive at a better conception of well-being and a more adequate consumption norm.

Diverse social scientific disciplines—anthropology, consumer science, economics, geography, history, psychology, and sociology—describe consumption practices and try to identify their causes and consequences.[4] Although it is important to understand why we consume the way we do and to be clear about the causal role, if any, of such values as frugality and pleasure in our consumption choices, my interest is in critically assessing currently held consumption norms and, if possible, improving them.

The first of these norms, materialism, assures us that well-being is being well off; it identifies well-being with buying, having, and displaying consumer goods, especially those that bring comfort and convenience. In America's consumer society, materialism is often perceived as a national characteristic. Though we poke fun at our materialist obsessions—"BORN TO SHOP"; "I SHOP, THEREFORE I AM!"; "NOTHING SUCCEEDS LIKE EXCESS!"; "SO MANY MALLS, AND SO LITTLE TRUNK SPACE!"—we do not often renounce them. According to Juliet B. Schor, "Americans spend three to four times as many hours a year shopping as their counterparts in Western European countries. Once a purely utilitarian chore, shopping has been elevated to the status of a national passion."[5] In his poem "The Return," Frederick Turner captures the consumerist nostalgia of American soldiers in Vietnam:

What we miss
are the bourgeois trivia of capitalism:
the smell of a new house, fresh drywall, resin
adhesive, vinyl, new hammered studs; ground coffee
in a friend's apartment in San Francisco, the
first day of the trip; the crisp upholstery
of a new car

....
                    It is the things
money *can* buy we remember, the innocence
of our unfallen materialism.[6]

The poem looks gently upon these goods and the wistful soldiers who recall them. But in other contexts, it is harder to see American materialism as innocent or "unfallen." Consider the consumerist manifesto that retailing analyst Victor Lebow issued in 1955 for an American economy enjoying a postwar boom: "Our enormously productive economy . . . demands that we make consumption our way of life, that we convert the buying and use of goods into rituals, that we seek our spiritual satisfaction, our ego satisfaction, in consumption. . . . We need things consumed, burned up, worn out, replaced, and discarded at an ever increasing rate."[7]

Although the "buying and use" of commodities may be essential to one kind of economic growth, most of us believe that commodities *by themselves* fail to give life reliable and ultimate meaning. As political economist Robert E. Lane suggests, it is not what we buy or own that brings us happiness but rather our work, our relations with our spouses and colleagues, and the well-being of our children.[8] Indeed, the world of consumer goods, and a life devoted to their pursuit, may insulate us from deeper challenges and human connections.

Antimaterialism, whether religious or nonreligious, feeds on the very real weaknesses of consumerist materialism. Some antimaterialists conceive the good life precisely so as to protect the self from disappointments in the changeable, frustrating world of bodily appetites and worldly possessions. The antimaterialist strives to free himself of all attachments to material goods, or at least to reduce significantly his level of material consumption. In its most extreme forms, antimaterialism forsakes the world in order to lay up "treasures in heaven," where "neither moth nor rust doth corrupt, and where thieves do not break through nor steal" (Matt. 6:20 King James).

More moderate forms of antimaterialism affirm the ultimate importance of this-worldly, but still nonmaterial, realities. Some prize inner rationality, self-possession, and self-sufficiency (as in Stoicism). Others emphasize the fulfillment that comes through personal relationships. Donella Meadows, for example, argues that people should "learn to meet nonmaterial needs such as love, respect, community, and identity through nonmaterial means, instead of through highly marketed and ultimately unsatisfying material substitutes."[9] This abjuring of material things in favor of intimate relationships may seem to require, in John Updike's words, a "vast and crushing" revision in our customary valuations of everyday "appurtenances" (as well as natural objects). In Updike's short story "Journey to the Dead," a man named Fredericks witnesses the signs of such a revision in the new dismissiveness of a dying friend:

> [Fredericks] got out and kissed [Arlene] on her upturned face, which in illness had become round and shiny, and explained that he hadn't wanted to run over the hose. "Ach, the hose!" she exclaimed with startling guttural force and a sweeping, humorous gesture. "Phooey to the hose!"
>
> Nevertheless, Fredericks went back and moved the hose so the next car would not run over it, at the same time trying to imagine how these appurtenances to our daily living, as patiently treasured and stored and

coiled and repaired as if their usefulness were eternal, must look to someone whose death is imminent. The hose. The flowers. The abandoned
trowel whose canary-yellow handle winks within weeds in the phlox border. The grass itself, and the sun and sky and trees like massive scuffed-
up stage flats—phooey to them. Their value was about to undergo a revision so vast and crushing Fredericks could not imagine it. Certainly he
could not imagine it in relation to the merry presence who entertained
them, sitting with her guests on the screened porch while her husband
cooked at the grill outside, in a cloud of gnats.[10]

Yet these various ideals of independence from the material world may
be just as misguided as the materialist effort to elevate the acquisition
and enjoyment of worldly goods to life's supreme aim. One obvious
concern is that there is a physical aspect of human well-being, a requirement of certain goods and services that meet basic needs—adequate
food, clothing, shelter, health care, and so on. The antimaterialists
might concede this point and allow for the modest satisfaction of these
needs. Still, their resulting ethic might be so austere that it condemns
much that makes life worth living.

It is true that we must avoid being obsessed with or possessed by
commodities. Yet we must also honestly recognize the positive role
some goods and services play in our lives; otherwise, we risk adopting a
critique of consumerism that is blindly at odds with our own considered
judgments. Nutritious and tastefully prepared food consumed with others can be good for both body and soul. (The setting of the Updike
passage cited earlier is a kind of "farewell" barbecue that the dying
woman and her husband hold for their friends.) Aesthetically attractive
dwellings and clothes enable us to shape and express who we are. Marriage rites include the exchange of rings. Although we do well to avoid
using presents to manipulate people, we sometimes express parental
love and nurture friendships through carefully selected material gifts.
We often take part in the wider community through phone, fax, and E-
mail. Air travel brings new ideas and new friends into our lives.

Rather than seek the good life by withdrawing to a self-sufficient
inner or transcendent world, many of us, when we are honest with ourselves, believe that we may realize our well-being when we satisfy *certain* worldly desires and utilize *certain* material means. As we—often
in the company of family, friends, or colleagues—meet human needs,
realize our best potentials, press against limits, and cope with bad for-
tune in humanly excellent ways, commodities can play an important
instrumental role.

We find, then, that although materialism and antimaterialism both
contain some truth, they are also guilty of exaggeration. Those who

endorse one of these views are typically engaged in an overreaction against the other, while others find themselves torn between the two.[11] Sometimes entire cultures vacillate between them, like a car that uncontrollably fishtails from side to side.[12] Generational changes in the United States since World War II illustrate the point:

> Burdened by college loans and facing a shifting job market, Gen X [Americans born between 1965–76] yearns for affluence. In that, it takes after its grandparents more than its parents. A generation ago, small was beautiful and materialism had fallen out of fashion. Only 31 percent of twentysomethings in 1973 agreed that money is "a very important personal value." Today 64 percent of Xers and matures [Americans born before 1946] say, "Material things, like what I drive and the house I live in, are really important to me." Only half of boomers [Americans born 1946-64] feel that way. Fewer twentysomethings seek "a simpler life," and, strikingly, a third of them agree that "the only meaningful measure of success is money."[13]

If, however, we are to have a reasonable consumption norm, the pair—materialism and antimaterialism—must be rejected together. We must transcend the false dichotomy presupposed in the question, "Is consumption a good to be maximized or a necessary evil to be minimized?"[14] We must seek to replace materialism and anti-materialism with a balanced and stable conception of the sources and meaning of well-being.

The Capabilities Approach

Given this evaluation of both materialism and antimaterialism, let us progress further toward an adequate consumption norm by investigating a philosophical interpretation of well-being and its relevance for assessing American consumption."[15] The conception of well-being that I present here derives largely from Aristotle's ethic of human flourishing and from the work of two contemporary philosophers, Amartya Sen and Martha C. Nussbaum, who have acknowledged their own debt to Aristotle in formulating what is known as the capabilities approach.[16]

According to this conception, well-being refers not to some one component of life, such as pleasure or the satisfaction of basic needs, but to a heterogeneous list of human conditions, activities, inner capacities, and external opportunities. To have well-being, to be and do well, is *to function* and *to be capable of functioning* in a plurality of humanly good ways. As applied to responsible adults—those with the ability to choose—the emphasis is on internal abilities and external opportunities for valuable activity: "The central feature of well-being is the ability to achieve valuable functionings."[17] With respect to those lacking the capacity to choose—the very young, the brain-damaged, the very old— the capabilities approach gives an account of well-being that employs the concept of valuable physical, mental, social, and "separateness" functionings.

The bodily components of well-being of those incapable of choice include being adequately healthy, nourished, clothed, sheltered, and mobile, as well as being free from physical pain and bodily attack. (The criterion of "adequacy," as applied to clothing and shelter, includes being able to appear in public and not be shamed by one's physical neediness.) In some circumstances responsible individuals willingly sacrifice some aspect of bodily well-being, as when a hunger striker allows herself to become malnourished. Such a person forgoes a component of healthy functioning. Notice, however, that she is not thereby *incapable* of being well-nourished. She is better off than someone who cannot acquire food or who, on account of illness, is unable to derive nourishment from the food he consumes. Thus we can say that the physical well-being of *responsible adults* is a matter of their certain capacities and opportunities for valuable physical functionings.

Although physical wellness is necessary for well-being, it is not sufficient. We must also include certain mental capabilities and functionings in our conception of well-being. Among these are the cognitive capacities for and activities of perceiving, imagining, reasoning, judging, and autonomously deciding. The latter embraces our being able to choose our causes and, more generally, a conception of the good life. Mental well-being also includes opportunities and capacities for what utilitarians value most: enjoying or finding pleasure—whether in other aspects of well-being, such as physical health, or in such things as art, nature, or moral goodness.[18]

Happiness, although contributory to well-being, is not sufficient, for it may occur with and even camouflage significant deprivation. That happiness or preference satisfaction is intrinsically good, *part* of well-being, seems to be one of our confident intuitions. But we commit what Alfred North Whitehead called the "fallacy of misplaced concreteness"[19] when we take the part to be the whole, one good to be identical with or an index of all goods. We see this fallacy most clearly and convincingly in what I have called elsewhere Sen's "small mercies argument."[20] Sen argues persuasively that neither happiness nor preference satisfaction is sufficient for well-being and can camouflage significant ill-being such as malnutrition and morbidity. Such distortion occurs when a person makes a deal with reality and reduces his or her desires to what seems feasible:

Judging importance by the mental metric of happiness or desire-fulfillment can take a deeply biased form due to the fact that the mental reactions often reflect defeatist compromises with harsh reality induced by hopelessness. The insecure sharecropper, the exploited landless laborer, the overworked domestic servant, the subordinate housewife, may all come to terms with their respective predicaments in such a way that grievance and discontent are submerged in cheerful endurance by the necessity of uneventful survival. The hopeless underdog loses the courage to desire a better deal and learns to take pleasure in small mercies. The deprivations appear muffled and muted in the metric of utilities.[21]

It is not that the satisfaction caused by the small mercy is not genuine or valuable—both immediately and in the long run—for the person. However, the example shows us that it would be unreasonable to say that pleasure or preference satisfaction is the only relevant criterion in evaluating what it is to live well. Information about amounts of happiness and preference satisfaction is necessary but not sufficient for knowing how well someone is doing. Moreover, the small mercy may cause the recipient to *believe* that she is doing well *generally* when in many ways she is objectively deprived. The drug Prozac, although perhaps therapeutic for some people when taken in the right doses, is a current fashionable means of inducing a pleasurable mental state that should not be identified with well-being.

Human well-being has a social as well as a physical and mental dimension. We believe our lives are not going well if we lack the deep personal relations of family and friendship as well as participation in wider social and ecological communities. It is largely from these relations that we derive a sense of purpose and self-respect.

A fourth aspect of well-being is what Nussbaum calls "separateness" but might be better termed "singularity": "Being able to live one's own life in one's very own surroundings and context."[22] In addition to social relations, human well-being depends on our being able to be "separate" or distinct from others in several ways. For our lives to go well, we must be able to choose for ourselves, especially with respect to matters that centrally constitute our identity, for instance, friendship, sexuality, marriage, parenting, employment,[23] and, more generally, our own conception of the good life.[24] We must also be able to have some singular relationships to particular persons, times, and places, and to have some things that are peculiarly ours. My well-being in the fullest sense requires that I have "some separateness of context, a little space to move around in, some special items to use or love."[25] Such personal possessions, such as family photographs or a favorite quilt, are not ends in themselves but rather things that contribute to each person's singular well-being and unique functioning.

What is the proper relation between these aspects of well-being? I would argue that the good life requires achieving a kind of *balance* among them. Although a particular consumption choice may contribute more to one valuable capability than to the others, the wise consumer strives for an overall consumption pattern that promotes balance and harmony among the four kinds of valuable capabilities (and functionings). Too much or too little of a good thing in one dimension may decrease our overall well-being in one or more of the others. The person obsessed with physical fitness will have little opportunity or capability for intellectual and social activity. The intellectual's books and the hacker's computer may stunt their owners' physical and social development and prevent full flourishing. My private possessions may distract me from civic participation. Within each dimension and among them, the wise consumer avoids the extremes of excess and deficit, and seeks moderation.

The ideal of balance has an additional application in our understanding of well-being. We do well to balance the times of our lives. This means, on the one hand, not unduly sacrificing present valuable capabilities for our future good and, on the other, not choosing to obtain certain aspects of well-being now when the likely long-term cost is significant loss of important capabilities. It also means that different "stages on life's way"—infancy, childhood, adolescence, maturity, old age—require different kinds of "balancing acts" because of typical changes in the potential, strength, and limits of our valuable powers. Likewise, the kind of balance that those with disabilities can attain will differ from that achieved by those with more comprehensive functionings. Sensitivity to these kinds of differences, however, is still compatible with the general ideal of being "in balance."

It might be objected that some "one-sided" lives can still go well or be well-chosen. What of the connoisseur whose single-minded devotion to acquisition results in poor health or failed friendships, but who assembles an art collection of unquestioned importance or beauty? Or what of the musical prodigy who willingly relinquishes some of the pleasures of childhood in order to cultivate her unique gifts?

There are, I think, four answers to this challenge. First, one may concede that well-being is not everything. A person's life may be well-chosen and worthwhile precisely because he has sacrificed his well-being, or indeed his life, for a noble cause—clan, country, or culture. When I do my moral duty and protect or promote the well-being of others, I may thereby lessen my own well-being. Likewise, some artistic accomplishments are not accompanied with and may only be achieved by surrendering good health or successful intimate relationships. But even as we honor those who embrace a higher good at the cost of their well-being, we usually regret that such a choice was required. We wish—correctly, I believe—that their moral or artistic accomplishments could have occurred without sacrificing their own well-being.

A second and similar response is appropriate if the imbalance is *among* the plural elements of well-being rather than between well-being and other achievements. It might be objected that more of one valuable capability, especially when chosen and enjoyed, compensates for less of the others. Couldn't a person's life go well—even very well—if she fully developed and exercised one valuable capability but did so at the cost of ignoring or shortchanging her other important potentials? The capabilities approach matches our considered judgment that this one-sided life also must be counted as less than full well-being even though the person exercises the valuable capability of choice and is markedly successful with respect to another well-being component such as physical well-being. Again, we give tribute to the ideal of balance when we affirm that the one-sided person's life would go even better if she could realize fully *all* her valuable capabilities.

The problem, of course, is that maximal realization of each element of well-being may not be possible; the only way to attain full achievement of one component may be to accept lesser achievement of others. A track analogy: The only way that an Olympic decathlete such as Jackie Joyner-Kersee could become an Olympic champion in the hurdles would be for her to forsake balance for specialized hurdle training. She could develop world-class hurdling ability only if she single-mindedly trained for that one event, thereby deemphasizing (if not neglecting altogether) skills relevant for other track events, such as the shot put. I concede that it is difficult to say which of the following has more well-being: the jack of all valuable capabilities but master of none or the one who masters one valuable capability at the expense of the others. In the track case, I do think it is instructive that the Olympic decathlon champion—and not the winners of individual events—is called "the world's best athlete." Likewise, we bestow special honor on those "well-rounded" persons who strive to realize in an integrated way *all* of their best potentials, even though this balance is attained by achieving less in any particular area than would have been the case if the person had been a "specialist." But it is not so clear whether such a balanced life illustrates more or less well-being than a life that does exceedingly well on one well-being dimension but falls far short on the others.

Third, it is also worth saying that absolute choices between different aspects of well-being are less often called for than we might think. Sometimes we are able to *emphasize* one good over another and still permit the other goods to make a significant contribution to our lives. Although less than full and complete well-being, this sort of balance contributes to a life's going well. Similarly, as I suggested above, the core ideal of balance can and should be realized in different ways at different times of our lives, depending on what is practically possible. Wynton Marsalis explains that after many years of playing exemplary jazz together, his group disbanded so that its members, now married with families, could spend more time at home. One hopes that each band member's attention to the social dimension of his well-being can be combined with some sort of continuation of his musical career. We see here diverse and age-appropriate specifications of the ideal of balance rather than one-sidedness at one stage of life being compensated for by the opposite one-sidedness at a later stage.

Finally, when consumption choices do disrupt the balance of our lives and result in a loss of well-being, the harm often arises not for the sake of some exalted achievement but, instead, from our own short-sightedness or self-deception. We foolishly consume what we know is (in the long run) bad for us. Bolstered by rationalizations, we myopically buy what will eventually harm us. We "convince" ourselves we need the fashionable shoes ("they are so well made," "they were on sale," "they go so well with my suit"), even though we know they will hurt our feet. We luxuriate in a dream vacation of opulent leisure, telling ourselves that "we deserve it" and "we only live once"; yet we know that our momentary enjoyment is purchased at the price of long-run financial difficulties. In such cases, we may reasonably conclude that the value of a life of sustained and balanced well-being exceeds the benefits of a consumption choice narrowly devoted to (one element of) present well-being.

Employing the Norm: Assessing American Consumption

The capabilities conception of well-being I have described provides the basis for a general and cross-cultural consumption norm: one consumption pattern or choice is better than another if it does better in protecting and promoting those capabilities and functionings that are the components of the person's well-being. The worth of commodities is relative to those capabilities that are ends in themselves. As Sen observes, "an absolute approach in the space of capabilities translates into a relative approach in the space of commodities, resources and incomes in dealing with some important capabilities, such as avoiding shame from failure to meet social conventions, participating in social activities, and retaining self-respect."[26]

Such a consumption norm has sufficient content to rule out the one-sidedness of materialism and antimaterialism and to provide determinate guidance in evaluating consumption choices. Yet this norm also has sufficient generality to permit quite diverse "balancing acts," depending on a person's specific resources, abilities, opportunities, and choices. What promotes, maintains, balances, weakens, or destroys the same aspects of well-being can and often does vary from person to person as well as from society to society. Some people can possess more commodities than others before such possession undermines their bodily health, practical rationality, or social participation by fostering imprudence and political indifference. To live well in an opulent, technologically advanced community requires different goods from those required to live well in a poor and traditional one. As Sen explains:

> To lead a life without shame, to be able to visit and entertain one's friends, to keep track of what is going on and what others are talking about, and so on, requires a more expensive bundle of goods and services in a society that is generally richer, and in which most people have, say, means of transport, affluent clothing, radios or television sets, and so on. Thus, some of the same capabilities (relevant for a "minimum" level of living) require more real income and opulence in the form of commodity possession in a richer society than in poorer ones. The same absolute levels of capabilities may thus have a greater relative need for incomes (and commodities).[27]

Wise consumption requires knowledge of ourselves and our society as well as choice in the light of that knowledge.

The capabilities concept of well-being, then, both provides a general orientation for assessing consumption and is sensitive to the ways in which individual and societal differences will require that this concept be specified and applied in different ways in different social and personal contexts.

How might such a consumption norm be applied to some typical American consumption patterns? Given its person and context sensitivity, what sort of guidance can a norm derived from the capabilities approach yield with respect to our consumption choices? To illustrate the salutary evaluative force of the capabilities norm, in this section I sketch with very broad strokes a general assessment of some current American consumption patterns and, in the next section, I employ the capabilities norm as a guide in the choice of housing.

Judged from the vantage point of the capabilities approach, Americans not surprisingly make both wise and unwise consumption choices. Sometimes we buy, use, and repair consumer goods prudently, in ways that maintain, restore, or enhance our well-being. However, even when

the *external* opportunities for well-being and flourishing are available—
and they often are not—many of us do not have the internal capacities
or motivation to seize those opportunities. Our consumption choices
and styles frequently prevent us from engaging in those activities that
make life worth living; even worse, our decisions sometimes destroy
the abilities on which those activities depend. However, rather than
blame our consumption ills on the current *level* of American consumption, it is better to say that Americans often have too much of some
things, and not enough of others, for their own good. Employing each
major component of the capabilities conception of well-being, let us
evaluate some representative American consumption patterns. I intend
this account to be illustrative and suggestive rather than comprehensive
and systematic. In particular, I offer only rough and impressionistic
judgments as to the relative proportions of personally beneficial and
harmful American consumption.

Physical Well-Being

First, how should we assess typical American consumer choices in
relation to the bodily component of healthy, well-nourished, decently
sheltered, and mobile functioning? On the one hand, the limited income
and wealth available to many of the poor do not permit them to attain
the level of minimally acceptable physical functioning. Thirty million
Americans are hungry in the richest nation in the world. Homelessness
continues to be a serious urban problem. The poorest strata often lack
the external opportunities and the internal abilities and motivation to
acquire and realize "basic capabilities," that is, minimally sufficient
amounts of the most valuable capabilities. Part of the problem here
is structural: many do not have the income needed to purchase or the
entitlements needed to command the kind of housing, food, and transportation required for basic capabilities and functioning. Our system of
production and consumption makes it increasingly difficult for poor
people, especially minorities and immigrants, to have the capability to
achieve well-being.

At the same time, those who enjoy economic advantages often do
not escape physical deprivations and threats to their bodily well-being.
Although some Americans eat foods that are nutritious, others habitu-
ally eat too much, too little, or the wrong things (for their own good).
Many adults have taken up exercise programs and have purchased the
apparel and equipment that facilitate these activities. Talented young
athletes participate in sports programs. However, increasing proportions of Americans—both adults and youth—are physically unfit. Poor
diets, tobacco and other drugs, and excessive television watching are

among the likely causes of this decline in health and fitness. Moreover, the demands of the workplace often take a heavy toll on the physical (and psychic) health of working Americans. Some jeopardize their health by working longer hours, taking a second job, creating households with two earners, or passing up vacations because they choose more income and a higher living standard over more leisure and a lower standard of living.[28]

Mental Well-Being

Let us turn to the mental components of well-being. Again the picture is mixed. On the one hand, as Robert Fullinwider argues, the Aristotelian virtues of discrimination, social deliberation, and wise judgment are often exercised when we select, use, and maintain those consumer goods involved in such diverse pastimes as gardening, recreation, weaving, and beer brewing.[29] Specialized ("niche") magazines, associations, and media programs—"car talk" and "sports talk"—enable their aficionados to express and hone the virtue of practical rationality. However, this valuable capability is unfortunately restricted to private life and is largely absent from one's life as a citizen. American men are much better in assessing NFL teams or hobby gear than proposals for health care reform.

Also disturbing are consumption choices, such as adolescent binge drinking, in which prudent deliberation and discriminating judgment are absent. Autonomy-destroying addiction is the cause and consequence of much American consumption. Drugs, tobacco, and excessive alcohol consumption undermine our free agency as well as damage us physically. And although advertising probably does not manipulate responsible adults to a degree that compromises their autonomy,[30] television programs and advertisements that target children are likely to shape excessively the preferences of the young. With respect to the happiness component of mental well-being, there is—as we saw earlier—much evidence that money and consumer goods by themselves do not bring lasting happiness and some evidence that they are one factor in a pervasive cultural malaise.

Social Well-Being

Some consumption patterns prevent our social potentialities from being realized or twist them in the service of getting and spending. Although dining together and exchanging gifts can express and enhance mutuality, "friendship" easily becomes a business tool, gifts a way of buying influence, and public service a means to private accumulation.

Primetime Live reveals that corporate enterprises, such as U.S. tobacco and defense contractors, regularly foot the bill for members of the U.S. Congress and their staffs to enjoy the recreational and culinary amenities of posh resorts in Barbados and on Florida's Captive Island. One critic observed, "The idea is 'We'll make you comfortable now, and you'll make us comfortable later (when you have the opportunity to vote on legislation that affects us).'"[31]

Finally, if Robert D. Putnam is right, it is not consumer goods as such but *one* consumer good—television—that is uniquely responsible for the disappearance of that nexus of social and political participation called "civic culture." The reason for the apparent increase in people bowling alone, distrusting their neighbors, and growing indifferent to civic and political affairs, argues Putnam, is that they are spending increasing amounts of leisure time watching television.[32] This is not to say that television programming or videos cannot be educational and entertaining. But indiscriminate and frequent television watching tends to weaken social skills and cause viewers to be passive, suspicious of others, and apolitical. Exaggerating "separateness" at the cost of our other valuable capabilities, television viewing may be invidiously compared with other household activities that it has replaced—for instance, conversation, games, music making, and reading to children.

Separateness

Americans often express their identities through what they buy and possess. For instance, Brian Brooks, a young architect, explains why his main concern upon graduating from college was buying the right car: "When people look at my car [a late-model Acura Vigor] that's me, that's Brian. . . . There's a certain amount of power and confidence that comes with it. . . . I was driving around in a rental car once, and I felt inferior to the world."[33] One advantage of America's cornucopia, at least in principle and for those with the resources, is that American consumers have the means to express (and invent) many identities. As hot-rodders did in an earlier epoch, consumers sometimes find ways to "customize" commodities that are standardized and mass produced. Or, like home brewers and clothes makers, they produce and consume personalized goods. Yet there are powerful social constraints upon and motivations for much of our consuming; as Judith Lichtenberg argues, we often consume (the way we do) because others consume (the way they do).[34] These conventional consumption patterns, as well as difficulties in customizing many consumer goods, deter many Americans from choosing to display or enhance their distinctiveness in what they buy and own.

Employing the Norm: The Choice of Housing

In addition to a norm for assessing current consumption patterns, the capabilities approach also supplies an orientation for making advantageous future consumption choices. To illustrate the salutary prescriptive force of the capabilities norm, let us suggest its application to the question of housing. Without presuming to give utterly novel housing guidelines, the capabilities norm of well-being will be successful if it clarifies and endorses one strand of our often contradictory everyday judgments about humanely good housing.

Although frequently neglected in the consumption debate, our choice of housing—which includes such things as the dwelling, utilities, and furnishings—is important, for it requires a far greater proportion of consumer dollars (31 percent) than any other major category of consumer expenditure. Many people, of course, have no choice but to settle for housing that is clearly at odds with even a modicum of well-being. Others could afford decent housing if only they changed their conception of the good life and their overall consumption pattern. Let us suppose, however, that an individual or family has or receives the resources to acquire a dwelling that protects and promotes the four aspects of well-being. What would be the *typical* characteristics—compatible with individual and societal variation—of such housing? The ultimate concern, of course, is not on housing features in themselves but on those characteristics that usually and for the most part facilitate the acquisition, maintenance, and realization of valuable capabilities.

First, the capabilities approach requires that housing options should be assessed with respect to their occupants' physical well-being. The neighborhood should be reasonably free of crime as well as the hazards posed by polluted air and water. Safe, accessible parks and playgrounds should offer opportunities for recreation. The dwelling itself should enable its occupants to be secure from the elements. Physical health requires good ventilation, sanitation, and sunlight as well as adequate space for sleeping, meal preparation, and personal hygiene.

"Livable" housing also protects and promotes the mental component of well-being. In its design and furnishings, good housing occasions aesthetic enjoyment. Maintaining and improving one's housing affords opportunities for the exercise of practical rationality.

Further, good housing safeguards and nurtures various forms of sociability and mutuality. Permitting and encouraging wider social participation, good housing is reasonably close to neighbors, work, schools, and cultural opportunities.

Finally, good housing expresses—through its design, furnishings, and such things as workshops or studies, gardens or basketball hoops—

the inhabitants specific and perhaps distinctive ideas of the good life. Moreover, a good dwelling is sufficiently commodious to provide each occupant with the personal space (and time) that is needed to be able to live one's distinctive life in one's own ambience. Such "separateness" may be best expressed by each occupant having his or her own room or part of a room.

Sometimes two or more components of well-being call for the same housing site or structure. A room with good sunlight, for example, can be both healthy and aesthetically pleasing. A shared bedroom can promote both mutuality and singularity. It will often prove difficult, however, to find housing that satisfies (equally) each component of this complex conception of well-being, for the elements of well-being can conflict with as well as support one another. There may be no neighborhood, for instance, that is both close to one's work and reasonably safe or near good schools. Moreover, the right house might be found, but its cost could be prohibitive—at least given the cost of other goods essential to the inhabitants' well-being. We must therefore employ practical rationality in order to address the advantages and disadvantages of each specific option, deliberate, and finally judge which abode (and larger consumer pattern) is, on balance, best for us.

Three Objections

The capabilities approach to consumption might be criticized in three ways; first, it fails to yield a norm to identify or condemn *over*consumption; second, it amounts to a merely personal ideal that fails to assess social structures; and, third, it presupposes an overly intrusive government. The first objection contends that the capabilities conception of well-being, although able to identify *under*consumption, lacks the resources to identify *over*consumption or criticize opulence. After all, the objection might proceed, you have conceded that some people's well-being—especially in affluent societies—would require abundant if not opulent goods and services. Although some people might have their best potentials damaged by too much or the wrong kinds of commodities, many others might flourish only through elevated levels of consumption. For instance, there would seem to be no way to criticize the connoisseur of fine wines, sports cars, or Impressionist paintings whose happiness really requires such expenditures. And if being able to appear in public without shame is a component of well-being and we accept that it takes more to live without shame in an affluent society than in a poor one, then there seems to be no basis for criticizing the millionaire bond trader Sherman McCoy and his wife, in Tom Wolfe's novel *Bon-*

fire of the Vanities, who must have a chauffeur and limousine in order to travel without shame to a dinner party just a few blocks away from their apartment.[35]

The capabilities norm of well-being does offer *some* basis for criticizing excessive consumption to the extent that it can be shown that the consumption choice in question undermines some other features of the consumer's well-being, for instance, her health or ability to choose. Hence, my friend might appropriately reprimand me for drinking habits that are either unsafe or addictive.[36] But suppose the consumer's choice—like Sherman McCoy's rental of a chauffeured limo—is not bad for him (in ways counted as harmful by the capabilities norm) and moreover seems to be part of his conception of the good life?[37]

What this objection shows, I believe, is not a deficiency in the capability norm of well-being but only that this norm cannot—by itself—supply a complete ethic of responsible consumption. For, I would argue, in addition to supplying a well-being norm, such an ethic would also interpret and justify our moral obligations to other people, social institutions, and the environment. If so, then there may be good reason to contend that Sherman McCoy's transportation choices violate his moral duties or prevent him from fulfilling his complex obligations.[38]

The second objection faults the capabilities approach for paying exclusive attention to personal choice and neglecting the ways in which the socioeconomic system closes (or opens) choice and damages (or promotes) individual well-being. The result, alleges the objection, is an uncritical acceptance, if not endorsement, of current institutions and policies. This criticism is analogous to and might be informed by a certain reading of Marx, which contends that problems of individual morality exist only because of a social failure to modify or replace those (unjust) societal structures that in turn create moral dilemmas. What is needed is not a norm for personal consumption but a political economy that explains and leads to the elimination of the roots of our present moral quandaries. If we are to have a consumption norm at all, it should be a *social* norm that enables us to assess the totality and deficiency of our present consumption-production system.

There is some truth in this objection, for we want to assess not only our best present options and choices but also the societal structures that open some options and close others.[39] Although it is important to make beneficial and responsible consumption choices in the present, it is also essential to assess available options, explain their proximate and, if possible, ultimate causes, and evaluate the consequences for well-being of alternative social structures. A social structure would be morally defective to the extent that it yielded options conducive to ill-being or not productive of well-being. Although the norm of well-being in this essay is proposed to guide *individual* choice, it can and should also be deployed to evaluate the effects that *social* institutions are likely to have on human options and well-being.

A third objection might reject the capabilities account of well-being as a consumption norm because it rests on the view that governments should dictate what people should buy and use. To promote and protect human well-being, governments should enforce some consumer choices and coercively proscribe others.

My quick response is that the present essay proposes a norm for personal consumer choice and neither offers nor implies a view of the nature and scope of governmental responsibility. However, just as the norm of well-being could be used to assess morally the causes and consequences of consumer choices, so the capabilities approach can and should consider the legitimate and illegitimate role of the state and other institutions in such matters. For instance, suppose the state were viewed as responsible for insuring that each citizen (and immigrant?) is able—if he or she so chooses—to live at a certain (minimal) level of well-being.

Many questions concerning the state's proper role in consumption choices would remain. That role surely would depend on the types of citizens and kinds of commodities involved. The persons in question can be foreign visitors and immigrants as well as citizens, and each group consists of individuals with different ages and capacities. Goods differ with respect to the risks and benefits—to self and others—that accompany their consumption. The state in turn has many ways to influence consumer choice. To employ Nussbaum's distinction, the state can "discipline," for instance by proscribing heroin, regulating tobacco, alcohol, and prescription drugs, and prescribing safety standards with respect to housing, food, clothing, and automobiles; and it can "enable," for instance by educating children about wise consumption and informing adults through nutritional and environmental labeling of consumer goods.[40] Falling outside of the discipline/enable dichotomy are such government actions as tax incentives and subsidies that noncoercively promote certain consumer choices with respect to housing, medicine, and food. A comprehensive capabilities approach to political philosophy would take up these and related questions.

Toward Responsible Consumption

In order to focus on the effects of consumption on our own well-being, I began this essay by setting aside other important questions about consumption choices: those involving our moral obligations toward the environment, societal institutions, and other people. In the course of my argument, moreover, I have suggested that the pursuit of higher goods and the exercise of our obligations do not necessarily require the sacrifice of well-being. Nonetheless, it is true that consumption choices that are ostensibly good for us often harm nature, society, or others and that the norm of our own well-being by itself is not sufficient for assessing these choices. A comprehensive approach to responsible consumption, which the capabilities approach aspires to be, would address the scope and weight of our various duties as well as the proper roles and limits of our various institutions. Some of the materials for such an assessment may be found in other essays in this volume.

Notes

I owe thanks to my colleagues at the Institute for Philosophy and Public Policy, especially Arthur Evenchik, Robert Fullinwider, Toby Linden, Mark Sagoff, and Jerome Segal, for illuminating discussions of these issues. David P. Crocker, Lawrence Crocker, Des Gasper, Michael Slote and Paul Streeten made valuable comments on earlier versions of the essay. I benefited from presenting the paper as the thirty-sixth Annual Hurst Lecture at the Department of Philosophy, American University, to the philosophy departments at Colorado State University, Swarthmore College, the University of Maryland, Southwestern University, and the Washington Moral Psychology Group. I also made presentations based on the paper at the University of Costa Rica, the World Bank, and the Boston Theological Institute/AAAS Conference on "Consumption, Population, & the Environment." I gratefully acknowledge support for this research from the National Endowment for the Humanities Grant #RO-22709-94 and from the Global Stewardship Initiative of the Pew Charitable Trusts. The views expressed are mine and not necessarily those of NEH or the Pew Charitable Trusts.

1. Robert L. Heilbroner and Lester Thurow, *Economics Explained* (Englewood Cliffs, N.J.: Prentice Hall, 1982), 80. See also Robert A. Blecker, "The Consumption Binge is a Myth," in *Understanding American Economic Decline*, ed. Michael A. Bernstein and David E. Adler (Cambridge, U.K.: Cambridge University Press, 1994), 276–309; Robert H. Frank and Philip J. Cook, *The Winner-Take-All Society* (Free Press, 1995), 213.

2. John Rawls's explanation and defense of the method of "reflective equilibrium" occur in *A Theory of Justice* (Cambridge, Mass.: Harvard University Press, 1971), 20–22, 46–53, 432, and 579.

3. Stanley Lebergott, "Pursuing Consumption Limits" (a paper presented to the conference "Consumption, Global Stewardship, and the Good Life," University of Maryland, College Park, September 29–October 2, 1994), 2. See also Stanley Lebergott, "What Principle?" *Report from the Institute for Philosophy & Public Policy* 15, no. 4 (Fall 1995): 22.

4. See, for example, Ben Fine and Ellen Leopold, *The World of Consumption* (London and New York: Routledge, 1993), and Daniel Miller, ed., *Acknowledging Consumption: A Review of New Studies* (London and New York: Routledge, 1995). The essays in part II, "Explaining and Assessing Consumption," of the present volume address the issue of the causes of consumption.

5. Juliet B. Schor, *The Overworked American: The Unexpected Decline of Leisure* (New York: Basic Books, 1992), 107. Colin Campbell argues (in this volume) that shopping may be less "a magpie-like desire to acquire as many material objects as possible" and more like escape into a world of fantasy and pleasure.

6. Frederick Turner, *The Return*, with a preface by George Steiner (Woodstock, Vt.: Countryman Press, 1981), 5–6, quoted in Chandra Mukerji, *From Graven Images: Patterns of Modern Materialism* (New York: Columbia University Press, 1983), xv.

7. Victor Lebow, *Journal of Retailing* (Spring 1995): 7, quoted in Alan Thein Durning, *How Much Is Enough: The Consumer Society and the Future of the Earth* (New York: W. W. Norton, 1992), 21–22.

8. See Robert E. Lane, "Does Money Buy Happiness," *Public Interest* 111 (Fall 1993): 59, 61.

9. Meadows's remarks are summarized in "Redefining the American Dream: The Search for Sustainable Consumption," Conference Report, Airlie, Virginia, 23–25 April 1995 (Merck Family Fund), 4. It should be noted that Meadows reportedly urged such nonmaterial concerns as means to the further end of reversing "growth of material and energy consumption."

10. John Updike, *The Afterlife and Other Stories* (New York: Fawcett Crest, 1994), 61–62.

11. In its survey on attitudes toward consumption, the Harwood Group finds that "Americans are ambivalent in their views on materialism." On the one hand "most of the people in the survey believe that we buy and consume too much." On the other hand, the same people have an "appreciation for the good things material wealth can bring . . . and just over half of those surveyed also agreed that 'material wealth is part of what makes this country great'" (Harwood Group, "Yearning for Balance: Views of Americans on Consumption, Materialism, and the Environment" [Merck Family Fund, July 1995], 6).

12. American cultural history may be interpreted as often extreme and even violent alternations between antimaterialism and materialism. See David E. Shi, *The Simple Life: Plain Living and High Thinking in American Culture* (New York and Oxford: Oxford University Press, 1985); Christopher Lasch, *The True and Only Heaven: Progress and its Critics* (New York and London: Norton, 1991); Michael Schudson, "Delectable Materialism, Second Thoughts on Consumer Culture" (in this volume); William Leach, *The Land of Desire: Merchants, Money, and the Rise of a New American Culture* (New York: Pantheon Books, 1993); and, Jackson Lears, *Fables of Abundance: A Cultural History of Advertising in America* (New York: Basic Books, 1994). William Leach, for example, tells the story of how American entrepreneurs, such as department store owner John Wanamaker of Philadelphia, projected and helped imple-

ment—often with religious arguments—a materialist vision in express opposition to American antimaterialist traditions.

13. Margot Hornblower, "Generation X Gets Real," *Time*, 9 June 1997, 66. For evidence that the "materialistic values" of American youth exhibited a "rapid rise . . . in the 1980s and only now [1997] is leveling off," see Wendy Rahn, "An Individual-Level Analysis of the Decline of Social Trust in American Youth," working paper, Center for the Study of Political Psychology, University of Minnesota (testimony presented to the National Commission on Civic Renewal, Washington, D.C., 25 January 1997).

14. Radford Byerly, "Consumption and Population Growth: Twin Challenges to Sustainable Development," Annual Meeting of the American Association for the Advancement of Science, Baltimore, Maryland, 8–13 February 1996).

15. The notion of moral inquiry as progressive specification of an initial "outline sketch" comes from Nussbaum's interpretation of Aristotle: "So much for our outline sketch for the good. For it looks as if we have to draw an outline first, and fill it in later. It would seem to be open to anyone to take things further and to articulate the good parts of the sketch." (*Nicomachean Ethics* 1098a20–26). See Martha C. Nussbaum, "Non-Relative Virtues: An Aristotelian Approach," in *Quality of Life*, ed. Martha C. Nussbaum and Amartya Sen (Oxford: Clarendon Press, 1993), 242–76.

16. See, for example, Nussbaum and Sen, eds., *The Quality of Life*; and, Martha C. Nussbaum and Jonathan Glover, eds., *Women, Culture and Development: A Study of Human Capabilities* (Oxford: Clarendon Press, 1995). For a bibliography of Sen and Nussbaum's extensive philosophical writings as well as an analysis and assessment of the "capabilities ethic" as a feature of the "capabilities approach" to development, see my essays: "Functioning and Capability: The Foundations of Sen's and Nussbaum's Development Ethic," *Political Theory* 20 (November 1992): 584–612; "Functioning and Capability: The Foundations of Sen's and Nussbaum's Development Ethic, Part 2," in *Women, Culture, and Development*, ed. Nussbaum and Glover; and *Florecimiento humano y desarrollo internacional: La nueva ética de capacidades humanas* (San José, Costa Rica: Editorial de la Universidad de Costa Rica, 1997). A complete bibliography of Sen's voluminous writings and important assessments of his contributions to social choice theory and economics occur in K. Basu, P. Pattanaik, and K. Suzumura, eds., *Choice, Welfare, and Development: A Festschrift in Honour of Amartya K. Sen* (Oxford: Clarendon Press, 1995). My account of well-being has also benefitted from Partha Dasgupta, *An Inquiry in Well-Being and Destitution* (Oxford: Clarendon Press, 1993); James Griffin, *Well-Being: Its Meaning, Measurement and Moral Importance* (Oxford: Clarendon Press, 1986); T. M. Scanlon, "Value, Desire, and Quality of Life," in *The Quality of Life*, ed. Nussbaum and Sen, 185–200; and T. M. Scanlon, "The Moral Basis of Interpersonal Comparisons," in *Interpersonal Comparisons of Well-Being*, ed. Jon Elster and John Roemer (Cambridge: Cambridge University Press, 1991), 17–44.

17. Amartya Sen, "Well-Being, Agency and Freedom: The Dewey Lectures 1984," *Journal of Philosophy* 82, no. 4 (1985): 200.

18. Sen distinguishes between our well-being and our "agency" achievement or the realization of our objectives. See Amartya Sen, "Well-Being, Agency and Freedom, 185–212; and *Inequality Reexamined* (Cambridge, Mass.: Harvard University Press, 1992), 56–72. Well-being and agency can vary together, for example, when my doing my moral duty makes me happy. In the capabilities approach, well-being does not by definition include moral goodness, but doing good *can* contribute to our well-being insofar as the former positively affects the latter. As Sen points out "The effect of 'other-regarding' concerns on one's well-being has to operate *through* some feature of the person's own being. Doing good may make a person contented or fulfilled, and these are functioning achievements of some importance. In this approach, functionings are seen as central to the *nature* of well-being, even though the *sources* of well-being could easily be external to the person" ("Capability and Well-Being," in *Quality of Life*, ed. Nussbaum and Sen, 36). But well-being and achieving our other goals also can go in different directions. Responsible adults, as we have seen, can choose to sacrifice their well-being for the sake of their causes or "agency" objectives. For a helpful discussion of five options for understanding the relation of "living well" and "doing right," see Thomas Nagel, *The View from Nowhere* (New York: Oxford University Press, 1986), 189–207.

19. Alfred North Whitehead, *Science and the Modern World* (New York: Macmillan, 1925), 200.

20. Crocker, "Functioning and Capability," 601.

21. Amartya Sen, *Resources, Values, and Development* (Cambridge, Mass.: Harvard University Press, 1984), 512 (footnote omitted). See also Sen, *On Ethics and Economics* (Oxford: Basil Blackwell, 1987), 45–46; "Well-Being, Agency and Freedom, 191. Cf. Jon Easter, "Sour Grapes—Utilitarianism and the Genesis of Wants," in *Utilitarianism and Beyond*, ed. Amartya Sen and Bernard Williams (Cambridge, U.K.: Cambridge University Press, 1982), 219–39. The version of Sen's small mercies argument cited undermines preference utilitarianism better than it does the hedonistic variety. Sen can effectively criticize the latter, however, by observing that uninterrupted drug-induced euphoria can be compatible with, may cause, and often camouflages the drug user's objective ill-being.

22. Nussbaum, "Human Capabilities, Female Human Beings," 85. Nussbaum's idea seems the same as Heidegger's concept of *Jemeinigkeit*. Misleadingly translated as "authenticity," the original meaning of the German term is closer to "my-owness." See Martin Heidegger, *Being and Time*, trans. John Macquarrie and Edward Robinson (New York and Evanston, Ill.: Harper & Row 1962), 67, 78, and 150.

23. Nussbaum, "Human Capabilities, Female Human Beings," 85.

24. The capability to choose a conception of the good life is both a mental and "separateness" component of well-being. It is the former because it specifies the general mental capacity of decision making. It is the latter insofar as the conception chosen is uniquely *mine* (although it may be similar in content to the basic ideals of others).

25. Nussbaum, "Human Capabilities, Female Human Beings," 80.

26. Sen, *Resources, Values and Development*, 343.

27. Amartya Sen, *The Standard of Living*, 1985 Tanner Lectures at Cambridge, with Contributions by Keith Hart, Ravi Muellbauer, and Bernard Williams, ed. Geoffrey Hawthorn (Cambridge, U.K.: Cambridge University Press) 18. Editors' note: portions of *The Standard of Living* appear as the 1987 postscript to Sen's essay in the present volume, 298–303, quote at 298. See also Sen, *Resources, Values and Development*, 335–38.

28. More empirical work is needed as to what extent people are working longer hours than earlier and, if they are, what explains it. Juliet B. Schor, who argues that Americans on average work the equivalent of one month a year more than they did twenty years ago, explains the putative increase in working time as due to firms, as a means of making greater profits, setting the hours and not permitting "flex time." See Schor, *The Overworked American*, 126–36. Others fault consumers, whose alleged desire to enhance their standard of living—as a means, for instance, to emulate others—results in their working increasingly more hours. Still others, such as Jerome M. Segal in this volume, submit structural features in the political economy, for example, a decline in public provision, to explain why increasingly more income is needed—and, thereby, hours are worked—merely to maintain one's standard of living. It should also be investigated to what extent people choose to work in jobs with longer hours as a means to professional advancement and achievement rather than as a means to protect or elevate their living standards. In her essay "Consuming Because Others Consume" (in this volume), Judith Lichtenberg evaluates explanatory theories of consumption.

29. Robert Fullinwider, "Consumption and the Good Life: Historical Perspectives," Institute for Philosophy and Public Policy, unpublished paper.

30. Claudia Mills, "Is Advertising Manipulative?" in *Values and Public Policy*, ed. Claudia Mills (Fort Worth, Texas: Harcourt Brace Jovanovich, 1992), 218–23.

31. ABC News Primetime Live, transcript 362, 11 August 1994.

32. Robert D. Putnam, "Bowling Alone: America's Declining Social Capital," *Journal of Democracy* 6, no. 10 (January 1995): 65–78; and, "The Strange Disappearance of Civic America," *American Prospect* 24 (Winter 1996): 34–48. In "What If Civic Life Didn't Die?" *American Prospect* (March/April 1996): 18–20, Michael Schudson challenges Putnam's argument that civic engagement is decreasing and, even if it were, Schudson contends that television viewing is not the best explanation. For evidence that declining levels of social trust are importantly due to a dramatic rise in materialist values, see Rahn, "An Individual-Level Analysis," 11–14.

33. Lonnae O'Neal Parker, "Looking Buff at Sam's: Carwash Is Place to Clean and Be Seen," *Washington Post*, 31 July 1995, A1, A7.

34. "Consuming Because Others Consume" (in this volume).

35. Paul Streeten follows Robert H. Frank in criticizing Sen with the Sherman McCoy case. See Robert H. Frank, review of Amartya Sen, *The Standard of Living*, in *Journal of Economic Literature* 27, no. 2 (1989): 666; Paul Streeten, "Poverty Concepts and Measurement," *Bangladesh Development Studies* 18, no. 3 (September 1990): 1–18, especially 9–14.

36. Although such reproaches are, arguably, part of my friend's duty to me, it does not follow that it is *morally* wrong for me to run personal risks and even undermine my own well-being—as long as such risks are central to my way of life and I am not thereby injuring someone else. See Amartya Sen, "The Right to Take Personal Risks" in *Values at Risk,* ed. Douglas MacLean (Totowa, N.J.: Rowman & Allanheld, 1986), 155–69.

37. The capabilities norm of well-being might yield criticism of McCoy inasmuch as his entire life is *constituted* by being "other-directed," by appearing to his peers in ways that *they* take to be nonshameful. Such a life does not go as well as it might for two reasons. First, autonomous choice is essentially absent, at least after McCoy's initial decision to be other-directed. Second, since McCoy's other-directed conduct is likely to undermine, as it does in the novel, other aspects of his well-being, we might urge him to choose a peer group that is more conducive to his life's going well. I owe these points to discussions with Mark Sagoff and Peter Levine.

38. In future work I will investigate whether (1) our moral obligations may be interpreted by the idea that we have a moral duty to protect and promote the well-being of others; (2) political morality, rather than being restricted to liberal neutralism, can be defended as primarily concerned with protecting and promoting human well-being; and (3) the capabilities approach to well-being can give us what we need with respect to the "duties of well-being." Cf. Joseph Raz, *The Morality of Freedom* (Oxford: Clarendon Press, 1986), and part I, "The Ethics of Well-being: Political Implications," *Ethics in the Public Domain: Essays in the Morality of Law and Politics* (Oxford: Clarendon Press, 1994), 3–176. See also William A. Galston, *Liberal Purposes: Goods, Virtues, and Diversity in the Liberal State* (Cambridge, U.K.: Cambridge University Press, 1991), especially chap. 8; and James Griffin, *Well-Being*, part 3, "Moral Importance."

39. See James A. Nash, "On the Subversive Virtue: Frugality" (in this volume).

40. Martha C. Nussbaum, "The Good As Discipline, the Good As Freedom" (in this volume).

20

"The Earth Is the Lord's and the Fullness Thereof": Jewish Perspectives on Consumption

Eliezer Diamond

In late-twentieth-century America anyone speaking in the public arena from a religious perspective has a difficult and delicate task. On the one hand, any mention of God and—even more so—organized religion is a source of discomfort to some. It may even trigger fears of a mix of proselytizing and political maneuvering often associated, correctly or not, with the Religious Right. On the other hand, to refrain from using religious language is to be dishonest and undermines the integrity of one's own commitments.

Because the content and methodology of Jewish religious thought is generally less well known than that of Christianity, it seems appropriate to preface this discussion with a brief description of Judaism's religious language. On the whole, Judaism is far more interested in the behavioral aspects of one's religious life than in the doctrinal ones. The set of directives that governs one's religious behavior is called in Hebrew *halakhah*; this term can be translated idiomatically as "the path" or "the way." These laws govern one's relations with God, with human kind, and with the cosmos, including the plant and animal worlds. This legal system, moreover, is not static; it contains within itself mechanisms for extending and modifying its own rulings. In this sense Judaism is particularly well suited to address questions of consumption; it offers specific, practical guidelines and a means for applying these to new and different circumstances. At the same time, Judaism's behavioral system is undergirded by an ideological matrix that, though ill defined and poorly organized, is crucial both for making sense of existing laws and for formulating new ones. In my presentation, I will present aspects of the theology underlying halakhah as it relates to consumption as well as actual applications of halakhah to this issue.

The Jewish view of consumption is informed by the belief that the earth is God's; in partaking of it, therefore, we are receiving a divine gift that must be utilized in accordance with God's will. This belief can be illustrated by the halakhic requirement that one recite a blessing before partaking of any food, acknowledging God as its creator. To fail to do so, says the Talmud, is the equivalent of misappropriating sancta,[1] which involves both taking what is not mine and profaning that which is holy, in other words, using that which is God's for purposes that God did not intend. Part of God's intention regarding human use of the world's resources is that there should be periods of activity alternating with times of rest and retreat. Thus, commenting on Genesis 2:15, "The Lord God took the man and placed him in the Garden of Eden, to work it (l'ovdah) and to tend [or: keep] it (l'shomrah)," the rabbis state the following: " 'To work it'—[as Scripture states elsewhere:] 'Six days shall you work' (Exod. 20:9); 'and to keep it' [as Scripture states elsewhere:] 'Observe [or: keep] the Sabbath day' (Deut. 5:12)."[2] Work is a transformative process, and therefore often consumes human and material resources;[3] tending or guarding is an act of preservation. The biblical imperative, as further amplified by rabbinic exegesis, is to find the appropriate balance between transformation and preservation. Part of this balance is established by pausing from work every seventh day.

This six-and-one cycle applies not only to weeks but, at least in the land of Israel, to years as well. Every seventh year is a year of rest for the land in which no cultivation of land is to take place (Lev. 25:3–5) and in which whatever grows of its own accord is to be distributed among the needy (Lev. 25:6–7). A few years back in the Jewish calendar, 5754 Anno Mundi (September 1993–August 1994) was a Sabbatical year; at least 3500 Israeli farmers refrained entirely from working their land for its duration; numerous others modified their farming practices to varying degrees in observance of the sabbatical year.

The limitations placed on Jewish individuals and society through the laws of Sabbath and the Sabbatical year, as well as restrictions governing one's diet and sexual behavior, are meant to help us come to terms with our limitedness, so that, rather than being seen as a curse, it is simply viewed as the starting point from which one constructs a meaningful life. "Who is wealthy?" ask the rabbis rhetorically. "One who is happy with one's lot"[4]. This perspective is an important corrective to a society in which success and meaning are often defined almost exclusively in monetary terms.

The opposite of "being happy with one's lot" is coveting, which is prohibited by the last of the Ten Commandments: "You shall not covet your neighbor's house: you shall not covet your neighbor's wife, or his male or female slave, or his ox or his ass, or anything that is your neighbor's" (Exod. 20:14; cf. Deut. 5:18). The prohibition against coveting is difficult to understand; as twelfth-century Spanish scholar Abraham ibn Ezra put it, "How can there be a person who does not desire in his heart whatever is desirable in his eyes?" Ibn Ezra explained the prohibition as follows:

> And now I will recount to you a parable [in order to explain the prohibition against coveting]: Know that a peasant of sound mind who sees a beautiful princess will not desire in his heart to lie with her, for he knows that this is impossible. . . . It is impossible [for the peasant to desire the princess] in the same way that a man does not desire to lie with his mother even if she is beautiful because he has been taught since childhood that she is forbidden to him. Similarly, every wise person must know that a person does not acquire a beautiful wife or wealth because of his intelligence but rather in accordance with what God has apportioned to him.[5]

Ibn Ezra seems to be making two central points. The first is that coveting involves the blurring of the boundaries that mark each person's integrity and individuality. Coveting reinforces the sense that what I need most is that which I do not have at present, and it may lead me to do whatever is necessary to obtain the object of my desire even if it involves sinning against others. As the late-fifteenth- and early-sixteenth-century Italian biblical commentator Ovadiah Sforno stated, "Coveting leads to theft."[6] On the other hand, when one has a clear sense of limits it is less likely that one will be preoccupied with what one does *not* have. Second, coveting involves a kind of hubris, an assumption that one deserves wealth, fame, or whatever it is that one desires. Only with the understanding that all that one has is a divine gift comes the acceptance of, and satisfaction with, one's own particular blessings.

The work of Colin Campbell makes it clear that the problem of coveting has much relevance to contemporary patterns of hyperconsumption.[7] Campbell argues convincingly for a link between the "dynamic and disacquiring nature of modern consumer behavior,"[8] and the form of pleasure seeking that developed beginning in the eighteenth century as an outgrowth of romanticism. This hedonism places a high value on daydreaming and fantasizing—in other words, coveting. Such pleasure seeking inevitably sends one in search of the pleasures one has not yet experienced and also dooms one to perpetual disillusionment, as the reality always falls short of the fantasy. This spurs one on to seek pleasure from yet another untapped source, and so the cycle continues. As Mark Sagoff has shown, this trend has been aided and abetted by political and economic models that concern themselves with personal preference to the exclusion of societal values.[9] The Bible's prohibition against coveting can be seen, then, as a useful corrective to the endlessly dissatisfied and acquisitive mentality that underlies much of our consumption. Halakhah concerns itself not only with balance in the individual and collective lives of the people; it also seeks balance, and equity, in the distribution and consumption of the fruits of labor. Thus, the biblical obligations of *peah*—leaving a corner of one's field for the poor at the time of harvest (Lev. 23:22)—and *ma'aser*—giving a tenth of one's harvest to the landless Levites (Deut. 14:27-29)—are expanded by the rabbis into an obligation to give between ten and twenty percent of one's income to the poor.[10]

Moreover, halakhah is careful to specify that familial and religious celebrations should include the poor, rather than being the occasion for conspicuous and excessive consumption; and should be restrained, so as not to create pressure on those others who are less well off in the community to spend beyond their means. An attempt to achieve the second goal was the formulation of sumptuary laws that limited conspicuous consumption within the community. The following is a ruling of the national Jewish Council of Lithuania, issued 4 September 1637:

> With respect to banquets: Inasmuch as people are spending too much money unnecessarily on festive meals every Jewish community and settlement which has a rabbi is expected to assemble its officers and rabbi and to consider the number of guests which it is suitable for every individual, in view of his wealth and the occasion, to invite to a festive meal. No one is permitted to come to a banquet unless he has been invited by the beadle. In a settlement where there is no rabbi the nearest Jewish court will enact such an ordinance for them.[11]

Although the frequent enactment of such ordinances indicates their observance more in the breach than in the practice, they nonetheless represent the aspirations toward which the community, or at least its leadership, strived. In at least one famous case present Jewish practice testifies to rabbinic success in limiting conspicuous consumption. The Talmud reports as follows:

> At first the carrying out of the dead was harder for his relatives than his death [because of astronomical burial costs] so they left [the corpse] and ran away until Rabban Gamliel [the patriarch of the Jewish community in early-second-century Palestine] came and adopted a simple style and they carried him out in garments of linen [that is, inexpensive garments], and

[then] all the people followed his example and carried out [the dead] in garments of linen.[12]

To this day a traditional Jewish burial is a simple, egalitarian affair, with the deceased buried in a plain pine coffin whether he or she is a scholar or a simpleton, rich or poor.

The first objective, sharing with the poor in times of celebration, is described elegantly and movingly by Maimonides in his evaluation of the relative merits of three obligations of the Purim festival, namely, to feast, to send gifts of food to one's friends, and to give gifts to the poor:

> Better for one to give many gifts to the poor than to have a sumptuous feast and send many gifts to one's acquaintances; for there is no greater or more elegant joy than to gladden the hearts of the poor, the orphan, the widow and the stranger in our midst. One who gladdens the hearts of these unfortunates is likened to the divine presence, as Scripture states: "[I] dwell . . . with the contrite and the lowly in spirit—reviving the spirits of the lowly, reviving the hearts of the contrite"[13] (Isa. 57:15).

Community leadership must be particularly careful to limit its consumption, for at least three reasons. First the people look to their leaders for models of appropriate behavior. Second, leaders who pursue opulent lifestyles often create, as a consequence, undue financial burdens for those they govern. Finally, the pursuit of wealth and pleasures is often a cause of moral corruption, something we can ill afford in our leaders. The classic text demanding that leadership restrain its consumption is Deuteronomy 17:16–17: "[The king] shall not keep many horses or send people back to Egypt to add to his horses, since the Lord has warned you, 'You must not go back that way again.' And he shall not have many wives, lest his heart go astray; nor shall he amass silver and gold to excess."

In rabbinic tradition, the call for restraint is tempered by the assumption that for leadership to be respected, it must have some of the trappings of majesty—and these cost money. Thus, for example, the rabbis interpret the verse, "And the priest who is exalted above his brothers" (Lev. 21:10), which refers to the high priest, to mean that he must be wealthier than any other priest, and if this is not the case, the situation is to be rectified through donations given to him by his fellows.[14] I suppose we have here an example of the viewpoint articulated by Tevye in *Fiddler on the Roof*: "When you're rich they think you really know." On the other hand, there are instances in which folk rabbis found the consumption of the official leadership excessive. The Talmud relates, for example, that the saintly Pinhas ben Yair was invited to dine at the official residence of Judah the Patriarch. When he reached the gate he saw several white mules, a rather rare and expensive breed, tethered there. Saying, "Must my fellow Jews feed all these?" he turned on his heel and left.[15]

One motive, then, for limiting consumption, is the need for balance in the personal and communal realms. Another is Judaism's concern for modesty (z'ni'ut). Indeed, a Talmudic passage suggests that the 613 commandments can be summed up by the following verse in Micah: "He has told you what is good, and what the Lord requires of you: Only to do justice, to love goodness and to walk modestly (hazne'ah lekhet) with your God; then your name will achieve wisdom" (Mic. 6:8). Modesty is broadly defined by the rabbis of the Talmud, and it includes refraining from consumption that is deemed excessive or overly conspicuous. Thus, the rabbinic tradition discourages one from eating in the marketplace,[16] from eating[17] and drinking[18] to excess, and from wearing clothes of such fine materials that they are likely to make one the center of attention.[19] Modesty includes living within one's means; one ought not, as a matter of course, rely upon the resources of others, whether in the form of loans or gifts.[20]

Yet another reason for limiting consumption is to facilitate mastery over one's physical and sensual appetites and thereby distance oneself from sinful or destructive behavior. The rabbis understand the verse "You shall be holy" (Lev. 19:2) as meaning, "You shall be abstemious."[21] Nahmanides, a medieval biblical exegete, explains further:

> The Torah forbids certain sexual relationships and various foods; on the other hand, it permits sex within marriage and the consumption of meat and wine. It is therefore possible that a hedonist may find license to become sexually profligate with his wife or wives, to be among those who swill wine and stuff themselves with meat, and to speak of all the vulgarities not specifically forbidden by the Torah; in this way one may technically remain within the bounds set by the Torah and yet be a vile person. Therefore, after specifying those activities which are completely forbidden, the Torah issues a general directive that we ought to separate ourselves from excess.[22]

Until now, we have spoken of moral and theological considerations in Judaism's concern with limiting consumption. Let us now consider two biblical directives, and their rabbinic glosses, that deal with limiting consumption out of a concern for sustainability, the environment, and the efficient use of resources.

The first is a series of verses in Deuteronomy: "If, along the road, you chance on a bird's nest, in any tree or on the ground, with fledglings or eggs and the mother sitting over the fledglings or on the eggs, do not take the mother together with her young. Let the mother go, and take only the young, in order that you may fare well and have a lengthy life" (Deut. 22:6–7). Deuteronomy itself does not give a reason for this prohibition, and its meaning was the subject of much rabbinic debate both in late antiquity and in the medieval period. Suffice it for our present purposes to note two comments of medieval provenience. The first is by the previously mentioned Nahmanides. He suggests as a rationale for the prohibition in Deuteronomy "that Scripture does not allow the total destruction of a species, although it allows us to slaughter some of its kind."[23] The second is by Don Isaac Abravanel, a fifteenth-century Spanish scholar:

> The Torah's intention is to prevent the possibility of untimely destruction and rather to encourage Creation to exist as fully as possible. For God made the continued existence of animals possible by enabling them to produce fruit, which are their fledglings, just as trees produce fruit. And God has commanded not to destroy that which generates progeny or produces fruit; rather, just as picking fruit is permitted while destroying the tree is forbidden—as Scripture states, "You shall eat from the tree but you shall not cut it down" (Deuteronomy 20:19)—similarly, God commanded that we take the fledglings, that are the fruit . . . but not destroy the tree itself. Instead, we should send away the mother so that we may partake of her offspring while the mother produces other progeny and thereby perpetuates God's creation.[24]

Abravanel's statement that "the Torah's intention is . . . to encourage Creation to exist as fully as possible"—although in context he seems to be speaking more in the quantitative than in the qualitative sense—can be seen as a theological version of today's calls to protect "biodiversity." Indeed, there are a number of rabbinic sources that address the question, Why did God create all that exists, particularly those creations that have no positive function from our perspective? Consider the following narrative:

> Once, while seated in his garden, David, king of Israel, saw a wasp eating a spider. David spoke up to the Holy One: Master of the universe, what benefit is there from these two You created in Your world? The wasp merely despoils the nectar of flowers—no benefit from it. The spider spins all year but makes no garments. The Holy One replied: David, you belittle my creatures! The time will come when you will have need of both of them.
> Later, while fleeing from King Saul, David took refuge in a cave, and the Holy One sent a spider, which spun a web across the cave's entrance, sealing it. When Saul came and saw the cave's entrance with the web across it, he said, "Surely no man has come in here, for had he done so,

he would have torn the web." So Saul went away without going into the cave.

As David left the cave and saw the spider, he blew it a kiss, saying, Blessed be your Creator, and blessed be you.

Subsequently, David found Saul asleep within a barricade [in the royal tent], with Abner [Saul's chief general] lying prone across the tent's entrances, his head in one entrance and his feet in the opposite entrance. Abner's knees were raised up, and so David was able to come in under them and pick up the cruse of water [see 1 Sam. 26:12]. As he was about to leave the way he came, Abner stretched out his legs, which were like two gigantic columns in size, pinning David down. David, beseeching the Holy One's compassion, prayed, "My God, my God, why have You forsaken me?" (Ps. 22:2). At that, the Holy One performed a miracle for him—He sent him a big wasp, which stung Abner's legs so that he again raised his knees, and thus David was free to leave.

In that instant, David said in praise of the Holy One: Master of the universe, "who can imitate your works, Your mighty acts?" (Deut. 3:24)—all your works are beautiful![25]

The above narrative acknowledges that the human assessment of nature's "utility" is not trustworthy because it is limited by the human perspective. Only the Creator, it is argued, can and does have a full understanding of the value of His creations. And while the usefulness ascribed to the wasp and the spider in the text is androcentric in nature, I do not think that the narrator means to limit the value of creation to its human utility. He is simply acknowledging that the worth of God's creation of which we are most aware is that from which we benefit. However, rather than assume that this constitutes the totality of a creature's value and purpose, this discovery should lead us to a humble admission of ignorance concerning the total worth of each and all of God's creatures. This latter notion is expressed strikingly in *Perek Shira* ("A Chapter of Hymns"), a work that probably originated in mystical circles and became part of some Jewish liturgies,[26] which describes all of creation—plants, animals, the land and the sea, the stars and the planets—as singing God's praises. Whatever the other significances of this text, it assumes that each part of creation expresses God's greatness in its own unique and therefore irreplaceable fashion.

The conclusion of Abravanel's remarks is also worth considering:

And this is the meaning of Scripture's concluding words, "in order that you may fare well and have a good life," meaning, this commandment is given not for the sake of the animal world but rather so that it shall be good for humankind when Creation is perpetuated so that one will be able to partake of it again in the future. This, too, is the meaning of "and [you will] have a lengthy life," namely, because you are destined to live for many years on this earth, you are reliant upon Creation perpetuating itself so that you will always have sufficient food.[27]

Abravanel sounds here a theme quite familiar to us from contemporary discourse, that ultimately it is in humankind's own best interests to ensure the viability of the ecosystem, for if it dies we die with it.[28] Extrapolating from this directive we could envision a biblical mandate to limit consumption to the degree necessary to create a sustainable economy. This concept is, of course, notoriously difficult to define and more often a source of heat than of light; nonetheless, in some branches of our economy, such as forestry and fishing, the application of this principle would seem relatively straightforward and not particularly controversial. That is, once it becomes clear to foresters and fishermen as well as to their clients that healthy future production depends on limiting the present harvesting of resources, rational self-interest, if not religious, moral, or environmental commitment, would dictate assent to employing restraint. Of course, once ancillary environmental concerns enter the picture—threats to endangered wildlife in areas designated for foresting or to alligators in a fishing region—we are again plunged into murky waters.[29] Moreover, the sustainability argument does not address the distinction that environmentalists make, for example, between forests on the one hand and tree farms on the other. There is a significant difference between ensuring sustainability and maintaining God's creation in its original beauty and complexity.

We are now ready to turn to a second set of biblical verses that many consider the locus classicus of Judaism's environmental concerns. This is not because these verses address environmental concerns any more fully than many other biblical texts, a number of which we have already cited. Rather, it is the result of these verses having become the springboard for most of the environmentally significant pronouncements in rabbinic tradition. Let us look first at the verses themselves:

> When in your war against a city you have to besiege it a long time in order to capture it, you must not destroy its trees, wielding the ax against them. You may eat of them, but you must not cut them down. Are the trees of the field human to withdraw before you into the besieged city? Only trees that you know do not yield food may be destroyed; you may cut them down for building siegeworks against the city that is waging war on you, until it has been reduced (Deut. 20:19–20).

Verse 19 prohibits cutting down fruit-bearing trees in a time of war. To what end was the felling of these trees intended? Biblical scholars have suggested that the Bible is alluding to the scorched-earth military tactics common in the ancient Near East.[30] In this view, there was no direct material advantage to be gained by those felling the trees; the intent was punitive or a form of psychological warfare. However, from the fact that the next verse apparently permits felling non-fruit-bearing trees only for some immediate positive use, namely, constructing siegeworks, it would appear that the prohibition of the previous verse includes cutting down fruit-bearing trees for a similar purpose. In short, then, fruit-bearing trees may not be cut down even for the purpose of using their wood because this would destroy forever their generative capabilities. This analysis is consistent with Abravanel's understanding of the requirement to send away the mother bird when taking her eggs or fledglings.

Rabbinic interpretation of these verses both extends and qualifies the biblical law. Extensions include the application of this prohibition, known in rabbinic parlance as *bal tashhit*, "you shall not destroy," to the entire material world. Thus, although it is Jewish practice to tear one's garment as a sign of mourning, one who tears one's garment "excessively"—the term is not quantified by the rabbis—is said to violate this prohibition.[31] This ruling, incidentally, raises interesting questions about the amount of resources an individual, or a society, is justified in expending for the sake of emotional catharsis—or, as it is more popularly known, escapist entertainment. Moreover, total destruction is understood to be not only forbidden but also inefficient. Thus the Talmud says that one who does not adjust the air flow of one's lamp properly, thereby causing unnecessary consumption of fuel, has violated the bal tashhit prohibition.[32]

However, the application of efficiency criteria also leads the rabbis to an important qualification of bal tashhit. According to one interpretation of a Talmudic passage,[33] if the transformative use of any raw materials—and this includes fruit-bearing trees—will produce more profit than its use in its present form, its transformative use is permitted. Thus, if a fruit-bearing tree will produce only $10 worth of fruit per year for the next ten years but its wood can be sold at present for $200, it may be cut down and its wood sold.

There are at least two problems with this interpretation, one technical and one ideological. The technical problem, which in fact is also an ideological one, arises in a case more complex than the example cited above. What if the long-term production of the tree will far outstrip any profit I can make from felling the tree at present, but, on the other hand, cutting down the tree now will lead to much more handsome short-term profits; are the short-term profits sufficient justification for felling the tree? Second, this analysis seems to have reduced the status of even the fruit-bearing tree to the status of Adam Smith's "stock,"[34] that is, potential raw material. What of what Holmes Rolston III calls the "natural value" of the tree?[35] Does this count for nothing? One is reminded of economists seeking to "price" pollution who found that some of their interviewees refused in principal to name a price they would be willing to accept in return for allowing certain types of pollution.[36] One feels that the sense of nature's pricelessness and irreplacability is missing from the above Talmudic text.

A responsum of Rabbi Moses Schreiber, an eighteenth-century Hungarian scholar, addresses this issue in part. Rabbi Schreiber rules, as do numerous authorities before him, that one may cut down fruit-bearing trees not only to use their wood but also because one wants to use the land on which they are standing. Nonetheless, says Schreiber, there is a difference between these two instances. In the case that one wishes to use the land, if it is at all possible to replant the trees elsewhere one is obligated to do so.[37] This responsum, then, evinces an awareness of the need to protect the continued existence of plant life in the face of residential and commercial development rather than treating plants simply as obstacles to be removed. Of course, Schreiber limits himself to requiring the protection of trees not actually used for economic development. Perhaps one could, and should, extend this requirement to replacing trees that are felled and insuring that areas that are cleared for residential and commercial development retain as much of their natural character as possible.

It should be clear from all of the above that Jewish tradition has much to say concerning the reasons for, and modes of, limiting consumption. Because most halakhic literature is written in Hebrew and, even once translated, its language and thought patterns seem arcane to many, its potential contribution to the discussion of consumption and other environmental issues has not been sufficiently appreciated. The foregoing essay constitutes a small contribution both to making the teachings of halakhah available to a broader audience and to pointing out some of the ways in which we might use its wisdom in thinking through problems that confront us as individuals, as communities, as nations, and as members of the human race.

Notes

1. Babylonian Talmud, Tractate Berakhot 35a.
2. Genesis Rabbah 16:5.
3. Cf. Mishnah Shabbat 7:2, which lists as one of the thirty-nine activities forbidden on the Sabbath "destroying in order to build."
4. Mishnah Avot 4:1.
5. Commentary (long version) to Exod. 20:14.

6. Commentary to Exod. 20:14.

7. Colin Campbell, *The Romantic Ethic and the Spirit of Modern Consumerism* (Oxford, U.K., and Cambridge, Mass.: Blackwell, 1987), 203.

8. Campbell, *The Romantic Ethic*, 203.

9. Mark Sagoff, *The Economy of the Earth: Philosophy, Law, and the Environment* (Cambridge, U.K., and New York: Cambridge University Press, 1988), 99–123.

10. See Maimonides' Laws of Gifts to the Poor, 7:5.

11. Cited in Jacob Rader Marcus, *The Jew in the Medieval World* (New York: Atheneum, 1983), 195.

12. Babylonian Talmud, Tractate Ketubot 8b.

13. See Maimonides' Laws of the Scroll of Esther, 2:17.

14. Babylonian Talmud, Yomah 18a.

15. Jerusalem Talmud, Tractate Demai 1:3.

16. Maimonides' Laws of Opinions, 5:2.

17. Maimonides' Laws of Opinions, 5:1.

18. Maimonides' Laws of Opinions, 5:3.

19. Maimonides' Laws of Opinions, 5:9.

20. Maimonides' Laws of Opinions, 5:10–12.

21. Sifre Kedoshim, Pericope 1, par. 2.

22. Nahmanides' commentary on the Torah, Lev. 19:2, s.v. "you shall be holy."

23. Nahmanides' commentary on the Torah, Deut. 22:6, s.v. "if you chance upon a bird's nest."

24. Abravanel's commentary on the Torah, Deut. 22:6, s.v. "if you chance upon a bird's nest."

25. Alphabet of Ben Sira.

26. See *Encyclopaedia Judaica* 13, cols. 273–75.

27. *Encyclopaedia Judaica* 13, cols. 273–75.

28. It is worth noting that at least one contemporary writer on environmental issues (M. Gerstenfeld, *Environment and Confusion* [Academon: Jerusalem, 1994], 61–62) has analyzed this passage in Deuteronomy in similar fashion.

29. See, for example, the issues raised by Holmes Rolston III, *Environmental Ethics: Duties to and Values in the Natural World* (Philadelphia: Temple University Press, 1988) regarding fishing (152) and forestry (122–23).

30. See Jeffrey H. Tigay, *The JPS Commentary: Deuteronomy* (Philadelphia/Jerusalem: Jewish Publication Society, 1996), 190.

31. Babylonian Talmud, Tractate Bava Kamma 91b.

32. Babylonian Talmud, Tractate Shabbat 67b.

33. Babylonian Talmud, Tractate Bava Kamma 91b; and see A. Levine, *Economics and Jewish Law: Halakhic Perspectives* (Hoboken, N.J.: Ktav, 1987), 160–68.

34. See Adam Smith, *An Inquiry into the Nature and Causes of the Wealth of Nations*, bk 2, chap. 1 (New York: Modern Library, 1937 [1776]).

35. Rolston, *Environmental Ethics*, 192–245.

36. See Sagoff, *The Economy of the Earth*, 74–98.

37. Responsa Hatam Sofer, Yoreh De'ah, No. 102.

21

The Ethics of Consumption: A Roman Catholic View

Charles K. Wilber

The social encyclicals and pastoral letters—from Pope Leo XIII's *Rerum Novarum* in 1891 through the U.S. Bishops' *Economic Justice for All: Pastoral Letter on Catholic Social Teaching and the U.S. Economy* to Pope John Paul II's *Centesimus Annus*—that form the foundation of Catholic Social Thought (CST) are fundamentally moral documents not economic treatises. The tradition of CST is rooted in a commitment to certain fundamental values—the right to human dignity, the need for human freedom and participation, the importance of community, and the nature of the common good. These values are drawn from the belief that each person is called to be a cocreator with God, participating in the redemption of the world and the furthering of the Kingdom. This requires social and human development where the religious and temporal aspects of life are not separated and opposed to each other.

As a result of these fundamental values two principles permeate CST. The first is a special concern for the poor and powerless that leads to a criticism of political and economic structures that oppress them. The second is a concern for certain human rights against both the collectivist tendencies of the state and the neglect of the free market.

Since *Rerum Novarum*, CST has taught that both state socialism and free-market capitalism violate these principles. State socialism denies the right of private property; excites the envy of the poor against the rich, leading to class struggle instead of cooperation; and violates the proper order of society by the state usurping the role of individuals and intermediate social groups.[1] Free-market capitalism denies the concept of the common good and the "social and public character of the right of property,"[2] including the principle of the universal destination of the earth's goods,[3] and violates human dignity by treating labor merely as a commodity to be bought and sold in the marketplace.[4] Pope John Paul II summarizes the thrust of CST when he says: "The individual today is often suffocated between two poles represented by the State and the marketplace. At times it seems as though he [or she] exists only as a producer and consumer of goods, or as an object of State administration. People lose sight of the fact that life in society has neither the market nor the State as its final purpose, since life itself has a unique value which the State and the market must serve."[5]

CST repudiates the position that the level of unemployment, the degree of poverty, the quantity of environmental destruction, and other such outcomes should be left to the dictates of the market. Emphasis on the common good means that the community has an obligation to ensure the right of employment to all persons,[6] to help the disadvantaged overcome their poverty,[7] and to safeguard the environment.[8]

Since the primary "signs of the times" that Pope John Paul II focuses on in *Centesimus Annus* (the latest statement of CST) is the collapse of communism in Eastern Europe, he emphasizes the limits to the role of the state and the utility of markets in providing incentives for production. However, this is a highly qualified endorsement, as when he says the efficiency of markets in fulfilling human needs is true only for those needs that are " 'solvent,' insofar as they are endowed with purchasing power, and for those resources which are 'marketable,' insofar as they are capable of obtaining a satisfactory price. But there are many human needs that find no place on the market."[9] Thus, markets do not adequately fulfill the needs of those who have little income or provide for nonmarketable goods, such as a clean environment and participation in the workplace. He also registers his fears that unrestrained markets result in environmental destruction,[10] promote a soulless consumerism,[11] and destroy the human environment needed by a community of persons.[12]

This brief review of CST shows that its focus from the beginning has been on the problems of poverty and marginalization of the disadvantaged, first in the industrial countries and then in the Third World. It is only in the last twenty-five years that concern about too much consumption by the rich rather than too little consumption by the poor has played a role in CST.

The Ethics of Consumption

While there are a number of reasons to be concerned with the ethics of consumption, there are three that have become prominent in CST. First, while it is recognized that consumption spending helps people by creating jobs, excessive consumption by some individuals and nations while other individuals and nations suffer from want is considered morally unacceptable. Income spent on luxuries could have been made available to others for their necessities. Typical is Pope Paul VI's statement: "the superfluous wealth of rich countries should be placed at the service of poor nations. . . . Otherwise their continued greed will certainly call down upon them the judgment of God and the wrath of the poor. . . ."[13] The problem of spending to buy products produced under sweatshop conditions is recognized but usually treated under the heading of the rights of workers and the obligations of employers.

Second, excessive consumption that threatens the earth's environment is also considered morally unacceptable. Pope John Paul II recently stated: "Equally worrying is the ecological question which accompanies the problem of consumerism and which is closely connected to it. In his [or her] desire to have and to enjoy rather than to be and to grow, man [or woman] consumes the resources of the earth and his [or her] own life in an excessive and distorted way."[14]

Third, treating consumption as the primary goal of life—that is, focusing on *having* instead of *being*—is seen as detrimental to human dignity. It is this third concern that I focus on in this essay. But first I want to compare CST to the mainstream economic theory that is dominant in our society.

In contrast to CST, economic theory is rooted in an individualist conception of society. Society is seen as a collection of individuals who have chosen to associate because it is mutually beneficial. The common good is simply the aggregate of the welfare of each individual. Individual liberty is the highest good, and, if individuals are left free to pursue their self-interest, the result will be the maximum material welfare.

Economic theory focuses on people as hedonists who want to maximize pleasure and minimize pain.[15] It assumes that pleasure comes primarily from the consumption of goods and services and that pain comes primarily from work and from parting with income. Thus, given resource constraints, the goal of the economy should be to maximize the production of goods and services. In short, more is better.

In modern industrial economies such as ours, it is perfectly rational for people to accept a philosophy of consumerism. People have little opportunity to choose meaningful work because the nature of jobs is determined by competitive pressures. The demand for labor mobility disrupts a satisfying sense of community. And the enjoyment of nature is attenuated by urbanization and the degradation of nature resulting from industrial and consumption practices. Thus, the only thing left under the individual's control is consumption. And it is true that con-

sumption can substitute, however inadequately, for the loss of meaningful work, community, and a decent environment. With enough income
people can buy bottled water, place their children in private schools,
buy a mountain cabin, and obtain the education necessary to get a more
interesting job.

However, when people are surveyed about their views on what the
economy should do, some surprising results emerge. For example, a
study by Tibor Scitovsky found that the simple increase in the amount
of consumption in the United States has not increased peoples' happiness.[16] Richard A. Easterlin discovered that a crucial component of such
an evaluation was the perception of one's relative situation.[17] Thus it
would seem to be exceptionally difficult for an economy to improve its
performance, for every relative gain would imply a relative loss, or no
net gain! This reality and the confusion in our society between growth,
which we place as a preeminent goal, and affluence, which by all standards we have clearly obtained, suggests that one of the problems our
society must deal with is "the poverty of affluence."[18]

The Catholic tradition condemns the materialist view of human welfare. In his 1968 encyclical, *Populorum Progressio*, Pope Paul VI
wrote:

> Increased possession is not the ultimate goal of nations or of individuals.
> All growth is ambivalent. It is essential if man [or woman] is to develop
> as a man [or woman], but in a way it imprisons man [or woman] if he [or
> she] considers it the supreme good, and it restricts his [or her] vision. Then
> we see hearts harden and minds close, and men [and women] no longer
> gather together in friendship but out of self-interest, which soon leads to
> oppositions and disunity. The exclusive pursuit of possessions thus be-
> comes an obstacle to individual fulfillment and to man's [or woman's] true
> greatness. Both for nations and for individual men [or women], avarice is
> the most evident form of moral underdevelopment.[19]

On the twentieth anniversary (1987) of *Populorum Progressio*, Pope
John Paul II wrote in *Sollicitudo Rei Socialis*: "All of us experience
first hand the sad effects of this blind submission to pure consumerism:
in the first place a crass materialism, and at the same time a radical
dissatisfaction because one quickly learns . . . that the more one possesses the more one wants, while deeper aspirations remain unsatisfied
and perhaps even stifled."[20] In his latest encyclical—*Centesimus
Annus*—marking the one-hundredth anniversary of *Rerum Novarum*,
Pope John Paul II writes: "It is not wrong to want to live better; what
is wrong is a style of life which is presumed to be better when it is
directed toward 'having' rather than 'being,' and which wants to have

more, not in order to be more but in order to spend life in enjoyment as an end in itself."[21]

Consumption and Human Welfare: An Alternative

It is not sufficient to simply reject the neoclassical economics position that satisfying individual preferences, as expressed in the market, is the only measure of economic welfare. Alternatives must be proposed and developed. Let me sketch out one possible alternative.[22]

Many working within the Roman Catholic tradition would argue that we must broaden our view of human welfare from that of the simple consumption of goods and services with consumer sovereignty as the goal. Instead, drawing upon cross-cultural studies that have attempted to find absolute needs or needs that are expressed in a variety of societies, three components of human welfare can be specified for an economy.[23]

The first is what Denis Goulet calls "life-sustenance," which corresponds generally to physiological needs or basic material goods. People need the basic goods that are necessary for life— adequate food, water, housing, clothing, and health care—and an economy is successful if it can provide them.

How can basic material goods be specified? One way is to differentiate among three types of goods. The first are necessities such as food and water. Within some limits these needs can be specified. The second type of goods are "enhancement goods," which make life more vital, more interesting, more worth living. Examples might be music, various forms of entertainment, some household goods, and so on. The third level of goods involves what are commonly known as luxury goods. Driving a Cadillac instead of a Chevrolet, buying a marble-topped table instead of a wooden one, and walking on a wool rug instead of a polyester one are all instances of consuming luxury goods. We can all agree that basic needs must be met. Most believe that enhancement goods are worthy of pursuit. There is less accord on luxury goods. Traditional economics in the United States has claimed that individual wants are unlimited and that luxury goods satisfy wants, as do basic goods. If individuals want Cadillacs and wool rugs, and if the economy can produce such luxuries, it ought to.

A second component of human welfare is esteem and fellowship. An economy should provide a sense of worth or dignity to its citizens. One's goods can be a measure of societal esteem, but surely there are other important elements. The institutions in which citizens work should support them physically and give them a sense of belonging and of contributing to an important undertaking. Society should have clubs, churches, or other entities that support the individual. If the family is the basic social and economic unit, as is the case in the United States, the economy should provide support for and encourage in families a sense of self-esteem that can help sustain them. Another term for this is fellowship; the economy should promote right relations among its participants and, to the extent it can, should keep life from being "nasty and brutish," while providing basic material goods to lengthen it. For no society can function smoothly, without disruptive tensions, if there is no fellowship among its members. If people are alienated from one another and society is fractured into myriad self-interested and self-centered individuals or groups, society will not long survive. If no genuine concern for one's neighbors exists and if empathy for others disappears, then each small self-reliant entity (whether this be family, occupational group, or individual) will eventually withdraw unto itself and live at odds with others. No social system that endorses or engenders such self-centeredness can prevail.

Even if material economic well-being were at the heart of social success, surely fellowship would be the lifeblood that sustains the community, the cohesion that makes one individual feel a closeness and a unity of purpose with all others in that society, whether known personally or not. Consequently, a key component of human welfare, in addition to the satisfaction of people's material needs, is the growth of widely shared esteem that yields a life-giving and life-sustaining fellowship. This implies an element of equity among citizens. No modern society that gave minimal income to most of the population, but fabulous wealth to a few families, could provide esteem or fellowship. Equity, of course, does not necessarily mean equality, but it does mean that there must be some consensus regarding the justness of the distribution of wealth and income.

The third component of human welfare is freedom. However, freedom is a difficult goal to specify clearly. It obviously does not mean that all individuals may do whatever they wish, for that would be anarchy and the death of society. At its weakest, an increase in freedom means that the range of options open to the individual or the group has increased, that there are more choices available. This has its physical side in choice of goods, but it can also operate in other spheres such as politics or religion.

There are three component parts to the goal of freedom. The first, and the one that is usually at the center of much economic theorizing in the United States, is the provision of consumer sovereignty. Individuals should be able to choose the goods that they wish to consume.

The second part is worker sovereignty. People must have a choice of jobs, ones they find meaningful and that enhance their human capacities. There must be mechanisms for finding peoples' preferences on work and creating the types of jobs required. A variety of mechanisms could satisfy this need: labor mobility among jobs of widely different character, control by workers over their job situations, or provision of capital resources to laborers to allow them to establish their own undertakings. Whatever the mechanisms, this characteristic is important because work plays an important part in human development.[24]

Third, a society must provide citizen sovereignty, a mechanism to aggregate peoples' preferences for community. What kind of community do people want? What kind of environment do they want? The concept of citizen sovereignty implies that a way to express preferences and to control communities is provided to the citizen. A number of mechanisms may be found that satisfy this requirement, in addition to the democratic voting procedures used in the United States. One way of enhancing citizen sovereignty could be through strengthening local groups for citizen participation in decision making, for example, parent–teacher organizations, zoning boards, and citizen review boards of police departments and other public agencies. Or perhaps local residents might participate in the operation of local industries in their areas, by electing representatives to firms' boards of directors to minimize the negative aspects of industrial production, such as noise and pollution. The absence of real citizen sovereignty generates conflicts among groups in society. The reality of such conflict has been denied over the recent past but is becoming a central element in local political debate. It can be either a destructive or a constructive force in charting the course of the economy.

In the light of traditional economists' claims about the importance of incentives for the operation of markets, is the treatment of human welfare in CST viable? It could be argued that this broadening of the concept of human welfare may be impossible because of: 1) the way markets create a bifurcation of people as consumers/workers, coupled with the competitive pressures that force business firms to become ever more efficient; and 2) the consumerism that is rooted in human greed and the workings of the business system.

Let me take the provision of meaningful work as an example. Because of competition, one firm cannot improve working conditions, raise wages, or democratize the workplace *if the result is an increase in production costs*. (The easy case is where improved working conditions are also more efficient and thus both workers and employers have an incentive to make the changes.) Competition from other firms will keep the costs from being passed on in higher prices and, thus, profits will decline. The bifurcation of people into consumers/workers means that what they prefer as consumers—lower prices—makes what they prefer as workers—better working conditions, higher wages, more meaningful work—less obtainable. Reliance on the market as the primary decision-making mechanism bifurcates the decision into separate areas. What people want as workers will not be ratified by those same people as consumers. Since competition is now worldwide, even a whole country faces difficulties in mandating workplace improvements that raise costs.

The problem is reinforced, first, by the fact that millions of Americans live in poverty and consume too little rather than too much and, second, by both human greed and the constant effort of business to promote consumption as the ultimate end of life. This creates constant pressure to reduce prices by reducing labor costs, undercutting attempts to improve the quality of work life.

Why do we accept this? The process, usually implicit, of teaching people that true happiness comes from consumption permeates our entire culture and begins at a very early age. Herbert Gintis and James H. Weaver provide a vivid example from an old Sears Roebuck Christmas catalog.

> Sears advertised . . . a new doll named Shopping Sheryl. Sheryl comes equipped with a supermarket which has a rotating checkout counter, a ringing cash register, a motorized check-out stand, shelves, cart, and groceries. Sheryl is a vinyl doll which picks things up with her magnetized right hand and grasps with her left hand. We can visualize Sheryl in her supermarket, picking and grasping, picking and grasping.
>
> This is really the final result of the evolutionary process. People have emerged from the muck and the ooze, overcome the hardships imposed by nature, built dwellings, invented agriculture, etc.—so that our children can have Shopping Sheryl and learn early in life that the true purpose of life is consumption.[25]

What Needs To Be Done?

Can anything be done to reduce the emphasis on consumption and to increase the possibilities for meaningful work and the restoration of community? I am not optimistic, but as a Christian and as an economist I would focus on two possibilities—the inculcation of more appropriate moral values and the judicious use of financial incentives.

Moral Values

First, we need to develop habits of morally constrained behavior, reinforced by cultural practices, so that short-run rewards become less important. We need values that transcend the narrow self-interest of the economic model as the guide for individual behavior. Is it possible to rebuild a moral consensus wherein we relearn habits of morally constrained behavior? Yes, this is a major point of CST, but economists must rethink their view of people as simply self-interested maximizers. They have made a major mistake in treating love, benevolence, and particularly public spirit as scarce resources that must be economized lest they be depleted. This is a faulty analogy because, unlike material factors of production, the supply of love, benevolence, and public spirit is not fixed or limited. As Albert O. Hirschman says: "first of all, these are resources whose supply may well increase rather than decrease through use; second, these resources do not remain intact if they stay unused."[26] These moral resources respond positively to practice, in a learning-by-doing manner, and negatively to nonpractice. Obviously there are limits; if overused they become ineffective.

A good example is a comparison of the system, which Richard M. Titmuss makes in *The Gift Relationship*, of blood collection for medical purposes in the United States and in Great Britain. In the United States, we gradually replaced donated blood with purchased blood. As the campaigns for donated blood declined, because purchased blood was sufficient, the amount of blood donated declined. In effect, our internalized benevolence toward those unknown to us, who need blood, began to atrophy from nonuse. In contrast, blood donations have remained high in England, where each citizen's obligation to others was constantly emphasized.

Titmuss questions the efficiency of market relationships based on purely monetary self-interest principles. Instead he hypothesizes that in some instances, such as blood giving, relying on internalized moral values (in this case, altruistic behavior) results in a more efficient supply and better quality of blood. Titmuss argues that the commercialization of blood giving produces a system with many shortcomings. A few of these shortcomings are the repression of expressions of altruism, increases in the danger of unethical behavior in certain areas of medicine, worsened relationships between doctor and patient, and shifts in the supply of blood from the rich to the poor. Furthermore, the commercialized blood market is bad even in terms of nonethical criteria.

> In terms of economic efficiency it is highly wasteful of blood; shortages, chronic and acute, characterize the demand-and-supply position and make illusory the concept of equilibrium. It is administratively inefficient and results in more bureaucratization and much greater administrative, accounting, and computer overheads. In terms of price per unit of blood to the patient (or consumer), it is a system which is five to fifteen times more

costly than voluntary systems in Britain. And, finally, in terms of quality, commercial markets are much more likely to distribute contaminated blood; the risks for the patient of disease and death are substantially greater. Freedom from disability is inseparable from altruism.[27]

It is noteworthy that since the AIDS crisis started in the United States, physicians regularly recommend that patients scheduled for nonemergency surgery donate their own blood in advance.

The commercialization of certain activities that historically were perceived to be within the realm of altruism results in a conceptual transformation that inhibits the expression of this altruistic behavior. Contrary to the commonly held opinion that the creation of a market increases the area of individual choice, Titmuss argues that the creation of a market may inhibit the freedom to give or not to give.

The supply of blood provides a clear illustration of the problem. A person is not born with a set of ready-made values; rather the individual's values are socially constructed through his being a part of a family, church, school, and particular society. If these groups expect and urge people to give their blood as an obligation of being members of the group, that obligation becomes internalized as a moral value. Blood drives held in schools, churches, and Red Cross facilities reinforce that sense of obligation. As commercial blood increases, the need for blood drives declines. Thus, the traditional reinforcement of that sense of obligation declines with the result that the embodied moral value atrophies. In addition, the fact that you can sell your blood creates an opportunity cost of donating it free. Finally, there is an information problem. As blood drives decline, it is rational for an individual to assume that there is no need for donated blood. The final outcome is that a person must overcome imperfect information, opportunity costs, and a lack of social approbation in order to choose to donate blood.

This suggests that the type of policy recommended will have implications for the type of society that will develop. Inherent in the type of policy suggested is a preference as to the motivational attitudes that are appropriate and should be encouraged. The motivations on which the results are based are also important; that is, *how* we achieve these results needs to be addressed.

I do not want to leave the impression that ethically based behavior and self-interest are always mutually exclusive. Proximity to self-interest alone does not defile morality. Moral values are often necessary counterparts in a system based on self-interest. There is not only a "vast amount of irregular and informal help given in times of need"[28] but also a consistent dependence on moral values upon which market mechanisms rely. Without a basic trust and socialized morality the economy would be much more inefficient.

It is easy to forget one of Adam Smith's key insights. It is true he claimed that self-interest leads to the common good if there is sufficient competition; but also, and more importantly, he claimed that this is true only if most people in society have internalized a general moral law as a guide for their behavior.[29] Peter Berger reminds us that "No society, modern or otherwise, can survive without what Durkheim called a 'collective conscience,' that is without moral values that have general authority."[30] Fred C. Hirsch reintroduces the idea of moral law into economic analysis: "Truth, trust, acceptance, restraint, obligation— these are among the social virtues grounded in religious belief which . . . play a central role in the functioning of an individualistic, contractual economy. . . . The point is that conventional, mutual standards of honesty and trust are public goods that are necessary inputs for much of economic output."[31]

People are capable of changing their values. In fact a principal objective of publicly proclaimed laws and regulations is to stigmatize certain types of behavior and to reward others, thereby influencing individual values and behavior codes. While families, churches, and schools play the most important role in shaping behavior and inculcating values, public laws have a role to play. For example, while law cannot make someone stop holding racist beliefs, it can punish certain types of racist *behavior*. With time that behavior, say refusing service in a restaurant, becomes delegitimized in public opinion.

Financial Incentives

The use of financial incentives to guide people's behavior is dear to an economist's heart. These range from the most general, such as a value-added tax on consumer goods, to highly targeted ones, such as excise taxes on luxury consumer goods or carbon taxes on the carbon content of goods.

However, extensive use of financial incentives will be very difficult if not impossible. Economic growth in the United States has been based on the value of individual consumption. The awesome power of modern advertising has spread the free market gospel—the good life comes from increases in consumption of individually marketable goods and services. People are urged to believe they must have individual washers and dryers instead of laundromats and private automobiles instead of public transportation. This phenomenon is particularly important when viewed in a worldwide context.

Large corporations have compounded the problem by competing through product innovation and differentiation resulting in an emphasis on stylistic and physical obsolescence. When goods are designed to be thrown away after use, or to be used less than their physical capacity because of style changes, or constructed to fall apart sooner than necessary, the result is increased waste of energy and natural resources *and* a need for people to continually buy more.

However, I am not completely without hope. Rising prices in the face of raw material shortages will force a reduction in some of these wasteful practices and coping with a worsening environment will leave fewer resources available for wasteful consumption. However, they will also create unemployment and a crisis in economic growth, not only in the United States but also around the world, if we do not plan ahead. If we wait and do nothing until the crisis is upon us, the adjustment will be painful indeed. Doing something in advance requires political action and, here, the record is not hopeful. President Carter tried to get a small tax increase on gasoline and was soundly defeated. His talk of limits was denounced as defeatist. President Clinton's idea of a carbon tax was a nonstarter. Political courage has always been a rare commodity but appears to be in particularly short supply today.

This, then, is the challenge we face: how do we move from a consumption-based economy to one that is also concerned about the quality of work and the importance of community without creating havoc in the world economy? The "conservative" majority pushes the ideas of smaller government and tax cuts and prefers to let people spend their money the way they want. This philosophy must be challenged with something other than the slightly milder version pushed by political "liberals."

Notes

1. Pope Leo XIII, *Rerum Novarum* (On the Condition of Workers), 15 May 1891, para. 7–8; and, Pope John Paul II, *Centesimus Annus* (100 Years After), 1 May 1991, para. 13–14.

2. Pope Pius XI, *Quadraesimo Anno* (On Reconstructing the Social Order), 15 May 1931, para. 46.

3. *Rerum Novarum*, para. 14; *Centesimus Annus*, para. 6.

4. *Rerum Novarum*, para. 31; *Quadraesimo Anno*, para. 83; *Centesimus Annus*, para. 33–35.

5. *Centesimus Annus*, para. 49.

6. *Centesimus Annus*, para. 15.

7. *Centesimus Annus*, para. 19, 40.

8. *Centesimus Annus*, para. 37.

9. *Centesimus Annus*, para. 34.

10. *Centesimus Annus*, para. 37.

11. *Centesimus Annus*, para. 36.

12. *Centesimus Annus*, para. 38.

13. Pope Paul VI, *Populorum Progressio* (On Promoting the Development of Peoples), 26 March 1967, para. 49.

14. *Centesimus Annus*, para. 37.

15. This is not quite accurate. Many economists would say that in maximizing their self-interest people might choose to help others because it makes them feel good. But in practice economists focus on people wanting more goods and services.

16. Tibor Scitovsky, *The Joyless Economy: An Inquiry into Human Satisfaction and Consumer Dissatisfaction* (New York: Oxford University Press, 1976). However, for an opposing view, see Stanley Lebergott, *Pursuing Happiness: American Consumers in the Twentieth Century* (Princeton, N.J.: Princeton University Press, 1993).

17. Richard A. Easterlin, "Does Economic Growth Improve the Human Lot? Some Empirical Evidence," in *Nations and Households in Economic Growth* (New York: Academic Press, 1974).

18. See Paul L. Wachtel, *The Poverty of Affluence: A Psychological Portrait of the American Way of Life* (New York: Free Press, 1983). An edited version of chapters 7 and 8 of this work appear in the present volume as Paul L. Wachtel, "Alternatives to the Consumer Society."

19. *Populorum Progressio*, para. 19.

20. Pope John Paul II, *Sollicitudo Rei Socialis* (On Social Concerns), 30 December 1987, para. 28.

21. *Centesimus Annus*, para. 36.

22. See Herbert Gintis and James H. Weaver, *The Political Economy of Growth and Welfare* (New York: MSS Modular Publications, Module 54, 1974), 1–26; Denis Goulet, *The Cruel Choice: A New Concept in the Theory of Development* (New York: Atheneum, 1971); Charles K. Wilber and Kenneth P. Jameson, *An Inquiry into the Poverty of Economics* (Notre Dame, Ind.: University of Notre Dame Press, 1983); and Amartya K. Sen, *Commodities and Capabilities* (Amsterdam: North-Holland Press, 1985).

23. See Goulet, *The Cruel Choice*.

24. See Pope John Paul II, *Laborem Exercens* (On Human Work), 14 September 1981.

25. Gintis and Weaver, *The Political Economy of Growth and Welfare*, 18.

26. Albert O. Hirschman, *Rival Views of Market Society* (New York: Viking, 1986), 155.

27. Richard M. Titmuss, *The Gift Relationship: From Human Blood to Social Policy* (London: Allen and Unwin, 1970), 205.

28. Kenneth Arrow, "Gifts and Exchange," *Philosophy and Public Affairs* 1 (Summer 1972): 345.

29. See Adam Smith, *Theory of Moral Sentiments* (Indianapolis, Ind.: Liberty Classics, 1976 [1759]) and *The Classical Economists and Economic Policy*, A. W. Coats (London: Methuen, 1971).

30. Peter Berger, "In Praise of Particularity: The Concept of Mediating Structures," *Review of Politics* 38 (1976): 134.

31. Fred C. Hirsch, *Social Limits to Growth* (Cambridge, Mass.: Harvard University Press, 1976), 141.

22

On the Subversive Virtue: Frugality

James A. Nash

One of the most interesting and largely unexamined problems in modern morality is the major demotion of frugality as a personal and social norm. An old and honored virtue, once near the heart of Christian ethics and some other normative approaches to economics, frugality has become one of the most neglected—and unnerving—norms in contemporary ethics. Though popular appeals for frugality may be increasing, ethically substantial interpretations and justifications of frugality have become quite rare. The decline of frugality is, however, much more than a matter of intellectual curiosity; it is a serious moral problem in itself if frugality is socially and ecologically significant.

Historically, frugality was a prime Christian economic norm. It was, for example, a prominent practice in the patristic and monastic traditions of East and West—though sometimes the practice went beyond the moderation characteristic of frugality to various degrees of austerity. Moreover, frugality combined with industry, honesty, reliability, equity, generosity, piety, and covenantal solidarity constituted the core of the classical "Protestant ethic," which Max Weber described, with some exaggeration, as "worldly asceticism."[1] These perspectives reflect the fears about the spiritual perils of prosperity and the commitment to frugal consumption "in the service of love" evident in the churches of the New Testament.[2] In gratitude to God, frugality was a rejection of vanity and envy and an expression of fidelity and social solidarity.

The norm of frugality—often in the guise of simplicity—exercised a strong but ambiguous and fluctuating influence on U.S. history. It was a prominent component in a "sustaining myth of national purpose," but it existed alongside a countermyth of progressive prosperity. Frugality was often honored more as an ideal than as a practice.[3]

Yet, in contemporary cultures that celebrate the prospects of progressive plenty, even the ideal is banished. For instance, frugality is notably absent from William J. Bennett's 800-plus-page bestseller, *The Book of Virtues*[4]—one sign of Bennett's political distortions of traditional morality. Frugality today is often greeted with amusement, ridicule, or even contempt. It is portrayed as unfashionable, unpalatable, and even unpatriotic. It is considered appropriate only under historical conditions of scarcity and is now anachronistic in the midst of high productivity. Thus, Peter Berger argues that frugality is economically and ethically dysfunctional—a vice—in the contemporary economic situation. "Epicureanism," he suggests, is now the moral alternative to frugality.[5]

In Christian contexts, frugality has certainly not been fully forgotten, but it has been significantly demoted—probably reflecting an accommodation to cultural values. Frugality is not featured, for example, in most modern manuals in Christian economic ethics or in various church statements on economic policy. Frugality remains as an undercurrent in contemporary Christian ethical and ecclesiastical thought, but that undercurrent generally flows with dramatically less power than it did historically.

This essay offers an ethical interpretation and justification of frugality. I argue that frugality is not an anachronistic or innocuous norm. On the contrary, frugality is a richly relevant and potentially transformative standard to combat excessive and unfair consumption *and* production (the dynamic that arouses most of our wants through marketing, in order to supply the demand it creates). Though I generally speak from a Christian perspective, frugality is not bound to that moral tradition. It is an economic discipline that can be justified in a variety of value systems, apart from an originating source of the norm. Solutions to major social and ecological problems depend on the revival of this virtue and its re-formation from a personal virtue into a social norm—as, indeed, it was intended to be in Puritanism[6] and its predecessors.

Frugality as Economic Subversion

I must first offer an interpretation of the contemporary economic and ecological context to which an ethically conscious frugality is a dissent or protest. A modern effort to revive this norm makes adequate sense only in this context.

Against this background, frugality is a subversive virtue, because it is a revolt against an economic system that depends upon intensive production and consumption to keep the system going and growing. Frugality is an encounter with an economics ethos that cannot afford frugality if that ethos is to thrive, and it resists, even undermines, the central assumptions of that ethos. Four basic and interrelated character- istics of this revolt or subversion are important to note here.

First, *frugality rejects the popular assumption that humans are insa- tiable creatures, ceaselessly acquisitive for economic gains and goods and egoistically committed to pleasure maximization.*[7] On this assump- tion, frugality is irrational, even unnatural. The function of economic enterprises is to respond to the indefinitely elastic demands of these mythical humans—and to re-create real humans in that image by con- stantly stimulating demands.

Yet, the practice of frugality is living refutation of this simplistic moral anthropology and its self-fulfilling prophecy. It is a witness to the fact that humans are not reducible to instinctive bundles of insatia- ble appetites and that excessive and unfair consumption is not so much a reflection of nature as a creation of culture. We *do* have the moral capacities to control and distribute consumption. Frugality reveals an- other side of human potential, as beings with powers of responsible control.

Second, *frugality is resistance to the temptations of consumer promo- tionalism—particularly the ubiquitous advertising that pressures us through sophisticated techniques to want more, bigger, better, faster, newer, more attractive, or state of the art products.* We are bombarded with an abundance of commercials creating dissatisfactions and ped- dling wares that promise to enhance our excitements and powers, re- duce our anxieties, and fulfill our aspirations. Commercials encourage impulse and therapeutic buying to improve self-esteem and social status. They stimulate feelings of envy and inadequacy unless we own given products. The more and bigger we can buy, the "better off" we are, since "consumerability" is the measure of meaning. Indeed, the more we boost sales, the "better off" the national and even world econ- omies will be.

This promotional system not only caters to our wants; more impor- tantly, it creates them, in order to provide goods and services to supply these demands. The dynamic seems to be fed more by the needs of competitive production than by the actual wants of consumers. In any case, shopping—accelerated by instant credit—is now the main means of recreation for millions. The pursuit of happiness has become the quest for acquisitions. The result is not only an abundance of benefits, but also a wealth of waste, irrelevancies, and perils to human welfare.

In contrast, by resisting these temptations and deceptions, frugality is again a witness to the fact that humans are far more than manipulatable consumers. It is an affirmation of human dignity—our moral potential, our deepest yearnings, our status as ends, not merely means—against consumer engineering. It is also an expression of purchasing power, with some potential for redirecting economic production to better means and ends.

Third, *frugality is a struggle against the various psychological and sociological dynamics, beyond market promotionalism, that stimulate overconsumption.* The causal factors in overconsumption appear to be numerous, complex, and interwoven. To some degree, they are self-generated, but they are also, and probably more so, culturally shaped. Certainly greed, gluttony, envy, and prodigality are implicated, but the causes are deeper and sometimes more sympathetic than these vices suggest.

Some of the main reasons for overconsumption appear to be the following: 1) A social ideology of rising expectations—driven by market forces and the belief that the good depends on more and better goods—creates feelings of relative deprivation and persistent discontent with present possessions.[8] 2) Changing socioeconomic conditions and technological developments continually create new perceived "needs"—electronic devices, for example—to function effectively and decently in the culture. 3) Higher discretionary income for many (despite stagnant or falling real wages for many others) has made possible extravagant expenditures. 4) Shopping has become an addiction for so-called shopaholics, compelling fixes of novelty with short-lived and diminishing gratifications.[9] 5) Ever-present hedonistic impulses are culturally encouraged, thus sanctioning and stimulating the quest for self-indulgent comforts and conveniences, new thrills and immediate pleasures. 6) Consumption patterns for many may be compensation for loneliness, powerlessness, insecurity, and ultimate vulnerability, given the decline of communal supports and transcendent values.[10] 7) Conformity to the values of one's reference group may stimulate excessive consumption in order to convey one's equal worth or status—even to the point of serious indebtedness for many. Conforming or imitative consumption is often motivated by the fear of social ostracism or the loss of social acceptability for the unfashionable.[11] 8) Competitive consumption relative to one's reference group is a flaunting of success, superiority, power, and importance, and it often creates a vicious spiral of ostentatious waste and indulgence as the competitors seek to surpass one another. This syndrome is the "invidious comparisons" "conspicuous consumption" analyzed nearly a century ago by Thorstein Veblen.[12]

The human reasons behind overconsumption are not always or even usually morally contemptible; they are often merely mournful, revealing the hollowness and stress of many affluent lives. They reflect the quest for self-esteem, social acceptance, personal satisfaction, and ultimate meaning, while being culturally conditioned to follow trails that frustrate these hopes. In contrast, frugality finds self-esteem, satisfaction, and meaning in resisting cultural pressures, curbing desires, and reducing consumption. Frugality is more than an alternative lifestyle; it is a countervision of being a purposeful and responsible human being in a purposeful and responsible society.

Fourth, ethically conscious frugality is a rejection of the prevailing ideology of indiscriminate, material economic growth. At this point we confront a fundamental feature of nearly all the prominent contemporary advocates of ethically conscious constraints on production and consumption.[13] From these perspectives, unconstrained *material* economic growth is a strategy for living beyond biophysical means—to the detriment particularly of poor people and nations, future generations, and nonhuman species. While this growth model provides a variety of values—from millions of jobs to vast tax revenues, from many important goods and services to philanthropic benefits—it also functions self-destructively through excessive and unfair use. It is a major factor in destroying the ecosystems on which the well-being of all social and economic systems finally depends. It presumes the practical inexhaustibility of the products and capacities of nature and human autonomy from the rest of nature. In reality, however, we live in an age of ecological scarcity[14]—prospectively at least, actually on many particulars. Everything is limited—from the biophysical resources necessary for human thriving to the technological powers to extend biophysical limits. Present patterns of economic activity appear to be approaching or surpassing some of these limits, locally and/or globally, in both nonrenewable resources (for example, fossil fuels and some industrially significant minerals) and renewable resources (for example, fisheries, forests, and croplands), as well as in wastes produced.[15] This pattern of superproduction and superconsumption is neither biophysically sustainable nor ethically acceptable.

The emphasis on biophysical limits and the economic infringements of these limits are foundational perceptions of empirical conditions in major contemporary rationales for frugality, including mine. These rationales depend, as do antagonistic interpretations, not only on empirical assessments but also on moral judgments—for example, the meaning of full human development and the material conditions necessary for it. By reading reality through different value lenses than their opponents, socially and ecologically sensitive frugalists argue that a new economics paradigm is needed and that frugality is a necessary condition for the ethical acceptability of that paradigm.

Thus, frugality is a revolt against some basic values of the Sumptuous Society. For the sake of personal, social, and ecological well-being, frugality rejects the gluttonous indulgence, compulsive acquisitiveness, conforming and competitive consumerism, casual wastefulness, and unconstrained material growth promoted by the peddlers of economic progress—and embraced in different degrees by all of us who have known the enticements of affluence.

With this interpretation of the economic and ecological context of frugality in mind, I now offer an interpretation of frugality itself.

What Is Frugality?

What is frugality? Frugality denotes moderation, temperance, thrift, cost-effectiveness, efficient usage, and a satisfaction with material sufficiency. As a norm for economic activity, both for individuals and societies, frugality means ethically disciplined production and consumption for the sake of some higher ends. It is a means, an instrumental value, not an end in itself. It generally implies both a reduction in the consumption of material goods *and* different patterns or kinds of consumption. Thus, frugality thrives not only on restrained consumption but also on conscientious conservation, optimal technical efficiency, comprehensive recycling, and an insistence on built-in durability and repairability. Overall, frugality should probably be understood as one dimension of stewardship, but if so, that dimension should be explicit and prominent, which it is not in most popular interpretations of stewardship. Indeed, if present at all, frugality is usually figleafed with a generic appeal for a stewardship without specified standards and responsibilities.[16]

Generally in contemporary thought, frugality is interpreted as strictly a personal virtue—a morally excellent trait or habit of individual behavior. A virtue issues in voluntary action. Not only means and ends but also right motives matter. As a virtue, frugality is a feature of individual character ethics.

But frugality should not be so constricted. Indeed, it was not in classical thought. Both Aristotle and Thomas Aquinas, for example, interpreted the virtues as having both personal and political dimensions, since humans are not atomistic entities but relational beings.[17] Thus, both frugal persons and frugal societies can be moral realities. Yet, when frugality is a social norm, emphases shift: the focus is on social ends and consequences rather than individual motives, on public decisions and structures more than personal character, on coercion as well as consent. Frugality is, then, a personal virtue only for those individuals who conscientiously practice it apart from social sanctions.

Nevertheless, both personal virtues and social norms are ethically necessary. In fact, voluntary commitments and social stimuli function interactively. Through incentives and disincentives, social structures can be a moral deterrent, making it difficult, if not impossible, for individuals to act virtuously; or they can be a moral catalyst, encouraging and enabling virtuous behavior. The simple act of recycling, for example, is not practical without recyclable products, recycling centers, public acceptance, and market potential, enabled by public policy. Frugal persons can flourish and function effectively only with the institutional supports of frugal societies.

Moreover, public policy in a participatory society depends on the dialectic of consent and coercion (which should be understood as embodying a range of intensity, beginning with mild social incentives and disincentives). A sufficient number of citizens must be virtuous, or willing to be virtuous, in order to have sufficient public consent to establish structures of coercion. In turn, such structures of coercion not only can change public behavior, but also, if perceived as reasonable and just, can shape personal values and virtues, thus enhancing the level of consent. Thus, frugality, like any other operative norm, depends on both moral education and public sanctions, on both character formation and social regulation, each shaping the capacities of the other.

Some might argue that temperance is a better word for the perspective and practices I am describing. This argument has considerable historical merit. In classical philosophy and theology, temperance was one of the four cardinal "natural" virtues. In Aristotle and Aquinas, temperance was the disciplined self-mastery (sophrosynē) of the bodily pleasures of touch and taste.[18] Like frugality, it referred to the mean between two vices or excesses, deficiency and indulgence.[19] It was the opposite of gluttony and greed, two of the seven "deadly" sins. Unfortunately, temperance was stripped of its classical meaning in the Prohibition campaign of the early twentieth century: it became synonymous with abstinence from alcoholic beverages. Consequently, temperance no longer has the rich breadth of meaning that it had in classical thought—though even then temperance referred generally to moderating the desires for food, drink, and sex.[20] (The last is certainly not what I would include under the category of frugality!) Thus, frugality seems to be the preferable word and concept here, because, unlike temperance, the meaning of frugality is generally restricted to a concern with economic activity. Philosophically, however, perhaps frugality can be understood as the economic subspecies of temperance.

Similarly, some might argue that "sufficiency" is a better term. This argument, too, has merit.[21] Frugality certainly includes regard for sufficiency, but this word does not seem to comprehend the full economic connotations and consequences of frugality. In fact, frugality may be a less popular concept than sufficiency precisely because the former is much clearer and more realistic than the latter in conveying the disciplined constraint and even sacrifice that are necessary as an adequate response to the economics–ecology dilemma. The same criticism applies, but even more forcefully, to Theodore Roszak's use of plenitude to give disciplined consumption honorific connotations.[22] Nevertheless, sufficiency and plenitude are useful concepts, perhaps best understood as ends to which frugality, as an instrumental norm, is the means.

The problem with verbal substitutions in this case seems more than semantic. It is rather that a lot of the proposed substitutions for frugality suggest a dilution of moral responsibilities. The common negative reactions to the word "frugality" are often really rejections of the positive moral values the word connotes.

Distortions of Frugality

Frugality often has been the victim of guilt by association. It has been linked to values and practices that are not inherent characteristics of frugality and that, in fact, distort its moral significance. The revival and reform of frugality depend on a dissociation from these distortions.

1) *Frugality is* not *austerity*—though if frugality is not chosen under certain conditions, biophysical limitations may impose austerity. For the balanced John Calvin, austerity is "too severe;" it "degrades" us into "blocks."[23] In praise of frugality, Calvin denounced both excess (extravagance, ostentation, prodigality, superfluity) *and* deficiency. This balance seems essential to the nature of frugality.

2) *Frugality is* not *a world-denying asceticism that makes some feel competitively righteous—but woefully deprived.* It is not the triumph of the spirit over the flesh. It is not the self-mortification and material denigration of some of the saints for the sake of spiritual purification, nor the elitist means by which some Puritans proved their divine election. These atomistic and ethereal distortions fail to reflect, as I shall argue, the communitarian and materialistic character of authentic frugality.

3) *Frugality is* not *a fixed formula for production and consumption.* It is not legalism. It does not entail the righteous rigidity and casuistic rules that preoccupy some of the frugal. Instead, frugality is a relative concept, expressing a fittingness to appropriate ends.[24] How much is enough depends on what, for whom, and for what purpose. Frugality allows for considerable variation in practices, depending on different needs, tastes, and talents; available resources; and social and ecological conditions. And surely there are a number of occasions for justifiable indulgence—perhaps a festive frugality.

Still, the relativity of frugality is troublesome. It can be interpreted, as it often was historically, as relative to social rank or status, justifying different standards in proportion to means.[25] Thus, it can be an open invitation to rationalizations of excess—one of the worst examples being the acquisitive Andrew Carnegie interpreting himself as a frugal man and audaciously advocating frugality for the poor.[26] Similarly, in Aristotle, nobles with the means for magnificence seem to be exempt from the standards of temperance; they are justified in grand expenditures for great achievements for the common good *and* for themselves.[27] In this context, while we cannot have fixed rules, advocates do need to develop operating principles of frugality—and these principles need to highlight just distribution (socially, intergenerationally, and ecologically) and place a burden of moral justification on frivolities for some in the absence of necessities for all.

4) *Frugality is* not *a strictly individualistic phenomenon.* Many rationales for frugality focus on the spiritual and moral well-being of the individual. The quest of acquisitions, for example, can harm the development of moral character and distract from ultimate obligations to God or the Good. This concern is appropriate but insufficient. Indeed, on individualistic assumptions, high levels of commodity consumption can probably be justified, so long as the individual is not physically, morally, or spiritually harmed. But humans do not exist as atomistic entities. We are social and ecological animals, and our moral responsibilities arise from this relational condition. Thus, appropriate levels of production and consumption should be determined not merely individualistically but also—and primarily—relationally. The measure of frugality is solidarity—the moral response to the fact of interdependence, the commitment to the common good, socially and ecologically, nationally and internationally.[28]

5) *Frugality is* not *the means to prosperity.* This is true normatively but, of course, not descriptively in Protestant history. The irony of frugality in Puritanism is that it helped make the pious prosperous! Though the manifest function of frugality was responsible consumption, the latent functions for some were the accumulation of capital and the production of profit—accompanied in some segments of the movement by corrupting dysfunctions, including the perceptions of wealth as the evidence of divine blessing and poverty of divine disfavor, the decline of covenantal solidarity, and the abandonment of frugality itself.[29] The moral purpose of frugality includes capital formation. Though it is not miserliness or hoarding, frugality surely includes saving and investing—reserving and increasing resources for future plans and needs, such as educational expenses or retirement. But frugality also has a

more comprehensive purpose, which includes just and generous sharing.

6) *Frugality is not a strategy for keeping the poor in their place.* This distortion can be found frequently. In mid-seventeenth-century Massachusetts, sumptuary laws, prohibiting displays of luxury by the poor or the parvenu, were designed not to institutionalize frugality but rather to preserve a stable, hierarchical order, to restrict social mobility.[30] Similarly, in contemporary debates about economic maldistribution, it is often argued that the globalization of North American standards of living would be ecologically disastrous. Yet, it is not always noted that it would be ethically discriminatory to tolerate a double track, in which the nations of the South restrict their production and consumption while the nations of the North continue their wanton prosperity.

Frugality, however, as a middle way, is inherently concerned about both overconsumption *and* underconsumption, particularly when the former is a contributing factor to the latter. Its objective is not to keep the poor in their place but to enable the poor to rise to a new and adequate place. On a planet with scarce resources and a rapidly rising human population, this objective seems to require both floors and ceilings on production and consumption. In general, the substantial reduction of production and consumption in the North may be necessary to enable sufficient production and consumption in the South. The primary moral claim of frugality is directed not at the poor but at the prosperous.

7) *Frugality is not a return to a rustic or pastoral ethos.* This way of life can have a moral integrity that warrants commendation—and it usually is frugal. But it is possible and appealing only for a comparatively few. It cannot be generalized in a nation of 260 million people, let alone on a planet rapidly approaching 6 billion. Nor can frugality be tied to a particular lifestyle; it is a universal norm, applicable to rural, suburban, and urban settings, local and global.

Moreover, this pastoral way of life is often more a quest for self-reliance in isolation or communes than the self-restraint for the sake of others that is characteristic of frugality. Frugality is the rejection of a new Gilded Age, but it is not thereby the restoration of an old and largely sentimentalized Arcadian Age.

8) *Frugality is not simplicity.* In U.S. cultural history, simplicity has been an equivocal concept, often with both moral and aesthetic applications—from plain clothing to unadorned architecture, from good taste to elementary technology, from functional furniture to unpretentious lifestyles, from an appreciation of natural beauties and wonders to a distaste for the ostentatious, from less-stressful jobs to less-complicated

choices. None of these multiple meanings, even though some are admirable, is an appropriate synonym for frugality.

More important, the common identification of simplicity and frugality makes frugality appear irrelevant to modernity. 'Tis not necessarily a gift to be simple; it is a curse when complex problems require complicated solutions. Frugality is not an anti-intellectual phenomenon. For example, both the concept and the practice of frugality are in themselves complex, requiring sophisticated reflection on responsible production and consumption. Nor is frugality an antitechnological phenomenon. It is quite compatible with a recognition of the ambiguities and great variations in the values of technologies. While some forms of technology are socially and ecologically perilous, others, like some medical innovations, can enhance the quality of life and expand human choices. Still others can improve energy and resource efficiency, reduce toxic emissions, and advance ecological knowledge. Frugality offers no wholesale indictment or exoneration of technology. It insists, instead, that ethically acceptable technologies must be "appropriate" to relevant values and social and ecological conditions.[31] Appropriateness, in fact, allows for different scales of technology, from small to large, low to high tech, depending on the situation.

Frugality As the Quest for Abundant Life

The norm of frugality arises in response to several basic questions about the adequacy of material provisions. These questions include: What is a good quality of life, and what kinds and amounts of goods are necessary or valuable for it? Are various goods significant benefits or liabilities to personal, communal, and ecological enhancement? How should we distinguish needs and wants? How much is enough in quantity to sustain a reasonable quality of life *and* to ensure that the rest of humanity and other species, present and future, have similar opportunities?

For Christians, the answers to these complex questions depend in part on struggling with the countercultural values encountered in scripture. They depend, for instance, on dealing with Jesus' radical critique of the idolatries commonly associated with wealth—the idea that one's treasures are indicators of ultimate values (Matt. 6:12). They will give heed to the wisdom in Jesus' parables of the rich, hoarding fool (Luke 12:15–21), the rich youth (Matt. 19:16–24; Luke 18:18–25), and the poor, generous widow (Luke 21:1–4), as well as to his disconcerting, hyperbolic teachings about alleviating materialistic anxiety (Luke 12:22–33; Matt. 6:25–33). In this view, there is an insatiable yearning that is morally legitimate in the human creature, but it is not the unquenchable greed for economic goods. Rather, it is the persistent desire for values like love and justice and ultimate meaning that are beyond economic calculations.

Christian answers depend, moreover, on compatibility with the biblical commitments to covenantal justice—which demands provisions for the basic needs and rights of all, including a "preferential option" for the economically vulnerable and powerless, as an expression of loyalty to the Lover of Justice (Ps. 99:4) and as the condition of harmony (shalom) in community (Is. 32:17).

Frugality is one strategic response to the above questions that fits faithfully with the moral norms in the biblical witness. But frugality also fits well with a practical and responsible involvement in resolving the socioeconomic and ecological problems of the age.

Frugality is an earth-affirming and enriching norm that delights in the non- and less-consumptive joys of the mind and flesh, especially the enhanced lives for human communities and other creatures that only constrained consumption and production can make possible on a finite planet. It is "sparing" in production and consumption—literally sparing of the scarce resources necessary for human communities and sparing of other species that are both values for themselves and instrumental values for human needs. Frugality minimizes harm to humans and other lifeforms, enabling thereby a greater thriving of all life. At its best, therefore, frugality can be described paradoxically as hedonistic self-denial, since it is a sensuous concern, or, as Alan Durning notes, "a true materialism that does not just care *about* things, but cares *for* them."[32]

This type of frugality seeks the plenitude of which Theodore Roszak speaks—the truly abundant life, the fruitfulness that the Latin root of frugality suggests. It is wanting more, but more of a different kind than economic abundance promises. It is a quest for *being* more rather than *having* more—that is, a qualitative rather than quantitative enrichment.[33] It is not shunning prosperity, but redefining prosperity in less consumption-oriented forms. It is a concern not for the wealth of nations per se, but for the welfare of nations and nature. From the perspective of frugality, wealth has moral significance only insofar as it contributes to just and sustainable welfare—and it seeks to redefine both wealth and welfare in qualitative ways that cannot be simply correlated with aggregate economic indicators such as gross national product.

Frugality certainly recognizes the great value of economic productivity. That is the foundation of human development. The quality of human life depends on a sufficient quantity of goods and services to satisfy basic biophysical needs and to enable the exercise of our unique creative powers, which, in turn, depends on sufficient kinds and amounts

of economic productivity. Frugality is committed to sufficient production, the just distribution of the products, and the reduction of wasteful
by-products in order to achieve full human development. It rejects indiscriminate material production, which has made the maximum accumulation of goods an end in itself and which serves not as a sign of but
as a substitute for human well-being. When the economic objective is
transformed into an end in itself, rather than the foundational means
for human development, what distinguishes human beings from other
mammals is that humans have the most voracious appetites and only
humans engage in mass production.

Thus, the essence of frugality is sacrifice for the sake of higher ends.
This sacrifice is real. Some comforts and pleasures, some lesser values
that might be acceptable in an atomistic context but not in a relational
one, must be given up. Frugality cannot be made pretty by denying the
values lost. Nevertheless, frugality is a form of sacrifice that promises
to bring fullness of being in solidarity.

As a norm of moderation, however, frugality does not demand as
great a sacrifice as some might contend the Christian ethic itself does
or go as far as some Christians believe that ethic demands vocationally
for them.[34] Frugality is clearly not "holy poverty" or asceticism. It is,
nonetheless, defensible as a faithful expression of Christian moral
norms. Moreover, the temperate character of frugality is a distinct advantage over other contenders in the context of moral pluralism. Unlike
asceticism or other severe norms of consumption, which seem to depend on assumptions concerning sacrifice that are limited to certain
Christian traditions, frugality is on common ground, the "natural law."
It is an ethical norm that can be rationally justified and universalized
in a morally pluralistic world, apart from appeals to epistemologically
privileged revelations or traditions. It is not dependent on a Christian
confession, even though that confession is a primary historical source
of the norm. A coherent case can be made for frugality as a rational and
just response to the economics-ecology dilemma. Indeed, that case
often is made by contemporary environmental and social analysts. Frugality provides a shared standard, perhaps part of a global ethic, for
strategic cooperation among practitioners of various moral traditions.

While the quest for frugality is a strategic response to the initial questions, it does not in itself provide intellectually satisfying answers. A
compelling case for frugality depends on comprehensive and coherent
answers to such basic questions as the relationship between the quality
of life and the quantity of goods. This task seems to be an indispensable
part of the mission of ethics in our time.

Frugality for Love, Justice, and Sustainability

Frugality in classical Christian ethical interpretations is an expression of love—seeking the good or well-being of others in response to their needs and to the God who is love. The source of the sacrificial dimension in frugality is love of neighbor, for love always entails giving up at least some of our self-interests and benefits for the sake of the welfare of others in communal relationships.

The connection between frugality and love is common in Puritanism. It is found in John Winthrop's "A Model of Christian Charity": "in brotherly affeccion," we are called "to abridge our selves of our superfluities for the supply of others necessities"[35] (though Winthrop is also careful here to remind his compatriots to stay in their stations). It is prominent in John Wesley's sermon "The Use of Money," famous for the homiletical maxim: "Gain all you can. Save all you can. Give all you can"[36] (with the emphasis on the last, at least for Wesley). William Penn focuses the connection sharply: "Frugality is good if Liberality be join'd with it. The first is leaving off superfluous Expences; the last bestowing them to the benefit of others that need."[37] For John Calvin, the "rule of moderation" is shaped by the "rule of love," as he spells out in nuanced detail. Frugal self-denial leads to liberal help of neighbors, and both are part of stewardly accountability to God.[38]

These Puritan positions on the frugality–love connection are rooted in a long stewardship tradition of the church catholic. Indeed, similar comments, sometimes even stronger, can be cited from such patristic theologians as John Chrysostom, Basil of Caesarea, Gregory of Nyssa, and Ambrose of Milan.[39] For all of these interpreters, frugality ought to be practiced for the sake of just and generous sharing. In the absence of such sharing, frugality is something else: miserliness or hoarding.

In this ethical tradition, distributive justice is one dimension of love; it is love apportioning benefits and burdens, on the basis of relevant similarities and differences, to ensure that all interested parties receive their due or proper share. All human beings, equally and universally in interdependent community, have moral rights to the material and other essential conditions for expressing their human dignity and for participation in defining and shaping the common good. These rights entail duties of justice by others in proportion to capacities.

This norm contrasts sharply with the present human condition. Radical disparities in economic capacities within and among nations are a fundamental feature of the modern world. These disparities raise important moral questions. If global ecological scarcity is our present or pending condition, is the extensive use of the world's finite resources by the affluent nations a significant factor, actually or potentially, in depriving poor nations of sufficient resources for their essential needs? The linkage between prosperity and poverty is complex and ambiguous. In the context of emerging global interdependence, some factors of prosperity often seem to contribute to poverty,[40] but a causal connection is not always clear or, in some cases, perhaps even present. In this ambiguous context, what are the moral responsibilities of the prosperous to the poor in patterns of consumption?

On the one hand, if a causal relationship exists and if the world's actual and potential material goods are insufficient to tolerate both profligate prosperity for some and economic adequacy for all, then distributive justice requires sufficient reduction of production and consumption of relevant goods in affluent nations in order to make available the material conditions for essential economic and social development in poor nations. In this case, frugality is a *necessary condition* of distributive justice—and, indirectly, of ecological integrity and population stability insofar as these depend on economic sufficiency for all.[41]

On the other hand, the deprivation of necessities for any is an issue of justice and a demand for frugality by the prosperous—whether or not ecological scarcity is a reality, whether or not a causal relationship exists between prosperity and poverty. In all cases, the wealthy must reduce the consumption of their bounty in order to share essentials with and enable sufficiency for the poor. Some might argue, however, that the case for justice here is unconvincing. Instead, the issue is understood as one of benevolent sharing or charitable generosity. If so, that standard is quite demanding in itself, even exceeding the minimal demands of justice! Frugality then would be an expression of love as benevolence.

A similar argument for frugality applies in the case of just responsibilities to future generations—or sustainability. Sustainability is living within the bounds of the regenerative, assimilative, and carrying capacities of the planet indefinitely. It is an extension of the covenant of solidarity to the future.

Yet, a primary characteristic of present patterns of using the planet as source and sink is *un*sustainability. The moral problem in excessive production and consumption is not only the damage done in the present but also the harm caused to future generations. A portion of humanity is receiving generous benefits by living beyond planetary means, while future generations will bear most of the risks and costs—from nuclear wastes and possible climate change to species' extinctions and soil erosion. In this context, frugality is an essential condition of sustainability.

It is the adaptation to biophysical limits for the sake of a just distribution to future generations.

Finally, the concern for the just treatment of nonhuman life presents another important argument for frugality—even in the absence of scarcity (though enhanced by it). This concern introduces a major moral limit to economic activity that advocates of unconstrained material growth generally do not recognize or accept. If biophysical scarcity were not a problem for human relations, and if nonhuman life-forms were nothing but economic instruments—simply "renewable resources" or "capital assets"—to enhance human wealth and welfare, then unconstrained material growth would not be a problem of distributive justice. But if other species are ends for themselves or otherwise moral claimants on moral agents, then obligations are imposed on the human community to restrict production and consumption in order to protect these ends. If this second option is true, then economic policies need to pursue the "biocentric optimum," rather than the "anthropocentric optimum," of the first option.[42] On this assumption,[43] profligate production and consumption are anthropocentric abuses of what exists for fair and frugal use in a universal covenant of justice. Counseling careful usage and, therefore, minimal harm to other life-forms, frugality is the earth-affirming instrument of distributive justice to ensure enough goods for all species.

Thus, frugality, as an expression of love, is an indispensable instrument of distributive justice and sustainability. Frugality imposes *positive duties*—providing goods and services to others from our provisions, such as private gifts or public funds. But it also entails *negative duties*—noninterference through constrained consumption so that enough scarce goods are available for others to make provisions for themselves. Both by positive and negative duties, frugality defines in part the character and conduct of just neighbors.

The Damning Drawback of Frugality

Frugality is not a major problem for the Sumptuous Society when it is only a personal virtue, even when practiced by several million earnest individuals or thousands of conclaves of the committed. Its social impact then is comparatively slight, and even its practical possibilities for individuals are limited by an antifrugal social context.

But if frugality became part of a social ethos, even generating sufficient consent to initiate some structures of coercion, it would likely cause severe economic dysfunctions in the current system. The damning drawback of frugality as a social norm is that it is a formula for market depression in a socioeconomic system that depends on stimulating the economy by encouraging increased consumption. Frugality implies significantly less economic stimuli. Thus, it would likely result in not only less production and fewer goods but also smaller investments, lower profits, lower wages, reduced revenues, decreased philanthropy, and higher unemployment. The social consequences could be serious, particularly for the poor and unemployed. Internationally, the repercussions could be no less serious, particularly for poor countries dependent on affluent countries for export markets and economic assistance. This superficial analysis of the effects of removing a major component of an interdependent system indicates the ambiguities of frugality—its long-term benefits and short-term liabilities. Frugality is an imperative for sustained human and biotic welfare, but it also could be a source of human agony under existing conditions.

This dilemma does not mean that ethics should forgo frugality as a social norm. The task of ethics is not to adapt reasonable norms to fit current practices but, rather, to challenge and enable societies to adapt their practices to fit these norms. Frugality simply does not fit the economic assumptions of the Sumptuous Society. Frugality points to a new economic paradigm that fits this norm, because this norm fits, as the consumptive model does not, the biophysical limits of the planet to which all societies—and norms—must adapt. Frugality offers the only potentially realistic means of resolving the economics–ecology dilemma.

Yet, for any ethics that claims consequences matter, the advocacy of frugality as a social norm is irresponsible apart from a concern for its potentially grievous socioeconomic effects, particularly the dangers of economic *in*sufficiency and social injustices, and a commitment to envision and advance the policy directions for preventing these effects. Social frugality need not have the predicted dire effects that opponents love to recite in generating fear. On the contrary, the simplistic "consume or decline" choice seems to be a myth.[44] In fact, the opposite seems to be the case. *Un*sustainable use often means increased *un*employment and reduced production in affected industries, such as is now occurring in fisheries and forestry in key places. But we need technical strategies to show the means and ends of economic conversion. These strategies will need to cover a variety of public policies, including trade restrictions to protect environments and workers globally and nationally, tax incentives and disincentives to affect supply and demand, public regulations to set limits on products and by-products, and full employment plans. Indeed, some strategies are already emerging—for instance, the proposals of the Worldwatch Institute in the annual *State of the World,* the steady state economy of Herman E. Daly,[45] and the ecologically restorative economics of Paul Hawken.[46] These deserve serious consideration, critical review, and creative responses.

The really perplexing problem, however, is not technical but moral: whether sufficient public consent can be generated to create fair and frugal economies. That will require as a start a lot of character formation.

Conclusion

This essay only points to the ethical potential and dilemmas of frugality. This norm deserves much greater theoretical development and practical interpretation than it has received in modern ethics. When freed from distortions, frugality seems to be one of the cardinal virtues for our age. As an expression of love, frugality is an indispensable instrument of social and ecological justice and sustainability.

Despite its mild-mannered reputation in ethics, frugality is a radical norm by current social standards—as the deep angst it evokes among some of the affluent suggests. It represents a revolt against some basic economic assumptions of the Sumptuous Society. But it is a positive, not a negative, norm, entailing sacrifices that are personally and relationally enriching. It is an alternative to the American Dream, a competing vision of the future—one that promises fullness of being in solidarity.

The present political prospects for the socialization of frugality are, of course, bleak. But we are not fated. Political possibilities can be transformed, particularly when serious initiatives are undertaken to create a widespread awareness of the values of frugality and the disvalues of alternatives. That is a major challenge to moral education.

Notes

1. Max Weber, *The Protestant Ethic and the Spirit of Capitalism* (New York: Charles Scribner's Sons, 1958), 95. Similarly, Ernst Troeltsch called it "ascetic Protestantism" or "secular asceticism" in *The Social Teachings of the Christian Church,* trans. Olive Wyon (New York: Harper Torchbooks, 1960), 814.

2. Wolfgang Schrage, *The Ethics of the New Testament,* trans. David E. Green (Philadelphia: Fortress Press, 1988), 102–6, 159–60.

3. David E. Shi, *The Simple Life: Plain Living and High Thinking in American Culture* (New York/Oxford: Oxford University Press, 1985), 49, 277.

4. William J. Bennett, *The Book of Virtues: A Treasury of Great Moral Stories* (New York: Simon and Schuster, 1994).

5. Peter Berger, "Vice and Virtue in Economic Life," in *Christian Social Ethics in a Global Era,* ed. Max Stackhouse et al. (Nashville: Abingdon Press, 1995), 79–91.

6. R. H. Tawney, *Religion and the Rise of Capitalism* (Harmondsworth, U.K.: Pelican Books, 1938), 111–22; and Shi, *The Simple Life,* 8–27.

7. For some refutations of this assumption, see Prentice L. Pemberton and Daniel Finn, *Toward a Christian Economic Ethic: Stewardship and Social Power* (Minneapolis: Winston Press, 1985), 134–36; Robert H. Nelson, *Reaching for Heaven on Earth: The Theological Meaning of Economics* (Lanham, Md.: Rowman & Littlefield, 1991), 5, 7, 282–83; Herman E. Daly and John B. Cobb Jr., *For the Common Good: Redirecting the Economy toward Community, the Environment, and a Sustainable Future* (Boston: Beacon Press, 1989), 5–7, 85–96; and M. Douglas Meeks, *God the Economist* (Minneapolis: Fortress Press, 1989), 158–67.

8. Paul L. Wachtel, *The Poverty of Affluence: A Psychological Portrait of the American Way of Life* (New York: Free Press, 1983), 10–16; Juliet B. Schor, *The Overworked American: The Unexpected Decline of Leisure* (New York: Basic Books, 1991), 115–25. Edited versions of chapters 7 and 8 of Wachtel's book and a new essay by Schor appear in the present volume.

9. Schor, *The Overworked American,* 108, 124–25.

10. Wachtel, *The Poverty of Affluence,* 65–71, 166–64.

11. Schor, *The Overworked American,* 134.

12. Thorstein Veblen, *The Theory of the Leisure Class* (New York: Dover Publications, 1931 [1899]).

13. See Daly and Cobb, *For the Common Good,* e.g., 296–97, 374; Herman E. Daly and Kenneth N. Townsend, eds., *Valuing the Earth: Economics, Ecology, Ethics* (Cambridge and London: MIT Press, 1993); John B. Cobb Jr., *Sustainability: Economics, Ecology, and Justice* (Maryknoll, N.Y.: Orbis Books, 1992); William Ophuls with A. Stephen Boyan Jr., *Ecology and the Politics of Scarcity Revisited: The Unraveling of the American Dream* (New York: W. H. Freeman, 1992); Christopher Lasch, *The True and Only Heaven: Progress and Its Critics* (New York and London: W. W. Norton, 1991), esp. 168–69, 530–32; Ian G. Barbour, *Ethics in an Age of Technology* (San Francisco: HarperSanFrancisco, 1993), 251–54, 256–57; Lester W. Milbrath, *Envisioning a Sustainable Society* (Albany:. State University of New York Press, 1989), 218–31; Theodore Roszak, *The Voice of the Earth* (New York: Simon and Schuster, 1992), esp. chap. 9; Erazim Kóhák, *The Embers and the Stars: A Philosophical Inquiry into the Moral Sense of Nature* (Chicago and London: University of Chicago Press, 1984), esp. 108; Schor, *The Overworked American,* 137–38, 164–65; Wachtel, *The Poverty of Affluence,* 48–54; and Alan Durning, *How Much Is Enough? The Consumer Society and the Future of the Earth* (New York and London: W. W. Norton, 1992). See in general the essays in the annual *State of the World* (New York: W. W. Norton, annual since 1984), especially Lester R. Brown, Christopher Flavin, and Sandra Postel, "Picturing a Sustainable Society" (1990), 187–90; Lester R. Brown, "The New World Order" (1991), 18–20; Lester R. Brown, "Launching the Environmental Revolution"

(1992), 174–90; Sandra Postel, "Carrying Capacity: Earth's Bottom Line" (1994), 3–21; and Alan Durning, "Asking How Much Is Enough" (1991), 153–69.

14. Ophuls, *Ecology and the Politics of Scarcity Revisited,* 17.

15. Frugalists are concerned about resource-intensive or material growth. They favor, of course, what might be called *qualitative* growth—growth in energy and resource efficiency, in ecologically compatible technologies, in cultural and natural aesthetic sensitivities, in human services, in patterns of economic justice, and in the breadth and depth of public responsibilities.

16. One notable exception in which frugality is evident is Douglas John Hall, *Imaging God: Dominion as Stewardship* (Grand Rapids, Mich.: Eerdmans/New York: Friendship Press, 1986), 1–13, 193–204.

17. Aristotle, *Nicomachean Ethics,* I.9, I.2, VII.10; Thomas Aquinas, *Summa theologiae,* I–II, Q 61.5, Q 62.4.

18. Aristotle, III.10–11, VII; Aquinas, I–II, Q 63.4; Q 60.5; Q 61.2–3.

19. Aristotle, II.6, 7, 9; Aquinas, I–II, Q 60.1, 4; Q 65.1.

20. Aristotle III.11; Aquinas, I–II, Q 60.5; Q 66.3.

21. On "sustainable sufficiency," see Robert L. Stivers, *Hunger, Technology and Limits to Growth: Christian Responsibility on Three Ethical Issues* (Minneapolis: Augsburg, 1984), 128–38. See the argument also of William E. Gibson, "The Lifestyle of Christian Faithfulness," in *Beyond Survival: Bread and Justice in Christian Perspective,* ed. Dieter T. Hessel (New York: Friendship Press, 1977), 127–36.

22. Roszak, *The Voice of the Earth,* 254–55.

23. John Calvin, *Institutes of the Christian Religion,* Library of Christian Classics, ed. John T. McNeill, trans. Ford Lewis Battles (Philadelphia: Westminster Press, 1960), 3.10.2–3

24. Cf. John V. Taylor, *Enough Is Enough* (London: SCM Press, 1976), 45–46.

25. Shi, *The Simple Life,* 35–36.

26. Shi, *The Simple Life,* 160–63.

27. Aristotle, IV.2.

28. Pope John Paul II, *Sollicitudo Rei Socialis* (On Social Concerns), 30 December 1987, 26, 38–39; see also Donal Dorr, "Solidarity and Integral Human Development," in *The Logic of Solidarity,* ed. Gregory Baum and Robert Ellsberg (Maryknoll, N.Y.: Orbis Books, 1989), 148–53.

29. See especially Tawney, *Religion and the Rise of Capitalism.*

30. Shi, *The Simple Life,* 15.

31. For an appropriately nuanced perspective on technology, see Barbour, *Ethics in an Age of Technology,* 4–25.

32. Durning, *How Much Is Enough?* 169.

33. See Pope John Paul II, *Sollicitudo Rei Socialis,* 28; *Centesimus Annus* (100 Years After), 1 May 1991, 36.

34. See Stivers, *Hunger, Technology and Limits to Growth,* 141–50.

35. Quoted in *Individualism and Commitment in American Life: Readings on the Themes of Habits of the Heart,* ed. Robert N. Bellah et al. (New York: Perennial Library, 1987), 22–27.

36. *John Wesley's Fifty-Three Sermons,* ed. Edward H. Sugden (Nashville: Abingdon, 1983), 632–46.

37. In *Fruits of Solitude* as quoted in J. Philip Wogaman, *Christian Ethics: A Historical Introduction* (Louisville: Westminster/John Knox Press, 1993), 142.

38. Calvin, 3.10.1–6; 3.7.5; 3.19.7–12.

39. See William J. Walsh and John P. Langan, "Patristic Social Consciousness: The Church and the Poor," in *The Faith That Does Justice,* ed. John C. Haughey (New York: Paulist Press, 1977), 113–51.

40. For example, Northern exploitation of Southern resources, Northern exports of toxic industries and wastes, trade inequities favoring the North, international debt burdens of Southern nations, the destructive and corrupting impacts of some multinational corporations, and the impoverishing effects in many nations of structural adjustments imposed by the World Bank, as well as the heritage of colonialism.

41. These widely recognized connections are a common theme in World Commission on Environment and Development, *Our Common Future* (New York: Oxford University Press, 1987); also Alan Durning, "Ending Poverty," in *State of the World 1990* (New York: W. W. Norton, 1990), 174–90.

42. See Herman E. Daly, "Elements of Environmental Macroeconomics," in *Sustainable Growth: A Contradiction in Terms?* Report of the Visser't Hooft Memorial Consultation (Geneva: Visser't Hooft Endowment Fund for Leadership Development, 1993), 47.

43. For a defense, see my *Loving Nature: Ecological Integrity and Christian Responsibility* (Nashville: Abingdon Press, 1991), chap. 6; and my "Biotic Rights and Human Ecological Responsibilities," *The Annual of the Society of Christian Ethics* (1993): 137–62.

44. Durning, *How Much Is Enough?* 105–16.

45. Besides *For the Common Good* with John Cobb, see his essays in *Valuing the Earth,* ed. Daly and Townsend, especially his response to criticisms and caricatures of the steady state, 365–81.

46. Paul Hawken, *The Ecology of Commerce: A Declaration of Sustainability* (New York: HarperBusiness, 1993).

23

Natural Resource Consumption: North and South

Allen L. Hammond

Consumption, especially of natural resources, is the focus of much current discussion. People living in industrialized countries—collectively known as the North—constitute a small fraction of the earth's human population, yet at present, they consume a large share of the world's natural resources. From the perspective of developing countries—the South—such consumption not only deprives them of resources needed for future development but also contributes disproportionately to the world's environmental degradation. These issues are controversial and complex.

The Resource Consumption Issue

Consumption in the North includes a wide variety of goods and services associated with a consumer culture, while in the South it focuses primarily on basic needs. Consumption patterns not only differ from North to South but also differ significantly from commodity to commodity. Industrialized countries are the largest consumers of energy, which is integral to the lifestyle of most countries of the North. Developing countries, however, consume the most wood and wood products, primarily as fuelwood and charcoal, and clear most of the forest land, primarily for agriculture. Patterns differ over time as well: in past centuries, industrialized countries cleared their forests; and in the next century, developing countries will become the largest users of energy.

The environmental consequences of natural resource consumption are often borne by people other than those to whom the benefits of that

437

consumption accrue.[1] The North has had a greater impact on the global commons than the South has had, by dominating the marine fisheries of the open ocean, many of which are now endangered, and contributing a larger share of the industrial chemicals now degrading the earth's stratospheric ozone shield. Northern consumption of fossil fuel has contributed disproportionately to the buildup of carbon dioxide in the atmosphere and hence to the threat of global climatic change.[2]

Consumption of metal, fiber, and food produced for the world market (dominated by the North) causes primarily local, not global, environmental degradation. As a group, the industrialized countries are the largest producers and consumers of most such materials and thus face the largest potential environmental impact. However, because of less efficient methods and technologies and fewer effective controls in the South, degradation is often relatively more severe there.

The environmental problems caused by natural resource consumption may be compounded when the people of the South claim their rightful share of the earth's natural resources and their countries become industrialized. In recent decades, consumption of most natural resources has grown faster in the South than in the North, although most per capita consumption levels are still far below those in the North.[3]

Nonetheless, the North's patterns of resource consumption are not environmentally sustainable even today, either for the region itself or as a model for the world. Stabilizing atmospheric concentrations of long-lived greenhouse gases such as carbon dioxide, for example, would require immediate 60 percent reductions in current emissions from human activity worldwide, and equity would suggest that such reductions should occur in those countries—primarily in the North—that have per capita emission levels or cumulative contributions well above the world average.[4] Maintaining current emissions levels, even with no growth, means eventually doubling and then quadrupling the atmospheric level of greenhouse gases, with the potential of committing the world to centuries of global warming, major change in precipitation patterns, increased variability in weather patterns, and significant sea level rise.[5]

Virtually all industrialized countries continue to release to the environment a massive quantity of toxic material—heavy metals, hazardous chemicals, and acidic gases. If such emissions continue, toxic material will accumulate in the environment and eventually reach levels that could degrade forests and other ecosystems, pose health hazards to humans, and overwhelm natural cycles, such as those that maintain the earth's protective stratospheric ozone layer. Altering the natural resource consumption patterns that drive these problems is likely to require either far more efficient and less polluting technology or significant change in lifestyles, or both.

The South, too, has some unsustainable patterns of consumption that directly threaten the livelihood of people who depend on natural resources and that potentially foreclose their availability to future generations. In specific areas, freshwater resources, soils, forests, and other productive natural resources are becoming severely depleted or degraded. Often, losses are a direct result of the struggle of severely impoverished people to earn a subsistence living by supplementing inadequate income with locally available natural resources in an unplanned manner. Achieving more sustainable resource consumption patterns will thus require development that alleviates poverty. Moreover, the urban areas and industrializing regions of the South are increasingly replicating the environmental problems associated with Northern resource consumption patterns—air and water pollution, release of toxic materials to the environment, and solid-waste disposal—even though per capita resource consumption remains relatively low.

The pattern of natural resource commodity consumption and its environmental consequences is closely associated with the pattern of economic relationships between North and South. Over the past two decades, most natural resource commodity prices have declined in real terms (adjusted for inflation), intensifying economic pressure on countries of the South, for whom such commodities constitute a principal export. At the same time, natural resource commodities have become less important to the economies of most Northern countries, whose primary exports are high-value manufactured goods and services. The result is an unequal distribution of the benefits derived from use of the earth's natural resources.

In recent decades, a number of developing countries have experienced more rapid economic growth than industrialized countries. In part, such growth reflects an increasing transfer of basic production to the South and the expansion of manufacturing in many developing countries. Thus, there has been an increasing shift in the South-to-North trade from raw natural resource commodities, such as roundwood, to lumber products; from copper ore to refined copper or even copper wire; from cotton lint to textiles; and from hides to shoes and other leather products. Such shifts reflect the process of development: they create additional economic value and employment in the South, although they may also increase the environmental burden. At the same time, the development of significant internal markets for processed and manufactured goods in developing countries means that an increasing proportion of their use of natural resources is to meet domestic needs in the South.

Even if such shifts are taken into account, altering patterns of natural resource consumption and addressing their environmental conse- quences in the South as well as in the North may require significant change in the economic relationships between the two regions. Change could be crucial if underlying problems, such as poverty, and a more equitable division of the earth's resources are to be addressed.

This essay examines patterns of natural resource consumption in in- dustrialized and developing countries and the extent to which they act as a barrier or potential barrier to economic and human development. It examines consumption trends and the environmental implications of current resource production and consumption for a number of specific resources and explores in a preliminary way the resource content of trade between North and South. Two case studies examine in greater detail aspects of natural resource consumption in the United States and India, seeking to illustrate the complexity of resource consumption is- sues and the difficulty of altering current patterns. Policy measures for altering natural resource consumption in ways that could reduce its en- vironmental and developmental impact are briefly considered. This essay thus attempts to provide a factual base for broader discussion of natural resource consumption issues.

Social and Historical Patterns

The background to this discussion includes a long history of eco- nomic relationships between Northern and Southern countries in which the latter's natural resources, often under the direct control of Northern governments or private entities, were exploited for Northern consump- tion. European colonies in Africa and Asia, U.S. commercial activity in Latin America, and Japanese activity in Asia are well-documented examples.[6] Colonial relationships enriched the North and often severely degraded the natural resource base of the South.

There are also aspects of Northern consumption that may appear self- indulgent to Southern countries still struggling to meet basic human needs for many of their people. In the United States, for example, resi- dential homeowners spend about $7.5 billion a year to care for their lawns.[7] Northern families in the United States and Japan spend about $9 billion a year on video games for their children.[8] In 1989–91, by comparison, U.S. foreign development aid of all kinds totaled $10.1 billion and that of Japan $9.7 billion.

There is enormous economic disparity between North and South. Per capita gross domestic product (GDP) and gross national product (GNP) are not reliable measures of natural resource consumption, but they do indicate the gap between North and South. Based on purchasing power parity, average 1991 GDP per capita is $18,988 for countries in the Organization for Economic Co-operation and Development (OECD), compared with just $2,377 for developing countries. Disparity is often larger than the averages suggest. For the United States and India, the two countries used here as case studies, the 1991 per capita GDP based on purchasing power is $22,130 and $1,150, respectively. Based on currency exchange rates, appropriate for commodities moving in international trade, the gap between North and South is larger still, with average GDPs of $21,215 and $836, respectively.

Although many developing economies have been growing more rapidly than industrial economies in recent decades in percentage terms, the absolute size of the gap between rich and poor (on a per capita GNP basis) continues to widen (see fig. 23.1). Such disparities in income and access to resources and technology between North and South cannot be ignored in a discussion of resource consumption.

Natural Resource Consumption and Development

Nonrenewable resources, by definition, are finite. Evidence suggests, however, that the world is not yet running out of most nonrenewable

Fig. 23.1. Trends in Gross National Product Per Capita, 1970–92

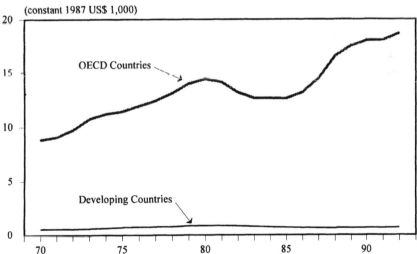

Sources: The World Bank, *The World Tables, 1993,* on diskette (Washington, D.C.: The World Bank, 1993); United Nations (UN) Population Division, *Interpolated National Populations, 1950–2025, 1992 Revision,* on diskette (New York: UN, 1993).

resources and is not likely to, at least in the next few decades. By a number of measures, reserves of energy and of subsoil minerals are more abundant, and real world prices for such commodities are generally lower today than twenty years ago, despite rising global consumption. Moreover, new technology is increasingly making possible substitutes for many traditional natural resource–based materials. Technology development is also yielding more efficient means of providing light, motive power, and other energy-related services. Such changes are paving the way to economies less dependent on natural resources. When shortages do emerge, experience and economic theory suggest that prices will rise, accelerating technological change and substitution.

Renewable resources, in contrast, are often thought to be indefinitely renewable. Yet some are location-specific or depend on finite resources such as land. As natural systems are asked to supply more and more and to absorb ever more waste and pollution, degradation of their productive capacity and even the possibility of ecosystem collapse cannot be ruled out. In many areas, exploitation of both biological and physical resources already exceeds the regenerative ability of natural systems. Thus, not only are many renewable resources increasingly scarce but also damage to the underlying systems that sustain or renew them threatens the near-term economic and human development of many nations.

Nonrenewable Resources

For minerals, economists distinguish between the resource base (all known resources) and reserves (that portion of a resource that can be produced at a profit at current prices). A traditional measure of the abundance of nonrenewable resources is the reserve-to-production ratio or reserve life index, which expresses the number of years of production at current annual rates that proven reserves will sustain. Since new resources are continually discovered and new process technologies increase the portion of those that can be economically recovered, estimates of reserves are continually adjusted. Nonetheless, the reserve-to-production ratio provides a snapshot of the perceived abundance of a mineral at a given time; changes in the ratio over time measure whether perceived abundance is increasing or decreasing.

A comparison of the world reserve-to-production ratios for nine major metals and for the three major fossil fuels shows that the ratio varies from about twenty years (for zinc, lead, and mercury) to well over one hundred years (for iron, aluminum, and coal). Petroleum reserves constitute a forty-year supply at current production levels. For most minerals, ratios generally increased over the 1970–90 period, despite rising consumption.[9] In many instances, if there were incentive to undertake the drilling needed to establish additional reserves, reserve figures could be higher.[10]

An alternative measure of resource abundance is provided by trends in supply and demand as measured by world commodity prices. Commodity prices are far more volatile measures than reserves, because they reflect a wide variety of market forces and (for oil) cartel actions, but the (inflation-adjusted) trend for major subsoil resources confirms that, in economic terms, they are less scarce than they were twenty years ago.[11]

An additional and critical factor for many nonrenewable resources is the prospect of substitution. In long-distance communication systems, copper is increasingly being replaced by optical fibers made of glass. Advanced plastics and composite materials are reducing the amount of iron and steel used in automobiles and the amount of aluminum used in airplanes. Increasing sophistication in the design of materials at a molecular level implies the ability to develop entirely new methods of meeting human needs and to engineer around any shortages of many minerals. Generally, this trend may imply that less and less of the economic value of final products will be attributable to raw materials. More efficient methods of converting fuel into electricity—from gas turbine/combined-cycle technologies to fuel cells—promise to reduce the energy needed to meet a given level of demand for power. In the next century, alternative technologies, such as biomass, solar, wind, and nuclear, may be able to supply a significant fraction of energy needs, reducing pressure on fossil fuel resources.

Deliberate policies could restrict demand still further or create more sustainable sources of supply. Recycling, for example, has already substantially reduced primary consumption of iron and aluminum in the United States. The use of demand management techniques in the U.S. utility sector, including regulatory provisions that reward utilities for investing in the energy efficiency of their customers, is considerably reducing the demand for electricity. Energy tax policies have successfully restrained demand for petrol in Europe. Similar measures may soon be seen in some parts of the developing world, where there are increasingly strong economic incentives for energy efficiency in the industrializing sectors.

Even without more resource-sparing policies, however, the cumulative effect of increasing reserves, more competition among suppliers, and technology trends that create substitutes suggests that global shortages of most nonrenewable resources are unlikely to check development in the early decades of the next century. Local shortfalls may occur, however, and the advanced technology that creates substitutes is largely under the control of the North. It is also clear that current rates of use of most nonrenewable resources are not indefinitely sustainable. Depletion of these resources today may limit opportunity for future generations.

Renewable Resources

Some renewable natural resources have identifiable economic value, but most of the biological and physical systems that sustain them lie outside the economic system. Thus economists assign a value to a stand of timber or to the annual fish catch or even to a quantity of water but not to the ecosystems or hydrological systems that produce and renew these resources. Other renewable natural resources such as sunlight, air, and a diversity of plants and animals are traditionally taken for granted as free goods of nature, which, along with the corresponding lack of price signals, may contribute to a lack of awareness of impending shortages. Yet it is the world's renewable resources and the resource base from which they stem that are most in danger of being severely degraded and depleted in some regions.

Clean Air

In a recent survey of twenty of the world's largest cities, all exceed the World Health Organization guidelines for at least one air pollutant, and fourteen exceed the guidelines for two pollutants.[12] Suspended particulate matter is the most prevalent form of pollution, often in combination with high concentrations of sulfur dioxide, a mix that is particularly hazardous to health. As urban areas expand, the number of people and sources of pollution threaten to outstrip even determined regulatory efforts. In developing countries, where urban areas are growing at 4 percent per year or more, the technical infrastructure for emissions controls often lags behind growth, and enforcement is lax. Clean air may become a rare resource for an increasingly large fraction of the earth's population.

Clean Water

In urban areas of the developing world, at least 170 million people lack access to clean water for drinking, cooking, and washing; in rural areas, more than 855 million lack clean water.[13] Water supplies are contaminated by disease-bearing human waste and, in some regions, by toxic chemicals and heavy metals that are hard to remove from drinking water with standard purification techniques. Use of polluted water spreads diseases that kill millions and sicken more than one billion each year; according to the World Bank, water pollution is the most serious environmental problem facing developing countries because of its direct effect on human welfare and economic growth.[14] Sewage and water treatment technologies are widely available but capital intensive. In addition, the capacity of rivers to support aquatic life and of coastal fisheries to maintain their productivity is threatened by pollution, loss of oxygen associated with the decomposition of pollutants, and algal blooms stimulated by nutrient runoff from areas of intensive fertilizer application. With surface waters increasingly polluted, many people have turned to groundwater sources, which in some places is drawing down aquifers faster than they can be replenished. Although opportunities exist to use and reuse water more efficiently, there is no substitute for water; new sources of supply (such as desalinization) tend to be expensive and energy intensive.

Fertile Soil

The Global Assessment of Soil Degradation study conducted for the United Nations Environment Programme found that in recent decades, nearly 11 percent of the earth's fertile soil has been so eroded, chemically altered, or physically compacted as to damage its original biotic function (its ability to process nutrients into a form usable by plants); about 3 percent of soil has been degraded virtually to the point where it can no longer perform that function.[15] In some regions, significant soil degradation is widespread—in Central America and Mexico, for example—affecting 25 percent of vegetated land. In some instances, loss of productivity has been made up by increasing the input of fertilizer, but yields are still lower than they would have been had soil degradation not occurred.[16] The continued loss of soil fertility, combined with rapidly rising populations in most of the developing world, poses the threat of insufficient food, fiber, and fuelwood supplies in the future. More intensive cultivation, higher-yield crop varieties, and novel (even synthetic) sources of food from biotechnology may ultimately substitute for losses in soil fertility and shortages of arable land. But substitutions could come at a high social cost, for example, reducing agricultural employment and food security for the poorest segments of developing societies.[17]

Biodiversity and Ecosystem Services

Life depends on a number of ecosystem services that are largely taken for granted. These services include microbial recycling of soil

nutrients, flood prevention and erosion control in watersheds, maintenance of the world's stocks of plants and animals, and replenishment
of atmospheric oxygen. Yet with ecosystems increasingly degraded or
converted for human use, their ability to provide services or to support
healthy, diverse communities of plants and animals is becoming more
and more jeopardized. In particular, loss of biodiversity appears to be
accelerating. Scientists estimate that 4 to 8 percent of tropical forest
species may face extinction over the next twenty-five years.[18] One expert believes that just under half of the world's 250,000 flowering plant
species occur only in areas that will be largely deforested or otherwise
disturbed over the next three decades.[19] Tropical forestland, a particularly rich habitat, was converted to other uses at an estimated rate of
15.4 million hectares (about 0.8 percent) per year during the 1980s.[20]
Wetlands are also under ever-growing pressure. Although no reliable
figures are available, damage to coral reefs appears to be on the rise.
Despite stepped-up efforts to create wildlife and nature preserves, germ
plasm banks, and genetically managed zoo populations, pressure on
habitats is a serious threat to the earth's genetic heritage and to the
ecosystems in which diversity flourishes.

Both nonrenewable and renewable resources are critical to development. But while local shortages of specific nonrenewable resources—
and some renewables such as fish or lumber—can often be compensated
for through imports, similar shortages of fresh air, freshwater, and viable ecosystems generally cannot. Shortages of renewable resources and
depletion of the resource base that supplies them can thus impede both
near-term development and long-term sustainability. Emerging shortages and their impact on development are concentrated especially, but
not exclusively, in developing countries.

Natural Resource Consumption and Environmental Degradation

Natural resource consumption patterns vary widely. To gain some insight into these patterns and their environmental consequences, it is
helpful to examine the trends in production and consumption of some
representative resources, both renewable and nonrenewable.[21]

Fossil Fuels

Worldwide, consumption of fossil fuel has risen (see figs. 23.2 and
23.3). The industrialized world's share has declined to less than 50 percent of the world total. Meanwhile, consumption has risen dramatically
in developing countries (by a factor of four over thirty years) and sub-

Fig. 23.2. Fossil Fuel Trends, Five-Year Averages, 1961–90: Consumption

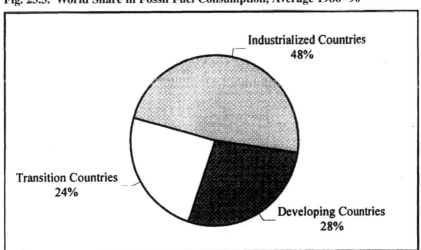

Source: Analysis by World Resources Institute based on data from United Nations Statistical Division (UNSTAT), *U.N. Energy Tape* (New York: UNSTAT 1992).

Fig. 23.3. World Share in Fossil Fuel Consumption, Average 1986–90

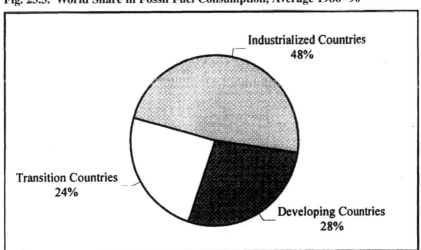

Source: Analysis by World Resources Institute based on data from United Nations Statistical Division (UNSTAT), *U.N. Energy Tape* (New York: UNSTAT 1992).

stantially in the former planned economies (by a factor of 2.4). Since the first oil shock, per capita consumption has declined moderately in industrialized countries but has risen rapidly in developing countries; industrial per capita levels are still very high (by a factor of nine) relative to those of the developing world (see table 23.1). Similar patterns hold for the production of fossil fuels among the three country classifications (see fig. 23.4).

An extraordinarily wide range of environmental degradation is associated with fossil fuel production, transport, and use. Local effects include land degradation from strip-mining of coal, the disposal of deep-coal mine tailings, and from oil and gas production and transport in fragile environments; freshwater pollution from acid mine drainage, oil

Table 23.1. Fossil Fuel Consumption (gigajoules/person)

Classification	1961-65	1966-70	1971-75	1976-80	1981-85	1986-90
Industrialized	115.82	142.53	165.70	169.52	153.81	160.06
Developing	7.37	8.26	10.34	12.91	14.53	17.28

Source: Analysis by World Resources Institute based on data from United Nations Statistical Division (UNSTAT), *U.N. Energy Tape* (New York: UNSTAT 1992).

Fig. 23.4. Fossil Fuel Trends, Five-Year Averages, 1961–90: Production

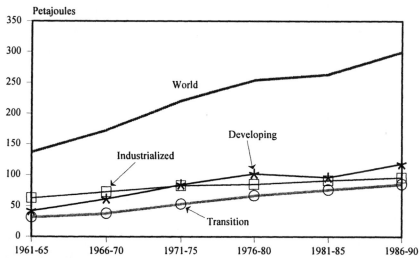

Source: Analysis by World Resources Institute based on data from United Nations Statistical Division (UNSTAT), *U.N. Energy Tape* (New York: UNSTAT 1992).

refinery operations, and improper disposal of used petroleum products; marine pollution from oil spilled or deliberately flushed out of tankers; and air pollution from fossil fuel combustion (sulfur dioxide and particulates), refinery operations (toxic emissions), coal combustion (dust and soot), and industrial and automobile fuels (urban smog). Regional effects include acid precipitation, primarily from coal and oil combustion, with its impact on monuments, buildings, forests and other vegetation, soil, and lakes. In addition, there is the potential global impact of climate change driven by greenhouse gases such as carbon dioxide, a product of all fossil fuel combustion, and methane emitted during the production, transport, and use of natural gas.

On a per capita basis, industrialized countries clearly contribute a disproportionate share of the impact of fossil fuel consumption on the global commons. Local effects accrue primarily in the country in which a fuel is consumed (most coal is consumed where it is mined). Acid precipitation, however, crosses national boundaries.

Metals and Minerals

Consumption patterns for aluminum and copper examined here to illustrate the general case of metals and other nonenergy minerals are similar to those for fossil fuel. Overall, the major regions have expanded their use of aluminum and copper, with consumption growing most rapidly in developing countries (ninefold growth for aluminum and fivefold for copper over thirty years) (see figs. 23.5 and 23.6). The industrialized world's share of global consumption has consequently been declining, although per capita consumption in that region is still much higher (by a factor of twenty for aluminum and seventeen for copper) than in the developing world (see figs. 23.7 and 23.8 and tables 23.2 and 23.3).

The story is quite different on the production side. Production of bauxite (the primary aluminum ore) has risen sharply in the industrialized world, which is approaching the share produced by the developing world (see fig. 23.9). The latter's share of copper production has risen slightly (see fig. 23.10).

Extraction, refining, dispersive use, and the disposal of metals and industrial minerals may cause significant local environmental problems. Mining can degrade land, creating quarries, vast open pits, and a huge amount of solid waste. During 1991, for example, more than 1,000 million metric tons of copper ore were dug up to obtain 9 million metric tons of metal.[22] Air pollution includes dust from mining, acidic gases from smelting and refining, and carbon dioxide from cement production. Fine particles of toxic trace metals that accumulate in soil and

Fig. 23.5. Metal Trends, Five-Year Averages, 1961–90: Aluminum Consumption

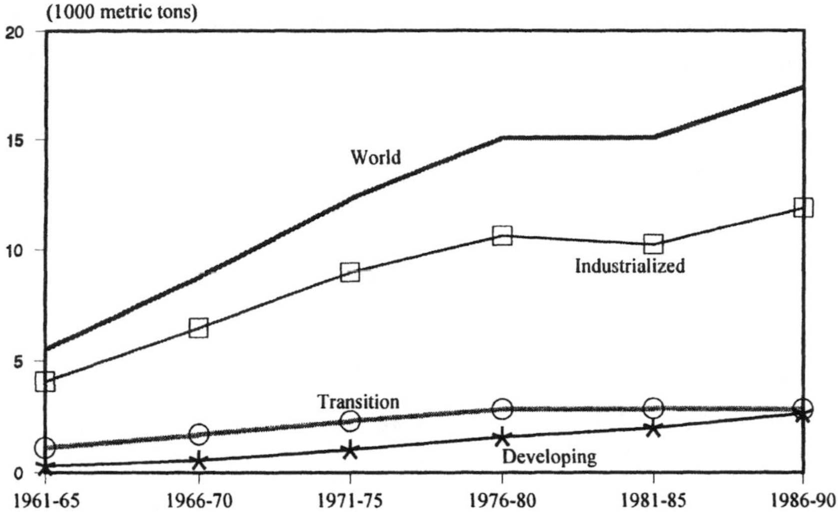

(1000 metric tons)

Sources: Analysis by World Resources Institute based on data from: World Bureau of Metal Statistics, *World Metal Statistics Yearbook, 1992* (Ware, U.K.: World Bureau of Metal Statistics, 1992); and Metallgesellschaft Aktiengesellschaft, *Metallstatistik 1961–71* and *Metallstatistik 1970–80* (Frankfurt, Germany: Metallgesellschaft A.G., 1972 and 1981).

aquatic ecosystems and in animal and human food chains are often dispersed during mining and refining operations; larger quantities are deliberately or inadvertently dispersed during use. Leaching from tailings or abandoned mines and the disposal of chemicals used in refining are significant sources of water pollution in mining regions. Improper use of minerals, for example in asbestos insulation, lead plumbing and gasoline additives, and lead- and chromium-based paints, can threaten human health.

A careful accounting of the environmental impacts from mineral consumption remains to be done. Preliminary studies suggest that use of heavy metals has left a significant, toxic legacy in the soil, ecosystems, and food chains of many industrial countries. The impact of the initial extraction of minerals falls on the producer states, both developing and industrialized; the primary benefit from their use accrues to the consumer states, still overwhelmingly the industrial countries.

Forest Products

Forests, extremely diverse biological communities, produce a range of products including firewood and charcoal, lumber, paper, and crops

Fig. 23.6. Metal Trends, Five-Year Averages, 1961–90: Copper Consumption

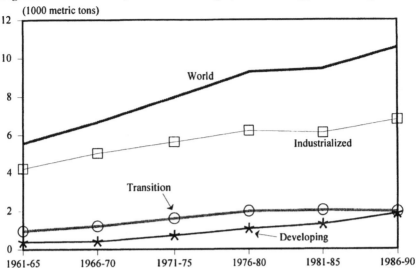

Sources: Analysis by World Resources Institute based on data from: World Bureau of Metal Statistics, *World Metal Statistics Yearbook, 1992* (Ware, U.K.: World Bureau of Metal Statistics, 1992); and Metallgesellschaft Aktiengesellschaft, *Metallstatistik 1961–71* and *Metallstatistik 1970–80* (Frankfurt, Germany: Metallgesellschaft A.G., 1972 and 1981).

such as coffee, oil palm, and rubber. The most common forest product in developing countries is firewood, the major source of cooking and heating fuel in most rural communities and in many major urban areas. Traditional fuels, largely firewood and brush, supply about 52 percent of all energy required in sub-Saharan Africa.[23] Charcoal produced from forests is also a major domestic energy source and, in countries such as Brazil, an important industrial fuel. Industrialized countries also use large amounts of wood as fuel, especially in the paper industry, but the most common wood products in the region are lumber, paper, and other industrial manufactures.

With careful planning of growth and harvesting, wood and other forest products are, in principle, renewable resources. But achieving renewability takes time, often decades, sometimes centuries. Without careful management, pressure for short-term exploitation can lead to tree removal, soil degradation, and conversion of woodland to other uses—a process more akin to mining than to sustainable harvesting.

Roundwood refers to any wood felled or harvested from trees, regardless of its final use. Globally, roundwood consumption has nearly doubled over thirty years, but the share of world consumption has fallen in

Fig. 23.7. World Share in Aluminum Consumption, Average 1986–90

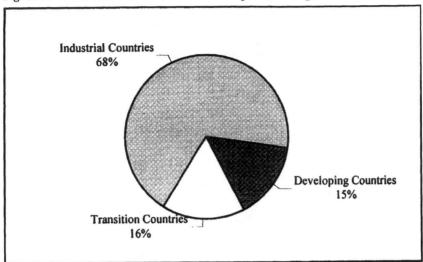

Sources: Analysis by World Resources Institute based on data from: World Bureau of Metal Statistics, *World Metal Statistics Yearbook, 1992* (Ware, U.K.: World Bureau of Metal Statistics, 1992); and Metallgesellschaft Aktiengesellschaft, *Metal-lstatistik 1961–71* and *Metallstatistik 1970–80* (Frankfurt, Germany: Metallgesell-schaft A.G., 1972 and 1981).

Table 23.2. Aluminum Consumption (metric tons/100 people)

Classification	1961-65	1966-70	1971-75	1976-80	1981-85	1986-90
Industrialized	5.99	9.00	11.89	13.50	12.56	14.13
Developing	0.13	0.23	0.37	0.51	0.58	0.69

Sources: Analysis by World Resources Institute based on data from : World Bureau of Metal Statistics, *World Metal Statistics Yearbook, 1992* (Ware, U.K.: World Bureau of Metal Statistics, 1992); and Metallgesellschaft Aktiengesellschaft, *Metal-lstatistik 1961–71* and *Metallstatistik 1970–80* (Frankfurt, Germany: Metallgesell-schaft A.G., 1972 and 1981).

transition and industrialized countries and risen in developing ones (see fig. 23.11). Global per capita consumption has grown slightly, with the level in industrialized countries remaining approximately 2.5 times that of developing countries (see table 23.4).

Production of roundwood has risen in all sectors of the world economy, but most rapidly in developing countries (see fig. 23.12). Gener-

Fig. 23.8. World Share in Copper Consumption, Average 1986–90

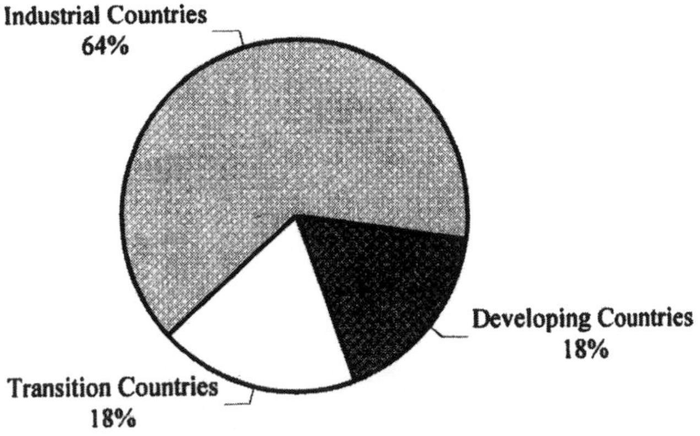

Industrial Countries
64%

Developing Countries
18%

Transition Countries
18%

Sources: Analysis by World Resources Institute based on data from: World Bureau of Metal Statistics, *World Metal Statistics Yearbook, 1992* (Ware, U.K.: World Bureau of Metal Statistics, 1992); and Metallgesellschaft Aktiengesellschaft, *Metallstatistik 1961–71* and *Metallstatistik 1970–80* (Frankfurt, Germany: Metallgesellschaft A.G., 1972 and 1981).

Table 23.3. Copper Consumption (metric tons/1,000 people)

Classification	1961-65	1966-70	1971-75	1976-80	1981-85	1986-90
Industrialized	6.17	7.00	7.46	7.90	7.50	8.06
Developing	0.17	0.17	0.26	0.34	0.38	0.48

Sources: Analysis by World Resources Institute based on data from : World Bureau of Metal Statistics, *World Metal Statistics Yearbook, 1992* (Ware, U.K.: World Bureau of Metal Statistics, 1992); and Metallgesellschaft Aktiengesellschaft, *Metallstatistik 1961–71* and *Metallstatistik 1970–80* (Frankfurt, Germany: Metallgesellschaft A.G., 1972 and 1981).

ally speaking, each region appears to consume its own production, although there are significant local exceptions. Japan, for example, imported about 60 percent of the roundwood it consumed in 1991, more than 20 percent of which came, until recently, from the state of Sabah in eastern Malaysia.[24] Relatively little roundwood is exported—the developing region presently exports less than 2 percent of its production, and the industrial region imports little more than 3 percent of its con-

Fig. 23.9. Metal Trends, Five-Year Averages, 1961–90: Bauxite Production

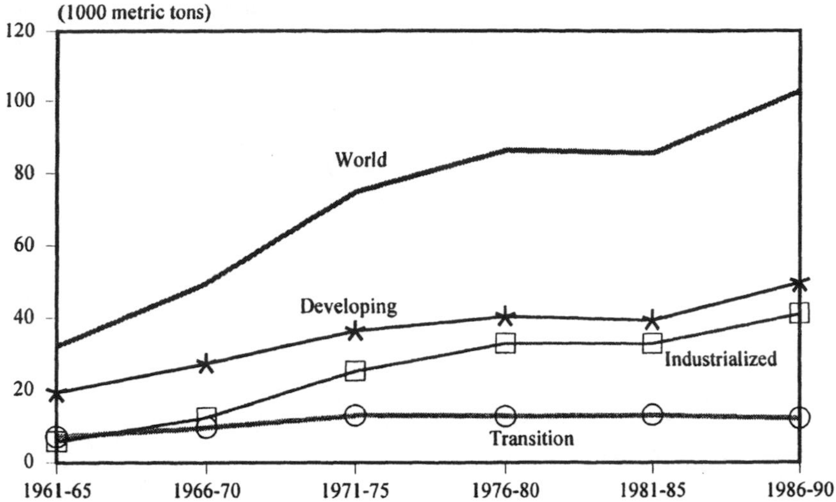

(1000 metric tons)

Sources: Analysis by World Resources Institute based on data from: World Bureau of Metal Statistics, *World Metal Statistics Yearbook, 1992* (Ware, U.K.: World Bureau of Metal Statistics, 1992); and Metallgesellschaft Aktiengesellschaft, *Metallstatistik 1961–71* and *Metallstatistik 1970–80* (Frankfurt, Germany: Metallgesellschaft A.G., 1972 and 1981).

sumption. Value-added exports of processed wood such as lumber, panels and veneers, pulp and paper, and furniture account for the bulk of wood-related trade; there is significant South-to-North trade in such products, particularly to Japan.

Consumption of forest resources can lead to environmental problems as well as loss of critical habitat and species. The severity of these problems depends on the method and extent of exploitation. In many parts of Asia and Africa, for example, fuelwood consumption exceeds supply, contributing to deforestation and devegetation. The demand for fuelwood and leaves and foliage used as cattle fodder is estimated to be six times the sustainable yield of India's forests. And the urban demand for firewood has contributed to severe shortages around most cities in Africa.[25]

Logging for timber, which in principle can be sustainable, often is not. Clearcutting, as practiced in North America, and similarly destructive methods in many tropical forests have destroyed habitat, contributed to the erosion of underlying soil and the degradation of watersheds, exacerbated flooding, and, in some cases, led to severe deforestation. The Food and Agriculture Organization (FAO) of the United Nations estimates that the area in tree plantations, a growing source of the

Fig. 23.10. Copper Trends, Five-Year Averages, 1961–90: Production

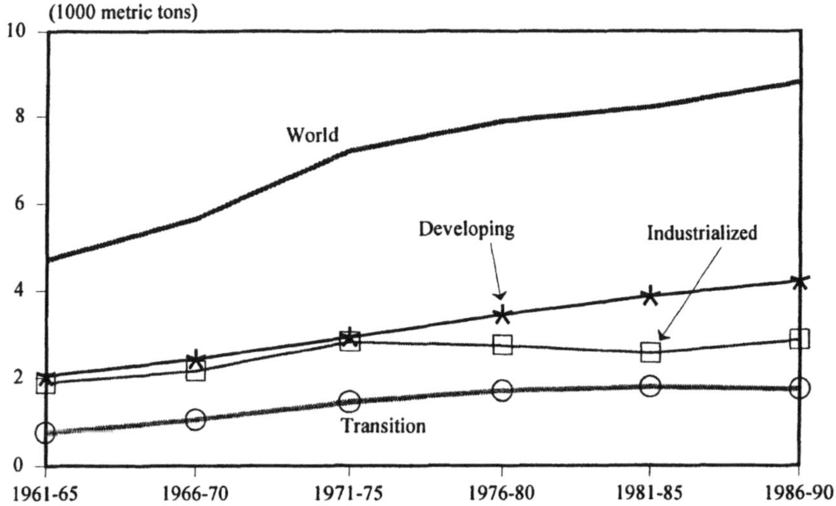

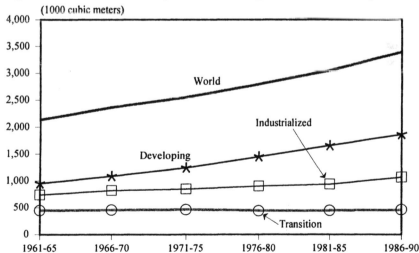

Sources: Analysis by World Resources Institute based on data from: World Bureau of Metal Statistics, *World Metal Statistics Yearbook, 1992* (Ware, U.K.: World Bureau of Metal Statistics, 1992); and Metallgesellschaft Aktiengesellschaft, *Metallstatistik 1961–71* and *Metallstatistik 1970–80* (Frankfurt, Germany: Metallgesellschaft A.G., 1972 and 1981).

Fig. 23.11. Roundwood Trends, Five-Year Averages, 1961–90: Consumption

Source: Analysis by World Resources Institute based on data from Food and Agriculture Organization of the United Nations (FAO), *Agrostat PC,* on diskette (Rome: FAO, 1992).

Table 23.4. Roundwood Consumption (cubic meters/person)

Classification	1961-65	1966-70	1971-75	1976-80	1981-85	1986-90
Industrialized	1.10	1.60	1.14	1.17	1.17	1.29
Developing	0.43	0.44	0.44	0.46	0.48	0.48

Source: Analysis by World Resources Institute based on data from Food and Agriculture Organization of the United Nations (FAO), *Agrostat PC,* on diskette (Rome: FAO, 1992).

Fig. 23.12. Roundwood Trends, Five-Year Averages, 1961–90: Production

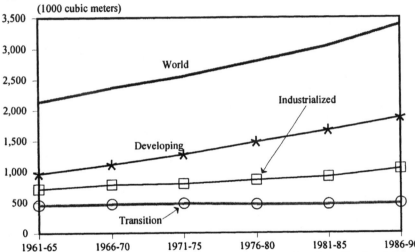

Source: Analysis by World Resources Institute based on data from Food and Agriculture Organization of the United Nations (FAO), *Agrostat PC,* on diskette (Rome: FAO, 1992).

world's lumber and paper, increased by almost 18 million hectares during the 1980s.[26] But tree plantations, although they may mitigate erosion, do not support the same level of biodiversity as natural forests. Pulp and paper mills are a significant source of water pollution. Paper is the largest component of municipal solid waste in most industrial countries, constituting more than one-third of such waste in the United States.[27]

Traditional agricultural practices (shifting cultivation) have little environmental impact on forestland when population density is low and fallow periods are long. As population increases and fallow periods decrease, however, shifting cultivation can degrade forestland and even lead to its permanent conversion to agriculture.

Trade Patterns and Trends in Natural Resources

An overview of global supply and demand patterns can be obtained from world trade matrices, showing the value in current U.S. dollars of exports and imports, for commodity classifications, by groups of countries. The trade patterns shown differ somewhat from those based on the volume or weight of the resources in question. Commodities are not treated individually but rather are grouped by standard international trade classifications (see table 23.5).

World Trade Patterns

Table 23.5 illustrates that industrial raw material is traded on a large scale within the industrialized world. Seventy percent of the North's imports comes from the North; only 25 percent comes from the South, though this constitutes about 65 percent of Southern exports of industrial raw materials. The share of the North's industrial raw material coming from the South has fluctuated but is now at its lowest level in almost thirty years; the share of Southern exports sent to the North has also declined somewhat. In contrast, the former planned economies have, on average, been shipping a growing proportion (65 percent in 1990) of their exports to industrial countries, even though the total amount is small compared to that from developing countries. The mineral fuel category of merchandise trade provides an extreme case of delivery of a primary, nonrenewable item from developing to industrialized countries. For decades, oil-exporting developing nations have shipped a fair amount of mineral fuel to industrialized countries, but by 1990, the volume and value had risen. Nearly three-fourths of Southern exports in this category were sent to OECD countries. In 1990, the exports of transitional countries (mainly from the former Soviet Union) were also sent, on a large scale, to OECD countries. This pattern had started earlier but was reinforced by much-reduced trade within transitional countries as Russia sought hard currency earnings. About 60 percent of the North's imports of mineral fuel by value came from the South in 1990, compared with about 34 percent from North-North trade.

More than 60 percent of all world trade in manufactured products takes place among the OECD countries. They have a surplus in trade with developing countries; a fairly steady fraction of their exports over

Table 23.5. World Trade Matrices, 1990[a]

Industrial Raw Material and Edible Oils[b]

Exports	Imports			
	OECD	Developing	Transition	Total
OECD	98,837	22,808	2,193	123,839
Developing	34,267	17,369	1,525	53,162
Transition	5,561	1,257	1,741	8,560
Total	138,665	41,436	5,459	185,560

Mineral Fuels[c]

Exports	Imports			
	OECD	Developing	Transition	Total
OECD	91,392	11,233	1,106	103,732
Developing	159,721	39,850	2,320	201,891
Transition	20,833	2,499	6,301	29,634
Total	271,946	53,583	9,727	335,257

Manufactures[d]

Exports	Imports			
	OECD	Developing	Transition	Total
OECD	1,578,007	377,995	41,688	1,997,690
Developing	278,812	143,390	5,969	428,172
Transition	26,936	12,600	33,709	73,244
Total	1,883,755	533,984	81,366	2,499,105

Source: United Nations (UN) Macroeconomic and Social Policy Analysis Division, unpublished data (New York: UN 1993).
Notes: a. These tabulations are in millions of current U.S. dollars and therefore are not free of inflation effects. The diagonal entries in the matrices would be zero for individual countries, but for groups of countries, as here, they indicate intratrade, that is, trade among countries in the respective groups. b. Standard International Trade Commodities (SITC) 2 and 4. c. SITC 3. d. SITC 5–9.

the last three decades, about 20 percent, flows to developing countries. This pattern is the reverse of the surplus of industrial raw material exports from developing to industrialized countries. An important trend, however, is that Southern exports of manufactured goods to the North are growing rapidly, while exports of industrial raw material to the North and imports of manufactured goods from the North are not.

Trade Pattern Implications

Trade patterns are complex and continuously changing. A degree of specialization does occur, with a significant share of raw material from the South going to the North and manufactured goods processed in the North returning to the South. As noted earlier, the terms of trade in this South-North-South cycle are generally unfavorable to the South. Yet generalizations can be misleading. For many natural resource commodities, for example, the largest supplier to the North is the North itself, although the pattern varies by country. Moreover, a significant portion of the South's natural resource exports is now in the form of processed or semimanufactured goods, with more of the value added retained in developing countries; trade in manufactured goods from South to North is also growing rapidly.

A Case Study in Resource Consumption Patterns: The United States

Historical Pattern

The United States consumes an enormous quantity of material. Apparent consumption, defined as domestic production plus recycling and imports and less exports, is the basis of the analysis reported here. In 1989 about 4.5 billion metric tons of natural resources were consumed in the United States—about 18 metric tons per person. Construction material (stone, sand, and gravel) accounted for 1.8 billion metric tons of the total, energy fuel for another 1.7 billion metric tons, and food (meats and grains) for about 317 million metric tons.[28] Consumption in 1989 also included 317 million metric tons of industrial minerals, 109 million metric tons of metal, 157 million metric tons of forestry products, 107 million metric tons of nonrenewable organic material such as asphalt and chemicals, and 6.7 million metric tons of natural fiber.[29]

The historical pattern for some of those materials contains several features of note (see fig. 23.13). Wood use has risen in the last decade after remaining relatively constant for the previous twenty years; paper use has been increasing since 1900. A decline in primary-metal consumption over the last few decades reflects increasing recycling and production from scrap (secondary metal), while an increase in consumption of nonfuel organic material reflects the rising use of plastic, synthetic fiber in textiles and carpets, synthetic rubber, and petrochemical products. Industrial minerals such as fertilizer and mineral feedstock

Fig. 23.13. U.S. Material Consumption Trends, 1900–89

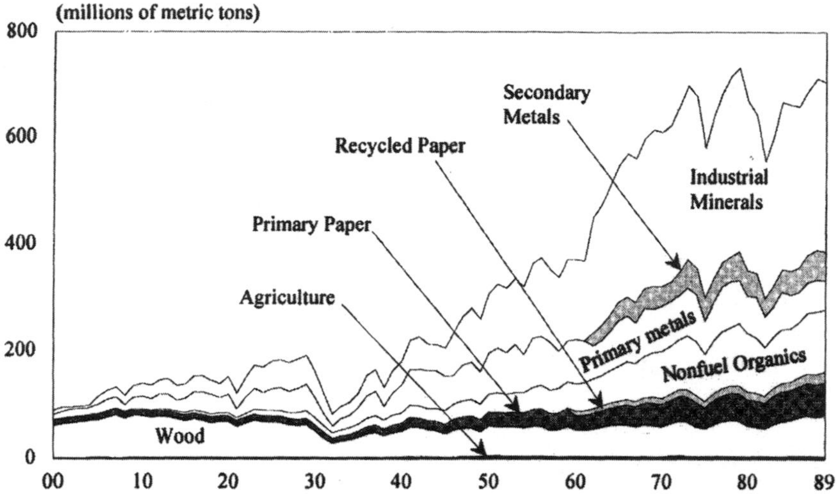

(millions of metric tons)

Source: U.S. Bureau of Mines, "Materials and the Economy," *Minerals Today* (April 1993), 15.

for the chemical industry have been used in relatively constant amounts since 1960.[30]

The intensity of natural resource consumption—measured either per capita or per unit of U.S. GNP—is declining for some commodities but not for all. Materials exhibiting the strongest current growth, such as plastic and paper, weigh much less than most of the metal and industrial minerals they are displacing. Thus, per capita consumption of forestry products, metal, and plastic—measured by weight—has been declining over the past twenty years, but per capita consumption measured by volume has been expanding slowly (see fig. 23.14). According to the U.S. Bureau of Mines, these trends reflect the growing use of more highly engineered and generally lighter material, packaging material, and paper, among other factors. Over the last decade, for example, the United States has used more plastic on a volume basis than all metals combined.[31] The rising volume of material consumption may partially explain the growing volume of postconsumer waste, despite reduced per capita consumption of primary metal.

Domestic and Imported Resources

Natural resource consumption in the United States is relatively high compared with average world consumption (see table 23.6). The ratio of U.S. per capita consumption to the world average varies from 1.5 for

Fig. 23.14. U.S. Material Intensity Trends

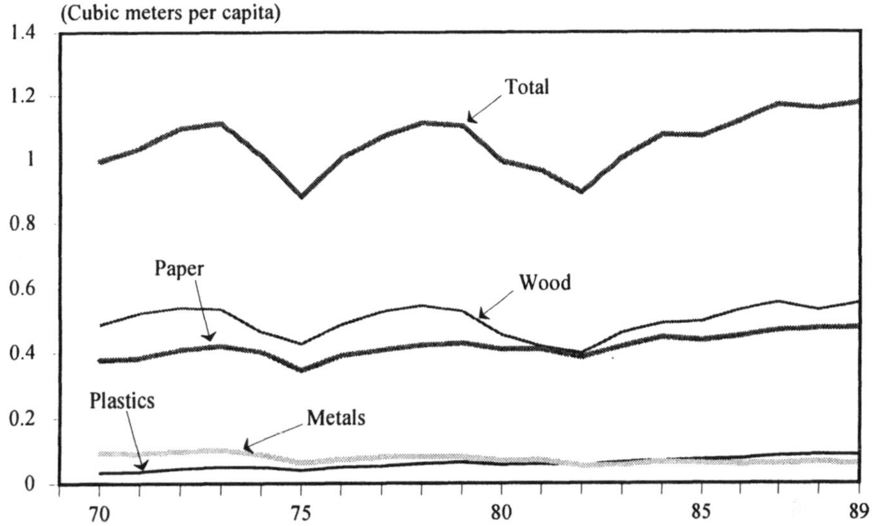

Source: U.S. Bureau of Mines, "Materials and the Economy," *Minerals Today* (April 1993), 16.
Notes: Wood covers lumber, plywood, veneer, and other forestry products. Metals include primary and secondary.

cement to 6.9 for plastic. Comparisons with consumption in developing countries shows even larger ratios.

With a few exceptions (notably petroleum), most of the natural resources consumed in the United States are from domestic sources. For many mineral and metal commodities, the United States provides 85 percent or more of its own raw material requirements. The major exceptions are bauxite (for aluminum) and potash, which are largely imported, and petroleum and iron ore, which are imported in significant quantity. Imports of these commodities come from industrial and transition countries as well as from developing countries. The United States is a net exporter of wood (but not of paper), coal, and grain.

The Distribution of Environmental Impacts

The predominantly domestic base for U.S. natural resource consumption creates local environmental impacts primarily within the United States. However, non-U.S. regions that export natural resources or natural resource–based products to the United States may also experience significant local environmental impact. In addition, there may be indirect or displacement effects of U.S. consumption, such as higher world

Table 23.6. U.S. and World Consumption of Selected Ores and Commodities, 1990

Ore/Commodity	U.S. Apparent Consumption (million metric tons)	Domestic Production[a] (percent)	World Production (million metric tons)	Per Capita Consumption U.S./World
Petroleum feedstocks[b] (quadrillion BTU)	1.3	62.3	4.1	6.7
Bauxite	12.0	5.0	109.6	2.3
Phosphate[c]	5.3	100.0	48.6	2.3
Salt	40.6	90.9	183.5	4.7
Potash[d]	5.5	31.4	29.3	4.0
Industrial sand and gravel	24.8	100.0	120.8	4.4
Iron ore	76.9	73.4	919.3	1.8
Plastic from petroleum feedstocks	25.4	See petro. feedstocks	78.3	6.9
Fibers from petroleum feedstocks	3.9	See petro. feedstocks	13.2	6.3
Aluminum[e]	5.3	See bauxite	18.0	6.2
Copper[f]	2.2	97.4	10.5	4.4
Iron and steel[g]	97.7	88.1	770.6	2.7
Nitrogen	14.9	84.9	97.1	3.3
Cement	81.3	86.0	1,152.8	1.5

Source: Analysis by U.S. Bureau of Mines based on data from: United States Bureau of Mines (USBM), *1990 Minerals Yearbook* (Washington, D.C.: USMB, 1993): United States Department of Energy (DOE), *Annual Energy Review, 1991* (Washington, D.C., DOE, Washington, D.C., 1992): and Donald G. Rogich and staff, "Material Use, Economic Growth, and the Environment," paper presented at the International Recycling Congress, Geneva, Switzerland, January 1993. Notes: a. Domestic production stated as a percent of apparent consumption. b. Ratio of U.S. per capita consumption and world per capita consumption includes petroleum and natural gas used for plastics and fibers from feedstocks. These amounts were assumed using 45.7 percent of total petroleum chemical feedstock consumption. Percent for domestic sources uses a weighted average of 22.2 percent natural gas and 77.8 percent petroleum. c. Phosphate-phosphorous pentoxide content of fertilizer. d. Potassium oxide content. e. World production is from primary sources only. f. World production is refined copper. g. World production is for raw steel.

oil prices due to large U.S. imports and, hence, additional coal or fuel-wood consumption in developing countries.

The global environmental impact of U.S. natural resource consumption presents a different picture. The United States is the world's leading producer of greenhouse gas emissions, which may result in global warming, and plays a significant role in degrading the global commons. Heavy fossil fuel consumption in the United States is not only the source of most U.S. greenhouse gas emissions but also a cause of acid precipitation in Canada.

Implications

Relative to GNP or population, U.S. consumption is expanding for some natural resource commodities, such as paper and plastic, and declining for others, such as primary metal. Domestic resources supply a large portion of that consumption for many raw materials and commodities. Nonetheless, U.S. consumption remains high, relative to world levels. It is therefore incumbent upon the United States to take a leadership role in seeking technologies and policies to use natural resources more efficiently and to minimize the environmental consequences of such use.

Of particular importance are global environmental problems such as emissions of greenhouse gases that can cause global warming. Here, the United States, as the world's largest consumer of fossil fuels, has a special responsibility. Yet, because many sectors of the U.S. economy are major contributors (directly and indirectly) to carbon dioxide emissions, significant changes in U.S. emissions would require widespread adjustments. And while this analysis suggests that the growth of U.S. carbon dioxide emissions may slow naturally, it will not cease in the near term without specific policy efforts. Stabilizing U.S. emissions at 1990 levels, while an important near-term goal, is far from enough; if the growing risk of climate change is to be reduced and the climate eventually stabilized, far greater reductions in emissions will be needed.

A Case Study in Resource Consumption Patterns: India

The consumption of natural resources and related environmental implications differ widely among various groups in India. The relative magnitude of resources required, directly and indirectly, to support the consumption of persons belonging to different income groups are analyzed using input-output methods and the environmental implications of these consumption patterns are discussed (see table 23.7).

Table 23.7. Direct and Indirect Per Capita Consumption in India, 1989–90 (Rupees/Annum)

Commodities	Rural		
	Bottom 50%	Mid 40%	Top 10%
Sugarcane	52.71	99.17	183.20
Cotton	50.21	65.48	70.43
Coal and lignite	21.51	37.27	80.63
Crude petroleum and natural gas	39.85	66.29	138.95
Iron ore	0.22	0.40	0.97
Other metallic minerals	1.27	2.47	6.07
Cement	2.42	4.21	11.81
Iron and steel	25.76	47.14	114.17
Electricity, gas, and water supply	81.05	136.36	264.63
All commodities	3,170.99	5,636.45	11,586.79
Population (in millions)	303.3	242.6	60.7
Percentage of population	37.4	29.9	7.5

Commodities	Urban		
	Bottom 50%	Mid 40%	Top 10%
Sugarcane	53.84	93.58	149.83
Cotton	60.70	105.62	213.99
Coal and lignite	40.40	94.27	237.79
Crude petroleum and natural gas	76.00	185.84	495.93
Iron ore	0.36	0.93	2.57
Other metallic minerals	2.30	6.13	16.29
Cement	3.56	8.13	28.52
Iron and steel	42.04	109.58	306.28
Electricity, gas, and water supply	150.11	346.35	830.90
All commodities	4,926.13	11,110.65	28,128.77
		81.8	
Population (in millions)	102.3	10.1	20.5
Percentage of population	12.6		2.5

Source: Analysis by the Indira Gandhi Institute for Development Research, Bombay, 1993.

Resource Use

Consumption of energy, minerals, and chemicals by upper-income groups (the top 50 percent of the population) account for a large portion of the country's total use. For minerals such as coal, iron ore, and crude petroleum, the resources required to support consumption by the lowest rural income group are only 8 to 10 percent of what is needed for the highest urban income group on a per capita basis. Hence a large portion of the global environmental impact such as emissions of carbon dioxide—as well as much of the local air and water pollution caused by industrial processes—is attributable to the urbanized upper-income groups. By international standards, however, per capita consumption is modest, well below average consumption in industrialized countries. Wide disparity between income groups largely reflects the virtual absence of consumption of nonfood items (other than clothing) by the poor. This inability to purchase market goods is a concern, because it drives the poor to meet their basic needs by relying primarily on the environment.

The Environmental Effects of Poverty

Poor people who cannot meet their subsistence needs through purchase are forced to use common property or private resources such as forests for food and fuel, pastures for fodder, and ponds and rivers for water. Though Indians have depended on such resources for millennia, the pattern of use has recently been modified by two major forces. Population growth has increased the pressure on natural resources, in some cases to the point of destruction. At the same time, natural resources are being used by higher-income urban dwellers in new ways. These two trends have hurt the poor.

Household tap water is available to 35 percent of urban households and only 18 percent of rural households in India.[32] Other residents share a community water tap or use wells, ponds, and rivers. Overuse of water resources by the poor, driven by population pressure, has resulted in some contamination and, where demand exceeds supply, exhaustion. Urban populations are also making growing use of rivers to dispose of untreated sewage and industrial effluent. The result is that the health of those dependent on untreated sources of water is increasingly at risk.

Those who can afford it buy cleaner commercial fuels—such as kerosene, liquified petroleum gas, or electricity—for cooking. The poor, however, must gather biofuel—wood, crop residue, and animal dung— from the local environment and risk the health effects of cooking with it, which include respiratory disease, anemia, and cancer. Women and children are the most exposed to risk.

As populations increase, the requirement for fuel may exceed the sustainable natural supply, leading to the gradual shrinkage of woodlands and the expenditure of more time and effort to collect fuel. At the same time, the urban or village need for wood in construction puts an additional demand on the same resource; those who can pay for wood are often supplied with chainsaws and trucks, technologies that make large-scale wood removal easy and are not available to the poor. Commercial markets for wood and paper products support the creation of contract woodlots, but planted forests do not supply the variety of non-timber resources on which the poor depend and may divert land and water that was formerly available for use by the poor. Commercial demands for crop residue and animal dung—as feedstock or as fuel for gasifiers and biogas generators—also deprive the poor of fuel.

Sanitation services are available to only 37 percent of urban and 8 percent of rural households in India.[33] Human waste, disposed of in open or common spaces, can spread pathogens through the air, in water supplies, and by direct contact. Waste-related health hazards increase as populations grow and affect the urban and rural poor most severely.

The poor are both agents and victims of environmental degradation. They suffer most directly the consequences of degradation, whether caused by their own actions or by the consumption of others. Moreover, the poor often have no alternative when the environmental resources they depend on are degraded—the environment is an integral and irreplaceable aspect of their life support system. Undependable food supplies, unsafe drinking water, polluted air, and unsanitary conditions contribute significantly to reduced life expectancy and high child mortality. These conditions, in turn, contribute to population growth as the poor make fertility decisions to compensate. Children are valuable—they gather fuel, collect drinking water, and care for aging relatives. But because many children die, it is necessary to have many. The result is a vicious cycle: a larger population leads to more poverty and more pressure on the environment.

Implications

The consumption patterns discussed above largely drive natural resource production and use in India. With the exception of iron ore and a few other commodities, most of the natural resources produced in India are also consumed within India (see table 23.8). The environmental consequences of consumption patterns include industrial pollution, a growing problem in India. Local pollution may worsen as consumption rises along with urban populations and incomes. More efficient use of energy and coal to generate electricity could limit pollution increases and also keep Indian contributions to the global buildup of greenhouse gases to a minimum. On a per capita basis, however, current levels of consumption and pollution are far lower than in industrial countries.

A far more difficult—and, from a global perspective, possibly more critical—problem is the vicious cycle of poverty, population growth, resource degradation, and more poverty. In addition to human degradation, this cycle degrades and threatens to exhaust renewable resources on which local populations depend. Thus, development and environmental goals are inextricably linked: development that alleviates poverty is essential if renewable resources—especially from common property—and sustainable livelihoods for a large fraction of the population are to be preserved in nations such as India. Consequently, policies that accelerate development can play a vital environmental role, if they are properly designed.

Policy Implications

The environmental and developmental impact of natural resource consumption makes many present consumption practices unsustainable. Industrialized countries need to consider how to reduce consumption and increase the efficiency of natural resource use. Most important, however, they need to mitigate significantly their impact on the global commons, exemplified by the buildup of greenhouse gases from the consumption of fossil fuel. In the Climate Convention signed at UNCED, industrialized countries made tentative commitments to stabilize emissions of greenhouse gases at 1990 levels; this is an important first step. But even if these commitments are fulfilled, the North will still be far from a sustainable consumption pattern on fossil fuel, and the region's potential impact on the global climate will continue to rise.

Developing countries would also benefit from more efficient use of natural resources. Even though per capita consumption is far lower in developing countries than in industrialized ones, their large and growing populations suggest that total natural resource use and related pollution problems will become significant both locally and globally. Most important, however, developing countries need to protect their endangered renewable-resource base, which will mean accelerating and targeting development in ways that can alleviate poverty and enable poor people to meet their basic needs in ways that do not degrade water, soil, or forest resources or reduce biodiversity.

Using the Price Mechanism

Because individuals and companies alike respond to price signals, governments have long used taxes and subsidies as economic policy levers. The same means can be used to encourage more efficient use of resources and to reduce environmental pressure from resource consumption. If the environmental costs of human economic activity were more adequately reflected in the prices paid for goods and services, for example, companies and ultimately consumers would have an economic incentive to adjust their behavior so as to reduce pollution and waste. Twenty years ago, the OECD agreed on this principle, called polluter pays, as a means of incorporating environmental externalities into the economic system in a way that does not give unfair advantage to the industries of one country over another. Though the idea of pollution and other green taxes is gaining attention, the polluter pays principle has never been systematically implemented in industrialized countries, and it remains controversial in many developing countries.

European countries have long used high taxes on petrol to restrain demand. More recently, taxes on the carbon content of all forms of fossil fuel have been proposed as a means of curbing growth in emissions of carbon dioxide.[34] One proposal in the United States calls for taxes of $30 per ton of carbon, and some analyses have suggested still higher taxes to hold U.S. emissions at 1990 levels. The extent to which a carbon tax would affect economic growth is a controversial question. Virtually all studies suggest that if the revenues were used to lower other taxes, a carbon tax could promote, rather than hinder, economic growth.[35] However, if imposed unilaterally, this kind of tax could alter a nation's economic competitiveness so that international cooperation may be required for such a policy to be implemented.

Taxes have been used or are being considered for many environmental purposes, among them reducing various forms of pollution, municipal solid waste, and congestion on urban highways, as well as encouraging recycling of materials. If such taxes were revenue neutral (revenues used to reduce other taxes), they could encourage both environmental protection and economic growth by shifting the tax burden away from more desirable economic activities, such as work (income taxes), employment (social security taxes), savings, and investment.[36]

Removing Subsidies That Encourage Unsustainable Use

Production of natural resource–related commodities is often subsidized in both industrialized and developing countries. Water supplied by public agencies for irrigation in the United States, for example, is 85 to 90 percent subsidized, on average.[37] The practice is widespread: the United States also subsidizes timber production and cattle grazing on public lands, Canada subsidizes hydroelectricity and timber production, and Germany subsidizes the production of coal. Such countries as Indonesia, the Philippines, and Papua New Guinea support timber production, in effect, by failing to charge concession holders an adequate royalty. India subsidizes irrigation water and electricity production.

Russia and most Central and Eastern European countries support energy production. Agriculture is also subsidized in many countries, for example through price supports in the United States and Europe and pesticide subsidies in the Philippines.[38]

Such subsidies encourage wasteful use of resources, often creating or exacerbating environmental problems. This is the result that underpricing energy has had throughout the former Soviet Union. Salinization from overirrigation is a major cause of land degradation in India and in some areas of the United States. Heavy use of coal in Germany has been a major contributor to air pollution and acid rain.

Eliminating or reducing such subsidies would confer both economic and environmental advantages and, just as with environmental taxes, send more appropriate price signals to businesses and consumers alike. It would reduce waste and pollution and ensure more efficient consumption of natural resources. It would free up fiscal resources that could be used to upgrade production and reduce pollution, diversify the economy, alleviate poverty, or support development in other ways. Of course, the elimination of subsidies, by weeding out inefficient or marginal enterprises, could raise unemployment. In developing countries, it could also have a serious impact on the livelihood of the poor. What is called for is the careful targeting of subsidies where they are most needed.

Measuring Consumption Costs Accurately

Accounting schemes that more accurately measure the environmental costs of economic activity at all levels could also help increase the efficiency of natural resource use and reduce related environmental impacts. For example, adjusting national accounts to include the costs of natural resource depletion or degradation might lead to more appropriate policies and resource management strategies.[39] At the level of the individual company, full-cost accounting would make management aware of the environmental cost of pollution and raw material use and encourage more responsible behavior. Frank Popoff, the chairman and chief executive officer of Dow Chemical Company, has called for industry to voluntarily adopt full-cost accounting in its own operations, suggesting that this could be the most important step down the path to sustainable development.[40] More widespread information about the environmental implications of individual consumption patterns might prove effective in reducing wasteful consumption, especially among the most wealthy segments of industrial society, and in encouraging the adoption of more sustainable lifestyles.

Development That Can Reduce Poverty

Much has been written about policies that could significantly aid development in the South, particularly the alleviation of poverty.[41] These include targeting human-capital investments in health care and education for the poorest segments of society, adopting legal reforms to extend land tenure and other rights to the rural poor and to legitimize the informal economies among the urban poor, and enhancing the status of women while increasing their participation in development.

More general efforts could be made to encourage economic growth and provide employment in developing countries. One possible—and highly controversial—policy lever is to reduce trade barriers in industrialized countries for goods imported from developing countries. This would likely increase Northern consumption of natural resources from the South, it might exacerbate local environmental problems in the South, and it would have an economic and social impact in the North. Yet such a policy could also powerfully stimulate development and reduce the overall environmental consequences of present consumption patterns in both North and South.

Japan, the United States, and the industrialized countries of Europe maintain barriers against most agricultural imports and significant subsidies for their own agricultural exports. These protectionist policies support a system of high-input, intensive agriculture that has major environmental and developmental impacts. The problems include pesticide and fertilizer runoff (a major source of water pollution), excessive soil erosion, and loss of biological diversity.

Agricultural protectionism imposes a heavy price on both industrial and developing countries. Within the OECD, for example, it costs domestic consumers and taxpayers an estimated $150 billion annually, more than double what farmers in OECD countries gain.[42] Trade barriers prevent market development and job creation among low-cost producers, perpetuating poverty, subsistence agriculture, and their environmental effects in developing countries. Lower world food prices also depress export income in developing countries and elsewhere, inhibiting needed investment in domestic agriculture.

Removal or substantial reduction of such protection would expand agricultural trade. Global liberalization of trade could increase income in developing countries by as much as $60 billion per year, reducing poverty and natural resource degradation.[43] Often the poorest segments in the developing world have not benefited from expanded agricultural trade; efforts must be made to ensure that in the future they do. There must also be a means of ensuring that expanded export production in the South is sustainable and does not simply transfer environmental problems from North to South. For example, pesticides are not yet as heavily used in developing as in industrial countries, but they are often applied in the South without adequate consideration of their effect on human health.

The Multi-Fibre Agreement and other trade barriers restrict imports of textiles, clothing, footwear, and other relatively labor-intensive products from developing countries that are low-cost producers and thus have a comparative advantage in the world market. These, like agricultural trade barriers, have the effect of lowering income in developing countries and raising consumer prices in industrialized countries. In the 1980s, for example, U.S. consumers paid about $18 billion per year in excess cost just for clothing and textiles.[44] Removing such trade barriers could increase employment, promote economic diversification in developing countries, and lower consumer costs in industrialized countries. It would require efforts to offset employment dislocation in the North and potential additional environmental problems in the South.

International Agreements

Regulation is still an essential policy mechanism for controlling pollution and other forms of environmental degradation in virtually every country. In dealing with global environmental problems, however, international agreements that harmonize approaches and ensure joint action play a critical role. The Vienna Convention and the subsequent Montreal Protocol on Substances That Deplete the Ozone Layer— which, as amended, required industrial countries to phase out production of chlorofluorocarbons (CFCs) by 1996—serve as successful prototypes of such agreements. Global CFC emissions are already beginning to decline. The global climate and biodiversity conventions signed in 1992, just coming into force, still require implementing agreements. Agreements will not be easy to achieve and enforce, but they have the potential to alter unsustainable patterns of natural resource consumption, restraining growth in fossil fuel consumption, for example, or channeling use of renewable resources into more sustainable patterns.

Additional international agreements or novel institutional arrangements may be needed to facilitate access to new technologies. At present, most technology development occurs in the North, increasingly in the private sector. Yet greater and more rapid access to technology, as well as policies that encourage development of new technology, are critical to enabling both the South and the North to make more efficient use of natural resources.[45]

Other kinds of international agreements can be used to protect natural resource commodities or to promote more sustainable production methods. One recent example is the international ban on trade in ivory, which has reduced the slaughter of elephants while causing some difficulty for countries that already manage their elephant herds sustainably. Proposals to reduce or halt consumption of other endangered commodities, such as tropical hardwoods, have also been proposed.

Conclusion

The world now faces a unique set of challenges related to sustainable resource use. On the one hand, it must find the means to foster development that interrupts the vicious cycle of poverty, population growth, and renewable resource degradation seen in many developing countries. On the other hand, it must also gather the will to alter unsustainable and environmentally damaging patterns of consumption in all countries, but especially industrial ones, which collectively have a huge impact on the global environment. Policy options exist for reducing pollution, for preventing the exhaustion of resources, and for shifting resource consumption to more sustainable patterns. Getting such policies accepted and implemented will not be easy, but these actions are nonetheless essential for achieving a sustainable future.

Notes

This essay is adapted from Allen L. Hammond et al., "Natural Resource Consumption," in *World Resources 1994–95* (New York and Oxford: Oxford University Press, 1994), 3–26 and is based on work by the author and by Lawrence Klein of the University of Pennsylvania and Kirit and Jyoti Parikh of the Indira Gandhi Institute of Development Research in Bombay.

1. Jyoti Parikh et al., "Consumption Patterns: The Driving Force of Environmental Stress," Indira Gandhi Institute of Development Research Discussion Paper No. 59 (Bombay: Indira Gandhi Institute of Development Research, 1991), 1–3.
2. World Resources Institute in collaboration with the United Nations Environment Programme and the United Nations Development Programme, *World Resources 1992–93* (New York: Oxford University Press, 1992), 206.
3. U. Hoffmann and D. Zivkovic, "Demand Growth for Industrial Raw Materials and its Determinants: An Analysis for the Period 1965–1988," United Nations Conference on Trade and Development Discussion Paper No. 50, Geneva, 1992, 33–43.
4. J. T. Houghton, G. J. Jenkins, and J. J. Ephraums, eds., *Climate Change:*

The IPCC Scientific Assessment (Cambridge: Cambridge University Press, 1990), appendix I.

5. S. Manabe and R. J. Stouffer, "Century-Scale Effects of Increased Atmospheric CO_2 on the Ocean-Atmosphere System," *Nature* 364, no. 6434 (1993): 215–17.

6. J. T. Thom, "Deforestation and Desertification in Twentieth-Century Arid Sahelien Africa," and C. L. Goucher, "The Impact of German Colonial Rule on the Forests of Togo," in *World Deforestation in the Twentieth Century*, ed. John Richards and Richard Tucker (Durham, N.C.: Duke University Press, 1988), 61–66 and 73–75; Madhav Gadgil and Ramachandra Guha, *This Fissured Land: An Ecological History of India* (Delhi: Oxford University Press, 1992), 113–214; Peter B. Evans, *Dependent Development: The Alliance of Multinational, State, and Local Capital in Brazil* (Princeton, N.J.: Princeton University Press, 1979), 55–83; Stephen D. Krasner, *Defending the National Interest: Raw Materials Investments and U.S. Foreign Policy* (Princeton, N.J.: Princeton University Press, 1978), 155–177; and Philip Hurst, *Rainforest Politics: Ecological Destruction in South-East Asia* (London: Zed Books, 1990), 245–51.

7. *The National Gardening Survey* (Burlington, Vt.: The National Gardening Association, June 1993), 27; and U.S. Environmental Protection Agency (EPA), *Lawn Care Pesticides White Paper* (Washington, D.C.: EPA, February 1993), 1–2.

8. Andrew Pollack, "Sega Takes Aim at Disney's World," *New York Times*, 4 July 1993, F6.

9. World Resources Institute (WRI), *World Resources Database* on diskette (Washington, D.C.: World Resources Institute, 1992).

10. George Miller, president, Mining Association of Canada, Ottawa, 1993 (personal communication).

11. *World Resources 1994–95* (New York: Oxford University Press, 1994), table 15.4.

12. United Nations Environment Programme and the World Health Organization, *Urban Air Pollution in Megacities of the World* (Oxford: Blackwell, 1992), 45.

13. World Bank, *World Development Report, 1992* (New York: Oxford University Press, 1992), 47.

14. World Bank, *World Development Report, 1992*, 45–46 and 48.

15. United Nations Environment Programme and the World Health Organization, *Urban Air Pollution in Megacities of the World*, 111–17.

16. United Nations Environment Programme and the World Health Organization, *Urban Air Pollution in Megacities of the World*, 111–17.

17. Paul Kennedy, *Preparing for the Twenty-First Century* (New York: Random House, 1993), 65–81.

18. W. V. Reid, "How Many Species Will There Be?" in *Tropical Deforestation and Species Extinction,* ed. Timothy Whitmore and Jeffrey Sayer (New York and London: Chapman and Hall, 1992), 63.

19. P. H. Raven, "Biological Resources and Global Stability," in *Evolution and Coadaptation in Biotic Communities,* ed. S. Kawano, J. H. Connell, and T. Hidaka (Toyko: University of Tokyo Press, 1988), 17–18.

20. Food and Agriculture Organization (FAO) of the United Nations, *Forest Resources Assessment, 1990: Tropical Countries* (Rome: FAO, 1993), ix.

21. The following sections feature quantitative global estimates of where a number of resources originate and where they are initially used (primary consumption). The analysis does not take into account value-added manufacture, export, and final consumption of goods and services containing natural resources in countries other than those where primary consumption occurs. The estimates may thus under- or overstate true consumption. Consumption and production data are presented as five-year averages in weight units. For this discussion, the industrialized world refers to OECD countries. All other countries, including China, are considered developing countries, except for the formerly centrally-planned or transition countries of Eastern Europe and the former Soviet Union.

22. H. Linneman et al., *Preliminary Conditions for International Commodity-Related Environmental Agreements* (research project on international commodity-related agreements) (Amsterdam: Free University, 1993), 77–80.

23. *World Resources 1994–95*, table 21.2.

24. FAO, *Agrostat PC* (Rome: FAO, 1993); "Malaysian Log Ban Could Reduce Japanese Imports," *Jakarta Post*, 14 May 1993, 8; and, FAO, *FAO Yearbook: Forest Products, 1991* (Rome: FAO, 1993), 3 and 9.

25. M. Bhagavan, "The Woodfuel Crisis in the SADCC Countries," *Ambio* 13, no. 1 (1984): 25.

26. K. D. Singh, "The 1990 Tropical Forest Resources Assessment," *Unasylva* 44, no. 174 (1993): 18.

27. EPA, *Characterization of Municipal Solid Waste in the United States: 1990 Update* (Washington, D.C.: EPA, 1990), 12.

28. World Resources Institute calculations.

29. Donald G. Rogich, "United States and Global Material Use Patterns," paper presented at the ASM International Conference on Materials and Global Environment, Washington, D.C., September 1993.

30. U.S. Bureau of Mines, "Minerals and the Economy," *Minerals Today* (April 1993): 14–18.

31. U.S. Bureau of Mines, "Minerals and the Economy," 14–18.

32. National Sample Survey Organization, *Sarvekshana: Journal of the National Sample Survey Organization* (New Delhi: Government of India Department of Statistics, April–June 1990).

33. National Sample Survey Organization, *Sarvekshana*.

34. Roger C. Dower and Mary Beth Zimmerman, *The Right Climate for Carbon Taxes: Creating Economic Incentives to Protect the Atmosphere* (Washington, D.C.: World Resources Institute, 1992).

35. Robert Repetto et al., *Green Fees: How a Tax Shift Can Work for the Environment and the Economy* (Washington, D.C.: World Resources Institute, 1992), 57–58, 60–61, and 69.

36. Repetto et al., *Green Fees*, 71 and 83–84.

37. Robert Repetto, *Skimming the Water: Rent-Seeking and the Performance of Public Irrigation Systems* (Washington, D.C.: World Resources Institute, 1986), 15.

38. Paul Faeth, ed., *Agricultural Policy and Sustainability: Case Studies from India, Chile, the Philippines, and the United States* (Washington, D.C.: World Resources Institute, 1993), 8–10.

39. Robert Repetto et al., *Wasting Assets: Natural Resources in the National Income Accounts* (Washington, D.C.: World Resources Institute, 1989), v and 6–11.

40. Frank Popoff and David T. Buzzelli, "Full-Cost Accounting," *Chemical and Engineering News* 71, no. 2 (11 January 1993): 8.

41. United Nations Development Programme, *Human Development Report, 1992* (New York: Oxford University Press, 1993), 7–8; and World Bank, *World Development Report, 1990* (New York: Oxford University Press, 1990), 4.

42. David Blandford, "The Costs of Agricultural Protection and the Difference Free Trade Would Make," in *Agricultural Protectionism in the Industrialized World*, ed. Fred H. Sanderson (Washington, D.C.: Resources for the Future, 1990), 407–09.

43. A. Salazar, P. Brandao, and W. Martin, "Implications of Agricultural Trade Liberalization for the Developing Countries," World Bank Policy Research Working Papers (Washington, D.C.: World Bank, 1993), 22 and 38.

44. World Bank, *World Development Report, 1987* (New York: Oxford University Press, 1987), 151.

45. George Heaton, Robert Repetto, and Rodney Sobin, *Transforming Technology: An Agenda for Environmentally Sustainable Growth in the 21st Century* (Washington, D.C.: World Resources Institute, 1991).

24

Consumption and Population

Nathan Keyfitz

It is easier to be loyal to a club than to the planet; the bylaws are shorter and one is personally acquainted with the members.

—Attributed to E.B. White

Humanity, a local species of minor consequence as little as ten thousand years ago when it included fewer than 10 million individuals, has spread over all parts of the planet, which it now dominates. Beginning with a position in the web of life not very different from that of other primates, its spread and achievement were made possible by the collective intelligence and knowledge that we call culture and by cooperative habits of work. Tools and technology have always been an important part of culture, but in the second half of this century technology seems to have taken a sudden jump forward. The dizzying rate of technological change in the past decades has confused our wisest minds so that forecasting what life will be like is impossible and every kind of social planning is in disarray.

The planet is being drastically modified to provide for more people and so that a larger fraction of them can live in the style we know as middle class. In order to make room for present and prospective numbers of people and to accommodate our modern high-consumption style of life, we have to modify or destroy the works of nature. Will we always be able to replace nature by works of humans that do the same job better?

On the path of population growth and consumption we are following we have to trust the parallel development of science. But every application of science has side effects; can we be sure that science will always be able to solve the problems resulting from its own creations? Leaving matters to nature cannot provide for the dense high-living society of the

476

future; most of us would starve today without modern arrangements of the planet. Does it matter that we turn the countryside over to corporate farming and live artificial lives in large crowded cities?

Like others, I cannot answer these questions. This essay is designed to provide at least some of the data and identify some of the relevant considerations. We start with a discussion of population and examine the prospects for its further increase.

Population

Population Numbers

According to the World Population Clock maintained by the U.S. Bureau of the Census, the total projected population of the world at the moment this essay is being written (2:30:51 PM EDT on 26 June 1997) is 5,850,602,392 persons.[1]

Compare the current total of 5.9 billion with the 1950 total of 2.5 billion. The 5-billion mark was passed in the late 1980s, so that there was a doubling over about forty years. With much less accuracy, various sources estimate a total population of about 10 billion, say plus or minus 2 billion, by the middle of the twenty-first century.

We are told also that the world population is now going up by about 6.6 million per month; which is about the same as the current population of New York City. In the last year there were 133 million births and 54 million deaths—a 79 million net increase.[2]

Fertility

The population of the world's largest country, China, was estimated at 1.2 billion in 1995. But its growth is slowing; table 24.1 shows percent increases from 1960 to 1990 and gives some forecasts for the twenty-first century. The rate of population growth declined steadily up

Table 24.1. Net Annual Increase in Population as Percent of Population for Mainland China

		Forecast:	
1960–1970	2.3	1990–2000	1.0
1970–1980	1.8	2040–2050	−0.3
1980–1990	1.4		

to 1990, and it is expected that this decline in rates will continue until there is an actual decline in total population at a level of about 1.5 billion people. Because the population has a young age distribution resulting from the high level of fertility in the past, mere replacement fertility, 2.1 children per woman, would not help reduce the rate of annual increase in population. So China persists in its draconian campaign for one-child families.

France, in contrast, is one of the few countries that has energetically resisted the downward trend in birth rates, as shown in table 24.2. France is a rich industrial country that has been devoting a substantial part of its national budget to family allowances and other means of raising the birthrate; China is a poor industrializing country, conscious of its poverty and the weight of its large population, doing its utmost to reduce its birthrate. Despite sharply contrasting cultures and policies, they have in common the downward trend in their rates of population increase: down somewhat over half in thirty years (estimated to the end of the century)—China drops from 2.3 percent per year to 1.0; France from 1.1 percent per year to 0.4. The largest part of the decrease in population growth is due to declining birthrates. Such figures suggest that a decline in the birthrate is inevitable, whether aided by or in spite of governmental effort.

Does this make concerted official and unofficial efforts to limit population superfluous? By no means. But the most effective policies are those that stimulate the growth and distribution of income, the spread of education, especially among women, and improvement in health. France has (unintentionally) brought its birthrate down by just such measures, pursued for their own sake. These measures are most effective when they are combined with the availability of contraceptives and information on their use.

But we also know that a high birthrate and rapidly increasing population make development harder. For one thing, capital is required to equip the additional people up to the level of those already present, and that reduces the capital available for innovation.[3] Hence, it is more than

Table 24.2. Net Annual Increase in Population as Percent of Population for France

		Forecast	
1960–1970	1.1	1990–2000	0.4
1970–1980	0.6	2040-2050	-0.6
1980–1990	0.5		

possible that if the situation were left to itself a high birthrate could delay the development that would control the birthrate. That is why it is dangerous to refrain from intervention by the standard measures of population control ranging from education to the provision of contraceptives. Of all the continents, Africa is the one to which this statement most clearly applies.

The Transience of Differential Fertility

When I started studying demographics there was a differential fertility proposition that went something like this: The urban, the wealthier, and the better-educated parts of a population bear fewer children than the rural, the poor, and the less-educated. The belief was that this differential was a permanent demographic feature of all societies. The few cases (including traditional China) where the rich had more children than the poor were classified as anomalies. No feature of social life seemed to be more firmly established than this. Interpreting the difference in intelligence test scores between rich and poor as a matter of genetics justified the argument that the genetic quality of the human race was deteriorating as a result of differential fertility.

One aspect of this hereditarian view that was not appreciated was the possibility that differential fertility was a passing feature that would stop or even be inverted once the whole country became essentially urban, well off, and educated. A transitory cross-sectional appearance could have been mistakenly taken as a longitudinal process persisting through time. One cannot be certain of this yet, but current data show that the differentials—between the urban, educated rich and the rural, uneducated poor—have sharply diminished. Birth control is used in all income groups. The traditional agricultural life encouraged many children, but present-day corporate farming does not. The corporate farm is operated not by the owner and his family but by a salaried manager who hires wage labor. The owner-operator needed sons to help him run the farm and to take over when he could no longer do the work himself; for the wage earner, children are an expense with little economic benefit. Today, city and country dwellers are hardly distinguishable in their ways of life. Formal education, at least up to secondary school graduation, is becoming a universal qualification for practically any job and part of the spreading middle-class way of life that I discuss later. Education, especially of women, lowers the birthrate everywhere.

A similar relation of cross-sectional to longitudinal forms applies to the world as a whole, among countries as within countries. Every country's population expands with modernization and runs through a growth cycle in which its population multiplies something like threefold, after which it stabilizes. It is in the rich, educated, and urban classes that the process begins. The more developed countries (MDCs) have followed such a pattern; don't the less developed countries (LDCs) have the right to expand first and then stabilize as well? This point reappears in the discussion of fairness below.

Mortality

Mortality has fallen steadily in most of the industrial countries, where life expectancy has increased by one or two years each decade. This is the mortality history of at least the past half-century or longer. Life expectancies in the more developed regions increased from 66.0 years in 1950–55 to 73.7 in 1985–90; in that time life expectancies in the less-developed regions rose nearly three times as fast, from 40.7 to 60.7 years. The increase in life expectancy in China was exceptional, from 40.8 to 69.4 years over the same period. This spectacular increase in the average life span of its vast population was due to the application of basic medicine by barefoot doctors with six months of training, using inoculations and antibiotics, as well as to the availability of more or less adequate diet for the whole population, at least in famine-free years. With these rudimentary measures it came close to catching up with the advanced countries by 1960.

But there is a limit to what can be achieved with standard medicine or even through a broader approach to influence behavior, such as exercise, smoking, alcohol, and diet. In 1964, the Surgeon General's Report showed that smoking caused not only lung cancer but also heart disease and other ailments. During less than a single generation, as the scientific findings were disseminated, smoking changed from a virtually universal male custom to the addiction of a minority. In the 1960s, noting that female longevity had come to exceed that of males by about five years, several scholars attributed the difference to smoking; now, with male smoking diminished and female increased, the difference has risen to almost eight years. That embarrassing outcome now leads to the conclusion that the change in smoking habits, and hence the effect of the anti-smoking campaign, was limited. The difference is biological: the female is the stronger sex!

Only recently have demographers started to think of a mortality-caused decline in population. Current Russian statistics show a concrete case of such a decline; life expectancy dropped two years during 1993 and another six years in 1994, and 1995 is expected to show an even further decline. Eberstadt shows that deterioration of the medical system in the former Soviet Union has occurred, but it cannot be the sole cause of this rise in mortality.[4] That is demonstrated by examining age incidence of the new high mortality, which is greatest for twenty- to fifty-year-old men, just the ages at which men make least use of hospitals and doctors. Analysis of the change by cause shows a rise in cardiovascular disease, alcoholism, and violent death through suicide and murder.

Can we in the West now take for granted the indefinite increase in life span of recent generations? Or, is the increase in Russian mortality a warning of what can happen in industrial society generally? The causes operating in Russia are not a likely danger for us, but other causes do affect us, arising out of our inextricable involvement with the biological processes of the planet and the way we are disturbing them.

While I cannot explore these questions fully here, there are some grim signs. The *New York Times* carried a report of the city's Department of Health showing a rise in mortality for men.[5] Life expectancy for New York men was 40.6 years at the beginning of the twentieth century, rose steadily and reached 68.5 in 1980, and then fell back to 68.0 in 1990. For women the rise continues, to 77.2 years in 1990. AIDS was important in the decline for men but not the entire cause.

Population Fairness

An ethical formulation of the population question might be "How much right to space on the planet do different countries have?" Or, if we may group countries, how much space for the LDCs versus the MDCs?

At the outset of UN calculations in 1950, the LDCs had double the population of the MDCs; at the present time they have about three times the population, and by 2020 they are expected to have more than four and one half times as many people as the MDCs. Going a little further on the same path, we can say that by 2050 the world population will be in the neighborhood of 10 billion, and the ratio of the population of the LDCs to that of the MDCs will be something like 5. The ratio will have multiplied by two and one-half since 1950. That promises to be the net distributional outcome of the fastest hundred years of expansion in world population history.

Many conclude from table 24.3 that the populations of Africa, Asia, and Latin America—the LDCs—are increasing beyond all bounds. But the information shown in table 24.3 is only a small slice of world history.

Something quite different appears when we take a thicker slice—not 100 years but 250. The six estimates of world population for 1800 show a range from 890 to 954 million—call the total at that time 925 million.[6] Then the increase over the 250 years from 1800 to 2050 will have been

**Table 24.3. Percent of World Population of the More Developed Countries
(MDC) and the Less Developed Countries (LDC), 1950–2020 (millions of persons)**

Year	Population	% LDC	% MDC	LDC/MDC
1950	2515	66.93	33.07	2.02
1960	3018	68.70	31.30	2.19
1970	3693	71.64	28.36	2.53
1980	4449	74.45	25.55	2.91
1990	5246	76.94	23.06	3.34
2000	6121	79.15	20.85	3.80
2010	6989	80.95	19.05	4.25
2020	7822	82.40	17.60	4.68

Source: Data from *World Demographic Estimates and Projections,* 1950–2025
(New York: United Nations, 1990).

from 925 million to about 10,000 million, that is, more than tenfold.
But for the first 150 years, the fastest increase was in the MDCs; their
response to the industrial revolution was a rapid increase in population.
From this long-time perspective there is nothing surprising in the present increase. What is disturbing is the large population from which the
new industrial revolution increase is taking off.

The demographic transition is the name given by Frank Notestein and
Kingsley Davis to the change from the pre-industrial high birth and
death rates to the low birth and death rates that followed the industrial
revolution.[7] It clearly is related to education and income, both of which
increased over that interval. Within an industrializing country it is the
upper class, then the middle class, and last the poor whose birthrate
declines. This differential fertility can be assimilated to the same set of
causes—whatever they are—that trigger the demographic transition in
whole countries. The point is that both are transient.

Globalization and Consumption Alternatives

High Tech Versus Mass Employment

A large population, with heavy unemployment both overt and dis-
guised, presents development policy with special problems. Rightly
seen, that population is the nation's most important asset. Each day of
delay in putting it to work is an irretrievable national loss.

The funds that governments receive in foreign aid, and those they handle through their control of the sale of raw materials, which are often used for the construction of high-tech factories, ought instead to be used to upgrade the technology of the village—better plows, better seed—and its infrastructure, especially roads, along with simple rural industry. Among many other benefits this will tend to keep people in the countryside. This has been understood all along in the more progressive LDCs.

Harry Tatsumi Oshima points out that Japan stressed agriculture when it was digging itself out of the ruins of World War II.[8] It had little capital, and that capital was too precious to spend on large factories; it was used to put the whole population to work. And with small capital the only thing most of the unemployed could do was grow food. Ultimately the food surplus they produced could support people in industry, and so development could take place. Adam Smith, Arthur Lewis, and many others recommended this as the path to be followed by the presently rich countries starting in the late eighteenth century.[9]

That may seem obvious enough, and yet the political dynamics of many countries give weight to a policy exactly the opposite. Indonesia's experts and its influential elite believe that putting up an aircraft factory will diffuse technology in aircraft and other industries. After all, look at the most advanced countries; what do you actually see there? High-tech factories, large cities, skyscrapers, modern factories with labor-saving equipment. Indonesia seems to think that going to "high tech" immediately will allow it to circumvent the hard work and misery of the original industrial revolution.

Unfortunately the number of people hired in such plants is infinitesimal in relation to the masses seeking work, and the continuing unemployment, besides being a threat to social stability, means not using the LDC's main asset, its surplus of labor. Thus whatever capital the government owns or can borrow should be used for building infrastructure that will facilitate employment, even if at the start this is necessarily at lower levels of productivity. So much for the classical theory of development, as interpreted by Oshima. Such a theory makes sense to a demographer trying to see how large unequipped populations can maintain themselves and produce maximum value for the community and greater well-being for more individuals and families.

But a new element has entered in recent years: the existence of large amounts of mobile capital seeking to maximize returns. Absentee capital cannot profitably invest in peasant farming because it is too difficult to collect the returns from thousands of small peasants. On the other hand, why shouldn't a factory in the United States, Japan, or Germany have the labor-intensive parts of a job performed in Mexico or Taiwan? Ship out the parts made by highly automated methods in the high-wage country and ship back the completed product. Boeing has subassemblies of its planes put together abroad, with something approaching half of the value of the plane being added by foreign labor. One manufacturer of a well-known brand of ladies' pyjamas has them entirely made by contract in China.

The effects of this new mobility of capital are varied. In the developed country the designer and manager, not to mention the shareholder, enjoy higher salaries and dividends; the customers who buy the product pay less for it; but the ordinary workers find themselves in competition with workers in low-wage countries. Governments of the LDCs like such investment because it provides foreign exchange and a larger tax base; workers in the plant do have jobs, but often under sweatshop conditions that would be illegal in the MDC. Briefly, it is immensely beneficial to managers and owners in the MDC and to labor in the LDC.

This global market has the effect of pushing wage levels for comparable jobs in the MDCs and the LDCs closer to one another. Since it has never been tried on such a scale before, we cannot be sure how strong the industry that it builds is. The former Soviet Union, Eastern Europe, and the LDCs all want such investment: it provides employment, inducts their workforce into factory discipline and gives them skills, trains local foremen and managers, and strengthens the foreign exchange position. There could be a shakedown as the LDCs compete for such investment, with the inevitable winners and losers. Some fear that such development is fragile, but it is reasonable to hope that when the flow of foreign investment slows down local sources will finance and lead the development process.

Globalization and Social and Ecological Problems

Most governments now recognize their responsibility for the environment, at least in principle. Of course their action depends on their being pushed by their citizens, as in a democracy it ought so to depend. Austrians push their government for a high level of environmental protection; when their government planned and built a nuclear plant the public uproar would not be satisfied without a referendum, and the referendum rejected the plant. The reactor was located at Hainburg, which is on the border with Slovakia, so that only half of the possible radioactive waste would fall on Austria, but that did not save it. The multibillion-schilling investment is idle to this day.

Americans also demand protection, though much less insistently. We are a tolerant people—old newspapers and other trash on the streets, weed-filled vacant lots, and smoke in the air do not disturb us overmuch. Nonetheless, few like to think of the damage our industries would do without the Environmental Protection Agency to hold them in check. Yet we cannot be sure that such protection will be maintained at present levels in the future. Taxes that would pay for environmental, as for social, protection are a handicap to competition in external markets, so the lower we make our taxes the better for our exports, the value of our dollar in foreign exchange markets, and the retention of our financial capital and our manufacturing plant. Producers can threaten to move their facilities abroad or actually move them. Taxes have to be kept low especially on the rich, who otherwise would move their capital to countries where it can secure a higher after-tax return. It would not pay to move for one burden alone, but if environmental protection is added to high taxes and minimum wages, then economic calculation sooner or later values the cost of moving at less than it values the burdens. In the end competition leads to a race to the bottom in respect to any kind of governmental regulation.

To summarize: with globalization the external force that guides and pushes governments is much less the identifiable transnational corporations, which it used to be fashionable to castigate, than a giant machine operated by numerous investors, whose motives are neither vicious nor benign, who merely seek to maximize their returns. Just as they are little moved by sentiments of national patriotism, so they take little account of the planetary ecosphere. The vast size of mutual funds and pension funds, plus the ability of financial operators to respond with the speed of a computer, makes any government stop and think before acting in a way that threatens the profits earned by its producers.

The global economic machine provides its enormous benefits in a competitive process in which the contenders cannot afford to pay attention to the impact of their production processes or of their products on the biosphere. They cannot afford to consider the comfort of their workers beyond what will directly contribute to output. For example, Shell Oil feels that it cannot afford to give up a profitable franchise, or otherwise to take account of the way its activities benefit and strengthen a cruel dictatorship that tramples on the human rights of Nigerians.

We have been treated to a flood of efforts to downsize government, to make it smaller by eliminating entire departments, supported with arguments about the ineffectiveness of government. Without government we will supposedly have a leaner, more efficient economy; but that, as the polls show, frightens the majority of citizens. It even frightens a more humane economist; Paul Samuelson speaks on television of the "ruthless economy" that is now taking us over.

But I submit that in a grim way, and taking account of globalization, the proponents of smaller government are right. If government is no longer able to provide welfare payments, protect the environment, set minimum wages, ensure decent working conditions, and take redistributive measures that will divide incomes more equitably than the market can do, then it might as well be reduced in size. For those who want social and environmental action even at some cost in growth the answer must be some way of controlling globalization. The trade-off is between more goods and stronger social measures, and for the moment the goods have it.

It is indeed often the case that environmental regulation does improve productivity, that longer annual vacations improve morale and so output, but it is too much to hope that a satisfactory level of protection will be obtained solely by entrepreneurial action, as Karl Polanyi says.[10] Some regulation, whether governmental or trade union, is needed.

There are efficient and inefficient ways of regulating air and other pollution. The inefficient ways include setting an upper limit on the pollution any plant can produce, allowing coal to be burned only five days a week, or banning all use of soft coal. The efficient way is to allow all polluting activities provided they are paid for at a suitable price. The price can be set to allow whatever degree of such activity in total is considered tolerable; one way of implementing this is to issue and then auction tradable permits totaling that amount. This would ensure that whatever pollution occurred was done by those enterprises that could make the most effective use of it. An appropriate way to use the money so collected would be to apply it to mitigate of the effects of the pollution that does occur.

The Expanding Middle Class

The condition of an economy, its rate of development, is usually measured by gross domestic product (GDP), which is a precise way of expressing the total of goods and services produced. But this is not the way that development comes to people. In their more concrete perception, development is progressing from walking to traveling by bicycle to traveling by car. In the transitions between these stages money is only an instrument; development is moving up the steps toward what can be called, for brevity, the middle-class lifestyle. This lifestyle consists, for example, of more and better food and the acquisition of artifacts such as radios, television sets, indoor toilets, refrigerators, and automobiles.

Imperfections in the GDP per capita as a measure of welfare—its lack of any clear relation to the environment, the difficulty of calculating its distribution, its awkwardness in incorporating consumption that does not pass through the market—encourages experimenting with a count of the middle class as an alternative measure of how well off a country is.

Not only is money an instrument to acquire goods but also the goods themselves are instruments to change people—to increase their capabilities and their freedoms. People want money and goods so that they can have good health, be informed, have friends and social involvement, and enjoy nature. Harvard economist Amartya Sen has broken through to this ultimate objective of economic growth.[11] And making it explicit brings out that at least some of the goods we choose are misdirected.

My discussion here is narrower, dealing only with the increasingly worldwide demand for a certain package of goods. I make no assertion that this middle-class package makes people happy or that it is the best thing for them, but I do assert that it is spreading rapidly and that it has an effect on the environment. It cannot be estimated with anything like the accuracy of GDP, but that is no argument for using GDP in circumstances where it is inappropriate.

The automobile seems to be the most characteristic artifact of the middle-class lifestyle. It distinguishes the middle-class Indian from the poor one who moves in a bullock cart. The Indian who has a car is also likely to travel by plane from time to time, have a solid (pukka) house rather than a thatch and bamboo cabin, and have contact outside the village or neighborhood by telephone, radio, and television. The automobile is the best single indicator I have come across of the way people live. Life expectancy is probably a better indicator of welfare; in this section I am speaking not of welfare but of consumption, a very different matter.

Table 24.4 shows the increase in numbers of motor vehicles in seven countries. The United States numbers rise at a low rate and almost in a straight line, the mark of a population saturated with motor cars and requiring only replacement. By 1980 it had 135 million registered vehicles for a population of 227 million, about 1.7 persons per vehicle. The latecomers among the industrial countries, Japan and Italy, rose the fastest. There are some doubts about the comparability of the numbers among countries and years not shown in my condensation of the table in the *Statistical Abstracts*. But one can accept broadly the net conclusion: for the thirty-two countries listed in the original table, the annual percent increase was 6.1. The pace continues through the early 1990s, when the half-billion mark was passed.

Looked at ecologically, it is middle-class methods of travel that have the greatest impact, followed by their dietary customs, homes, and living arrangements, with smaller impact for clothing and entertainment other than travel.

Ownership of three artifacts is compared in table 24.5. Automobiles

Table 24.4. Motor Vehicles in thousands in Use in Seven Industrialized Countries, Each Having at Least 100,000 in 1960

Country	1958	1968	1977	Avg. Annual % Increase 1958–1977
United States	68,300	99,563	135,155	3.6
Canada	3,573	7,747	11,333	6.3
France	5,976	14,048	19,340	6.4
W. Germany	3,914	12,222	21,410	9.4
Italy	848	8,968	17,607	17.3
Japan	766	12,430	31,379	21.6
United Kingdom	5,915	12,670	16,460	5.5

Source: Data from *Statistical Abstracts of the United States* (Washington, D.C.: Government Printing Office). Data for 1958 from 1960 edition; data for 1968 from 1970 edition; data for 1977 from 1980 edition.

Table 24.5. Absolute Number of Three Artifacts (in hundred thousands) in 32 Industrialized Countries Over a 20-Year Period of Time from About 1960 to About 1980, and Average Annual Percentage Increase between Those Dates

Artifact	1960	1980	% increase
Automobiles	102	316	6.1
Televisions	73	295	9.8
Telephones	116	382	6.5

show the slowest growth at a little over 6 percent. A more or less fixed percentage increase corresponds to an accelerating absolute increase, and what counts for the ecology of the planet is not percentages of increase but absolute amounts, although such percentages grow 2 or 3 times faster than GDP per capita.

For none of the fifteen MDCs listed by the *Economist* for 1995 is the increase in GDP as high as 4 percent, and among twenty-five LDCs listed, thirteen are higher than 5 percent—the median for the LDCs is about 5 percent.[12] Bear in mind that it is the total GDP that the *Economist* publishes—individual welfare for the LDCs would require a deduction of about 1–3 percent to allow for population growth. A study of the correlation of this spread with the increase of GDP, as among countries in a given interval of time, could be instructive (see table 24.6).

As I said, the increase in percentage is relatively constant over the successive five-year periods, except for television, which only came into use at the beginning of the period, following which its initial high rate of growth slowed to the long-term rate. While automobiles do affect the environment, televisions and telephones do not, and our interest in them here is solely as indicators of middle-class families, who will travel by plane and otherwise have an environmental effect.

Unfortunately most of the numbers I was able to secure refer to Europe and Japan, where presumably saturation is approaching. Table 24.7 shows the few LDCs available. The point of all this is to estimate the number of persons worldwide who are middle class and the rate at which they are increasing in the MDCs and the LDCs. Table 24.7 indi-

Table 24.6. Average Percentage Increase in Three Artifacts in 32 Industrialized Countries (5-Year Intervals)

Artifact	1958–63	1963–68	1968–73	1973–78
Automobiles	6.9	7.0	6.2	6.1
Televisions	13.3	9.2	6.9	7.8
Telephones	6.0	6.7	7.4	5.6

Table 24.7. Average Annual Percentage Increase Over 20 Years for Three Artifacts, for Those Less Developed Countries for Which Data Are Available

Country	Motor Vehicles	Televisions	Telephones
Argentina	8.0	21.2	3.5
Brazil	12.4	16.1	9.1
Chile	7.7		5.6
Colombia	7.2	15.4	9.5
India	7.0		
Indonesia	10.2		
Mexico	9.6	17.2	11.8
Philippines	8.4		
Venezuela	8.6	11.3	8.4

Source: Data from Statistical Abstracts of the United States (Washington, D.C.: Government Printing Office). Data from the 1960, 1970, and 1980 editions.

cates that the rate of increase of automobiles is about 7 to 10 percent per year for the LDCs. The increase for the mature economies of the MDCs, moving toward saturation, is clearly lower, typically 3 to 5 percent.

There are two ways to interpret such data in allocating ecological responsibility to the MDCs and the LDCs. At the present time the preponderance of automobiles is in the MDCs, so the population of the LDCs cannot be blamed as the chief culprit for problems such as global warming. To make statements about the future on that basis would imply that the LDCs are going to stay where they are. But if we see the LDCs as growing economically and becoming more middle class, then the size of population at which they stabilize during the twenty-first century is important indeed.

One cheering feature of economic advance is that it moves more and more to the consumption of services rather than hard commodities and toward smaller, lighter, more efficient hard commodities. These observations, with respect to the shift toward services, originally due to Australian economist Colin Clark,[13] are repeated by everyone who writes on the subject. The assertion that services are coming to dominate the economy is difficult to understand when one cannot find household help or a good tailor. Among the services that have expanded are those provided by doctors, lawyers, and accountants, each the possessor of a high level of human capital.

If development is the spread of a certain way of life that I call middle class, and if it is thought to be indicated by possession of a motor car, then the total middle class would be 1 billion, assuming the number of Americans per car—two—is replicated for the 500 million cars in the world. Alternatively, one might simply use MDC and LDC for middle class and poor, and say that of the world total estimated at 5,246 million people some 23 percent are in the MDCs, so on this way of calculating there would be 1.2 billion middle-class people in the world.

David Riesman and Howard Roseborough[14] speak of a standard package of consumer goods that every family needs for respectable living; in modern society, whatever consumption is in common between the owner of a small, moderately successful business, the skilled worker and the unskilled worker with a steady job whose wife also works.

Leaving out a few eccentrics, each of these families lives in a solid house or apartment rather than in a tin-roofed squatter settlement; owns one or two cars, a refrigerator, a telephone, and a television set; takes a summer vacation; gets away on long weekends; and has no more than two or three children. A house so furnished is the stage on which the middle-class lifestyle is mainly enacted.

The chief event in world history of the past century, rarely mentioned as such in text books, is the expansion of the middle class and its evolution. At one time the middle class included many small, independent entrepreneurs; now their descendants have lost their independence and become clerical supervisors, assembly line workers, and managers of the local McDonald's.

The middle-class consumer culture with which we are surrounded is so familiar that most of the time we do not notice it, and when our attention is drawn to it we think it inevitable, the only reasonable way of living. Yet in fact, as wealth increased our culture could have developed along quite different lines. We could, for example, be living like minor aristocrats and landholders of earlier ages. We could be hiring the poor as our servants; the minimum wage of $10,000 per year could easily be afforded by many families that call themselves middle class, but they prefer to spend the same money on goods.

Even within the present developed countries, middle-class life is not a constant. The Austrian GDP per capita is about equal to the American. For 1993 the averages were $24,580 for the United States and $22,790 for Austria[15]; rates of increase of GDP for 1995 were 1.3 and 1.2 percent respectively.[16]

However, although income was about the same, time allocation and expenditure are not. From the Austrian housewife's walk in the early morning to buy the essential fresh bread for breakfast from a baker two blocks away, to her husband spending late afternoons in a café talking to friends, time means something different in the two countries. In Austria, there is money to subsidize local bus transport, which is used not only by the poor but also by the middle class. For Austrians, driving is less important and the quality of the air more important; they accept a gasoline tax the equivalent of $2 per gallon while the United States canceled a tax of less than 4 cents per gallon. Diets are somewhat different, with the Austrian eating more pork and the American more beef; the grain costs of the latter are double those of the former.

The Austrian takes more pride in his or her work. U.S. taxi drivers, hoping that something better will come along, view their job as a last-resort way of keeping alive; Austrian taxi drivers see themselves as having a respectable career. I found in response to my questioning that such people are more likely than their U.S. counterparts to be homeowners and are more willing to talk about their children, of which there are fewer than in the United States. Those employed in other service activities—such as tailors and booksellers—feel the same pride in their careers. There is less mobility in Austria; people are not trying to find a way to escape into a new line of work, but are more interested in perfecting themselves in their chosen work. All this is a way of saying that for Austrians, and for Europeans generally, one's job, whatever it is, is a way of life, and not merely a means of making money. Is this merely the mark of a static society?

Although Austrians may have a stronger work ethic, a limited amount of work suffices. Six weeks of paid vacations a year are standard, and Austrians receive pay for innumerable saint's days and national holidays, including the week between Christmas and New Year's. Novelty is less important in Austria, where people are satisfied to live in carefully maintained one hundred-year-old houses. People often are born, live and die in the same premises. Gracious surroundings are worth paying for by individuals and the community and flowers are planted on vacant lots, on street corners, and in window boxes.

Austrians pay higher social security taxes than Americans. At 7.4 percent, Austrian unemployment is higher than that in the United States (5.6 percent).[17] But the Austrian unemployed are better supported by insurance, given more extensive training, and helped in other ways. Beyond these differences, the United States has a proportionately higher number of televisions, reported rapes, and drug crimes than Austria, while Austria has a higher rate of male suicide.

I mention all this to show that the middle-class way of life is, in various respects, institutionalized differently in different countries. And today it is changing everywhere. But there is a common denominator: the middle-class family has a car, refrigerator, and meat two or three times a day.

The Middle-Class Lifestyle Is Not Inevitable

Built around the automobile and the television set as made and used in America, that middle-class style in general is diffusing around the world. It is becoming the unquestioned ideal, or norm, everywhere.

Without departing radically from the way we presently choose to use our wealth, we have some options on individual commodities. We need not take our carbohydrates and proteins in the form of meat but could consume more of them as potatoes and bread and beans as South Americans (poor and affluent alike) have done from pre-Columbian times and by doing so use much less land. Residents of some Western countries prefer a quickly and cheaply built wooden house that will last for forty years to a more solid stone house that will last one hundred years; U.S. statistics show that about one-quarter of our wood is used for construction; stone is environmentally costless and durable, but initially expensive.

If money is highly discounted the wooden house is cheaper; without discounting the stone house could well cost less. Most environmental issues hinge on people's evaluation of future costs against present ones.

A people living on their credit cards, that is, on their future income, should not disregard the rate of interest in the choices they make.

When a pious Indian or Burmese has done his life's work and amassed what wealth he feels he needs, he may well settle down to a life of meditation and prayer. If that is the ideal in South Asia, the corresponding ideal in the West leans more to world tours by plane or travels on their own continent by car and trailer. When a Burmese friend of mine retired to meditate at about age sixty, his community regarded him as a little more pious than average, not as an eccentric. Similarly the American flying or driving unnecessary miles is not regarded as odd or wasteful by his friends, just lucky that he can afford it. Sustainability requires a very different set of values from those that now determine the American middle-class style of life and toward which the rest of the world is moving.

But many would say that the middle-class style is not an arbitrary or problematic standard, as I claim it is. They point to the fact that these "middle-class goods"—telephones, cars, televisions, and so on—are demanded in the marketplace and that people all over the world are deserting their indigenous cultures to seek the benefits and the goods of the Western middle class. The automobiles and air travel would not be produced unless people wanted them.

That is a grossly incomplete story. We have to ask why people want these goods. And the answer is in part that they are persuaded by the powerful instruments of present-day public communication. If the consumer knew just what he or she wanted, advertising would consist of mere lists of the goods that stores stock and the stores' opening and closing hours. And beyond explicit advertising is the whole apparatus of novels, films, sitcoms, and soap operas that extol a particular style of life. Imagine the same skill put into publicity for Buddhist meditation!

But the motivation for the purchase of goods does not affect their impact on the ecosphere. It is equally negative whether goods are in some sense necessary or whether the satisfaction they give depends on the envy of neighbors. And insofar as their production is driven by the search for profit, I can only agree with Lord Keynes' hopeful forecast for 1984: "The love of money as a possession—as distinct from the love of money as a means to the enjoyment and realities of life—will be recognized for what it is, a somewhat disgusting morbidity, one of those semi-criminal, semi-pathological propensities which one hands over with a shudder to the specialists in mental disease."[18]

All this is unimportant for a small and sparse population, but the world is fast moving toward one larger—10 billion—and denser—more and more concentrated in megacities. We recall that a main object of this chapter is to find an equitable arrangement between the MDCs and the LDCs. The middle class is still largely in the MDCs. I estimate 80 percent of the middle class resides in MDCs.[19] If most of the population in the LDCs is ecologically harmless, then how can we in the MDCs in good conscience urge the LDCs to cut their birthrate in return for our controlling our pollution? Is not the obligation solely on our side, to cut our effluents?

The answer is no, for the question as phrased is looking at the past. If one looks at the future and sees the immense aspiration for development—defined as the middle-class lifestyle—on the part of the population of the LDCs and the energetic steps that most of them are taking to fulfill this aspiration, then one is in a position to contemplate the future realistically. That realistic future is one in which the already immense populations, especially of Asia, rapidly move into the middle class, say at the rate of some 6 percent per year. The likely kind of middle-class consumption of the future, along with the vast numbers of Asians and others who will be able to afford it, is more than anything determinative of what kind of planet our grandchildren will inhabit.

Diffusion of a Single World Culture

America was the fountainhead of the middle-class style of life in the past and it can be expected to continue to lead in the future. First the style passes a considerable way down the income levels in the United States, then it jumps the Atlantic and in Europe starts at the top and works down.

The diffusion applies in both production and consumption: producers in countries of labor surplus substitute capital for labor in higher than optimum proportions at the same time that consumers substitute modern for traditional goods prematurely and so save less than they might for investment. This transition from one way of life to another includes the limiting of family size, as having fewer children makes it possible to afford more modern goods.

Thorstein Veblen, like other keen observers, never thought that individuals make independent consumption choices.[20] "With the exception of the instinct of self-preservation, the propensity for emulation is probably the strongest and the most alert and persistent of the economic motives proper." Knowing that the way of life they adopt will be widely imitated, and that their high consumption damages the environment, what moral obligations rest on the better off of rich countries?

Little Shortage of Inputs but Great Excess of Unwanted Outputs

The big worry used to be that industrial society was using up the earth's limited raw materials. Now we know that with substitutions and new discoveries the worry was unnecessary. Even the price of oil is down, and it would fall further if Iraq were allowed to ship out some of its plentiful supplies. Using up all the oil on the planet will take a very long time.

Industrial societies have enormous power with which to process the minerals and other elements of the environment; they put the soil, the metals, the oil, and forests through a vast machine that converts everything and adapts it to human use. The output includes useful or at least salable goods, but there are also chemical wastes, superfluous fertilizers and pesticides, household garbage, emissions from the burning of fossil fuels, and nuclear fuel that has been used to the point where it is too diluted for input to a reactor but still concentrated enough to be extremely dangerous.

It is these unwanted goods—I'll follow Kenneth Boulding and call them bads—rather than scarcity that set the limits of population, especially of the number of people who can live as the majority of those in the MDCs live. It being recognized that this is the essence of the environmental problem, much effort now goes into treating effluents, usually at the "end of the pipe," leaving the process that generates them unaffected.

There are four ways of reducing the impact of bads on the environment and allowing more people to live well.

Cleaning the Output at the End of the Pipe

Leaving the process that generates effluents unaffected, one can process these bads after they are produced, usually at considerable expense and often unsatisfactorily.

Increasing Mechanical Efficiency

The end of the pipe is too late. What we need to do is re-engineer the entire process, right back to the raw material, so that as far as possible the wastes will not be produced in the first place. That is a large task, not only for industry but also for science, since the new kind of engineering is blocked by many gaps in theoretical knowledge.

Nonetheless, securing the same ultimate consumer artifacts with less undesired outputs is proceeding. Mechanical efficiency in motor cars, generating stations, electric motors, is part of it; housing and automobiles that are more durable is another part. Natural gas generates energy with less emissions and its use is spreading, much of it transported by sea in liquid form. One can think of many other changes that would provide the identical style of living, the same desired output, with smaller amounts of the undesired waste.

Raising Use Efficiency

So much for whatever efficiency can be attained with no alteration in the target style of life. But incentives to consumers to demand efficient products that will provide the same service as at present will not go far enough if middle-class lifestyle becomes worldwide.

The way to do better is by more radical changes than merely stepping up mechanical efficiency. Changes are required that would secure essentially the same objectives, but using different means. What are these changes, toward what can be called use efficiency, that go beyond mechanical efficiency? Some examples will give the idea.

If the object is shelter and warmth, an apartment with one or two walls exposed to the weather saves fuel compared with a detached house having five surfaces exposed. Mass transportation saves fuel compared with individual automobiles and, in some situations, could get passengers there as comfortably and more quickly, but mass transportation is rendered difficult by spatially dispersed housing. German per capita fuel consumption is 543 gallons, compared to 1029 gallons in the United States.[21] These are substitutions that can hardly be called painful, but their impact on the environment is profound.

Lifestyle Change

But even with these changes, a population of 10 billion could not be accommodated in the style of life described as middle class without irreparable damage to the environment. That style would have to be more radically changed than indicated above. There would have to be sharp decreases in the amount of transportation by whatever means, fewer square meters of housing per person, and less meat in our diet. This not only changes the mechanical efficiency and the use efficiency by which more benign means are chosen for attaining given objectives, the two changes suggested above, but also changes the objectives themselves. Nothing less than changes in the style of life would be involved. Persuading people to live differently in the interest of the planet would be no easy task.

However produced, the unwanted outputs are external to the producing agent. Poisonous waste can be poured into the Love Canal; the North Shore of Alaska can be opened for drilling. In these cases, whatever harm is done is external; it is the cheap way of solving a disposal problem and does no particular harm to the doer. Environmental regulation, whether it takes the form of a simple ban or, more efficiently, rations the pollution by auctioning tradable permits, must be mandated by government or it will not happen. This is not to underestimate the activities of conscientious citizens—the ship *Rainbow Warrior* is an example on the edge of legality—but that activity is limited by the fact that citizens have other things to worry about. And so do corporations, even though they are concerned about the regard in which they are held by the public. There are few instances where tradable permits to pollute have been used, but the achievements of regulation are numerous—for instance, New Yorkers appreciate especially the cleanup of the Hudson River.

Citizen pressure on governments to regulate and on corporations to behave responsibly is increasing, and now we find that a full majority in the United States are concerned about the environmental threats. The Harris Poll reports that U.S. citizens are concerned about air pollution (considered "very serious" by 60 percent), water pollution (71 percent), contaminated soil (54 percent), loss of species (49 percent), loss of rain forest (63 percent), global warming (47 percent), and loss of ozone (56 percent).[22] Besides those who thought the problem "very serious," there were presumably others less strongly concerned but who still wanted to see something done. On the whole, citizens of European countries, also polled by Harris, reported concern at about the same level; other continents are much less interested.

So in the end protection is left to governments, acting on behalf of their citizens, and, indeed, governments acted fairly energetically for a while. In the last decade, however, as we saw above, globalization has come to constrain all governments.

Toward a New Style of Life

The Global Diffusion of Our Style of Life: Can We Stand Success?

The global population has now reached nearly 6 billion, and the modern middle-class style of life, largely originated in the United States, has reached about one billion. All seem quick to adapt, to incorporate the new technologies into their daily lives. None of us can imagine communication without cellular phones and modems, medicine without antibiotics, long-distance travel except by air, or doing our daily activities except by automobile. Yet all of these belong to the twentieth century, mostly to the last half of it.

Wisdom starts by realizing that such consumption is only one direction for the meaning of life, that it is contrary to most ideals of all past ages and all other cultures, that alternative possibilities exist also for us, some of which would offer greater satisfaction with less stress on nature. These other possibilities ought now to be a main subject of education, for high consumption is already sufficiently taught. Yet schools are pressed to teach subjects that will be helpful in earning a living—vocational instruction in short. We usually neglect to teach youngsters about the possibilities for consuming in more environmentally responsible or prudent ways.

I repeat that all this is taking place in a time and country where national income, productivity per capita, and supply of goods have never been greater but where inequality in distribution is allowed to widen. The high end of the income distribution is rising fastest, and lighter taxes are urged for those benefiting most. I say that all this has the appearance of irrationality born of confusion; there may be some villainy in it, but that is secondary to the general confusion.

The suddenness with which the new style of life has emerged and the changes in the planet that have already appeared leave us bewildered not only about how we ought to behave toward one another, what moral code is now appropriate, but equally about how to behave toward the environment. For almost all of history there was plenty of room for more people; the human race was rightly seen as fragile, too easily destroyed by plague or other catastrophe. It was right to encourage maximum childbearing, to see contraception and abortion as immoral and even to make them illegal. With current population levels, a catastrophe that would wipe us out is made more, not less, likely by further increase of population. Until this century, in most places we were not numerous enough to damage forests and fisheries, and we did not have the technology to pollute air and water. With our present numbers and technology we are damaging (though some would say only modifying) the environment on a massive scale.

Out of all the alternative styles that history has tried, all the life objectives imagined in utopias or portrayed by philosophers, it is the high-consumption, North American style of life that has become the standard for the billion who have attained it and the ideal for the 5 billion that aspire to it. This spread of a new standard is part of the configuration to which we fail to adapt. Those who have attained it are so worried about losing it that they have less wish than ever to help the homeless, the disabled, and the hungry. The poor peasant, who would divide his humble fare with an impoverished neighbor, is not always matched by the middle-class citizen of today. All too common is the Malthusian answer: If I help these panhandlers today there will be more of them coming around tomorrow. If that statement is true, it is because in the vast populations of contemporary cities social relations are of secondary importance to individual comfort and security.

We can rightly be encouraged by some of the directions in which behavior has been changed to accord with our new situation. Adults in America have largely stopped smoking and efforts are being made to avoid acquisition of the habit among teenagers. Modified behavior is checking the spread of AIDS in the United States. Sensible restraint in the use of antibiotics by doctors and by patients enables each new drug discovered to last that much longer before the disease becomes resistant. The practices of recycling waste and cleaning up water and air are making consumption less destructive and life healthier in Europe and America.

It is true that in many LDCs there is less public concern than there might be for the environmental degradation to which they are subject. Yet we do see less childbearing and the start of more fostering of the countryside and more environmental concern in the LDCs. Indonesia's allocation of funds for public works in its villages was a start. In due course such measures should put fewer people into the already overcrowded cities.

Hopeful steps have been taken toward solution of the environment problem: we are learning to fit ourselves—through collective action as well as voluntary individual changes to our lifestyle—into the planetary web of life. Both MDCs and LDCs are at least learning what they ought to do, even if their performance lags. On the one hand, because of the direct effects of the MDCs' lifestyle, and the example it sets for the LDCs, consumption that is more personally and environmentally responsible is the responsibility of the MDCs. On the other hand, further reduction in the prospective growth of population has to be the responsibility of the LDCs, which on present trends will grow 174 percent by 2050, while the MDCs will increase only 2 percent.

The consumer goods that typify our lives—television sets and modems, antibiotics and other pharmaceuticals, pills that make birth control easy, mass travel by air, daily use of the automobile—are all relatively recent inventions. All of these belong to the twentieth century, their mass use to the second half of it. The global economy steps up the diffusion of these entities worldwide. Should we be surprised at some initial confusion as society struggles to adapt?

Notes

I am greatly indebted for suggestions made by the editor and referees.

1. U.S. Bureau of the Census, as given on the World Wide Web site <http://www.census.gov/cgi-bin/ipc/popclockw>. Many other items in this chapter are taken from this site, the home page of which is <http://www.census.gov/>.

2. U.S. Bureau of the Census website.

3. Ansley J. Coale and Edgar M. Hoover, *Population Growth and Economic Development in Low-Income Countries* (Princeton, N.J.: Princeton University Press, 1958).

4. See Nicholas Eberstadt, *The Tyranny of Numbers: Mismeasurement and Misrule* (Washington, D.C.: AEI Press, 1995).

5. *New York Times*, 27 April 1996, 25.

6. Joel E. Cohen, *How Many People Can the Earth Support?* (New York: W. W. Norton, 1996).

7. Frank Notestein, "Population: The Long View," in *Food for the World*, ed. T. W. Schultz, Norman Wait Harris Memorial Fund Lectures (Chicago: University of Chicago Press, 1945); Kingsley Davis, "The World Demographic Transition: World Population in Transition," *The Annals,* vol 237, ed. Kingsley Davis (Philadelphia: The American Academy of Political and Social Science, 1945): 1–11.

8. Harry Tatsumi Oshima, *A Labor-Intensive Strategy for South-East Asia and Priorities* (New York: Asia Society, 1973).

9. See W. Arthur Lewis, "Economic Development with Unlimited Supplies of Labor," *The Manchester School*, vol. 22 (May 1954): 139–91; Adam Smith, *An Inquiry into the Nature and Causes of the Wealth of Nations* (New York: Modern Library, 1937 [1776]); Oshima, *A Labor-Intensive Strategy.*

10. Karl Polanyi, *The Great Transformation* (New York: Rinehart, 1944).

11. Amartya Sen, *Inequality Reexamined* (Cambridge, Mass.: Harvard University Press, 1992).

12. *Economist*, 13–19 April 1996.

13. Colin Clark, *The Conditions of Economic Progress* (London: Macmillan, 1940) and *The Economics of 1960* (London: Macmillan, 1962).

14. See David Riesman with Howard Roseborough, "Careers and Consumer Behavior," in *Consumer Behavior,* vol. 2, ed. Lincoln Clark (New York: NYU Press, 1995) and Howard Roseborough, "Sociology of Consumer Spending," (Ph.D. diss., Harvard University, 1958).

15. *Statistical Abstracts of the United States* (Washington, D.C.: U.S. Department of Commerce, 1995), 855.

16. *The Economist*, 13–19 April 1996.

17. *The Economist*, 13–19 April 1996.

18. John Maynard Keynes, *Essays in Persuasion* (London: Macmillan, 1931), part v.

19. *Statistical Abstracts*, 1995, 857.

20. Thorstein Veblen, *The Theory of the Leisure Class* (New York: Dover Publications, 1994 [1899]), chap. 5.

21. *New York Times,* 23 July 1996, D1.

22. Riley E. Dunlap, George H. Gallup Jr., and Alex M. Gallup, *Health of the Planet: A George H. Gallup Memorial Survey* (Princeton, N.J.: The George H. Gallup International Institute, 1993).

25

A Global Resources Dividend

Thomas W. Pogge

Article 25: Everyone has the right to a standard of living adequate for the health and well-being of himself and of his family, including food, clothing, housing and medical care.

Article 28: Everyone is entitled to a social and international order in which the rights and freedoms set forth in this Declaration can be fully realized.

Universal Declaration of Human Rights

Radical Inequality and our Responsibility

One great challenge to any morally sensitive person today is the extent and severity of global poverty. Hundreds of millions are born into abject poverty and remain poor, dependent, and uneducated all their lives.[1] These persons are so poor and so cut off from minimally adequate nutrition, hygiene, and medicines that some 20 million of them die each year of starvation or easily curable diseases.[2] Most of these deaths occur in ordinary times, where extreme poverty makes persons highly vulnerable to even very minor misfortunes. Being so routine as well as temporally and spatially dispersed, this suffering is barely perceived by the rest of the world. We are more familiar with famines and epidemics triggered by photogenic catastrophes, such as cyclones, earthquakes, droughts, and (civil) wars. But even in these cases, the root cause of most of the suffering is the poverty of those affected. Among the rest of us, droughts and earthquakes do not trigger famines and epidemics.[3]

The circumstances of the global poor contrast sharply with those of many others who are vastly better off in most respects, such as personal security; rights, freedom, and opportunities; political influence; income, wealth, and leisure time; sanitation and hygiene; life expectancy and infant mortality; and access to education, health care, food, clothing, and shelter.[4]

There are two ways of conceiving this privation as a moral challenge to us. One might assign a positive responsibility to us, based on the fact that we could improve the circumstances of the poor: Since they are truly suffering and we are so much better off, we should sacrifice some of our own time, energy, and wealth so as to help them.[5] Alternatively, one might ascribe a negative responsibility to us, based on the fact that we participate in, and profit from, the unjust and coercive imposition of severe poverty.

These two views differ in important ways. The positive formulation is more broadly applicable, and it is thus easier to show its relevance. All that needs to be shown is that the poor are very badly off, that we are very much better off, and that we could relieve some of their suffering without significant losses to our own well-being. But this ease comes at a price: Some who accept the positive formulation nevertheless feel entitled to focus on leading their own lives without bothering with worthy causes, especially when the demands these causes make on them are significant. Many feel entitled, at least, to support good causes of their choice—their church, neighborhood council, or alma mater, perhaps, or medical research, animal rights, or the environment—rather than putting themselves out for total strangers half a world away, with whom they share no bond of community or culture beyond the very tenuous one of a common humanity. It is of some importance, therefore, to investigate whether we might bear a negative responsibility for world poverty by participating in its unjust perpetuation. This is important for us, insofar as we want to gain a moral orientation in this world, and important also for the poor, because it is likely that global poverty would not continue so persistently if we more affluent world citizens ascribed a negative responsibility for it to ourselves.

Some believe that the mere fact of *radical* inequality can ground a claim of negative responsibility. The modifier "radical" may be defined as involving five elements:

1. Those at the bottom are very badly off in absolute terms.
2. They are also very badly off in relative terms—very much worse off than many others.
3. The inequality is persistent: It is difficult or impossible for those at the bottom substantially to improve their lot; and most of those at the top never experience life at the bottom for even a few months and have no vivid idea of what it is like to live in that way.
4. The inequality is pervasive: It concerns not merely some aspects

of life, such as the climate or access to natural beauty or high culture, but most aspects or all.
5. The inequality is avoidable: Those at the top can improve the circumstances of those at the bottom without becoming badly off themselves.

It is clear that the phenomenon of global poverty exemplifies radical inequality as defined.[6] But I do not believe that these five conditions suffice to ground more than a merely positive responsibility. And I suspect that most citizens of the developed West—those I want to convince—would also find them insufficient. They might appeal to the following parallel: Suppose that we discovered persons on Venus who are very badly off and much worse off than we are, and suppose we could help them without great cost to ourselves. One could say that by refusing such help we would become participants in the coercive maintenance of an unjust state of affairs—even profiteers, by embezzling the aid we were required to give. But those who allow any moral significance to the distinction between positive and negative responsibility will hardly find this charge convincing, because we do not in this case seem to contribute at all to the perpetuation of the radical inequality. This point, of course, could be further disputed. But let me accept the Venus argument. Assuming that radical inequality is not a *sufficient* condition for a negative responsibility by those at the top for the circumstances of those at the bottom, let us then seek out more plausible bases for negative responsibility.

Obviously, radical inequality is not a *necessary* condition for negative responsibility either.[7] I will here, however, confine myself to radical inequalities by asking under what conditions a radical inequality manifests an injustice for which those at the top share negative responsibility. I see three plausible approaches to this question, which invoke, respectively, the effects of shared institutions, uncompensated exclusion from the use of natural resources, and the effects of a common and bloody history. These approaches belong to diverse and competing philosophical traditions. Nevertheless, we need not decide among them here, if, as I shall argue, the following two theses are true. First, the conditions for assigning negative responsibility for injustice, as specified by all three approaches, are fulfilled by the existing problem of global poverty, which therefore manifests what might be called a *core injustice*. Second, the status quo can be reformed in a way that all three approaches would recognize as an important step toward a just world order.

If these two theses can be supported, then there is hope for a coalition, focused on the topic of global justice, among the adherents of the most important approaches in Western political philosophy. This coalition would express a limited consensus,[8] according to which the present world order is grievously unjust and would become considerably more just through the introduction of the Global Resources Dividend, which I describe below.

Three Grounds of Negative Responsibility

The Effects of Shared Institutions

The first approach[9] holds that those at the top share a *negative* responsibility for the poverty of those at the bottom if and only if—in addition to the five conditions of radical inequality—three further elements are present:

6. Everyday conduct of those at the top often strongly affects the circumstances of those at the bottom in a way that shows that both coexist under a single scheme of social institutions.
7. This institutional scheme is implicated in the radical inequality by avoidably producing the poverty of those at the bottom, in this sense: It is not the case that every practicable institutional alternative would also generate such severe and extensive poverty.
8. The radical inequality cannot be traced to extrasocial factors (such as genetic handicaps or natural disasters) that, as such, affect different human beings differentially.

Present radical global inequality fulfills the sixth condition: the global poor live in the context of a worldwide state system based on internationally recognized territorial domains, interconnected through a global network of market trade and diplomacy. Thanks to our vastly superior military and economic strength, we citizens of the developed countries enjoy a position of overwhelming political dominance in this system, and, through this system, we also dramatically affect the circumstances of the global poor—via investments, loans, military aid, trade, sex tourism, culture exports, and much else. Their very survival often depends decisively (for example, through the price of their foodstuffs or their opportunities to find work) upon our demand behavior, which may determine such things as whether local landowners will grow cash crops (coffee, cotton, flowers) for export or food for local consumption.[10] It is quite impossible to trace the effects of even a single one of our buying decisions, because these effects produce further effects indefinitely and also interact with the effects of billions of other decisions. So I am not claiming that we are responsible for the effects of our individual economic decisions and ought to make such decisions in light of all their ever so remote effects. Such a demand would be completely unrealistic. Nor am I making the dubious and utopian suggestion that global interdependence should be undone by isolating states or groups of states from one another. Rather, the relevance of the sixth condition consists in bringing out that—in sharp contrast to the Venus case—we are causally deeply entangled in the misery of the poor and cannot extricate ourselves from this involvement so long as their misery continues.

The seventh condition involves tracing the circumstances of individuals to the structure of social institutions rather than merely to the conduct of individual or collective agents. This exercise is important insofar as feasible alternative institutional frameworks differ in morally significant ways in how they affect the lives of human beings. The idea is not easy to grasp when social institutions endure over long periods, as the core features of our global institutional scheme have done.[11] Their constancy makes us experience these features as natural and unalterable, like the physical core features of our planet, and thus renders their moral significance all but invisible to common sense and often to political philosophers as well. Thus we speak of good and bad luck when someone is born into a rich or poor country or family just as when someone is born well endowed or disabled. But the parallel between social and natural factors holds only with respect to the starting positions persons occupy within a given distribution, not for the distribution itself. The distributional profile of genetic endowments is not—not yet, anyway—under human control; but the distributional profile of social benefits and burdens can be considerably reshaped through global institutional reform.[12] We tend to be blind to this possibility, because the constancy of our global order—the lack of observable alternatives elsewhere in space or in time—makes it quite hard to appreciate and hard also to ascertain how particular institutional reforms would affect human lives.

The explanatory importance of social institutions has been powerfully illustrated recently by numerous domestic regime changes in the countries of Eastern Europe, for example. These changes have shown that institutional choices, such as that between socialism and capitalism, can have a dramatic impact on the distribution of income and wealth, education and health care, rights and liberties, and quality of life. But, curiously, our new familiarity with institutional change on the national level has made it even harder to appreciate its importance for the global level. Dramatic differences in standard of living across countries draw our attention to local factors—such as national institutions, cultures, resources, climates, environments, levels of development— that help furnish country-specific explanations and/or explanations of international variations. But these national factors do not tell the whole story. Country-specific explanations of persistent poverty, for instance, do not add up to an explanation of the global incidence of poverty—just as explanations of particular suicides do not add up to an explanation of the suicide rate.[13] And the obvious fact that national factors are important for explaining *where* poverty occurs does not entail that these factors are also important for explaining how extreme and how widespread poverty is worldwide.[14] These reflections lend support to the idea that we should connect the severe poverty of people in Nigeria, Bangladesh, and Brazil, say, not only with such obvious local factors as tyrannical rulers, climatic hazards, and ancient hatreds but also with our global institutional framework. This framework is important for explaining morally significant global rates and levels. These cannot be explained by national factors alone, because the effects of national factors are strongly influenced by global factors and because national factors are themselves shaped within, and partly by, their global institutional context. I will do more to show the importance of global institutions in section 3 of this essay, "A Moderate Proposal," where I sketch an institutional alternative that would have quite different distributional effects and would also exert different influences upon the development of national institutions and cultures.

Global poverty fulfills the eighth condition because the global poor, if only they had been born into different social circumstances, would be just as able and likely to lead healthy, happy, and productive lives as the rest of us. The root cause of their suffering is their abysmal social starting position, including the social context into which they are born, which does not give them much of a chance to become anything but poor, vulnerable, and dependent—unable to give their children a better start than they had had themselves.

When the three additional conditions are fulfilled, then it makes sense to call those who are very badly off in absolute and in relative terms radically deprived. Here the word "deprived" indicates that they do not merely lack what they need to lead a fulfilling human life but that what they need is withheld from them through human agency. These persons are not merely poor and often starving, but they are being impoverished and starved by our common institutional arrangements, which inescapably shape their lives. We, the more powerful and advantaged participants in the global framework, deprive them of what they need because we—whether intentionally or not—impose this framework upon them rather than some feasible institutional alternative that would not generate such severe and widespread poverty.

This thought brings out why, according to the first view, global poverty has the special moral urgency we associate with negative responsibility and why we should take it much more seriously than otherwise similar suffering that arises from genetic handicaps, natural disasters, accidents, addiction, or in the absence of interdependence. The distribution of social positions within any social system is significantly affected by how this system is structured and organized, by its ground rules or social institutions, which we create, shape, and uphold and also can modify significantly through institutional reforms.

The first approach can be presented in a consequentialist guise, as in Jeremy Bentham, or in a contractarian guise, as in John Rawls or Jürgen Habermas.[15] In both cases, the central thought is that social institutions are to be assessed in a forward-looking way, on the basis of their effects. In the current international order, some 1.3 billion human beings are born into social starting positions in which their life prospects are extremely low. Their misery could be justified only if there were no superior institutional alternative under which this sort of misery would be avoided. If, as I will try to show, there is such an alternative, then the misery of these persons can be ascribed to our global institutional scheme and therefore, in the last analysis, to ourselves. Even Charles Darwin writes, in reference to his native Britain: "If the misery of our poor be caused not by laws of nature, but by our own institutions, great is our sin."[16]

Uncompensated Exclusion from the Use of Natural Resources

The second approach adds, in place of conditions 6–8, only one condition to the five of radical inequality:

9. Those at the top enjoy significant advantages in the use of a single natural resource base from whose benefits those at the bottom are largely, and without compensation, excluded.

Our current world is characterized by a highly uneven appropriation of wealth from our planet. Affluent persons today employ and consume vastly more of the world's resources, such as fossil fuels, minerals, air, water, and land than the very poor; and they do so unilaterally, without giving any compensation to the global poor for their disproportionate appropriation. Though the affluent often pay for the resources they use—for example, for imported crude oil—these payments go to other affluent people, such as the Saudi family or the Nigerian kleptocracy (who can use these funds to entrench their undemocratic rule), with very little, if anything, trickling down to the global poor. So the question remains: Why should the members of a global elite be entitled to use up the world's natural resources on mutually agreeable terms while excluding the global poor from the benefits?

Although accepting that all inhabitants of the earth ultimately have equal claims to its resources, defenders of capitalist institutions have developed conceptions of justice that support rights to unilateral appropriation and discretionary disposal of a disproportionate share of resources. They argue that a practice permitting unilateral appropriation of disproportionate shares is justified if all are better off under this practice than they would be if such appropriation were limited to proportional shares.

For John Locke, persons in a state of nature are subject to the moral constraint that their unilateral appropriations must always leave "enough, and as good" for others, that is, must be confined to a proportional share.[17] This constraint, the so-called Lockean proviso, may however be lifted with universal consent. Locke subjects such a lifting to a second-order proviso, which requires that the ground rules of human coexistence may be changed only if everyone will be better off under the new rules than under the old, that is, only if everyone can *rationally* consent to the alteration. And he claims that the lifting of the enough-and-as-good constraint through the general acceptance of money (which does not exist in the state of nature[18]) satisfies the second-order proviso: A day laborer in England feeds, lodges, and is clad better than a king of a large fruitful territory in the Americas.[19]

It is hard to believe that Locke's claim was true in his time. In any case, it is surely false on the global plane today. Hundreds of millions are born into a world in which all available resources are already owned by others. It is true that many of them can rent out their labor power and then buy natural resources on the market on the same terms as the affluent. But their educational and employment opportunities are almost always so restricted that, no matter how hard they work, they can barely earn enough for the survival of their family and certainly cannot secure anything like a proportionate share of the world's natural resources.[20] While the global poor are thus largely excluded from natural resources, condemned to watching helplessly as the affluent distribute the abundant natural wealth of this planet among themselves, they do get their proportional share of the burdens resulting from the degradation of our natural environment—a disproportionate share even, in that they generally lack the knowledge and the means to protect themselves. Many of the global poor are today just about as badly off, economically, as human beings could be while still alive. It is not true, then, that all strata of humankind, and the poorest in particular, are better off with universal rights to unilateral appropriation and pollution than without the same; and our world, therefore, does not meet the requirements for lifting of the Lockean proviso. The exclusion of the poor from a proportionate share of resources therefore manifests an injustice that citizens of the affluent states and the "elites" of the poor countries impose by force. Accepting this exclusion voluntarily would be rational for the global poor only if they were compensated for it by being effectively guaranteed an adequate share of the benefits that others derive from their unilateral appropriations. I investigate this possibility further in section 3 of this essay ("A Moderate Proposal").

The Effects of a Shared and Bloody History

The third approach adds one condition to the five of radical inequality:

10. The social starting positions of those at the bottom and those at the top have emerged from a single historical process that was pervaded by massive grievous wrongs.

Conquest and colonization, with severe oppression, enslavement, even genocide, have destroyed or severely traumatized the native institutions and cultures of four continents. This history continues to have a significant impact on the circumstances of the global poor. This is not meant to be an argument for reparations. I am not claiming (or denying) that those whose ancestors took part in these crimes bear some special historical responsibility or that those whose ancestors were victims of these crimes have an historical claim to restitution. The thought is rather that we should not tolerate such radical inequalities in social starting positions if the allocation of these positions depends upon historical processes in which all important moral (and legal) rules and principles were massively violated. Even if (the two preceding subsections notwithstanding) radical inequality is morally acceptable when it comes about pursuant to "rules of the game"—perhaps pursuant to libertarian ground rules that permit unlimited unilateral appropriation—that are morally at least somewhat plausible and are observed at least for the most part, such radical inequality cannot be considered morally acceptable when such rules were in fact massively violated through crimes of all kinds, whose momentous effects can obviously not be surgically neutralized decades and centuries later.[21] A morally deeply tarnished history should not be allowed to result in *radical* inequality.[22]

Friends of the current socioeconomic distribution sometimes invoke the claim that standards of living in Africa and Europe, for example, would be just about the same if Africa had never been colonized. Even if this claim were both clear and true, it would still be ineffective against the argument I have sketched, because this argument applies to persons and not to continents or societies. If world history had progressed without colonization and enslavement, then there would perhaps now be affluent persons living in Europe and poor ones in Africa. But these would be different persons from the ones who are now actually living there. We can therefore not tell starving Africans that *they* would be starving and that *we* would be affluent even if the crimes of colonialism had never occurred. Without these crimes there would not be this now existing radical inequality, which consists in the fact that *these* persons are affluent and *those* are very poor.

Having found this existing radical inequality unjust on account of its genesis, the third approach will draw the same conclusion as the other two: we, the more affluent, have a negative responsibility and duty to stop collaborating in the coercive maintenance of this inequality.

A Moderate Proposal

Let me now try to sketch a practicable modification of the present global order that can be backed by all three approaches. This will support my second thesis that the status quo can be reformed in a way that all three approaches would recognize as an important step toward a just world order. But it is also needed to close gaps in my argument for the first thesis (that we share a negative responsibility for an unjust status quo): The sketch should show that the existing radical inequality can be traced to the structure of our global economic order (condition 7). And it should also show that condition 5 is fulfilled; for, according to all three approaches, the status quo is unjust only if we can improve the circumstances of the global poor without thereby having to share their fate.

I am orienting my proposal to the second approach, because the other two approaches would support virtually any reform that would improve the circumstances of the global poor. The second approach narrows the field by suggesting a more specific idea: Those, usually the affluent, who make more extensive use of the resources of our planet should compensate those who, involuntarily, use very little. This idea does not require that we conceive of global resources as the common heritage of humankind, to be controlled through a global democratic process and their full value to be equally divided among all members of the human species. My reform proposal is far more modest than this in that it accepts the existing state system[23] and, in particular, leaves each national government in control of the (persons and) natural resources of its territory. Modesty is important, because the proposed institutional alternative should be feasible, that is, both realistic—capable of gaining the approval and support especially in the wealthy countries that is necessary to implement it—and also practicable—capable of sustaining itself by eliciting enough cooperation and support from its participants in the world as we know it. I hope that my Global Resources Dividend, or GRD, satisfies these two desiderata by staying reasonably close to the institutional arrangements now in place and by being evidently responsive to the moral concerns implicit in all three approaches.

The GRD proposal envisions that neither states nor their governments shall have full libertarian property rights over the natural resources in their territory but, instead, can be required to share a small part of the value of any resources they decide to use or sell.[24] I call the payment they are required to make a *dividend* not merely to avoid the odious connotations of *tax* and *fee*, but mainly to suggest that the global poor own an inalienable stake in all limited natural resources.[25] As in the case of preferred stock, this stake confers no right to participate in decisions about whether or how natural resources are to be used; therefore it does not interfere with national control over resources or eminent domain. But it does entitle its holder to a share of the economic benefits from the use of the resource in question, if in fact the decision is to use it. Under my proposal, the Saudis, for example, would continue fully to control their crude oil reserves. They would not be required to pump oil or to allow others to do so. But if they did choose to do so, they would be required to pay a linear dividend on any crude oil extracted, whether for their own use or for sale abroad. This idea could be extended to limited resources that are not destroyed through use but merely eroded, worn down, or occupied, such as air and water polluted by industrial discharges or land used in agriculture and ranching. The dividend could be applied even to the use of limited resources that can be reused indefinitely without deterioration (such as metals), but a one-time charge at the time of extraction is obviously much less cumbersome.

In light of the vast extent of global poverty today, one may think that a massive GRD would be necessary to solve the problem. But I do not think this is so. Current radical inequalities are the cumulative result of decades and centuries in which the more affluent societies and groups have used their advantages in capital and knowledge to expand these advantages ever further. These inequalities demonstrate the power of long-term compounding rather than overwhelmingly powerful centrifugal tendencies of our global market system. It is then quite possible that, if radical inequalities have once been eradicated, quite a small GRD may, in the context of a fair and open world market system, be sufficient continuously to balance those ordinary centrifugal tendencies of markets enough to forestall the re-emergence of radical deprivation.

The great magnitude of the problem does suggest, however, that initially more, perhaps as much as 1 percent of the world's social product, may be needed, so that it does not take all too long until accumulated poverty is dismantled and an acceptable distributional profile is reached. To get a concrete sense of the magnitudes involved, let us then consider this higher figure, on the understanding that a lower one should be substituted if this would better advance the interests of the globally worst off in the long run or if, sometime in the future, less is needed to maintain a world free from severe poverty. A 1 percent GRD would currently raise about $300 billion annually. This is equivalent to roughly $250 per person in the poorest quintile, vastly more than their current average annual income.[26] Such an amount, if well targeted and effectively spent, would make a phenomenal difference to them even within a few years.[27] However, the amount is rather small for the rest of us: comparable to the annual defense budget of the United States alone (about $250 billion), and a good bit less than the market price (about $420 billion) of the current annual crude oil production.

Let us stay with the case of crude oil for a moment and examine the likely effects of a $2 per barrel GRD on crude oil extraction. This dividend would be paid by the governments of the countries that own oil reserves and choose to extract them. They would try to pass along as much as possible of this cost, through higher world market prices, to the end users of petroleum products.[28] Some of the GRD on crude oil would thus fall upon the Japanese, who have no oil of their own, but import a large amount. This point significantly mitigates the concern that the GRD proposal might be arbitrarily biased against some affluent societies, the resource rich, and in favor of others. The GRD's pollution component further mitigates this concern, as the Japanese would also pay the GRD on their fossil fuel emissions.

Presumably, not all of the cost could be passed along in this way, because a $2 per barrel rise in the world market price of crude oil would entail a welcome reduction in demand, even if potential substitutes (gas, coal, uranium) were also affected. Therefore, the new equilibrium price could turn out to be less than $2 above the current one. Hence, those who own and extract oil reserves would end up bearing some of the GRD burden. Reduced oil consumption would also diminish the GRD revenue from oil, which at present consumption levels (68.6 million barrels per day) would be $50 billion annually. Even so, the crude oil example shows how nearly one-sixth of even the high initial goal of 1 percent of the world's social product can comfortably be achieved. The cost would be minor: The price of petroleum products would be about a nickel per gallon higher,[29] while the gains of those who own and pump crude oil would fall slightly.

The initial goal could thus be fully achieved by targeting a limited number of resources and pollutants. These should be chosen carefully, with an eye to all the collateral effects of such choices. Several desiderata come into play: While designing the GRD is inevitably difficult and complicated, the dividend itself should be easy to understand and to apply. It should, for instance, be based on resources and pollutants whose extraction or discharge is reasonably easy to monitor or estimate, in order to ensure that every society is paying its fair share and also to assure everyone that this is so. Such transparency also helps fulfill the second desideratum of keeping overall collection costs low. Third, the GRD should have only a small impact on the price of basic foodstuffs and other goods consumed to satisfy basic needs. Thus, although some uses of land and water should presumably be targeted, one might specifically exempt water used for human consumption as well as land used in the production of basic staples. Fourth, the GRD should encourage conservation and environmental protection for the sake of our own and future generations. It should, for instance, target the extraction of nonrenewable resources liable to run out within a few decades in preference to that of resources of which we have an abundant supply; and it should target the discharging of pollutants that will persist for centuries in preference to that of equally harmful pollutants that decay more quickly.

Intelligent targeting of GRD liabilities thus makes it possible—without major changes to our global economic system—to raise a revenue stream that is clearly sufficient to eradicate world hunger within a few years. What is perhaps surprising is that the collateral effects of raising this revenue may well be positive on the whole, on account of the GRD's benefits for environmental protection and conservation.[30] These benefits are hard to secure in a less concerted way because of familiar collective-action problems ("tragedy of the commons"): Each society has little incentive to restrain its consumption and pollution, because the opportunity cost of such restraint falls on it alone while the depletion and pollution costs of consumption are spread worldwide and into the future as well.[31]

It may be objected that the global poor are also end users of natural resources and of products associated with pollution, so that some of the GRD will, in the final analysis, be borne by them. However, since the global poor will continue to account for a very small share of global consumption and are the sole intended beneficiaries of the entire GRD scheme, they are bound to be far better off with the GRD modification than without.[32] They will, however, be subject to the same incentives toward conservation and environmental protection as the rest of us, and this is as it should be.[33]

Proceeds from the GRD are to be used for raising the world's minimum standard of living,[34] emancipating the present and future global poor, and ensuring that all human beings will be able to meet their own basic needs with dignity. The goal is not merely to improve the nutrition, medical care, and sanitary conditions of the global poor but also to make it possible that they can *themselves* effectively defend and realize their basic interests against the rest of humankind, compatriots and foreigners. This capacity presupposes that they are freed from bondage and relations of personal dependence, that they are able to read and write and to learn a profession, that they are able to participate as equals in politics and in the labor market, and that their status is protected by appropriate legal rights that they can understand and effectively enforce through an open and fair legal system.

Rules for the disbursement of GRD funds are to be designed so as to optimize their contribution to the stated goal in the long run. The effort to formulate such rules must draw upon the expertise of economists and international lawyers. And it may be necessary to redesign the GRD in the light of practical experience. But let me nevertheless make a few provisional suggestions. The qualification "in the long run" indicates that smaller short-term benefits should not outweigh greater long-term costs. This means, in particular, that incentive effects must be taken into account. The political and economic elite of any poor country stands to gain from GRD funds in various ways and therefore has an interest in ensuring that its country receives GRD funds. The rules should be designed to take full advantage of this incentive—making it clear to such elites that, if they want to benefit from their society's receipt of GRD funds, they must cooperate in making these funds effective toward enhancing the circumstances and opportunities of the domestic poor.[35]

In an ideal world of fully cooperating, just, and efficient governments, GRD funds could be spent through the governments of the poorer societies. Those funds would enable these governments to eradicate poverty in their territories in whatever way is most effective: by maintaining lower (including negative) tax rates, higher tax exemptions, and/or higher domestic spending (for education, health care, microloans, infrastructure, land reform, and so forth) than would otherwise be possible. Insofar as these governments would actually do this, the entire GRD scheme would require no central bureaucracy and certainly nothing like a world government. Governments could simply transfer the GRD amounts to one another through some facilitating organization, such as an appropriately reorganized World Bank. Acceptance of GRD payments would of course be voluntary: A society might reject, perhaps for religious or cultural reasons, greater affluence and could then democratically choose to renounce its GRD share for the benefit of poverty eradication elsewhere.

In the real world, corrupt governments in the poorer states pose a significant problem. Such governments might be inclined, for instance, to use GRD funds to underwrite indispensable services while diverting any domestic tax revenue saved to the rulers' personal use. Any government that behaved in this way would not be entitled to GRD funds. The whole point of the GRD is, after all, to secure for the poorest persons, not for the poorest states, their fair share of the value of natural resources. In such cases it might still be possible to find other ways of spending the targeted funds for the benefit of the poor in the country in question: by making cash payments directly to the local poor or their organizations or by funding development programs administered through existing UN agencies (UNICEF, UNDP, WHO) or suitable non-governmental organizations (Oxfam). When, in extreme cases, GRD funds could not be used effectively to reduce poverty in a particular country, then there would be no reason to spend them there. They should rather be spent where they can make more of a difference in reducing poverty and disadvantage.[36]

With regard to each GRD-eligible country there are then the following possibilities: GRD funds may be allocated to this country or withheld and allocated to others instead. If allocated, funds could be paid to the government or to official or private organizations and then be transferred directly to the poor or be spent on other poverty eradication measures. Mixtures are, of course, also possible. Rules for deciding these matters should be clear and straightforward and their administration should be cheap and transparent. These rules are to be designed, and possibly revised, with an eye to optimizing their effects. In particular, a poor society that has shown greater effectiveness in eradicating domestic poverty should, other things being equal, receive larger GRD shares; and the more effective its government has been in supporting the effort, the more of this country's GRD share should go directly to its government. This arrangement would give governments and national elites a strong incentive to work toward the eradication of domestic poverty. This incentive may not always prevail. In some poor countries there may well be factions of the ruling elite for whom this incentive would be outweighed by their interest in keeping their poorer compatriots destitute, uneducated, powerless, dependent, and, hence, exploitable. Still, the envisioned GRD rules would make it harder for such factions, which cancel or reduce the country's GRD share, to maintain themselves in power. The incentive would thus shift the political balance of forces in the right direction. With the GRD in place, reforms would be pursued more vigorously and in more countries, and would succeed more often and sooner, than without it. The GRD would stimulate a peaceful international competition in effective poverty eradication.

This beneficial incentive must not be undermined by taking domestic income distribution into account in calculating GRD shares. It may seem that, of two countries with the same population size and per capita income, the one with more severe poverty (more poor people or poorer poor people) should receive, other things being equal, a larger GRD flow. But this would give governments a perverse incentive secretly to tolerate, and even to promote, domestic poverty in order to receive larger GRD payments. This incentive is bad, because governments might act on it and also because it could generate appearance and assurance problems as governments might, rightly or wrongly, be thought to act or be accused of acting on it. Countries' shares of GRD funds should thus be based only on their per capita income.[37] For countries with equal per capita income and equal effectiveness, GRD receipts should be proportional to population size.[38]

While conventional development programs have an aura of handouts and dependence, the GRD avoids any appearance of arrogant generosity: It merely incorporates into international law the moral claim of the poor to partake in the benefits from the use of the world's resources. It implements a moral right—and one that can be justified in multiple ways: namely also prospectively, by reference to its effects, and retrospectively, by reference to the genesis of the current economic distribution.

While development aid is often viewed as redistributive, GRD payments should not be conceived in this way. Calling them redistributive would suggest that they correct some initial distribution while the institutional mechanisms that generate this distribution are taken for granted and left in place. What I advocate, by contrast, is that we should recognize the existing economic institutions as unjust and should support their reform, aiming for modified institutions that would engender a different distribution of benefits and burdens and would thereby greatly reduce, if not eliminate, the moral need for corrective *re*distributions.[39]

A related contrast to development aid is that GRD payments are a matter of entitlement rather than charity and—there being no matching of "donors" and recipients—are not conditional upon rendering political or economic favors to a donor or upon adopting a donor's favored political or economic institutions. This feature would greatly contribute to making any well-functioning GRD scheme much more efficient than conventional development aid, which generally has far more to do with dominant political and economic interests in the donor country than with the fulfillment of basic needs in the recipient countries.[40]

You may prefer to receive such comparative efficiency judgments from economists rather than from a philosopher. I, too, would be very glad if economists were willing to teach us more about possible reforms of our global economic order that could effectively eradicate global poverty. The problem is that, on the whole, economists pay very little attention to this question, though they have much (conflicting) advice on what economic policies LDC governments should pursue within the existing global framework. Having said this, I should mention a proposal somewhat similar to my own, which Nobel laureate James Tobin has recently repeated at the international conference on global poverty in Copenhagen. He proposes a 1/2 percent tax on currency transactions in order to discourage currency speculation. The specific intent of the tax is to reduce speculative exchange rate fluctuations and thereby to enable national governments and central banks better to adapt their monetary policy to domestic economic conditions.[41] Even if this tax were to reduce the volume of currency transactions—which is currently about $1.5 trillion *per day!*—by 95 percent, it would still raise $137 billion annually. While acknowledging that "raising revenues for international purposes was not a primary motivation of my proposal," Tobin does suggest that the funds should be so used.[42] It is quite possible that his proposal is pragmatically superior to mine, at least if massive clandestine exchange activity in offshore investment havens can be effectively suppressed. The funds might be cheaper to collect and the rich countries could be more easily won over to the proposal. On the other hand, the Tobin tax has no environmental payoff and also lacks a moral rationale connecting payers and recipients. Why should those who engage in currency transactions, of all people, be made to pay for global poverty eradication? These differences pale, however, beside the shared conviction that such an institutional reform is feasible and should be attempted. The Tobin tax, too, would be a great gain for global justice. It is high time, in any case, that economists, jurists, political scientists, politicians, the media, and all of us seriously consider and discuss such proposals.

We must now deal with the objection that the GRD scheme simply would not work: Since the funds raised through the GRD are spent in the poorest countries and regions, many of the wealthier and more powerful states would lose by complying. The moral motives we can expect from the populations and governments of these states will not be sufficient in all cases to secure compliance.[43] And noncompliance by some would undermine others' willingness to participate. Instituting a GRD would therefore require significant further institutional reforms, including central enforcement mechanisms.

I agree that the GRD scheme would have to be backed by sanctions. But sanctions could be decentralized: Once the agency facilitating the

flow of GRD payments reported that a country has not met its obligations under the scheme, all other countries would be required to impose
duties on imports from, and perhaps also similar levies on exports to,
this country in order to raise funds equivalent to its GRD obligations
plus the cost of these enforcement measures. Such decentralized sanctions would stand a very good chance of discouraging small-scale
defections. Our world is now, and is likely to remain, highly interdependent economically; most countries export and import between 10 and
50 percent of their gross domestic product. None of them would benefit
from shutting down foreign trade for the sake of avoiding a GRD obligation of around 1 percent of GDP. And each would have reasons to
meet its GRD obligation voluntarily: to retain full control over how
the funds are raised, to avoid the additional payments for enforcement
measures, and to avoid the negative publicity associated with noncompliance.

Such a scheme of decentralized sanctions could work only so long as
both the United States and the European Union (EU) continue to com-
ply with and participate in the sanction mechanism. I assume that both
would do this, provided they could be brought to commit themselves to
something like the GRD regime in the first place. This condition, which
is decisive for the success of the proposal, will be addressed below. It
should be clear, however, that the refusal of the United States and/or
the EU to participate in the eradication of global poverty would not
alter the fact that conditions 5 and 7 are fulfilled. We citizens of wealthy
countries obviously cannot argue that, because we prevent any reforms
of the global economy that would reduce our advantage, the misery of
the global poor is unavoidable and manifests no injustice. To be sure,
none of us can single-handedly reform the existing world order. But
this incapacity supports no more than the following thought: There is
a practicable alternative to the present world order under which the
socioeconomic position of the worst off would be much better. But the
majority of the rich and mighty are blocking the required reform. In
view of the grievous injustice of the existing order, I should try to convert my peers and use some of the resources that the present order puts
at my disposal to mitigate some of its worst effects.

By sketching the GRD proposal in some detail, I hope to have clarified and made more familiar the idea that our global institutional
scheme is involved in the production of radical deprivation. Faced with
massive poverty, hunger, and abuse in LDCs, we are tempted toward
explanations in terms of differences in national institutions. And such
explanations certainly have a role to play—in explaining, for example,
why some LDCs have developed so much more rapidly than others.
What I have tried to show is that we should not rest content with such

national explanations, that our global institutional framework also plays an important role in the production of radical inequality. This is difficult to see, for at least two reasons: There has never been a genuine succession of economic regimes on the global plane, as states have always been recognized as full and sovereign owners of "their" resources. And the available national explanations seem to do the explanatory job all on their own. My sketch of the GRD scheme is supposed to help overcome these difficulties. It constitutes a genuine, albeit hypothetical, alternative to the existing global economic framework. This alternative would, quite obviously, have very different distributional effects. It would also make a difference to what kinds of national regimes emerge, and in what frequencies. This shows that the existing global economic arrangements are involved in the production of radical deprivation, that world hunger and poverty cannot be explained by reference to national factors alone.

The Moral Argument for the Proposed Reform

By showing that conditions 1–10 are fulfilled, I hope to have demonstrated that current world poverty manifests a grievous injustice that can and should be abolished through institutional reform, for example, through introduction of a GRD. To make my argument as transparent and criticizable as possible, I will now restate it in the following six steps:

A. If a society or comparable social system, regulated by a single set of social institutions, is characterized by radical inequality, then its institutional scheme is prima facie unjust and hence stands in need of justification. Here the burden of proof is on those who wish to defend these institutions and their coercive imposition as compatible with justice.

Perhaps this first premise can best be defended by showing how very weak it is in three respects: It applies only if the inequality occurs within *one* institutional framework, so that the everyday conduct of those at the top has a strong and lasting impact on the circumstances of those at the bottom (condition 6). Moreover, the first premise applies only if the existing inequality is radical, that is, involves truly extreme poverty and extreme differentials in standards of living (conditions 1–5). Finally, the first premise does not flatly exclude institutional schemes under which such radical inequalities persist, but merely demands that they be justified. And—seeing that social institutions are,

after all, created and imposed, perpetuated or reformed, by human beings—this demand can hardly be refused with any plausibility.

B. A justification of radical inequality among the participants in an
   institutional scheme would need to show either:
   B1   that condition 10 is unfulfilled, perhaps because the existing
         radical inequality came about fairly, through an historical
         process that transpired in accordance with morally plausible
         rules that were generally observed; or
   B2   that condition 9 is unfulfilled, because the worst off can ade-
         quately benefit from the use of natural resources through ac-
         cess to a proportional share or through a superior substitute;
         or
   B3   that condition 8 is unfulfilled, that is, that the existing radical
         inequality can be traced to extrasocial factors (such as ge-
         netic handicaps or natural disasters) that, as such, affect dif-
         ferent persons differentially;[44] or
   B4   that condition 7 is unfulfilled, because any proposed alterna-
         tive to the existing institutional scheme either is impractica-
         ble, that is, cannot be stably maintained in the long run; or
         cannot be instituted in a morally acceptable way even with
         the good will of all concerned; or would not significantly
         improve the circumstances of the worst off; or would have
         other morally significant disadvantages that offset any im-
         provement in the circumstances of the worst off.[45]

This second premise, too, is quite weak. It gives the defender of the
status quo four justificatory options and leaves him the choice of which
one to attempt. In particular, such a defender is free to try out each of
the three criteria of justice introduced in the second section above, even
though he can hardly subscribe to all three of them at once.

C. Our current global institutional scheme fulfills the antecedent condition of premise A.
D. Our current global institutional scheme therefore stands in need
   of justification, from A and C.
E. Current global radical inequality can be given no justification of
   forms B1, B2, and B3. A justification of form B4 fails as well,
   because modifying the existing global economic order through the
   introduction of a GRD provides an alternative that is practicable,
   can, with some goodwill by all concerned, be instituted in a morally acceptable way, would significantly improve the circum-

stances of the worst off, and would not have disadvantages of comparable moral significance.

F. Our current global institutional framework is therefore unjust, from D, B, and E.

Five Further Remarks About the Argument

In presenting this argument, I have not attempted to satisfy the strictest demands of logical form, which would have required various qualifications and repetitions. I have merely tried to clarify the structure of the argument in order to make clear how it can be assessed. To attack it from within, one would need to refute premise C, give a justification of forms B1, B2, or B3, or show that my reform proposal does run into one of the four problems listed under B4. To attack it from the outside, one would need to argue against the moral premises A or B, that is, one would need to show that institutional schemes within which radical inequalities occur sometimes do not stand in need of justification or can be justified in a way that differs from the four (B1–B4) I have described.

The conclusion of the argument is reached only if all ten of the conditions introduced earlier are fulfilled. When this is so, then all three approaches agree in their assessment, and current global poverty thus manifests a core injustice. Adherents of these different and competing moral conceptions can then work together to eradicate this injustice. If they are advantaged and influential participants in the current international order, they will accept some shared negative responsibility for its injustice, which gives them a strong moral reason to work with others toward its reform and toward protecting those victimized by this order from its worst effects.

Even if one accepts this reasoning, one might still retort that we have competing moral reasons of a more particularistic kind as well, which make it at least permissible for us to give precedence to the fight against poverty and injustice at home, within our own country. I have three things to say in response to this common view.

Other things remaining the same, the introduction of a GRD would indeed reduce the standard of living of the poor in the developed countries. In the case of affluent countries structured in a just way this would pose no problem, because even the poorest persons in these countries would still be reasonably well off and certainly much better off than the (no longer quite so poor) worst off in the poorer countries. There exist some economically unjust affluent countries in which some persons live in harsh poverty. But the responsibility for their poverty (and for its worsening after the introduction of a GRD) surely rests with those who are politically influential in these countries. For under the GRD proposal, each society retains full sovereignty over its domestic economic system. If it wants to reform its economy so as to reduce domestic inequality, it is always free to do so through tax reforms, subsidies, incentives, and so forth. It would clearly be absurd to exempt *unjust* affluent countries from the GRD.[46] By doing so, one would confer a further gain upon the wealthy in these countries, over and above the gain they now presumably derive from the injustice of the national economic order they uphold, and give them an incentive to promote poverty and injustice at home so as to get their country exempted from the GRD.

It is true, of course, that we stand in special relations to some persons and are thereby more strongly bound—both nonmorally and morally—to them than to others. I have especially strong moral reasons to work for the education of *my* children, the success of *my* firm or university, and the justice and culture of *my* country. And, likewise, we and our government have especially strong moral reasons to promote the interests of our own society and compatriots, even if foreigners are worse off. I need not deny this claim, only qualify it. Partiality is legitimate only in the context of a *fair* competition. This idea is familiar and widely accepted in the domestic case. It is perfectly all right for persons to concentrate on promoting the interests of themselves and their relatives, provided they do so on a "level playing field" where substantive fairness is continually preserved. Partiality toward one's family is decidedly not acceptable when we, qua citizens, face political decisions in which that playing field itself is at stake. It would be morally wrong, for example, even (or perhaps especially) if one's children are white boys, to use one's political influence to oppose equal access to higher education for women or blacks. Whenever we act politically—even merely as voters—we are to leave particularistic reasons aside and focus exclusively on justice and the common good. Most citizens in the developed West understand and accept this point without question. It should not be all that hard to make them understand that for closely analogous reasons (1) national partiality is morally acceptable only on condition that the fairness of international relations is continually preserved, and (2) it is morally wrong for us and our political representatives to use our vastly superior bargaining power to impose upon the global poor an unjust international economic order that tends to perpetuate their poverty and inferiority.[47]

The problem of global poverty is not the only injustice in this world. And so one might think that, even if it is the worst injustice, we should be entitled to give precedence to other injustices that concern us more directly, for example, the injustice of our own domestic socioeconomic institutions. I accept that as participants in some injustice we have a reason to give priority to the struggle against it. As a U.S. citizen one has, other things being equal, more reason to work for the reform of U.S. institutions than for the reform of Canadian or Korean ones. But this priority is irrelevant here, because we are participants in both national and global institutional schemes, both of which are unjust. And— however one may want to conduct such comparisons—the injustice of the global order is surely vastly greater than that of our national one. And there is surely no moral reason for giving precedence to the reform of smaller over that of larger institutional schemes when one is a participant in both.

Is the Reform Proposal Realistic?

Even if the GRD proposal is practicable, and even if it could be implemented with the goodwill of all concerned, there remains the problem of generating this goodwill, especially on the part of the rich and mighty. Without the support of the United States and the European Union, global poverty will certainly not be eradicated in our lifetimes. How realistic is the hope of mobilizing such support? I have two answers to this question.

First, even if this hope is not realistic, it is still important to understand that present world poverty manifests a grievous injustice according to all the major Western approaches in political philosophy. We are not merely distant witnesses of a problem unrelated to ourselves, with a weak, positive duty to help mitigate this problem, perhaps through occasional donations. Rather, we are, both causally and morally, intimately involved in the fate of the poor, in particular by imposing upon them an economic order that regularly produces severe poverty, and/or effectively excludes them from the benefits of natural resources, and/ or upholds a radical inequality that resulted from an historical process pervaded by massive crimes. In light of this involvement, we have a strong, negative duty to stop contributing to, and profiting from, the maintenance of the status quo and also to help work out and implement plausible reforms. If no plausible and implementable reform can be found, then we may in the end be unable to do more than mitigate the misery of the poor. But even then a difference would remain, because the point of our donations would then no longer be to help the needy but to protect victims of an injustice, in which we ourselves participate, from its worst effects and also to reduce the extent to which we profit from this injustice. And duties of this last kind are, other things being equal, much more stringent than those of the first.

My second answer is that the hope may not be so unrealistic after all.

My provisional optimism is based on two considerations. The first is
that moral convictions can have real effects even in international politics, as even some political realists admit, albeit with regret.[48] Sometimes these are the moral convictions of politicians. But it seems rather
more common for politics to be influenced by the moral convictions of
citizens, who influence, and are themselves influenced by, the mass
media. One dramatic example of this is the suppression of the slave
trade in the nineteenth century. After a massive mobilization of its domestic population, which was predominantly morally motivated, Britain
was in the forefront of this effort. The British actively enforced a ban
on the entire maritime slave trade irrespective of a vessel's ownership,
registration, port of origin, or destination. They bore the whole cost of
their enforcement efforts and could not hope to gain significant benefits
from it. In fact, the British bore additional opportunity costs in the form
of lost trade, especially with Latin America.[49] Such a mobilization may
also be possible for the sake of eradicating world poverty, if two conditions are met: if the citizens of the more powerful states can be
convinced of a moral conclusion that really can be supported in a convincing way and if a path can be shown that makes only modest demands on each of us.[50]

The GRD proposal satisfies the first condition.[51] As I have shown, this
proposal can be anchored broadly in the three main, though mutually
incompatible, strands of the Western intellectual tradition, the tradition
that matters most, since most of the burdens, relative to the status quo,
of the GRD would, directly or indirectly, fall upon the people of the
developed West. The GRD also has the morally significant advantage of
shifting consumption in ways that restrain global pollution and resource
depletion in the interest of all human beings and of future generations
in particular. Because it can be backed by these four important and
mutually independent moral rationales, the GRD proposal is well positioned to benefit from the fact that moral reasons can have effects in the
world. If some help could be secured from other disciplines, such as
economics, political science, and law, toward translating, specifying,
and defending the idea, then moral acceptance of the GRD may gradually emerge and become widespread in the developed West.

Eradicating global poverty through institutional reform also involves
more realistic demands than a solution through private initiatives and
bilateral development aid. To be sure, private donations and some development projects have prevented much suffering while attempts at institutional reform have thus far led nowhere.[52] But it is not realistic to
hope that the problem of world poverty will be solved once and for all
in the foreseeable future through an expansion of private initiatives and
bilateral development aid. This does not mean, of course, that we should

shun donations or oppose development aid. It means only that we should also reflect on the possibility of a global order that would not lead to the kind of massive and severe poverty that must then continually be mitigated through donations, development aid, and debt relief. Continual mitigation of poverty leads to fatigue, aversion, even contempt. It demands of the more affluent citizens and governments that they rally to the cause again and again while knowing full well that most similarly situated persons and governments contribute nothing or very little, that their own contributions are legally optional and that, no matter how much they give, they could for just a little more always save yet another child from disease or malnutrition.

These last two factors may well be important for explaining the inefficiency of traditional development aid (mentioned in note 40). This inefficiency is not merely due to lack of goodwill on the part of the governments of the donor countries. It is due also to their competitive situation: Every affluent state must be concerned not to place itself at a competitive disadvantage vis-à-vis the others by granting purely altruistic development aid. And many, therefore, feel morally entitled to reject the demand for greater concern for the truly deprived by pointing out that their competitors, too, do not meet such demands. This hypothesis supports the optimistic assumption that the affluent states would be prepared, in joint reciprocity, to commit themselves to more than what they tend to do each on its own. Analogous considerations apply to the contribution of the GRD to environmental protection and the conservation of resources. When many parties decide separately then the solution that would be best for all is not achieved. Each party gets (almost) the full benefit of its pollution and wastefulness while the resulting harms are shared by all ("tragedy of the commons"). An additional point is that national development aid and environmental protection measures must be politically fought for or defended year after year, while acceptance of the GRD regime would require only one, albeit rather more far-reaching, political decision.

The other optimistic consideration has to do with prudence. The times when we could afford to ignore developments in the "less-developed countries" are over for good. The economic development of the LDCs will have great influence upon our environment, and their military and technological development will be accompanied by various serious dangers, among which those associated with nuclear, biological/ genetic, and chemical weapons and technologies are only the most obvious. Here we must think not only of weapons and technologies that the more powerful states possess already but also of those that will be developed in the next decades and centuries and then presumably find their way into the hands of other governments and groups. The transnational imposition of externalities and risks will more and more become a two-way street. No state or group of states, however rich and mighty, will be able effectively to insulate itself from external influences, such as military and terrorist attacks, illegal immigration, epidemics, the drug trade, pollution and climate change, price fluctuations, and scientific-technological and cultural innovations. Hence it is increasingly in our interest that stable democratic institutions, in which governmental power is effectively constrained through procedural rules and basic rights, should emerge in the less-developed regions. Large parts of the populations of these countries have only the most minimal education, often not even the ability to read and write, and have no assurance that they will be able to meet even their most basic needs. In these countries, democratic institutions are much less likely than explosive mixtures of religious and ideological fanaticism, revolutionary movements, death squads, and politicized militaries. To expose ourselves to the occasional explosions of these mixtures would be increasingly dangerous and also more costly in the long run than the introduction of the proposed GRD.

This prudential consideration has a moral side as well. A future that is pervaded by radical inequalities and hence instability would endanger not only the security of ourselves and our children but also the long-term survival of our society, values, and culture. Moreover, such a future would endanger the security of all other human beings and their children as well as the survival of their societies, values, and cultures. And so the interest in peace, in a future world in which different societies, values, and cultures can coexist and interact peacefully, is obviously also, and importantly, a moral interest.

Realizing our prudential and moral interest in a peaceful and ecologically sound future will—and here I go beyond my earlier modest proposal—require supranational institutions and organizations that limit the sovereignty rights of states more severely than is currently the case. The most powerful states could try to impose such limitations upon all the rest while exempting themselves. It is quite doubtful, however, that today's great powers will summon the political will to make this attempt before it is too late. It is doubtful also whether such an attempt could succeed. For it would provoke the bitter resistance of many other states, which would try very hard, through rearmament, to gain membership in the club of great powers themselves. For such a project, the "elites" in many LDCs could probably mobilize their populations quite easily.

It might then make more sense for all concerned to work toward supranational institutions and organizations that limit the sovereignty rights of all states equally.[53] But this solution can work only if at least a large majority of the states participating in these institutions and organizations are stable democracies. This presupposes, in turn, that the citizens of these states can satisfy their basic needs, can attain a decent standard of education, and are assured of a reasonable income.

The current direction of geopolitical development points toward a world in which a steadily growing number of militarily and technologically advanced states and groups constitute a steadily growing danger for ever larger parts of humankind. Deflecting this development in a more reasonable direction realistically requires considerable support from those other 80 percent of the world's population who want to reduce our economic hegemony and participate in our high standard of living. Through the introduction of the GRD, or some similar reform, we can gain such support by showing in a tangible way that our relations to the rest of the world are not devoted solely to cementing our economic hegemony and that the poor of this world will be able peacefully to achieve a considerable improvement in their circumstances. In this way, and only in this way, can we refute the conviction, which is understandably widespread in the LDCs, that we will not be concerned about their misery until they have the economic and military power to do us serious harm. And only in this way can we undermine the popular support that aggressive political movements of all kinds can derive from this conviction.

This second consideration shows that the GRD proposal can also be supported by prudential arguments and might therefore succeed even if the political effectiveness of moral and ecological arguments were to prove insufficient. It is therefore of some moral importance to develop and present also the prudential arguments as clearly and convincingly as possible.

Conclusion

We are familiar, through charity appeals for example, with the assertion that it lies in our power to save the lives of many or, by doing nothing, to let these people die. We are less familiar with the notion of a negative responsibility, according to which most of us do not merely let persons starve, but also participate actively in starving them.[54] It is not surprising that our initial reaction to this even more unpleasant assertion is indignation and even hostility. Rather than think it through or discuss it, we want to forget it or put it aside as plainly absurd. At the very least we want to demand that an assertion so dramatically opposed to our commonsense judgments be proved in every detail and with the utmost stringency.

I have not here been able to deliver so rigorous a proof. It is extremely difficult to estimate whether a proposed modification of our global order is practicable and, if so, what its long-term effects would be on the incidence of radical inequality. Economists may be able to offer more precise estimates on this score and to work out a more detailed reform proposal; but a stringent proof is not to be expected even from them. The morally reasonable reaction to this essay must nevertheless, I believe, be constructive. Even if its argumentation falls short of strict proof, it must raise considerable doubts about our commonsense prejudices, which we should in any case treat with suspicion given how strongly our self-interest is engaged in this matter. The great moral importance of reaching the correct judgment on this issue also counsels against lightly dismissing the assertion defended here. The essential data about the lives and deaths of the global poor in our current world are, after all, indisputable. In view of very considerable global interdependence, it is extremely unlikely that their poverty is due exclusively to local factors and that no reform of our global order could affect either that poverty or these local factors. No less incredible is the view that ours is the best of all possible global orders as far as poverty is concerned. We should collaborate across disciplines to conceive a comprehensive solution to the problem of global poverty and across borders for the political implementation of this solution.

Notes

Work on this essay was supported by a 1993–94 Laurance S. Rockefeller fellowship at the Princeton University Center for Human Values. I would also like to thank those who have commented on its earlier versions as presented to the conference, "Consumption, Global Stewardship, and the Good Life," at the University of Maryland, to a conference in memory of Professor Tscha Hung in Beijing, and to a colloquium on international justice in Graz, Austria—in particular, Susan Wolf and Paul Streeten; Ted Hondrich and Rudolf Haller; Peter Koller, Anton Leist, and Alexander Somek. For additional help in composing the final version I would further like to thank Marko Ahtisaari, Brian Barry, David A. Crocker, Sidney Morgenbesser, Brian Orend, Steffen Wesche, and Peter Unger. Their good objections have led to substantial clarifications.

1. The United Nations Development Programme reports that "about 1.3 billion people [24 percent of world population] live below the poverty line," defined as "that income and expenditure level below which a minimum, nutritionally adequate diet plus essential non-food requirements are not affordable" (United Nations Development Programme, *Human Development Report 1995* [New York: Oxford University Press, 1995], 16 and 223). This includes 350 million (or 40 percent of the population) in India, 105 million (10 percent) in China, 93 million (80 percent) in Bangladesh, 72 million (47 percent) in Brazil,

and about 300 million in Ethiopia, Vietnam, the Philippines, Nigeria, Pakistan, and Indonesia (*The Economist*, British edition, 25 June 1994, 130). About 70 percent of the global poor are female.

2. If the United States had its fair share of these deaths, it would lose one million citizens a year to poverty—about as many every three weeks as it lost during the entire Vietnam War. In this century, many more premature deaths globally were caused by peacetime poverty than by all wars combined.

3. Cf. Amartya Sen, *Poverty and Famines* (Oxford: Clarendon Press, 1981).

4. Although it is important to my argument that we are quite well off and very much better off than the global poor, I do not discuss how standards of living should be defined, compared, and measured. This topic has received a great deal of academic attention in recent years, most notably, perhaps, from Ronald Dworkin, James Griffin, Martha C. Nussbaum, Derek Parfit, John Rawls, Thomas Scanlon, and Amartya Sen. I avoid this issue not only for reasons of space but also because I am certain that any plausible specification would sustain the claims I want to make. There is also the fear that all the debate about definition and measurement, and perhaps any encoding of inequalities in numerical terms, may perplex and diminish our appreciation of what would otherwise be an overwhelmingly obvious and monstrous fact. We read that the average income in some countries is less than 1 percent of ours; but this figure obscures the fact that many persons there cannot earn anywhere near this average income and must constantly reckon with the possibility that their children may die of simple diarrhea because they cannot afford a 15-cent oral rehydration pack. (Some 3 million children annually die in this way, another 3.5 million of pneumonia, 1 million of measles, and so on; see James P. Grant, *The State of the World's Children 1993* [New York: Oxford University Press, 1993].) In any case, we must keep in mind that what, in this essay, I blandly call "poverty" has many aspects over and above low income and wealth.

5. This mode of argument goes back to Peter Singer; see "Famine, Affluence and Morality" in *Philosophy and Public Affairs* 1 (1972): 229–43. It has been developed further in Henry Shue, *Basic Rights: Subsistence, Affluence, and U.S. Foreign Policy* (Princeton: Princeton University Press, 1980), and Shelly Kagan, *The Limits of Morality* (Oxford: Oxford University Press, 1989). Among the latest contributions, with detailed bibliographies, are Garrett Cullity, "International Aid and the Scope of Kindness," *Ethics* 105 (1994): 99–127, and Peter Unger, *Living High and Letting Die: Our Illusion of Innocence* (New York: Oxford University Press, 1996).

6. The first four points are amply documented by numerous intergovernmental and nongovernmental agencies and organizations. The fifth point can be substantiated through the institutional reform I propose in the third section, and also through the many successes in protection that organized citizens of developed countries have achieved by helping to supply seeds, wells, fuel-efficient stoves, and microloans and by helping to promote basic capabilities (reading, writing, accounting, marketing, and so on) and basic knowledge (for example, about hygiene, nutrition, prophylaxis, birth control, irrigation, and the law).

7. One may be negatively responsible for harms and injuries one has inflicted upon others, for example.

8. One might call this an overlapping consensus, but it differs from what Rawls has in mind by being on a higher level and also more concrete. Rawls envisions that the adherents of different conceptions of the good agree on an entire conception of justice together with the basic structure it entails under present circumstances [John Rawls, *Political Liberalism* (New York: Columbia University Press, 1993), chap. 4]. I envision that the adherents of different conceptions of justice reach a morally based agreement on a program for reforming a core injustice. This second model is especially important in contexts like the international one, where there is little chance for agreement on a full conception of justice. I would like to develop this model further, especially by also taking account of moral conceptions prevalent in other cultures.

9. For a concise exposition of the first approach, see Thomas Nagel, "Poverty and Food: Why Charity Is Not Enough" in *Food Policy: The Responsibility of the United States in the Life and Death Choices*, ed. Peter Brown and Henry Shue (New York: Free Press, 1977), 54–62 ; and perhaps also Onora O'Neill, "Lifeboat Earth," in *International Ethics*, ed. Charles Beitz et al. (Princeton, N.J.: Princeton University Press, 1985), 262–81, and Thomas Pogge, *Realizing Rawls* (Ithaca, N.Y.: Cornell University Press, 1989), §24.

10. We tend to underestimate global interdependence because of its one-sidedness. Our circumstances are only mildly affected by developments abroad and hardly at all by developments in the poorer countries.

11. Talk of "our global institutional scheme" sounds forbiddingly abstract, and I cannot hope to explicate this notion fully here. To convey at least a rough idea, one should mention, first and foremost, the institution of the modern state. The land surface of our planet is divided into a number of clearly demarcated and nonoverlapping national territories. Human beings are matched up with these territories so that (at least for the most part) each person belongs to exactly one territory. Any person or group effectively controlling a preponderant share of the means of coercion within such a territory is recognized as the legitimate government of both the territory and the persons belonging to it. It is entitled to rule "its" people through laws, orders, and officials, to adjudicate conflicts among them, and also to exercise ultimate control over all resources within the territory ("eminent domain"). It is also entitled to represent these persons against the rest of the world: to bind them through treaties and contracts, to regulate their relations with outsiders, to declare war in their name, to represent them through diplomats and emissaries, and to control outsiders access to the country's territory. In this second role, a government is considered continuous with its predecessors and successors: bound by the undertakings of the former, and capable of binding the latter through its own undertakings. There are, of course, various minor deviations and complications, as well as many further, more peripheral features of our global order, some of which have undergone significant change over time. (One important modification was the succession of international trading regimes marked by the agreement at Bretton Woods, which was associated with noticeable changes in overall prosperity and its distribution.) But its central and most consequential features have been remarkably stable for centuries. Much about the circumstances of the global poor

can be understood by comprehending fully the role of only these central features.

12. It is bad luck to be born into a family that is too poor to feed one. But the fact that a quarter of all children are born into such families is not bad luck but bad organization.

13. Émile Durkheim, *Suicide: A Study in Sociology*, trans. John A. Spaulding and George Simpson, ed. George Simpson (New York: Free Press, 1966).

14. Drawing this false inference exemplifies a fallacy that used to be quite common, for instance, in the controversy over the heritability of IQ. But the point is now well understood. Even if genetic differences are by far the most important factor in explaining interpersonal differences in vulnerability to a certain disease, it may still be true that the overall incidence of this disease could be dramatically reduced through a change in the environment. And even if more than 90 percent of the observed variation in female adult height in some village is due to hereditary factors (there being a very high correlation between a woman's height and the average height of her two parents), it is still quite possible that all woman villagers would be much taller if, when they were growing up, the village had had an adequate food supply or girls had not been disadvantaged compared to boys.

15. Habermas's commitment to this first approach is brought out in his universalization principle, according to which social norms are to be assessed by considering what effects and side effects their universal observance would have upon the interests of each individual person (see Jürgen Habermas, *Moralbewußtsein und kommunikatives Handeln* [Frankfurt: Suhrkamp, 1983], 103).

16. Quoted in Stephen Jay Gould, "The Moral State of Tahiti—and of Darwin," *Natural History* 10 (1991): 19. This quote is remarkable, because Darwin is often claimed by those who find it either desirable or unavoidable that human life should be a competitive struggle for survival.

17. John Locke, "An Essay Concerning the True Original, Extent, and End of Civil Government" in *John Locke: Two Treatises of Government*, ed. Peter Laslett (Cambridge: Cambridge University Press, 1988 [1689]), §27 and §33. See also Robert Nozick, *Anarchy, State, and Utopia* (New York: Basic Books, 1974).

18. Locke, "An Essay Concerning the True Original," §36.

19. Locke, "An Essay Concerning the True Original," §41 and §37; cp. Nozick, *Anarchy, State, and Utopia*, 175–77 and chapter 4.

20. An important element in this restriction is the constraint on their freedom of movement that results from the fact that states successfully claim and enforce their right to exclude foreigners from their territory.

21. This is so not only because we cannot collect the necessary data about all these crimes and estimate their effects upon the present world but also because different persons would have come to exist had these crimes not occurred (cf. Thomas Schwartz, "Obligations to Posterity" in *Obligations to Future Generations*, ed. Richard I. Sikora and Brian Barry [Philadelphia: Temple University Press, 1978], 3–13; and Derek Parfit, *Reasons and Persons* [Oxford: Oxford University Press, 1984], chap. 16).

22. Even Nozick suggests that in such a case Rawls's difference principle, which is focused on the eradication of poverty, may be a morally plausible solution (Nozick, *Anarchy, State, and Utopia*, 231). He does, however, make this suggestion in the context of the assumption that the offspring of the victims of past crimes are likely to be overrepresented among the current poor. The third approach, as I have sketched it, is not committed on this point. It deems it unjust to allow innocent persons to be victims of radical inequality when this inequality came about through historical processes pervaded by crimes—even if these crimes had been committed by ancestors of the current poor. I believe that Nozick, too, would accept this point on reflection, because the kinship liability involved in denying it does not fit into his overall position. He would then agree with the central idea of the third approach: Radical inequality can be compatible with justice only if it came about pursuant to morally plausible rules that were actually observed.

23. In contrast to Thomas Pogge, "Cosmopolitanism and Sovereignty," *Ethics*, 103 (1992): 48–75, where the prevailing conception of sovereignty is criticized.

24. Compare the far more radical idea that on a Lockean account "each individual has a right to an equal share of the basic non-human means of production" (that is, means of production other than labor that are not themselves produced: resources in the sense of my GRD), as presented in Hillel Steiner, "The Natural Right to the Means of Production," *Philosophical Quarterly* 27 (1977): 49, and developed further in G. A. Cohen, "Self-Ownership, World Ownership, and Equality: Part II," *Social Philosophy and Policy* 3 (1986): 87–95.

25. When first making the proposal (in Thomas Pogge, "An Egalitarian Law of Peoples," *Philosophy and Public Affairs* 23 [1994]:195–224), I did speak of a "global resources tax"—misleadingly, as taxes and fees are not usually understood as payments deriving from (partial) ownership.

26. It is difficult to estimate the average annual per capita income among the poorest quintile of world population. Sixty dollars would seem to be a reasonable guess. Since the purchasing power of money (converted at market exchange rates) is about five times greater in the poorest countries, their annual per capita purchasing power would then be equivalent to that of $300 in the rich countries. This squares with Partha Dasgupta's statement that most in the poorest quintile have annual per capita purchasing power below $275 and all below $370 in 1985 U.S. dollars (Partha Dasgupta, *An Inquiry into Well-Being and Destitution* [Oxford: Clarendon Press, 1993], 79f.). It also squares with the statement that 1.3 billion persons have purchasing power of below $1 per day (United Nations Development Programme, *Human Development Report 1996* [New York: Oxford University Press, 1996], 27). Mr. Selim Jahan, deputy director of the UNDP *Human Development Report* office in New York City, has confirmed orally that the figure of $1 per day represents purchasing power, not income. With such incredibly low incomes it is not surprising that most in the poorest quintile, 800 million, do not get enough food (United Nations Development Programme, *Human Development Report 1995*, 16). Note that estimates

in terms of annual income still understate the economic inequality. For, to earn these incomes, the global poor must generally spend a much greater proportion of their time at work than we do. So the inequality in incomes per hour is greater than that in annual incomes. The inequality is greater still when quality of work is taken into account. And it is further aggravated by the even more extreme wealth inequality—the global poor own essentially nothing of the world's wealth and thus have no reserves for even minor emergencies.

27. Since part of this money would be spent not merely *on* but also *in* the poorest countries and regions, its impact would be significantly enhanced by multiplier effects.

28. The cost of raising the GRD would be quite small. No new administrative capacities would need to be developed at the national level, as national tax systems are already in place and oil extraction is already either taxed or nationalized. Global monitoring costs would also be low, as extraction and pollution activities are relatively easy to quantify.

29. We would also pay slightly more for any other goods and services that contain crude oil components. But, with few exceptions (such as airline tickets), these increases would be negligible.

30. It may be thought that the GRD would have the collateral effect of dampening economic activity. But I do not see why it should. The funds raised through the GRD scheme do not, after all, disappear: They are spent by, and for the benefit of, the global poor and thereby generate effective market demand that spurs economic activity.

31. Here I should concede that the rich countries could hope to negotiate a (for them) cheaper solution to this collective action problem: We could institute a national resources dividend and try to induce other states to do the same. This would probably involve some side payments to less-developed countries (LDCs). But these could be narrowly focused on their governments and rulers and would, in any case, need to include only those LDCs whose developmental decisions might otherwise adversely affect the global environment. We have seen this strategy at work in recent treaties under which some LDC governments have been forgiven some of their foreign debt in exchange for undertaking certain environmental initiatives in their territory.

32. Even if we disregard multiplier effects and assume that only one-quarter of total GRD revenue reaches persons in the poorest quintile, their average annual income would still improve by over $60, that is, would double compared to the status quo (cp. note 26 above). This improvement would simply overwhelm minor price increases.

33. Consider this analogy: If we taxed gasoline an extra 50¢ per gallon in the United States and paid the full revenue to the poorest 40 percent in the form of a flat tax credit, then the poor would certainly be much better off than before even if they stuck to their driving habits. However, they would presumably not stick to their driving habits. They would use less gasoline and thereby make themselves even better off while reducing pollution and slowing oil depletion.

34. This minimum could be defined in terms of some substantial fraction of world population. The exact choice of fraction does not make much of a practi-

cal difference, as focusing on the poorest 5 percent, say, would rather soon bring them up to the level of the sixth percentile and would then begin improving the circumstances of an ever-growing fraction of world population. Given the extremely heavy concentration of global income today, it is quite possible that adoption of the GRD reform would ensure that, in the long run, incomes at each of the bottom sixty or seventy percentiles would be higher than they would have been under a continuation of current institutional arrangements.

35. This assumes, plausibly, in my view, that the local costs of such rule design (that the circumstances of the poor are sometimes not improved at all, rather than a little) are outweighed by its global benefits (that national elites develop a stronger interest in the eradication of poverty, in order to qualify their country for GRD funds).

36. The GRD scheme involves, then, a secondary conditionality. Obligations toward the global poor are primary and unconditional, but obligations toward the governments of poor countries are derivative. They can, therefore, be made conditional, but not arbitrarily so: An obligation toward such a government can be made conditional only upon this government's effectiveness in combating poverty in its territory.

37. This could give governments an incentive toward keeping per capita income low. But this incentive would be overwhelmed by opposing interests: A government's power depends in many ways on its country's overall prosperity.

38. Or perhaps proportional to the size of the adult population, if effective population control efforts might otherwise be discouraged.

39. For a more extensive discussion of the term redistribution and its tendentious connotations, see Pogge, *Realizing Rawls*, 32, 34f., 238, 276, and, "Cosmopolitanism and Sovereignty," 52.

40. There are various studies showing how development aid often benefits those capable of reciprocation, that is, the "elites" in the politically more important developing countries. In addition, such aid is often focused on expensive high-visibility projects in which firms of the donor country can profitably participate. For more on this theme and for relevant references, see the cover story "Why Aid Is an Empty Promise," *The Economist*, 7 May 1994, 13–14 and 21–24.

41. James Tobin, "A Currency Transactions Tax, Why and How," unpublished typescript (1994); Barry Eichengreen, James Tobin, and Charles Wyplosz, "Two Cases for Sand in the Wheels of International Finance," *Economic Journal* 105 (1995): 162–72; cp. James Tobin, "A Proposal for International Monetary Reform," *Eastern Economic Journal* 4 (1978): 153–59.

42. James Tobin, "A Tax on International Currency Transactions" in United Nations Development Programme, *Human Development Report 1994* (New York: Oxford University Press, 1994), 70.

43. These claims might be supported by pointing to how lax many states have been about paying their much smaller membership dues to the UN.

44. It is important to realize that the unequal distribution of property in natural resources, unlike that of natural genetic endowments, is *not* such an extrasocial factor. The geographical distribution of natural resources (for instance, that

the Middle East holds a large part of the world's crude oil reserves) is, of course, an extrasocial fact. But this fact does not as such affect different persons differentially, but does so only insofar as it is combined with another, clearly social, factor: namely, that our global order assigns to national societies and governments exclusive rights to ownership and control over natural resources on their territory.

45. Showings of types B2 and B4 generally will justify only the extent of existing inequality, not its allocation (that is, the existing role distribution: that *these* persons are poor and *those* wealthy).

46. Just as it would be absurd to grant affluent adults who do not feed their children well an exemption from their taxes.

47. This argument is more fully developed in Thomas Pogge, "The Bounds of Nationalism," in *Canadian Journal of Philosophy*, supplementary volume (forthcoming). For a complementary argument, to the effect that unqualified partiality constitutes a loophole in our morality, see Thomas Pogge, "Loopholes in Moralities," *Journal of Philosophy* 89 (1992): 84– 98.

48. It is not a coincidence, I believe, that political realism had its heyday (with Hans Morgenthau, George Kennan, and Henry Kissinger) in the Cold War era. During this time, the pragmatic imperatives of prevailing and winning were, or seemed, so absolutely compelling that they tended to overwhelm all other considerations. In periods when states feel more secure, it is much more likely that their governments and citizens can be moved by moral considerations, even in their foreign policy.

49. Seymour Drescher, *Capitalism and Antislavery: British Mobilization in Comparative Perspective* (London: Macmillan, 1986). For a relevantly similar, though somewhat more contestable, account about the U.S. retreat from Vietnam, see Howard Zinn, *A People's History of the United States* (New York: Harper, 1980), chap. 18.

50. Obviously, a lot more could and should be said about the various similarities and dissimilarities between this case and the proposed GRD reform. But here I have merely wanted to point out that there do seem to be significant counterexamples to the claim that governments never act contrary to what they take to be in their own, or their society's, best interest.

51. To show this fully, one would need to respond to the objection that instituting the GRD would be an immoral imposition of our Western values upon a pluralistic world. As explained elsewhere (Pogge, *Realizing Rawls*, 267–73, and "An Egalitarian Law of Peoples," 215–18), I find this objection implausible, mainly because there can be no "neutral" global order, nor a "neutral" role that the developed Western states could play in regard to how the world economy is structured: Our political and economic policies and decisions unavoidably codetermine the structure and development of global institutions. Even if the objection had some merit, the Western countries should at least jointly propose (something like) the GRD regime.

52. Witness the proposals for a new international economic order, which UNCTAD and the UN General Assembly debated extensively in the 1970s but without result, for an international tax on carbon dioxide emissions and for an

agreement, which was to have been included in the Law of the Sea Treaty, to use the value of ocean-floor resources "to benefit all peoples, with special regard for the needs of the least developed countries."

53. This vision jars, I admit, with our current notions of state sovereignty—with which I had said my GRD proposal would be compatible. It involves a more democratic world order, a greater role for central organizations, and more world government than we have at present—though nothing like a world government on the model of current national governments. But this vision is not part of my GRD proposal. It merely describes what I take to be another important potential benefit for us of the GRD scheme.

I am not naive enough to believe that this proposal would be popular in all countries, let alone with all current governments. Implementing it could well require economic sanctions and even military interventions. My point is that its implementation, assuming I am right to believe that it could gain significant support in most LDCs, would at least be morally and politically feasible, while instituting a technology control regime unilaterally would be neither. So long as the developed world shows itself essentially indifferent to the immense and massive suffering of the global poor, it will be much easier for hard-liners in the LDCs to gain and hold power and to win support for ambitious weapons and technology programs. "Only through such programs," they can plausibly say to their compatriots, "can we become a potential threat to the peoples of the affluent states, and only if we constitute a potential threat to them will they pay any attention to our society."

54. We participate *indirectly* because we contribute to the imposition of a grievously unjust world order. The responsibility of persons for the injustice of any institutional scheme in which they participate will vary. The more influential and privileged persons are within the scheme, the greater will be their negative responsibility for any grievously unjust institutions they help to uphold and do not work to reform. The greater also will be the contribution they should be willing to make toward helping to reform unjust and also toward upholding just social institutions. Responsibility here links up not with blameworthiness but with wrongness: Privileged and influential participants in a grievously unjust institutional scheme who help support the scheme without working toward its reform act wrongly. They may nevertheless, in some cases, not be blameworthy on account of such conduct, if it is due, for instance, to genuine and excusable factual or moral error.

26

Consumption, Appropriation, and Stewardship

David Wasserman

This essay examines how acts of consumption are morally constrained by a consumer's obligations to others. Political theorists since Locke have examined the justification for removing resources "from the common" and claiming ownership of them. They have paid less attention to those acts by which people remove or alter common resources without making any proprietary claim. But acts of this second kind are of special concern in a world where the depletion and despoliation of common resources is an object of moral and political concern. When emissions from Northern factories destroy atmospheric ozone, or when fishing fleets from poor countries destroy the great coral reefs, resources that no one claims to own are taken out of the commons. Various theories of justice specify restraints on the distribution of resources and regard certain disparities as unacceptable. Can such theories also be used to specify restraints on the consumption of resources? When are disparities in the consumption of resources morally significant?

For the purposes of this discussion, it will be useful to have a single term that encompasses not only the act of asserting or establishing ownership of a resource but also the act of consuming resources without any proprietary claim. Let us describe both kinds of acts as forms of *appropriation.*

There are two ways in which ownership and consumption have been seen as relevantly similar for purposes of political justice. The first concerns the relative amounts appropriated by different nations and citizens; the second, the harm caused by appropriation.

Consider the complaint that citizens of the United States comprise only 5 percent of the world's population but consume 40 percent of its resources. In one respect, this complaint is similar to those that are made about massive inequalities in the ownership of land or other scarce resources: it assumes that consumption, like ownership, is rival or exclusive. This assumption is often valid. There may be a limited supply of the resource consumed, as in the case of many fuel sources; or the consumption of one good may reduce the limited supply of another, as the use of fluorocarbons destroys ozone, the production of beef destroys grain, and the harvesting of fruits and vegetables starves the animals that feed on them.

But the real objection, I think, is not that some consume *more* than others—if it were, then we would actively defend the rights of present nonconsumers to destroy their fair share of coral reefs or atmospheric ozone. Rather, the objection is that consumption by some causes *harm* to others. Although the kind of harm alleged in standard complaints about consumption is the loss or depletion of vital resources, there are other forms of harm as well. Consumption, like ownership, may cause harm cumulatively, as it does when the combined exhaust from a large number of motor vehicles exceeds toxic levels of air pollution. And consumption, like ownership, may cause less tangible harms, for example, as it does by contributing to coercive, exploitative, or other demeaning relationships between groups or individuals.

With these distinctions in place, this essay will consider how well restrictions on harming can ground plausible limits on consumption, without recourse to a theory of justice committed to a particular type of distribution. I will focus on the most familiar restriction of this kind, the so-called Lockean proviso: that we may appropriate resources so long as "there is enough, and as good, left in common for others."[1] I will examine several interpretations of, and variations on, the Lockean proviso discussed in the recent literature.

As stated, the proviso might appear to be a distributional constraint, limiting the amount that can be appropriated on the basis of the amount left for others. But even understood this way, it is not a constraint on the *ultimate* distribution of ownership or consumption: even if initial appropriations do leave as much and as good for others to appropriate, differences in ability, preference, and luck can result in vast disparities in ownership and consumption. And as we will see, the proviso has not always been interpreted as distributional, even in a narrower sense. Some argue that it does not require the initial appropriator to leave all others with "enough" resources *to make similar appropriations;* others argue that even if an appropriator does leave "enough," the appropriation may be prohibited because of other adverse consequences. For many commentators, the proviso is really no more than Locke's awkward first attempt at formulating a principle that restricts appropriations if they cause certain kinds of harms, of which resource depletion is only, and not always, one.

The strength and plausibility of the proviso as a constraint on consumption depends on how broadly we construe the harm associated with appropriation. I will argue that although restrictions on harming do not appear to yield fully independent constraints on consumption, they suggest the importance of justifying the appropriation of unclaimed resources. Following G. A. Cohen, I will argue that one critical question in the political justice of appropriation is how we should regard the world's resources as initially held or owned.

Finally, I will explore two related approaches to this question: each person can be regarded as holding the world's resources as a trustee for each other or as a steward for all people. On a trusteeship or stewardship account, no part of the world's resources is up for grabs, but neither is every appropriation hostage to universal consent. The success of these accounts, however, requires the development of a freestanding notion of trusteeship or stewardship, which does not rely on a specific system of legal rights or set of religious beliefs. The difficulties in developing such freestanding notions appear to be formidable.

License to Appropriate: Interpreting the Lockean Proviso

Locke may have seen his proviso merely as a ban on gratuitous hoarding or a special restriction for a few scarce commodities, not as a general constraint on the appropriation of natural resources. His image of natural bounty was the superabundant stream, whose capacity exceeds any possible demand, from which we cannot help but leave "as much and as good," however much we drink.[2] Hillel Steiner suggests that Locke failed to see the implications of the proviso because he did not recognize the truth, "painfully apparent to us today," that "no world can be one of unlimited natural resources."[3]

Robert Nozick argues, however, that scarcity need not have dire implications for appropriation under the proviso, since it can be interpreted in different ways. One line of interpretation suggests that an appropriation is not permitted if it precludes similar appropriations of the same resources by others; another finds that an appropriation is permitted as long as it does not leave nonappropriators worse off than they would have been without that appropriation, because it compensates them for the lost resources or lost opportunity to appropriate them.[4]

Nozick regards the first interpretation as the stronger, since it requires that others be able to make similar appropriations, not merely that they be compensated for losing that opportunity. It is only on the first interpretation, Nozick argues, that scarcity imposes severe constraints on ownership. As we will see, however, the comparative strength of the two interpretations depends on the baseline from which we assess the harm that, under the second interpretation, needs to be compensated. If we take a broad view of the harm for which compensation is owed, to include such adverse effects as the loss of natural landscapes or political autonomy, the second interpretation may turn out to be more stringent than the first, because compensation may be impossible.

"Enough and As Good": The First Interpretation

Nozick himself rejects the first interpretation, because he does not believe that the ultimate depletion of a specific resource must preclude its initial appropriation. Nozick argues that the first interpretation would prohibit any ownership in a world with limited resources, like ours: since further appropriations would eventually leave nothing to appropriate, the recursive application of the proviso would preclude all appropriations back to the first.[5] Some critics of absolute property rights would not regard this as a reductio ad absurdum. Steiner, for example, argues that in a world with scarce resources, overlapping generations, and unbounded population, a principle of equal liberty prohibits individual ownership of *any* natural resource.[6]

This interpretation of the proviso would have even more drastic consequences for the consumption of scarce, nonrenewable resources: we could not consume at all if any level of consumption would lead to eventual exhaustion of this particular resource. In this case, the consequences of the proviso *would* be a reductio: we can hardly expect the inhabitants of a planet with a limited, nonrenewable oxygen supply to stop breathing.

Fortunately, however, many vital natural resources in our world, while perhaps not "superabundant," are renewable, so that their consumption by one person does not necessarily preclude their consumption by another. For the consumption of those resources, the first interpretation of the proviso may have less drastic consequences, since the prospects for renewal are far better for many resources that are consumed, like oxygen, than for many resources that are owned, like land. We can leave "enough and as good" for others if we do not consume those resources beyond their capacity for renewal, even if we consume beyond our subsistence needs. Of course, the need to assure sustainability may impose severe limits on what we may deplete or despoil. But those limits are being extended by modern technology.

Admittedly, some future generation may contain too many people to permit the same level of consumption. But this possibility arguably would not constrain present consumption as long as the resources available for future generations were not depleted by the present one. If our consumption results in no lasting depletion, then we leave "enough and as good" for future generations even if, because of their size, their members have far smaller shares.

Alternatively, we might feel that the obligation to leave "enough and as good" could only be satisfied by leaving enough to give the members of future generations shares equal to our own, even if those generations were of much larger size. But if so, we might regard later generations as having a correlative obligation to keep their size within reasonable bounds: present consumers can only be expected to leave "enough and as good" for a limited number of successors.[7]

There is, however, a more basic challenge to the first interpretation of the proviso, especially as it applies to consumption. To insist on the nondepletion of specific resources, regardless of the effect of depletion on well-being, seems fetishistic. A reasonable condition on appropriation, it might appear, should focus instead on the risk of harm from depletion and the prospect of compensation for that harm. We are led, then, to the second interpretation of the proviso.

The Second Interpretation

The second interpretation of the Lockean proviso permits some to appropriate to the exclusion of others if those who appropriate adequately compensate those who cannot and thereby leave them no worse off for the appropriation. This interpretation avoids Herbert Spencer's conclusion that equal ownership of resources would be required to prevent the impoverishment or enslavement of latecomers, because it provides latecomers with compensation for any loss due to their inability to make similar appropriations.

The possibility of compensation seems to increase the latitude for appropriation. But critics have claimed that compensation is not possible in a world of unlimited population growth, since appropriators can have no idea how many nonappropriators they will need to compensate then. As Steiner argues: "an appropriator can [not] know, and therefore compensate for, the loss of well-being incurred in consequence of their being deprived of the use of the appropriated object—by persons who do not yet exist."[8]

For consumption, however, the constraints do not appear as severe: the possibility of resource renewal limits the need for compensation while the possibility of resource substitution makes compensation more feasible. If our consumption results in no lasting depletion, we have nothing for which to compensate. While we must compensate others for our consumption of nonrenewable resources, we may be entitled to assume, as under the first interpretation of the proviso, that later generations and other nations will match our restrained consumption with restrained procreation so as to make compensation feasible.

But the prospects for compensation depend to some extent on what counts as an adequate substitution. Do we, for example, fully compensate others when we deplete a scarce and valuable resource but discover or create a substitute that is equally useful for present purposes? Even if our only concern is with the material adequacy of the substitute good, this is a difficult question to answer.

What about *potential* uses of the depleted resource? What, for example, if that resource could be used in some future circumstances in ways that the substitute good could not? A technological pessimist would argue that we cannot regard a synthetic good as an adequate substitute for a natural resource, because we cannot anticipate the full range of contingencies in which that resource might be used. On the other hand, the substitute good might prove useful in circumstances where the depleted resource would not be. Can we assess the adequacy of the replacement, and of compensation, by comparing the utility of the original and substitute resources across all possible circumstances? Must the substitute good be as useful in all circumstances, or only in some probability-weighted average?

A technological optimist would not be daunted by these questions. He would argue that if we had to eliminate any risk of harm, compensation would never be possible and we would be consigned, at best, to bare subsistence. He would claim that technology often permits us to satisfy a less extreme but highly risk-averse standard, requiring a very favorable balance of expected benefits to risks.

Even if the optimist is right, however, the question remains unanswered of what harms the appropriator must compensate for. Suppose that appropriators provided compensation in the form of substitute goods that adequately protected nonappropriators from the vicissitudes of nature but limited their prospects for development. Would that be compensation enough?

The Choice of a Baseline

The question of what constitutes an adequate substitute thus raises the broader question of the appropriate baseline for assessing harm. As Nozick recognizes, the strength of the second interpretation depends on the baseline chosen. Nozick appears to favor a state-of-nature baseline,[9] which would allow the North to consume at a level that would preclude the South from ever rising above its level of preindustrial subsistence. Even Nozick's baseline, however, would prohibit many of the practices by which the North achieved its present ascendancy, like the destruction of subsistence economies by mineral extraction industries.

This baseline reduces the Lockean proviso to a bounded first-come, first-served rule, which would let people in the most-developed nations acquire ownership of as much as they wanted, so long as they did not make less-developed nations and later generations any worse off than they would have been in a preindustrial state. It would impose even fewer constraints on consumption. Northern nations could deplete some resources as long as they produced enough others so that Southern nations and future generations were as well off as they would have been without economic development. The North could consume resources at a rate that would consign the South to permanent underdevelopment.

But if we reject a state-of-nature baseline, it may be difficult to find an alternative. Cohen argues that without arbitrary restrictions on the alternative baselines to be considered, the Lockean proviso would prohibit not only full private ownership but also virtually any other form of appropriation, since there will almost always be some baseline under which some other person would have been better off than he is with the present appropriation—for instance, if that person had appropriated the resource first.[10] In particular, if we regard the world's resources as held in common, so that all must consent to any appropriation, then any division of resources that might result from hypothetical bargaining could serve as a baseline. Cohen concludes that this makes the Lockean proviso, and perhaps any restriction on harming, useless as a criterion for appropriation.

Extending the Notion of Harming

We may be able to salvage the state-of-nature baseline, and thereby save the second interpretation of the proviso from fatal indeterminacy, by taking account of less tangible harms. We have been focusing narrowly on harm that results from the unavailability of natural resources to non-appropriators. But there are other effects of appropriation, that may harm nonappropriators without depriving them of resources:

1) Harms from the depletion of natural resources besides their resulting unavailability to others

Robert Eliot has suggested that Nozick's state-of-nature baseline might be considerably more stringent than it appears, because people may be left worse off than they would otherwise be by the destruction of primeval forests, pastoral landscapes, and the like brought about by high levels of consumption.[11] Nozick might deny that such losses would leave people worse off, because he assumes that well-being can be measured in economic terms (an odd assumption for a philosopher otherwise so deferential to the way individuals value their own outcomes) and that the economic surplus yielded by appropriation would permit others to be fully compensated.[12] But if the loss of noneconomic value is regarded as noncompensable, the appropriations causing the loss will be prohibited even by the second version of Locke's proviso: those who do not appropriate will be worse off, not because they are denied the opportunity for similar appropriation but because they have lost something irreplaceable. To the extent that we see the loss or degradation of natural resources as noncompensable, the second interpretation of the proviso will be as strict as the first. It may even be stricter, since it would not be satisfied by assuring that each person was left the same amount of the same type of resources to despoil. If we ravage the earth and pollute the atmosphere, we do not leave others with "as much and as good," however much is left for them to ravage and pollute.

Although Eliot's proposal would make the state-of-nature baseline more constraining than Nozick regards it, it would also raise difficult questions about what counts as an irreplaceable loss. The Lockean proviso could hardly require people to leave the natural world in a pristine state—to leave "nothing but footprints"—because the cost of such self-restraint might well be extinction. Eliot points out several ambiguities in a less stringent proviso: in deciding how much, if any, of the past and future impact of human settlement and migration is to be incorporated into the baseline for assessing individual appropriations. Moreover, any constraint that was limited to environmental harms, to the destruction of ecosystems and places of natural beauty, might permit other intangible harms, such as economic dependence and exploitation.

2) Harms from the appropriation of natural resources apart from their depletion or destruction

The consumption of natural resources by the North affects not only the resources that the South has to consume but also the relationship between North and South. Even if we do not condemn as an injustice the simple disparity in prosperity that results from appropriation, we may regard various predictable effects of that disparity as harms. Thus, to alter Locke's example, imagine that instead of drinking the water from a superabundant stream the man diverts some of it to generate power. He leaves enough for everyone else to do likewise, but they lack the skill or interest. His power supply enables him to produce a whole array of modern labor-saving devices and consumer goods with but a small amount of other renewable resources. Although the others can easily subsist on the natural resources he has left undepleted, they live an austere life, and they crave his comfort and luxury. He offers them manufactured goods in exchange for long hours of work as factory hands or domestic servants, and many of them accept. If we regard this relationship as exploitative and demeaning, then we may have a basis for condemning that appropriation as harmful.

It is, admittedly, difficult to subsume this harm under the Lockean proviso, since the exploited may still be left with "enough and as good in common" in terms of material good and even in terms of such intangible goods as pastoral landscapes and primeval forests. As Brian Barry argues: "Most of the disparities in national prosperity are not accounted for by the abundance or lack of natural resources. They flow, rather, from differences in the stock of productive capital, in the infrastructure of transport and communication facilities, and in the training and education of the work force, the abilities of managers, and so on."[13]

It may be possible to attribute these very disparities to the North's initial appropriation of natural resources. But to condemn the disparities themselves as harms that preclude the initial appropriation is to rely on a theory of distributive justice that finds such disparities unacceptable. And while we might not need such a theory to condemn the full range of harms associated with those disparities—the destruction of traditional cultures, the dispossession of communities, and the creation of demeaning relationships between nations and between individuals—those harms may have too attenuated a connection to the original appropriation to be a basis for rejecting it. To attribute the harms wrought by industrialization, or by the globalization of capital, to the initial appropriations of natural resources is to ignore the role of subsequent history, of a myriad of other agents and social forces, in bringing about those harms. It is to treat the initial appropriations like the consumption of a forbidden fruit that cast us out of a preindustrial Eden.

Is "Enough and As Good" Enough? Beyond Nonharming to Mutual Trusteeship and Stewardship

We have seen that restrictions on harming are unlikely by themselves to impose plausible, independent limits on appropriation. Too much depends on how we construe harm, which, in turn, depends on debatable views about what kinds of environmental impact and social relationships are acceptable. And even if we could agree on the kinds of effects that count as harmful, it would be implausible to attribute them in any direct way to initial acts of appropriation.

The inquiry into a baseline for harming, however, suggests a different source of constraints on appropriation: our conception of how the world's unclaimed resources are initially held or owned. Our understanding of the moral status of those resources may impose limits on appropriation without recourse to a baseline for assessing harm or a consensus on the acceptability of particular distributions of resources or social goods.

Cohen suggests that if we reject the idea that the world's resources are simply up for grabs, we can treat them as collectively owned in one of two ways: as jointly owned, with each person having an equal, nonseverable interest in the whole and veto power over appropriations by others, or as equally divisible, with each person having the right to remove her own share or receive compensation for it. The latter is the more familiar form of collective ownership in modern societies. For example, if a divorcing couple owns property in common, each spouse has the right to demand partition, either by the literal division of the property or, where that is impractical, by a "buyout" of his or her interest.

Both forms of collective ownership have unacceptable consequences: If we regard the world as jointly owned, Locke's "wild Indian" would need unanimous consent to eat the fruits and venison around him and, thus, might starve "notwithstanding the plenty God had given him." [14] But if we regarded the world as divisible into equal shares, we would have to tolerate the great disparities in prosperity that would arise from the freedom of individuals to withdraw their "shares" and enhance them with their very disparate abilities. [15]

This dilemma only arises, however, if we restrict ourselves to the two forms of collective ownership conceived by Cohen. A notion of mutual trusteeship or joint stewardship may offer a more attractive alternative. The former treats all of us as holding the world's resources as trustees for each other. Because others hold those resources in trust for us, they must allow us reasonable appropriations; because we hold those resources in trust for them, we must marshall and develop those resources for their benefit as well as our own. Our duties to others are not incurred by specific acts of appropriation; rather, both our license to consume and our duties to provide for others arise from this relationship of mutual solicitude.

Mutual trusteeship is more demanding than Cohen's notion of ownership in common, since it does not permit individuals to remove "their" shares. But it is less demanding than Cohen's notion of joint ownership, since it does not give individuals a veto on each others' appropriation of resources. All are required to benefit others, none are subject to the others' whims.

A trusteeship approach treats our obligations to each other as grounded not only in our residence within the same national boundaries, or in our achievement of a given level of economic and social interaction or interdependence, or in any tacit agreement, but in the simple fact that we "cohabit" a single planet and live off its resources.[16] The notion of trusteeship requires an equality of concern for our cohabitants that may be consistent with a variety of distributive schemes.

For the trusteeship approach to offer a firm foundation for a theory of justice in consumption, however, it must assign the individual trustees clear, dischargeable duties. The legal concept of trusteeship is attractive because it recognizes settings in which individuals have a broad, flexible duty to maintain resources for the benefit of certain people or purposes. But expanding the classes of beneficiaries and trustees to include the world's present and future population might seem to threaten the coherence of the concept.

There is, however, a well-established public trust doctrine in the area of land-use law that recognizes the government's obligation to manage certain resources—such as rivers, seashores, and the air—in the public interest. The government cannot auction off such resources to the highest bidder or develop them for their most remunerative uses but must maintain them in a manner that ensures public access and preserves their aesthetic, moral, cultural, and historical qualities. This doctrine has been successfully applied to prevent private appropriation or development of areas of singular natural beauty and ecological or historical significance.

But the public trust doctrine is embedded in a legal system that recognizes extensive private property rights, to which public trusteeship is an important exception. The idea that all the world's resources are held in trust makes the exception the rule and takes the notion of trusteeship out of the conceptual framework from which it arguably derives its meaning. The mandate of the public trustee is, in theory, circumscribed by a system of private property and welfare rights that provides for most of the material needs of the public; the trustee does not need to use trust property toward the satisfaction of those needs and make the difficult allocative decisions that would require. Moreover, the trustee's role has been clarified by a long history of constitutional adjudication on the powers and duties of state agents.

The role of mutual trusteeship for the world's resources lacks both the limitations on trust property and the division of labor that make the role of a public land trustee reasonably well defined. It lacks an account of the resources to which individual trustees are assigned and of the standards by which they are to preserve, develop, or "invade" those resources. Nor is it clear how the legal notion of trusteeship, even as extended to public lands, would provide the resources for such an account.

Finally, it is hard to see how trusteeship can be mutual if it is extended to future generations, whose actions cannot affect the material well-being of the present generation—a recalcitrant asymmetry. A notion of mutual trusteeship that did not include future generations, however, would seem too narrow to limit appropriation adequately. The interests of future generations would guide the present "trustees" only to the extent that the welfare of those generations was a matter of concern to present people—a very thin reed on which to rest a policy of resource conservation.

If the notion of mutual trusteeship seems too indeterminate and too difficult to apply across generations, perhaps we can understand the moral status of the world's resources more clearly in terms of the notion of stewardship. Sylvia Schwartzchild finds the conception of "ownership qua stewardship" in Locke's Second Treatise, coexisting uneasily with his more familiar conception of private property. Stewardship, Schwartzchild argues, is "intimately connected with the notion of possessing something originally obtained as a gift."[17] We obtain dominion over nature as a gift from God, and our duties as stewards reflect "the continuing moral obligation the recipient has to the will of the donor."[18] In Locke's view, Schwartzchild claims, owning such gift property is "fundamentally a form of guardianship."[19] She argues that Locke's labor theory of value, in which a person acquires a good by mixing his labor with it, can be seen in part as an account of "how someone could justly use and benefit from a communal property without violating their [other owners'] inclusive rights, on the one hand, and without himself being excluded from the property on the other."[20]

But if the notion of mutual trusteeship requires a legal context it cannot take with it in its global application, the notion of stewardship is embedded in theology. It seems to derive its appeal from the idea of a Creator who appoints us guardians of the world's resources and holds us accountable for their proper use. Schwartzchild wonders if that role can survive "[i]f a shared belief in God can no longer be assumed."[21] More broadly, it is not clear whether a notion of stewardship can be detached from its theological moorings without losing much of its moral appeal.

Schwartzchild suggests that we can view an individual's fundamental rights in his body and his holdings as a gift from a "reasonable community," a community that might well impose conditions on their use such as Rawls's difference principle. But for purposes of grounding a notion of stewardship, the "community" may be a less suitable donor than God. God's benevolence provides a clear basis for defining stewardship duties: those duties depend on the objects of God's benevolence, his understanding of their good, and his division of labor for promoting their good. These critical details are part of many, if not most, theologies.

It is far less obvious how we would determine the stewardship duties that a "reasonable community" would impose. If we regard such a community as composed of rationally self-interested members, then the strings it attached to its "gifts" of resources would depend on how much the members knew about their own conditions and on the vagaries of self-interested calculation. But if we endowed the members of the community with a moral commitment to each other, to future generations, or to nature, then "the community" would become little more than a repository for our considered moral judgments instead of an independent source of moral constraints.[22]

In light of these obvious difficulties, it might be unrealistic to expect a fully adequate account of how the world's resources are initially held or owned. But if our uncertainty cannot be resolved, it can at least keep us from assuming that things "come into the world already owned." We should, perhaps, take seriously the suggestion Nozick offers as a reductio and see the world's resources as a kind of mysterious manna, an anonymous gift with indeterminate recipients. This will not tell us how those resources should be assigned, but it will protect us from complacency about our entitlement to what we own and what we consume.

Notes

1. John Locke, *Two Treatises of Government,* ed. Peter Laslett (Cambridge: Cambridge University Press, 1960 [1690]), II, sec. 27. On a literal reading of Locke, any consumption of natural resources might be regarded as conferring ownership: a person acquires ownership of a natural resource by mixing her labor with it and consumption necessarily mixes the consumer's labor with the resource consumed (*Two Treatises,* II, sec. 27). For Locke, it might seem that consumption conferred ownership regardless of the consumer's intent—to modify the sign in the antique shop, "you consume it, you own it." Some recent commentators have concluded, though, that Locke cannot be taken literally in treating labor mixing as sufficient for ownership. See, for example, Thomas Mautner, "Locke on Original Appropriation," *American Philosophical Quarterly* 19 (1982): 259–70; Karl Olivecrona, "Locke's Theory of Appropriation," *Philosophical Quarterly* 24 (1974): 220–34. They have suggested that the mixing condition must be interpreted in light of its underlying rationales.

Locke had two rationales for his "mixing" condition, neither of which would require that all consumption be treated as ownership. The incorporation rationale, as we have seen, applies to consumption only insofar as the goods consumed are rendered permanently inaccessible to others. Much consumption would not have such enduring impact and, thus, would arguably not constitute ownership.

A second rationale, that of value enhancement, would rarely apply to consumption, since our transformation of resources by breathing, ingesting, or burning them would rarely enhance their value or give us any independent claim to their residues. (There are exceptions, of course, like a pair of jeans worn out by Mick Jagger.) There is a scholarly debate about whether Locke himself saw value enhancement as a necessary or a sufficient condition for the ownership of once-common resources.

2. Locke, *Two Treatises*, II, sec. 33.

3. Hillel Steiner, "Slavery, Socialism, and Private Property," in *Property*, ed. John W. Chapman and J. Roland Pennock (New York: New York University Press, 1980), 253.

4. Robert Nozick, *Anarchy, State, and Utopia* (Cambridge, Mass.: Harvard University Press, 1974), 175–77. Actually, Nozick does not describe the contrasting interpretations in quite this way, but as G. A. Cohen observes, what he does say is confused, and the distinction in the text seems a fair reconstruction of what he intended to say. See Cohen, "Self-Ownership, World-Ownership, and Equality," in *Justice and Equality Here and Now*, ed. Frank Lucash (Ithaca, N.Y.: Cornell University Press, 1983), 108–35.

5. Nozick, *Anarchy, State, and Utopia*, 175–76.

6. Steiner, "Slavery, Socialism, and Private Property," 254–61.

7. We might regard the obligations of the present generation as conditioned on the restraint of later generations. But this would have the odd result that the present generation would not know whether it was obliged and that even reckless consumption by the present generation would be (retroactively) permitted if future generations turned out to violate their obligations of self-restraint (and their violations were not caused, justified, or excused by the actions of the present generation). It makes more sense to treat the present generation as obligated to leave "enough and as good" for future generations of reasonable size, where "reasonable size" might be significantly larger than the present population but could not exceed the earth's carrying capacity.

8. Steiner, "Slavery, Socialism, and Private Property," 253.

9. Nozick, *Anarchy, State, and Utopia*, 177.

10. Cohen, "Self-Ownership," 132–33.

11. Robert Eliot, "Future Generations, Locke's Proviso and Libertarian Justice," *Journal of Applied Philosophy* 3 (1986): 217–27.

12. Nozick, *Anarchy, State, and Utopia*, 177.

13. Brian Barry, "Do Countries Have Moral Obligations? The Case of World Poverty," *The Tanner Lectures on Human Values,* vol. 2 (Salt Lake City: University of Utah Press, 1981), 36.

14. Locke, *Two Treatises*, II, sec. 26.

15. G. A. Cohen, "Self-Ownership, World Ownership, and Equality: Part II," *Social Philosophy and Policy* 3 (1986): 77–96.

16. Like any other conception of cross-generational obligation, the notion of trusteeship must somehow deal with the causal asymmetries of past, present, and future generations.

17. Sylvia Schwartzchild, "Locke's Two Conceptions of Property," *Social Theory and Practice* 14 (1988): 146.

18. Schwartzchild, "Locke's Two Conceptions," 147.

19. Schwartzchild, "Locke's Two Conceptions," 146.

20. Schwartzchild, "Locke's Two Conceptions," 153.

21. Schwartzchild, "Locke's Two Conceptions," 161–62.

22. In "Contemporary Property Rights, Lockean Provisos, and the Interests of Future Generations," *Ethics* 105 (1995): 791–818, Clark Wolfe revives the notion of "usufructuary rights" to capture the limits on ownership that emerge from the application of the Lockean proviso, understood as a prohibition on harming: "While there is no one else whose claims supersede those of current owners, such owners simply do not possess any valid claim to degrade, consume, or destroy resources in which future persons may have an important stake" (812). But we unavoidably degrade, consume, and destroy resources in which future persons may have an important stake, and the critical issue is how much we may do so—how we must balance our stake against theirs. The notion of usufructuary rights may reflect the necessity of balancing those interests, but it cannot tell us how to do so.

27

Consumption As a Topic for the North-South Dialogue

Luis A. Camacho

In this essay, I want to address several issues: (1) What are the consequences for the South of mass consumption in the North? (2) What is the relation between Northern consumption and mass destitution in the South, and is it a reciprocal relation? (3) Is there an ongoing discussion in the South on the influence of patterns of Northern consumption and, if there is one, what can we learn from it ? (4) Is there something like a contemporary perspective on consumption typical of the South?

A preliminary remark may be useful: "North" and "South," like "West" and "East" before them, are to be taken as very imprecise designations. In addition to the truism that there is no correspondence between geography and economics (New Zealand is in the geographic South but in the economic North; Russia is in the geographic North but in the economic South), there is another, more important fact: intraregional differences are almost as great as regional ones. So the label "typical of the South" is only an approximation. The only justification for the use of these terms is usual practice and lack of a better terminology.

In the context of a global market, and for the South, consumption means loss of control in three ways: (1) Consumption is deemed a phenomenon imposed from above, or from outside, regarding which the individual can do little if anything; (2) consumption is something some people can engage in and others cannot, as if predestined by some kind of divine design; (3) consumption becomes a way of life that replaces or is at odds with political involvement. Consumption is thus one of the aspects of powerlessness for the majority of the population, either because most people have very limited access to it or because they are

552

condemned to remain within the status of mere consumers, without any influence on events.

A parallel may be drawn here with discussions going on today concerning free-market liberalism, globalization, and privatization. The issue of foreign influence and native values is at stake. The idea being defended by political scientists and philosophers is that countries once inhabited by self-employed owners of small farms are increasingly and rapidly becoming societies of low-paid workers laboring for big companies, most of them transnationals, while a small percentage of the population reaps huge profits from all kinds of deals under the guise of privatization. This process, in turn, is supposedly based on the exigencies of globalization. It is easy to see the consequences: many companies with large numbers of low-paid workers coexist with shiny malls full of expensive items for the privileged few. Consumption in this context is seen by many as the expression of a gross materialism on the part of the elites that is deleterious to human liberty and dignity. Others see it as a tool for the erosion of political sovereignty.

It is obvious that consumption is fostered and promoted by globalization. In fact, the first encounter with globalization for most people in the South has to do precisely with this aspect of everyday life: more consumer items on supermarket shelves and more commercial advertisements. Globalization is supposed to mean, among other things, better products and services. But globalization on the shelf and in the home is limited in its first stages, in fact very limited—not only by physical constraints but also by the purchasing capacity of buyers. Every individual cannot be an infinite consumer—certainly not in Latin America, where the first distinction to be made regarding consumption is between those who can engage in it at will and those who are excluded from it or nearly so.

Philosophers tend to ask about meaning, in this case the meaning of the changes taking place today. Do we need mammoth malls with thousands of goodies brought in from distant lands in hundreds of freighters instead of the family-owned corner stores, stocked with essential items, that once dotted the landscape of towns and cities? What are the political and ethical implications of these changes?

Such questions lead us to explore the less visible phases of globalization. These phases are, in fact, far less trivial than the initial one, because they are related to a very important problem: *jobs*, both created and destroyed in the process. If new brands of merchandise are available at competitive prices, local factories may sell less and may be forced to lay off employees. Here those in favor of globalization usually argue that if factories can compete in the international market, in fact globalization will mean more jobs. No doubt this is sometimes the case.

But it is frequently asserted that the only conditions for success of both small and large companies are their compliance with global standards and their connection with global networks.[1]

This line of reasoning presupposes that all companies are on the same footing and that all of them have the same opportunities. But this assumption is usually false. Big companies in big countries have profited from large national markets and from their connection with the agencies of powerful governments; small companies in small countries do not have the same experience or clout. Today, efficient small companies end up being bought by large companies from large countries; this has been the case with many long-established Costa Rican firms since the implementation of the Mexico–Costa Rica Free Trade Agreement. The Costa Rican firms were simply bought by Mexican companies that took advantage of the new possibilities, perhaps as part of a strategy to compensate for their losses at home as a consequence of the recent political and economic turmoil in Mexico. Instead of foreign competition for local companies, what we have now is a situation where there is no competition but substitution of local companies with others.

Have the customers benefited? Not necessarily. In the best of cases the situation remains *almost* the same: same products, same prices, same jobs, just different owners. In many cases, however, the customers find strange, new brands instead of familiar ones. These new brands sometimes have different specifications because they were made for other markets and simply transferred to the new ones. In the process, jobs held by nationals are lost because of decisions made in other countries. For many people in small countries that have been left completely at the mercy of international firms, globalization thus means a painful loss of personal security. And because nothing is sold where people cannot buy, the major job losses that occur with the takeover of local markets by international companies will be the undoing of the whole process. At that point, once the local economy has been ruined, one can foresee the departure of foreign companies.

For Third-World countries, globalization has implications for sovereignty that are very different from those in industrialized nations. This explains why many people consider *globalization* just a misnomer for a process that has nothing to do with the literal meaning of the word. Every day countries like Costa Rica are unilaterally subjected to all kinds of quotas and restrictions for their products while they themselves are unable to deploy protectionist measures to defend their interests against powerful, industrialized nations. Some of these restrictions are so outrageous that they have become well known internationally, as is the case with the privileges obtained by the sugar lobby in the United States. Recently Costa Rica was forced to sign an agreement with European countries in order to be able to sell its bananas there; Chiquita Brands, an American company and a large contributor to Republican candidates, lobbied Congress in order to impose severe sanctions on Costa Rica because it considered itself to be negatively affected by the agreement with Europe.[2] What "globalization" is there if a small country is forced to use an American company for the marketing of its products under the threat of sanctions imposed by the U.S. Congress? Another good example can be taken from the textile industry: Costa Rican garment factories cannot export to the United States unless they submit to a quota system; in addition, they are forced to buy in the United States the fabrics used in the production of garments.[3] Such impositions are unilateral and affect the prices of the products. No wonder many ask themselves, Where is the globalization being touted as the panacea for all economic problems?

As a consequence, "globalization" is perceived merely as a clever ploy to open up all national markets to all kinds of products from industrialized nations, without any comparable reciprocity.

Twenty years ago in Latin America many theorists tried to explain the underdevelopment of the South by pointing to its extreme dependency on developed countries. One answer to this dependency, they argued, was the creation of a nonconsumerist society. Such a society would affirm local traditions against the encroachments of modernization and insist that development in imitation of the North was not necessarily the best course for the nonindustrial world. But this "dependence theory" was undoubtedly one-sided. In stressing Southern dependency, it failed to consider the ways in which relations between developed and underdeveloped regions are reciprocal; and in placing so strong an emphasis on external dependency, it tended to miss the internal contradictions that are characteristic of the developing world. Nonetheless, the theory performed a useful function by asking what an alternative model of development, and thus an alternative society, might look like. It is not difficult to locate examples of wasteful consumption, on the one hand, and severe deprivation on the other. But is there not a third option, one that would be open to the majority?

Unfortunately, in the South today, a privileged minority engage in ostentatious consumption while large sectors of the population remain in dire poverty. Patterns of wasteful consumption by elites in the South tend to mimic and exaggerate typical consumption in the North.

The promotion of high consumption in the South is advantageous to Northern industrial and service companies. It has been argued that, conversely, consumption patterns in the North are likewise beneficial to Southern countries, since their exports sold in the North provide them with badly needed hard currencies. In fact, the rationale for signing

North–South trade agreements like NAFTA is that an increase in international commerce is good business for all concerned.

But if we delve into the matter more carefully, we find that, without corrective measures, possible benefits do not outweigh present conditions. More consumption as a result of new conditions in international trade does not necessarily mean less poverty. For millions of destitute persons in the world, consumption is primarily something that a few inhabitants of their countries can engage in as a privilege, while at the same time it is denied or severely restricted to the rest, either because of rampant unemployment or because of the great disparity between wages and prices. Hence, the first disaggregation of the idea of "consumption" from a Southern perspective involves not the distinction between good and bad consumption but, instead, the distinction between consumption as a real *option* for some and as an unfulfilled *desire* for most.

It has now become clear: as seen from the North, consumption is associated with the pleasures of shopping and perhaps with the depression resulting from not finding happiness in what can be bought; as seen from the South, consumption is connected with the ostentation of the rich, daydreams of the poor, and food riots by hungry crowds.

In the South, the external signs of the latest onslaught in the battle for a consumerist society are very visible: huge, enclosed malls take the place of open shopping centers, which in turn had replaced small grocery stores; flashy cars substitute for inexpensive public transportation; for a small minority, designer clothes take the place of traditional garb. Malls are especially interesting, because they represent such a violent imposition on local conditions—both climatological and social. Only a profound distortion of the economy and of social values (together with a modification of political conditions) can explain the existence of these huge, air-conditioned buildings in countries where the temperature is comfortable all year round. English is the written language of the malls, in countries where people do not speak it; giant parking lots accommodate dozens of cars, though most of the surrounding roads are filled with potholes. The visual impact of these monstrous buildings is likewise remarkable: both their size and style—or lack thereof—amount to a violation of the landscape. To attract customers, they are often built in populated neighborhoods, which instantly become noisy, exhaust-filled places and lose any human intimacy they may have had in the past.

Everything inside the malls is geared toward selling and buying; all human transactions are reduced to a single function, and the scale of the whole enterprise seems to foster the limited behavior conducive to buying as much as possible. However, because prices in Southern malls tend to be astronomical, a substantial majority of the population is reduced to gawking without buying. The few remaining traditional small grocery stores, and even the more modern supermarkets that began to sprout in the 1950s, were and continue to be visited by people with specific needs and wants as well as the money to pay for what they buy. These malls, on the contrary, give rise to a new phenomenon: the reduction of most people to passive onlookers, who dream of the day when they will be able to buy many gadgets the purpose of which they do not yet fully understand.

If *Homo sapiens* becomes *Homo oeconomicus* inside the malls, there by necessity appears what Ivan Illich calls *Homo miserabilis*, the type of person who is reduced to a marginal condition, not because she cannot perform as an economic agent in another type of society but because the social conditions are such that she is forced to remain on the periphery of the new economy. It is hard to imagine hordes of visitors crowding into supermarkets and grocery stores just to look and to long for the time when they will be able to buy. Yet this has become an everyday occurrence in Third-World malls. Physically similar to the ones in the North, they are very different socially.

The combination of closed spaces, great variety of imported goods, and English labels is probably intended to give the visitor the impression that she or he is somewhere in the North and not in a country where shanty towns and beggars are all too common. For many years now, movies, magazines, and television sitcoms have depicted a blissful part of the world where most people live in happiness amid plenty of goods and services; now the malls are exactly those blissful places. The North has moved South.

But now let us take a look at the other side of the coin. If the presence of Northern consumption patterns in the South is so obvious and disruptive, is there something like a Southern presence in the North? Here I can only offer a highly speculative suggestion. It is likely that for many people in the North, the picture of destitution in the South operates as a deterrent to change, as a powerful image of what they might become if they do not keep doing what they do every day: working endless hours in jobs that may be meaningless and oppressive, engaging in a constant rush to nowhere in order to obtain the income required to meet their ever-expanding needs. So, in the same way that consumption in the North as a utopian dream for the South has become a powerful motive for action in the South, perhaps destitution in the South has also become a motive for action—something to avoid—in the North. This symmetry is worth exploring. In both cases, these images seem to be the motives for the wrong type of action: an individualistic pursuit of the worst features of industrial society for some, an impediment to change toward more meaningful lives for others. And just as showy shops full of consumer goods are the visible part of the North in the South, homeless people and inner-city slums may be taken as the presence of the South in the North.

Unfortunately, the questions I have addressed about the relation between North and South have largely been bypassed in recent discussions and debates. What we often find in their stead is the complaint that the South has too many people and the North too much consumption. This slogan has become a powerful political weapon because of its simplicity and its facile use of imagery. It has been voiced in important international gatherings and in policy documents. As usually happens with oversimplified visions, it hides a complex web of related problems; at the same time, it becomes either an excuse for avoiding action or a slogan for the justification of hasty policies. The North is said to consume more than it needs and the South to need more than it consumes. But since there is a North in the South, external problems of unequal relations become internal contradictions.

In the North, it is easy to imagine that one of the reasons for worker dissatisfaction is the perception that the labor of millions of people contribute to the prolongation of a system that, on a global scale, perpetuates the destitution of the many and the destruction of precious resources. One could argue at this point that a better distribution of consumption would alleviate both the pressure on the environment and the political tensions arising from the needs of destitute masses and that, therefore, a solution should be found combining the high-tech self-sufficiency proposed for postindustrial regions and the low-tech subsistence consumption proposed for preindustrial ones.

In most industrialized countries the transition from subsistence agriculture to a high-consumption society took place a long time ago, so that it is not present in the memories of citizens today. In underdeveloped countries, on the contrary, such a process has taken place recently, so that the memory of subsistence agriculture is still present to many of its citizens. Where some of the mammoth malls are being built, family-run agricultural plots were in production not too long ago. When the external debt crisis hit Latin America in the early 1980s and real income fell precipitously, grain production rose in many places. Lots of people went back to their plots to grow corn and beans. Will they have such a possibility in the next crisis? More important, is consumption somehow related to such crises?

Expensive consumption has been looked upon with suspicion by many Latin American thinkers as one of the causes of the recurrence of economic crises. It is seen as a grave danger for the well-being of society, which is thought to be more secure in a simple life of frugality. One finds such a concern in the 1973 book *The Poverty of Nations*, by the late Costa Rican politician José ("Pepe") Figueres (1906–90), who served twice as president of that country. Figueres saw the consumption of expensive imported goods as an obstacle to the all-important task of creating decent jobs for the population, especially for landless peasants. The cover illustration of his book seems to summarize this idea: it is a reproduction of a 1936 drawing by a local artist depicting a barefooted peasant trying to cross a city street with the heavy burden of a sack of coffee beans on his back while a luxury car passes by. Coffee exports make it possible for a member of the elite to buy the imported car. But this luxury item contributes nothing either to the productive capacity of the country or to the improvement of the conditions of the peasant.

There is a final aspect of the Southern perspective that merits some attention. In spite of all the adverse conditions in which they live, millions of poor people survive with very low levels of consumption. How do they manage to survive? How is it possible to find laughter and joy in poverty? If these mechanisms of survival in the South were well understood in the North, perhaps the fear associated with personal and social change, sometimes perceived as threatening, would abate. Consumption, then, provides a point of entry to a complex set of realities—especially in a world where survival may well be a shared problem.

Notes

This essay is an extended version of a paper of the same title that appeared in the *Report from the Institute for Philosophy and Public Policy* 15, no. 4, 1995, which was, in turn, an adaptation of a talk given at the conference "Consumption, Global Stewardship, and the Good Life," at the University of Maryland, October 1994.

1. Rosabeth Moss Kanter argues that compliance with global standards and connection with global networks will become necessary and sufficient conditions for the success of companies. See "Thriving Locally in the Global Economy," *Harvard Business Review*, 73, no. 5 (September–October 1995): 151–60.

2. See "Banana Republican," *Time*, 22 January 1996, 36–37. The subtitle reads, "Carl Lindner is an empire builder who invests in U.S. lawmakers and harvests favors from them."

3. See, for example, "País llevará lío textil a OMC," in the Costa Rican daily newspaper *La Nación*, 2 February 1996, 16A.

Index of Names

Index of Subjects

acid rain, 463
acquisitive society thesis, 147
adaptation-level theory, 201
addiction, 227, 254, 419; and consuming the earth, 27, 146, 149
advertising: and autonomy, 379; and children, 379; and consumer promotionalism, 417–19; costs of, 202, 215–16n6; creation of wants, 25–26, 132–33, 176, 187, 493; and day-dreaming, 154n12; defense of, 277–79; frugality as resistance to, 417–19; Galbraith's critique of, 272–79, 283–84; government promotion of condoms, 333; and identity formation, 132–33; image of the good life, 1, 227, 273, 413; Lasch's critique of, 261; Puritan critique of, 253–55. *See also* dependence effect
aesthetic, 253–54, 399, 357–58; affluence effect, 243n47; critique of consumerism, 134, 261–62; ideals of, 150, 266; of time, 352–53; value, 161, 257, 262, 492
affluent society. *See* consumer society
Africa, 97, 440, 451, 454, 479, 481, 509–10
agriculture, 269–70, 469–70; and biological limits to, 76; and cropland, 71, 78–81, 91n18, 97–98, 420, 437, 511; and development, 483;

and environmental effects of, 86–88, 95–96, 98; and extensification, 97–98; and farm employment, 81; and farmers, 41, 64, 69, 269; and fertilizer use, 85–88; and Green Revolution, 82, 98–99; and International Rice Research Center, 98; and irrigation, 82, 100, 468–69; productivity of, 4, 11, 19, 35, 41, 69, 71–74, 76–77, 83, 85–90, 98–100; sustainability in, 95–110; traditional, 456. *See also* diet; food; pesticides
alchemists, 54, 55, 57, 59, 61
alcohol: alcoholism, 481; consumption, 26, 378, 379; and taxation, 107
Alcohol, Drug Abuse, and Mental Health Administration, 219
altruism, 411–12
Amazonia, 71
American Dream, 1, 6, 136–37, 433
American Revolution, 260
anarchy, 408
answering machines, 158, 159
antimaterialism: in American history, 386n12; critique of, 13, 158–59, 250–68, 370, 377, 423, 428; definition of, 369–70, 386n9; as distortion of frugality, 416, 423; explanation of, 139–40, 148–49, 152n2, 155

565

About the Contributors

Luis A. Camacho is professor in the School of Philosophy and vice president for academic affairs at the University of Costa Rica. He is the president of the Costa Rican Philosophical Association. His writings in logic, philosophy of science, and development ethics have appeared in Costa Rica, Mexico, Argentina, the United States, Sweden, and the Netherlands.

Colin Campbell is reader in sociology and head of the department at the University of York, England. He is the author of *Toward a Sociology of Irreligion, The Romantic Ethic and the Spirit of Modern Consumerism,* and, most recently, *The Myth of Social Action.* His work has been published in many journals including *Sociological Analysis, The American Sociological Review,* and *Sociological Theory.*

David A. Crocker is senior research scholar at the Institute for Philosophy and Public Policy and School of Public Affairs at the University of Maryland. His book, *Florecimiento humano y desarrollo internacional: La nueva ética de las capacidades humanas,* will be published in Costa Rica. He is the president of the International Development Ethics Association and the author of many articles on development ethics.

Eleonora Curlo is assistant professor of marketing, Baruch College.

Herman E. Daly is professor of public policy at the School of Public Affairs at the University of Maryland. He previously served as senior economist in the Environment Department of the World Bank and as alumni professor of economics at Louisiana State University. He has written more than one hundred articles in professional journals and anthologies as well as four books, the most recent being *Beyond Growth: The Economics of Sustainable Development.*

Rabbi Eliezer Diamond is Rabbi Judah Nadich Assistant Professor of Talmud and Rabbinics at the Jewish Theological Seminary of America. He has published widely in scholarly and popular journals and is presently completing a book on fasting and asceticism in rabbinic culture.

Robert Goodland is environmental adviser at the World Bank and the author of many of the World Bank's environmental policies. A tropical ecologist specializing in environmental assessment of development—especially energy—projects, he is the president of the International Association of Impact Assessment. The author of seventeen books, he is currently writing a study of the "Big Dams Debate."

Allen L. Hammond is director of the Resource and Environmental Information Program of the World Resources Institute. He has served as editor-in-chief for three volumes of the *World Resources* series (1990–91, 1992–93, 1994–95) and three volumes of the *Information Please Environmental Almanac* (1992, 1993, 1994). He has written or edited fourteen books, published more than 130 articles in technical journals, and written extensively for general circulation magazines and newspapers. He currently conducts research on environmental indicators and long-term sustainability issues and is writing a book on the latter topic.

Nathan Keyfitz is professor emeritus of population and sociology at Harvard University. He has been awarded eight honorary degrees in three countries and is a member of the National Academy of Sciences and the American Academy of Arts and Sciences. In 1993 the Austrian government awarded him its Medal for Science. He is the author of *Applied Mathematical Demography* and *Introduction to the Mathematics of Population.*

Robert E. Lane is Eugene Meyer Professor Emeritus of Political Science at Yale University and a member of the Senior Common Room, Nuffield College, Oxford. His most recent book is *The Market Experience.* He is currently working on a book tentatively entitled *Well-Being: The Contribution of Market Democracies.*

Judith Lichtenberg is associate professor of philosophy at the University of Maryland and senior research scholar at the Institute for Philosophy and Public Policy at the University of Maryland. She is the editor of *Democracy and the Mass Media,* and the author of many articles on ethics and political philosophy.

Toby Linden was a research assistant at the Institute for Philosophy and Public Policy at the University of Maryland and is currently an educational consultant.

David Luban is Frederick Haas Professor of Law and Philosophy at the Georgetown University Law Center and research scholar at the Institute for Philosophy and Public Policy. He is the author of several books, including *Lawyers and Justice: An Ethical Study* and *Legal Modernism,* as well as more than fifty papers in professional journals.

James A. Nash is the executive director of the Churches' Center for Theology and Public Policy, a national ecumenical research center in Washington, D.C. He is also lecturer in social and ecological ethics at Wesley Theological Seminary and has served as executive director of the Massachusetts Council of Churches. He is the author of *Loving Nature: Ecological Integrity and Christian Responsibility.*

Martha C. Nussbaum is Ernst Freund Professor of Law and Ethics at the University of Chicago Law School. Her writings include *The Fragility of Goodness: Luck and Ethics in Greek Tragedy and Philosophy, Love's Knowledge: Essays on Philosophy and Literature, Therapy of Desire: Theory and Practice in Hellenistic Ethics,* and *Poetic* Justice. She is coeditor (with Amartya Sen) of *The Quality of Life* and (with Jonathan Glover) of *Women, Culture and Development.*

Thomas W. Pogge is professor of philosophy at Columbia University. His most recent publications include *Realizing Rawls,* "Loopholes in Moralities," "Cosmopolitanism and Sovereignty," "An Egalitarian Law of Peoples," "How Should Human Rights be Conceived," "Kant on Ends and the Meaning of Life," and "The Bounds of Nationalism."

Mark Sagoff is senior research scholar at the Institute for Philosophy and Public Policy at the University of Maryland. He is the author of *Economy of the Earth: Philosophy, Law, and the Environment* and has published numerous articles on philosophy, law, and economics. In 1991, he was selected to be a Pew Scholar in Conservation and the Environment and, in 1994, elected president of the International Society of Environmental Ethics.

Juliet B. Schor is senior lecturer on economics and director of women's studies at Harvard University, as well as a member of the editorial board of the *Journal of Applied Economics.* She is the author of *The Overworked American: The Unexpected Decline of Leisure,* and coeditor (with Jong-il You) of *Changing Production Relations: A Global Perspective* and (with Stephen A. Marglin) *The Golden Age of Capitalism.* She is also the author of numerous articles on consumption, leisure, and macroeconomic policy.

Michael Schudson is professor of communication and adjunct professor of sociology at the University of California, San Diego. He is the author of a number of books and many articles on journalism, advertising, political culture, and public knowledge, including *Discovering the News*; *Advertising, the Uneasy Persuasion*; *Watergate in American Memory*; and *The Power of News*. He is presently completing a history of the "public sphere" in the United States.

Jerome M. Segal is research scholar at the Institute for Philosophy and Public Policy at the University of Maryland. He is the author of *Agendy and Alienation: A Theory of Human Presence,* and of the forthcoming *Graceful Simplicity.* He is also the director of the Jewish Peace Lobby.

Amartya Sen is the master of Trinity College at Cambridge University and Lamont University Professor and Professor of Economics and Philosophy at Harvard University. He is a past president of the Econometric Society, the International Economic Association, the Indian Economic Association, and the American Economic Association. He is the author or editor of numerous papers and books—most recently *Inequality Reexamined* and, with Jean Drèze, *India: Economic Development and Social Opportunity.*

Alan Strudler is assistant professor of legal studies, the Wharton School, University of Pennsylvania.

Paul L. Wachtel is CUNY Distinguished Professor in the Doctoral Program in Clinical Psychology at the City University of New York. He has written widely on psychological theory and the integration of the major schools of psychotherapy and on the applications of psychological theory to social issues. He is the author of *The Poverty of Affluence.*

Paul E. Waggoner has worked at the Connecticut Agricultural Experiment Station, New Haven, since 1951, and served as director from 1972 to 1987. He is a member of the National Academy of Sciences. His studies encompass evaporation from foiliage, mathematical simulation of plant disease, the effect of climate change upon agriculture and water resources, and global food supply.

David Wasserman is research scholar at the Institute for Philosophy and Public Policy at the University of Maryland.

Charles K. Wilber is professor of economics at the University of Notre Dame. He has published more than one hundred articles and a number of books, including *An Inquiry into the Poverty of Economics* and *Beyond Reaganomics: A Further Inquiry into the Poverty of Economics,* both coauthored with Kenneth Jameson.